Major Problems in
American History
Volume I

MAJOR PROBLEMS IN AMERICAN HISTORY SERIES

GENERAL EDITOR

THOMAS G. PATERSON

Major Problems in American History

Volume I
To 1877

DOCUMENTS AND ESSAYS

EDITED BY

ELIZABETH COBBS HOFFMAN

SAN DIEGO STATE UNIVERSITY

JON GJERDE

UNIVERSITY OF CALIFORNIA, BERKELEY

HOUGHTON MIFFLIN COMPANY
Boston   New York

Editor in Chief: Jean L. Woy
Sponsoring Editor: Colleen Shanley Kyle/Mary Dougherty
Senior Development Editor: Frances Gay
Senior Project Editor: Christina M. Horn
Associate Production/Design Coordinator: Christine Gervais
Manufacturing Manager: Florence Cadran
Senior Marketing Manager: Sandra McGuire

Cover image: *California News* (1850), by William Sidney Mount. The Long Island Museum of American Art, History and Carriages. Gift of Mr. and Mrs. Ward Melville.

Printed in the U.S.A.

Library of Congress Control Number: 2001131500

ISBN: 0-618-06133-9

123456789-CRS-05 04 03 02 01

For
Victoria and Gregory Shelby
and
Christine and Kari Gjerde

Contents

C H A P T E R 3
Colonial New England and the Middle Colonies in British America
Page 70

C H A P T E R 6
Competing Visions of Empire in the Early National Period
Page 163

C H A P T E R 7
Westward Movement, the Market Revolution, and Indian Removal
Page 196

CHAPTER 8
*Nationalism, Sectionalism, and Expansionism
in the Age of Jackson*
Page 228

C H A P T E R   1 1

*Commercial Development and Immigration
in the North at Midcentury*

Page 327

C H A P T E R   1 4
The Civil War
Page 418

CHAPTER 15
Reconstruction, 1865–1877
Page 449

Preface

History is a matter of interpretation. Individual scholars rescue particular stories from the welter of human experience, organize them into a pattern, and offer arguments to suggest how these phenomena reflected or reshaped human society at a given moment. This means that yet other historians might select different stories, organize them into a pattern, and arrive at a contrasting interpretation of the same period of time or even the same event. All scholars use evidence, but the choice and interpretation of evidence is to some extent inevitably an expression of personal judgment. History is not separate from historians.

The goal of *Major Problems in American History* is to place meat on this barebones description of how the study of the past "works." Like most instructors, we want students to learn and remember the "important" facts, yet at the same time we want to make clear that historians often disagree on what is important. And, even when historians do agree on what is worthy of commentary, they often disagree on what a certain piece of evidence signifies. For example, scholars know that the Declaration of Independence was written in 1776 but may well debate why the colonists felt compelled to take this dramatic step.

The two volumes that make up this book bring together primary documents and secondary sources on the major debates in American history. The primary sources give students evidence to work with. They represent a mix of the familiar and unfamiliar. Certain pieces are a "must" in any compilation for a survey course because they had a powerful, widely noted impact on American history, such as Tom Paine's *Common Sense,* Lincoln's Second Inaugural, *Brown* v. *Board of Education,* or the manifesto of the National Organization for Women. We have also selected pieces that evoke the mood of the period and the personal experiences of individuals who reflected their times but may not have changed them. Included are statements by pioneer women on the frontier, immigrant workers, African American soldiers and educators, eyewitnesses to the terrors of World War II, children in rebellion against their parents during the 1960s, and so on. These documents often show conflicting points of view, from the "bottom up," as well as the "top down." We hope that they will give both students and professors a wide variety of reference points for classroom discussion, as well as help students become familiar with some principal facts of the topic under discussion.

The secondary sources in these volumes fulfill a somewhat different goal, which is to expose students to the elemental historical debates for each broad period. We have chosen, therefore, to focus on classic debates, often combining very recent essays with more seasoned pieces by eminent historians who set the terms of discussion for an entire generation or more. Our purpose is to make the interpretive contrasts as clear as possible for students who are just learning to distinguish interpretation from fact and to discern argument within description. This book seeks to stimulate classroom debate by providing clearly delineated, alternative approaches to historical problems. In addition, the essays often make direct reference to one of the primary documents, demonstrating to students how historians integrate evidence in an interpretation. Sometimes historians refer to one another, pointing to the process of revisionism.

Volume I, prepared by Jon Gjerde, encompasses American history from its beginnings through Reconstruction. It grapples with certain momentous events that occurred in specific chronological periods, such as the encounter between indigenous people and European empires in the fifteenth century, the American Revolution, the Constitution, the Civil War, and Reconstruction. Yet this volume also considers regional developments over a long period of time in the North, South, and West that created distinct subcultures and ultimately led to collision in the mid-nineteenth century. Finally, Volume I addresses topics of reform, religious change, and the transformation of gender relations in the nineteenth century. Our goal is to provide a balance between topical and chronological problems, between social history and political history, and between the voices of everyday folk and the elite. The book also seeks to give students a fair representation of the different categories that scholars today use to organize the historical story, including gender, race, class, ethnicity, and region.

This book follows the same general format as other volumes in the *Major Problems in American History* series. Each chapter begins with a short introduction that orients the student to the topic. In these volumes for the U.S. history survey course, we have included a new section called "Questions to Think About" after the chapter introduction, to help students focus their reading of the subsequent material. Next come eight to ten primary documents, followed by two essays that highlight contrasting interpretations. Headnotes at the start of the document and essay sections help readers know what to look for and identify key themes and debates. Each chapter concludes with a "Further Reading" section. This selected bibliography is intentionally brief, to tempt readers into further research without overwhelming them. In addition, we have included at the beginning of these two volumes an "Introduction to Students" that gives suggestions on how to read primary and secondary sources and critically analyze their content, point of view, and inferences. The introduction encourages students to draw their own conclusions and use evidence to back up their reasoning.

Many friends and colleagues have contributed to these volumes. We especially wish to thank Robin Einhorn, David Henkin, James Kettner, and Mary Ryan of the University of California, Berkeley; William Cheek, Sarah Elkind, John Putman, Harry McDean, and Andrew Wiese of San Diego State University; Brian Balogh of the University of Virginia; Drew Cayton of Miami University of Ohio; Eric Hinderaker of the University of Utah; Phil Morgan of Johns Hopkins; Bruce Schulman of Boston University; James Stewart of Macalaster College; and Louis Warren of the University of California at Davis.

We received detailed and extremely helpful reviews from Elizabeth Ansnes, San Jose State University; Robert Buzzanco, University of Houston; Brian Greenberg, Monmouth University; Steven Hahn, Northwestern University; Marianne

Holdzkum, Ohio State University; Eugene E. Leach, Trinity College, Hartford; Daniel J. McIrney, Utah State University; Thomas C. Rust, Montana State University—Billings; and Karin Wulf, American University. We are very grateful to them. We also received valuable assistance from our graduate students, Chris Agee, Dee Bielenberg, Walter Gustafson, David Johnson, Leland Smith, and Wendy Warren. Thomas G. Paterson, the editor of the *Major Problems* series, provided support and timely advice. The editors at Houghton Mifflin, Colleen Shanley Kyle, Frances Gay, Christina Horn, and Jean Woy, helped to keep us on track as we struggled to complete the manuscript amidst the many competing priorities within academia. We are grateful for their kind encouragement and helpful recommendations.

The life of the mind is exceptionally fulfilling, but it is happiest when set within the life of the family. We wish to express our deep gratitude to our spouses, Ruth Gjerde and Daniel Hoffman, for their love and patience. We dedicate the book to our four children and the young people of their generation, for whom it is written. To paraphrase the poet Emily Dickinson, this is our letter to their world.

E. C. H.
J. G.

Introduction to Students: How to Read Primary and Secondary Sources

College study encompasses a number of subjects. Some disciplines, such as mathematics, are aimed at problems and proofs. Students learn methods to discover the path to a correct answer. History is different. Unlike math, it is focused much more on interpretation and imagination. Historians study and analyze sources to construct arguments about the past. They generally understand that there is no "right" answer, even if there are some arguments that are more convincing than others. They search less for a proof than an interpretation, less for absolute truth than for understanding. A historical imagination is useful in creating these interpretations. People in the past thought and acted differently than we do today. Their views of science, of religion, of the place of women and men—to cite only a few examples—were not the same as our views. When we as historians create an argument about the past, we must imagine a world unlike the one we now inhabit.

The "problems" in U.S. history on which this text focuses, then, are different from math "problems." They are a series of issues in the American past that might be addressed, discussed, and debated, but not necessarily solved. The text provides readers with two types of tools to grapple with these problems. The first is the *primary source,* which is a piece of evidence that has survived from the period we are analyzing. Primary sources come in a variety of forms, including pictures, artifacts, and written texts. And they may have survived in a number of ways. Archaeologists might uncover pieces of evidence when they undertake digs of lost civilizations; ethnologists might transcribe stories told by people; economists might take bits of evidence to create numerical measures of past behavior; and historians might scrutinize surviving written sources. This volume by and large presents written texts, varying from political tracts to private letters. Some of the texts, however, are transcriptions, that is, texts written by someone who noted what another person said.

As historians, we must be critical of primary sources for a number of reasons. First of all, we must consider whether a source is really from the historical period we are studying. You might have occasionally read stories in the newspaper about paintings that had been attributed to famous artists but were discovered to be frauds painted by an unknown copyist. When the fraud is discovered, the painting's value plummets. The same can be said for a primary source. If it is not valid, it is not as valuable. A letter alleged to have been written by George Washington clearly is not of much use for revealing his innermost thoughts if we discover the document was written in 1910. But we should also be aware of the opposite: not all pieces of evidence have survived to the present. We might ask if there is a bias in the likelihood of one point of view surviving and another being lost. Or we might ask if some points of view were not given as much voice in the era we are studying. The experiences of slaveholders, for example, might have been more commonly written and published than those of slaves. Because they were rarely given the opportunity to publish their thoughts, slaves—in addition to others such as Native Americans and women—have bequeathed us some sources that have survived as transcriptions. As essential as these sources are in reconstructing the past, as historians we must be critical of them as well. Did the people writing down the spoken words accurately set them to paper or did they inject their own thoughts?

Once we consider the validity of sources and understand that some sources were more likely to survive than others, another reason to critique the sources is that they are not "objective" portrayals of the past. By nature, they are points of view. Like anyone in a society, the writer of each primary source provides us with his or her viewpoint and thus gives us a window through which to view his or her world, complete with its biases. When we read about the American Revolution, for example, we will see many different perspectives on the events leading up to the Declaration of Independence by the American colonies. Those who opposed independence saw the events in a very different light from those who led the independence movement. We have often read about the advocates of independence who saw the British as threats to American freedom. Theirs is a story of realizing that the American colonies would be better off as an independent nation and bringing this vision to fruition. Americans for generations have viewed this as a truly heroic episode in U.S. history. But many contemporaries were not as sure that independence was the correct course of action. Many British American colonists opposed independence because they felt they were more secure if they remained in the British Empire. Countless members of Indian nations were suspicious of the intentions of the American "patriots" and remained loyal to the king. African American slaves were often leery of the aims of their patriot owners. The fact that people had different viewpoints allows us to grapple with the multiple perspectives of the past. In the end, there is no single story that encompasses the American past, but rather a series of competing narratives.

When you are reading the documents in this volume, then, you are urged to criticize each document. We are certain that these are valid sources, and so you should be especially critical of the point of view contained in each document. Consider both the document and its author. Who wrote or spoke the words in the document? What was his or her reason for expressing the thoughts? Given the background and motivations of the authors, what are their perspectives and potential biases? How do they see the world differently from the way others do? And why do you think these different perspectives exist? Whose viewpoint do you agree with most? Why? It is not too much to say that the student of history is similar to a detective who seeks out sources and clues that illuminate the lives and events of the past.

In addition to primary sources, each chapter in this volume contains two essays that represent what we call a *secondary source*. Secondary sources are the written work of historians who have conducted painstaking research in primary sources. Historians work with an array of primary sources that they uncover and use as evidence to construct an argument that addresses one of the major problems in American history. A secondary source is so named because it is one step removed from the primary source. As you will notice, the writers of the essays in each chapter do not necessarily reach similar conclusions. On the contrary, they illustrate differing opinions about why events occurred and what they mean for us today.

Hence secondary sources, like primary sources, do not provide us with the "truth," even to the extent that they are based on verifiable facts. Rather, historians' conclusions vary just as your ideas about the documents might differ from those of someone else in your class. And they differ for a number of reasons. First, interpretations are influenced by the sources on which they depend. Occasionally, a historian might uncover a cache of primary sources heretofore unknown to other scholars, and these new sources might shed new light on a topic. Here again historians are like detectives.

Second and more important, however, historians carry their own perspectives to the research. As they read secondary sources, analyze primary texts, and imagine the past, historians usually develop arguments that differ in emphasis from those developed by others. As they combine their analyses with their own perspectives, they create an argument to explain the past. Historians' individual points of view and even society's dominant point of view influence their thinking. If analyzing sources resembles working as a detective, writing history is similar to being a judge who attempts to construct the most consistent argument from the sources and information at hand. And historians can be sure that those who oppose their viewpoints will analyze their use of sources and the logic of their argument. Those who might disagree with them—and that might include you—will criticize them if they make errors of fact or logic.

The essays were selected for this text in part because they reflect differing conclusions with which you may or may not agree. For example, what caused the Civil War? For decades, historians have given us a number of answers. Some have said the war could have been prevented if politicians had been more careful to avoid sectional divisions or if the U.S. political system had been suitable for compromise. Others have observed that the divisions that developed between North and South over time became so acute that they could not be compromised away. A civil war in their view was well nigh inevitable. Or what are we to make of the "Age of Jackson"? Some historians have celebrated this period as a flowering of American democracy. The increased voting rights for men fostered raucous political parades that celebrated the American freedoms. Others have noted that these rights were given only to white men and that the "freedoms" were in name only. Or how do we make sense of the Vietnam War nearly forty years after the first American troops landed? Was it a terrible mistake that undermined confidence in the United States both at home and abroad, or was it, in President Reagan's words, a "noble cause"?

An important question left unanswered in all of these chapters is what do *you* think is the correct interpretation? In the end, maybe you don't agree completely with any of the essayists. In fact, you might wish to create your own argument that uses primary sources found here and elsewhere and that accepts parts of one essay and parts of another. When you do this, you have become a historian, a person who attempts to analyze texts critically, someone who is actively engaged in the topic. If that occurs, this volume is a success.

When we discuss the discipline of history with people, we typically get one of two responses. One group of people says something like "I hated history in school."

The other group says something like "history was my favorite subject when I went to school." Invariably the people who hated history cite all the boring facts that they had to memorize. In contrast, those who loved history remember a teacher or professor who brought the subject alive by invoking the worlds of people in the past. As we have tried to indicate in this short overview, history is not about memorizing boring facts but rather an active enterprise of thought and interpretation. Historians are not rote learners; studying history does not entail simply memorization. Instead, historians are detectives and judges, people who interpret and imagine what happened in history and why, individuals who study the past in order to understand the world in which they live in the present. Facts are important, but they are only building blocks in a larger enterprise of interpretation. In sum, our intent with this text is to show how primary and secondary sources can be utilized to aid you in understanding and interpreting major problems in the American past. It is also aimed at keeping that group of people who hates studying history as small as possible and enlarging that second group who considers history their passion. Frankly, it's more fun to talk to the latter.

Major Problems in
American History
Volume I

Conquest and Colliding Empires

Tisquantum, a member of the Patuxet nation, lived a life that exemplifies the intricate connections between his native people and the European invaders. In 1605, he was kidnapped by an Englishman who was exploring the coasts of Canada and New England and was carried off to England. There, he learned the English language. He eventually returned to America on another voyage of exploration in 1614 and was kidnapped again and taken to southern Spain. His abductors intended to sell him into slavery, but he was rescued by Catholic friars, with whom he lived until 1618. He returned once again to the New England coast, only to discover that his entire nation had been destroyed by disease some years before. Shortly after his return, he met a group of English colonists who called themselves Pilgrims; they were astounded when he spoke to them in English. He befriended the Pilgrims and taught them how to survive in the American wilderness—he was a participant in the first "thanksgiving"— and he became their trading partner. In late 1622, Tisquantum, whom we know today as Squanto, was attacked by what the English called "Indian fever" and died. Tisquantum's life, as remarkable as it was, illustrates many of the experiences of native people following contact with Europeans: slavery, disease, war, and trade.

While Tisquantum lived in a changing world, American Indian society had not been static before it came into contact—and conflict—with Europeans. To the contrary, the process of change had begun centuries before Squanto stumbled upon the Pilgrims. Native people had lived for millennia in what eventually was known as the Americas. Complex civilizations developed and evolved. The Aztec empire, located in what is today Mexico, was characterized by its military power. It was at the peak of its power when its people first encountered Europeans. Other complex societies, such as the Anasazi culture in the regions now called Arizona and New Mexico and the Hopewell culture in present-day Illinois, ascended in power and then mysteriously declined. Native people hunted, gathered, and grew an array of foods, including potatoes, squash, beans, and maize, that nourished millions of people in what would become the United States. In short, the Americas were not an empty land when the Europeans arrived.

Yet the Indians' world changed even more dramatically beginning with the landfall of Christopher Columbus and his crew in 1492. Over the course of the centuries that followed, people from Europe, the Americas, and Africa together would create a "new world." This creation involved both an interaction between peoples of striking differences and a brutality of remarkable proportions. Perhaps at no other time did peoples with such different worldviews and social practices meet. Indians and

1

Europeans differed not only in appearance but also in such matters as work roles between women and men, notions of private property, religious belief, and governmental structures. Some of the new arrivals simply observed these differences, whereas others used them to justify conflict and savagery.

The earliest European explorers were interested in gaining riches in the Americas. Once they realized the abundance of wealth that the Americas offered, they sought to amass it. Spanish conquistadors, for example, conquered the Aztec empire in 1519 and gained untold riches from it. Soon, native people found themselves enslaved to provide labor for burgeoning mines. Between 1545 and 1660, over seven million pounds of silver were extracted from American lands by slaves for the Spanish empire. As other European states recognized the economic possibilities, they too searched for land and riches. France, the Netherlands, Sweden, and England all attempted to build empires. These empires came into conflict with one another and in contact with indigenous peoples. This contact between Americans and Europeans often resulted in conflict and war. Perhaps even more important than overt conflict was a mysterious and hidden exchange of disease. As native people were exposed to an array of diseases ranging from smallpox to influenza with which they had had little prior contact, they suffered epidemics that weakened their societies and therefore their ability to contest additional European incursions. Like Squanto, the native peoples became traders, but they also became slaves and victims of strange new diseases. Their home in effect had become a new world for them as well as for the Europeans.

QUESTIONS TO THINK ABOUT

What advantages did the Europeans possess that enabled them to defeat the Indians? How would the story of Indian-European contact have differed if Indians had been better able to resist disease? In what ways did Europeans of different nationalities treat Indians? Were religious leaders different from those seeking material gain in the ways in which they interacted with Indians?

DOCUMENTS

The initial interactions between Indians and Europeans involved a strange combination of terror and wonder, as these documents indicate. Christopher Columbus, in Document 1, recounts his first meeting with the people in the Caribbean and his sense of the economic possibility of the Indies. In its description of the Indians, his letter betrays an odd blending of tenderness and a brutal assessment of their potential uses. In Document 2, a Spanish priest, Fray Bernardino de Sahagun, describes the conquest of the Aztecs by Spanish conquistadors in 1519. Document 3 was written by Bartolomé de Las Casas, the first Spanish priest ordained in the Americas, in 1542. De Las Casas disparages the exploitation and enslavement of the native people. Although Europeans wrote most of the documents in this chapter, Document 4 is an exception. It is a transcription of an oral tradition that describes the arrival of the Dutch on Manhattan Island. Document 5 provides a French account of relationships with Native Americans that attempts to describe "good" and "bad" people and depicts their religion and patterns of life. Document 6 is an English description of native people in what is now New England in 1634, shortly before the bloody Pequot War. Note how author William Wood, an early settler in Massachusetts Bay, pays particular attention to the varying conditions of which they fix little sharpened stakes. Even these, they dare not use. . . . I gave them of everything which I had, as well cloth as many other things, without accepting aught therefor—; but such they are, incurably timid. It is true that since they have become more assured, and are losing that terror, they are artless and generous with what they have, to such a degree as no one would believe but him who had seen it. Of anything they have, if it be asked for, they never say no, but do rather invite the person to accept it, and show as much lovingness as though they would give their hearts. And whether it be a thing of value, or one of little worth, they are straightways content with whatsoever trifle of whatsoever kind may be given them in return for it. I forbade that anything so worthless as fragments of broken platters, and pieces of broken glass, and strap-buckles, should be given them; although when they were able to get such things, they seemed to think they had the best jewel in the world, for it was the hap of a sailor to get, in exchange for a strap, gold to the weight of two and a half castellanos, and others much more for other things of far less value. . . . They took even pieces of broken barrel-hoops, and gave whatever they had, like senseless brutes. . . . I gave gratuitously a thousand useful things that I carried, in order that they may conceive affection, and furthermore may be made Christians; for they are inclined to the love and service of their Highnesses and of all the Castilian nation, and they strive to combine in giving us things which they have in abundance, and of which we are in need. And they knew no sect, nor idolatry; save that they all believe that power and goodness are in the sky, and they believed very firmly that I, with these ships and crew, came from the sky; and in such opinion they received me at every place where I landed. . . . They are men of very subtle wit, who navigate all those seas, and who give a marvellously good account of everything. . . . As I have already said, they are the most timorous creatures there are in the world, so that the men who remain there are alone sufficient to destroy all that land, and the island is without personal danger for them if they know how to behave themselves. It seems to me that in all those islands, the men are all content with a single wife; and to their chief or king they give as many as twenty. The women, it appears to me, do more work than the men. Nor have I been able to learn whether they held personal property, for it seemed to me that whatever one had, they all took share of, especially of eatable things. Down to the present, I have not found in those islands any monstrous men, as many expected, but on the contrary all the people are very comely; nor are they black like those in Guinea, but have flowing hair; and they are not begotten where there is an excessive violence of the rays of the sun. . . . And in conclusion, to speak only of what has been done in this voyage, which has been so hastily performed, their Highnesses may see that I shall give them as much gold as they may need, with very little aid which their Highnesses will give me; spices and cotton at once, as much as their Highnesses will order to be shipped, and as much as they shall order to be shipped of mastic,—which till now has never been found except in Greece, in the island of [Chios], and the Seignory [of Genoa] sells it for what it likes; and aloe-wood as much as they shall order to be shipped; and slaves as many as they shall order to be shipped,—and these shall be from idolators. And I believe that I have discovered rhubarb and cinnamon, and I shall find that the men whom I am leaving there will have discovered a thousand other things of value; as I made no delay at any point, so long as the wind gave me an opportunity of sailing, except only in the town of Navidad till I had left things safely arranged and well established. And in truth I should have done much more if the ships had served me as well as might reasonably have been expected. . . . Since thus our Redeemer has given to our most illustrious King and Queen, and to their famous kingdoms, this victory in so high a matter, Christendom should take gladness therein and make great festivals, and give solemn thanks to the Holy Trinity for the great exaltation they shall have by the conversion of so many peoples to our holy faith; and next for the temporal benefit which will bring hither refreshment and profit, not only to Spain, but to all Christians. This briefly, in accordance with the facts. Dated, on the caravel, off the Canary Islands, the 15 February of the year 1493.

At your command,
THE ADMIRAL.

2. Fray Bernardino de Sahagun Relates an Aztec Chronicler's Account of the Spanish Conquest of the Aztecs, 1519

[In 1519, at the town of Cholula,] there arose from the Spaniards a cry summoning all the noblemen, lords, war leaders, warriors, and common folk; and when they had crowded into the temple courtyard, then the Spaniards and their allies blocked the entrances and every exit. There followed a butchery of stabbing, beating, killing of the unsuspecting Cholulans armed with no bows and arrows, protected by no shields . . . with no warning, they were treacherously, deceitfully slain. . . .

[As Cortés and his army approached Tenochtitlán, the people of the city] rose in tumult, alarmed as if by an earthquake, as if there were a constant reeling of the face of the earth.

Shocked, terrified, Moctezuma himself wept in the distress he felt for his city. Everyone was in terror; everyone was astounded, afflicted. Many huddled in groups, wept in foreboding for their own fates and those of their friends. Others, dejected, hung their heads. Some groups exchanged tearful greetings; others tried mutual encouragement. Fathers would run their hands over their small boys' hair and, smoothing it, say, "Woe, my beloved sons! How can what we fear be happening in your time?" Mothers, too: "My beloved sons, how can you live through what is in store for you?" . . .

The iron of [the Spaniards'] lances . . . glistened from afar; the shimmer of their swords was as of a sinuous water course. Their iron breast and back pieces, their helmets clanked. Some came completely encased in iron—as if turned to iron. . . . And ahead of them . . . ran their dogs, panting, with foam continually dripping from their muzzles. . . .

Moctezuma's own property was then brought out . . . precious things like necklaces with pendants, arm bands tufted with quetzal feathers, golden arm bands, bracelets, golden anklets with shells, rulers' turquoise diadems, turquoise nose rods; no end of treasure. They took all, seized everything for themselves . . . as if it were theirs. . . .

[In 1520, the Spanish occupied Tenochtitlán, took Moctezuma hostage, and finally strangled him. Then] they charged the crowd with their iron lances and

From an anonymous Aztec chronicler in Fray Bernardino de Sahagun, *General History of Things in New Spain* (1582).

hacked us with their iron swords. They slashed the backs of some. . . . They hacked at the shoulders of others, splitting their bodies open. . . . The blood of the young warriors ran like water; it gathered in pools. . . . And the Spaniards began to hunt them out of the administrative buildings, dragging out and killing anyone they could find . . . even starting to take those buildings to pieces as they searched.

[The Aztecs, led by Moctezuma's brother, Cuitlehuac, counterattacked, and trapped the Spanish in Moctezuma's palace. One night two months later, Cortés and his army tried to escape. But they were so burdened with loot that two-thirds of them died trying to cross the aqueducts leading out of the city.]

That night, at midnight, the enemy came out, crowded together, the Spaniards in the lead, the Tlaxcallans following. . . . Screened by a fine drizzle, a fine sprinkle of rain, they were able undetected to cross the canals . . . just as they were crossing, a woman drawing water saw them. "Mexicans! Come, all of you. . . . They are already leaving! They are already secretly getting out!" Then a watcher at the top of the temple . . . also shouted, and his cries pervaded the entire city. . . .

The canal was filled, crammed with them. Those who came along behind walked over . . . on corpses. . . . It was as if a mountain of men had been laid down: they had pressed against one another, smothered one another. . . .

[Then] at about the time that the Spaniards had fled from Mexico . . . there came a great sickness, a pestilence, the smallpox. It . . . spread over the people with great destruction of men. It caused great misery. . . . The brave Mexican warriors were indeed weakened by it. It was after all this had happened that the Spaniards came back.

[By the time the Spanish returned in 1521, Cuitlehuac had died of smallpox. He was succeeded by Cuauhtémoc. Tenochtitlán held out against the Spanish siege for 75 days. Finally the Spanish took the city, destroying it and killing hundreds of thousands of Aztec citizens. Many of them were already sick and starving. Cuauhtémoc was forced to surrender, and later executed.] Fighting continued, both sides took captives, on both sides there were deaths . . . great became the suffering of the common folk. There was hunger. Many died of famine. . . . The people ate anything—lizards, barn swallows, corn leaves, saltgrass. . . . Never had such suffering been seen. . . . The enemy pressed about us like a wall . . . they herded us. . . . The brave warriors were still hopelessly resisting. . . .

Finally the battle just quietly ended. Silence reigned. Nothing happened. The enemy left. All was quiet, and nothing more took place. Night fell, and the next day nothing happened, either. No one spoke aloud; the people were crushed. . . . So ended the war.

3. Father Bartolomé de Las Casas Disparages the Treatment of the Indians, 1542

God has created all these numberless people to be quite the simplest, without malice or duplicity, most obedient, most faithful to their natural Lords, and to the Christians, whom they serve; the most humble, most patient, most peaceful and calm, without

"Of the Island of Hispanola," in Bartolomé de Las Casas, *Very Brief Account of the Devastation of the Indies* (1542), trans. F. A. McNutt (Cleveland: The Arthur H. Clark Company, 1909), 312–319.

should come on immediately. These arriving in numbers, and having themselves
viewed the strange appearance, and observing that it was actually moving towards
the entrance of the river or bay; concluded it to be a remarkably large house in which
the Mannitto (the Great or Supreme Being) himself was present, and that he probably
was coming to visit them. By this time the chiefs were assembled at York island, and
deliberating in what manner in which they should receive their Mannitto on his arrival. Every measure was taken to be well provided with plenty of meat for a sacrifice. The women were desired to prepare the best victuals. All the idols or images
were examined and put in order, and a grand dance was supposed not only to be an
agreeable entertainment for the Great Being, but it was believed that it might, with
the addition of a sacrifice, contribute to appease him if he was angry with them. The
conjurers were also set to work, to determine what this phenomenon portended, and
what the possible result of it might be. To these and to the chiefs and wise men of the
nations, men, women, and children were looking up for advice and protection. Distracted between hope and fear, they were at a loss what to do; a dance, however, commenced in great confusion. While in this situation, fresh runners arrive declaring it to
be a large house of various colours, and crowded with living creatures. It appears
now to be certain, that it is the great Mannitto, bringing them some kind of game,
such as he had not given them before, but other runners soon after arriving declare
that it is positively a house full of human beings, of quite a different colour from that
of the Indians, and dressed differently from them; that in particular one of them was
dressed entirely in red, who must be the Mannitto himself. They are hailed from the
vessel in a language they do not understand, yet they shout or yell in return by way of
answer, according to the custom of their country; many are for running off to the
woods, but are pressed by others to stay, in order not to give offence to their visitor,
who might find them out and destroy them. The house, some say, large canoe, at last
stops, and a canoe of a smaller size comes on shore with the red man, and some others
in it; some stay with his canoe to guard it. The chiefs and wise men, assembled in
council, form themselves into a large circle, towards which the man in red clothes approaches with two others. He salutes them with a friendly countenance, and they return the salute after their manner. They are lost in admiration; the dress, the manners,
the whole appearance of the unknown strangers is to them a subject of wonder; but
they are particularly struck with him who wore the red coat all glittering with gold
lace, which they could in no manner account for. He, surely, must be the great Mannitto, but why should he have a white skin? Meanwhile, a large *Hackhack* is brought
by one of his servants, from which an unknown substance is poured out into a small
cup or glass, and handed to the supposed Mannitto. He drinks—has the glass filled
again, and hands it to the chief standing next to him. The chief receives it, but only
smells the contents and passes it on to the next chief, who does the same. The glass or
cup thus passes through the circle, without the liquor being tasted by any one, and is
upon the point of being returned to the red clothed Mannitto, when one of the Indians,
a brave man and a great warrior, suddenly jumps up and harangues the assembly on
the impropriety of returning the cup with its contents. It was handed to them, says he,
by the Mannitto, that they should drink out of it, as he himself had done. To follow
his example would be pleasing to him; but to return what he had given them might
provoke his wrath, and bring destruction on them. And since the orator believed it for
the good of the nation that the contents offered them should be drunk, and as no one
else would do it, he would drink it himself, let the consequence be what it might; it

was better for one man to die, than that a whole nation should be destroyed. He then took the glass, and bidding the assembly a solemn farewell, at once drank up its whole contents. Every eye was fixed on the resolute chief, to see what effect the unknown liquor would produce. He soon began to stagger, and at last fell prostrate on the ground. His companions now bemoan his fate, he falls into a sound sleep, and they think he has expired. He wakes again, jumps up and declares, that he has enjoyed the most delicious sensations, and that he never before felt himself so happy as after he had drunk the cup. He asks for more, his wish is granted; the whole assembly then imitate him, and all become intoxicated.

After this general intoxication had ceased, for they say that while it lasted the whites had confined themselves to their vessel, the man with the red clothes returned again, and distributed presents among them, consisting of beads, axes, hoes, and stockings such as the white people wear. They soon became familiar with each other, and began to converse by signs. The Dutch made them understand that they would not stay here, that they would return home again, but would pay them another visit the next year, when they would bring them more presents, and stay with them awhile: but as they could not live without eating, they should want a little land of them to sow seeds, in order to raise herbs and vegetables to put into their broth. They went away as they had said, and returned in the following season, when both parties were much rejoiced to see each other. . . . As the whites became daily more familiar with the Indians, they at last proposed to stay with them, and asked only for so much ground for a garden spot as, they said, the hide of a bullock would cover or encompass, which hide was spread before them. The Indians readily granted this apparently reasonable request; but the whites then took a knife, and beginning at one end of the hide, cut it up to a long rope, not thicker than a child's finger, so that by the time the whole was cut up, it made a great heap; they then took the rope at one end, and drew it gently along, carefully avoiding its breaking. It was drawn out into a circular form, and being closed at its ends, encompassed a large piece of ground. The Indians were surprised at the superior wit of the whites but did not wish to contend with them about the little land, as they had still enough themselves. The white and red men lived contentedly together for a long time, though the former from time to time asked for more land, which was readily obtained, and thus they gradually proceeded higher up the Mahicannittuck, until the Indians began to believe that they would soon want all their country, which in the end proved true.

5. Father Paul Le Jeune Reports on His Encounters with the Indians, 1634

On the Belief, Superstitions, and Errors of the Montagnais Savages

I have already reported that the Savages believe that a certain one named Atachocam had created the world, and that one named Messou had restored it. I have questioned upon this subject the famous Sorcerer and the old man with whom I passed the

Reuben Gold Thwaites, ed., *The Jesuit Relations and Allied Documents: Travels and Explorations of the Jesuit Missionaries in New France, 1610–1791* (Cleveland: The Burrows Brothers Company, 1897), VI: 157, 159, 161, 201, 203, 205, 225, 229, 231, 233, 243, 245, 247; VII: 35, 37, 39, 41, 43. This document can also be found in Robert Marcus and David Burner, eds., *America Firsthand* (St. Martin's Press/Bedford Books, 1989), 12–18.

Winter; they answered that they did not know who was the first Author of the world,—that it was perhaps Atachocam, but that was not certain; that they only spoke of Atachocam as one speaks of a thing so far distant that nothing sure can be known about it; . . .

As to the Messou, they hold that he restored the world, which was destroyed in the flood; whence it appears that they have some tradition of that great universal deluge which happened in the time of Noë. . . .

They also say that all animals, of every species, have an elder brother, who is, as it were, the source and origin of all individuals, and this elder brother is wonderfully great and powerful. . . . Now these elders of all the animals are the juniors of the Messou. Behold him well related, this worthy restorer of the Universe, he is elder brother to all beasts. . . .

Their Religion, or rather their superstition, consists besides in praying; but O, my God, what prayers they make! . . .

. . . I have heard them pray for the Spring, or for deliverance from evils and other similar things; and they express all these things in the form of desires, crying out as loudly as they can, "I would be very glad if this day would continue, if the wind would change," etc. I could not say to whom these wishes are addressed, for they themselves do not know, at least those whom I have asked have not been able to enlighten me. . . .

On the Good Things Which Are Found Among the Savages

If we begin with physical advantages, I will say that they possess these in abundance. They are tall, erect, strong, well proportioned, agile; and there is nothing effeminate in their appearance. Those little Fops that are seen elsewhere are only caricatures of men, compared with our Savages. . . .

As to the mind of the Savage, it is of good quality. I believe that souls are all made from the same stock, and that they do not materially differ; hence, these barbarians having well formed bodies, and organs well regulated and well arranged, their minds ought to work with ease. Education and instruction alone are lacking. Their soul is a soil which is naturally good, but loaded down with all the evils that a land abandoned since the birth of the world can produce. . . .

Moreover, if it is a great blessing to be free from a great evil, our Savages are happy; for the two tyrants who provide hell and torture for many of our Europeans, do not reign in their great forests,—I mean ambition and avarice. As they have neither political organization, nor offices, nor dignities, nor any authority, for they only obey their Chief through good will toward him, therefore they never kill each other to acquire these honors. Also, as they are contented with a mere living, not one of them gives himself to the Devil to acquire wealth.

They make a pretence of never getting angry, not because of the beauty of this virtue, for which they have not even a name, but for their own contentment and happiness. . . .

They are very much attached to each other, and agree admirably. You do not see any disputes, quarrels, enmities, or reproaches among them. Men leave the arrangement of the household to the women, without interfering with them; they cut, and decide, and give away as they please, without making the husband angry. . . .

On Their Vices and Their Imperfections

The Savages, being filled with errors, are also haughty and proud. Humility is born of truth, vanity of error and falsehood. They are void of the knowledge of truth, and are in consequence, mainly occupied with thought of themselves. They imagine that they ought by right of birth, to enjoy the liberty of Wild ass colts, rendering no homage to any one whomsoever, except when they like. . . . All the authority of their chief is in his tongue's end; for he is powerful in so far as he is eloquent; and, even if he kills himself talking and haranguing, he will not be obeyed unless he pleases the Savages. . . .

I have shown in my former letters how vindictive the Savages are toward their enemies, with what fury and cruelty they treat them, eating them after they have made them suffer all that an incarnate fiend could invent. This fury is common to the women as well as to the men, and they even surpass the latter in this respect. I have said that they eat the lice they find upon themselves, not that they like the taste of them, but because they want to bite those that bite them.

These people are very little moved by compassion. When any one is sick in their Cabins, they ordinarily do not cease to cry and storm, and make as much noise as if everybody were in good health. They do not know what it is to take care of a poor invalid, and to give him the food which is good for him; if he asks for something to drink, it is given to him, if he asks for something to eat, it is given to him, but otherwise he is neglected; to coax him with love and gentleness, is a language which they do not understand. As long as a patient can eat, they will carry or drag him with them; if he stops eating, they believe that it is all over with him and kill him, as much to free him from the sufferings that he is enduring, as to relieve themselves of the trouble of taking him with them when they go to some other place. . . .

The Savages are slanderous beyond all belief; I say, also among themselves, for they do not even spare their nearest relations, and with it all they are deceitful. . . .

Lying is as natural to Savages as talking, not among themselves, but to strangers. Hence it can be said that fear and hope, in one word, interest, is the measure of their fidelity. I would not be willing to trust them, except as they would fear to be punished if they failed in their duty, or hoped to be rewarded if they were faithful to it. They do not know what it is to keep a secret, to keep their word, and to love with constancy,—especially those who are not of their nation, for they are harmonious among themselves, and their slanders and raillery do not disturb their peace and friendly intercourse. . . .

What One Must Suffer in Wintering with the Savages

. . . Now, when we arrived at the place where we were to camp, the women, armed with axes, went here and there in the great forests, cutting the framework of the hostelry where we were to lodge; meantime the men, having drawn the plan thereof, cleared away the snow with their snowshoes, or with shovels which they make and carry expressly for this purpose. Imagine now a great ring or square in the snow, two, three or four feet deep, according to the weather or the place where they encamp. This depth of snow makes a white wall for us, which surrounds us on all sides, except the end where it is broken through to form the door. The framework having been brought, which consists of twenty or thirty poles, more or less, according to the size of the cabin, it is planted, not upon the ground but upon the snow; then they throw upon these poles, which converge a little at the top, two or three rolls of bark sewed together, beginning at the bottom, and behold, the house is made. The ground inside, as well as the wall of snow which extends all around the cabin, is covered with little branches of fir; and, as a finishing touch, a wretched skin is fastened to two poles to serve as a door, the doorposts being the snow itself. . . .

You cannot stand upright in this house, as much on account of its low roof as the suffocating smoke. . . .

This prison, in addition to the uncomfortable position that one must occupy upon a bed of earth, has four other great discomforts,—cold, heat, smoke, and dogs.

6. William Wood Describes Indian Responses to the English, 1634

Of Their Wondering at the First View of Any Strange Invention

These Indians being strangers to arts and Sciences, and being unacquainted with the inventions that are common to a civilized people, are ravisht with admiration at the first view of any such sight: They tooke the first Ship they saw for a walking Iland, the Mast to be a Tree, the Saile white Clouds, and the discharging of Ordinance for Lightning and thunder, which did much trouble them, but this thunder being over, and this moving Iland stedied with an Anchor, they manned out their cannowes to goe and picke strawberries there, but being saluted by the way with a broad side, they cried out, what much hoggery, so bigge walke, and so bigge speake, and by and by kill; which caused them to turne back, not daring to approach till they were sent for. They doe much extoll and wonder at the English for their strange Inventions, especially for a Wind-mill, which in their esteeme was little lesse than the worlds wonder, for the strangenesse of his whisking motion, and the sharpe teeth biting the corne (as they terme it) into such small peeces. . . . [T]he Indian seeing the plow teare up more ground in a day, than their Clamme shels could scrape up in a month, desire to see the workemanship of it, and viewing well the coulter and share, perceiving it to be iron, told the plow-man, hee was almost Abamocho, almost as cunning as the Devill. . . .

Of the Pequants and Narragansetts, Indians Inhabiting Southward

The Pequants be a stately warlike people, of whom I never heard any misdemeanour; but that they were just and equall in their dealings; not treacherous either to their Country-men, or English: Requiters of courtesies, affable towards the English. Their next neighbours the Narragansetts, be at this present the most numerous people in those parts, the most rich also, and the most industrious; being the storehouse of all such kind of wild Merchandize as is amongst them. These men are the most curious minters of their Wampompeage and Mowhakes, which they forme out of the inmost wreaths of Perwinkle-shels. The Northerne, Easterne, and Westerne Indians fetch

William Wood, *New England's Prospect* (London: 1634), 61–62, 77–78, 94–97.

all their Coyne from these Southerne Mint-masters. From hence they have most of their curious Pendant & Bracelets; from hence they have their great stone-pipes, which wil hold a quarter of an ounce of Tobacco, which they make with steele-drils and other instruments; such is their ingenuity & dexterity, that they can imitate the English mold so accurately, that were it not for matter and colour it were hard to distinguish them. . . . Since the English came, they have employed most of their time in catching of Beavers, Otters, and Musquashes, which they bring downe into the Bay, returning backe loaded with English commodities, of which they make a double profit, by selling them to more remote Indians, who are ignorant of what they make them pay. . . .

Of the Aberginians or Indians Northward

First of their [the Indians'] stature, most of them being between five or six foot high, straight bodied, strongly composed, smooth-skinned, merry countenanced, of complexion something more swarthy than Spaniards, black haired, high foreheaded, black eyed, out-nosed, broad shouldered, brawny armed, long and slender handed, out breasted, small waisted, lank bellied, well thighed, flat kneed, handsome grown legs, and small feet. . . .

. . . [T]he reason is rendered why they grow so proportionable and continue so long in their vigor (most of them being fifty before a wrinkled brow or gray hair bewray their age) is because they are not brought down with suppressing labor, vexed with annoying cares, or drowned in the excessive abuse of overflowing plenty, which oftentimes kills them more than want, as may appear in them. For when they change their bare Indian commons for the plenty of England's fuller diet it is so contrary to their stomachs that death or a desperate sickness immediately accrues, which makes so few of them desirous to see England. . . .

Of Their Women, Their Dispositions, Employment, Usage by Their Husbands, Their Apparell, and Modesty

To satisfy the curious eye of women readers, who otherwise might think their sex forgotten or not worthy a record, let them peruse these few lines wherein they may see their own happiness, if weighed in the woman's balance of these ruder Indians who scorn the tutorings of their wives or to admit them as their equals—though their qualities and industrious deservings may justly claim the preeminence and command better usage and more conjugal esteem, their persons and features being every way correspondent, their qualifications more excellent, being more loving, pitiful, and modest, mild, provident, and laborious than their lazy husbands.

Their employments be many: first their building of houses, whose frames are formed like our garden arbors, something more round, very strong and handsome, covered with close-wrought mats of their own weaving which deny entrance to any drop of rain, though it come both fierce and long, neither can the piercing north wind find a cranny through which he can convey his cooling breath. They be warmer than our English houses. . . . And as is their husbands' occasion, these poor tectonists [builders or carpenters] are often troubled like snails to carry their houses on their backs, sometime to fishing places, other times to hunting places, after that to a planting place where it abides the longest.

Another work is their planting of corn, wherein they exceed our English husbandmen, keeping it so clear with their clamshell hoes as if it were a garden rather than a corn field, not suffering a choking weed to advance his audacious head above their infant corn or an undermining worm to spoil his spurns. Their corn being ripe they gather it, and drying it hard in the sun convey it to their barns, which be great holes digged in the ground in form of a brass pot, sealed with rinds of trees, wherein they put their corn, covering it from the inquisitive search of their gourmandizing husbands who would eat up both their allowed portion and reserved seed if they knew where to find it. . . .

Another of their employments is their summer processions to get lobsters for their husbands, wherewith they bait their hooks when they go afishing for bass or codfish. This is an everyday's walk, be the weather cold or hot, the waters rough or calm. They must dive sometimes over head and ears for a lobster, which often shakes them by their hands with a churlish nip and bids them adieu. The tide being spent, they trudge home two or three miles with a hundredweight of lobsters at their backs, and if none, a hundred scowls meet them at home and a hungry belly for two days after. Their husbands having caught any fish, they bring it in their boats as far as they can by water and there leave it: as it was their care to catch it, so it must be their wives' pains to fetch it home, or fast. Which done, they must dress it and cook it, dish it, and present it, see it eaten over their shoulders; and their loggerships having filled their paunches, their sweet lullabies scramble for their scraps. In the summer these Indian women, when lobsters be in their plenty and prime, they dry them to keep for winter, erecting scaffolds in the hot sunshine, making fires likewise underneath them (by whose smoke the flies are expelled) till the substance remain hard and dry. In this manner they dry bass and other fishes without salt, cutting them very thin to dry suddenly before the flies spoil them or the rain moist them, having a special care to hang them in their smoky houses in the night and dankish weather.

In summer they gather flags [probably cattail], of which they make mats for houses, and hemp and rushes, with dyeing stuff of which they make curious baskets with intermixed colors and protractures [drawings or designs] of antic imagery. . . . In winter they are their husbands' caterers, trudging to the clam banks for their belly timber, and their porters to lug home their venison which their laziness exposes to the wolves till they impose it upon their wives' shoulders. They likewise sew their husbands' shoes and weave coats of turkey feathers, besides all their ordinary household drudgery which daily lies upon them, so that a big belly hinders no business, nor a childbirth takes much time. . . .

For their carriage it is very civil, smiles being the greatest grace of their mirth; their music is lullabies to quiet their children, who generally are as quiet as if they had neither spleen or lungs. . . .

Since the English arrival, comparison hath made them miserable, for seeing the kind usage of the English to their wives, they do as much condemn their husbands for unkindness and commend the English for their love, as their husbands—commending themselves for their wit in keeping their wives industrious—do condemn the English for their folly in spoiling good working creatures. . . .

In a word, to conclude this woman's history, their love to the English hath deserved no small esteem, ever presenting them something that is either rare or desired, as strawberries, hurtleberries, raspberries, gooseberries, cherries, plums, fish, and other such gifts as their poor treasury yields them. . . . I have often heard men cast upon the English there, as if they should learn of the Indians to use their wives in the like manner and to bring them to the same subjection—as to sit on the lower hand and to carry water and the like drudgery. But if my own experience may out-balance an ill-grounded scandalous rumor, I do assure you, upon my credit and reputation, that there is no such matter, but the women find there as much love, respect, and ease as here in old England.

7. John Mason Gives a Puritan Account of the Pequot War, 1637

To the Honourable the General Court of Connecticut.
Honoured Gentlemen, . . .

In the Beginning of May 1637 there were sent out by Connecticut Colony Ninety Men under the Command of Capt. John Mason against the Pequots, with Onkos an Indian Sachem living at Mohegan, who was newly revolted from the Pequots. . . .

In the Morning, we awaking and seeing it very light, supposing it had been day, and so we might have lost our Opportunity, having purposed to make our Assault before Day; rowsed the Men with all expedition, and briefly commended ourselves and Design to God, thinking immediately to go to the Assault; the Indians shewing us a Path, told us that it led directly to the Fort. . . . Then Capt. Underhill came up, who Marched in the Rear; and commending ourselves to God, divided our Men: There being two Entrances into the Fort, intending to enter both at once: Captain Mason leading up to that on the North East Side; who approaching within one Rod, heard a Dog bark and an Indian crying Owanux! Owanux! which is Englishmen! Englishmen! We called up our Forces with all expedition, gave Fire upon them through the Pallizado; the Indians being in a dead indeed their last Sleep: Then we wheeling off fell upon the main Entrance, which was blocked up with Bushes about Breast high, over which the Captain passed, intending to make good the Entrance, encouraging the rest to follow. Lieutenant Seeley endeavoured to enter; but being somewhat cumbred, stepped back and pulled out the Bushes and so entred, and with him about sixteen Men: We had formerly concluded to destroy them by the Sword and save the Plunder.

Whereupon Captain Mason seeing no Indians, entred a Wigwam; where he was beset with many Indians, waiting all opportunities to lay Hands on him, but could not prevail. At length William Heydon espying the Breach in the Wigwam, supposing some English might be there, entred; but in his Entrance fell over a dead Indian;

John Mason, *A Brief History of the Pequot War: Especially of the Memorable Taking of Their Fort at Mistick in Connecticut in 1637 [1656]* (Boston: S. Kneeland and T. Green, 1736). This document can also be found in Charles Orr, ed., *History of the Pequot War: The Contemporary Accounts of Mason, Underhill, Vincent and Gardner* (Cleveland: The Helman-Taylor Co., 1897; reprint, New York: AMS Press, 1980), 11–12, 15–21, 23–31, 44–46.

but speedily recovering himself, the Indians some fled, others crept under their Beds: The Captain going out of the Wigwam saw many Indians in the Lane or Street; he making towards them, they fled, were pursued to the End of the Lane, where they were met by Edward Pattison, Thomas Barber, with some others; where seven of them were Slain, as they said. The Captain facing about, Marched a slow Pace up the Lane he came down, perceiving himself very much out of Breath; and coming to the other End near the Place where he first entred, saw two Soldiers standing close to the Pallizado with their Swords pointed to the Ground: The Captain told them that We should never kill them after that manner: The Captain also said, We must Burn them; and immediately stepping into the Wigwam where he had been before, brought out a Firebrand, and putting it into the Matts with which they were covered, set the Wigwams on Fire. Lieutenant Thomas Bull and Nicholas Omsted beholding, came up; and when it was thoroughly kindled, the Indians ran as Men most dreadfully Amazed.

And indeed such a dreadful Terror did the Almighty let fall upon their Spirits, that they would fly from us and run into the very Flames, where many of them perished. And when the Fort was thoroughly Fired, Command was given, that all should fall off and surround the Fort; which was readily attended by all; only one Arthur Smith being so wounded that he could not move out of the Place, who was happily espied by Lieutenant Bull, and by him rescued. . . .

Thus were they now at their Wits End, who not many Hours before exalted themselves in their great Pride, threatning and resolving the utter Ruin and Destruction of all the English, Exulting and Rejoycing with Songs and Dances: But God was above them, who laughed his Enemies and the Enemies of his People to Scorn, making them as a fiery Oven: Thus were the Stout Hearted spoiled, having slept their last Sleep, and none of their Men could find their Hands: Thus did the Lord judge among the Heathen, filling the Place with dead Bodies!

And here we may see the just Judgment of God, in sending even the very Night before this Assault, One hundred and fifty Men from their other Fort, to join with them of that Place, who were designed as some of themselves reported to go forth against the English, at that very Instant when this heavy Stroak came upon them where they perished with their Fellows. So that the Mischief they intended to us, came upon their own Plate: They were taken in their own snare, and we through Mercy escaped. And thus in little more than one Hour's space was their impregnable Fort with themselves utterly Destroyed, to the Number of six or seven Hundred, as some of themselves confessed. There were only seven taken captive, and about seven escaped.

Of the English, there were two Slain outright, and about twenty Wounded: Some Fainted by reason of the sharpness of the Weather, it being a cool Morning, and the want of such Comforts and Necessaries as were needful in such a Case. . . .

And was not the Finger of God in all this? . . . What shall I say: God was pleased to hide us in the Hollow of his Hand; I still remember a Speech of Mr. Hooker at our going abroad; That they should be Bread for us. And thus when the Lord turned the Captivity of his People, and turned the Wheel upon their Enemies; we were like Men in a Dream; then was our Mouth filled with Laughter, and our Tongues with Singing; thus we may say the Lord hath done great Things for us among the Heathen, whereof we are glad. Praise ye the Lord!

❦ E S S A Y S

Although the effects of the European invasion of the Americas on Indian society were profound, indigenous peoples had resided in what would become the United States for millennia. Their societies and cultures had undergone constant change. Scholars thus have puzzled over the best way of understanding the American Indian world prior to, during, and after its first contact with Europeans. James H. Merrell, who teaches history at Vassar College, argues that a "new world" was created for Indians when they encountered Europeans and Africans in the Carolinas and Virginia. Merrell stresses that the vast changes that contact brought about created a new order not unlike that encountered by the Europeans and Africans who crossed the ocean. In contrast, Neal Salisbury, a historian at Smith College, emphasizes the flux that had characterized the societies of indigenous peoples prior to contact with Europeans and Africans. Indian society, he argues, had been in transition prior to contact, as it would be afterward.

The Indians' New World

JAMES H. MERRELL

In August 1608 John Smith and his band of explorers captured an Indian named Amoroleck during a skirmish along the Rappahannock River. Asked why his men—a hunting party from towns upstream—had attacked the English, Amoroleck replied that they had heard the strangers "were a people come from under the world, to take their world from them." Smith's prisoner grasped a simple yet important truth that students of colonial America have overlooked: after 1492 native Americans lived in a world every bit as new as that confronting transplanted Africans or Europeans.

The failure to explore the Indians' new world helps explain why, despite many excellent studies of the native American past, colonial history often remains "a history of those men and women—English, European, and African—who transformed America from a geographical expression into a new nation." One reason Indians generally are left out may be the apparent inability to fit them into the new world theme, a theme that exerts a powerful hold on our historical imagination and runs throughout our efforts to interpret American development. . . . [S]cholars have analyzed encounters between peoples from the Old World and conditions in the New, studying the complex interplay between European or African cultural patterns and the American environment. Indians crossed no ocean, peopled no faraway land. It might seem logical to exclude them.

The natives' segregation persists, in no small degree, because historians still tend to think only of the new world as the New World, a geographic entity bounded by the Atlantic Ocean on the one side and the Pacific on the other. Recent research suggests that process was as important as place. Many settlers in New England recreated familiar forms with such success that they did not really face an alien environment until long after their arrival. Africans, on the other hand, were struck by the shock of the new at the moment of their enslavement, well before they stepped on

James H. Merrell, "The Indians' New World: The Catawba Experience," *William and Mary Quarterly,* 3rd ser., 41, no. 4 (October 1984): 537–539, 541–546, 549–560, 564–565. Reprinted by permission of William and Mary Quarterly.

board ship or set foot on American soil. If the Atlantic was not a barrier between one world and another, if what happened to people was more a matter of subtle cultural processes than mere physical displacements, perhaps we should set aside the maps and think instead of a "world" as the physical and cultural milieu within which people live and a "new world" as a dramatically different milieu demanding basic changes in ways of life. Considered in these terms, the experience of natives was more closely akin to that of immigrants and slaves, and the idea of an encounter between worlds can—indeed, must—include the aboriginal inhabitants of America.

For American Indians a new order arrived in three distinct yet overlapping stages. First, alien microbes killed vast numbers of natives, sometimes before the victims had seen a white or black face. Next came traders who exchanged European technology for Indian products and brought natives into the developing world market. In time traders gave way to settlers eager to develop the land according to their own lights. These three intrusions combined to transform native existence, disrupting established cultural habits and requiring creative responses to drastically altered conditions. Like their new neighbors, then, Indians were forced to blend old and new in ways that would permit them to survive in the present without forsaking their past. By the close of the colonial era, native Americans as well as whites and blacks had created new societies, each similar to, yet very different from, its parent culture.

The range of native societies produced by this mingling of ingredients probably exceeded the variety of social forms Europeans and Africans developed. Rather than survey the broad spectrum of Indian adaptations, this [essay] considers in some depth the response of natives in one area, the southern piedmont. . . . Avoiding extinction and eschewing retreat, the Indians of the piedmont have been in continuous contact with the invaders from across the sea almost since the beginning of the colonial period. . . .

. . . [T]hese groups [the piedmont peoples] shared a single history once Europeans and Africans arrived on the scene. Drawn together by their cultural affinities and their common plight, after 1700 they migrated to the Catawba Nation, a cluster of villages along the border between the Carolinas that became the focus of native life in the region. Tracing the experience of these upland communities both before and after they joined the Catawbas can illustrate the consequences of contact and illuminate the process by which natives learned to survive in their own new world.

For centuries, ancestors of the Catawbas had lived astride important aboriginal trade routes and straddled the boundary between two cultural traditions, a position that involved them in a far-flung network of contacts and affected everything from potting techniques to burial practices. Nonetheless, Africans and Europeans were utterly unlike any earlier foreign visitors to the piedmont. Their arrival meant more than merely another encounter with outsiders; it marked an important turning point in Indian history. Once these newcomers disembarked and began to feel their way across the continent, they forever altered the course and pace of native development.

Bacteria brought the most profound disturbances to upcountry villages. When Hernando de Soto led the first Europeans into the area in 1540, he found large towns already "grown up in grass" because "there had been a pest in the land" two years before, a malady probably brought inland by natives who had visited distant Spanish posts. The sources are silent about other "pests" over the next century, but soon after the English began colonizing Carolina in 1670 the disease pattern became all too clear. Major epidemics struck the region at least once every generation—in 1698, 1718, 1738, and 1759—and a variety of less virulent illnesses almost never left native settlements.

Indians were not the only inhabitants of colonial America living—and dying—in a new disease environment. The swamps and lowlands of the Chesapeake were a deathtrap for Europeans, and sickness obliged colonists to discard or rearrange many of the social forms brought from England. Among native peoples long isolated from the rest of the world and therefore lacking immunity to pathogens introduced by the intruders, the devastation was even more severe. John Lawson, who visited the Carolina upcountry in 1701, when perhaps ten thousand Indians were still there, estimated that "there is not the sixth Savage living within two hundred Miles of all our Settlements, as there were fifty Years ago." The recent smallpox epidemic "destroy'd whole Towns," he remarked, "without leaving one *Indian* alive in the Village." Resistance to disease developed with painful slowness; colonists reported that the outbreak of smallpox in 1759 wiped out 60 percent of the natives, and, according to one source, "the woods were offensive with the dead bodies of the Indians; and dogs, wolves, and vultures were . . . busy for months in banqueting on them."

Survivors of these horrors were thrust into a situation no less alien than what European immigrants and African slaves found. The collected wisdom of generations could vanish in a matter of days if sickness struck older members of a community who kept sacred traditions and taught special skills. When many of the elders succumbed at once, the deep pools of collective memory grew shallow, and some dried up altogether. In 1710, Indians near Charleston told a settler that "they have forgot most of their traditions since the Establishment of this Colony, they keep their Festivals and can tell but little of the reasons: their Old Men are dead." Impoverishment of a rich cultural heritage followed the spread of disease. Nearly a century later, a South Carolinian exaggerated but captured the general trend when he noted that Catawbas "have forgotten their ancient rites, ceremonies, and manufactures."

The same diseases that robbed a piedmont town of some of its most precious resources also stripped it of the population necessary to maintain an independent existence. In order to survive, groups were compelled to construct new societies from the splintered remnants of the old. The result was a kaleidoscopic array of migrations from ancient territories and mergers with nearby peoples. While such behavior was not unheard of in aboriginal times, population levels fell so precipitously after contact that survivors endured disruptions unlike anything previously known.

The dislocations of the Saponi Indians illustrate the common course of events. In 1670 they lived on the Staunton River in Virginia and were closely affiliated with a group called Nahyssans. A decade later Saponis moved toward the coast and built a town near the Occaneechees. When John Lawson came upon them along the Yadkin River in 1701, they were on the verge of banding together in a single village with Tutelos and Keyauwees. Soon thereafter Saponis applied to Virginia officials for permission to move to the Meherrin River, where Occaneechees, Tutelos, and others joined them. In 1714, at the urging of Virginia's Lt. Gov. Alexander Spotswood, these groups settled at Fort Christanna farther up the Meherrin. Their friendship with Virginia soured during the 1720s, and most of the "Christanna Indians" moved to the Catawba Nation. For some reason this arrangement did not satisfy them, and many returned to Virginia in 1732, remaining there for a decade before choosing to migrate north and accept the protection of the Iroquois.

Saponis were unusual only in their decision to leave the Catawbas. Enos, Occaneechees, Waterees, Keyauwees, Cheraws, and others have their own stories to tell, similar in outline if not in detail. With the exception of the towns near the confluence of Sugar Creek and the Catawba River that composed the heart of the Catawba Nation, piedmont communities decimated by disease lived through a common round of catastrophes, shifting from place to place and group to group in search of a safe haven. Most eventually ended up in the Nation, and during the opening decades of the eighteenth century the villages scattered across the southern up-country were abandoned as people drifted into the Catawba orbit.

No mere catalog of migrations and mergers can begin to convey how profoundly unsettling this experience was for those swept up in it. While upcountry Indians did not sail away to some distant land, they, too, were among the uprooted, leaving their ancestral homes to try to make a new life elsewhere. The peripatetic existence of Saponis and others proved deeply disruptive. A village and its surrounding territory were important elements of personal and collective identity, physical links in a chain binding a group to its past and making a locality sacred. Colonists, convinced that Indians were by nature "a shifting, wandring People," were oblivious to this, but Lawson offered a glimpse of the reasons for native attachment to a particular locale. "In our way," he wrote on leaving an Eno-Shakori town in 1701, "there stood a great Stone about the Size of a large Oven, and hollow; this the *Indians* took great Notice of, putting some Tobacco into the Concavity, and spitting after it. I ask'd them the Reason of their so doing, but they made me no Answer." Natives throughout the interior honored similar places—graves of ancestors, monuments of stones commemorating important events—that could not be left behind without some cost.

The toll could be physical as well as spiritual, for even the most uneventful of moves interrupted the established cycle of subsistence. Belongings had to be packed and unpacked, dwellings constructed, palisades raised. Once migrants had completed the business of settling in, the still more arduous task of exploiting new terrain awaited them. Living in one place year after year endowed a people with intimate knowledge of the area. The richest soils, the best hunting grounds, the choicest sites for gathering nuts or berries—none could be learned without years of experience, tested by time and passed down from one generation to the next. Small wonder that Carolina Indians worried about being "driven to some unknown Country, to live, hunt, and get our Bread in."

Some displaced groups tried to leave "unknown Country" behind and make their way back home. In 1716 Enos asked Virginia's permission to settle at "Enoe Town" on the North Carolina frontier, their location in Lawson's day. Seventeen years later William Byrd II came upon an abandoned Cheraw village on a tributary of the upper Roanoke River and remarked how "it must have been a great misfortune to them to be obliged to abandon so beautiful a dwelling." The Indians apparently agreed: in 1717 the Virginia Council received "Divers applications" from the Cheraws (now living along the Pee Dee River) "for Liberty to Seat themselves on the head of Roanoke River." Few natives managed to return permanently to their homelands. But their efforts to retrace their steps hint at a profound sense of loss and testify to the powerful hold of ancient sites.

Compounding the trauma of leaving familiar territories was the necessity of abandoning customary relationships. Casting their lot with others traditionally considered foreign compelled Indians to rearrange basic ways of ordering their existence. Despite frequent contacts among peoples, native life had always centered in kin and town. The consequences of this deep-seated localism were evident even to a newcomer like John Lawson, who in 1701 found striking differences in language, dress, and physical appearance among Carolina Indians living only a few miles apart. Rules governing behavior also drew sharp distinctions between outsiders and one's own "Country-Folks." Indians were "very kind, and charitable to one another," Lawson reported, "but more especially to those of their own Nation." A visitor desiring a liaison with a local woman was required to approach her relatives and the village headman. On the other hand, "if it be an *Indian* of their own Town or Neighbourhood, that wants a Mistress, he comes to none but the Girl." Lawson seemed unperturbed by this barrier until he discovered that a "Thief [is] held in Disgrace, that steals from any of his Country-Folks," "but to steal from the *English* [or any other foreigners] they reckon no Harm."

Communities unable to continue on their own had to revise these rules and reweave the social fabric into new designs. What language would be spoken? How would fields be laid out, hunting territories divided, houses built? How would decisions be reached, offenders punished, ceremonies performed? When Lawson remarked that "now adays" the Indians must seek mates "amongst Strangers," he unwittingly characterized life in native Carolina. Those who managed to withstand the ravages of disease had to redefine the meaning of the term *stranger* and transform outsiders into insiders. . . .

Muskets and kettles came to the piedmont more slowly than smallpox and measles. Spanish explorers distributed a few gifts to local headmen, but inhabitants of the interior did not enjoy their first real taste of the fruits of European technology until Englishmen began venturing inland after 1650. Indians these traders met in upcountry towns were glad to barter for the more efficient tools, more lethal weapons, and more durable clothing that colonists offered. Spurred on by eager natives, men from Virginia and Carolina quickly flooded the region with the material trappings of European culture. In 1701 John Lawson considered the Wateree Chickanees "very poor in *English* Effects" because a few of them lacked muskets.

Slower to arrive, trade goods were also less obvious agents of change. The Indians' ability to absorb foreign artifacts into established modes of existence hid the revolutionary consequences of trade for some time. Natives leaped the technological gulf with ease in part because they were discriminating shoppers. If hoes were too small, beads too large, or cloth the wrong color, Indian traders refused them. Items they did select fit smoothly into existing ways. Waxhaws tied horse bells around their ankles at ceremonial dances, and some of the traditional stone pipes passed among the spectators at these dances had been shaped by metal files. Those who could not afford a European weapon fashioned arrows from broken glass. Those who could went to great lengths to "set [a new musket] streight, sometimes shooting away above 100 Loads of Ammunition, before they bring the Gun to shoot according to their Mind."

Not every piece of merchandise hauled into the upcountry on a trader's packhorse could be "set streight" so easily. Liquor, for example, proved both impossible to resist and extraordinarily destructive. Indians "have no Power to refrain this Enemy," Lawson observed, "though sensible how many of them (are by it) hurry'd into the other World before their Time." And yet even here, natives aware of the risks sought to control alcohol by incorporating it into their ceremonial life as a device for achieving a different level of consciousness. Consumption was usually restricted to men, who "go as solemnly about it, as if it were part of their Religion," preferring to drink only at night and only in quantities sufficient to stupefy them. When ritual could not confine liquor to safe channels, Indians went still further and excused the excesses of overindulgence by refusing to hold an intoxicated person responsible for his actions. "They never call any Man to account for what he did, when he was drunk," wrote Lawson, "but say, it was the Drink that caused his Misbehaviour, therefore he ought to be forgiven."

Working to absorb even the most dangerous commodities acquired from their new neighbors, aboriginal inhabitants of the uplands, like African slaves in the lowlands, made themselves at home in a different technological environment. Indians became convinced that "Guns, and Ammunition, besides a great many other Necessaries, . . . are helpful to Man" and eagerly searched for the key that would unlock the secret of their production. At first many were confident that the *"Quera,* or good Spirit," would teach them to make these commodities "when that good Spirit sees fit." Later they decided to help their deity along by approaching the colonists. In 1757, Catawbas asked Gov. Arthur Dobbs of North Carolina "to send us Smiths and other Tradesmen to teach our Children."

It was not the new products themselves but the Indians' failure to learn the mysteries of manufacture from either Dobbs or the *Quera* that marked the real revolution wrought by trade. During the seventeenth and eighteenth centuries, everyone in eastern North America—masters and slaves, farmers near the coast and Indians near the mountains—became producers of raw materials for foreign markets and found themselves caught up in an international economic network. Piedmont natives were part of this larger process, but their adjustment was more difficult because the contrast with previous ways was so pronounced. Before European contact, the localism characteristic of life in the uplands had been sustained by a remarkable degree of self-sufficiency. Trade among peoples, while common, was conducted primarily in commodities such as copper, mica, and shells, items that, exchanged with the appropriate ceremony, initiated or confirmed friendships among groups. Few, if any, villages relied on outsiders for goods essential to daily life. . . .

By forcing Indians to look beyond their own territories for certain indispensable products, Anglo-American traders inserted new variables into the aboriginal equation of exchange. Colonists sought two commodities from Indians—human beings and deerskins—and both undermined established relationships among native groups. While the demand for slaves encouraged piedmont peoples to expand their traditional warfare, the demand for peltry may have fostered conflicts over hunting territories. Those who did not fight each other for slaves or deerskins fought each other for the European products these could bring. As firearms, cloth, and other items became increasingly important to native existence, competition replaced comity at the foundation of trade encounters as villages scrambled for the cargoes of merchandise. . . .

. . . The mask [of the natives' control of their own destiny] came off when, in 1715, the traders—and the trade goods—suddenly disappeared during the Yamassee War.

The conflict's origins lay in a growing colonial awareness of the Indians' need for regular supplies of European merchandise. In 1701 Lawson pronounced the Santees "very tractable" because of their close connections with South Carolina. Eight years later he was convinced that the colonial officials in Charleston "are absolute Masters over the *Indians* . . . within the Circle of their Trade." Carolina traders who shared this conviction quite naturally felt less and less constrained to obey native rules governing proper behavior. Abuses against Indians mounted until some men were literally getting away with murder. When repeated appeals to colonial officials failed, natives throughout Carolina began to consider war. Persuaded by Yamassee ambassadors that the conspiracy was widespread and convinced by years of ruthless commercial competition between Virginia and Carolina that an attack on one colony would not affect relations with the other, in the spring of 1715 Catawbas and their neighbors joined the invasion of South Carolina.

The decision to fight was disastrous. Colonists everywhere shut off the flow of goods to the interior, and after some initial successes Carolina's native enemies soon plumbed the depths of their dependence. In a matter of months, refugees holed up in Charleston noticed that "the Indians want ammunition and are not able to mend their Arms." The peace negotiations that ensued revealed a desperate thirst for fresh supplies of European wares. Ambassadors from piedmont towns invariably spoke in a single breath of restoring "a Peace and a free Trade," and one delegation even admitted that its people "cannot live without the assistance of the English." . . .

By the end of the colonial period delicate negotiations across cultural boundaries were as familiar to Catawbas as the strouds they wore and the muskets they carried. But no matter how shrewdly the headmen loosened provincial purse strings to extract vital merchandise, they could not escape the simple fact that they no longer held the purse containing everything needed for their daily existence. In the space of a century the Indians had become thoroughly embedded in an alien economy, denizens of a new material world. The ancient self-sufficiency was only a dim memory in the minds of the Nation's elders.

The Catawba peoples were veterans of countless campaigns against disease and masters of the arts of trade long before the third major element of their new world, white planters, became an integral part of their life. Settlement of the Carolina uplands did not begin until the 1730s, but once underway it spread with frightening speed. In November 1752, concerned Catawbas reminded South Carolina governor James Glen how they had "complained already . . . that the white People were settled too near us." Two years later five hundred families lived within thirty miles of the Nation and surveyors were running their lines into the middle of native towns. "[T]hose Indians are now in a fair way to be surrounded by White People," one observer concluded.

Settlers' attitudes were as alarming as their numbers. Unlike traders who profited from them or colonial officials who deployed them as allies, ordinary colonists had little use for Indians. Natives made poor servants and worse slaves; they obstructed settlement; they attracted enemy warriors to the area. Even men who respected Indians and earned a living by trading with them admitted that they made unpleasant neighbors. "We may observe of them as of the fire," wrote the South Carolina trader James Adair after considering the Catawbas' situation on the eve of the American Revolution, "'it is safe and useful, cherished at proper distance; but if too near us, it becomes dangerous, and will scorch if not consume us.'"

A common fondness for alcohol increased the likelihood of intercultural hostilities. Catawba leaders acknowledged that the Indians "get very Drunk with [liquor] this is the Very Cause that they oftentimes Commit those Crimes that is offencive to You and us." Colonists were equally prone to bouts of drunkenness. In the 1760s the itinerant Anglican minister, Charles Woodmason, was shocked to find the citizens of one South Carolina upcountry community "continually drunk." More appalling still, after attending church services "one half of them got drunk before they went home." Indians sometimes suffered at the hands of intoxicated farmers. In 1760 a Catawba woman was murdered when she happened by a tavern shortly after four of its patrons "swore they would kill the first Indian they should meet with."

Even when sober, natives and newcomers found many reasons to quarrel. Catawbas were outraged if colonists built farms on the Indians' doorstep or tramped across ancient burial grounds. Planters, ignorant of (or indifferent to) native rules of hospitality, considered Indians who requested food nothing more than beggars and angrily drove them away. Other disputes arose when the Nation's young men went looking for trouble. As hunting, warfare, and other traditional avenues for achieving status narrowed, Catawba youths transferred older patterns of behavior into a new arena by raiding nearby farms and hunting cattle or horses.

Contrasting images of the piedmont landscape quite unintentionally generated still more friction. Colonists determined to tame what they considered a wilderness were in fact erasing a native signature on the land and scrawling their own. Bridges, buildings, fences, roads, crops, and other "improvements" made the area comfortable and familiar to colonists but uncomfortable and unfamiliar to Indians. "The Country side wear[s] a New face," proclaimed Woodmason proudly; to the original inhabitants, it was a grim face indeed. "His Land was spoiled," one Catawba headman told British officials in 1763. "They have spoiled him 100 Miles every way." Under these circumstances, even a settler with no wish to fight Indians met opposition to his fences, his outbuildings, his very presence. Similarly, a Catawba on a routine foray into traditional hunting territories had his weapon destroyed, his goods confiscated, his life threatened by men with different notions of the proper use of the land.

To make matters worse, the importance both cultures attached to personal independence hampered efforts by authorities on either side to resolve conflicts. Piedmont settlers along the border between the Carolinas were "people of desperate fortune," a frightened North Carolina official reported after visiting the area. "[N]o officer of Justice from either Province dare meddle with them." Woodmason, who spent even more time in the region, came to the same conclusion. "We are without any Law, or Order," he complained; the inhabitants' "Impudence is so very high, as to be past bearing." Catawba leaders could have sympathized. Headmen informed colonists that the Nation's people "are oftentimes Cautioned from . . . ill Doings altho' to no purpose for we Cannot be present at all times to Look after them." "What they have done I could not prevent," one chief explained. . . .

The Indians would have to find some way to get along with these unpleasant neighbors if the Nation was to survive. As Catawba population fell below five hundred after the smallpox epidemic of 1759 and the number of colonists continued to climb, natives gradually came to recognize the futility of violent resistance. During the last decades of the eighteenth century they drew on years of experience in dealing with Europeans at a distance and sought to overturn the common conviction that Indian neighbors were frightening and useless. . . .

Catawbas took one of the first steps along the road to accommodation in the early 1760s, when they used their influence with colonial officials to acquire a reservation encompassing the heart of their ancient territories. This grant gave the Indians a land base, grounded in Anglo-American law, that prevented farmers from shouldering them aside. Equally important, Catawbas now had a commodity to exchange with nearby settlers. These men wanted land, the natives had plenty, and shortly before the Revolution the Nation was renting tracts to planters for cash, livestock, and manufactured goods.

Important as it was, land was not the only item Catawbas began trading to their neighbors. Some Indians put their skills as hunters and woodsmen to a different use, picking up stray horses and escaped slaves for a reward. Others bartered their pottery, baskets, and table mats. Still others traveled through the upcountry, demonstrating their prowess with the bow and arrow before appreciative audiences. The exchange of these goods and services for European merchandise marked an important adjustment to the settlers' arrival. In the past, natives had acquired essential items by trading peltry and slaves or requesting gifts from representatives of the Crown. But piedmont planters frowned on hunting and warfare, while provincial authorities— finding Catawbas less useful as the Nation's population declined and the French threat disappeared—discouraged formal visits and handed out fewer presents. Hence the Indians had to develop new avenues of exchange that would enable them to obtain goods in ways less objectionable to their neighbors. Pots, baskets, and acres proved harmless substitutes for earlier methods of earning an income.

Quite apart from its economic benefits, trade had a profound impact on the character of Catawba-settler relations. Through countless repetitions of the same simple procedure at homesteads scattered across the Carolinas, a new form of intercourse arose, based not on suspicion and an expectation of conflict but on trust and a measure of friendship. When a farmer looked out his window and saw Indians approaching, his reaction more commonly became to pick up money or a jug of whiskey rather than a musket or an axe. The natives now appeared, the settler knew, not to plunder or kill but to peddle their wares or collect their rents. . . .

On that August day in 1608 when Amoroleck feared the loss of his world, John Smith assured him that the English "came to them in peace, and to seeke their loves." Events soon proved Amoroleck right and his captor wrong. Over the course of the next three centuries not only Amoroleck and other piedmont Indians but natives throughout North America had their world stolen and another put in its place. Though this occurred at different times and in different ways, no Indians escaped the explosive mixture of deadly bacteria, material riches, and alien peoples that was the invasion of America. Those in the southern piedmont who survived the onslaught were ensconced in their new world by the end of the eighteenth century.

Population levels stabilized as the Catawba peoples developed immunities to once-lethal diseases. Rents, sales of pottery, and other economic activities proved adequate to support the Nation at a stable (if low) level of material life. Finally, the Indians' image as "inoffensive" neighbors gave them a place in South Carolina society and continues to sustain them today.

Vast differences separated Catawbas and other natives from their colonial contemporaries. Europeans were the colonizers, Africans the enslaved, Indians the dispossessed; from these distinct positions came distinct histories. Yet once we acknowledge the differences, instructive similarities remain that help to integrate natives more thoroughly into the story of early America. By carving a niche for themselves in response to drastically different conditions, the peoples who composed the Catawba Nation shared in the most fundamental of American experiences. Like Afro-Americans, these Indians were compelled to accept a subordinate position in American life yet did not altogether lose their cultural integrity. Like settlers of the Chesapeake, aboriginal inhabitants of the uplands adjusted to appalling mortality rates and wrestled with the difficult task of "living with death." Like inhabitants of the Middle Colonies, piedmont groups learned to cope with unprecedented ethnic diversity by balancing the pull of traditional loyalties with the demands of a new social order. Like Puritans in New England, Catawbas found that a new world did not arrive all at once and that localism, self-sufficiency, and the power of old ways were only gradually eroded by conditions in colonial America.

The Indians' Old World

NEAL SALISBURY

Scholars in history, anthropology, archaeology, and other disciplines have turned increasingly over the past two decades to the study of native peoples during the colonial period of North American history. The new work in Indian history has altered the way we think about the beginning of American history and about the era of European colonization. Historians now recognize that Europeans arrived, not in a virgin land, but in one that was teeming with several million people. Beyond filling in some of the vast blanks left by previous generations' overlooking of Indians, much of this scholarship makes clear that Indians are integral to the history of colonial North America. In short, surveys of recent textbooks and of scholarly titles suggest that Native Americans are well on their way to being "mainstreamed" by colonial historians.

Substantive as this reorientation is, it remains limited. Beyond the problems inherent in representing Indian/non-Indian interactions during the colonial era lies the challenge of contextualizing the era itself. Despite opening chapters and lectures that survey the continent's native peoples and cultures, most historians continue to represent American history as having been set in motion by the arrival of European explorers and colonizers. They have yet to recognize the existence of a North

Neal Salisbury, "The Indians' Old World: Native Americans and the Coming of the Europeans," *William and Mary Quarterly,* 3rd ser., 53, no. 3 (July 1996): 435–437, 439–441, 443, 449, 451–455, 457–458. Reprinted by permission of William and Mary Quarterly.

American—as opposed to English or European—background for colonial history, much less to consider the implications of such a background for understanding the three centuries following Columbus's landfall. Yet a growing body of scholarship by archaeologists, linguists, and students of Native American expressive traditions recognizes 1492 not as a beginning but as a single moment in a long history utterly detached from that of Europe. These findings call into question historians' synchronic maps and verbal descriptions of precontact Indians—their cultures, their communities, their ethnic and political designations and affiliations, and their relations with one another. Do these really describe enduring entities or do they represent epiphenomena of arbitrary moments in time? If the latter should prove to be the case, how will readings of Indian history in the colonial period be affected? . . .

. . . [I]ndigenous North Americans exhibited a remarkable range of languages, economies, political systems, beliefs, and material cultures. But this range was less the result of their isolation from one another than of the widely varying natural and social environments with which Indians had interacted over millennia. What recent scholars of precolonial North America have found even more striking, given this diversity, is the extent to which native peoples' histories intersected one another.

At the heart of these intersections was exchange. By exchange is meant not only the trading of material goods but also exchanges across community lines of marriage partners, resources, labor, ideas, techniques, and religious practices. Longer-distance exchanges frequently crossed cultural and linguistic boundaries as well and ranged from casual encounters to widespread alliances and networks that were economic, political, and religious. For both individuals and communities, exchanges sealed social and political relationships. Rather than accumulate material wealth endlessly, those who acquired it gave it away, thereby earning prestige and placing obligations on others to reciprocate appropriately. And as we shall see, many goods were not given away to others in this world but were buried with individuals to accompany them to another. . . .

By the twelfth century, agricultural production had spread over much of the Eastern Woodlands as well as to more of the Southwest. In both regions, . . . more complex societies were emerging to dominate widespread exchange networks. In the Mississippi Valley and the Southeast, the sudden primacy of maize horticulture is marked archaeologically in a variety of ways—food remains, pollen profiles, studies of human bone (showing that maize accounted for 50 percent of people's diets), and in material culture by a proliferation of chert hoes, shell-tempered pottery for storing and cooking, and pits for storing surplus crops. These developments were accompanied by the rise of what archaeologists term "Mississippian" societies, consisting of fortified political and ceremonial centers and outlying villages. The centers were built around open plazas featuring platform burial mounds, temples, and elaborate residences for elite families. Evidence from burials makes clear the wide social gulf that separated commoners from elites. Whereas the former were buried in simple graves with a few personal possessions, the latter were interred in the temples or plazas along with many more, and more elaborate, goods such as copper ornaments, massive sheets of shell, and ceremonial weapons. Skeletal evidence indicates that elites ate more meat, were taller, performed less strenuous physical activity, and were less prone to illness and accident than commoners. Although most archaeologists' conclusions are informed at least in part by models developed

by political anthropologists, they also draw heavily from Spanish and French observations of some of the last Mississippian societies. These observations confirm
that political leaders, or chiefs, from elite families mobilized labor, collected tribute,
redistributed agricultural surpluses, coordinated trade, diplomacy, and military activity, and were worshipped as deities.

The largest, most complex Mississippian center was Cahokia, located not far
from the confluence of the Mississippi and Missouri rivers, near modern East St.
Louis, Illinois, in the rich floodplain known as American Bottoms. By the twelfth
century, Cahokia probably numbered 20,000 people and contained over 120 mounds
within a five-square-mile area. . . . One key to Cahokia's rise was its combination
of rich soil and nearby wooded uplands, enabling inhabitants to produce surplus
crops while providing an abundance and diversity of wild food sources along with
ample supplies of wood for fuel and construction. A second key was its location,
affording access to the great river systems of the North American interior.

Cahokia had the most elaborate social structure yet seen in North America.
Laborers used stone and wooden spades to dig soil from "borrow pits" (at least nineteen have been identified by archaeologists), which they carried in wooden buckets
to mounds and palisades often more than half a mile away. The volume and concentration of craft activity in shell, copper, clay, and other materials, both local and
imported, suggests that specialized artisans provided the material foundation for
Cahokia's exchange ties with other peoples. Although most Cahokians were buried
in mass graves outside the palisades, their rulers were given special treatment. At a
prominent location in Mound 72, the largest of Cahokia's platform mounds, a man
had been buried atop a platform of shell beads. Accompanying him were several
group burials: fifty young women, aged 18 to 23, four men, and three men and three
women, all encased in uncommonly large amounts of exotic materials. As with the
Natchez Indians observed by the French in Louisiana, Cahokians appear to have
sacrificed individuals to accompany their leaders in the afterlife. Cahokia was surrounded by nine smaller mound centers and several dozen villages from which it
obtained much of its food and through which it conducted its waterborne commerce
with other Mississippian centers in the Midwest and Southeast. . . .

At the outset of the twelfth century, the center of production and exchange in
the Southwest was in the basin of the San Juan River at Chaco Canyon in New
Mexico, where Anasazi culture achieved its most elaborate expression. A twelve-
mile stretch of the canyon and its rim held twelve large planned towns on the north
side and 200 to 350 apparently unplanned villages on the south. The total population was probably about 15,000. The towns consisted of 200 or more contiguous,
multistoried rooms, along with numerous kivas (underground ceremonial areas),
constructed of veneered masonry walls and log beams imported from upland areas
nearly fifty miles distant. The rooms surrounded a central plaza with a great kiva.
Villages typically had ten to twenty rooms that were decidedly smaller than those
in the towns. Nearly all of Chaco Canyon's turquoise, shell, and other ornaments
and virtually everything imported from Mesoamerica are found in the towns rather
than the villages. Whether the goods were considered communal property or were
the possessions of elites is uncertain, but either way the towns clearly had primacy.
Villagers buried their dead near their residences, whereas town burial grounds were
apparently located at greater distances, although only a very few of what must have

been thousands of town burials have been located by archaeologists. Finally, and of particular importance in the arid environment of the region, the towns were located at the mouths of side canyons where they controlled the collection and distribution of water run-off. . . .

The canyon was the core of an extensive network of at least seventy towns or "outliers," as they are termed in the archaeological literature, and 5,300 villages located as far as sixty miles from the canyon. . . . Facilitating the movement of people and goods through this network was a system of roads radiating outward from the canyon in perfectly straight lines, turning into stairways or footholds rather than circumventing cliffs and other obstacles. . . .

When Europeans reached North America . . . the continent's demographic and political map was in a state of profound flux. A major factor was the collapse of the great centers at Cahokia and Chaco Canyon and elsewhere in the Midwest and Southwest. Although there were significant differences between these highly centralized societies, each ran up against the capacity of the land or other resources to sustain it. This is not to argue for a simple ecological determinism for, although environmental fluctuations played a role, the severe strains in each region resulted above all from a series of human choices that had brought about unprecedented concentrations of people and power. Having repudiated those choices and dispersed, midwestern Mississippians and Anasazis formed new communities in which they retained kinship, ceremonial, and other traditions antedating these complex societies. At the same time, these new communities and neighboring ones sought to flourish in their new political and environmental settings by establishing, and in some cases endeavoring to control, new exchange networks.

Such combinations of continuity and change, persistence and adaptability, arose from concrete historical experiences rather than a timeless tradition. The remainder of this [essay] indicates some of the ways that both the deeply rooted imperatives of reciprocity and exchange and the recent legacies of competition and upheaval informed North American history as Europeans began to make their presence felt.

Discussion of the transition from pre- to postcontact times must begin with the sixteenth century, when Indians and Europeans met and interacted in a variety of settings. When not slighting the era altogether, historians have viewed it as one of discovery or exploration, citing the achievements of notable Europeans in either anticipating or failing to anticipate the successful colonial enterprises of the seventeenth century. Recently, however, a number of scholars have been integrating information from European accounts with the findings of archaeologists to produce a much fuller picture of this critical period in North American history.

The Southeast was the scene of the most formidable attempts at colonization during the sixteenth century, primarily by Spain. Yet in spite of several expeditions to the interior and the undertaking of an ambitious colonizing and missionary effort, extending from St. Augustine over much of the Florida peninsula and north to Chesapeake Bay, the Spanish retained no permanent settlements beyond St. Augustine itself at the end of the century. Nevertheless, their explorers and missionaries opened the way for the spread of smallpox and other epidemic diseases over much of the area south of the Chesapeake and east of the Mississippi. . . .

As in the Southeast, Spanish colonizers in the sixteenth-century Southwest launched several ambitious military and missionary efforts, hoping to extend New Spain's domain northward and to discover additional sources of wealth. The best-documented encounters of Spanish with Pueblos—most notably those of Coronado's expedition (1540–1542)—ended in violence and failure for the Spanish who, despite vows to proceed peacefully, violated Pueblo norms of reciprocity by insisting on excessive tribute or outright submission. In addition, the Spanish had acquired notoriety among the Pueblos as purveyors of epidemic diseases, religious missions, and slaving expeditions inflicted on Indians to the south, in what is now northern Mexico.

The Spanish also affected patterns of exchange throughout the Southwest. Indians resisting the spread of Spanish rule to northern Mexico stole horses and other livestock, some of which they traded to neighbors. By the end of the sixteenth century, a few Indians on the periphery of the Southwest were riding horses, anticipating the combination of theft and exchange that would spread horses to native peoples throughout the region and, still later, the Plains and the Southeast. In the meantime, some Navajos and Apaches moved near the Rio Grande Valley, strengthening ties with certain pueblos that were reinforced when inhabitants of those pueblos sought refuge among them in the face or wake of Spanish *entradas*.

Yet another variation on the theme of Indian-European contacts in the sixteenth century was played out in the Northeast, where Iroquoian-speaking villagers on the Mississippian periphery and Archaic hunter-gatherers still further removed from developments in the interior met Europeans of several nationalities. At the outset of the century, Spanish and Portuguese explorers enslaved several dozen Micmacs and other Indians from the Nova Scotia–Gulf of St. Lawrence area. Three French expeditions to the St. Lawrence itself in the 1530s and 1540s followed the Spanish pattern by alienating most Indians encountered and ending in futility. Even as these hostile contacts were taking place, fishermen, whalers, and other Europeans who visited the area regularly had begun trading with natives. As early as the 1520s, Abenakis on the coast of Maine and Micmacs were trading the furs of beavers and other animals for European goods of metal and glass. By the 1540s, specialized fur traders, mostly French, frequented the coast as far south as the Chesapeake; by the 1550s or soon thereafter, French traders rendezvoused regularly with Indians along the shores of upper New England, the Maritimes, and Quebec and at Tadoussac on the St. Lawrence.

What induced Indians to go out of their way to trap beaver and trade the skins for glass beads, mirrors, copper kettles, and other goods? Throughout North America since Paleo-Indian times, exchange in the Northeast was the means by which people maintained and extended their social, cultural, and spiritual horizons as well as acquired items considered supernaturally powerful. Members of some coastal Indian groups later recalled how the first Europeans they saw, with their facial hair and strange clothes and traveling in their strange boats, seemed like supernatural figures. Although soon disabused of such notions, these Indians and many more inland placed special value on the glass beads and other trinkets offered by the newcomers. Recent scholarship on Indians' motives in this earliest stage of the trade indicates that they regarded such objects as the equivalents of the quartz, mica, shell, and other sacred substances that had formed the heart of long-distance exchange in North America for millennia and that they regarded as sources of physical and spiritual well-being, on earth and in the afterlife. Indians initially altered and wore many of the utilitarian goods they received, such as iron axe heads and copper pots, rather than use them for their intended purposes, Moreover, even though the new objects might pass through many hands, they more often than not ended up in graves, presumably for their possessors to use in the afterlife. Finally, the archaeological findings make clear that shell and native copper predominated over the new objects in sixteenth-century exchanges, indicating that European trade did not suddenly trigger a massive craving for the objects themselves. While northeastern Indians recognized Europeans as different from themselves, they interacted with them and their materials in ways that were consistent with their own customs and beliefs.

By the late sixteenth century, the effects of European trade began to overlap with the effects of earlier upheavals in the northeastern interior. Sometime between Jacques Cartier's final departure in 1543 and Samuel de Champlain's arrival in 1603, the Iroquoian-speaking inhabitants of Hochelaga and Stadacona (modern Montreal and Quebec City) abandoned their communities. The communities were crushed militarily, and the survivors dispersed among both Iroquois and Hurons. Whether the perpetrators of these dispersals were Iroquois or Huron is a point of controversy, but either way the St. Lawrence communities appear to have been casualties of the rivalry, at least a century old, between the two confederations as each sought to position itself vis-à-vis the French. The effect, if not the cause, of the dispersals was the Iroquois practice of attacking antagonists who denied them direct access to trade goods; this is consistent with Iroquois actions during the preceding two centuries and the century that followed.

The sudden availability of many more European goods, the absorption of many refugees from the St. Lawrence, and the heightening of tensions with the Iroquois help to explain the movement of most outlying Huron communities to what is now the Simcoe County area of Ontario during the 1580s. This geographic concentration strengthened their confederacy and gave it the form it had when allied with New France during the first half of the seventeenth century. Having formerly existed at the outer margins of an arena of exchange centered in Cahokia, the Hurons and Iroquois now faced a new source of goods and power to the east.

The diverse native societies encountered by Europeans as they began to settle North America permanently during the seventeenth century were not static isolates lying outside the ebb and flow of human history. Rather, they were products of a complex set of historical forces, both local and wide ranging, both deeply rooted and of recent origin. Although their lives and worldviews were shaped by long-standing traditions of reciprocity and spiritual power, the people in these communities were also accustomed—contrary to popular myths about inflexible Indians—to economic and political flux and to absorbing new peoples (both allies and antagonists), objects, and ideas, including those originating in Europe. Such combinations of tradition and innovation continued to shape Indians' relations with Europeans, even as the latter's visits became permanent.

The establishment of lasting European colonies, beginning with New Mexico in 1598, began a phase in the continent's history that eventually resulted in the displacement of Indians to the economic, political, and cultural margins of a new order. But during the interim natives and colonizers entered into numerous relationships in which they exchanged material goods and often supported one another diplomatically or militarily against common enemies. These relations combined native and European modes of exchange. While much of the scholarly literature emphasizes the subordination and dependence of Indians in these circumstances, Indians as much as Europeans dictated the form and content of their early exchanges and alliances. Much of the protocol and ritual surrounding such intercultural contacts was rooted in indigenous kinship obligations and gift exchanges, and Indian consumers exhibited decided preferences for European commodities that satisfied social, spiritual, and aesthetic values. Similarly, Indians' long-range motives and strategies in their alliances with Europeans were frequently rooted in older patterns of alliance and rivalry with regional neighbors. Such continuities can be glimpsed through a brief consideration of the early colonial-era histories of the Five Nations Iroquois in the Northeast, the Creeks in the Southeast, and the Rio Grande Pueblos in the Southwest.

Post-Mississippian and sixteenth-century patterns of antagonism between the Iroquois and their neighbors to the north and west persisted, albeit under altered circumstances, during the seventeenth century when France established its colony on the St. Lawrence and allied itself with Hurons and other Indians. France aimed to extract maximum profits from the fur trade, and it immediately recognized the Iroquois as the major threat to that goal. In response, the Iroquois turned to the Dutch in New Netherland for guns and other trade goods while raiding New France's Indian allies for the thicker northern pelts that brought higher prices than those in their own country (which they exhausted by midcentury) and for captives to replace those from their own ranks who had died from epidemics or in wars. During the 1640s, the Iroquois replaced raids with full-scale military assaults (the so-called Beaver Wars) on Iroquoian-speaking communities in the lower Great Lakes, absorbing most of the survivors as refugees or captives. All the while, the Iroquois elaborated a vision of their confederation, which had brought harmony within their own ranks, as bringing peace to all peoples of the region. For the remainder of the century, the Five Nations fought a grueling and costly series of wars against the French and their Indian allies in order to gain access to the pelts and French goods circulating in lands to the north and west.

Meanwhile, the Iroquois were also adapting to the growing presence of English colonists along the Atlantic seaboard. . . . After the English supplanted the Dutch in New York in 1664, Iroquois diplomats established relations with the proprietary governor, Sir Edmund Andros, in a treaty known as the Covenant Chain. The Covenant Chain was an elaboration of the Iroquois' earlier treaty arrangements with the Dutch, but, whereas the Iroquois had termed the Dutch relationship a chain of iron, they referred to the one with the English as a chain of silver. The shift in metaphors was appropriate, for what had been strictly an economic connection was now a political one in which the Iroquois acquired power over other New York Indians. After 1677, the Covenant Chain was expanded to include several English colonies, most notably Massachusetts and Maryland, along with those colonies' subject Indians. The upshot of these arrangements was that the Iroquois cooperated with their colonial partners in subduing and removing subject Indians who impeded settler expansion. The Mohawks in particular played a vital role in the New England colonies' suppression of the Indian uprising known as King Philip's War and in moving the Susquehannocks away from the expanding frontier of settlement in the Chesapeake after Bacon's Rebellion.

For the Iroquois, such a policy helped expand their "Tree of Peace" among Indians while providing them with buffers against settler encroachment around their homelands. The major drawback in the arrangement proved to be the weakness of English military assistance against the French. This inadequacy, and the consequent suffering experienced by the Iroquois during two decades of war after 1680, finally drove the Five Nations to make peace with the French and their Indian allies in the Grand Settlement of 1701. Together, the Grand Settlement and Covenant Chain provided the Iroquois with the peace and security, the access to trade goods, and the dominant role among northeastern Indians they had long sought. That these arrangements in the long run served to reinforce rather than deter English encroachment on Iroquois lands and autonomy should not obscure their pre-European roots and their importance in shaping colonial history in the Northeast.

In the southeastern interior, . . . descendants of refugees from Coosa and neighboring communities regrouped in clusters of Creek *talwas* (villages), each dominated by a large talwa and its "great chief." In the late seventeenth century, these latter-day chiefdom/provinces forged alliances with English traders, first from Virginia and then from Carolina, who sought to trade guns and other manufactured goods for deerskins and Indian slaves. In so doing, the Creeks ensured that they would be regarded by the English as clients rather than as commodities. The deerskin trade proved to be a critical factor in South Carolina's early economic development, and the trade in Indian slaves significantly served England's imperial ambitions vis-à-vis Spain in Florida. After 1715, the several Creek alliances acted in concert as a confederacy—the Creek Nation—on certain occasions. As a result, they achieved a measure of success in playing off these powers and maintaining neutrality in their conflicts with one another. While much differentiates Creek political processes in the colonial period from those of the late Mississippian era, there are strong elements of continuity in the transformation of Mississippian chiefdoms into great Creek talwas.

In the Southwest, the institution of Spanish colonial rule on the Rio Grande after 1598 further affected exchange relations between Pueblo Indians and nearby Apaches and Navajos. By imposing heavy demands for tribute in the form of corn, the Spanish prevented Pueblo peoples from trading surplus produce with their non-farming neighbors. In order to obtain the produce on which they had come to depend, Apaches and Navajos staged deadly raids on some pueblos, leaving the inhabitants dependent on the Spanish for protection. In retaliation, Spanish soldiers captured Apaches and Navajos whom they sold as slaves to their countrymen to the south. From the beginning, the trading pueblos of Pecos, Picuris, and Taos most resented Spanish control and strongly resisted the proselytizing of Franciscan missionaries. From the late 1660s, drought and disease, intensified Apache and Navajo raids, and the severity of Spanish rule led more and more Indians from all pueblos to question the advantages of Christianity and to renew their ties to their indigenous religious traditions. Spanish persecution of native religious leaders and their backsliding followers precipitated the Pueblo Revolt of 1680, in which the trading

Pueblos played a leading role and which was actively supported by some Navajos and Apaches.

When the Spanish reimposed their rule during the 1690s, they tolerated traditional Indian religion rather than trying to extirpate it, and they participated in interregional trade fairs at Taos and other villages. The successful incorporation of Pueblo Indians as loyal subjects proved vital to New Mexico's survival as a colony and, more generally, to Spain's imperial presence in the Southwest during the eighteenth and early nineteenth centuries.

As significant as is the divide separating pre- and post-Columbian North American history, it is not the stark gap suggested by the distinction between prehistory and history. For varying periods of time after their arrival in North America, Europeans adapted to the social and political environments they found, including the fluctuating ties of reciprocity and interdependence as well as rivalry, that characterized those environments. They had little choice but to enter in and participate if they wished to sustain their presence. Eventually, one route to success proved to be their ability to insert themselves as regional powers in new networks of exchange and alliance that arose to supplant those of the Mississippians, Anasazis, and others.

To assert such continuities does not minimize the radical transformations entailed in Europeans' colonization of the continent and its indigenous peoples. Arising in Cahokia's wake, new centers at Montreal, Fort Orange/Albany, Charleston, and elsewhere permanently altered the primary patterns of exchange in eastern North America. The riverine system that channeled exchange in the interior of the continent gave way to one in which growing quantities of goods arrived from, and were directed to, coastal peripheries and ultimately Europe. In the Southwest, the Spanish revived Anasazi links with Mesoamerica at some cost to newer ties between the Rio Grande Pueblos and recently arrived, nonfarming Athapaskan speakers. More generally, European colonizers brought a complex of demographic and ecological advantages, most notably epidemic diseases and their own immunity to them, that utterly devastated Indian communities; ideologies and beliefs in their cultural and spiritual superiority to native peoples and their entitlement to natives' lands; and economic, political, and military systems organized for the engrossment of Indian lands and the subordination or suppression of Indian peoples.

Europeans were anything but uniformly successful in realizing their goals, but the combination of demographic and ecological advantages and imperial intentions, along with the Anglo-Iroquois Covenant Chain, enabled land-hungry colonists from New England to the Chesapeake to break entirely free of ties of dependence on Indians before the end of the seventeenth century. Their successes proved to be only the beginning of a new phase of Indian-European relations. By the mid-eighteenth century, the rapid expansion of land-based settlement in the English colonies had sundered older ties of exchange and alliance linking natives and colonizers nearly everywhere east of the Appalachians, driving many Indians west and reducing those who remained to a scattering of politically powerless enclaves in which Indian identities were nurtured in isolation. Meanwhile, the colonizers threatened to extend this new mode of Indian relations across the Appalachians. An old world, rooted in indigenous exchange, was giving way to one in which Native Americans had no certain place.

FURTHER READING

James Axtell, *The Invasion Within: The Contest of Cultures in Colonial North America* (1986).

Alfred W. Crosby, *The Columbian Exchange: Biological and Cultural Consequences of 1492* (1972).

Brian Fagan, *Kingdoms of Gold, Kingdoms of Jade: The Americas Before Columbus* (1991).

Francis Jennings, *The Founders of America: From the Earliest Migrations to the Present* (1993).

Karen O. Kupperman, *Settling with the Indians: The Meeting of English and Indian Cultures in America, 1580–1640* (1980).

William and Carla Phillips, *The Worlds of Christopher Columbus* (1992).

Daniel K. Richter, *The Ordeal of the Longhouse: The Peoples of the Iroquois League in the Era of European Colonization* (1992).

David J. Weber, *The Spanish Frontier in North America* (1993).

Richard White, *The Middle Ground: Indians, Empires, and Republics in the Great Lakes Region, 1650–1815* (1991).

CHAPTER
2

The Southern Colonies
in British America

On April 26, 1607, a group of ships bearing 128 men sailed into Chesapeake Bay and began the settlement of Jamestown, the first successful English plantation in the Americas. The English had attempted to form colonies beginning in the sixteenth century in locations as varied as present-day Maine and Virginia, but all had failed. Jamestown probably would have failed as well but for some fortunate circumstances. The colony's early years were horrific. The colonists were more interested in finding precious metals than in feeding themselves. Equally dangerous, they encountered a variety of new diseases in the swampland on which Jamestown was located. Many were gentlemen who felt it below their station to clear fields or build stockades. Nine months after their arrival, only thirty-eight of the English adventurers remained alive.

A series of developments, however, led the Jamestown colony out of its privation. After several more years of starvation and disease, the colonists began planting West Indian tobacco in 1611. Within two decades, tobacco exports grew to 1.5 million pounds. Tobacco was a demanding crop. It rapidly depleted the soil, which increased the demand for land, and it required intensive labor, which led to the importation of unfree workers. Colonists, including former indentured servants, increasingly looked to the land controlled by Indians, leading to conflict between the two groups. This was the basis of the demands in Bacon's Rebellion in 1676. Although the bound laborers tended to be European indentured servants in the early years, African slaves later began to replace them. Legal distinctions between servants and slaves at first were imprecise, but over time the status of African slaves in relation to English servants deteriorated. This decline in status coincided with an increase in the slave population. By 1690, the Chesapeake area contained more African slaves than European servants.

A series of other colonies that followed the Virginia pattern were subsequently formed. Maryland (founded in 1634), the Carolinas (1669), and Georgia (1732) joined profitable British colonies in the Caribbean and were based in large part on staple crops, increasingly tended by African slaves. Unlike the Chesapeake area, which continued to grow tobacco, South Carolina and Georgia relied on indigo, a purple dye, and on rice, whereas the Caribbean colonies produced sugar. Which crops were grown profoundly influenced the workers' lives. Sugar production was particularly toilsome, and rice demanded different rhythms of labor. In all of these colonies, however, the slave population grew until the Caribbean colonies and South Carolina had an African majority. In most regions of the South, colonies with slaves ultimately became slave colonies.

By the eighteenth century, race, status, and degree of freeness profoundly divided the inhabitants of the southern colonies. As wealthy planters profited from the labor of a slave population, they began to cultivate an ideal of paternalism that rested on the notion that planters and slaves alike were knit into a world based on reciprocity and obligation. In the growing slave quarters, a slave community was forged. Families were formed, children were socialized, and the community attempted to temper the horrors of slavery. To be sure, only a minority of white people owned slaves, but the nonslaveholding class too was influenced by the institution. If their "white" race gave them privilege, they were nonetheless expected to defer to the colony's slaveholding elite.

Q U E S T I O N S   T O   T H I N K   A B O U T

Historians have been deeply divided over the reasons why Africans became slaves and Europeans were servants. One school of thought focuses on an inherent racism within English society that differentiated Africans from Europeans and justified the enslavement of the former. Another school argues that decisions were made according to the price and availability of unfree laborers. Which makes the most sense? How did the increasing complexity of the colonial South change the relationships between rich and poor; black, red, and white; free and unfree?

D O C U M E N T S

The life of an English indentured servant could be difficult, as Document 1 indicates. In this letter to his parents, Richard Frethorne recounts the trials of living in seventeenth-century Virginia and pleads to return to England. In contrast, in Document 2, George Alsop contends that the indentured servants enjoy good fortune. You might wish to consider why these two accounts differ so much. Document 3 is the "declaration in the name of the people" issued by Nathaniel Bacon in 1676 that documents the misdeeds of Governor William Berkeley. Note how Bacon condemns Berkeley for favoring the Indians over the English. Document 4 is a selection of Virginia laws from 1660 to 1705 that illustrate the ways in which the position of African slaves hardened when compared with that of English servants. Document 5, the secret diary of William Byrd, a wealthy slaveholder in Virginia, illustrates a strange blend of devotion to God and learning with cruelty to slaves. Document 6 is a 1757 narrative written by Olaudah Equiano that describes the terror of enslavement in Africa, the journey to the West Indies, and the bewilderment and cruelties faced by slaves. Not all people in the southern colonies were masters, servants, or slaves. Document 7 gives the not-so-complimentary observations of Reverend Charles Woodmason, an Anglican minister who passed through the Carolina backcountry in 1768.

1. Richard Frethorne, an Indentured Servant, Laments His Condition in Virginia, 1623

Loving and kind father and mother, my most humble duty remembered to you hoping in God of your good health, as I my self am at the making hereof, this is to let you understand that I your Child am in a most heavy Case by reason of the nature of the Country is such that it Causeth much sickness, as the scurvy and the bloody flux [dysentery], and divers other diseases, which maketh the body very poor, and Weak, and when we are sick there is nothing to Comfort us; for since I came out of the ship, I never ate any thing but peas and loblollie (that is water gruel) as for deer or venison I never saw any since I came into this land, there is indeed some fowl, but We are not allowed to go and get it, but must Work hard both early and late for a mess of water gruel, and a mouthful of bread, and beef, a mouthful of bread for a penny loaf must serve for 4 men which is most pitiful if you did know as much as I, when people cry out day, and night, Oh that they were in England without their limbs and would not care to lose any limb to be in England again, yea though they beg from door to door, for we live in fear of the Enemy every hour, yet we have had a Combat with them on the Sunday before Shrovetide, and we took two alive, and make slaves of them. . . . [W]e are fain to get other men to plant with us, and yet we are but 32 to fight against 3000 if they should Come, and the nighest help that We have is ten miles of us, and when the rogues overcame this place last, they slew 80 persons. How then shall we doe for we lie even in their teeth, they may easily take us but that God is merciful, and can save with few as well as with many; as he showed to Gilead and like Gilead's soldiers if they lapped water, we drink water which is but Weak, and I have nothing to Comfort me, nor there is nothing to be gotten here but sickness, and death, except that one had money to lay out in some things for profit; But I have nothing at all, no not a shirt to my backe, but two Rags nor no Clothes, but one poor suit, nor but one pair of shoes, but one pair of stockings, but one Cap, but two bands, my Cloak is stolen by one of my own fellows. . . . I am not half a quarter so strong as I was in England, and all is for want of victuals, for I do protest unto you, that I have eaten more in a day at home than I have allowed me here for a Week. You have given more than my day's allowance to a beggar at the door. . . . [I]f you love me you will redeem me suddenly, for which I do entreat and beg, and if you cannot get the merchants to redeem me for some little money then for God's sake get a gathering or entreat some good folks to lay out some little sum of money, in meal, and Cheese and butter, and beef, any eating meat will yield great profit, . . . and look whatsoever you send me be it never so much, look what I make of it. I will deal truly with you. I will send it over, and beg the profit to redeem me, and if I die before it Come I have entreated Goodman Jackson to send you the worth of it, who hath promised he will. If you send you must direct your letter to Goodman Jackson, at James Town, a Gunsmith. . . . Good Father do not forget me, but have mercy and pity my miserable Case. I know if you did but see me you would weep to see me, for I have but one suit, but it is a strange one, it is very well guarded, wherefore for

Richard Frethorne to his mother and father, March–April, 1623. From Susan M. Kingsbury, ed., *Records of the Virginia Company,* IV (Washington, D.C.: U.S. Government Printing Office, 1935), 58–62.

God's sake pity me. I pray you to remember my love to all my friends, and kindred, I hope all my Brothers and sisters are in good health, and as for my part I have set down my resolution that certainly Will be, that is, that the Answer of this letter will be life or death to me, there good Father send as soon as you can, and if you send me any thing let this be the mark.

RICHARD FRETHORNE
Martin's Hundred

2. George Alsop Argues That Servants in Maryland Profit from Life in the Colonies, 1666

The necessariness of Servitude proved, with the common usage of Servants in Mary-Land, together with their Priviledges.

. . . There is no truer Emblem of Confusion either in Monarchy or Domestick Government, then when either the Subject, or the Servant, strives for the upper hand of his Prince, or Master, and to be equal with him, from whom he receives his present subsistace: Why then, if Servitude be so necessary that no place can be governed in order, nor people live without it, this may serve to tell those which prick up their ears and bray against it, That they are none but Asses, and deserve the Bridle of a strict commanding power to rein them in: For I'me certainly confident, that there are several Thousands in most Kingdoms of Christendom, that could not at all live and subsist, unless they had served some prefixed time, to learn either some Trade, Art, or Science, and by either of them to extract their present livelihood.

Then methinks this may stop the mouths of those that will undiscreetly compassionate them that dwell under necessary Servitudes. . . .

. . . [L]et such, where Providence hath ordained to life as Servants, either in England or beyond Sea, endure the pre-fixed yoak of their limited time with patience, and then in a small computation of years, by an industrious endeavour, they may become Masters and Mistresses of Families themselves. And let this be spoke to the deserved praise of Mary-Land. That the four years I served there were not to me so slavish, as a two years Servitude of a Handicraft Apprenticeship was here in London. . . .

They whose abilities cannot extend to purchase their own transportation over into Mary-Land, (and surely he that cannot command so small a sum for so great a matter, his life must needs be mighty low and dejected) I say they may for the debarment of a four years sordid liberty, go over into this Province and there live plentiously well. And what's a four years Servitude to advantage a man all the remainder of his dayes, making his predecessors happy in his sufficient abilities, which he attained to partly by the restrainment of so small a time? . . .

The Merchant commonly before they go aboard the Ship, or set themselves in any forwardness for their Voyage, has Conditions of Agreements drawn between

George Alsop, "A Character of the Province of Maryland, 1666," in C. C. Hall, ed., *Narratives of Early Maryland* (New York: Charles Scribner's Sons, 1910; copyright renewed Barnes and Noble, 1946), 354–360.

him and those that by a voluntary consent become his Servants, to serve him, his Heirs or Assigns, according as they in their primitive acquaintance have made their bargain, some two, some three, some four years; and whatever the Master or Servant tyes himself up to here in England by Condition, the Laws of the Province will force a performance of when they come there: Yet here is this Priviledge in it when they arrive. If they dwell not with the Merchant they made their first agreement withall, they may choose whom they will serve their prefixed time with; and after their curiosity has pitcht on one whom they think fit for their turn, and that they may live well withall, the Merchant makes an Assignment of the Indenture over to him whom they of their free will have chosen to be their Master, in the same nature as we here in England (and no otherwise) turn over Covenant Servants or Apprentices from one Master to another. Then let those whose chaps are always breathing forth those filthy dregs of abusive exclamations, . . . against this Country of Mary-Land, saying, That those which are transported over thither, are sold in open Market for Slaves, and draw in Carts like Horses; which is so damnable as untruth, that if they should search to the very Center of Hell, and enquire for a Lye of the most antient and damned stamp, I confidently believe they could not find one to parallel this: For know, That the Servants here in Mary-Land of all Colonies, distant or remote Plantations, have the least cause to complain, either for strictness of Servitude, want of Provisions, or need of Apparel: Five dayes and a half in the Summer weeks is the alotted time that they work in; and for two months, when the Sun predominates in the highest pitch of his heat, they claim an antient and customary Priviledge, to repose themselves three hours in the day within the house, and this is undeniably granted to them that work in the Fields.

In the Winter time, which lasteth three months (*viz.*) December, January, and February, they do little or no work or imployment, save cutting of wood to make good fires to sit by, unless their Ingenuity will prompt them to hunt the Deer, or Bear, or recreate themselves in Fowling, to slaughter the Swans, Geese, and Turkeys (which this Country affords in a most plentiful manner:) For every Servant has a Gun, Powder and Shot allowed him, to sport him withall on all Holidayes and leasurable times, if he be capable of using it, or be willing to learn. . . .

. . . He that lives in the nature of a Servant in this Province, must serve but four years by the Custom of the Country; and when the expiration of his time speaks him a Freeman, there's a Law in the Province, that enjoyns his Master whom he hath served to give him Fifty Acres of Land, Corn to serve him a whole year, three Sutes of Apparel, with things necessary to them, and Tools to work withall; so that they are no sooner free, but they are ready to set up for themselves, and when once entered, they live passingly well.

The Women that go over into this Province as Servants, have the best luck here as in any place of the world besides; for they are no sooner on shoar, but they are courted into a Copulative Matrimony, which some of them (for aught I know) had they not come to such a Market with their Virginity might have kept it by them until it had been mouldy. . . .

In short, touching the Servants of this Province, they live well in the time of their Service, and by their restrainment in that time, they are made capable of living much better when they come to be free; which in several other parts of the world I have observed, That after some servants have brought their indented and limited time to a just and legal period by Servitude, they have been much more incapable of supporting themselves from sinking into the Gulf of a slavish, poor, fettered, and intangled life, then all the fastness of their pre-fixed time did involve them in before.

3. Nathaniel Bacon Recounts the Misdeeds of the Virginia Governor, 1676

Declaration of Nathaniel Bacon in the Name of the
People of Virginia, July 30, 1676

1. For having, upon spacious pretences of public works, raised great unjust taxes upon the commonalty for the advancement of private favorites and other sinister ends, but no visible effects in any measure adequate; for not having, during this long time of his government, in any measure advanced this hopeful colony either by fortifications, towns, or trade.
2. For having abused and rendered contemptible the magistrates of justice by advancing to places of judicature scandalous and ignorant favorites.
3. For having wronged his Majesty's prerogative and interest by assuming monopoly of the beaver trade and for having in it unjust gain betrayed and sold his Majesty's country and the lives of his loyal subjects to the barbarous heathen.
4. For having protected, favored, and emboldened the Indians against his Majesty's loyal subjects, never contriving, requiring, or appointing any due or proper means of satisfaction for their many invasions, robberies, and murders committed upon us.
5. For having, when the army of English was just upon the track of those Indians, who now in all places burn, spoil, murder and when we might with ease have destroyed them who then were in open hostility, for then having expressly countermanded and sent back our army by passing his word for the peaceable demeanor of the said Indians, who immediately prosecuted their evil intentions, committing horrid murders and robberies in all places, being protected by the said engagement and word past of him the said Sir William Berkeley, having ruined and laid desolate a great part of his majesty's country, and have now drawn themselves into such obscure and remote places and are by their success so emboldened and confirmed by their confederacy so strengthened that the cries of blood are in all places, and the terror and consternation of the people so great, are now become not only a difficult but a very formidable enemy who might at first with ease have been destroyed.
6. And lately, when, upon the loud outcries of blood, the assembly had, with all care, raised and framed an army for the preventing of further mischief and safeguard of this his Majesty's colony.

"Nathaniel Bacon Esq'r, His Manifesto Concerning the Present Troubles in Virginia, 1676," *Virginia Magazine of History and Biography* 1 (1894): 55–61.

7. For having, with only the privacy of some few favorites without acquainting the people, only by the alteration of a figure, forged a commission, by we know not what hand, not only without but even against the consent of the people, for the raising and effecting civil war and destruction, which being happily and without bloodshed prevented; for having the second time attempted the same, thereby calling down our forces from the defense of the frontiers and most weakly exposed places.

8. For the prevention of civil mischief and ruin amongst ourselves while the barbarous enemy in all places did invade, murder, and spoil us, his Majesty's most faithful subjects.

Of this and the aforesaid articles we accuse Sir William Berkeley as guilty of each and every one of the same, and as one who has traitorously attempted, violated, and injured his Majesty's interest here by a loss of a great part of this his colony and many of his faithful loyal subjects by him betrayed and in a barbarous and shameful manner exposed to the incursions and murder of the heathen. And we do further declare these the ensuing persons in this list to have been his wicked and pernicious councillors, confederates, aiders, and assisters against the commonalty in these our civil commotions.

Sir Henry Chichley	*Nicholas Spencer*
Lt. Col. Christopher Wormeley	*Joseph Bridger*
Phillip Ludwell	*William Claiburne, Jr.*
Robt. Beverley	*Thomas Hawkins*
Ri: Lee	*William Sherwood*
Thomas Ballard	*John Page Clerke*
William Cole	*John Cluffe Clerk*
Richard Whitacre	

John West, Hubert Farrell, Thomas Reade, Math. Kempe.

And we do further demand that the said Sir William Berkeley with all the persons in this list be forthwith delivered up or surrender themselves within four days after the notice hereof, or otherwise we declare as follows.

That in whatsoever place, house, or ship, any of the said persons shall reside, be hid, or protected, we declare the owners, masters, or inhabitants of the said places to be confederates and traitors to the people and the estates of them is also of all the aforesaid persons to be confiscated. And this we, the commons of Virginia, do declare, desiring a firm union amongst ourselves that we may jointly and with one accord defend ourselves against the common enemy. And let not the faults of the guilty be the reproach of the innocent, or the faults or crimes of the oppressors divide and separate us who have suffered by their oppressions.

These are, therefore, in his Majesty's name, to command you forthwith to seize the persons abovementioned as traitors to the King and country and them to bring to Middle Plantation and there to secure them until further order, and, in case of opposition, if you want any further assistance you are forthwith to demand it in the name of the people in all the countries of Virginia.

Nathaniel Bacon
General by consent of the people.

4. Virginia's Statutes Illustrate the Declining Status of African American Slaves, 1660–1705

1660–1661, Act XXII.

English running away with negroes.

   BEE itt enacted That in case any English servant shall run away in company with any negroes who are incapable of makeing satisfaction by addition of time, *Bee itt enacted* that the English so running away in company with them shall serve for the time of the said negroes absence as they are to do for their owne by a former act.

1662, Act XII.

Negro womens children to serve according to the condition of the mother.

   WHEREAS some doubts have arrisen whether children got by any Englishman upon a negro woman should be slave or ffree, *Be it therefore enacted and declared by this present grand assembly,* that all children borne in this country shalbe held bond or free only according to the condition of the mother, *And* that if any christian shall commit ffornication with a negro man or woman, hee or shee soe offending shall pay double the ffines imposed by the former act.

1705, Chap. XLIX.

   IV. *And also be it enacted, by the authority aforesaid, and it is hereby enacted,* That all servants imported and brought into this country, by sea or land, who were not christians in their native country, (except Turks and Moors in amity with her majesty, and others that can make due proof of their being free in England, or any other christian country, before they were shipped, in order to transportation hither) shall be accounted and be slaves, and as such be here bought and sold notwithstanding a conversion to christianity afterwards. . . .

   VII. *And also be it enacted, by the authority aforesaid, and it is hereby enacted,* That all masters and owners of servants, shall find and provide for their servants, wholesome and competent diet, clothing, and lodging, by the discretion of the county courts and shall not, at any time, give immoderate corrections neither shall, at any time, whip a christian white servant naked, without an order from a justice of the peace. . . .

   X. *And be it also enacted,* That all servants, whether, by importation, indenture, or hire here, as well feme coverts, as others, shall, in like manner, as is provided, upon complaints of misusage, have their petitions received in court, for their wages and freedom. . . .

   XI. And for a further christian care and usage of all christian servants, *Be it also enacted, by the authority aforesaid, and it is hereby enacted,* That no negroes, mulattos, or Indians, although christians, or Jews, Moors, Mahometans, or other

The Statutes at Large: Being a Collection of all the Laws of Virginia, from the First Session of the Legislature, in the year 1619, Volumes I, II, III by William Waller Hening, © 1823.

infidels, shall, at any time, purchase any christian servant, nor any other, except of their own complexion, or such as are declared slaves by this act. . . .

XV. *And also be it enacted, by the authority aforesaid, and it is hereby enacted,* That no person whatsoever shall buy, sell, or receive of, to, or from, any servant, or slave, any coin or commodity whatsoever, without the leave, licence, or consent of the master or owner of the said servant, or slave. . . .

XVII. *And also be it enacted, by the authority aforesaid, and it is hereby enacted, and declared,* That in all cases of penal laws, whereby persons free are punishable by fine, servants shall be punished by whipping, after the rate of twenty lashes for every five hundred pounds of tobacco, or fifty shillings current money, unless the servant so culpable, can and will procure some person or persons to pay the fine. . . .

XVIII. And if any women servant shall be delivered of a bastard child within the time of her service aforesaid, *Be it enacted, by the authority aforesaid, and it is hereby enacted,* That in recompense of the loss and trouble occasioned her master or mistress thereby, she shall for every such offence, serve her said master or owner one whole year after her time by indenture, custom, and former order of court, shall be expired; or pay her said master or owner, one thousand pounds of tobacco; and the reputed father, if free, shall give security to the church-wardens of the parish where that child shall be, to maintain the child, and keep the parish indemnified; or be compelled thereto by order of the county court, upon the said church-wardens complaint. . . .

And if any woman servant shall be got with child by her master, neither the said master, nor his executors administrators, nor assigns, shall have any claim of service against her, for or by reason of such child; but she shall, when her time due to her said master, by indenture, custom or order of court, shall be expired, be sold by the church-wardens, for the time being, of the parish wherein such child shall be born, for one year, or pay one thousand pounds of tobacco; and the said one thousand pounds of tobacco, or whatever she shall be sold for, shall be emploied, by the vestry, to the use of the said parish. And if any woman servant shall have a bastard child by a negro, or mulatto, over and above the years service due to her master or owner, she shall immediately, upon the expiration of her time to her then present master or owner, pay down to the church-wardens of the parish wherein such child shall be born, for the use of the said parish, fifteen pounds current money of Virginia, or be by them sold for five years, to the use aforesaid: And if a free christian white woman shall have such bastard child, by a negro, or mulatto, for every such offence, she shall, within one month after her delivery of such bastard child, pay to the church-wardens for the time being, of the parish wherein such child shall be born, for the use of the said parish fifteen pounds current money of Virginia, or be by them sold for five years to the use aforesaid: And in both the said cases, the church-wardens shall bind the said child to be a servant, until it shall be of thirty one years of age.

XIX. And for a further prevention of that abominable mixture and spurious issue, which hereafter may increase in this her majesty's colony and dominion, as well by English, and other white men and women intermarrying with negros or mulattos, as by their unlawful coition with them, *Be it enacted, by the authority aforesaid, and it is hereby enacted,* That whatsoever English, or other white man or woman, being free, shall intermarry with a negro or mulatto man or woman, bond or free, shall, by judgment of the county court, be committed to prison, and there remain, during the space of six months, without bail or mainprize, and shall forfeit and pay ten pounds current money of Virginia, to the use of the parish, as aforesaid.

XX. *And be it further enacted,* That no minister of the church of England, or other minister, or person whatsoever, within this colony and dominion, shall hereafter wittingly presume to marry a white man with a negro or mulatto woman; or to marry a white woman with a negro or mulatto man, upon pain of forfeiting and paying, for every such marriage the sum of ten thousand pounds of tobacco.

5. William Byrd Describes His Views Toward Learning and His Slaves, 1709–1710

[February 22, 1709] I rose at 7 o'clock and read a chapter in Hebrew and 200 verses in Homer's Odyssey. I said my prayers and ate milk for breakfast. I threatened Anaka with a whipping if she did not confess the intrigues between Daniel and Nurse, but she prevented by a confession. I chided Nurse severely about it, but she denied, with an impudent face, protesting that Daniel only lay on the bed for the sake of the child. I ate nothing but beef for dinner. . . .

[June 10, 1709] I rose at 5 o'clock this morning but could not read anything because of Captain Keeling, but I played at billiards with him and won half a crown of him and the Doctor. George B-th brought home my boy Eugene. . . . In the evening I took a walk about the plantation. Eugene was whipped for running away and had the [bit] put on him. I said my prayers and had good health, good thought, and good humor, thanks be to God Almighty. . . .

[September 6, 1709] . . . About one o'clock this morning my wife was happily delivered of a son, thanks be to God Almighty. I was awake in a blink and rose and my cousin Harrison met me on the stairs and told me it was a boy. We drank some French wine and went to bed again and rose at 7 o'clock. I read a chapter in Hebrew and then drank chocolate with the women for breakfast. I returned God humble thanks for so great a blessing and recommended my young son to His divine protection.

[October 6, 1709] I rose at 6 o'clock and said my prayers and ate milk for breakfast. Then I proceeded to Williamsburg, where I found all well. I went to the capitol where I sent for the wench to clean my room and when I came I kissed her and felt her, for which God forgive me. Then I went to see the President, whom I found indisposed in his ears. I dined with . . . on beef. Then we went to his house and played at piquet where Mr. Clayton came to us. We had much to do to get a bottle of French wine. About 10 o'clock I went to my lodgings. I had good health but wicked thoughts, God forgive me. . . .

[December 1, 1709] I rose at 4 o'clock and read two chapters in Hebrew and some Greek in Cassius. I said my prayers and ate milk for breakfast. I danced my dance. Eugene was whipped again for pissing in bed and Jenny for concealing it. . . .

Louis B. Wright and Marion Tinling, eds., *The Secret Diary of William Byrd of Westover, 1709–1712* (Richmond, Va.: Dietz Press, 1941), 7, 46, 79–80, 90–91, 113, 159, 192.

[December 3, 1709] I rose at 5 o'clock and read two chapters in Hebrew and some Greek in Cassius. I said my prayers and ate milk for breakfast. I danced my dance. Eugene pissed abed again for which I made him drink a pint of piss. I settled some accounts and read some news. . . .

[March 31, 1710] I rose at 7 o'clock and read some Greek in bed. I said my prayers and ate milk for breakfast. Then about 8 o'clock we got a-horseback and rode to Mr. Harrison's and found him very ill but sensible. . . . In the morning early I returned home and went to bed. It is remarkable that Mrs. Burwell dreamed this night that she saw a person that with money scales weighed time and declared that there was no more than 18 pennies worth of time to come, which seems to be a dream with some significance either concerning the world or a sick person. In my letters from England I learned that the Bishop of Worcester was of opinion that in the year 1715 the city of Rome would be burned to the ground, that before the year 1745 the popish religion would be routed out of the world, that before the year 1790 the Jews and Gentiles would be converted to the Christianity and then would begin the millennium.

[June 17, 1710] . . . I set my closet right. I ate tongue and chicken for dinner. In the afternoon I caused L-s-n to be whipped for beating his wife and Jenny was whipped for being his whore. In the evening the sloop came from Appomattox with tobacco. I took a walk about the plantation. I said my prayers and drank some new milk from the cow. . . .

6. Olaudah Equiano, an African, Recounts the Horrors of Enslavement, 1757

One day, when all our people were gone to their works as usual, and only I and my dear sister were left to mind the house, two men and a woman got over our walls, and seized us both, and they stopped our mouths, and ran off with us into the nearest wood. Here they tied our hands, and continued to carry us as far as they could, till night came on, when we reached a small house, where the robbers halted for refreshment, and spent the night. We were then unbound, but were unable to take any food; and, being quite overpowered by fatigue and grief, our only relief was some sleep, which allayed our misfortune for a short time. The next morning we left the house, and continued travelling all the day. . . . When we went to rest the following night they offered us some victuals; but we refused it; and the only comfort we had was in being in one another's arms all that night, and bathing each other with our tears. But alas! we were soon deprived of even the small comfort of weeping together. The next day proved a day of greater sorrow than I had yet experienced; for my sister and I were then separated, while we lay clasped in each other's arms. It was in vain that we besought them not to part us; she was torn from me, and immediately carried away, while I was left in a state of distraction not to be described. I cried and grieved continually; and for several days I did not eat any thing but what they forced into my mouth. . . .

From Olaudah Equiano, *The Life of Olaudah Equiano*, 1789.

The first object which saluted my eyes when I arrived on the coast was the sea, and a slave ship, which was then riding at anchor, and waiting for its cargo. These filled me with astonishment, which was soon converted into terror when I was carried on board. . . . I was now persuaded that I had gotten into a world of bad spirits, and that they were going to kill me. Their complexions too differing so much from ours, their long hair, and the language they spoke, (which was very different from any I had ever heard) united to confirm me in this belief. . . . When I looked round the ship too and saw a large furnace of copper boiling, and a multitude of black people of every description chained together, every one of their countenances expressing dejection and sorrow, I no longer doubted of my fate; and, quite overpowered with horror and anguish, I fell motionless on the deck and fainted. When I recovered a little I found some black people about me, who I believed were some of those who brought me on board, and had been receiving their pay; they talked to me in order to cheer me, but all in vain. I asked them if we were not to be eaten by those white men with horrible looks, red faces, and loose hair. They told me I was not; . . . Soon after this the blacks who brought me on board went off, and left me abandoned to despair. I now saw myself deprived of all chance of returning to my native country, or even the least glimpse of hope of gaining the shore, which I now considered as friendly; and I even wished for my former slavery in preference to my present situation, which was filled with horrors of every kind, still heightened by my ignorance of what I was to undergo. I was not long suffered to indulge my grief; I was soon put down under the decks, and there I received such a salutation in my nostrils as I had never experienced in my life: so that, with the loathsomeness of the stench, and crying together, I became so sick and low that I was not able to eat, nor had I the least desire to taste any thing. I now wished for the last friend, death, to relieve me; but soon, to my grief, two of the white men offered me eatables; and, on my refusing to eat, one of them held me fast by the hands, and laid me across I think the windlass, and tied my feet, while the other flogged me severely. I had never experienced any thing of this kind before; and although, not being used to the water, I naturally feared that element the first time I saw it, yet nevertheless, could I have got over the nettings, I would have jumped over the side, but I could not; and, besides, the crew used to watch us very closely who were not chained down to the decks, lest we should leap into the water: and I have seen some of these poor African prisoners most severely cut for attempting to do so, and hourly whipped for not eating. This indeed was often the case with myself. In a little time after, amongst the poor chained men, I found some of my own nation, which in a small degree gave ease to my mind. I inquired of these what was to be done with us; they gave me to understand we were to be carried to these white people's country to work for them. I then was a little revived, and thought, if it were no worse than working, my situation was not so desperate: but still I feared I should be put to death, the white people looked and acted, as I thought, in so savage a manner; for I had never seen among any people such instances of brutal cruelty; and this not only shewn towards us blacks, but also to some of the whites themselves. One white man in particular I saw, when we were permitted to be on deck, flogged so unmercifully with a large rope near the foremast that he died in consequence of it; and they tossed him over the side as they would have done a brute. This made me fear these people the more; and I expected nothing less than to be treated in the same manner. I could not help expressing my fears and apprehensions to some of my countrymen: I asked them if these people had no country, but lived in this hollow place (the ship): they told me they did not, but came from a distant one. "Then," said I, "how comes it in all our country we never heard of them?" They told me because they lived so very far off. I then asked where were their women? had they any like themselves? I was told they had "and why," said I, "do we not see them?" they answered, because they were left behind. I asked how the vessel could go? they told me they could not tell; but that there were cloths put upon the masts by the help of the ropes I saw, and then the vessel went on and the white men had some spell or magic they put in the water when they liked in order to stop the vessel. I was exceedingly amazed at this account, and really thought they were spirits. I therefore wished much to be from amongst them, for I expected they would sacrifice me: but my wishes were vain. . . .

. . . At last we came in sight of the island of Barbadoes, at which the whites on board gave a great shout, and made many signs of joy to us. We did not know what to think of this; but as the vessel drew nearer we plainly saw the harbour, and other ships of different kinds and sizes; and we soon anchored amongst them off Bridge Town. Many merchants and planters now came on board, though it was in the evening. They put us in separate parcels, and examined us attentively. They also made us jump, and pointed to the land, signifying we were to go there. We thought by this we should be eaten by these ugly men as they appeared to us; and, when soon after we were all put down under the deck again, there was much dread and trembling among us, and nothing but bitter cries to be heard all the night from these apprehensions, insomuch that at last the white people got some old slaves from the land to pacify us. They told us we were not to be eaten, but to work, and were soon to go on land, where we should see many of our country people. This report eased us much; and sure enough, soon after we were landed, there came to us Africans of all languages. We were conducted immediately to the merchant's yard, where we were all pent up together like so many sheep in a fold, without regard to sex or age. As every object was new to me every thing I saw filled me with surprise. What struck me first was that the houses were built with stories, and in every other respect different from those in Africa: but I was still more astonished on seeing people on horseback. I did not know what this could mean; and indeed I thought these people were full of nothing but magical arts. . . . We were not many days in the merchant's custody before we were sold after their usual manner, which is this:—On a signal given (as the beat of a drum), the buyers rush at once into the yard where the slaves are confined, and make choice of that parcel they like best. The noise and clamour with which this is attended, and the eagerness visible in the countenances of the buyers, serve not a little to increase the apprehensions of the terrified Africans, who may well be supposed to consider them as the ministers of that destruction to which they think themselves devoted. In this manner, without scruple, are relations and friends separated, most of them never to see each other again. I remember in the vessel in which I was brought over, in the men's apartment, there were several brothers, who, in the sale, were sold in different lots; and it was very moving on this occasion to see and hear their cries at parting. . . .

While I was thus employed by my master I was often a witness to cruelties of every kind, which were exercised on my unhappy fellow slaves. I used frequently to have different cargoes of new negroes in my care for sale; and it was almost a constant practice with our clerks, and other whites, to commit violent depredations on the chastity of the female slaves; and these I was, though with reluctance, obliged to submit to at all times, being unable to help them. When we have had some of these slaves on board my master's vessels to carry them to other islands, or to America, I have known our mates to commit these acts most shamefully, to the disgrace, not of Christians only, but of men. I have even known them gratify their brutal passion with females not ten years old; . . . And yet in Montserrat I have seen a negro man staked to the ground, and cut most shockingly, and then his ears cut off bit by bit, because he had been connected with a white woman who was a common prostitute: as if it were no crime in the whites to rob an innocent African girl of her virtue; but most heinous in a black man only to gratify a passion of nature, where the temptation was offered by one of a different colour, though the most abandoned woman of her species. Another negro man was half hanged, and then burnt, for attempting to poison a cruel overseer. Thus by repeated cruelties are the wretched first urged to despair, and then murdered, because they still retain so much of human nature about them as to wish to put an end to their misery, and retaliate on their tyrants!

7. Reverend Charles Woodmason Complains About Life in the Carolina Backcountry, 1768

Sunday, August 7 It is impossible that any Gentleman not season'd to the Clime, could sustain this—It would kill 99 out of 100—Nor is this a Country, or place where I would wish any Gentleman to travel, or settle, altho' Religion and the State requires a Number of Ministers—Their Ignorance and Impudence is so very high, as to be past bearing—Very few can read—fewer write—Out of 5000 that have attended Sermon this last Month, I have not got 50 to sign a Petition to the Assembly. They are very Poor—owing to their extreme Indolence for they possess the finest Country in America, and could raise but ev'ry thing. They delight in their present low, lazy, sluttish, heathenish, hellish Life, and seem not desirous of changing it. Both Men and Women will do any thing to come at Liquor, Cloaths, furniture, &c. &c. rather than work for it—Hence their many Vices—their gross Licentiousness Wantonness, Lasciviousness, Rudeness, Lewdness, and Profligacy they will commit the grossest Enormities, before my face, and laugh at all Admonition.

Last Sunday I distributed the last Parcel of Mr. Warings Tracts on Prayer. It is very few families whom I can bring to join in Prayer, because most of them are of various Opinions the Husband a Churchman, Wife, a Dissenter, Children nothing at all. My Bibles and Common Prayers have been long gone, and I have given away to amount of £20 of Practical Books, besides those I received of the Society—Few or no Books are to be found in all this vast Country, beside the Assembly, Catechism, Watts Hymns, Bunyans Pilgrims Progress—Russells—Whitefields and Erskines Sermons. Nor do they delight in Historical Books or in having them read to them, as do our Vulgar in England for these People despise Knowledge. . . .

Richard J. Hooder, ed., *The Carolina Backcountry on the Eve of the Revolution: The Journal and Other Writings of Charles Woodmason, Anglican Itinerant* (Chapel Hill: University of North Carolina Press, 1953), 52, 60–61.

Saturday, September 3 Many of these People walk 10 or 12 Miles with their Children in the burning Sun—Ought such to be without the Word of God, when so earnest, so desirous of hearing it and becoming Good Christians, and good Subjects! How lamentable to think, that the Legislature of this Province will make no Provision—so rich, so luxurious, polite a People! Yet they are deaf to all Solicitations, and look on the poor White People in a Meaner Light than their Black Slaves, and care less for them. Withal there is such a Republican Spirit still left, so much of the Old Leaven of Lord Shaftsbury and other the 1st principal Settlers still remains, that they seem not at all disposed to promote the Interest of the Church of England. . . .

It will require much Time and Pains to New Model and form the Carriage and Manners, as well as Morals of these wild Peoples—Among this Congregation not one had a Bible or Common Prayer—or could join a Person or hardly repeat the Creed or Lords Prayer—Yet all of 'em had been educated in the Principles of our Church. . . .

. . . In few Years, I hope to bring about a Reformation, as I already have done in several Parts of the Country.

✒ E S S A Y S

Although the system of unfree labor colored all aspects of the colonial South, it was not a static institution. One issue that has concerned historians for some time is the different paths taken by African slaves and European servants. Both entered the colonies as unfree laborers, but only the Africans ultimately endured perpetual servitude. These two essays grapple with another issue: the changing relationships between slave and slaveholder over the course of the colonial era. Both argue that the ethos of patriarchalism that dominated in the seventeenth- and early-eighteenth-century colonial South gave way in the eighteenth century to a paternalist ethos, yet they differ on causes and outcomes of this shift. Kathleen M. Brown, professor of history at the University of Pennsylvania, concentrates on the anxiety of the planter class and the ways in which enslaved people used the paternalism that resulted to their own advantage. Philip D. Morgan, who teaches history at Johns Hopkins University, also considers the transition from patriarchalism to paternalism and the many-sided relationships between free and nonfree, black and white. He argues that paternalism was less austere and was based on a reciprocal relationship of obligation between slave and slaveholder. Yet he also notes that the transition to paternalism changed the relationships between poor whites and enslaved blacks, a change that would have critical implications for the future.

The Anxious World of the Slaveowning Patriarch

KATHLEEN M. BROWN

In 1711, Lucy Parke Byrd argued with her husband, William Byrd II, about her plan to pluck her eyebrows before their journey to the colonial capital in Williamsburg. Threatening not to accompany her husband, she attempted to override his objections to her beauty regimen. That she failed we can glean from William Byrd's

Kathleen M. Brown, *Good Wives, Nasty Wenches, and Anxious Patriarchs: Gender, Race, and Power in Colonial Virginia* (Chapel Hill: University of North Carolina Press, 1998), 319–326, 350, 355–356, 360–361, 364–366. Published for the Omohundro Institute of Early American History and Culture. Copyright © 1998 by the University of North Carolina Press. Used by permission of the publisher.

entry in his secret journal for that day. "I refused, however, and got the better of her, and maintained my authority," he noted smugly. The couple departed from their Westover home later that morning with Lucy Byrd's eyebrows unplucked and William Byrd's position as head of household and master over his wife confirmed. Not only had Byrd's taste in female fashion held the day, but his desire to have his wife accompany him during his round of social, political, and business dealings in Williamsburg prevailed.

For colonial gentlemen like Byrd, authority was a delicate project, much like a house built upon an unstable foundation. To keep such a structure standing, the owner had to be extremely sensitive to fine cracks and imperfections, shoring up the edifice to prevent the entire house from tumbling down. Conscious of being colonials whose dependent and marginal relationship to London diminished their status, Byrd and his peers could never achieve enough success to reassure themselves that the foundation of their identity would not collapse. Maintaining authority thus required constant vigilance against even small usurpations of power such as the forbidden plucking of eyebrows, for tiny fissures not only indicated larger weaknesses in the construction but constituted a nagging reminder of contradictions inherent in colonial masculinity.

Marriage, parenthood, slaveownership, and electoral politics all tested a man, requiring him to behave with equanimity in a variety of social contexts. A man who was simultaneously a husband, father, slaveowner, and Council member needed to respond appropriately to the different challenges inherent in each relationship. Ultimately, each tried the same quality: his ability to communicate power over others by appearing to have power over himself. Authority derived not simply from a man's power over his wife, children, slaves, and lesser men but also from his ability to subdue within himself those qualities he attributed to subordinates: passion, weakness, and dependence.

By the mid-eighteenth century, elite male identity in Virginia had a complex historical, political, and emotional architecture. From the outset, the project of establishing colonies emerged from a gendered context of imperial rivalry, debates about woman's nature, and desires for far-off lands. English explorers became English men through encounters with Indians in which differences between English and Indian gender performances provided a language of self-definition and a means of expressing struggles for power. When English settlers began importing Africans to produce tobacco, gender figured prominently in the legal and political language used to distinguish slaves from free people, reflecting the importance of relationships between enslaved women and their masters to definitions of slavery. It was not until Bacon's challenge to Berkeley in 1676, however, that questions about what it meant to be a Virginian and to constitute political authority in a colonial society came to a head. The reaction against white women and the repudiation of black masculinity provided the basis for a fragile alliance of white men and the assertion of an authentic colonial identity. In this sense, Bacon's Rebellion was the crucible for colonial masculinity.

Eighteenth-century planters gentrified Bacon's legacy of masculinity, incorporating it into their mimicry of the material and emotional world of the English gentry. Domestic tranquillity became the ideal of planters who dreamed of hegemonic authority over compliant wives, children, and slaves and of unquestioned political leadership over less privileged men. An appropriate emotional lexicon for men aspiring to self-mastery, domestic tranquillity also promised to detach power from coercion, delivering authority on a silver platter to men who need never raise their voices in anger or lift the lash to inflict punishment. Self-mastery and harmonious, if not affectionate, familial relations thus went hand in hand, swathing the violent history of planter power in an insulating layer of emotional serenity.

Virginia planters, however, were perhaps more successful politically than they were domestically. Compared to the political leadership of other British colonies, the Old Dominion's elite enjoyed a relatively stable tenure throughout most of the eighteenth century. Both the political legacy of Nathaniel Bacon and the state's implication in slavery provided the colony's gentry with a firm foundation for political dominance that was not easily challenged.

At the root of planter domestic authority and political success lay slavery, the most difficult relationship for planters to translate into an English idiom. Slaves intermittently threatened to disturb gentry equanimity, forcing planters to respond as either a "fool or a fury," as Byrd once observed. Coercion thus permeated master-slave relations to a much greater degree than it did other social relations, offering a graphically violent showcase for planter authority and state power. Dismemberments, hangings, and burnings of slaves provided planters with a foundation for authority rooted in the infliction of pain. As long as planters could exercise power over slave bodies, other domestic and political relationships need not be regularly disrupted by violence.

Historians usually discuss the authority exercised by elite white men over their wives, children, slaves, and social and economic inferiors as if each relationship existed in isolation from the others. The terms describing authority are frequently defined imprecisely, if at all, and often assume completely different meanings for scholars investigating the history of different social relations. To those explicating political theory, "patriarchy" connotes state power under the rule of an absolute monarchy, whereas "paternalism" signifies reciprocal yet still deferential social relations under a weaker crown. To historians of the family, "patriarchy" means the rule of the father over his wife, children, and dependent household members but is often used interchangeably with "paternalism," by which is meant a softer, more affectionate familial system. For feminist scholars, however, "patriarchy" and "paternalism" both describe a male-dominated political and economic order, with the latter appearing, at least on the surface, to be characterized by greater mutuality and reciprocity in domestic relationships between men and women. Studies of slavery have provided perhaps the most sophisticated explanation for paternalism, yet scholars still disagree about the specific connotations of each term.

Despite different usage, most analysts share the assumption that paternalism represents a qualitative improvement in human relationships over patriarchy, gradually displacing more coercive social relations sometime during the late eighteenth century. Historians use the words "warm," "soft," "mellow," "affectionate," "companionate," and "face-to-face" to describe a paternalistic world of heightened intimacy and emotion in which the crasser, sharper edges of patriarchy have been smoothed or "domesticated," and the "impersonal" relations of a class society have not yet taken hold. The unstated assumption behind this use of language is that paternalistic social relations accompany a flowering of domestic life and emotional intimacy characterized by face-to-face contact. This view both celebrates "modern" family relations and is nostalgic for the lost intimacy of preindustrial society. It is also based upon generalizations inappropriate for female slaves, for whom paternalism's face-to-face style presented graver dangers than less intimate relations with masters.

An eighteenth-century planter's authority cannot be easily described using either of these terms exclusively. Before 1750, it would not be unusual for the same individual to court a woman with tender words, threaten to disinherit his child, whip a slave, and offer rum to social subordinates at a militia muster. Was such a man a patriarch or a paternalist? If we were to examine only his relationship with his wife-to-be, we might conclude that harmonious domestic relations had supplanted crude patriarchal authority. Similarly, if we noted only the whipping or the disinheritance, we might come to a very different conclusion. In the instance of our fictional planter, the coexistence of paternalistic language and patriarchal tactics suggests a more complicated relationship between styles of authority often taken to be distinct.

The overlapping of different kinds of authoritative relations within the life of a single individual complicates matters further. Within the plantation house, for example, a man frequently shifted his primary identity from father to husband, master to gentry patron, host to plantation manager. Ideally, he strove to move from role to role effortlessly, conducting himself so that each identity complemented the others and augmented his authority. Although elite men enjoyed some separation of roles—the long ride to Williamsburg undoubtedly provided some men with the opportunity to don their political faces—their authority sprang from the accumulated clout of being husband and father, landowner and slaveholder, planter and politician. It is tempting to conclude that Virginia's elite planters wore many different hats, but it is perhaps more accurate to say that they wore one, appropriate for many different occasions.

By the beginning of the eighteenth century, as we have already seen, Virginia's planter class had reason to consider themselves patriarchs. Planter power coalesced in 1705 with the reorganization of the colony's law codes. In that year, legislators rewrote Virginia's statutes to create a comprehensive body of slave laws that reiterated and extended the master's powers over his slaves. Within five years, lawmakers reinforced a statute forbidding infanticide by threatening severe punishments to those who concealed the death of a bastard child. The consolidation of the power of the father with that of political patron and slaveholder launched Virginia's elite planters on a nearly fifty-year reign of social and economic supremacy.

During this high-water mark of planter authority, elite men derived their power from five main sources: landownership, control over sexual access to women, rights to the labor of slaves and servants, formal access to political life, and the ability to create and manipulate symbols signifying these other sources of power. Planters such as William Byrd and Landon Carter, who kept extensive diaries, depicted their daily exertions of authority in graphic physical terms. Slaves could be whipped, shackled, or medicated; wives and enslaved women could be compelled to engage in sexual intercourse; children's diets and bodily functions required careful monitoring. Although men like Byrd and Carter tended to write self-consciously about their authority as being public and political, their management of the bodies in their households was perhaps the most vivid expression of their power.

If ever Virginia gentlemen were patriarchs, it was between 1700 and 1750. Yet, even at the peak of their power, planters compared themselves unfavorably to their English counterparts and worried that their domestic authority was being usurped.

Some of their anxiety was a consequence of unrealistic expectations for hegemonic power, the tortured perfectionism of colonials who could never achieve enough of an English inflection. They were, after all, more successful as a ruling class than almost any other colonial elite, although they seemed to take little comfort in this achievement. Perhaps the collective disappointments of daily life proved too great for such ambitious, anxious men. Much to the frustration of would-be patriarchs, dependents did not passively await the planter's imprimatur on their bodies. Rather, enslaved people ran away, wives disobeyed, and children ignored their father's words of advice. Even voters, over whom planters had the least physical power but the steadiest symbolic authority, might turn a man out of office.

The ethos of self-mastery and domestic tranquillity that began to appear in eighteenth-century planter journals and letters reflected the limits of coercive power exercised on bodies, but it did not signify an end to that power. Planters continued to practice regimes of corporal punishment on recalcitrant slaves and, less frequently, disobedient servants and children even as quiet displays of sacrosanct authority, rooted in the planter's appearance of self-governance, gradually crept into elite discussions of power. Such a style represented domestic authority as unimpeachable by denying the existence of challenges that might undermine it. The quieter ideal also signaled the rise of a new technology of elite male power in which planters portrayed themselves as the guardians of reason and tranquillity, whereas white women, slaves of both sexes, children, and disorderly common folk were described as being unable to control their passions. Paternalistic styles of authority may have partially masked the cruder side of planter power, but they never fully displaced it.

By the eighteenth century, elite planters believed habitual self-control, rooted in rural plantation life, was the key to exercising power over others. Male planters diligently applied this maxim to their emotional lives early in the century and, with increasing difficulty as the century progressed, to their drinking, eating, spending, and gambling habits. With authority resting in the ability to control one's emotions, many planters placed great value on keeping anger and grief in check.

Gentlemen on both sides of the Atlantic associated emotional restraint with class position, race, and gender identity. Elite men interpreted control over emotions such as anger, sadness, and lust as the triumph of reason over passion. White women of all classes, lower-class white men, and enslaved men and women, many writers believed, were less capable of governing their appetites than elite men. Through control over self, gentlemen reminded themselves, they would have control over others. White women also made use of this discourse of reason and passion, as seen in the poem by Elizabeth Pratt. Maria Byrd, second wife of William II, articulated a similar association between slaves and passion in a letter to her son William III in which she reprimanded him for his neglect of his children's education and upbringing. His daughter's "chief time is spent with servants and Negro children her play fellows," complained Mrs. Byrd, "from whom she had learnt a dreadfull collection of words, and is intolerably passionate."

Beliefs in the efficacy of self-restraint and attempts to weave it into a technology of power contained special benefits for colonial men. Most were already battling feelings of vulnerability to elite patrons and merchants in London and worried about losing touch with London political networks. It may have been reassuring to efface within oneself all vestiges of the qualities one associated with other vulnerable individuals—wives, children, and slaves—and to insist, emphatically, that these others were repositories of unreasonable passions. Already prone to try too hard to be like English gentlemen, men like William Byrd II made a science of emotional and physical self-containment; Byrd recorded his emotional fluctuations in the same detail he did his diet, his daily physical exercise, his bowel movements, and his sexual encounters. If self-control was a quality to be admired in gentlemen, Byrd seemed to believe, he would perform the part flawlessly, striving toward the artful effortlessness expressed by Alexander Pope in an epigram on graceful writing: "True ease in writing comes from Art, not Chance/As one moves easily who has learned to dance." As we have already noted, many of Virginia's elite planters claimed that their rural estates presented the ideal environment for achieving this elusive goal.

Byrd recorded his daily battles for emotional self-restraint in the cryptic code of his secret diary. After the death of his nine-month-old son, Byrd tersely compared his own and his wife's reactions:

> I rose at 6 o'clock and as soon as I came out news was brought that the child was very ill. We went out and found him just ready to die and he died about 8 o'clock in the morning. God gives and God takes away; blessed be the name of God. . . . My wife was much afflicted but I submitted to His judgement better, notwithstanding I was very sensible of my loss, but God's will be done.

In the days to come, Byrd expressed concern over the intensity of his wife's grief and noted differences in their ability to submit to God's will. On the day after the boy's death, Byrd noted, "My wife had several fits of tears for our dear son but kept within the bounds of submission." Although Byrd claimed to have "submitted to His judgement better," his restraint seems to have exacted a toll; during the boy's last day of illness, Byrd developed "gripes" in his stomach, which tormented him for nearly two weeks after his son's death. This was the same illness, moreover, that afflicted him when worry, regret, grief, or anger threatened to overwhelm his efforts to control his emotions.

Despite his efforts at self-control, Byrd's life did not even come close to the domestic ideal of tranquillity to which many elite Virginians aspired. Lucy and William fought frequently and bitterly. Byrd recorded one such exchange in which he barely retained control of himself: "My wife flew into such a passion that she hoped she would be revenged of me. I was moved very much at this but only thanked her for the present lest I should say things foolish in my passion." Several days later, although they had patched up their differences, Byrd wrote angrily, "I was out of humor with my wife for her foolish passions, of which she is often guilty, for which God forgive her and make her repent and amend." After intervening in his wife's violent corrections of his slave Jenny, Byrd recorded a similarly upsetting outburst: "She lifted up her hands to strike me but forebore to do it. She gave me abundance of bad words and endeavored to strangle herself, but I believe in jest only. However after acting a mad woman a long time she was passive again." Byrd's diary is littered with similar references to quarrels he claimed were started by his wife's passion and descriptions of her fits of tears and hysteria. In his view, passions unchecked, which he usually attributed to women, were nearly always the source of domestic discord. . . .

Although master-slave relationships more frequently featured coercion than did other social relations involving elite planters, slaves successfully moved their masters toward a paternalistic style of authority by midcentury. Planters also had their reasons for preferring persuasion and personal ties to physical punishment, but the paternalism they envisioned was quite different from that of their slaves. Whereas enslaved people advanced a moral economy in which reasonable work conditions, adequate provisions, and respect for family ties all became part of a concept of just treatment within slavery, planters sought docile, respectful, and efficient obedience that confirmed their sense of righteous mastery. . . .

White planters' attitudes about race, honor, and sexuality found expression in myriad ways that were annoying and humiliating for enslaved people. Byrd reported with amusement that, while staying at a friend's house, he threw a pan of water out his window, drenching a slave woman. High society parties in Williamsburg occasionally included raffles of slaves; at one such event, a black woman described as "fit for house business" was raffled off along with her child. Elite women described their black female servants as dirty and ugly and associated skill and tractability with light skin. Infusing an age-old epigram with new racial and social significance, one white woman communicated what she saw as an enslaved woman's limited potential for obedient and efficient domestic service by referring to the permanence of her color: "Julitt will never be washt white."

Most important to this matrix of dishonor, however, was the intertwining of race and sexuality in white male planters' attitudes toward their slaves. Although it is possible only to conjecture about the frequency with which white men visited slave quarters for the specific purpose of sexually exploiting enslaved women, there is evidence that this did indeed happen—and that its occurrence was enmeshed in attitudes about sexual domination, slave promiscuity, and sexual dishonor. As a married man approaching the age of seventy, Byrd frequently engaged in sexual activity with enslaved women, perhaps as many as nine times during a period of eighteen months. These were the only incidents of sexual activity he recorded during this time. Byrd was not alone. His brother-in-law, John Custis, allegedly maintained a long-term relationship with an enslaved woman named Alice by whom he fathered a son. The boy, Christoforo John, received special mention in his father's will.

Many historians have interpreted the sexual interests of white planters in their dependent female slaves as evidence of intimacy or racial fluidity, indicative of white people's willingness to relate to their slaves as human beings. These analyses fail to account for the skewed gender pattern of interracial sexuality among the Virginia gentry—white men and enslaved women—and for the way it reinforced the power relations encoded in legally sanctioned gender and racial hierarchies. Although it would be wrong to assume that all such relationships were a product of coercion, it is important to note that all occurred in a context where coercion was never far beneath the surface. Female slaves stood relatively disempowered compared to their masters both as black women and as unfree people. Their patterns of sexual interaction with white masters were thus part of a larger field of power relations in which masters expressed power sexually and viewed sexual activity as an expression of male power.

Confronted with the considerable power of planters, enslaved people repackaged and redirected patriarchal authority, making absolute dominance impossible. As a young planter, William Byrd frequently found himself foiled by his slaves' collaboration, despite his attempts to reinforce his authority with harsh punishments. Byrd's slave Jenny, for example, tried twice to save the slave Eugene from further punishment for bed-wetting by concealing the soiled linens; a whipping from Byrd, moreover, did not discourage her from making the second attempt. Byrd's maid Anaka, who had herself stolen rum from the liquor cellar, collaborated with the white woman "Nurse" to give the black maid Prue access to the cellar. . . .

Planters' desires for domestic harmony offered enslaved people an opportunity to extract concessions conducive to family life, but the same ideal also provided masters with an overarching rationale for intervening in slaves' disputes. Articulated hopes for a serene domestic environment, moreover, were not incompatible with other tactics, including the denial of family privileges and outright coercion. Planters like Byrd occasionally involved themselves in the conflicts of enslaved people at the request of one of the parties in an effort to restore peace. Byrd injected himself into the troubled relations of married slaves, imposing a monogamous standard to which even he did not adhere. He recorded in his secret diary for 1710 that he "caused L——s——n to be whipped for beating his wife and Jenny was whipped for being his whore." Byrd also intervened in relationships that threatened to breed more serious conflicts. He reported that he ordered "Johnny to be whipped for threatening to strike Jimmy and caused Moll also to be whipped and made them renounce one the other." Occasionally, Byrd's deeper motive for enforcing tranquil relations—the maintenance of his own authority—surfaced in his dealings with enslaved people. "At night I talked with my people and refused to let P——p——l go to see his wife," he wrote in an entry for August 1720. Although, in this instance, Byrd denied a family privilege to a slave, his actions were not inconsistent with his previous efforts to foster domestic harmony. In both situations, he attempted to impose his will upon slaves he referred to as "my people," curbing their rights to vent anger against each other and forbidding them to leave the premises of Westover to visit spouses.

Byrd's interventions in enslaved peoples' relationships were part of a larger effort to protect his own use of "discipline" from being confused with mere violence. Like gifts of liquor and evening visits to the quarters, such interventions blunted the sharpest edges of patriarchal authority and may have prevented the escalation of master-slave conflicts into episodes of violent resistance or running away. On several occasions, as already noted, challenges to Byrd's exclusive right to use violence came not just from enslaved people but from his own wife. Byrd correctly perceived that physical contests between Lucy Byrd and the female slaves in his household did nothing to enhance white authority and much to diminish it, threatening to turn the exercise of discipline into a brawl. The subjection of enslaved people to Lucy Byrd's intensely corporal exercise of authority also disrupted his own attempts to achieve peaceful order in the household. Although Byrd himself had sometimes resorted to cruel punishments of enslaved people, he had done so as an expression of will, a flexing of patriarchal muscle that underscored more genteel manifestations of power. Uncontrolled outbursts of violence—which to Byrd meant all violent acts initiated by others—undermined his attempts to rule effortlessly over household members, disturbing his calculus of persuasion, warning, and inflicted pain.

Of all the social relations constituting and trying planters' authority, master-slave relationships were the least distanced from outright coercion. Planter efforts to achieve a genteel, restrained authority over their households somewhat mitigated the physical cruelty inherent in slavery, cushioning it with reciprocity and rhetorical, if not actual, gestures toward recognizing the existence of slave families. Planters' efforts to cultivate intimate personal relationships with enslaved people, however, supplemented rather than precluded the use of cruel punishments. Paternalism only represented an improvement of conditions for slaves if enslaved people themselves made it so. Evening walks around the plantation grounds to talk with laborers, gifts of liquor, and intervention in slave relationships allowed masters intimate access to enslaved peoples' lives, increasing the dangers of unwanted sexual contact for enslaved women. Eighteenth-century paternalism thus left an ambiguous legacy, offering a tissue-thin layer of protection from harsh corporal punishment and leaving enslaved women more vulnerable to the sexual desires of their masters. . . .

Virginia's elite planters were at the height of their powers as a class during the first half of the eighteenth century. Compared to their seventeenth-century counterparts, they enjoyed longer lives, more stable families, larger estates, and greater security. Compared to gentlemen in other parts of the British Empire, they were a political success story, a stable regime whose most serious challenge at mid-century came from the crown rather than from below.

Despite these considerable achievements and their very real control over most of their society's resources, Virginia's elite planters were never able to allay self-doubts about the security and legitimacy of their positions. Even the most powerful of planters occasionally lost an election, fell victim to fluctuating tobacco prices, or failed to make a suitable impression on a metropolitan contact. Domestic authority, moreover, also proved elusive. In the relationships most fundamental to their patriarchal identities, men like William Byrd, Landon Carter, and Joseph Ball met with disobedience and recalcitrance. Wives refused to obey their husbands, children flouted their father's will, and slaves ran away. These acts of defiance troubled Virginia's gentlemen as much as, if not more than, their public failures because they occurred in a context in which planters' legal, economic, and coercive power was virtually untrammeled. If they were not patriarchs in their own households, many men seem to have wondered, could they hope to be gentlemen in the eyes of the colony's voters, their gentry peers, or London society? . . .

Relationships between masters and slaves proved to be the most difficult to recast according to the ethic of domestic tranquillity. Although the ideal of slave family integrity had begun to enter planter discourse by the 1730s, allowing slaves to press claims to remain near family members, violence and brutality continued to punctuate the relationship. Planters were more likely to inflict corporal punishment on enslaved people than they were on wives and white children. They were also more likely to experiment on their bound laborers with harsh medicines. Rhetoric about domestic harmony rarely protected enslaved people from the violence inherent in slavery.

Although the master-slave relationship was distinctive because of the violent technologies of power that lay at its core, it remained connected to other relationships of power in slaveowning households. The sexual exploitation of enslaved women, for example, was closely akin to planter conceptualizations of sex and power more generally. Planters who viewed sexual intercourse as a natural outgrowth of male dominance and female appetite easily transformed such an expression of power into domination over slave women. Perhaps most important, slavery allowed planters to showcase their coercive power without disturbing ideals for harmonious relationships with white family members. Far from proving incompatible with the ethos of domestic tranquillity, the coercion of slaves may have made such ideals possible, providing planters with a suitable foil for the serene authority they hoped to wield over wives and children.

In the absence of any significant erosion of the economic and political foundations of planters' power between 1700 and 1750, it would be mistaken to conclude that paternalistic styles represented a lesser authority than patriarchal ones. An examination of the full complement of planters' social relations reveals paternalism—in the guise of the ideals of domestic tranquillity—to be one face of patriarchy, not a softer replacement of it. Rooted in coercion, slavery remained a perpetual reminder of the limits of domestic harmony and gentility, compelling planters to confront the fact that much of their authority depended upon their ability to inflict pain.

The Effects of Paternalism Among Whites and Blacks

PHILIP D. MORGAN

The free and the unfree engaged in endless and varied encounters. To comprehend these kaleidoscopic contacts between masters and slaves, whites and blacks requires complex formulations. However cruelly whites exploited blacks, their fates were intricately intertwined. However much masters treated their slaves as chattels, the humanity of their property could not be ignored or evaded. However total the masters' exercise of power, negotiation and compromise were necessary to make slavery function. However sincerely planter patriarchs stressed mutuality and reciprocity, their authority ultimately rested on force. However sentimentally and benevolently some late-eighteenth-century masters viewed slaves, their relentless denial of rights to bondmen increasingly placed slaves outside society. However unequivocally daily existence brought blacks and whites together, growing race consciousness and class distinctions thrust them apart. However deep a chasm opened between whites and blacks, channels of communication arose to bridge it. However fundamentally slavery was the result of interaction between master and slave, nonslaveholders intruded to shape the institution's character. The intricacy of eighteenth-century white-black relations defies easy definition. . . .

The dominant social ethos and cultural metaphor of seventeenth- and early-eighteenth-century Anglo-America, patriarchalism, embodied the ideal of an organic social hierarchy. Invoking the Great Chain of Being, one Virginia lawyer argued in 1772: "Societies of men could not subsist unless there were a subordination of one to another. . . . That in this subordination the department of slaves must be filled by some, or there would be a defect in the scale of order." Deeply ingrained assumptions about the workings not only of society but also of politics elevated the role of father to mythic heights. From this perspective, patriarchs anchored a social system based on the protection that the powerful offered the weak, just as monarchs defined a political system where royal power defended the people in return for their obedience

Philip D. Morgan, *Slave Counterpoint: Black Culture in the Eighteenth-Century Chesapeake and Lowcountry* (Chapel Hill: University of North Carolina Press, 1998), 257–260, 273–276, 284–286, 294–296, 300–302, 310–313, 315–317. Copyright © 1998 by the University of North Carolina Press. Used by permission of the publisher.

and loyalty. Indeed, masters might draw a precise parallel, as Henry Laurens once did when he reflected, "Never was an absolute Monarch more happy in his Subjects than at the Present time I am." Suffusing the thought of the age, the patriarchal outlook was an austere code, emphasizing control, obedience, discipline, and severity. Yet patriarchalism also involved protection, guardianship, and reciprocal obligations. It defined the gentleman planter's self-image and constituted the ideals and standards by which slaveholding behavior was judged. . . .

. . . Patriarchalism was reformulated over the course of the eighteenth century. Masters began to speak less of duties and obligations, more of individual rights, particularly property rights. Slaves were more and more defined as people without rights; and, because they were viewed increasingly as property, they were said to enhance their owners' independence. Whereas the patriarchal ethos held that even the lowliest person was part of an organic society, the denial of rights could place the slave completely outside society. In part because slaves were being seen as perpetual outsiders, masters could emphasize solicitude rather than authority, sentiments rather than severity, in their governance. This shift in emphasis was partly a response to political events but also resulted from the development of a more affectionate family life, the rise of evangelicalism, the growth of romanticism, and the increase of humanitarianism. It was a reflection in the realm of ideas of broad-gauged changes affecting Revolutionary America. Austere patriarchalism slowly gave way to mellow paternalism. . . .

The duality of growing separation and common bonds applied as much to the relationship of plain white folk and blacks as it did to large planters and their slaves. Because in the late seventeenth century poor whites associated closely and openly with slaves, the growing gap between them was notable. Relations between poor whites and blacks were also part of a larger tangled web that enmeshed patriarchs, plain folks, and slaves. The existence of a large group of plain white folks, for example, encouraged planters to seek their support and recognition. To the degree that nonslaveholders honored slaveholders, they enhanced the large planters' social legitimacy. Slaves in turn saw proud, free white men defer to powerful masters, reinforcing in their eyes the authority of large planters. Paradoxically, the ties established between patriarchs and plain folks could strengthen those between grandees and slaves. . . .

One of the reasons why slavery with all its attendant ambiguities could be readily assimilated into the early modern Anglo-American world was a long-standing patriarchal tradition that had clearly defined the relationship between master and servant. Manuals of household government in sixteenth- and seventeenth-century England spoke of servants as they did of wives and children. All were subservient members of the family, living under the authority of the paterfamilias. Gentlemen were not to let their care stop at their own children. "Let it reach to your menial servants," they were instructed, for "though you are their master, you are also their father." The relationship between master and servant received the highest ideological sanction in the concept of patriarchalism. Patriarchal doctrines can be found, as one historian has argued, in all strata of thought in seventeenth-century England, "from well-ordered and self-conscious theories . . . to the unstated prejudices of the inarticulate masses." A deep respect for rank and hierarchy infused the very marrow of the early modern British American world, and at its core lay the authority of the father-figure in his household.

Many eighteenth-century masters of slaves conspicuously defined themselves in light of this venerable tradition. None more so perhaps than William Byrd II, who in a famous passage took a quasi-spiritual view of his role, likening himself to a biblical patriarch amid his bondmen and bondwomen. Similarly, it required little imagination for a South Carolina planter to "fancy [him]self one of the Patriarchs of old . . . being surrounded with near 200 Negroes who are guided by my absolute Command." As the most dependent members of the patriarchal family, slaves were, according to the Reverend Thomas Bacon of Maryland, "an immediate and necessary part of our household." He emphasized that "next to our children and brethren by blood, our servants, and especially our slaves, are certainly in the nearest relation to us." A Jesuit priest echoed his Anglican counterpart when he stated, "Charity to Negroes is due from all[,] particularly their Masters." As members of Christ, he continued, black slaves were "to be dealt with in a charitable, Christian, paternal manner."

Plantation owners in the eighteenth-century South were especially prone to think of themselves as all-powerful father figures. Plantation America was a remarkably underinstitutionalized world. An attenuated social and economic infrastructure enhanced the authority of the household head. Moreover, household authority expanded rather than contracted over the colonial period in the South. Even though early modern Britain and Western Europe are generally thought to have had a more hierarchical social structure than colonial America, Carole Shammas rightly notes that "a notably higher proportion of people in the Americas," particularly in plantation America, "fell into the category of legal dependents." Not accidentally, "the first thing" Robinson Crusoe did "in the advancement of his New World plantation was to purchase "a negro slave, and an European servant"; he soon had prospects of becoming "a rich and thriving man" in his "new Plantation." Crusoe was later shipwrecked en route to Africa to acquire more slaves. Marooned, Crusoe establishes "two plantations." Crusoe is generally good to Friday, but, as Christopher Hill points out, the first word he taught him was "Master." Eventually, Crusoe acquires both native and foreign labor and begins to envisage himself in monarchical terms. Since the "whole country" was his property, Crusoe mused, he had "undoubted right of dominion," and since "my people," as he significantly termed them, were "perfectly subjected," he was "absolute lord and lawgiver." The family was the foundation of the plantation social order, and its head was lord, master, a monarch in miniature. In a sequel, Crusoe returns bearing goods, to be told he "was a father" to his people. He himself was "pleased" with "being the patron of those people I placed there, and doing for them in a kind of haughty majestic way, like an old patriarchal monarch; providing for them, as if I had been father of the whole family, as well as of the plantation." Defoe had shrewdly caught the tenor of idealized plantation life.

Patriarchalism cannot be dismissed as mere propaganda or apologetics—although, like all ideological rationalizations, it contained its share of self-serving cant; rather, it was an authentic, if deeply flawed, worldview. Its familial rhetoric was not just a smokescreen for exploitation, because patriarchalism offered no guarantee of benevolence. It was no sentimental self-image, but rather a harsh creed. Patriarchs in ancient Rome exercised the right to dispatch wives, children, and slaves. In Virginia, a law of 1669 allowed masters the Roman "power of the father" over the life and death of a slave, but later legislation balanced the interests of the state, masters, and white nonslaveholders with minimal protections for slaves. Although the despotic powers of masters were moderated, the cruel and authoritarian core of patriarchalism helps explain why patriarchs could ignore the enormity of what they did to their slave families. Fathers, after all, do not normally sell their children. But when patriarchs spoke of their family, both white and black, their protective domination contained little of the warmth or tenderness associated with modern familial relations. . . .

. . . [A] more enlightened patriarchalism [emerged] in the second half of the eighteenth century. . . . Patriarchal doctrines and strategies were transformed more generally in at least three major directions. First, although late-eighteenth-century masters continued to stress order and authority, they were more inclined to emphasize their solicitude toward and generous treatment of their dependents. Second, no self-respecting patriarch would speak cloyingly of his kindness toward his slaves, but gradually masters began to express such sentiments and came in return to expect gratitude, even love, from their bondpeople. Their outlook became far more sentimental. Third, patriarchs rarely boasted of the submissiveness or docility of their bondpeople, but gradually masters began to create the fiction of the contented and happy slave. This shift in patriarchal strategies—greater softness, more reciprocity, less authoritarianism—had complex origins. In part it was a response to political and military events, but it owed far more to broader developments—a more affectionate family environment, the rise of evangelicalism, romanticism, and humanitarianism, and a growing emphasis on private property rights. Gradually it blossomed in the nineteenth century into full-blown paternalism.

Late-eighteenth-century masters sometimes appealed to rather than threatened their slaves. This change of emphasis may be attributed in part to the temporary disruption of the masters' power caused by the Revolutionary crisis. During wartime and in the early postwar years, in particular, masters often had little control over their slaves. Threats were useless; exhortations became commonplace. Thus, there was the spectacle of a South Carolina slave, resident in Saint Augustine in 1784, telling his master's envoy that he was prepared to return home "willingly . . . but not at present." The master's spokesman was reduced to hoping that he "might be able to persuade him" to return earlier than the slave intended. Or there was Maria Byrd's Wat, a Virginia slave who had aided the British during the war and resided in New York in the spring of 1783. Byrd assured Wat that he could "come home with Safety." She had heard that he "wishes much to return, and his wife and Children are very anxious to see him"; these were her "inducements for wishing him to come back." She was prepared to overlook past actions; indeed, she was even prepared to engage Wat's services in recovering her other lost slaves. For these "good offices," Wat would receive a "handsome" reward. She did not expect that any of her absent slaves would "return willingly whatever they may pretend to." But "to make them more happy if they are sent me," she wanted them to know that no slaves, to her knowledge, had been punished on their return and that her slaves "may rely on the best usage."

The seeming loyalty of many other slaves who did not flee their masters during the Revolutionary war, however, contributed to the growing myth that slaves might be content in their condition. In the summer of 1776, Henry Laurens proudly recorded that his slaves "to a Man are strongly attached to me . . . hitherto not one of them has attempted to desert." These claims of loyalty may be more important for what they say of the owners' perceptions than what they record of the slaves' behavior. But, after the war had ended, Laurens contrasted the "faithless" behavior of his white servants with the "fidelity" of his slaves, "a very few instances excepted." As a result, he noted, "we are endeavouring to reward those and make the whole happy." Making them happy was a prescient remark. Late in life, Laurens took great pride in his various labor-saving experiments that reduced the arduousness of his slaves' labor. These "improvements," he maintained, "are the pleasure of my life, more particularly as they contribute to bring my poor blacks to a level with the happiest peasants to be found in Europe"—a refrain that would echo down the corridors of Southern history.

A more caring attitude toward slaves also arose as the strength of their family ties became recognizable to masters and as family life in general became more egalitarian and affectionate. In 1764, James Habersham was "affected" by the death of one of his slave women, not just because she had been a favorite of his late wife or because she had nursed two of his daughters, but because she had left behind an "inconsolable" husband. Eight years later, he recalled that he had buried almost eighty slaves during his lifetime and in each case had "acquiessed in the Dispensation of divine Providence." However, he found it impossible to "divest myself of Humanity," as he put it, at the events surrounding a recent slave death. It concerned a slave boy bitten by a rabid dog. "The Cries and Intreaties of the Mother begging her Child to be put to Death," wrote the shaken master, "the dreadfull shreiks of the Boy, and his more than pretty Behaviour in his taking leave of all around him, has rung such a Peal in my Ears, that I never can forget." Late-eighteenth-century masters seemed much more respectful of slave family ties than their predecessors. Gangs were often sold "in families" rather than individually, and many a prospective purchaser stated a preference for family units. When a South Carolina slave patron became "dissatisfied and desirous of being sold," his master was quick to assure prospective buyers that the man's wife had also to be sold "for a principle of humanity *alone,*" because "they were very unwilling to be separated." . . .

Enlightened patriarchalism had limits. Where it collided with self-interest and commercial advantage, the slave invariably lost. According to one early-nineteenth-century observer, Georgia slaves were "considered nothing more than perishable property, and interest not principle clothes and feeds them." Similarly, in the early nineteenth century, a South Carolina master was willing to speak cynically of the conflict between his slaves' desire for freedom and his property rights. He described the motivations of his runaways and his own response in this way: "Liberty is sweet and in that they are right—property is comfortable and if I can stop them, I will also be right."

A sense of the flexibility and ultimate rigidity of enlightened patriarchalism is unwittingly captured in the self-justifying remarks of a loyalist slaveholder. "In this land of Nominal freedom and actual Slavery," he had been able, he admitted, to "justify the keeping my fellow beings in bondage" by alleviating the "too common weight of the[ir] chains." He explained that he "scarce used the rod except for theft and other crimes" and, for his slaves' "encouragement," provided ample supplies of corn, meat two or three times a week, and a regular and adequate clothing allowance. Not that his "slaves are used better than any others," he acknowledged, for "some Masters I know, and I hope there are many, treat theirs with the utmost humanity." At the same time, however, he was proud of how he had secured his slaves' respect. "By selling a few, who proved obstinately bad," he had "brought the others to consider their being sold" as the "greatest punishment I can inflict." He had found that the "greatest incitement to their duty" lay in their "hopes of living and dying on my property without being separated from their families, connexions, and friends." It hardly became this generous-spirited master—and, presumably, by the lights of eighteenth-century Anglo-American masterdom, he was exactly that—to rail at the possibility that his slaves might be confiscated and be "subject to the most humiliating circumstance of human nature—that of being sold like the *Brutes that perish.*"

As this master implies, humane treatment did not have to conflict with economic benefit, nor did modes of control have to be crudely coercive. Masters employed a variety of positive incentives to achieve their aims. In fact, compassion could maximize profits and enhance the masters' investment in their slaves. The threat of sale was perhaps even more effective than the whip in keeping slaves in line. When the duc de La Rochefoucauld-Liancourt visited the Lowcountry in the late eighteenth century, he encountered planters willing to laud the advantages of their new approach. One "excellent master to his negroes" claimed, "against the opinion of many others, that the plantations of mild and indulgent masters thrive most, and that the negroes are more faithful and laborious" than those who belonged to severe masters.

Paradoxically, masters felt that they could show more indulgence toward their slaves as they increasingly placed them outside civil society. As North Americans affirmed the absolute value of individual liberty, the only effective way to justify slavery was to exclude its victim from the community of man. When all free inhabitants were seen as enjoying certain unalienable rights, slaves had to be defined as lacking all rights. Moreover, as liberty was predicated on the acquisition and maintenance of private property, so slaveowners' rights to their slaves became inviolable. Slaves enhanced the independence of their owners. Arbitrarily deprive someone of his or her possessions, and that person became a slave. Whereas the patriarchal ethos held that even the lowliest person was part of an organic society, the denial of rights to slaves and the conception of private property as a basic natural right placed slaves outside society altogether. Ironically, as slavery became more firmly entrenched, masters could show more benevolence toward their dependents.

In thoroughgoing patriarchal households, the subjection of slaves was absolute and unquestioned. The master was first cause, prime mover, almost a demigod. Restraint, order, and authority were constant watchwords. Gradually, however, new values infiltrated his patriarchal citadel. Masters began to view themselves less as harsh taskmasters grandly presiding over their estates and more as benefactors providing for their dependents. They preferred to see their relationship with their slaves grounded less in the tradition of divine right than in voluntary, consensual terms. Austere, rigid patriarchalism gave way to warm, mellow paternalism. By the early nineteenth century, William Moultrie reflected on the changes that had occurred. "I am very much pleased to see the treatment of the slaves in the country is altered so much," he observed, particularly noting the "tenderness and humanity" now extended to slaves. Slavery would soon be viewed as a benign institution; slaves would, in George Fitzhugh's exaggerated words, be enveloped in "domestic affection"; before long, it would be the master for whom pity would be invoked as "the greatest slave" of all. . . .

Plain Folk and Slaves

In general, the distance between plain white folk and black slaves grew progressively wider throughout the course of the eighteenth century. In the middle to late seventeenth century, black slaves and the poorer sections of the white community, particularly servants, associated closely and openly. By the turn of the eighteenth century, however, cooperation and alliances between white servants and black slaves began to dissolve, in part because of actions taken by the planter class, in part because servant numbers declined, and in part because the black population became more numerous and alien. Most of these processes remained at work well into the eighteenth century. Yet, the ruling class was never completely successful in wooing lower-class whites to their cause; the importation of twenty thousand convicts into the Chesapeake during the eighteenth century meant that servant ranks were never negligible—at least in that region; and, as the black population creolized, so it again became possible for lower-class whites and blacks to identify with one another. The gap between lower-class whites and blacks widened in the second half of the eighteenth century, but more slowly than before.

The growing divide that separated lower-class whites from blacks had its limits. However much the ruling class attempted to separate the races, plain white folk and slaves still shared their lives in ways impermissible for a planter-patriarch and his bondpeople. Slaves and plain white folk not only lived nearer to one another but were more likely to work alongside one another, speak the same dialect, have their children play together, commit crimes jointly, and run away together. Contacts between plain white folk and slaves were also more regular and frequent in some places than others. They were more evident in the Chesapeake than in the Lowcountry; in both regions, they were more evident on the periphery and in towns than in plantation heartlands. Contacts between plain white folk and slaves also fluctuated over time. Even though the gap between the two gradually widened over the eighteenth century, the Revolutionary crisis proved that some poor whites and slaves could still cooperate.

Shared labor helped create common bonds. The duc de La Rochefoucauld-Liancourt thought that the small planters of Virginia treated their slaves better than did large planters because they "share[d] with them the toils of the fields." He added, "Although they do not clothe and feed them well, yet [they] treat them . . . as well as they do themselves." One of Henry Laurens's slaves, Sampson, a recent African immigrant, offers similar testimony from South Carolina. Absenting himself from Laurens's Mepkin plantation only a few days after his arrival, Sampson went to the Santee and, in Laurens's words, "fell in with a poor worthless fellow who entertained him near 8 months." Fearful that he would be discovered, the white man sent Sampson back to Laurens. But Sampson was no longer the same man, for, during his absence, he had "learned to make Indigo or at least to work at it and to speak tolerable good English." What is more, when Laurens returned Sampson to Mepkin, he immediately ran off again "to his former range which proves," his master acknowledged, "that he had not been unkindly treated there."

In addition to their work, plain white folk and blacks shared even the items they wore and the language they spoke. When Devereaux Jarrett, of modest slave-holding stock in Virginia, wanted to "be counted somebody," he got himself "an old wig, which, perhaps being cast off by the master had become the property of his slave, and from the slave it was conveyed to me." A nonelite white man had no reservations about wearing an item that had previously adorned the head of a black slave. Plain folk and blacks also shared a patois. Ebenezer Hazard observed that "the common country people" of South Carolina "talk very much like Negros," while the "better sort" used only "a little of that dialect." Similarly, another Low-country traveler encountered an illiterate German overseer and his wife, who "by living with the Negroes . . . had become so accustomed to the swearing and cursing . . . that they had to do themselves violence to refrain from it during my presence." Those who lived together swore together.

From cradle to grave, plain white folk and black slaves lived near one another. Thus, although a patriarch's child might occasionally play with slaves of the same age, such contact was almost inevitable for the children of plain white folk. Charles Drayton became aware of such activity when his slave boy Jack, waiting on an overseer at an outlying plantation, came to Drayton Hall with a broken arm and dislocated shoulder, the product of his "idly riding about the fields with the ov[erseer's] son." Growing up in a poor white home might mean sharing living space with blacks, certainly living close to them, sharing much the same diet and clothes. Death, too, might bring lowly white and slave together, as in the scene described by a visitor to Maryland's Eastern Shore: "Last evening at dark the corps [of overseer Nathan Cullins] was put in a plain coffin, and conveyed to the grave, by four negroes, and one carrying a spade and shovel—No other person attended." A white overseer went to his grave unrecognized, except by the blacks with whom he labored. . . .

Although white solidarity could never be assumed in eighteenth-century Virginia or South Carolina, and although a surprising level of cooperation between lower-class whites and blacks persisted through the century, the trend was in the opposite direction. Proximity of estate induced some plain white folk to throw their lot with slaves, but more often it spurred most to put as much distance as possible between themselves and bondpeople. The eighteenth century was a crucible in which the deep and increasingly reciprocal contempt felt between lower-class whites and blacks was forged. That contempt had not emerged in fully polished form by 1800, but the essentials were in place.

The gentry helped foster lower-class contempt for slaves by aligning plain folk on their side. At the end of the seventeenth century, gentlemen busily created a legal framework that gave advantages to lower-class whites at the expense of blacks. Throughout the eighteenth century, as Edmund Morgan has shown in Virginia, the status of plain white folk rose. In part, this improvement was inadvertent, a consequence of a broadly based, rising prosperity; but ruling class efforts to reduce taxes and to involve plain folk in the political process worked to the same end. More directly relevant to their interests as slaveholders, the gentry held out inducements to lower-class whites in order that they might support and police their respective slave societies. The gentry was not uniformly successful where patrolling was concerned, but the capture of runaways seems to have been a particularly rewarding activity. Eighteenth-century Virginia county court records list several thousand claims for the capture of runaways. The vast majority of claimants were individuals outside the gentry, whereas almost two-thirds of the captured blacks belonged to members of the gentry. The ruling class had recruited plain white folk to support its interests. . . .

The resentments of poor whites toward slaves were spontaneously generated, not just encouraged from above. After all, many poor whites accurately perceived that slaves posed a threat to their livelihoods. In the Lowcountry this menace was most acute in Charleston, where a variety of white artisans expressed indignation at competition from black workers. Over the course of the eighteenth century, ship-wrights, chimney sweeps, house carpenters, brick-layers, cordwainers, master coopers, and master tailors banded together in turn to complain that blacks were taking their jobs. Their inability to halt this process was hardly designed to make them look kindly on their black counterparts. In the countryside, skilled and semi-skilled white labor increasingly felt the pressure of black competition as native-born slaves assumed positions ranging from boatman to blacksmith, wheelwright to wagoner. The nature of rural life, however, made it difficult for white laborers to organize and protest. One exception was a group of South Carolina patroons who in 1744 complained of "several Planters and others in this Province, who did order, permit and appoint their Negro Slaves to be constantly employed to go as Masters or Patroons of their Pettiaugers or small vessels without any White man on board to take any charge or care of such vessels, which hindered the Petitioners from being constantly employed there."

If plain white folk could befriend slaves and yet just as easily persecute them viciously, this ambivalence was not solely a white prerogative. Slaves sometimes turned against their erstwhile allies. They might, for example, be instrumental in the arrest of poor whites. In 1723, two York County planters claimed expenses for the capture of a runaway white servant through the combined efforts of their slaves. Sixteen years later, a witness in a Virginia county court case reported that at four o'clock in the morning he had heard "an uproar without amongst the People" and had found that his slaves had apprehended a white man who was robbing their meat house. In 1790, two whites visited the Nomini Hall estate in Lancaster County and asked directions of Robert Carter's overseer. Because it was night, the overseer was suspicious, but he let them pass. They made their way to the granary, where Carter's slave Solomon "got up and took his axe in his hand, went out and called them to, and asked them to go into his House, and warm themselves. . . . [T]hey accepted of his invitation—Solomon gave them some Bread, made them a good Fire, they laid down on some boards and fell asleep—Solomon suspecting they were the men that lately escaped from Northumberland Jail" went to the over-seer and rounded up a number of slaves sufficient to arrest his two unsuspecting visitors. Friendly, trusting slaves were not always what they seemed.

Slaves adopted even subtler methods to provoke hostility from plain white folk. An overseer employed by Landon Carter complained that Carter's waiting man, Nas-sau, had "refused to bleed him." When Carter confronted the slave, Nassau denied the story, saying the overseer had "only asked a vomit of him and he gave him one." Nassau was then sent to the sick man on his "honor not to touch a drop of Spirits" and with instructions to use both blister and lancet if necessary. Apparently, Nassau broke his promise and got drunk; perhaps that helps explain why the overseers died two days later. Slaves persecuted by word as well as by action. Morgan Godwyn observed that slaves contemptuously taunted the Irish with the claim "that if the Irishman's country had first lighted in the Englishman's way, he might have gone no further to look for Negro's." As Eugene Genovese has remarked, it was probably slaves who coined the term "po'r white trash." . . .

Relations between plain white folk and slaves are instructive in two important ways. The rift that progressively opened between the two was portentous for North America's future. Throughout the eighteenth century, whites gradually moved toward a sense of communal solidarity and purpose through their debasement of blacks. White unity was never fully achieved, but Chesapeake and Lowcountry slave societies moved steadily to a position where, functionally, they rested on a rationale of racial superiority. At the same time, lower-class whites had an ameliorative effect on the character of the two emerging slave systems. Where a large group of plain folk existed, as preeminently in Virginia, but to a lesser degree also in South Carolina, masters courted their support and generally received their recognition. The master class thus gained in legitimacy and respect, and the society as a whole could afford to have pretensions to culture and civilization. By contrast, the absence of a substantial class of nonslaveholding whites, as in many slave societies of the Caribbean and Dutch East Indies, helps explain why slavery in these places became so brutal and degrading to slaves and masters. Lower-class whites played a vital role in determining the nature of any slave society.

Encounters between whites and blacks in the eighteenth-century South were never simple or straightforward. As much as masters treated slaves as chattels, they were unable to ignore their inescapable humanity. As much as they devised barbarous laws to hamstring their slaves, they also sought ways to mitigate the impact of legislation. As much as they subjected slaves to personal domination, they also offered them personal protection. As much as they inflicted unspeakable cruelties on slaves, they also established warm and caring relationships with them. As much as they viewed slaves as animals, they never doubted slaves' desire for liberty and capacity to rebel. As much as they spoke the language of commercial capitalism, they also talked of reciprocal obligations and mutuality. As much as plain white folk and slaves became implacable foes, they also continued to share much and to cooperate. White-black relations in the eighteenth century were riven with ambiguities.

These paired polarities were not immutable. For most of the eighteenth century, control and discipline were the masters' watchwords. To be sure, masters acknowledged their obligations to provide and protect, but they were also quick to judge and punish. They were often brutal, whipping and dismembering their slaves almost at will. Yet, at least these severe taskmasters viewed slaves as integral parts of society, as members of their households. But new ways of thinking gradually emerged. By the late eighteenth century, masters began to augment their threats with appeals, temper their severity with solicitude, expect not just obedience but gratitude, and manumit not just for faithful service but out of respect and regard for their slaves. At the same time, masters who saw themselves less as taskmasters than as benefactors increasingly viewed slaves, not as organic members of society, but as outside civil society altogether. Just as the masters' worldview became more exclusive, so the everyday world of whites and blacks became more fissured. The distance between plain white folk and black slaves, for example, grew wider through the eighteenth century.

FURTHER READING

David Galenson, *White Servitude in Colonial America* (1981).

Rhys Isaac, *The Transformation of Virginia, 1740–1790* (1982).

Winthrop D. Jordan, *White over Black: American Attitudes Toward the Negro* (1986).

Allan Kulikoff, *Tobacco and Slaves: The Development of Southern Cultures in the Chesapeake, 1680–1800* (1986).

Daniel C. Littlefield, *Rice and Slaves: Ethnicity and the Slave Trade in Colonial South Carolina* (1981).

Sidney Mintz, *Sweetness and Power: The Place of Sugar in Modern History* (1985).

Edmund S. Morgan, *American Slavery, American Freedom: The Ordeal of Colonial Virginia* (1975).

Peter H. Wood, *Black Majority: Negroes in Colonial South Carolina from 1670 Through the Stono Rebellion* (1974).

CHAPTER

3

Colonial New England

and the Middle Colonies

in British America

In September of 1620, some one hundred English people boarded the Mayflower and set sail for Virginia. Most of those aboard ship were dissenters from the Church of England who called themselves Pilgrims. After nine long weeks at sea, battling sickness and Atlantic storms, they lay anchor near Cape Cod, hundreds of miles away from their intended destination. Shortly thereafter, they met Squanto, described in Chapter 1. A few years after the Mayflower's arrival, another wave of English settlers, known as Puritans, arrived in Massachusetts. Meanwhile, small colonies of Dutch and Swedish settlers, who were particularly interested in trading with the Indians, gained toeholds to the south. Although England eventually seized both New Netherlands and New Sweden, the ethnic diversity brought by these early colonization efforts would endure. In 1681, King Charles II granted William Penn a huge tract of land, which became known as Pennsylvania, or "Penn's woods." Pennsylvania too would become a site of religious and ethnic diversity. From these modest beginnings, the colonial regions of New England (the colonies of Massachusetts, Connecticut, Rhode Island, and New Hampshire) and the Middle Colonies (New York, Pennsylvania, Delaware, and New Jersey) would grow to power and influence.

From very early on, colonial New England and the Middle Colonies had several prominent features. First, religious belief deeply colored the aspirations and daily life of many colonists. Ironically, the Puritans' quest to create "holy communities" in Massachusetts led to religious conflict and encouraged some to flee westward and form their own colonies in Rhode Island and Connecticut. A variety of religious groups made use of Penn's promise of religious tolerance in the Middle Colonies and created additional communities into the eighteenth century. In the mid-eighteenth century, many colonists would be stirred to religious rebirth by a movement known as the Great Awakening. Second, ethnic diversity characterized the Middle Colonies, and this did not diminish over time; if anything, it increased. In the eighteenth century, immigrants from Ireland, Scotland, and Germany joined English colonists in settling the rich farmland of Pennsylvania. As the century progressed, they participated in *a westward migration that brought them into contact—and often into conflict—with Indians. A third characteristic was an interest in trade; even though the Dutch traders were conquered by the British, their economic aspirations for a trading empire endured. By the eighteenth century, merchants from the Middle Colonies and New England dominated colonial trade. Fleets of ships, owned and operated by American colonists, plied their trade throughout the Atlantic world.*

The endurance of these features led the economies of New England and the Middle Colonies to develop in ways that differed from those of the southern colonies. Slavery existed in all the British American colonies, but plantation agriculture never took root in the soils of the North. Rather, people in these colonies either farmed or joined a growing mercantile and artisanal class that provided services or made goods for the whole colonial economy. These activities changed the society and culture of the northern colonies as well as their economy. Religious goals tended to give way to economic ones; as some historians have pointed out, "puritans" became "yankees." Americans also began to focus on the economic opportunity that their society offered to Europe's poor. More than one American observed that their colony was "the best poor man's country" in the world. The emblematic colonist now was not a Puritan divine, but someone such as Ben Franklin, a self-made man who celebrated the virtues of thrift, self-control, and patience.

☛ Q U E S T I O N S   T O   T H I N K   A B O U T

Historians have been fascinated by the transformation of religious colonies into secular societies. What psychological anxieties might have resulted from this transition? In what ways might these anxieties have been manifested in society? How did the population of the northern colonies differ from that of the South in terms of occupation and ethnic background? How did this contribute to a colonial world different from that of the plantation South?

☛ D O C U M E N T S

The first five documents illustrate the early hopes of creating a colonial society and the tensions and failures that punctuated the first century of settlement. The Pilgrims and Puritans were very concerned about creating an ideal society in New England. Whereas the Pilgrims wrote a contract called the Mayflower Compact in 1620, Puritan leaders also put down their beliefs about the proper organization of their society, as evidenced in Document 1. Written by Governor John Winthrop in 1630, *A Model of Christian Charity* asks the people to work together to create a godly society. Unfortunately, the hopes of fostering such a society were often challenged. Document 2, written by Pilgrim William Bradford, is an explanation of what happens when wickedness—in this case, bestiality—occurred and how it might be explained. When Pennsylvania was founded, William Penn wrote an account of the colony, which is Document 3, that described its attributes and, more importantly, encouraged people to move there. Document 4 is an account of another challenge to New England society: the Salem witchcraft outbreak in 1692. Notice how the accused and accusers explained the events in court by invoking supernatural behavior. In the mid-eighteenth century, a religious revival known as the Great Awakening burst forth, again in part as a result of tensions in society. Document 5 is a segment from a sermon by Reverend Jonathan Edwards that graphically depicts hell and the possibility that sinners will find themselves there for eternity. The next two documents illustrate the economic changes in northern society that were reflected in society. In Document 6, Benjamin Franklin provides us with a blueprint for living with frugality and industriousness. While Franklin eschewed the acquisition of wealth for the sake of opulence, Document 7 is from a diary by a Scottish traveler named Alexander Hamilton, who noted in 1744 that northerners were increasingly buying material goods and displaying these goods in their homes. In Document 8, a German immigrant named Gottlieb Mittelberger tells how Germans coming to America often faced a frightful journey and then had to serve terms as unfree laborers to pay off the costs of their passage. Mary Jemison, whose narrative is found in Document 9, moved from northern Ireland as a girl. But her life was abruptly altered when she was abducted by the Shawnee Indians and ultimately integrated into the Seneca nation, with whom she lived for the remainder of her life.

1. Governor John Winthrop Provides a Model of Christian Charity, 1630

1. For the persons, we are a Company professing ourselves fellow members of Christ. . . .

2. for the work we have in hand, it is by a mutual consent through a special over-ruling providence, and a more than an ordinary approbation of the Churches of Christ to seek out a place of Cohabitation and Consortship under a due form of Government both civil and ecclesiastical. . . .

3. The end is to improve our lives to do more service to the Lord the comfort and increase of the body of christ whereof we are members that ourselves and posterity may be the better preserved from the Common corruptions of this evil world. . . .

4. for the means whereby this must be effected, they are 2fold, a Conformity with the work and end we aim at, these we see are extraordinary, therefore we must not content ourselves with usual ordinary means whatsoever we did or ought to have done when we lived in England, the same must we do and more also where we go: That which the most in their Churches maintain as a truth in profession only, we must bring into familiar and constant practice, as in this duty of love we must love brotherly without dissimulation, we must love one another with a pure heart fervently we must bear one another's burdens, we must not look only on our own things, but also on the things of our brethren, neither must we think that the lord will bear with such failings at our hands as he doth from those among whom we have lived. . . .

. . . [F]or we must Consider that we shall be as a City upon a Hill, the eyes of all people are upon us; so that if we shall deal falsely with out god in this work we have undertaken and so cause him to withdraw his present help from us, we shall be made a story and a by-word through the world, we shall open the mouths of enemies to speak evil of the ways of god and all professors for God's sake; we

John Winthrop, *A Model of Christian Charity*, 1630, in Massachusetts Historical Society, *Collections*, 3rd ser., VII (1838), 3–48; reprinted in Massachusetts Historical Society, *Winthrop Papers*, II (Boston: Massachusetts Historical Society, 1931), 282–295.

shall shame the faces of many of gods worthy servants, and cause their prayers to be turned into Curses upon us till we be consumed out of the good land whether we are going.

2. Governor William Bradford Mourns a Wickedness That Breaks Forth, 1642

Marvilous it may be to see and consider how some kind of wickednes did grow and breake forth here, in a land wher the same was so much witnesed against, and so narrowly looked unto, and severly punished when it was knowne; as in no place more, or so much, that I have known or heard of; insomuch as they have been some-what censured, even by moderate and good men, for their severitie in punishments. And yet all this could not suppress the breaking out of sundrie notorious sins, (as this year, besides other, gives us too many sad presidents and instances,) espetially drunkennes and un[cleannes]; not only in continencie betweene persons unmaried, for which many both men and women have been punished sharply enough, but some maried persons allso. But that which is worse, even sodomie and bugerie, (things fearful to name,) have broak forth in this land, oftener then once. I say it may justly be marveled at, and cause us to fear and tremble at the consideration of our corrupte natures, which are so hardly bridled, subdued, and mortified; nay, cannot by any other means but the powerful worke and grace of Gods spirite. . . .

. . . Ther was a youth whose name was Thomas Granger; he was servant to an honest man of Duxbery, being about 16 or 17 years of age. (His father and mother lived at the same time at Sityate.) He was this year detected of buggery (and indicted for the same) with a mare, a cowe, [two] goats, five sheep, [two] calves, and a turkey . . . And accordingly he was cast by the jury, and condemned, and after executed about the 8 of Sept[ember,] 1642. A very sade spectakle it was; for first the mare, and then the cowe, and the rest of the lesser catle, were [killed] before his face, ac-cording to the law, Levit: 20 15. and then he him selfe was executed. The catle were all cast into a great and large pitte that was digged of purpose for them, and no use made of any part of them.

Upon the examenation of this person, and also of a former that had made some sodomiticall attempts upon another, it being demanded of them how they came first to the knowledge and practice of shuch wickednes, the one confessed he had long used it in old England; and this youth last spoaken of said he was taught it by an other that had heard of shuch things from some in England when he was ther, and they kept catle togeather. By which it appears how one wicked person may infecte many; and what care all ought to have what servants they bring into their families.

But it may be demanded how came it to pass that so many wicked persons and profane people should so quickly come over into this land, and mixe them selves amongst them? seeing it was religious men that begane the work, and they came for religions sake.

William Bradford, *History of Plymouth Plantation, 1620–1647,* II (Boston: Massachusetts Historical Society, 1912), 308–310, 328–330.

3. William Penn Promotes His Colony, 1681

Since (by the good providence of God) a country in *America* is fallen to my lot, I thought it not less my duty than my honest interest to give some public notice of it to the world, that those of our own, or other nations, that are inclined to transport themselves or families beyond the seas, may find another country added to their choice. . . . But before I come to treat of my particular concernment, I shall take leave to say something of the benefit of *plantations* or *colonies* in general, to obviate a common objection.

Colonies, then, are the seeds of nations begun and nourished by the care of wise and populous countries, as conceiving them best for the increase of human stock, and beneficial for commerce.

Some of the wisest men in history have justly taken their fame from this design and service. . . .

Nor did any of these ever dream it was the way of decreasing their people or wealth. For the cause of the decay of any of those states or empires was not their *plantations,* but their *luxury and corruption of manner.* . . . I deny the vulgar opinion against *plantations, that they weaken* England. They have manifestly enriched and so strengthened her, which I briefly evidence thus:

1st. Those that go into a foreign *plantation*, their industry there is worth more than if they stayed at home, the product of their labor being in commodities of a superior nature to those of this *country.* . . .

2dly. More being produced and imported than we can spend here, we export it to other countries in *Europe,* which brings in money or the growth of those countries, which is the same thing. And this is [to] the advantage of the *English* merchants and seamen.

3dly. Such as could not only not *marry* here, but hardly live and allow themselves clothes, do marry there, and bestow thrice more in all necessaries and conveniencies (and not a little in ornamental things, too) for themselves, their wives, and children, both as to apparel and household stuff. . . .

4thly. But let it be considered *that the plantations employ many hundreds of shipping and many thousands of seamen,* which must be in diverse respects an advantage to *England,* being an island, and by nature fitted for navigation above any country in *Europe.* This is followed by other depending trades, as *shipwrights, carpenters, sawyers, hewers.* . . .

The place lies 600 miles nearer the sun than *England;* for *England* begins at the 50th degree and ten minutes of north latitude, and this place begins at forty, which is about the latitude of *Naples* in *Italy,* or *Montpellier* in *France.* I shall say little in its praise to excite desires in any, whatever I could truly write as to the soil, air, and water. This shall satisfy me, that by the *blessing* of God and the honesty and industry of man, it may be a good and fruitful land.

Jean R. Soderlund, ed., *William Penn and the Founding of Pennsylvania, 1680–1684: A Documentary History* (Philadelphia: University of Pennsylvania Press, 1983), 58–60, 62–65.

For *navigation* it is said to have two conveniencies: the one by lying nine score miles upon *Delaware* River. . . . The other convenience is through *Chesapeake Bay*.

For timber and other wood, there is variety for the use of man.

For *fowl, fish,* and *wild deer,* they are reported to be plentiful in those parts. Our *English* provision is likewise now to be had there at reasonable rates. The commodities that the country is thought to be *capable* of, are *silk, flax, hemp, wine, cider, wood, madder, licorice, tobacco, potashes,* and *iron,* and it does actually produce *hides, tallow, pipe-staves,* beef, pork, sheep, wool, corn, as *wheat, barley, rye,* and also *furs,* as your *peltry, minks, raccoons, martens,* and such like; store of *furs* which is to be found among the *Indians,* that are profitable commodities in *Europe.*

The way of trading in those countries is thus: they send to the southern plantations *corn, beef, pork, fish,* and *pipe-staves,* and take their growth and bring for *England,* and return with *English* goods to their own country. Their *furs* they bring for *England,* and either sell them here, or carry them out again to other parts of *Europe,* where they will yield a better price. And for those that will follow *merchandise* and *navigation,* there is conveniency, and *timber sufficient for shipping.* . . .

These persons that Providence seems to have most fitted for plantations are,

1st. Industrious *husbandmen* and *day laborers,* that are hardly able (with extreme labor) to maintain their families and portion their children.

2dly. Laborious *handicrafts,* especially *carpenters, masons, smiths, weavers, tailors, tanners, shoemakers, shipwrights,* etc. . . .

3dly. A plantation seems a fit place for those *ingenious spirits* that being low in the world, are much clogged and oppressed about a livelihood. . . .

4thly. A fourth sort of men to whom a *plantation* would be proper, takes in those that are *younger brothers* of small inheritances. . . .

Lastly, there are another sort of persons, not only fit for, but necessary in *plantations,* and that is, *men of universal spirits* that have an eye to the good of posterity, and that both understand and delight to promote good discipline and just government among a plain and well intending people. Such persons may find *room in colonies for their good counsel and contrivance,* who are shut out from being of much use or service to great nations under settled customs. These men deserve much esteem, and would be hearkened to. . . .

To conclude, I desire all my dear country folks, who may be inclined to go into those parts, to consider seriously the premises, *as well the present inconveniences as future ease and plenty,* that so none may move rashly or from a fickle but solid mind, *having above all things, as eye to the providence of God, in the disposal of themselves.* And I would further advise all such at least, to have the permission, if not the good liking of their near relations, for that is both natural, and a duty incumbent upon all; and by this means will natural affection be preserved, and a friendly and profitable correspondence be maintained between them. In all which *I beseech Almighty God to direct us, that His blessing may attend our honest endeavor, and then the consequence of all our undertaking will turn to the glory of His great name, and the true happiness of us and our posterity.* Amen.

4. Massachusetts Officials Describe the Outbreak of Witchcraft in Salem, 1692

Mr. Parris had been some years a Minister in Salem-Village, when this sad Calamity (as a deluge) overflowed them, spreading it self far and near: . . .

It was the latter end of February 1691, when divers young Persons belonging to Mr. Parris's Family, and one or more of the Neighbourhood, began to Act, after a strange and unusual manner, *viz.* as by getting into Holes, and creeping under Chairs and Stools, and to use sundry odd Postures and Antick Gestures, uttering foolish, ridiculous Speeches, which neither they themselves nor any others could make sense of; the Physicians that were called could assign no reason for this; but it seems one of them, having recourse to the old shift, told them he was afraid they were Bewitched; upon such suggestions, they that were concerned applied themselves to Fasting and Prayer, which was attended not only in their own private Families, but with calling in the help of others.

March the 11th. Mr. Parris invited several Neighbouring Ministers to join with him in keeping a Solemn day of Prayer at his own House; the time of the exercise those Persons were for the most part silent, but after any one Prayer was ended, they would Act and Speak strangely and Ridiculously, yet were such as had been well Educated and of good Behaviour, the one, a Girl of 11 or 12 years old, would sometimes seem to be in a Convulsion Fit, her Limbs being twisted several ways, and very stiff, but presently her Fit would be over.

A few days before this Solemn day of Prayer, Mr. Parris's Indian Man and Woman made a Cake of Rye Meal, with the Childrens Water, and Baked it in the Ashes, and as is said, gave it to the Dog; this was done as a means to Discover Witchcraft, soon after which those ill affected or afflicted Persons named several that they said they saw, when in their Fits, afflicting of them.

The first complain'd of, was the said Indian Woman, named Tituba. She confessed that the Devil urged her to sign a Book, which he presented to her, and also to work Mischief to the Children, etc. She was afterwards Committed to Prison, and lay there till Sold for her Fees. The account she since gives of it is, that her Master did beat her and otherways abuse her, to make her confess and accuse (such as he call'd) her Sister-Witches, and that whatsoever she said by way of confessing or accusing others, was the effect of such usage; her Master refused to pay her Fees, unless she would stand to what she had said.

The Children complained likewise of two other Women, to be the Authors of their Hurt, *Viz.* Sarah Good, who had long been counted a Melancholy or Distracted Woman, and one Osburn, an Old Bed-rid Woman; which two were Persons so ill thought of, that the accusation was the more readily believed; and after Examination before two Salem Magistrates, were committed:

March the 19th, Mr. Lawson (who had been formerly a Preacher at the said Village) came thither, and hath since set fourth in Print an account of what then passed, about which time, as he saith, they complained of Goodwife Cory, and

"An Impartial Account of the Most Memorable Matters of Fact, Touching the Supposed Witchcraft in New England," in George Lincoln Burr, *Narratives of the Witchcraft Cases* (New York: Barnes and Noble Books, 1914), 341–344.

Goodwife Nurse, Members of the Churches at the Village and at Salem, many others being by that time Accused.

March the 21*st,* Goodwife Cory was examined before the Magistrates of Salem, at the Meeting House in the Village, a throng of Spectators being present to see the Novelty. Mr. Noyes, one of the Ministers of Salem, began with Prayer, after which the Prisoner being call'd, in order to answer to what should be Alledged against her, she desired that she might go to Prayer, and was answered by the Magistrates, that they did not come to hear her pray, but to examine her.

The number of Afflicted were at that time about Ten, *Viz.* Mrs. Pope, Mrs. Putman, Goodwife Bibber, and Goodwife Goodall, Mary Wolcott, Mercy Lewes (at Thomas Putmans) and Dr. Griggs Maid, and three Girls, *Viz.* Elizabeth Parris, Daughter to the Minister, Abigail Williams his Neice, and Ann Putman, which last three were not only the beginners, but were also the chief in these Accusations. These Ten were most of them present at the Examination, and did vehemently accuse her of Afflicting them, by Biting, Pinching, Strangling, etc. And they said, they did in their Fits see her likeness coming to them, and bringing a Book for them to Sign; Mr. Hathorn, a Magistrate of Salem, asked her, why she Afflicted those Children? she said, she did not Afflict them; he asked her, who did then? she said, "I do not know, how should I know?" she said, they were Poor Distracted Creatures, and no heed to be given to what they said; Mr. Hathorn and Mr. Noyes replied that it was the Judgment of all that were there present, that they were bewitched, and only she (the Accused) said they were Distracted: She was Accused by them, that the Black Man Whispered to her in her Ear now (while she was upon Examination) and that she had a Yellow Bird, that did use to Suck between her Fingers, and that the said Bird did Suck now in the Assembly; order being given to look in that place to see if there were any sign, the Girl that pretended to see it said, that it was too late now, for she had removed a Pin, and put it on her Head, it was upon search found, that a Pin was there sticking upright. When the Accused had any motion of their Body, Hands or Mouth, the Accusers would cry out, as when she bit her Lip, they would cry out of being bitten, if she grasped one hand with the other, they would cry out of being Pinched by her, and would produce marks, so of the other motions of her Body, as complaining of being Prest, when she lean'd to the seat next her, if she stirred her Feet, they would stamp and cry out of Pain there. After the hearing the said Cory was committed to Salem Prison, and then their crying out of her abated.

5. Jonathan Edwards Pictures Sinners in the Hands of an Angry God, 1741

. . . This that you have heard is the case of every one of you that are out of Christ. That world of misery, that lake of burning brimstone, is extended abroad under you. There is the dreadful pit of the glowing flames of the wrath of God; there is hell's wide gaping mouth open; and you have nothing to stand upon, nor any thing

"Sinners in the Hands of an Angry God," Enfield, July 8, 1741 (Salem, Mass.: G. Roulstone, 1786), 1st ser., no. 19618.

to take hold of; there is nothing between you and hell but the air; 'tis only the power and mere pleasure of God that holds you up.

You probably are not sensible of this; you find you are kept out of hell, but don't see the hand of God in it, but look at other things, as the good state of your bodily constitution, your care of your own life, and the means you use for your own preservation. But indeed these things are nothing; if God should withdraw his hand, they would avail no more to keep you from falling, than the thin air to hold up a person that is suspended in it.

Your wickedness makes you as it were heavy as lead, and to tend downwards with great weight and pressure towards hell; and, if God should let you go, you would immediately sink, and swiftly descend and plunge into the bottomless gulf; and your healthy constitution, and your own care and prudence, and best contrivance, and all your righteousness, would have no more influence to uphold you and keep you out of hell, than a spider's web would have to stop a falling rock. . . .

The God that holds you over the pit of hell, much as one holds a spider or some loathsome insect over the fire, abhors you, and is dreadfully provoked. His wrath towards you burns like fire; he looks upon you as worthy of nothing else but to be cast into the fire. He is of purer eyes than to bear you in his sight; you are ten thousand times as abominable in his eyes as the most hateful, venomous serpent is in ours. You have offended him infinitely more than ever a stubborn rebel did his prince, and yet 'tis nothing but his hand that holds you from falling into the fire every moment. . . .

O sinner! Consider the fearful danger you are in! 'Tis a great furnace of wrath, a wide and bottomless pit, full of fire and of wrath that you are held over in the hand of that God whose wrath is provoked and incensed as much against you as against many of the damned in hell. You hang by a slender thread, with the flames of Divine wrath flashing about it, and ready every moment to singe it and burn it asunder. . . .

It would be dreadful to suffer this fierceness and wrath of Almighty God one moment; but you must suffer it to all eternity. There will be no end to this exquisite, horrible, misery. . . .

How dreadful is the state of those that are daily and hourly in danger of this great wrath and infinite misery! But this is the dismal case of every soul in this congregation that has not been born again, however moral and strict, sober and religious, they may otherwise be. Oh! that you would consider it, whether you be young or old!

6. Benjamin Franklin Celebrates a Life of Thrift and Industry (c. 1730–c. 1750), 1793

I now opened a small stationer's shop. I had in it blanks of all kinds; the correctest that ever appeared among us. . . .

I began now gradually to pay off the debt I was under for the printing-house. In order to secure my credit and character as a tradesman, I took care not only to be in *reality* industrious and frugal, but to avoid the appearances to the contrary. I dressed plain, and was seen at no places of idle diversion. . . . And, to show that I was not above my business, I sometimes brought home the paper I purchased at the

Benjamin Franklin, *Autobiography* (London: Hutchinson & Co., 1903), 81–92.

stores, through the streets on a wheelbarrow. Thus being esteemed an industrious, thriving young man and paying duly for what I bought, the merchants who imported stationery solicited my custom: others proposed supplying me with books, and I went on prosperously. . . .

At the time I established myself in Pennsylvania, there was not a good book-seller's shop in any of the colonies to the southward of Boston. In New York and Philadelphia, the printers were indeed stationers; but they sold only paper, almanacs, ballads, and a few common school-books. Those who loved reading were obliged to send for their books from England; the members of the Junto had each a few. We had left the ale-house, where we first met, and hired a room to hold our club in. I proposed that we should all of us bring our books to that room, where they would not only be ready to consult in our conferences, but become a common benefit, each of us being at liberty to borrow such as he wished to read at home. This was accordingly done, and for some time contented us.

Finding the advantage of this little collection, I proposed to render the benefit from the books more common by commencing a public subscription library. . . . So few were the readers at that time in Philadelphia, and the majority of us so poor that I was not able with great industry to find more than fifty persons, mostly young trades-men, willing to pay down for this purpose forty shillings each, and ten shillings per annum. With this little fund we began. The books were imported. The library was opened one day in the week for lending them to subscribers, on their promissory notes to pay double the value if not duly returned. The institution soon manifested its utility, was imitated by other towns, and in other provinces. The libraries were aug-mented by donations, reading became fashionable; and our people having no public amusements to divert their attention from study, became better acquainted with books, and in a few years were observed by strangers to be better instructed and more intelligent than people of the same rank generally are in other countries. . . .

The objections and reluctances I met with in soliciting the subscriptions made me soon feel the impropriety of presenting one's self as the proposer of any useful project that might be supposed to raise one's reputation in the smallest degree above that of one's neighbours, when one has need of their assistance to accom-plish that project. I therefore put myself as much as I could out of sight, and stated it as a scheme of a *number of friends,* who had requested me to go about and pro-pose it to such as they thought lovers of reading. In this way my affair went on more smoothly, and I ever after practised it on such occasions; and, from my fre-quent successes, can heartily recommend it. The present little sacrifice of your vanity will afterwards be amply repaid. If it remains a while uncertain to whom the merit belongs, some one more vain than yourself may be encouraged to claim it, and then even envy will be disposed to do you justice, by plucking those assumed feathers, and restoring them to their right owner.

This library afforded me the means of improvement by constant study, for which I set apart an hour or two each day, and thus repaired in some degree the loss of the learned education my father once intended for me. Reading was the only amusement I allowed myself. I spent no time in taverns, games, or frolics of any kind; and my industry in my business continued as indefatigable as it was necessary. . . . My cir-cumstances, however, grew daily easier. My original habits of frugality continuing, and my father having, among his instructions to me when a boy, frequently repeated a proverb of Solomon, *"Seest thou a man diligent in his calling, he shall stand before kings, he shall not stand before mean men."* I thence considered industry as a means of obtaining wealth and distinction, which encouraged me—though I did not think that I should ever literally *stand before kings,* which, however, has since happened; for I have stood before *five,* and even had the honour of sitting down with one, the King of Denmark, to dinner.

7. Dr. Alexander Hamilton Depicts the Material Acquisitions of Northern Colonists, 1744

New York

Saturday, June 16th. . . .

I found the city less in extent, but by the stir and frequency upon the streets, more populous than Philadelphia. I saw more shipping in the harbour. The houses are more compact and regular, and in general higher built, most of them after the Dutch model, with their gavell ends fronting the street. There are a few built of stone; more of wood, but the greatest number of brick, and a great many covered with pantile and glazed tile with the year of God when built figured out with plates of iron, upon the fronts of several of them. The streets in general are but narrow, and not regularly disposed. The best of them run parallel to the river, for the city is built all along the water, in general.

This city has more of an urban appearance than Philadelphia. Their wharfs are mostly built with logs of wood piled upon a stone foundation. In the city are several large public buildings. There is a spacious church, belonging to the English congregation, with a pretty high, but heavy, clumsy steeple, built of freestone. . . .

Schenectady

. . . In the city are about 4,000 inhabitants, mostly Dutch or of Dutch extract.

The Dutch here keep their houses very neat and clean, both without and within. Their chamber floors are generally laid with rough plank, which in time, by constant rubbing and scrubbing, becomes as smooth as if it had been planed. Their chambers and rooms are large and handsome. They have their beds generally in alcoves, so that you may go thro' all the rooms of a great house and see never a bed. They affect pictures much, particularly scripture history, with which they adorn their rooms. They set out their cabinets and *buffets* much with china. Their kitchens are likewise very clean, and there they hang earthen or delft plates and dishes all round the walls, in manner of pictures, having a hole drilled thro' the edge of the plate or dish, and a loop of ribbon put into it to hang it by; but notwithstanding all this nicety and cleanliness in their houses they are in their persons slovenly and dirty. They live here very frugally and plain, for the chief merit among them seems to be riches, which they spare no pains or trouble to acquire, but are a civil and hospitable people in their way, but at best rustic and unpolished. . . .

Dr. Alexander Hamilton, *Hamilton's Itinerarium: Being a Narrative of a Journey . . . from May to September, 1744,* ed. Albert Bushnell Hart (St. Louis: The De Vinne Press, 1907), 51, 87–88, 182–183, 197.

Nantucket Fall . . .

While I waited for the chocolate which I had ordered for breakfast, Angell gave me an account of his religion and opinions, which I found were as much out of the common road as the man himself. I observed a paper pasted upon the wall, which was a rabble of dull controversy betwixt two learned divines, of as great consequence to the publick as *The Story of the King and the Cobbler* or *The Celebrated History of the Wise Men of Gotham*. This controversy was intituled *Cannons to batter the Tower of Babel*. Among the rest of the chamber furniture were several elegant pictures, finely illuminated and coloured, being the famous piece of *The Battle for the Breeches, The Twelve Golden Rules*, taken from King Charles I's study, of blessed memory (as he is very judiciously styled), *The Christian Coat of Arms*, &c., &c., &c., in which pieces are set forth divine attitudes and elegant passions, all sold by Overton, that inimitable ale-house designer at the White Horse without Newgate. . . .

New London . . .

I went home at six o'clock, and Deacon Green's son came to see me. He entertained me with the history of the behaviour of one Davenport, a fanatick preacher there, who told his flock in one of his enthusiastic rhapsodies, that in order to be saved they ought to burn all their idols. They began this conflagration with a pile of books in the publick street, among which were Tillotson's *Sermons*, Beveridge's *Thoughts*, Drillincourt on *Death*, Sherlock, and many other excellent authors, and sang psalms and hymns over the pile while it was a-burning. They did not stop here, but the women made up a lofty pile of hoop petticoats, silk gowns, short cloaks, cambrick caps, red-heeled shoes, fans, necklaces, gloves, and other such apparel, and, what was merry enough, Davenport's own idol, with which he topped the pile, was a pair of old wore-out plush breeches.

8. Gottlieb Mittelberger, a German, Portrays the Difficulties of Immigration, 1750

When the ships have weighed anchor for the last time, usually off Cowes in Old England, then both the long sea voyage and misery begin in earnest. For from there the ships often take eight, nine, ten, or twelve weeks sailing to Philadelphia, if the wind is unfavorable. But even given the most favorable winds, the voyage takes seven weeks.

During the journey the ship is full of pitiful signs of distress—smells, fumes, horrors, vomiting, various kinds of sea sickness, fever, dysentery, headaches, heat, constipation, boils, scurvy, cancer, mouth-rot, and similar afflictions, all of them caused by the age and the highly-salted state of the food, especially of the meat, as well as by the very bad and filthy water, which brings about the miserable destruction and death of many. Add to all that shortage of food, hunger, thirst, frost, heat, dampness, fear, misery, vexation, and lamentation as well as other troubles. Thus,

Gottlieb Mittelberger, *Reise nach Pennsylvania (Journey to Pennsylvania)*, 1756.

for example, there are so many lice, especially on the sick people, that they have to be scraped off the bodies. All this misery reaches its climax when in addition to everything else one must also suffer through two to three days and nights of storm, with everyone convinced that the ship with all aboard is bound to sink. In such misery all the people on board pray and cry pitifully together. . . .

Among those who are in good health impatience sometimes grows so great and bitter that one person begins to curse the other, or himself and the day of his birth, and people sometimes come close to murdering one another. Misery and malice are readily associated, so that people begin to cheat and steal from one another. And then one always blames the other for having undertaken the voyage. Often the children cry out against their parents, husbands against wives and wives against husbands, brothers against sisters, friends and acquaintances against one another.

But most of all they cry out against the thieves of human beings! Many groan and exclaim: "Oh! If only I were back at home, even lying in my pig-sty!" Or they call out: "Ah, dear God, if I only once again had a piece of good bread or a good fresh drop of water." Many people whimper, sigh, and cry out pitifully for home. . . .

When at last after the long and difficult voyage the ships finally approach land, when one gets to see the headlands for the sight of which the people on board had longed so passionately, then everyone crawls from below to the deck, in order to look at the land from afar. And people cry for joy, pray, and sing praises and thanks to God. The glimpse of land revives the passengers, especially those who are half-dead of illness. Their spirits, however weak they had become, leap up, triumph, and rejoice within them. . . .

When the ships finally arrive in Philadelphia after the long voyage only those are let off who can pay their sea freight or can give good security. The others, who lack the money to pay, have to remain on board until they are purchased and until their purchasers can thus pry them loose from the ship. In this whole process the sick are the worst off, for the healthy are preferred and are more readily paid for. The miserable people who are ill must often still remain at sea and in sight of the city for another two or three weeks—which in many cases means death. Yet many of them, were they able to pay their debts and to leave the ships at once, might escape with their lives. . . .

This is how the commerce in human beings on board ship takes place. Every day Englishmen, Dutchmen, and High Germans come from Philadelphia and other places, some of them very far away, sometime twenty or thirty or forty hours' journey, and go on board the newly arrived vessel that has brought people from Europe and offers them for sale. From among the healthy they pick those suitable for the purposes for which they require them. Then they negotiate with them as to the length of the period for which they will go into service in order to pay off their passage, the whole amount of which they generally still owe. When an agreement has been reached, adult persons by written contract bind themselves to serve for three, four, five, or six years, according to their health and age. The very young, between the ages of ten and fifteen, have to serve until they are twenty-one, however.

Many parents in order to pay their fares in this way and get off the ship must barter and sell their children as if they were cattle. Since the fathers and mothers often do not know where or to what masters their children are to be sent, it frequently happens that after leaving the vessel, parents and children do not see each other for years on end, or even for the rest of their lives.

9. Mary Jemison Recounts Her Experience of Capture and Becoming Seneca, 1755

. . . Our family, as usual, was busily employed about their common business. Father was shaving an axe-helve at the side of the house; mother was making preparations for breakfast;—my two oldest brothers were at work near the barn; and the little ones, with myself, and the woman and her three children, were in the house.

Breakfast was not yet ready, when we were alarmed by the discharge of a number of guns, that seemed to be near. Mother and the women before mentioned, almost fainted at the report, and every one trembled with fear. . . .

. . . They first secured my father, and then rushed into the house, and without the least resistance made prisoners of my mother, Robert, Matthew, Betsey, the woman and her three children, and myself, and then commenced plundering. . . .

The party that took us consisted of six Indians and four Frenchmen, who immediately commenced plundering, as I just observed, and took what they considered most valuable; consisting principally of bread, meal and meat. Having taken as much provision as they could carry, they set out with their prisoners in great haste, for fear of detection, and soon entered the woods. . . .

Early the next morning the Indians and Frenchmen that we had left the night before, came to us; but our friends were left behind. It is impossible for any one to form a correct idea of what my feelings were at the sight of those savages, whom I supposed had murdered my parents and brothers, sister, and friends, and left them in the swamp to be devoured by wild beasts! But what could I do? . . .

My suspicions as to the fate of my parents proved too true; for soon after I left them they were killed and scalped, together with Robert, Matthew, Betsey, and the woman and her two children, and mangled in the most shocking manner. . . .

After a hard day's march we encamped in a thicket, where the Indians made a shelter of boughs, and then built a good fire to warm and dry our benumbed limbs and clothing; for it had rained some through the day. . . .

In the course of the night they made me to understand that they should not have killed the family if the whites had not pursued them. . . .

At the place where we halted, the Indians combed the hair of the young man, the boy and myself, and then painted our faces and hair red, in the finest Indian style. We were then conducted into the fort, where we received a little bread and were then shut up and left to tarry alone through the night. . . .

The morning at length arrived, and our masters came early and let us out of the house. . . .

. . . [I]t was not long before I was in some measure relieved by the appearance of two pleasant looking squaws of the Seneca tribe, who came and examined me attentively for a short time, and then went out. After a few minutes absence they returned with my former masters, who gave me to them to dispose of as they pleased. . . .

At night we arrived at a small Seneca Indian town, at the mouth of a small river, that was called by the Indians, in the Seneca language, She-nan-jee. . . .

A Narrative of the Life of Mrs. Mary Jemison (1824; reprint, American Scenic and Historic Preservation Society, 1982).

Having made fast to the shore, the Squaws left me in the canoe while they went to their wigwam or house in the town, and returned with a suit of Indian clothing, all new, and very clean and nice. My clothes, though whole and good when I was taken, were now torn in pieces, so that I was almost naked. They first undressed me and threw my rags into the river; then washed me clean and dressed me in the new suit they had just brought, in complete Indian style; and then led me home and seated me in the center of their wigwam.

I had been in that situation but a few minutes, before all the Squaws in the town came in to see me. I was soon surrounded by them, and they immediately set up a most dismal howling, crying bitterly, and wringing their hands in all the agonies of grief for a deceased relative. . . .

"Oh our brother! Alas! He is dead—he has gone; he will never return! Friendless he died on the field of the slain, where his bones are yet lying unburied! Oh, who will mourn his sad fate? No tears dropped around him; oh no! No tears of his sisters were there! . . .

. . . His spirit has seen our distress, and sent us a helper whom with pleasure we greet. Dickewamis has come: then let us receive her with joy! She is handsome and pleasant! Oh! She is our sister, and gladly we welcome her here. In the place of our brother she stands in our tribe. With care we will guard her from trouble; and may she be happy till her spirit shall leave us."

In the course of that ceremony, from mourning they became serene—joy sparkled in their countenances, and they seemed to rejoice over me as over a long lost child. I was made welcome amongst them as a sister to the two Squaws before mentioned, and was called Dickewamis; which being interpreted, signifies a pretty girl, a handsome girl, or a pleasant, good thing. That is the name by which I have ever since been called by the Indians.

I afterwards learned that the ceremony I at that time passed through, was that of adoption. The two squaws had lost a brother in Washington's war, sometime in the year before, and in consequence of his death went up to Fort Pitt, on the day on which I arrived there, in order to receive a prisoner or an enemy's scalp, to supply their loss.

. . . If they receive a prisoner, it is at their option either to satiate their vengeance by taking his life in the most cruel manner they can conceive of; or, to receive and adopt him into the family, in the place of him whom they have lost. All the prisoners that are taken in battle and carried to the encampment or town by the Indians, are given to the bereaved families, till their number is made good.

⬛ E S S A Y S

As farms were established and cities were formed, Americans in the northern colonies fostered an economic development that remarkably changed their society. Historians have puzzled over the meaning of these changes in the minds of colonial Americans. James A. Henretta, who teaches at the University of Maryland, argues that farmers in the colonial North were "pre-capitalist" people who measured their success by how well they provided resources for the next generation. Traditional in orientation, they did not think of themselves as individuals, but rather as people who were part of a group. In contrast, T. H. Breen, a historian at Northwestern University, observes that colonial

Americans were less concerned with self-sufficiency than with becoming part of an "empire of goods." Americans were consumers, and in order to consume, they needed to accumulate wealth. Breen argues that Americans' patterns of consumption fostered identities that not only tied them to the British Empire, but enabled them to perceive common bonds with other colonists.

The Northern Colonies as a
Family-Centered Society

JAMES A. HENRETTA

The history of the agricultural population of pre-industrial America remains to be written. As a result of quantitative investigations of wealth distribution and social mobility; of rates of birth, marriage, and death; and of patterns of inheritance, office-holding, and church membership, there is an ever-growing mass of data that delineates the *structures* of social existence in the small rural communities that constituted the core of American agricultural society in the North before 1830. But what of the *consciousness* of the inhabitants, the mental or emotional or ideological aspects of their lives? And what of the relationship between the two? Can a careful statistical analysis of people's lives—a precise description of their patterns of social action—substantiate at least limited statements as to their motivations, values, and goals? . . .

This process of production and capital formation derived much of its emotive and intellectual meaning from the cultural matrix—from the institutional character of the society. Work was arranged along familial lines rather than controlled communally or through a wage system. This apparently simple organizational fact was a crucial determinant of the historical consciousness of this farming population. For even as the family gave symbolic meaning and emotional significance to subsistence activities, its own essence was shaped by the character of the productive system. There was a complex relationship between the agricultural labor and property system of early America and its rural culture; and it is that matrix of productive activities, organizational structures, and social values which the following analysis attempts (in a very preliminary fashion) to reconstruct.

Because the primary economic unit—the family—was also the main social institution, production activities had an immense impact on the entire character of agrarian life. Family relationships could not be divorced from economic considerations; indeed, the basic question of power and authority within the family hinged primarily on legal control over the land and—indirectly—over the labor needed to work it. The parents (principally the husband) enjoyed legal possession of the property—either as freeholders, tenants, or sharecroppers—but they were dependent on their children for economic support in their old age. Their aim, as Greven has pointed out, was to control the terms and the timing of the transfer of economic resources to the succeeding generation.

The intimate relationship between agricultural production and parental values, between economic history and family history, is best approached through a series

---

James A. Henretta, "Families and Farms: *Mentalité* in Pre-Industrial America," *William and Mary Quarterly*, 3rd ser., 35 (1978): 3, 21–32. Reprinted by permission of William and Mary Quarterly.

of case studies. The first of these small family dramas began in 1739 with the arrival in Kent, Connecticut, of Joseph Fuller. At one time or another Fuller was an investor in an iron works, a "typical speculative proprietor," and a "rich squatter" who tried to deceive the Connecticut authorities into granting him (and his partner Joshua Lassell) 4,820 acres of provincial land. Fuller's energy, ambition, and activities mark him as an entrepreneur, even a "capitalist." Yet his behavior must be seen in the widest possible context, and the motivation assessed accordingly. When this restless man arrived in Kent at the age of forty (with his second wife), he was the father of seven sons, aged two to sixteen; thirteen years later, when his final petition for a land grant was rejected, he had nine sons, aged eleven to twenty-nine years, and five daughters. With fourteen children to provide with land, dowries, or currency, Fuller *had* to embark on an active career if he wished to keep his children (and himself and his wife in their old age) from a life of landless poverty.

In the event, fecundity overwhelmed the Fullers' financial ingenuity. None of the children of Joseph Fuller ever attained a rating on the tax list equal to the highest recorded for their father, and a similar pattern prevailed among the sons of the third generation. The total resources of the Fuller "clan" (for such it had become) grew constantly over time—with nine second- and twelve third-generation males appearing on the tax lists of Kent—but their per capita wealth declined steadily. The gains of one generation, the slow accumulation of capital resources through savings and invested labor, had been dispersed among many heirs.

Such divisions of limited resources inevitably roused resentment and engendered bitter battles within farm families. Ultimately, the delicate reciprocal economic relationship between parents and children might break down completely. Insufficiency of land meant that most children would have to be exiled—apprenticed to wealthier members of the community or sent out on their own as landless laborers— and that parents would have to endure a harsh old age, sharing their small plot with the remaining heir. High fertility and low mortality threatened each generation of children with the loss of class status; the unencumbered inheritance of a freehold estate was the exception, not the rule.

Even in these circumstances—as a second example will suggest—the ideal for many dispossessed children remained property ownership and eventual control of the transfer process with regard to their own offspring. "My parents were poor," an "Honest Farmer" wrote to the *Pennsylvania Packet* in 1786,

> and they put me at twelve years of age to a farmer, with whom I lived till I was twenty one. . . . I married me a wife—and a very working young woman she was—and we took a farm of forty acres on rent. . . . In ten years I was able to buy me a farm of sixty acres on which I became my own tenant. I then, in a manner, grew rich and soon added another sixty acres, with which I am content. My estate increased beyond all account. I bought several lots of out-land for my children, which amounted to seven when I was forty-five years old.
>
> About this time I married my oldest daughter to a clever lad, to whom I gave one hundred acres of my out-land.

Was this "success story" typical? Did the "Honest Farmer" minimize the difficulties of his own ascent and exaggerate the prospects of his seven children, each of whom would have to be provided with land, livestock, or equipment? It is clear, at any rate, that this Pennsylvanian enjoyed a crucial advantage over Joseph Fuller;

he could accumulate capital through the regular sale of his surplus production on the market, and offer economic assistance to his children. His grandchildren, moreover, would grow up in the more fully developed commercial economy of the early nineteenth century. Ten years of work as a farm laborer—and an intense commitment to save—would now yield a capital stock of five hundred dollars. With this sum invested in equipment, livestock, and supplies, it would then be feasible to rent a farm, "with the prospect of accumulating money at a rate perhaps double that possible by wage work." To begin with less than five hundred dollars was to increase dependence on the landlord—to accept a half-and-half division of the produce rather than a two-thirds share. In either case, there was a high financial and psychological price to be paid. For many years these young adults would be "dependent," would work as wage laborers without security, as sharecroppers without land, or as mortgagors without full independence; their labor would enrich freeholders, landlords, and bankers even as it moved them closer to real economic freedom.

This process is readily apparent in a third case study, an archetypical example of the slow but successful accumulation of productive agricultural property in the mid-nineteenth century. In 1843 a young farmer in Massachusetts bought an old farm of 85 acres for $4,337; "in order to pay for it, I mortgaged it for $4,100, paying only $237, all that I had, after buying my stock." Nine years later it was clear that some progress had been made, for he had "paid up about $600 on the mortgage, and laid out nearly $2,000 in permanent improvements on my buildings and farm." This hard-working farmer was "a little nearer the harbor than I was when I commenced the voyage," but he was still $3,500 in debt and had interest payments of $250 to make each year. These obligations might be met in ten or fifteen years, but by then new debts would have to be incurred in order to provide working capital for his children. This farmer would die a property owner, but at least some of his offspring would face a similarly time-consuming and difficult climb up the agricultural ladder.

Two features of the long-term process of capital formation through agricultural production revealed by these case studies stand out as particularly important, one static and the other dynamic. The recurrent factor was the continual pressure of population on the existing capital stock; the rate of natural increase constantly threatened to outstrip the creation of new productive resources: cleared land, machinery, housing, and livestock. This danger is demonstrable in the case of the Fuller clan, and its specter lurks in the prose of the "Honest Farmer" and his younger accumulation-oriented counterpart in Massachusetts. Economic prosperity was the result of unremitting labor by each generation. Only as farm parents began consciously to limit their fertility were they able to pass on sizable estates to their children—and this occurred primarily after 1830.

What changed—from the seventeenth to the early nineteenth century—was the increased rate of capital formation stemming from the expansion of the market economy; the growing importance of "unearned" profits because of the rise in the value of land and of other scarce commodities; and the extent to which middlemen dominated the processes of agricultural production and of westward migration. These three developments were interrelated. All were aspects of an increasingly important system of commercial agriculture that generated antagonistic social relationships and incipient class divisions. These alterations brought greater prosperity to those farmers whose geographic locations and cultural values were conducive to market activity. The new structural possibilities undoubtedly induced other producers (who might otherwise have been content with their subsistence existence) to raise their output, perhaps even to alter their mode of production by hiring labor or purchasing farm machinery. Certainly, the boom in land values enabled those settlers with substantial estates to reap windfall profits. They had not always purchased their land with speculative resale in mind, but they benefited nonetheless from social and economic forces beyond their control: the surge in population and in agricultural prices both in the American colonies and in Western Europe. Finally, there were individuals and groups who sought to manage the new system of production and exchange. By the mid-eighteenth century, merchants and land speculators had appeared as crucial factors in the westward movement of population, and within another fifty years bankers and mortgage companies were also extracting a share of agricultural production. At some times and places the monetary liens imposed by middlemen and substantial landowners were justified; they represented fair returns for services rendered. More often, the farm population—especially those of its members who were young or landless—paid a disproportionate price for access to the productive system because bankers, speculators, and merchants were able to use their political and economic power to set the terms of exchange in order to gain a greater share of the growing wealth of the society than was warranted by their entrepreneurial contribution.

Even as this process of economic specialization and structural change was taking place, the family persisted as the basic unit of agricultural production, capital formation, and property transmission. This is a point of some importance, for it suggests that alterations in the macro-structure of a society or an economic system do not inevitably or immediately induce significant changes in its micro-units. Social or cultural change is not always systemic in nature, and it proceeds in fits and starts. Old cultural forms persist (and sometimes flourish) within new economic structures; there are "lags" as changes in one sphere of life are gradually reconciled with established values and patterns of behavior.

And so it was in the case of the pre-industrial yeoman family. Changes in societal structure did not alter the basic character of the farm family (although the proportion of such families in the population steadily decreased). As the case studies suggest, the agricultural family remained an extended lineal one; each generation lived in a separate household, but the character of production and inheritance linked these conjugal units through a myriad of legal, moral, and customary bonds. Rights and responsibilities stretched across generations. The financial welfare of both parents and children was rooted in the land and in the equipment and labor needed to farm it. Parents therefore influenced their children's choice of marriage partners. Their welfare, or that of their other children, might otherwise be compromised by the premature division of assets which an early marriage entailed. The line was more important than the individual; the patrimony was to be conserved for lineal purposes.

The historical significance of these lineal values was immense. The emphasis on the line or upon the welfare of the entire family, for example, inhibited the emergence of individualism. When the member of this agricultural society traced the contours of their cultural landscape, they began with the assumption . . . that the basic unit was a family, "a little commonwealth," not a man (and still less a woman) "for himself," in their disparaging phrase. This stress on family identity also shaped the character—and often confined the scope—of entrepreneurial activity and capitalist enterprise. . . . Religious membership was also circumscribed by cultural values, especially in the Congregational churches of New England. . . .

Nevertheless, lineal values were not always dominant. And they were often affected by the emergent market economy; indeed, the commercial family-capitalism of the early modern period and the small father-son businesses of the nineteenth century represented striking adaptations of the lineal ideal. Equally significant alterations took place in rural areas, in response to the pressure of population on agricultural resources. In the seventeenth century many settlers had attempted to identify the family with a specific piece of land, to ensure its continued existence by rooting it firmly in space. Thus, in 1673, Ebenezer Perry of Barnstable, Massachusetts, entailed his land to his son Ebenezer and to the latter's "eldest son surviving and so on to the male heirs of his body lawfully begottten forever." Other early inhabitants of Massachusetts preferred to bequeath the family homestead to the youngest son—ultimogeniture—both because this would allow elder siblings to leave the farm at an early age and because the youngest son often came to maturity just as the parents were ready to retire. In either case, the transmission of property was designed to link one generation with the next, and both with "family land."

When the pressure on family resources made it impossible to provide all surviving sons with a portion of the original family estate, the settlers devised alternative strategies of heirship. Some parents uprooted the family and moved to a newly settled area where it would be possible to maintain traditional lineal ties between generations. "The Squire's House stands on the Bank of [the] Susquehannah . . . ," Philip Fithian reported from the frontier region of northeastern Pennsylvania in 1775. "He tells me . . . he will be able to settle all his Sons and his fair Daughter *Betsy* on the Fat of the Earth." Other farmers remained in the old community and sought desperately to settle their children on nearby lands. The premature death of one son brought the Reverend Samuel Chandler of Andover, Massachusetts, to remember that he had "been much distressed for land, for his children," and to regret that "he took so much care . . . [for] one is taken away and needs none." From nearby Concord, Benjamin Barrett petitioned the General Court for a grant of land in New Hampshire, since he and many other residents were "without land for their posterity"; yet when this request was granted, none of the petitioners migrated to the new settlement. When Barrett died in 1728, the income from these western lands helped to settle two sons on his Concord estate and two younger sons on farms in nearby Worcester County.

This imaginative use of western land rights to subsidize the local settlement of offspring may have been fairly widespread. Of the forty-one men who were the original purchasers of proprietary shares in Kent, Connecticut, twenty-five did not become inhabitants of the town but sold their rights to residents, relatives, and neighbors. Still, the limited availability of arable land in the older communities of New England and the Middle Colonies ruled out this option for most parents. The best they could do was to finance migration of some children while keeping intact the original farmstead. Both in Newtown, Long Island, and in German areas of Pennsylvania in the eighteenth century, fathers commonly willed the family farm to the eldest son, requiring him to pay a certain sum of money to his younger brothers and his sisters. In other cases, the farm was "sold" to one son or son-in-law, with the "profits" of the transaction being divided among the other children—daughters usually receiving one-half the amount bestowed on the sons.

These attempts by individual farmers to preserve a viable family estate reflected a set of values that was widespread in the community and which eventually received a formal legal sanction. When the appraisers of intestate property in Concord, Massachusetts, reported that a property could not be divided "without Spoiling the Whole," the probate court granted the farm intact to one heir (usually the eldest son), requiring him to compensate his brothers and sisters for their shares in the estate. Such rulings confirmed the societal norm: even as New England parents wrote wills that divided their lands, they encouraged or directed their children to reconstitute viable economic units, with regard to both size and access. As Mark Hasket of Rochester, Massachusetts, wrote in his will: "my sons shall not any of them debar or hinder one another from having a way over each others Land when and where there may be ocation [occasion] for it."

There were other respects in which the central position of the lineal family (rather than the conjugal unit or the individual) was reflected in the legal system. On the death of her husband, a wife normally received the "right" to one-third of the real property of the estate. Yet this control was strictly limited: it usually lapsed upon remarriage and, even more significant, did not include the privilege of sale. The widow's "third" had to be preserved intact, so that upon her death the property could revert to the heirs of the estate. More important than the economic freedom of the widow—her rights as an individual—was the protection of the estate and the line of succession. These deeply held values were preserved even in the more diverse, money-oriented economy of eastern Massachusetts in the eighteenth century; the law was changed to permit widows to sell family property, but the court carefully regulated such transactions to ensure that the capital of the estate would be used for the support of the child-heirs. Property was "communal" within the family, with the limits of alienation strictly limited by custom or by law. Even as the link to the land was broken the intimate tie between the estate and the lineal family was reaffirmed.

These traditional notions of family identity were subjected to considerable strain by the mid-nineteenth century. The psychological dimensions of the economic changes that diminished the importance of the family farm as the basic productive unit are revealed, in an oblique fashion, in the naming patterns practiced by parents in Hingham, Massachusetts. During the colonial period, most parents in this agricultural settlement did not perceive their children as "unique *per se.*" If a child died, his or her existence was perpetuated indirectly, for the same forename was normally given to the next infant of the same sex, especially when the dead child carried the same name as one of the parents. This necronymic pattern, with its obvious emphasis on the line rather than the individual, persisted in Hingham until the 1840s. So also did the tendency of parents to name their first children after themselves—to entail the parental name, as it were, and thus to stress the continuity between generations. As economic change altered the structure and character of Hingham society, these lineal conceptions of identity gradually yielded to more individualistic ones. After 1800 first sons were given the same forenames as their fathers but a distinctive middle name. This was a subtle and complex compromise, for these middle names were often family names as well (the mother's surname, for example)—yet another manifestation of the persistence of traditional forms in a time of transition.

It is significant that this shift toward a distinctive personal identity—toward individualism—has been traced in Hingham, Massachusetts, one of the oldest English settlements in America, and not on the frontier. A similar development may have resulted from (or accompanied) the westward movement, but it is equally likely . . . that lineal family values were *more* important than individualism in the new farming communities of the old Northwest. For farm families usually trained and encouraged their children "to succeed *them*, rather than to 'succeed' by rising in the social system." The young adults of thriving farm communities were not forced to confront the difficult problems of occupational choice and psychological identity as were those from depressed and overcrowded rural environments or growing cities. The dimensions of existence had expanded in the East, even as the eighteenth-century patterns of farm life, community stratification, and family identity were being recreated, in a modified form, in the new settlements of the West.

In some of these older and crowded communities in New England and the Middle States, lineal family values remained important well into the nineteenth century because they were consistent, at least temporarily, with rural industrialization and an emergent market economy. Fathers and mature sons continued to farm the (now depleted or subdivided) land while mothers, daughters, and younger sons turned their talents and energies to the production of textiles, shoes, and other items. The period between 1775 and 1815 was "the heyday of domestic manufactures" in America.

The family factory assumed major economic importance as a result of the commercial dislocations produced by the War for Independence; household production of linen and woolen cloth was increased to compensate for the lack of English imports. Subsequently, this enlarged productive capacity was systematically organized by American entrepreneurs. In some cases, merchants sought out new markets for household manufactures and then capitalized part of the productive process itself; providing necessary materials and credit through the "putting out" system. Tens of thousands of "Negro shoes" were sold to southern slaveholders by Quaker merchants from Lynn, Massachusetts; and this productive network extended far back into the New England countryside. An even more important product of the rural family factory was wearing apparel. In New York State the production of textiles increased steadily until 1825, when the per capita output of household looms amounted to 8.95 yards.

This extraordinary household output was made possible not only by the existence of a regional or national market—the product of a mature merchant-directed commercial capitalism—but also by the peculiar evolution of the factory system. By the late eighteenth century certain operations which were difficult in the home— such as fulling, carding, dyeing, and spinning in the case of textile production—had been assumed, with constantly increasing efficiency, by small mills. This process of specialization was as yet incomplete; eventually the weaving of cloth (as well as the preparation of the yarn) would be removed from the home and placed in the factory. For the moment—indeed for more than a generation—this final stage in the "evolution of the simple household industry into the . . . factory system" was held in abeyance by technological constraints, and the family factory reigned supreme. Rural industrialization expanded the productive capacity of the society and systematically integrated female labor into the market economy; but it did so without removing the family from the center of economic life.

One result was to perpetuate, for another generation, the delicate and reciprocally beneficial economic relationship between eastern farm parents and their offspring. The intergenerational exchange of youthful labor for an eventual inheritance had been threatened in the mid-eighteenth century by land scarcity, which diminished the financial security of aging parents and their ability or willingness to assist their children. Some young adults implicitly rebuked their parents by migrating; others stayed and exercised a gentle form of coercion. Nineteen percent of all first births registered in Concord, Massachusetts, in the 1740s were premaritally conceived, and the proportion rose to 40 percent in Concord, Hingham, and many other northern communities by the end of the century. "If they were again in the same circumstances," one observer noted, these young men and women "would do the same again, because otherwise they could not obtain their parents' consent to marry." Once the legal and financial concessions were extracted from reluctant parents, marriage quickly followed. Both parents and children shunned illegitimacy; both accepted the cultural norm of stable family existence.

Whatever their economic weakness and vulnerability to youthful persuasion, parents retained significant power over their offspring. Affective bonds remained strong, and they were augmented by the power of the state. Young men who wished to work outside the household unit before they attained their legal majority were obliged to buy their economic freedom, undertaking in written contracts to pay their parents a certain sum in return for the privilege. Similarly, the first New England mill girls turned at least a portion of their earnings over to their parents; they were working outside the home but not for themselves as unattached individuals. The lineal family remained predominant, in large part because there were few other institutions in early nineteenth-century America that could assume its social and economic functions—few schools, insurance companies, banks, or industries to provide training and capital for the new generation, and comfort and security for the old. Only a major structural change in the society itself—the widespread appearance of non-familial social, economic, and political organizations—would undermine the institutions of lineage; until this occurred there were simply no "alternatives to the family as a source of provision for the number of crucially important needs."

The lineal family—not the conjugal unit and certainly not the unattached individual —thus stood at the center of economic and social existence in northern agricultural society in pre-industrial America. The interlocking relationship between the biological life cycle and the system of agricultural (and domestic) production continued to tie the generations together even as the wider economic structure was undergoing a massive transformation and as the proportion of farming families in the population was steadily declining. Most men, women and children in this yeoman society continued to view the world through the prism of family values. This cultural outlook—this inbred pattern of behavior—set certain limits on personal autonomy, entrepreneurial activity, religious membership, and even political imagery. Lineal family values did not constitute, by any means, the entire world view—the *mentalité* —of the agricultural population, but they did define a central tendency of that consciousness, an abiding core of symbolic and emotive meaning; and, most important of all, they constituted a significant and reliable guide to behavior amid the uncertainties of the world.

The Northern Colonies as an Empire of Goods

T. H. BREEN

Just before Christmas 1721 William Moore, described in court records as "a Pedler or Petty Chapman," arrived in the frontier community of Berwick, Maine. Had Moore bothered to purchase a peddler's license, we would probably know nothing of his visit. He was undone by success. His illicit sales drew the attention of local authorities, and they confiscated Moore's "bagg or pack of goods." From various witnesses the magistrates learned that the man came to Berwick with "sundry goods and Merchandizes for Saile & that he has Travelled from town to town Exposeing said Goods to Sale and has Sold to Sundry persons."

The people of Berwick welcomed Moore to their isolated community. One can almost imagine the villagers, most of them humble farmers, rushing to Phillip Hubbard's house to examine the manufactured goods that the peddler had transported from Boston. Daniel Goodwin, for example, purchased "a yard and halfe of Stuff for handcarchiefs." Sarah Gooding could not forgo the opportunity to buy some muslin, fine thread, and black silk. She also bought "a yard and Quarter of Lase for a Cap." Patience Hubbard saw many things that she wanted, but in the end she settled for a "pare of garters." Her neighbor, Sarah Stone, took home a bundle of "smole trifles." None of the purchases amounted to more than a few pennies.

Colonial American historians have understandably overlooked such trifling transactions. They have concentrated instead on the structure of specific communities, and though they have taught us much about the people who lived in villages such as Berwick, they have generally ignored the social and economic ties that connected colonists to men and women who happened to dwell in other places. But Moore's visit reminds us that Berwick was part of an empire—an empire of goods. This unfortunate peddler brought the settlers into contact with a vast market economy that linked them to the merchants of Boston and London, to the manufacturers of England, to an exploding Atlantic economy that was changing the material culture not only of the well-to-do but also of average folk like Sarah Stone and Patience Hubbard. . . .

. . . [A] major obstacle to fresh analysis of the Anglo-American empire of the eighteenth century is the almost unshakable conviction that the colonists were economically self-sufficient. Modern historians who do not agree on other points of interpretation have found themselves defending this hardy perennial. Before World War II, it was common to encounter in the scholarly literature the resourceful yeoman, an independent, Jeffersonian figure who carved a farm out of the wilderness and managed by the sweat of his brow to feed and clothe his family. This is the theme of patriotic mythology. These were men and women who possessed the "right stuff."

In recent years this self-sufficient yeoman has recruited some enthusiastic new support. James A. Henretta, in an influential essay entitled "Families and Farms," offered perhaps the most coherent argument for this position. These colonial farmers,

T. H. Breen, "An Empire of Goods: The Anglicization of Colonial America, 1690–1776," *Journal of British Studies,* 25 (1986): 467–468, 479–481, 485–489, 492–498. Copyrighted 1986 by The North American Conference on British Studies. Reprinted by permission of The University of Chicago Press and the author.

he insisted, were not agrarian entrepreneurs who focused their energies on maximizing profit. To the contrary, they represented a "precapitalist" way of life. They saw themselves not so much as individuals as members of lineal families or of little communities. Since their primary goals were to provide for the welfare of dependents, to pass productive land on to future generations, and to achieve economic security, these colonial farmers studiously avoided the risks associated with the market economy. They rejected innovation in favor of tradition. They were deaf to market incentives. Within their households they attempted to satisfy as many of their material needs as possible, and when they required something they could not produce, they preferred to deal with neighbors rather than outside merchants. In other words, from this perspective, subsistence was not the result of personal failure or physical isolation. It was a positive expression of precapitalist values, a *mentalité,* that was slowly and painfully being eroded by the advance of commercial capitalism. If this is correct, we might as well forget about the consumer society. It hardly seems likely that a few imported English baubles would have turned the heads of such militantly self-sufficient farmers.

This thesis struck a responsive chord among some American historians. They saw the essay as an important statement in a much larger critique of capitalism in the United States, and they claim to have discovered this precapitalist mentality throughout American history, in urban as well as rural situations, in the South as well as the North. For them, colonial yeoman become "cultural heroes," warriors in what James T. Lemon has ironically termed "a desperate rear-guard action" against the encroachment of capitalism. . . .

Though these embattled precapitalist farmers flourish in the pages of learned journals, they have proved remarkably difficult to find in the historical record. Colonial historians who have gone in search of precapitalist colonial America have discovered instead entrepreneurial types, men and women shamelessly thrusting themselves into the market economy. Joyce Appleby reviewed this literature and announced that "evidence mounts that prerevolutionary America witnessed a steady commercialization of economic life: trades of all kinds increased; frontier communities quickly integrated themselves into market networks; large and small farmers changed crops in response to commercial incentives; new consuming tastes and borrowing practices proliferated." James T. Lemon experienced no better luck than did Appleby in discovering a precapitalist mentality. This careful student of Pennsylvania agriculture stated that, "far from being opposed to the market, 'independent' farmers eagerly sought English manufactured goods and in other ways acted as agents of capitalism." . . .

The argument for self-sufficiency encounters other problems as well. Henretta originally posed his interpretation as a dichotomous proposition: either colonial Americans toiled to preserve the "lineal family," or they strove to participate fully in the market economy. But, surely, there is some middle ground. No one seriously maintains that the people who settled New England and the Middle Colonies were unconcerned about the well-being of family members. They knew how difficult it was to survive a hard winter. They planned ahead as best they could. They also worried about their children's futures, about providing education, about dowries for daughters and land for sons. Such human concerns would hardly seem to be the monopoly of precapitalists. Love of family certainly did not cool the enthusiasm of Pennsylvania farmers for commercial agriculture, nor for that matter did the sale of wheat on the world market unloose an outpouring of corrosive economic individualism. . . .

Having liberated ourselves from the myth of self-sufficiency, we can return with fresh appreciation to the world of consumption. Between 1700 and 1770, the population of the mainland colonies rose approximately eightfold, from roughly 275,000 to 2,210,000. During the decade of the 1760s, it jumped almost 40 percent. Such extraordinarily rapid growth must have strained economic and political institutions. At any given time the majority of this population consisted of young people, boys and girls who were consumers but not yet full producers in this agricultural economy. And yet, contrary to Malthusian expectations, the eighteenth-century colonists were remarkably prosperous. They managed to raise the value of their exports to the mother country by some 500 percent during this period. The importation of British goods rose at an even faster rate. In 1700 the average American annually purchased British imports valued at just under a pound sterling. By 1770 the per capita figure had jumped to £1.20, a rise made all the more impressive when set against the population explosion. What this meant is each succeeding generation of colonial American farmers possessed more British imports than their fathers had. Gloria L. Main discovered that even in New England, the poorest region of the continent, "parents of each generation succeeded in raising their children in material circumstances no worse and possibly a little better than that enjoyed by themselves."

These numbers alone reveal why British merchants and manufacturers were increasingly drawn to this robust American market. Over the course of the eighteenth century, the center of Britain's commercial gravity shifted west, away from traditional linkages to the Continent to new ports such as Liverpool and Glasgow that catered to the colonial consumer demand. In other words, as the American buyers became more dependent on British suppliers, the British business community became more dependent on the colonial market. "It was thus hard facts," explains Jacob M. Price, "and not imagination that made British manufacturers so sensitive to the opening and closing of the North American market at the time of the nonimportation agreements of the 1760's and 1770's."

The Americans were only slowly integrated into the British consumer economy. The key decade in this commercial process appears to be the 1740s. Before that time, colonial demand for imports rose, but not very rapidly. . . .

During the 1740s, the American market suddenly took off. British goods flooded the colonies, and though war occasionally disrupted trade, business always rebounded. Journals carried more and more advertisements for consumer goods. Stores popped up in little New England country villages and along the rivers of the Chesapeake. Carolinians demanded consumer goods; so too did the wheat farmers and the Indian traders of the Middle Colonies. Everywhere the pace of business picked up. By 1772 the Americans were importing British manufactures in record volume. As in the mother country, this market was driven largely by demand. To pay for these goods the colonists produced more and more tobacco, rice, indigo, wheat, fish, tar—indeed, anything that would supply the income necessary to purchase additional imports. The Staple Colonies maintained direct trade links with England and Scotland, but in New England and the Middle Colonies the consumer challenge forced merchants to peddle local products wherever there was a market. Pennsylvania merchants carried ever larger amounts of wheat and flour to southern

Europe. New Englanders relied on the West Indian trade to help pay the bill for British manufactures. As one New Yorker explained in 1762, "Our importation of dry goods from England is so vastly great, that we are obliged to betake ourselves to all possible arts to make remittances to the British merchants. It is for this purpose we import cotton from St. Thomas's and Surinam; lime-juice and Nicaragua wood from Curacoa [sic]; and logwood from the bay, &c. and yet it drains us of all the silver and gold we can collect."

This consumer revolution affected the lives of all Americans. To be sure, the social effect was uneven, and the British imports initially flowed into the households of the well-to-do. These are the goods that catch our eyes in modern museums and restored colonial homes. Not surprisingly, we know a good deal about the buying habits of the gentry. Their lives were often well documented, and the fine pieces of china and silver that came into their possession are more apt to have survived to the present than were the more ordinary items that found their way into modest households. The general pattern of cultural diffusion seems clear enough. Poorer colonists aped their social betters, just as wealthy Americans mimicked English gentlemen. However slowly these new tastes may have been communicated, they eventually reached even the lowest levels of society. In her study of colonial Maryland, for example, Lorena Walsh discovered that, "by the 1750s, even the poorer sorts were finding a wide variety of non-essentials increasingly desirable. At the lowest levels of wealth this meant acquiring more of the ordinary amenities families had so long foregone—tables, chairs, bed steads, individual knives and forks, bed and table linens, and now-inexpensive ceramic tableware." A similar transformation of material culture was occurring in other regions.

Perhaps the central item in this rapidly changing consumer society was tea. In the early decades of the eighteenth century, tea began to appear in the homes of wealthier Americans. It may have replaced stronger drinks such as the popular rum punch, and by the 1740s proper ladies and gentlemen regularly socialized over tea. Taking tea became a recognized ritual requiring the correct cups and saucers, sugar bowls, and a collection of pots. By mid-century lesser sorts insisted on drinking tea, and though their tea services may not have been as costly as those of the local gentry, they performed the ritual as best they could. Even the poor wanted tea. One historian found that, during a confrontation with city officials that occurred in 1766, the residents of the Philadelphia poor house demanded Bohea tea. For all these Americans, drinking tea required cups that could hold extremely hot liquids and that, in turn, forced them to import the technically advanced ceramics that originated in Staffordshire. Not until well after the Revolution were American potters able to produce cups of such high quality at competitive prices. What catches our attention is how colonial Americans were increasingly drawn into the marketplace. A decision to buy tea led to other purchases. English glasses held imported wines. English cloth fashioned into dresses and coats looked better with imported metal buttons. One had to serve imported sugar in the appropriate imported pewter or silver bowl.

The consumer revolution also introduced choice into the lives of many Americans. With each passing generation the number of imported goods available to the colonists expanded almost exponentially. In the 1720s, for example, the newspapers carried advertisements for at most a score of British manufactures. Usually, these were listed in general categories, such as dry goods, and one has the impression that even urban merchants carried a basic and familiar stock. But after the 1740s American shoppers came to expect a much larger selection, and merchants had to maintain ever larger inventories. When Gottlieb Mittelberger, a German minister, traveled through Pennsylvania in the early 1750s, he could not believe how many imported items he saw for sale: wine, spices, sugar, tea, coffee, rice, rum, fine china, Dutch and English cloth, leather, linen cloth, fabrics, silks, damask, and velvet. "Already," Mittelberger declared, "it is really possible to obtain all the things one can get in Europe in Pennsylvania, since so many merchant ships arrive there every year." Individual merchants placed journal advertisements during the 1760s announcing the arrival from the mother country of hundreds of items. During some busy months, more than 4,000 separate goods appeared in the newspaper columns. Advertisers now broke down general merchandise groups by color and design. The consumer revolution exposed the colonists not only to a proliferation of goods but also to an ever escalating descriptive language. No doubt, as time passed, colonial buyers became more discerning, demanding increasingly better quality and wider variety.

For many consumers—particularly for women—the exercise of choice in the marketplace may have been a liberating experience, for with choice went a measure of economic power. One could literally take one's business elsewhere. We have come to think of consumerism as a negative term, as a kind of mindless mass behavior, but for the colonists of the mid-eighteenth century, shopping must have heightened their sense of self-importance. It was an arena in which they could ask questions, express individuality, and make demands. One could plausibly argue that, by exposing colonists to this world of consumer choice, the British reinforced the Americans' already strong conviction of their own personal independence. . . .

These colonial stores, wherever they appeared, provided an important link between the common people of America and the mother country. Unfortunately, we do not know much about these scattered places of business. Most were probably small, no larger than a garage in a home today. Such certainly was the store operated by Jonathan Trumbull in rural Connecticut. But despite their modest size, these buildings—sometimes a room in the merchant's home—held an amazing variety of goods. As Glenn Weaver, Trumbull's biographer, explains, a sampling of the merchant's ledger books during the 1730s and 1740s reveals an amazingly full stock of imports: "Pepper, lace, gloves, gunpowder, flints, molasses, rum, *Watts' Psalms,* mohair, drugs, tiles, paper, garlix (a kind of cloth), pots, pans, 'manna,' cord, pails, needles, knives, indigo, logwood, earthenware, raisins, thimbles, buckles, allspice, tea, buttons, mace, combs, butter, spectacles, soap, brimstone, nails, shot, sewing silk, sugar, wire, looking glasses, tape, 'Italian crape,' 'allam,' pewter dishes, etc." One wonders what items were hidden in Weaver's "etc." He seems already to have listed just about everything that a Connecticut farm family might have desired. . . .

Along the roads of mid-eighteenth-century America also traveled the peddlers, the chapmen, and the hawkers, figures celebrated in folklore but ignored almost completely by serious historians. The failure to explore the world of these itinerant salesmen is unfortunate, for they seem to have accounted for a considerable volume of trade. The peddlers made up a sizable percentage of James Beckman's customers, and he was one of the most successful import merchants in New York City. In Boston Thomas Hancock took good care of his "country chaps," making certain British merchants and manufacturers supplied them with the items that the colonists actually wanted to buy. These travelers seem to have hawked their goods along city streets as well as country highways. Men as well as women peddled their wares. A New York law setting conditions for this sort of business specifically mentioned "he" and "she," indicating that in this colony at least people of both sexes carried consumer goods from town to town.

But whatever their gender, itinerants sometimes traveled far, popping up everywhere, ubiquitous denizens of village taverns. When Alexander Hamilton journeyed through the northern colonies in 1744, for example, he regularly encountered peddlers. "I dined att William's att Stonington, [Connecticut,] with a Boston merchant name Gardiner and one Boyd, a Scotch Irish pedlar," Hamilton scribbled. "The pedlar seemed to understand his business to a hair. He sold some dear bargains to Mrs. Williams, and while he smoothed her up with palaber, the Bostoner amused her with religious cant. This pedlar told me he had been some time agoe att Annapolis[, Maryland]." In Bristol, Rhode Island, Hamilton and his black servant were taken for peddlers because they carried large "portmanteaux," and the local residents rushed out into the street to inspect their goods. The number of peddlers on the road appears to have been a function of the general prosperity of the colonial economy. In other words, they do not seem to have represented a crude or transitional form of merchandising. As the number of stores increased, so too did the number of peddlers. In fact, the two groups often came into conflict, for the peddlers operating with little overhead could easily undercut the established merchant's price. Shopkeepers petitioned the various colonial legislatures about this allegedly unfair competition. In turn, the lawmakers warned the peddlers to purchase licenses, some at substantial fees, but judging from the repetition of these regulations in the statutes, one concludes that the peddlers more than held their own against the rural merchants. . . .

One can only speculate about the motivation of the colonial buyer. The psychology of eighteenth-century consumption was complex, and each person entered the market for slightly different reasons. Some men and women wanted to save money and time. After all, producing one's own garments—a linen shirt, for example— was a lengthy, tedious process, and the purchase of imported cloth may have been more cost effective than was turning out homespun. Beauty also figured into the calculus of consumption. An imported Staffordshire plate or a piece of ribbon brought color into an otherwise drab environment. Contemporary merchants certainly understood that aesthetics played a major role in winning customers. In 1756, for example, one frustrated English supplier wrote to the Philadelphia merchant John Reynall, "There is no way to send goods with any certainty of sale but by sending Patterns of the several colours in vogue with you." No doubt, some Americans realized that ceramic plates and serving dishes were more sanitary to use than were the older wooden trenchers. In addition, consumer goods provided socially mobile Americans with boundary markers, an increasingly recognized way to distinguish betters from their inferiors, for though the rural farmer may have owned a tea cup, he could not often afford real china. In whatever group one traveled, however, one knew that consumer goods mediated social status. Their possession gave off messages full of meanings that modern historians have been slow to comprehend. Finally, just as it is today, shopping in colonial times was entertaining. Consumer goods became topics of conversation, the source of a new vocabulary, the spark of a new kind of social discourse.

. . . British imports provided white Americans with a common framework of experience. Consumption drew the colonists together even when they themselves were unaware of what was happening. Men and women living in different parts of the continent purchased a similar range of goods. The items that appeared in New England households also turned up in the Carolinas. The rice planters of Charleston probably did not know that northern farmers demanded the same kinds of imports. They may not have even cared. But however tenuous communication between mid-eighteenth-century colonists may have been, there could be no denying that British manufacturers were standardizing the material culture of the American colonies. Without too much exaggeration, Staffordshire pottery might be seen as the Coca-Cola of the eighteenth century. It was a product of the metropolitan economy that touched the lives of people living on the frontier of settlement, eroding seventeenth-century folkways and bringing scattered planters and farmers into dependence on a vast world market that they did not yet quite comprehend.

Herein lies a paradox[:] . . . The road to Americanization ran through Anglicization. In other words, before these widely dispersed colonists could develop a sense of their own common cultural identity, they had first to be integrated fully into the British empire. Royal government in colonial America was never large enough to effect Anglicization. Nor could force of arms have brought about this cultural redefinition. Such a vast shift in how Americans viewed the mother country and each other required a flood of consumer goods, little manufactured items that found their way into gentry homes as well as frontier cabins. . . .

The extent of this imperialism of goods amazed even contemporaries. In 1771, William Eddis, an Englishman living in Maryland, wrote home that "the quick importation of fashions from the mother country is really astonishing. I am almost inclined to believe that a new fashion is adopted earlier by the polished and affluent American than by many opulent persons in the great metropolis. . . . In short, very little difference is, in reality, observable in the manners of the wealthy colonist and the wealthy Briton." Eddis may have exaggerated, but probably not much. Students of the book trade, for example, have discovered that the colonists demanded volumes printed in England. Indeed, so deep was the Anglicization of American readers that "a false London imprint could seem an effective way to sell a local publication." Newspaper advertisements announced that merchants carried the "latest English goods." By the mid-eighteenth century, these imported items had clearly taken on symbolic value. Put simply, pride of ownership translated into pride of being part of the empire, a sentiment that was reinforced but not created by the victory of the British army over the French in the Seven Years' War.

So long as the king of England ruled over an empire of goods, his task was relatively easy. The spread of the consumer society, at least before the Stamp Act Crisis, tied the colonists ever closer to the mother country. This is what Benjamin Franklin tried to communicate to the House of Commons. He observed that before 1763 the Americans had "submitted willingly to the government of the Crown, and paid, in all their courts, obedience to acts of parliament." It cost Parliament almost nothing, Franklin explained, to maintain the loyalty of this rapidly growing population across the Atlantic. The colonists "were governed by this country at the expense only of a little pen, ink, and paper. They were led by a thread. They had not only a respect, but an affection, for Great Britain, for its laws, its customs and manners, and even a fondness for its fashions, that greatly increased the commerce." No American, of course, had a greater fondness for cosmopolitan fashion than did Franklin. And in 1763 he could not comprehend why anyone would want to upset a system that seemed to operate so well.

◆ *F U R T H E R   R E A D I N G*

Bernard Bailyn, *Voyagers to the West* (1986).

Paul Boyer and Stephen Nissenbaum, *Salem Possessed: The Social Origins of Witchcraft* (1994).

Richard Bushman, *The Refinement of America: Persons, Houses, Cities* (1992).

Jon Butler, *Awash in a Sea of Faith: Christianizing the American People* (1990).

Joyce Goodfriend, *Before the Melting Pot: Society and Culture in Colonial New York City, 1664–1730* (1992).

Gary B. Nash, *The Urban Crucible: Social Change, Political Consciousness, and the Origins of the American Revolution* (1979).

Laurel Thatcher Ulrich, *Good Wives: Image and Reality in the Lives of Women in Northern New England, 1650–1750* (1982).

C H A P T E R
4

The American Revolution

When the French and Indian War concluded with the Treaty of Paris in 1763, the map of North America was radically redrawn. Because France lost the war, it was forced to relinquish vast territories in Canada to Britain. France's Indian allies faced defeat as well. For years, Indian nations had successfully played off the English and the French. When the French were removed, this strategy was no longer feasible. Pontiac, an Ottawa chief, realized this fact shortly after the war's conclusion. He forged an alliance with neighboring Indian nations and laid siege to Fort Detroit. When Pontiac was defeated, his people's situation became, if anything, worse than before.

The winners seemingly were the British Empire and its American subjects. The empire had expanded, and white Americans thirsted after the opportunities for trade, farming, and land speculation promised by the new acquisitions of land. As one Bostonian put it, the "garden of the world [with] all things necessary for the conveniency and delight of life" awaited. Thirteen years after the Treaty of Paris, however, the people of thirteen of the colonies in North America were so disgusted with their position in the empire that they declared their independence. How this could have happened is one of the most important questions in American history.

The first step in the journey to separation was the British response following the end of the French and Indian War. The war had been expensive—the national debt had doubled during the war—and British officials were determined to recoup some of their losses through a reorganization of the empire. Accordingly, they enacted a series of measures that attempted to regulate settlement and trade and to increase the tax burden of the colonists. The Proclamation of 1763, for example, forbade colonists to live west of a line drawn at the crest of the Appalachian Mountains. The Sugar Act of 1764 was the first in a series of acts that attempted to enforce more rigorously the rules of trade within the British Empire. And the Stamp Act of 1765 levied direct taxes on a variety of items ranging from newspapers to legal documents.

If British officials felt that these were just actions made necessary by the costs of empire, many Americans perceived this reorganization in a very different light. They saw the Proclamation of 1763 as an effort to restrict economic growth and the Stamp Act as the first step in imposing direct taxation on the colonies. The response of many was to protest in the streets and to speak out in political assemblies. As early as 1765, a secret organization called the Sons of Liberty was formed to resist British initiatives. Though the British ultimately repealed the Stamp Act, they still felt the need to increase revenue from and control over their American colonies. A series of additional acts, including the Townshend Acts (1767), the Tea Act (1773), and the "Intolerable Acts" (1774), were passed, and the colonial response continued to bewilder British officials. Legislation was followed by protest, which often resulted in more legislation. Colonial rhetoric grew more shrill, and events like the Boston Massacre in 1770, which followed the quartering of troops in Boston, and the Boston Tea Party in 1773, which followed the Tea Act, only served to ratchet up the tension between the mother country and its unruly colonies. By 1774, King George III had concluded that "blows must decide." When independence was declared in 1776, the colonists had already engaged in battles with the British.

   American leaders differed in their views of the reorganization of the empire. Many focused on the ways their rights as English people were being ignored. If they had no direct representation in Parliament, were not these efforts at direct taxation intolerable? If they had no say in the levels of taxation, was not this patently unjust? Even more serious was the argument that imperial policy was only part of a larger plot to deny the liberties not only of colonists, but of all English people. From this perspective, their protests were attempts to restore the constitution of English society before this conspiracy was put in place. Although colonists looked backward to a time when the empire was operating properly, they increasingly looked forward to the possibilities of an independent America. Many Americans were taken with the idea that they could best control the "garden of the world" that lay to the west.

QUESTIONS TO THINK ABOUT

The Revolution affected virtually everyone in American society. How did it alter the lives of various groups—men and women; Indians, slaves, and European immigrants; loyalists and patriots—in different ways? Do the British measures leading up to the Revolution in retrospect look reasonable? If so, how can one explain the American response to them? Would you characterize the Revolution as a conflict that looked forward or backward?

DOCUMENTS

These documents illustrate how the American colonists moved toward independence. Document 1 is the Resolutions of the Stamp Act Congress, which was convened in 1765 and which argued that no taxes could be imposed on the colonists without their consent. Document 2 is a description of the "Boston Massacre" in 1770. It recounts the events that led up to the "horrid massacre" and shows how colonists used the event to vilify the British soldiers. In Document 3, Thomas Jefferson in 1774 summarizes the rights of British America and describes the difficulties that the British Empire was creating for Americans. A speech by Patrick Henry in 1775, Document 4, provides us with an example of the fiery rhetoric that flourished as the colonies neared their declaration of independence. Document 5 is a selection from Thomas Paine's powerful pamphlet *Common Sense*. Written in 1776, this pamphlet was among the most popular tracts advocating American independence and a republican system of government. Many people were moved by the rhetoric of independence and political change. Documents 6 through 8 provide three brief examples of the ways in which German immigrants, women, and enslaved African Americans used the ideas of natural rights. The most famous document in this group is Document 7, Abigail Adams's reminder to her husband, John Adams, to "remember the ladies." However, not all Americans favored independence from Britain, as the next two documents illustrate. Joseph Brant, in Document 9, depicts the loyalty that many Indians felt toward the king of England. Yet Brant, who is of the Mohawk nation, also warns of the costs of war that Indian loyalists were paying. Document 10 illustrates how a group of white loyalists some years later, like Brant, explained their aid to the British cause and the damages that they faced because of "republican tyranny."

1. Congress Condemns the Stamp Act, 1765

The members of this Congress, sincerely devoted with the warmest sentiments of affection and duty to His Majesty's person and Government, inviolably attached to the present happy establishment of the Protestant succession, and with minds deeply impressed by a sense of the present and impending misfortunes of the British colonies on this continent: having considered as maturely as time will permit the circumstances of the said colonies esteem it our indispensable duty to make the following declarations of our humble opinion respecting the most essential rights and liberties of the colonists, and of the grievances under which they labour, by reason of several late Acts of Parliament.

I. That His Majesty's subjects in these colonies owe the same aliegiance to the Crown of Great Britain that is owing from his subjects born within the realm, and all due subordination to that august body the Parliament of Great Britain.

II. That His Majesty's liege subjects in these colonies are intitled to all the inherent rights and liberties of his natural born subjects within the kingdom of Great Britain.

III. That it is inseparably essential to the freedom of a people and the undoubted right of Englishmen, that no taxes be imposed on them but with their own consent, given personally or by their representatives.

IV. That the people of these colonies are not, and from their local circumstances cannot be, represented in the House of Commons in Great Britain.

V. That the only representatives of the people of these colonies are persons chosen therein by themselves and that no taxes ever have been, or can be constitutionally imposed on them, but by their legislatures.

VI. That all supplies to the Crown being free gifts of the people it is unreasonable and inconsistent with the principles and spirit of the British Constitution, for the people of Great Britain to grant to His Majesty the property of the colonists.

VII. That trial by jury is the inherent and invaluable right of every British subject in these colonies.

VIII. That the late Act of Parliament, entitled *An Act for granting and applying certain stamp duties, and other duties, in the British colonies and plantations in America, etc.,* by imposing taxes on the inhabitants of these colonies; and the said Act, and several other Acts, by extending the jurisdiction of the courts of Admiralty beyond its ancient limits, have a manifest tendency to subvert the rights and liberties of the colonists.

"Resolutions," October 19, 1765, in John Almon, ed., *Collection of Interesting, Authentic Papers Relative to the Dispute Between Great Britain and North America* (London, 1777), 27.

IX. That the duties imposed by several late Acts of Parliament, from the peculiar circumstances of these colonies, will be extremely burthensome and grievous; and from the scarcity of specie, the payment of them absolutely impracticable.

X. That as the profits of the trade of these colonies ultimately center in Great Britain, to pay for the manufactures which they are obliged to take from thence, they eventually contribute very largely to all supplies granted there to the Crown.

XI. That the restrictions imposed by several late Acts of Parliament on the trade of these colonies will render them unable to purchase the manufactures of Great Britain.

XII. That the increase, prosperity, and happiness of these colonies depend on the full and free enjoyments of their rights and liberties, and an intercourse with Great Britain mutually affectionate and advantageous.

XIII. That it is the right of the British subjects in these colonies to petition the King or either House of Parliament.

Lastly, That it is the indispensable duty of these colonies to the best of sovereigns, to the mother country, and to themselves, to endeavour by a loyal and dutiful address to His Majesty, and humble applications to both Houses of Parliament, to procure the repeal of the Act for granting and applying certain stamp duties . . . and of the other late Acts for the restriction of American commerce.

2. The Town of Boston Denounces the "Boston Massacre," 1770

What gave occasion to the melancholy event of that evening seems to have been this. A difference having happened near Mr. Grays ropewalk, between a soldier and a man belonging to it, the soldier challenged the ropemakers to a boxing match. The challenge was accepted by one of them, and the soldier worsted. He ran to the barrack in the neighborhood, and returned with several of his companions. The fray was renewed, and the soldiers were driven off. They soon returned with recruits and were again worsted. This happened several times, till at length a considerable body of soldiers was collected, and they also were driven off, the ropemakers having been joined by their brethren of the contiguous ropewalks. By this time Mr. Gray being alarmed interposed, and with the assistance of some gentlemen prevented any further disturbance. To satisfy the soldiers and punish the man who had been the occasion of the first difference, and as an example to the rest, he turned him out of his service; and waited on Col. Dalrymple, the commanding officer of the troops, and with him concerted measures for preventing further mischief. Though this affair ended thus, it made a strong impression on the minds of the soldiers in general, who thought the honor of the regiment concerned to revenge those repeated repulses. For this purpose they seem to have formed a combination to commit some outrage upon the inhabitants of the town indiscriminately; and this was to be done on the evening of the 5th instant or soon after; as appears by the depositions of the following persons, viz.:

A Short Narrative of the Horrid Massacre in Boston. Printed by Order of the Town of Boston. Republished with Notes and Illustrations by John Doggett, Jr. (New York, 1849), 13–19, 21–22, 28–30.

William Newhall declares, that on Thursday night the 1st of March instant, he met four soldiers of the 29th regiment, and that he heard them say, "there were a great many that would eat their dinners on Monday next, that should not eat any on Tuesday."

Daniel Calfe declares, that on Saturday evening the 3d of March, a camp-woman, wife to James McDeed, a grenadier of the 29th, came into his father's shop, and the people talking about the affrays at the ropewalks, and blaming the soldiers for the part they had acted in it, the woman said, "the soldiers were in the right;" adding, "that before Tuesday or Wednesday night they would wet their swords or bayonets in New England people's blood."

Samuel Drowne declares that, about nine o'clock of the evening of the fifth of March current, standing at his own door in Cornhill, he saw about fourteen or fifteen soldiers of the 29th regiment, who came from Murray's barracks, armed with naked cutlasses, swords, &c., and came upon the inhabitants of the town, then standing or walking in Cornhill, and abused some, and violently assaulted others as they met them; most of whom were without so much as a stick in their hand to defend themselves, as he very clearly could discern, it being moonlight, and himself being one of the assaulted persons. . . .

These assailants, who issued from Murray's barracks (so called), after attacking and wounding divers persons in Cornhill, as above-mentioned, being armed, proceeded (most of them) up the Royal Exchange lane into King street; where, making a short stop, and after assaulting and driving away the few they met there, they brandished their arms and cried out, "Where are the boogers! where are the cowards!" . . . The outrageous behavior and the threats of the said party occasioned the ringing of the meeting-house bell near the head of King street, which bell ringing quick, as for fire, it presently brought out a number of inhabitants, who being soon sensible of the occasion of it, were naturally led to King street, where the said party had made a stop but a little while before, and where their stopping had drawn together a number of boys, round the sentry at the Custom House. Whether the boys mistook the sentry for one of the said party, and thence took occasion to differ with him, or whether he first affronted them, which is affirmed in several depositions,—however that may be, there was much foul language between them, and some of them, in consequence of his pushing at them with his bayonet, threw snowballs at him, which occasioned him to knock hastily at the door of the Custom House. From hence two persons thereupon proceeded immediately to the main-guard, which was posted opposite to the State House, at a small distance, near the head of the said street. The officer on guard was Capt. Preston, who with seven or eight soldiers, with fire-arms and charged bayonets, issued from the guard house, and in great haste posted himself and his soldiers in front of the Custom House, near the corner aforesaid. In passing to this station the soldiers pushed several persons with their bayonets, driving through the people in so rough a manner that it appeared they intended to create a disturbance. . . .

The said party was formed into a half circle; and within a short time after they had been posted at the Custom House, began to fire upon the people.

Captain Preston is said to have ordered them to fire, and to have repeated that order. One gun was fired first; then others in succession, and with deliberation, till ten or a dozen guns were fired; or till that number of discharges were made from the guns that were fired. By which means eleven persons were killed and wounded, as above represented.

3. Thomas Jefferson Specifies the Rights of British Americans, 1774

[The deputies are to set forth to the King the rights of the colonies and of the invasions of them from the time of their first settlement and . . .]

To remind him that our ancestors, before their emigration to America, were the free inhabitants of the British dominions in Europe, and possessed a right, which nature has given to all men, of departing from the country in which chance, not choice, has placed them, of going in quest of new habitations, and of there establishing new societies, under such laws and regulations as, to them, shall seem most likely to promote public happiness. . . . America was conquered, and her settlements made and firmly established, at the expense of individuals, and not of the British public. Their own blood was spilt in acquiring lands for their settlement, their own fortunes expended in making that settlement effectual. For themselves they fought, for themselves they conquered, and for themselves alone they have right to hold. No shilling was ever issued from the public treasures of his Majesty, or his ancestors, for their assistance, till of very late times, after the colonies had become established on a firm and permanent footing. That then, indeed, having become valuable to Great Britain for her commercial purposes, his Parliament was pleased to lend them assistance against an enemy who would fain have drawn to herself the benefits of their commerce, to the great aggrandisement of herself, and danger of Great Britain. . . . We do not, however, mean to underrate those aids, which, to us, were doubtless valuable, on whatever principles granted: but we would shew that they cannot give a title to that authority which the British Parliament would arrogate over us; and that may amply be repaid by our giving to the inhabitants of Great Britain such exclusive privileges in trade as may be advantageous to them, and, at the same time, not too restrictive to ourselves. . . .

. . . History has informed us, that bodies of men as well as of individuals, are susceptible of the spirit of tyranny. A view of these acts of Parliament for regulation, as it has been affectedly called, of the American trade, if all other evidences were removed out of the case, would undeniably evince the truth of this observation. Besides the duties they impose on our articles of export and import, they prohibit our going to any markets Northward of Cape Finisterra, in the kingdom of Spain, for the sale of commodities which Great Britain will not take from us, and for the purchase of others, with which she cannot supply us; and . . . have raised their commodities called for in America, to the double and treble of what they sold for, before such exclusive privileges were given them, and of what better commodities of the same kind would cost us elsewhere; and, at the same time, give us much less for what we carry thither, than might be had at more convenient ports. That these acts prohibit us from carrying, in quest of other purchasers, the surplus of our tobaccos, remaining after the consumption of Great Britain is supplied: so that we must leave them with the British merchant, for whatever he will please to allow us, to be by him re-shipped to foreign markets, where he will reap the benefits of making sale of them for full

Thomas Jefferson, "A Summary View of the Rights of British America" (1774), in *The Complete Jefferson,* ed. S. K. Padover (New York: Duell, Sloan, and Pearce, 1943).

value. That, to heighten still the idea of Parliamentary justice, and to show with what moderation they are like to exercise power, where themselves are to feel no part of its weight, we take leave to mention to his Majesty, certain other acts of the British Parliament, by which they would prohibit us from manufacturing, for our own use, the articles we raise on our own lands, with our own labor. By an act passed in the fifth year of the reign of his late Majesty, King George the second, an American subject is forbidden to make a hat for himself, of the fur which he has taken, perhaps, on his own soil; an instance of despotism, to which no parallel can be produced in the most arbitrary ages of British history. By one other act, passed in the twenty-third year of the same reign, the iron which we make, we are forbidden to manufacture; and, heavy as that article is, and necessary in every branch of husbandry, besides commission and insurance, we are to pay freight for it to Great Britain, and freight for it back again, for the purpose of supporting, not men, but machines, in the island of Great Britain. . . . American lands are made subject to the demands of British creditors, while their own lands were still continued unanswerable for their debts; from which, one of these conclusions must necessarily follow, either that justice is not the same thing in America as in Britain, or else, that the British Parliament pay less regard to it here than there. . . .

. . . The abolition of domestic slavery is the great object of desire in those colonies, where it was, unhappily, introduced in their infant state. But previous to the enfranchisement of the slaves we have, it is necessary to exclude all further importations from Africa. Yet our repeated attempts to effect this by prohibitions, and by imposing duties which might amount to a prohibition, having been hitherto defeated by his Majesty's negative: thus preferring the immediate advantages of a few British corsairs, to the lasting interests of the American States, and to the rights of human nature, deeply wounded by this infamous practice. . . .

With equal inattention to the necessities of his people here has his Majesty permitted our laws to lie neglected, in England, for years neither confirming them by his assent, nor annulling them by his negative. . . . And, to render this grievance still more oppressive, his Majesty, by his instructions, has laid his Governors under such restrictions, that they can pass no law, of any moment, unless it have such suspending clause. . . .

. . . After dissolving one House of Representatives, they have refused to call another, so that, for a great length of time, the legislature provided by the laws, has been out of existence. From the nature of things, every society must, at all times, possess within itself the sovereign powers of legislation. The feelings of human nature revolt against the supposition of a State so situated, as that it may not, in any emergency, provide against dangers which, perhaps, threaten immediate ruin. . . .

That we shall, at this time also, take notice of an error in the nature of our land holdings, which crept in at a very early period of our settlement. . . . The fictitious principle, that all lands belong originally to the King, [our ancestors who migrated hither] were early persuaded to believe real, and accordingly took grants of their own lands from the Crown. And while the Crown continued to grant for small sums and on reasonable rents, there was no inducement to arrest the error, and lay it open to public view. But his Majesty has lately taken on him to advance the terms of purchase and of holding, to the double of what they were; by which means, the acquisition of lands being rendered difficult, the population of our country is likely to be checked. It is time, therefore, for us to lay this matter before his Majesty, and to declare, that he has no right to grant lands of himself. From the nature and purpose of civil institutions, all the lands within the limits, which any particular party has circumscribed around itself, are assumed by that society, and subject to their allotment; this may be done by themselves assembled collectively, or by their legislature, to whom they may have delegated sovereign authority; and, if they are allotted in neither of these ways, each individual of the society may appropriate to himself such lands as he finds vacant, and occupancy will give him title. . . .

That these are our grievances, which we have thus laid before his Majesty, with that freedom of language and sentiment which becomes a free people, claiming their rights as derived from the laws of nature, and not as the gift of their Chief Magistrate. Let those flatter, who fear: it is not an American art. To give praise where it is not due might be well from the venal, but would ill beseem those who are asserting the rights of human nature. They know, and will, therefore, say, that Kings are the servants, not the proprietors of the people. Open your breast, Sire, to liberal and expanded thought. Let not the name of George the third, be a blot on the page of history. . . . This, Sire, is the advice of your great American council, on the observance of which may perhaps depend your felicity and future fame, and the preservation of that harmony which alone can continue, both to Great Britain and America, the reciprocal advantages of their connection. It is neither our wish nor our interest to separate from her.

4. Patrick Henry Warns the British to Maintain American Liberties, 1775

Sir, we have done everything that could be done to avert the storm which is now coming on. We have petitioned; we have remonstrated, we have supplicated; we have prostrated ourselves before the throne, and have implored its interposition to arrest the tyrannical hands of the ministry and Parliament. Our petitions have been slighted; our remonstrances have produced additional violence and insult; our supplications have been disregarded; and we have been spurned, with contempt, from the foot of the throne. In vain, after these things, may we indulge the fond hope of peace and reconciliation? There is no longer any room for hope. If we wish to be free—if we mean to preserve inviolate those inestimable privileges for which we have been so long contending—if we mean not basely to abandon the noble struggle in which we have been so long engaged, and which we have pledged ourselves never to abandon until the glorious object of our contest shall be obtained, we must fight! I repeat sir, we must fight! An appeal to arms and to the God of Hosts is all that is left us! . . .

It is in vain, sir, to extenuate the matter. Gentlemen may cry, "Peace, Peace!"— but there is no peace. The war is actually begun! The next gale that sweeps from the north will bring to our ears the clash of resounding arms! Our brethren are already in the field! Why stand we here idle? What is it that gentlemen wish? What would they have? Is life so dear, or peace so sweet, as to be purchased at the price of chains and slavery? Forbid it, Almighty God! I know not what course others may take; but as for me, give me liberty, or give me death!

Patrick Henry, "Give Me Liberty, or Give Me Death" speech (1775).

5. Thomas Paine Advocates the
"Common Sense" of Independence, 1776

In the following pages I offer nothing more than simple facts, plain arguments, and common sense; and have no other preliminaries to settle with the reader, than that he will divest himself of prejudice and prepossession, and suffer his reason and his feelings to determine for themselves; that he will put *on,* or rather that he will not put *off* the true character of a man, and generously enlarge his views beyond the present day. . . .

. . . Now is the seed-time of continental union, faith and honor. The least fracture now will be like a name engraved with the point of a pin on the tender rind of a young oak; the wound will enlarge with the tree, and posterity read it in full grown characters. . . .

As much hath been said of the advantages of reconciliation, which, like an agreeable dream, hath passed away and left us as we were, it is but right, that we should examine the contrary side of the argument, and inquire into some of the many material injuries which these colonies sustain, and always will sustain, by being connected with, and dependant on Great-Britain. . . .

I have heard it asserted by some, that as America hath flourished under her former connexion with Great-Britain, that the same connexion is necessary towards her future happiness, and will always have the same effect. Nothing can be more fallacious than this kind of argument. We may as well assert that because a child has thrived upon milk, that it is never to have meat, or that the first twenty years of our lives is to become a precedent for the next twenty. But even this is admitting more than is true, for I answer roundly, that America would have flourished as much, and probably much more, had no European power had any thing to do with her. The commerce, by which she hath enriched herself, are the necessaries of life, and will always have a market while eating is the custom of Europe. . . .

It has lately been asserted in parliament, that the colonies have no relation to each other but through the parent country, *i. e.* that Pennsylvania and the Jerseys, and so on for the rest, are sister colonies by the way of England; this is certainly a very round-about way of proving relationship, but it is the nearest and only true way of proving enemyship, if I may so call it. France and Spain never were, nor perhaps ever will be our enemies as *Americans,* but as our being the *subjects of Great-Britain.*

But Britain is the parent country, say some. Then the more shame upon her conduct. Even brutes do not devour their young, nor savages make war upon their families; wherefore the assertion, if true, turns to her reproach; but it happens not to be true, or only partly so, and the phrase *parent* or *mother country* hath been jesuitically adopted by the king and his parasites, with a low papistical design of gaining an unfair bias on the credulous weakness of our minds. Europe, and not England, is the parent country of America. This new world hath been the asylum for the persecuted lovers of civil and religious liberty from *every part* of Europe. Hither have they fled, not from the tender embraces of the mother, but from the cruelty of the monster;

Thomas Paine, *The Essential Thomas Paine* (London: Penguin Books, 1986), 36–40, 43–45, 48–49, 54–57, 59.

and it is so far true of England, that the same tyranny which drove the first emigrants from home, pursues their descendants still. . . .

. . . Not one third of the inhabitants, even of this province, are of English descent. Wherefore I reprobate the phrase of parent or mother country applied to England only, as being false, selfish, narrow and ungenerous. . . .

. . . Our plan is commerce, and that, well attended to, will secure us the peace and friendship of all Europe; because, it is the interest of all Europe to have America a *free port.* Her trade will always be a protection, and her barrenness of gold and silver secure her from invaders. . . .

. . . It is the true interest of America to steer clear of European contentions, which she never can do, while by her dependance on Britain, she is made the make-weight in the scale of British politics. . . .

As to government matters, it is not in the power of Britain to do this continent justice: The business of it will soon be too weighty, and intricate, to be managed with any tolerable degree of convenience, by a power so distant from us, and so very ignorant of us; for if they cannot conquer us, they cannot govern us. . . .

Small islands not capable of protecting themselves, are the proper objects for kingdoms to take under their care; but there is something very absurd, in supposing a continent to be perpetually governed by an island. In no instance hath nature made the satellite larger than its primary planet, and as England and America, with respect to each other, reverses the common order of nature, it is evident they belong to different systems; England to Europe, America to itself. . . .

. . . No man was a warmer wisher for reconciliation than myself, before the fatal nineteenth of April 1775, but the moment the event of that day was made known, I rejected the hardened, sullen tempered Pharaoh of England for ever; and disdain the wretch, that with the pretended title of FATHER OF HIS PEOPLE can unfeelingly hear of their slaughter, and composedly sleep with their blood upon his soul.

But admitting that matters were now made up, what would be the event? I answer, the ruin of the continent. And that for several reasons.

First, The powers of governing still remaining in the hands of the king, he will have a negative over the whole legislation of this continent. And as he hath shewn himself such an inveterate enemy to liberty, and discovered such a thirst for arbitrary power; is he, or is he not, a proper man to say to these colonies, *"You shall make no laws but what I please."* And is there any inhabitant in America so ignorant, as not to know, that according to what is called the *present constitution,* that this continent can make no laws but what the king gives leave to; and is there any man so unwise, as not to see, that (considering what has happened) he will suffer no law to be made here, but such as suit *his* purpose. We may be as effectually enslaved by the want of laws in America as by submitting to laws made for us in England. . . .

But where, says some, is the King of America? I'll tell you. Friend, he reigns above, and doth not make havoc of mankind like the Royal Brute of Britain. Yet that we may not appear to be defective even in earthly honors, let a day be solemnly set apart for proclaiming the charter; let it be brought forth placed on the divine law, the word of God; let a crown be placed thereon, by which the world may know, that so far we approve of monarchy, that in America THE LAW IS KING. . . .

Some, perhaps, will say, that after we have made it up with Britain, she will protect us. Can we be so unwise as to mean, that she shall keep a navy in our harbours for that purpose? Common sense will tell us, that the power which hath endeavoured to subdue us, is of all others the most improper to defend us. . . .

Another reason why the present time is preferable to all others, is, that the fewer our numbers are, the more land there is yet unoccupied, which instead of being lavished by the king on his worthless dependants, may be hereafter applied, not only to the discharge of the present debt, but to the constant support of government. No nation under heaven hath such an advantage at this. . . .

As to religion, I hold it to be the indispensable duty of all government, to protect all conscientious professors thereof, and I know of no other business which government hath to do therewith, Let a man throw aside that narrowness of soul, that selfishness of principle, which the niggards of all professions are so unwilling to part with, and he will be at once delivered of his fears on that head. Suspicion is the companion of mean souls, and the bane of all good society. For myself, I fully and conscientiously believe, that it is the will of the Almighty, that there should be diversity of religious opinions among us: It affords a large field for our Christian kindness. Were we all of one way of thinking, our religious dispositions would want matter for probation; and on this liberal principle, I look on the various denominations among us, to be like children of the same family, differing only, in what is called, their Christian names. . . .

These proceedings may at first appear strange and difficult; but, like all other steps which we have already passed over, will in a little time become familiar and agreeable; and, until an independence is declared, the Continent will feel itself like a man who continues putting off some unpleasant business from day to day, yet knows it must be done, hates to set about it, wishes it over, and is continually haunted with the thoughts of its necessity.

6. German Americans Support the American Revolution, 1776

—Remember—and remind your families—, you came to America, suffering many hardships, in order to escape servitude and enjoy liberty.

—Remember, in Germany serfs ["leibeigene"] may not marry without the consent of their master, . . . they are regarded as little better than black slaves on West Indian islands. . . .

—Remember the forced labor ["Frondienst"] which subjects, especially peasants, must in some places still perform for their overlords. . . .

—Remember the almost unbearable taxes with which the princes burden their subjects. . . .

—Remember, how in many places a farmer is not permitted to shoot the deer which devastates his freshly sown fields. . . .

Staatsbote (Philadelphia), March 9, 1776. Translated by Willi Paul Adams. Reprinted in Bernard Bailyn and John B. Hench, eds., *The Press and the American Revolution* (Boston: Northeastern University Press, 1981).

—Remember, how in times of war soldiers drive the citizen and farmer almost out of his house, occupy his best rooms and his beds, and make the owner himself sleep on straw or on a bench.

—Remember that the administration of Britain and its Parliament intends to treat Americans the same way, or worse.

7. Abigail Adams Asks Her Husband to "Remember the Ladies," 1776

Braintree March 31 1776

I wish you would ever write me a Letter half as long as I write you; and tell me if you may where your Fleet are gone? What sort of Defence Virginia can make against our common Enemy? Whether it is so situated as to make an able Defence? Are not the Gentery Lords and the common people vassals, are they not like the uncivilized Natives Brittain represents us to be? I hope their Riffel Men who have shewen themselves very savage and even Blood thirsty; are not a specimen of the Generality of the people. . . .

I have sometimes been ready to think that the passion for Liberty cannot be Eaquelly Strong in the Breasts of those who have been accustomed to deprive their fellow Creatures of theirs. Of this I am certain that it is not founded upon that generous and christian principal of doing to others as we would that others should do unto us. . . .

The Town in General is left in a better state than we expected, more oweing to a precipitate flight than any Regard to the inhabitants, tho some individuals discoverd a sense of honour and justice and have left the rent of the Houses in which they were, for the owners and the furniture unhurt, or if damaged suffcent to make it good.

Others have committed abominable Ravages. The Mansion House of your President is safe and the furniture unhurt whilst both the House and Furniture of the Solisiter General have fallen a prey to their own merciless party. . . .

I feel very differently at the approach of spring to what I did a month ago. We knew not then whether we could plant or sow with safety, whether when we had toild we could reap the fruits of our own industery, whether we could rest in our own Cottages, or whether we should not be driven from the sea coasts to seek shelter in the wilderness, but now we feel as if we might sit under our own vine and eat the good of the land. . . .

. . . I long to hear that you have declared an independancy—and by the way in the new Code of Laws which I suppose it will be necessary for you to make I desire you would Remember the Ladies, and be more generous and favourable to them than your ancestors. Do not put such unlimited power into the hands of the Husbands. Remember all Men would be tyrants if they could. If perticuliar care and attention is not paid to the Laidies we are determined to foment a Rebellion, and will not hold ourselves bound by any Laws in which we have no voice, or Representation.

Adams Family Correspondence, I (Cambridge: Harvard University Press, 1963), 369–370.

That your Sex are Naturally Tyrannical is a Truth so thoroughly established as to admit of no dispute, but such of you as wish to be happy willingly give up the harsh title of Master for the more tender and endearing one of Friend. Why then, not put it out of the power of the vicious and the Lawless to use us with cruelty and indignity with impunity. Men of Sense in all Ages abhor those customs which treat us only as the vassals of your Sex. Regard us then as Beings placed by providence under your protection and in immitation of the Supreem Being make use of that power only for our happiness.

8. African Americans Petition for Freedom, 1777

To the Honorable Counsel & House of [Representa]tives for the State of Massachusitte Bay in General Court assembled, Jan. 13, 1777.

The petition of A Great Number of Blackes detained in a State of slavery in the Bowels of a free & Christian Country Humbly shuwith that your Petitioners apprehend that thay have in Common with all other men a Natural and Unaliable Right to that freedom which the Grat Parent of the Unavers hath Bestowed equalley on all menkind and which they have Never forfuted by any Compact or agreement whatever—but thay wher Unjustly Dragged by the hand of cruel Power from their Derest friends and sum of them Even torn from the Embraces of their tender Parents—from A populous Pleasant and plentiful contry and in violation of Laws of Nature and off Nations and in defiance of all the tender feelings of humanity Brough[t] hear Either to Be sold Like Beast of Burthen & Like them Condemnd to Slavery for Life—Among A People Profesing the mild Religion of Jesus A people Not Insensible of the Secrets of Rationable Being Nor without spirit to Resent the unjust endeavours of others to Reduce them to a state of Bondage and Subjection your honouer Need not to be informed that A Life of Slavery Like that of your petitioners Deprived of Every social privilege of Every thing Requiset to Render Life Tolable is far worse then Nonexistance.

[In imitat]ion of the Lawdable Example of the Good People of these States your petiononers have Long and Patiently waited the Evnt of petition after petition By them presented to the Legislative Body of this state and cannot but with Grief Reflect that their Sucess hath ben but too similar they Cannot but express their Astonishment that It has Never Bin Consirdered that Every Principle from which Amarica has Acted in the Cours of their unhappy Deficultes with Great Briton Pleads Stronger than A thousand arguments in favowrs of your petieners they therfor humble Beseech your honours to give this peti[ti]on its due weight & consideration and cause an act of the Legislatur to be past Wherby they may Be Restored to the Enjoyments of that which is the Naturel Right of all men—and their Children who wher Born in this Land of Liberty may not be heald as Slaves after they arive at the age of Twenty one years so may the Inhabitance of thes Stats No longer chargeable with the inconsistancey of acting themselves the part which they condem and oppose in others Be prospered in their present Glorious struggle for Liberty and have those Blessing to them, &c.

Donald McQuade et al., eds., *The Harper American Literature,* 2d ed. (New York: HarperCollins, 1990).

9. Mohawk Leader Joseph Brant Commits the Loyalty of His People to Britain, 1776

Brother Gorah [British Secretary of State Lord Germain]:

We have cross'd the great Lake and come to this kingdom with our Superintendant Col. Johnson from our Confederacy the Six Nations and their Allies, that we might see our Father the Great King, and joyn in informing him, his Councillors and wise men, of the good intentions of the Indians our bretheren, and of their attachment to His Majesty and his Government.

Brother: The Disturbances in America give great trouble to all our Nations, as many strange stories have been told to us by the people in that country. The Six Nations who always loved the King, sent a number of their Chiefs and Warriors with their Superintendant to Canada last summer, where they engaged their allies to joyn with them in the defence of that country, and when it was invaded by the New England people, they alone defeated them.

Brother: In that engagement we had several of our best Warriors killed and wounded, and the Indians think it very hard they should have been so deceived by the White people in that country, the enemy returning in great numbers, and no White people supporting the Indians, they were obliged to retire to their vilages and sit still. We now Brother hope to see these bad children chastised, and that we may be enabled to tell the Indians, who have always been faithfull and ready to assist the King, what His Majesty intends.

Brother: The Mohocks our particular Nation, have on all occasions shewn their zeal and loyalty to the Great King; yet they have been very badly treated by his people in that country, the City of Albany laying an unjust claim to the lands on which our Lower Castle is built. . . . We have been often assured by our late great friend Sʳ William Johnson who never deceived us, and we know he was told so that the King and wise men here would do us justice; but this notwithstanding all our applications has never been done, and it makes us very uneasie. . . . We have only therefore to request that his Majesty will attend to this matter: it troubles our Nation & they cannot sleep easie in their beds. Indeed it is very hard when we have let the Kings subjects have so much of our lands for so little value, they should want to cheat us in this manner of the small spots we have left for our women and children to live on. We are tired out in making complaints & getting no redress. We therefore hope that the Assurances now given us by the Superintendant may take place, and that he may have it in his power to procure us justice.

Brother: We shall truly report all that we hear from you, to the Six Nations at our return. We are well informed there has been many Indians in this Country who came without any authority, from their own, and gave much trouble. We desire Brother to tell you this is not our case. We are warriors known to all the Nations, and are now here by approbation of many of them, whose sentiments we speak.

Brother: We hope these things will be considered and that the King or his great men will give us such an answer as will make our hearts light and glad before we

E. B. O'Callaghan, ed., *Documents Relative to the Colonial History of the State of New York* (Albany: Weed, Parsons, 1853–1887), 8: 670–671.

go, and strengthen our hands, so that we may joyn our Superintendant Col. Johnson in giving satisfaction to all our Nations, when we report to them, on our return; for which purpose we hope soon to be accomodated with a passage.

Dictated by the Indians and taken down by

Jo: CHEW, Sec^y

10. Loyalists Plead Their Cause to the King, 1782

Relying with the fullest confidence upon national justice and compassion to our fidelity and distresses, we can entertain no doubts but that Great Britain will prevent the ruin of her American friends, at every risk short of certain destruction to herself. But if compelled, by adversity or misfortune, from the wicked and perfidious combinations and designs of numerous and powerful enemies abroad, and more criminal and dangerous enemies at home, an idea should be formed by Great Britain of relinquishing her American colonies to the usurpation of congress, we thus solemnly call God to witness, that we think the colonies can never be so happy or so free as in a constitutional connexion with, and dependence on Great Britain; convinced, as we are, that to be a British subject, with all its consequences, is to be the happiest and freest member of any civil society in the known world—we, therefore, in justice to our members, in duty to ourselves, and in fidelity to our posterity, must not, cannot refrain from making this public declaration and appeal to the faithful subjects of every government, and the compassionate sovereign of every people, in every nation and kingdom of the world, that our principles are the principles of the virtuous and free; that our sufferings are the sufferings of unprotected loyalty, and persecuted fidelity; that our cause is the cause of legal and constitutional government, throughout the world; that, opposed by principles of republicanism, and convinced, from recent observation, that brutal violence, merciless severity, relentless cruelty, and discretionary outrages are the distinguished traits and ruling principles of the present system of congressional republicanism, our aversion is unconquerable, irreconcileable.—That we are attached to monarchical government, from past and happy experience—by duty, and by choice. That, to oppose insurrections, and to listen to the requests of people so circumstanced as we are, is the common interest of all mankind in civil society. That to support our rights, is to support the rights of every subject of legal government; and that to afford us relief, is at once the duty and security of every prince and sovereign on earth. Our appeal, therefore, is just; and our claim to aid and assistance is extensive and universal. But if, reflecting on the uncertain events of war, and sinking under the gloomy prospect of public affairs, from the divisions and contests unhappily existing in the great councils of the nation, any apprehensions should have been excited in our breasts with respect to the issue of the American war, we humbly hope it cannot, even by the most illiberal, be imputed to us as an abatement of our unshaken loyalty to our most gracious sovereign, or of our unalterable predilection in favor of the British nation and government, whom may God long protect and preserve, if, in consequence thereof, we thus humbly implore that your majesty, and the

Hezekiah Niles, ed., *Principles and Acts of the Revolution in America* (Baltimore: W. O. Niles, 1822), 393–397.

parliament, would be graciously pleased, in the tenderness of our fears, and in pity to our distresses, to solicit, by your ambassadors at the courts of foreign sovereigns, the aid of such powerful and good allies, as to your majesty and parliament, in your great wisdom and discretion, may seem meet. Or if such a measure should in any manner be thought incompatible with the dignity and interest of our sovereign and the nation, we most humbly and ardently supplicate and entreat, that, by deputies or ambassadors, nominated and appointed by your majesty's suffering American loyalists, they may be permitted to solicit and obtain from other nations that interference, aid and alliance, which, by the blessing of Almighty God, may, in the last fatal and ultimate extreme, save and deliver us, his majesty's American loyalists, who, we maintain, in every one of the colonies, compose a great majority of the inhabitants, and those too the first in point of opulence and consequence, from the ruinous system of congressional independence and republican tyranny, detesting rebellion as we do, and preferring a subjection to any power in Europe, to the mortifying debasement of a state of slavery, and a life of insult, under the tyranny of congressional usurpation.

☞ *E S S A Y S*

Historians have for decades debated the meaning of the Revolution for American society. They have argued as to whether it was a war to determine "home rule" (whether the colonies should be independent of Britain) or a war to determine "who should rule at home" (who the rulers in the new country would be). And they have disputed the degree to which the Revolution was a radical departure on the part of Americans or a conservative attempt to reassert control over their political world. These two essays address the last of these questions. Bernard Bailyn, a professor at Harvard University, argues that the colonists perceived a concerted effort by elements in England to strip Americans of their liberty. This conspiracy, the colonists thought, might consume all of the British Empire, and therefore, their revolution was an attempt to reestablish the liberties of English people. In contrast, Gordon Wood, a historian at Brown University, emphasizes the radicalism of the American Revolution. He argues that American revolutionaries not only resented the corruption within the British Empire, but also assaulted the bonds of a traditional monarchical society. As a result, the Revolution set in motion processes of change that would transform the arrangements of state and society and would propel the new country in radical new directions.

The American Revolution as a Response to British Corruption

BERNARD BAILYN

. . . The colonists believed they saw emerging from the welter of events during the decade after the Stamp Act a pattern whose meaning was unmistakable. They saw in the measures taken by the British government and in the actions of officials in the colonies something for which their peculiar inheritance of thought had prepared

Reprinted by permission of the publisher from Bernard Bailyn, *The Ideological Origins of the American Revolution* (Cambridge, Mass.: The Belknap Press of Harvard University Press), 94–96, 99–101, 105–107, 112–114, 116–119, 122–128, 132–133, 138, 140–143. Copyright © 1967, 1992 by the President and Fellows of Harvard College.

them only too well, something they had long conceived to be a possibility in view of the known tendencies of history and of the present state of affairs in England. They saw about them, with increasing clarity, not merely mistaken, or even evil, policies violating the principles upon which freedom rested, but what appeared to be evidence of nothing less than a deliberate assault launched surreptitiously by plotters against liberty both in England and in America. The danger to America, it was believed, was in fact only the small, immediately visible part of the greater whole whose ultimate manifestation would be the destruction of the English constitution, with all the rights and privileges embedded in it.

This belief transformed the meaning of the colonists' struggle, and it added an inner accelerator to the movement of opposition. For, once assumed, it could not be easily dispelled: denial only confirmed it, since what conspirators profess is not what they believe; the ostensible is not the real; and the real is deliberately malign.

It was this—the overwhelming evidence, as they saw it, that they were faced with conspirators against liberty determined at all costs to gain ends which their words dissembled—that was signaled to the colonists after 1763, and it was this above all else that in the end propelled them into Revolution.

Suspicion that the ever-present, latent danger of an active conspiracy of power against liberty was becoming manifest within the British Empire, assuming specific form and developing in coordinated phases, rose in the consciousness of a large segment of the American population before any of the famous political events of the struggle with England took place. No adherent of a nonconformist church or sect in the eighteenth century was free from suspicion that the Church of England, an arm of the English state, was working to bring all subjects of the crown into the community of the Church; and since toleration was official and nonconformist influence in English politics formidable, it was doing so by stealth, disguising its efforts, turning to improper uses devices that had been created for benign purposes. . . .

Reinforcement for this belief came quickly. . . . [T]he passage of the Stamp Act was not merely an impolitic and unjust law that threatened the priceless right of the individual to retain possession of his property until he or his chosen representative voluntarily gave it up to another; it was to many, also, a danger signal indicating that a more general threat existed. For though it could be argued, and in a sense proved by the swift repeal of the act, that nothing more was involved than ignorance or confusion on the part of people in power who really knew better and who, once warned by the reaction of the colonists, would not repeat the mistake—though this could be, and by many was, concluded, there nevertheless appeared to be good reason to suspect that more was involved. For from whom had the false information and evil advice come that had so misled the English government? From officials in the colonies, said John Adams, said Oxenbridge Thacher, James Otis, and Stephen Hopkins—from officials bent on overthrowing the constituted forms of government in order to satisfy their own lust for power, and not likely to relent in their passion. Some of these local plotters were easily identified. To John Adams, Josiah Quincy, and others the key figure in Massachusetts from the beginning to the end was Thomas Hutchinson who by "serpentine wiles" was befuddling and victimizing the weak, the avaricious, and the incautious in order to increase his notorious engrossment of public office. In Rhode Island it was, to James Otis, that "little, dirty, drinking, drabbing, contaminated knot of thieves, beggars, and transports . . . made up of Turks, Jews, and other infidels, with a few renegado Christians and Catholics"—the Newport junto, led by Martin Howard, Jr., which had already been accused by Stephen Hopkins and others in Providence of "conspiring against the liberties of the colony."

But even if local leaders associated with power elements in England had not been so suspect, there were grounds for seeing more behind the Stamp Act than its ostensible purpose. The official aim of the act was, of course, to bring in revenue to the English treasury. But the sums involved were in fact quite small, and "some persons . . . may be inclined to acquiesce under it." But that would be to fall directly into the trap, for the smaller the taxes, John Dickinson wrote in the most influential pamphlet published in America before 1776, the more dangerous they were, since they would the more easily be found acceptable by the incautious, with the result that a precedent would be established for making still greater inroads on liberty and property.

> Nothing is wanted at home but a PRECEDENT, the force of which shall be established by the tacit submission of the colonies. . . . If the Parliament succeeds in this attempt, other statutes will impose other duties . . . and thus the Parliament will levy upon us such sums of money as they choose to take, *without any other* LIMITATION *than their* PLEASURE. . . .

But even this did not exhaust the evidence that a design against liberty was unfolding. During the same years the independence of the judiciary, so crucial a part of the constitution, was suddenly seen to be under heavy attack, and by the mid-1760's to have succumbed in many places.

This too was not a new problem. The status of the colonial judiciary had been a controversial question throughout the century. The Parliamentary statute of 1701 which guaranteed judges in England life tenure in their posts had been denied to the colonies, in part because properly trained lawyers were scarce in the colonies, especially in the early years, and appointments for life would prevent the replacement of ill-qualified judges by their betters, when they appeared; and in part because, judicial salaries being provided for by temporary legislative appropriations, the removal of all executive control from the judiciary, it was feared, would result in the hopeless subordination of the courts to popular influences. The status of the judiciary in the eighteenth century was therefore left open to political maneuvering in which, more often than not, the home government managed to carry its point and to make the tenure of judges as temporary as their salaries. Then suddenly, in the early 1760's, the whole issue exploded. In 1759 the Pennsylvania Assembly declared that the judges of that province would thereafter hold their offices by the same permanence of tenure that had been guaranteed English judges after the Glorious Revolution. But the law was disallowed forthwith by the crown. Opposition newspapers boiled with resentment; angry speeches were made in the Assembly; and a pamphlet appeared explaining in the fullest detail the bearing of judicial independence on constitutional freedom. . . .

All the colonies were affected. In some, like New Jersey, where the governor's incautious violation of the new royal order led to his removal from office, or like North Carolina, where opposition forces refused to concede and managed to keep up the fight for permanent judicial tenure throughout the entire period from 1760 to 1776, the issue was directly joined. In others, as in Massachusetts, where specific Supreme Court appointments were vehemently opposed by anti-administration interests, the force of the policy was indirect. But everywhere there was bitterness at the decree and fear of its implications, for everywhere it was known that judicial tenure "at the will of the crown" was "dangerous to the liberty and property of the subject," and that if the bench were occupied by "men who depended upon the smiles of the crown for their daily bread," the possibility of having an independent judiciary as an effective check upon executive power would be wholly lost. . . .

Meanwhile an event even more sinister in its implications had taken place in the colonies themselves. On October 1, 1768, two regiments of regular infantry, with artillery, disembarked in Boston. For many months the harassed Governor Bernard had sought some legal means or excuse for summoning military help in his vain efforts to maintain if not an effective administration then at least order in the face of Stamp Act riots, circular letters, tumultuous town meetings, and assaults on customs officials. But the arrival of troops in Boston increased rather than decreased his troubles. For to a populace steeped in the literature of eighteenth-century English politics the presence of troops in a peaceful town had such portentous meaning that resistance instantly stiffened. It was not so much the physical threat of the troops that affected the attitudes of the Bostonians; it was the bearing their arrival had on the likely tendency of events. . . . The mere rumor of possible troop arrivals had evoked the age-old apprehensions. "The raising or keeping a standing army within the king-dom in time of peace, unless it be with the consent of Parliament, is against the law," the alarmed Boston Town Meeting had resolved. It is, they said,

> the indefeasible right of [British] subjects to be *consulted* and to give their *free consent in person* or by representatives of their own free election to the raising and keeping a standing army among them; and the inhabitants of this town, being free subjects, have the same right derived from nature and confirmed by the British constitution as well as the said royal charter; and therefore the raising or keeping a standing army without their consent in person or by representatives of their own free election would be an infringe-ment of their natural, constitutional, and charter rights; and the employing such army for the enforcing of laws made without the consent of the people, in person or by their representatives, would be a grievance.

But the troops arrived, four regiments in all: in bold, stark actuality a standing army—just such a standing army as had snuffed out freedom in Denmark, classi-cally, and elsewhere throughout the world. True, British regulars had been intro-duced into the colonies on a permanent basis at the end of the Seven Years' War; that in itself had been disquieting. But it had then been argued that troops were needed to police the newly acquired territories, and that they were not in any case to be regularly garrisoned in peaceful, populous towns. No such defense could be made of the troops sent to Boston in 1768. No simple, ingenuous explanation would suffice. The true motive was only too apparent for those with eyes to see. One of the classic stages in the process of destroying free constitutions of government had been reached. . . .

And then, a few weeks later, came the Boston Massacre [in 1770]. Doubts that the troops in Boston constituted a standing army and that it was the purpose of stand-ing armies to terrify a populace into compliance with tyrannical wills were silenced by that event. . . . The acquittal of the indicted soldiers did not alter the conviction that the Massacre was the logical work of a standing army, for it accentuated the par-allel with the English case which also had concluded with acquittal; and in Boston too there was suspicion of judicial irregularities. How the murderers managed to escape was known to some, it was said, but was "too dark to explain."

Unconstitutional taxing, the invasion of placemen, the weakening of the judiciary, . . . standing armies—these were major evidences of a deliberate assault of power upon liberty. Lesser testimonies were also accumulating at the same time: small episodes in themselves, they took on a large significance in the context in which they were received. Writs of assistance in support of customs officials were working their expected evil: "our houses, and even our bedchambers, are exposed to be ransacked, our boxes, trunks, and chests broke open, ravaged and plundered by wretches whom no prudent man would venture to employ even as menial servants." Legally convened legislatures had been "adjourned . . . to a place highly inconvenient to the members and greatly disadvantageous to the interest of the province"; they had been prorogued [discontinued] and dissolved at executive whim. Even the boundaries of colonies had been tampered with, whereby *"rights of soil"* had been eliminated at a stroke. When in 1772 the Boston Town Meeting met to draw up a full catalogue of the "infringements and violations" of the "rights of the colonists, and of this province in particular, as men, as Christians, and as subjects," it approved a list of twelve items, which took seventeen pamphlet pages to describe.

But then, for a two-year period, there was a détente of sorts created by the repeal of the Townshend Duties, the withdrawal of troops from Boston, and the failure of other provocative measures to be taken. It ended abruptly, however, in the fall and winter of 1773, when, with a rush, the tendencies earlier noted were brought to fulfillment. In the space of a few weeks, all the dark, twisted roots of malevolence were finally revealed, plainly, for all to see.

The turning point was the passage of the Tea Act and the resulting Tea Party in Boston in December 1773. Faced with this defiant resistance to intimidation, the powers at work in England, it was believed, gave up all pretense of legality— "threw off the mask," John Adams said in a phrase that for a century had been used to describe just such climactic disclosures—and moved swiftly to complete their design. In a period of two months in the spring of 1774 Parliament took its revenge in a series of coercive actions no liberty-loving people could tolerate: the Boston Port Act, intended, it was believed, to snuff out the economic life of the Massachusetts metropolis; the Administration of Justice Act, aimed at crippling judicial processes once and for all by permitting trials to be held in England for offenses committed in Massachusetts; the Massachusetts Government Act, which stripped from the people of Massachusetts the protection of the British constitution by giving over all the "democratic" elements of the province's government—even popularly elected juries and town meetings—into the hands of the executive power; the Quebec Act, which, while not devised as a part of the coercive program, fitted it nicely, in the eyes of the colonists, by extending the boundaries of a "papist" province, and one governed wholly by prerogative, south into territory claimed by Virginia, Connecticut, and Massachusetts; finally, the Quartering Act, which permitted the seizure of unoccupied buildings for the use of troops on orders of the governors alone even in situations, such as Boston's, where barracks were available in the vicinity.

Once these coercive acts were passed there could be little doubt that "the system of slavery fabricated against America . . . is the offspring of mature deliberation." To the leaders of the Revolutionary movement there was, beyond question, "a settled, fixed plan for *enslaving* the colonies, or bringing them under arbitrary government, and indeed the nation too." By 1774 the idea "that the British government—the *King, Lords,* and *Commons*—have laid a regular plan to enslave America, and that they are now deliberately putting it in execution" had been asserted, Samuel Seabury wrote wearily but accurately, "over, and over, and over again." The less inhibited of the colonial orators were quick to point out that "the MONSTER of a standing ARMY" had sprung directly from "a PLAN . . . *systematically* laid, and pursued by the British *ministry,* near twelve years, for enslaving America." . . .

But who, specifically, were these enemies, and what were their goals? Josiah Quincy, at the center of affairs in London in the winter of 1774–75, was convinced "that all the measures against America were planned and pushed on by Bernard and Hutchinson." But most observers believed that local plotters like Hutchinson were only "creatures" of greater figures in England coordinating and impelling forward the whole effort. . . . A . . . general version of this view was that a Stuart-Tory party, the "corrupt, Frenchified party in the nation," as it was described in 1766— "evil-minded individuals," Jonathan Mayhew believed, "not improbably in the interests of the houses of Bourbon and the Pretender"—was at work seeking to reverse the consequences of the Glorious Revolution. It was a similar notion that in all probability accounts for the republication of Rapin's *Dissertation on . . . the Whigs and Tories* in Boston in 1773; and it was this notion that furnished Jefferson with his ultimate understanding of the "system" that sought to destroy liberty in America. Still another explanation, drawing no less directly on fears that had lain at the root of opposition ideology in England since the turn of the century, emphasized the greed of a "monied interest" created by the crown's financial necessities and the power of a newly risen, arrogant, and irresponsible capitalist group, that battened on wars and stock manipulation. . . .

The most common explanation, however—an explanation that rose from the deepest sources of British political culture, that was a part of the very structure of British political thought—located "the spring and cause of all the distresses and complaints of the people in England or in America" in "a kind of fourth power that the constitution knows nothing of, or has not provided against." This "overruling arbitrary power, which absolutely controls the King, Lords, and Commons," was composed, it was said, of the "ministers and favorites" of the King, who, in defiance of God and man alike, "extend their usurped authority infinitely too far," and, throwing off the balance of the constitution, make their "despotic will" the authority of the nation.

> For their power and interest is so great that they can and do procure whatever laws they please, having (by power, interest, and the application of the people's money to *placemen* and *pensioners*) the whole legislative authority at their command. So that it is plain (not to say a word of a particular reigning arbitrary *Stuarchal* power among them) that the rights of the people are ruined and destroyed by ministerial *tyrannical* authority, and thereby . . . become a kind of slaves to the ministers of state.

This "junto of courtiers and state-jobbers," these "court-locusts," whispering in the royal ear, "instill in the King's mind a divine right of authority to command his subjects" at the same time as they advance their "detestable scheme" by misinforming and misleading the people. . . .

No fear, no accusation, had been more common in the history of opposition politics in eighteenth-century England; none was more familiar to Americans whose political awareness had been formed by the literature of English politics. It had, moreover, a special resonance in New England and elsewhere in the colonies where people generally were acquainted with the Biblical Book of Esther and hence had a special model for a ministerial conspiracy in the story of that "tyrannic *bloodthirsty* MINISTER OF STATE," Haman, at the court of Ahasuerus. . . .

But why were not these manipulators of prerogative satisfied with amassing power at home? Why the attention to faraway provinces in America? Several answers were offered, besides the general one that power naturally seeks to drive itself everywhere, into every pocket of freedom. One explanation was that the court, having reached a limit in the possibilities of patronage and spoils in the British Isles, sought a quarrel with the colonies as an excuse for confiscating their wealth. "The long and scandalous list of placemen and pensioners and the general profligacy and prodigality of the present reign exceed the annual supplies. England is drained by taxes, and Ireland impoverished to almost the last farthing. . . . America was the only remaining spot to which their oppression and extortion had not fully reached, and they considered her as a fallow field from which a large income might be drawn." When the colonists' reaction to the Stamp Act proved that "raising a revenue in America quietly" was out of the question, it was decided to destroy their power to resist: the colonies were to be "politically broken up." And so the Tea Act was passed, not to gain a revenue but, as in the case of the Massacre, to provoke a quarrel. The ministry wished "to see America in arms . . . because it furnished them with a pretense for declaring us rebels; and persons conquered under that character forfeit their all, be it where it will or what it will, to the crown." . . .

That by 1774 the final crisis of the constitution, brought on by political and social corruption, had been reached was, to most informed colonists, evident; but if they had not realized it themselves they would soon have discovered it from the flood of newspapers, pamphlets, and letters that poured in on them from opposition sources in England. Again and again reports from the home country proclaimed that the English nation had departed, once and for all and completely, from the true principles of liberty. . . . The long-awaited signs of the total degeneration of the moral qualities necessary to preserve liberty were unmistakable, and these English radicals said so, vigorously, convincingly, in a series of increasingly shrill pamphlets and letters that were read avidly, circulated, published and republished, in America.

But it was not only the radicals. A wide range of public figures and pamphleteers, known and read in America, carried forward the cries of corruption that had been heard in earlier years and directed them to the specific political issues of the day. . . .

The fact that the ministerial conspiracy against liberty had risen from corruption was of the utmost importance to the colonists. It gave a radical new meaning to their claims: it transformed them from constitutional arguments to expressions of a world regenerative creed. For they had long known—it had been known everywhere in the English-speaking world in the eighteenth century—that England was one of the last refuges of the ancient gothic constitution that had once flourished everywhere in the civilized world. And now, in the outpourings of colonial protest, it was again repeated, but with new point and urgency, that by far "the greatest part of the human race" already lies in "total subjection to their rulers." Throughout the whole continent of Asia people are reduced "to such a degree of abusement and degradation" that the very idea of liberty is unknown among them. In *Africa,* scarce any human beings are to be found but barbarians, tyrants, and slaves: all equally remote from the true dignity of human nature and from a well-regulated state of society. Nor is *Europe* free from the curse. Most of her nations are forced to drink deep of the bitter cup. And in those in which freedom seem to have been established, the vital flame is going out. Two kingdoms, those of *Sweden* and *Poland,* have been betrayed and enslaved in the course of one year. The free towns of *Germany* can remain free no longer than their potent neighbors shall please to let them. *Holland* has got the forms if she has lost the spirit of a free country. *Switzerland* alone is in the full and safe possession of her freedom.

And if now, in this deepening gloom, the light of liberty went out in Britain too—in Britain, where next to "self-preservation, political liberty is the main aim and end of her constitution"—if, as events clearly portended and as "senators and historians are repeatedly predicting . . . continued corruption and standing armies will prove mortal distempers in her constitution"—what then? What refuge will liberty find? . . .

This theme, elaborately orchestrated by the colonial writers, marked the fulfillment of the ancient idea, deeply embedded in the colonists' awareness, that America had from the start been destined to play a special role in history. The controversy with England, from its beginning in the early 1760's, had lent support to that belief, so long nourished by so many different sources: the covenant theories of the Puritans, certain strands of Enlightenment thought, the arguments of the English radicals, the condition of life in the colonies, even the conquest of Canada. It had been the Stamp Act that had led John Adams to see in the original settlement of the colonies "the opening of a grand scene and design in providence for the illumination of the ignorant and the emancipation of the slavish part of mankind all over the earth." And Jonathan Mayhew, celebrating the conclusion of the same episode, had envisioned future streams of refugees escaping from a Europe sunk in "luxury, debauchery, venality, intestine quarrels, or other vices." It was even possible, Mayhew had added, "who knows?" that "our liberties being thus established, . . . on some future occasion . . . we or our posterity may even have the great felicity and honor to . . . keep Britain herself from ruin."

Now, in 1774, that "future occasion" was believed to be at hand. After the passage of the Coercive Acts it could be said that "all the spirit of patriotism or of liberty now left in England" was no more than "the last snuff of an expiring lamp," while "the same sacred flame . . . which once showed forth such wonders in Greece and in Rome . . . burns brightly and strongly in America." Who ought then to suppress as "whimsical and enthusiastical" the belief that the colonies were to become "the foundation of a great and mighty empire, the largest the world ever saw to be founded on such principles of liberty and freedom, both civil and religious . . . [and] which shall be the principal seat of that glorious kingdom which Christ shall erect upon earth in the latter days"? America "ere long will build an empire upon the ruins of Great Britain; will adopt its constitution purged of its impurities, and from an experience of its defects will guard against those evils which have wasted its vigor and brought it to an untimely end." The hand of God was "in America now giving a new epocha to the history of the world." . . .

What would an independent American nation be? A republic, necessarily—and properly, considering the character and circumstances of the people. But history clearly taught that republics were delicate polities, quickly degenerating into anarchy and tyranny; it was impossible, some said, to "recollect a single instance of a nation who supported this form of government for any length of time or with any degree of greatness." Others felt that independence might "split and divide the empire into a number of petty, insignificant states" that would easily fall subject to the will of "some foreign tyrant, or the more intolerable despotism of a few American demagogues"; the colonies might end by being "parceled out, Poland-like."

But if what the faint-hearted called "the ill-shapen, diminutive brat, INDEPENDENCY" contained within it all that remained of freedom; if it gave promise of growing great and strong and becoming the protector and propagator of liberty everywhere; if it were indeed true that "the cause of America is in a great measure the cause of all mankind"; if "'Tis not the concern of a day, a year, or an age; posterity are virtually involved in the contest, and will be more or less affected even to the end of time by our proceedings now"—if all of this were true, ways would be found by men inspired by such prospects to solve the problems of a new society and government. And so let every lover of mankind, every hater of tyranny,

> stand forth! Every spot of the old world is overrun with oppression. Freedom hath been hunted round the globe. Asia and Africa have long expelled her. Europe regards her like a stranger, and England hath given her warning to depart. O! receive the fugitive, and prepare in time an asylum for mankind.

The American Revolution as a Radical Departure

GORDON S. WOOD

The Revolution brought to the surface the republican tendencies of American life. The "Suddenness" of the change from monarchy to republicanism was "astonishing." "Idolatry to Monarchs, and servility to Aristocratical Pride," said John Adams in the summer of 1776, "was never so totally eradicated from so many Minds in so short a Time." Probably Adams should not have been astonished, for the truncated nature of American society with its high proportion of freeholders seemed naturally made for republicanism. Yet adopting republicanism was not simply a matter of bringing American culture more into line with the society. It meant as well an opportunity to abolish what remained of monarchy and to create once and for all new, enlightened republican relationships among people.

Such a change marked a real and radical revolution, a change of society, not just of government. People were to be "changed," said the South Carolina physician and historian David Ramsay, "from subjects to citizens," and "the difference is immense. Subject is derived from the latin words, *sub* and *jacio,* and means one who is under the power of another; but a citizen is an unit of a mass of free people, who, collectively, possess sovereignty. Subjects look up to a master, but citizens are so far equal, that none have hereditary rights superior to others. Each citizen of a free state contains, within himself, by nature and the constitution, as much of the common sovereignty as another." Such a republican society assumed very different sorts of human relationships from that of a monarchy.

Gordon S. Wood, *The Radicalism of the American Revolution* (New York: Vintage Books, Random House, 1992), 169–181, 183–187. Copyright © 1992 by Gordon Wood. Used by permission of Alfred A. Knopf, a division of Random House, Inc.

By the late 1760s and early 1770s a potentially revolutionary situation existed in many of the colonies. There was little evidence of those social conditions we often associate with revolution (and some historians have desperately sought to find): no mass poverty, no seething social discontent, no grinding oppression. For most white Americans there was greater prosperity than anywhere else in the world; in fact, the experience of that growing prosperity contributed to the unprecedented eighteenth-century sense that people here and now were capable of ordering their own reality. Consequently, there was a great deal of jealousy and touchiness everywhere, for what could be made could be unmade; the people were acutely nervous about their prosperity and the liberty that seemed to make it possible. With the erosion of much of what remained of traditional social relationships, more and more individuals had broken away from their families, communities, and patrons and were experiencing the anxiety of freedom and independence. Social changes, particularly since the 1740s, multiplied rapidly, and many Americans struggled to make sense of what was happening. These social changes were complicated, and they are easily misinterpreted. Luxury and conspicuous consumption by very ordinary people were increasing. So, too, was religious dissent of all sorts. The rich became richer, and aristocratic gentry everywhere became more conspicuous and self-conscious; and the numbers of poor in some cities and the numbers of landless in some areas increased. But social classes based on occupation or wealth did not set themselves against one another, for no classes in this modern sense yet existed. The society was becoming more unequal, but its inequalities were not the source of the instability and anxiety. Indeed, it was the pervasive equality of American society that was causing the problems. . . .

. . . [B]ecause such equality and prosperity were so unusual in the Western world, they could not be taken for granted. The idea of labor, of hard work, leading to increased productivity was so novel, so radical, in the overall span of Western history that most ordinary people, most of those who labored, could scarcely believe what was happening to them. Labor had been so long thought to be the natural and inevitable consequence of necessity and poverty that most people still associated it with slavery and servitude. Therefore any possibility of oppression, any threat to the colonists' hard-earned prosperity, any hint of reducing them to the poverty of other nations, was especially frightening; for it seemed likely to slide them back into the traditional status of servants or slaves, into the older world where labor was merely a painful necessity and not a source of prosperity. "The very apprehension thereof, cannot but cause extreme uneasiness." "No wonder," said Gadsden, "that throughout *America,* we find these men extremely anxious and attentive, to the cause of liberty." These hardworking farmers and mechanics were extraordinarily free and well off and had much to lose, and "this, therefore, naturally accounts for these people, in particular, being so united and steady, everywhere," in support of their liberties against British oppression. . . .

America was no doubt "the best poor Man's Country in the World." But the general well-being and equality of the society set against the gross inequality and flagrant harshness of both white servitude and especially black slavery made many people unusually sensitive to all the various dependencies and subordinations that still lurked everywhere in their lives. Thus in 1765 at the outset of the imperial crisis John Adams's fearful and seemingly anachronistic invocation of an older feudal world of "servants and vassals" holding "their lands, by a variety of duties and services . . . in a state of servile dependence on their lords," could at once arouse the colonists' anxieties over the potentialities, however inchoate and remote, of a dependent world in their own midst. They repeatedly put into words their widespread sense that very little stood between their prosperous freedom and out-and-out oppression. Indeed, they told themselves over and over that if ever they should agree to a parliamentary tax or allow their colonial assemblies to be silenced, "nothing will remain to us but a dredful expectation of certain slavery." The tenants of one of the New York landlords may have seemed to the landlord's agent to be "silly people" by their resisting a simple extension of the services required of them out of "fear [of] drawing their Posterity into Bondage," but they knew the reality of the eighteenth-century world. They knew the lot of ordinary people elsewhere, and they knew especially the lot of white and black dependents in their own society, and thus they could readily respond to images of being driven "like draft oxen," of being "made to serve as bond servants," or of foolishly sitting "quietly in expectation of a m[aste]r's promise for the recovery of [their] liberty." The immense changes occurring everywhere in their personal and social relationships—the loosening and severing of the hierarchical ties of kinship and patronage that were carrying them into modernity—only increased their suspicions and apprehensions. For they could not know then what direction the future was taking.

By the middle of the century these social changes were being expressed in politics. Americans everywhere complained of "a Scramble for Wealth and Power" by men of "worldly Spirits." Indeed, there were by the early 1760s "so many jarring and opposite Interests and Systems" that no one in authority could relax, no magistrate, no ruler, could long remain unchallenged. More and more ordinary people were participating in electoral politics, and in many of the colonies the number of contested elections for assembly seats markedly increased. This expansion of popular politics originated not because the mass of people pressed upward from below with new demands but because competing gentry, for their own parochial and tactical purposes, courted the people and bid for their support by invoking popular whig rhetoric. Opposition factions in the colonial assemblies made repeated appeals to the people as counterweights to the use of royal authority by the governors, especially as the older personal avenues of appeal over the heads of the governors to interests in England became clogged and unusable. But popular principles and popular participation in politics, once aroused, could not be easily put down; and by the eve of the Revolution, without anyone's intending or even being clearly aware of what was happening, traditional monarchical ways of governing through kin and patronage were transformed under the impact of the imperial crisis. "Family-Interests," like the Livingstons and De Lanceys in New York, or the Pinckneys and Leighs of South Carolina, observed one prescient British official in 1776, "have been long in a gradual Decay; and perhaps a new arrangement of political affairs may leave them wholly extinct." Those who were used to seeing politics as essentially a squabble among gentlemen were bewildered by the "strange metamorphosis or other" that was taking place.

With the weakening of family connections and the further fragmentation of colonial interests, crown officials and other conservatives made strenuous efforts to lessen popular participation in politics and to control the "democratic" part of the colonists' mixed constitutions. Some royal governors attempted to restrict the expansion of popular representation in the assemblies, to limit the meetings of the assemblies, and to veto the laws passed by the assemblies. Other officials toyed with plans for remodeling the colonial governments, for making the salaries of royal officials independent of the colonial legislatures, and for strengthening the royal councils or upper houses in the legislatures. Some even suggested introducing a titled nobility into America in order to stabilize colonial society. But most royal officials relied on whatever traditional monarchical instruments of political patronage and influence they had available to them to curb popular disorder and popular pressure—using intricate maneuvering and personal manipulation of important men in place of whig and republican appeals to the people.

After 1763 all these efforts became hopelessly entangled in the British government's attempts to reform its awkwardly structured empire and to extract revenue from the colonists. All parts of British policy came together to threaten each colonist's expanding republican expectations of liberty and independence. In the emotionally charged atmosphere of the 1760s and 1770s, all the imperial efforts at reform seemed to be an evil extension of what was destroying liberty in England itself. Through the manipulation of puppets or placemen in the House of Commons, the crown—since 1760 in the hands of a new young king, George III—was sapping the strength of popular representation in Parliament and unbalancing the English constitution. Events seemed to show that the crown, with the aid of a pliant Parliament, was trying to reach across the Atlantic to corrupt Americans in the same way.

Americans steeped in the radical whig and republican ideology of opposition to the court regarded these monarchical techniques of personal influence and patronage as "corruption," as attempts by great men and their power-hungry minions to promote their private interests at the expense of the public good and to destroy the colonists' balanced constitutions and their popular liberty. . . .

By adopting the language of the radical whig opposition and by attacking the monarchical abuse of family influence and patronage, however, the American revolutionaries were not simply expressing their resentment of corrupt political practices that had denied some of them the highest offices of colonial government. They actually were tearing at the bonds holding the traditional monarchical society together. Their assault necessarily was as much social as it was political.

But this social assault was not the sort we are used to today in describing revolutions. The great social antagonists of the American Revolution were not poor vs. rich, workers vs. employers, or even democrats vs. aristocrats. They were patriots vs. courtiers—categories appropriate to the monarchical world in which the colonists had been reared. Courtiers were persons whose position or rank came artificially from above—from hereditary or personal connections that ultimately flowed from the crown or court. Courtiers, said John Adams, were those who applied themselves "to the Passions and Prejudices, the Follies and Vices of Great Men in order to obtain their Smiles, Esteem, and Patronage and consequently their favors and Preferments." Patriots, on the other hand, were those who not only loved their country but were free of dependent connections and influence; their position or rank came naturally from their talent and from below, from recognition by the people. "A real patriot," declared one American in 1776, was "the most illustrious character in human life. Is not the interest and happiness of his fellow creatures his care?"

Only by understanding the hierarchical structure of monarchical society and taking the patriots' assault on courtiers seriously can we begin to appreciate the significance of the displacement of the loyalists—that is, of those who maintained their allegiance to the British crown. The loyalists may have numbered close to half a million, or 20 percent of white Americans. As many as 80,000 of them are estimated to have left the thirteen colonies during the American Revolution, over six times as many émigrés per 1,000 of population as fled France during the French Revolution. Although many of these American émigrés, unlike the French émigrés, did not have to abandon their nation and could remain as much British subjects in Canada or the West Indies or Britain itself as they had been in one of the thirteen colonies, nevertheless, the emigration of the loyalists had significant effects on American society.

It was not how many loyalists who were displaced that was important; it was who they were. A disproportionate number of them were well-to-do gentry operating at the pinnacles of power and patronage—royal or proprietary officeholders, big overseas dry-goods merchants, and rich landowners. Because they commanded important chains of influence, their removal disrupted colonial society to a degree far in excess of their numbers. . . .

To eliminate those clusters of personal and familial influence and transform the society became the idealistic goal of the revolutionaries. Any position that came from any source but talent and the will of the people now seemed undeserved and dependent. Patrimonialism, plural officeholding, and patronage of all sorts—practices that had usually been taken for granted in a monarchical society—came under attack. . . .

It is in this context that we can best understand the revolutionaries' appeal to independence, not just the independence of the country from Great Britain, but, more important, the independence of individuals from personal influence and "warm and private friendship." The purpose of the Virginia constitution of 1776, one Virginian recalled, was "to prevent the undue and overwhelming influence of great landholders in elections." This was to be done by disfranchising the landless "tenants and retainers" who depended "on the breath and varying will" of these great men and by ensuring that only men who owned their own land could vote.

A republic presumed, as the Virginia declaration of rights put it, that men in the new republic would be "equally free and independent," and property would make them so. Property in a republic was still conceived of traditionally—in proprietary terms—not as a means of personal profit or aggrandizement but rather as a source of personal authority or independence. It was regarded not merely as a material possession but also as an attribute of a man's personality that defined him and protected him from outside pressure. A carpenter's skill, for example, was his property. Jefferson feared the rabble of the cities precisely because they were without property and were thus dependent.

All dependents without property, such as women and young men, could be denied the vote because, as a convention of Essex County, Massachusetts, declared in 1778, they were "so situated as to have no wills of their own." Jefferson was so keen on this equation of property with citizenship that he proposed in 1776 that the new state of Virginia grant fifty acres of land to every man that did not have that many. Without having property and a will of his own—without having independence—a man could have no public spirit; and there could be no republic. For, as Jefferson put it, "dependence begets subservience and venality, suffocates the germ of virtue, and prepares fit tools for the designs of ambition."

In a monarchical world of numerous patron-client relations and multiple degrees of dependency, nothing could be more radical than this attempt to make every man independent. What was an ideal in the English-speaking world now became for Americans an ideological imperative. Suddenly, in the eyes of the revolutionaries, all the fine calibrations of rank and degrees of unfreedom of the traditional monarchical society became absurd and degrading. The Revolution became a full-scale assault on dependency. . . .

Of course, the revolutionary leaders did not expect poor, humble men—farmers, artisans, or tradesmen—themselves to gain high political office. Rather, they expected that the sons of such humble or ungenteel men, if they had abilities, would, as they had, acquire liberal and genteel republican attributes, perhaps by attending Harvard or the College of New Jersey at Princeton, and would thereby rise into the ranks of gentlemen and become eligible for high political office. The sparks of genius that they hoped republicanism would fan and kindle into flame belonged to men like themselves—men "drawn from obscurity" by the new opportunities of republican competition and emulation into becoming "illustrious characters, which will dazzle the world with the splendor of their names." Honor, interest, and patriotism together called them to qualify themselves and posterity "for the bench, the army, the navy, the learned professions, and all the departments of civil government." They would become what Jefferson called the "natural aristocracy"—liberally educated, enlightened gentlemen of character. For many of the revolutionary leaders this was the emotional significance of republicanism—a vindication of frustrated talent at the expense of birth and blood. For too long, they felt, merit had been denied. In a monarchical world only the arts and sciences had recognized talent as the sole criterion of leadership. Which is why even the eighteenth-century *ancien régime* called the world of the arts and sciences "the republic of letters." Who, it was asked, remembered the fathers or sons of Homer and Euclid? Such a question was a republican dagger driven into the heart of the old hereditary order. "Virtue," said Thomas Paine simply, "is not hereditary."

Because the revolutionaries are so different from us, so seemingly aristocratic themselves, it is hard for us today to appreciate the anger and resentment they felt toward hereditary aristocracy. We tend to ignore or forget the degree to which family and monarchical values dominated colonial America. But the revolutionaries knew only too well what kin and patrimonial officeholding had meant in their lives. Up and down the continent colonial gentry like Charles Carroll of Maryland had voiced their fears that "all power might center in *one family*" and that offices of government "like a precious jewel will be handed down from *father* to *son*." Everywhere men expressed their anger over the exclusive and unresponsive governments that had distributed offices, land, and privileges to favorites. . . .

The Revolution's assault on patriarchy inevitably affected relationships within the family, as decisions concerning women's and daughters' rights were made that conservatives later regarded as "tending to loosen the bands of society." Changes in the family begun earlier found new republican justifications and were accelerated—showing up even in paintings. In earlier-eighteenth-century family portraits fathers had stood dominantly above their wives and children; now they were portrayed on the same plane with them—a symbolic leveling. With the Revolution men lost some of their earlier patriarchal control over their wives and property. Although wives continued to remain dependent on their husbands, they did gain greater autonomy and some legal recognition of their rights to hold property separately, to divorce, and to make contracts and do business in the absence of their husbands. In the colonial period only

New Englanders had recognized the absolute right to divorce, but after the Revolution all the states except South Carolina developed new liberal laws on divorce.

Women and children no doubt remained largely dependent on their husbands and fathers, but the revolutionary attack on patriarchal monarchy made all other dependencies in the society suspect. Indeed, once the revolutionaries collapsed all the different distinctions and dependencies of a monarchical society into either freemen or slaves, white males found it increasingly impossible to accept any dependent status whatsoever. Servitude of any sort suddenly became anomalous and anachronistic. In 1784 in New York, a group believing that indentured servitude was "contrary to . . . the idea of liberty this country has so happily established" released a shipload of immigrant servants and arranged for public subscriptions to pay for their passage. As early as 1775 in Philadelphia the proportion of the work force that was unfree— composed of servants and slaves—had already declined to 13 percent from the 40 to 50 percent that it had been at mid-century. By 1800 less than 2 percent of the city's labor force remained unfree. Before long indentured servitude virtually disappeared.

With the post-revolutionary republican culture talking of nothing but liberty, equality, and independence, even hired servants eventually became hard to come by or to control. White servants refused to call their employers "master" or "mistress"; for many the term "boss," derived from the Dutch word for master, became a euphemistic substitute. The servants themselves would not be called anything but "help," or "waiter," which was the term the character Jonathan, in Royall Tyler's 1787 play *The Contrast,* preferred in place of "servant." . . .

By the early nineteenth century what remained of patriarchy was in disarray. No longer were apprentices dependents within a family; they became trainees within a business that was more and more conducted outside the household. Artisans did less "bespoke" or "order" work for patrons; instead they increasingly produced for impersonal markets. This in turn meant that the master craftsmen had to hire labor and organize the sale of the products of their shops. Masters became less patriarchs and more employers, retail merchants, or businessmen. Cash payments of wages increasingly replaced the older paternalistic relationship between masters and journeymen. These free wage earners now came and went with astonishing frequency, moving not only from job to job but from city to city. This "fluctuating" mobility of workers bewildered some employers: "while you were taking an inventory of their property," sighed one Rhode Islander, "they would sling their packs and be off."

Although both masters and journeymen often tried to maintain the traditional fiction that they were bound together for the "good of the trade," increasingly they saw themselves as employers and employees with different interests. Although observers applauded the fact that apprentices, journeymen, and masters of each craft marched together in the federal procession in Philadelphia on July 4, 1788, the tensions and divergence of interests were already visible. Before long journeymen in various crafts organized themselves against their masters' organizations, banned their employers from their meetings, and declared that "the interests of the journeymen are separate and in some respects opposite of those of their employers." Between 1786 and 1816 at least twelve major strikes by various journeymen craftsmen occurred— the first major strikes by employees against employers in American history.

One obvious dependency the revolutionaries did not completely abolish was that of nearly a half million Afro-American slaves, and their failure to do so, amidst all their high-blown talk of liberty, makes them seem inconsistent and hypocritical in our eyes. Yet it is important to realize that the Revolution suddenly and effectively ended the cultural climate that had allowed black slavery, as well as other forms of bondage and unfreedom, to exist throughout the colonial period without serious challenge. With the revolutionary movement, black slavery became excruciatingly conspicuous in a way that it had not been in the older monarchical society with its many calibrations and degrees of unfreedom; and Americans in 1775–76 began attacking it with a vehemence that was inconceivable earlier.

For a century or more the colonists had taken slavery more or less for granted as the most base and dependent status in a hierarchy of dependencies and a world of laborers. Rarely had they felt the need either to criticize black slavery or to defend it. Now, however, the republican attack on dependency compelled Americans to see the deviant character of slavery and to confront the institution as they never had to before. It was no accident that Americans in Philadelphia in 1775 formed the first anti-slavery society in the world. As long as most people had to work merely out of poverty and the need to provide for a living, slavery and other forms of enforced labor did not seem all that different from free labor. But the growing recognition that labor was not simply a common necessity of the poor but was in fact a source of increased wealth and prosperity for ordinary workers made slavery seem more and more anomalous. Americans now recognized that slavery in a republic of workers was an aberration, "a peculiar institution," and that if any Americans were to retain it, as southern Americans eventually did, they would have to explain and justify it in new racial and anthropological ways that their former monarchical society had never needed. The Revolution in effect set in motion ideological and social forces that doomed the institution of slavery in the North and led inexorably to the Civil War.

With all men now considered to be equally free citizens, the way was prepared as well for a radical change in the conception of state power. Almost at a stroke the Revolution destroyed all the earlier talk of paternal or maternal government, filial allegiance, and mutual contractual obligations between rulers and ruled. The familial image of government now lost all its previous relevance, and the state in America emerged as something very different from what it had been.

FURTHER READING

Edward Countryman, *The American Revolution* (1985).

Marc Egnal, *A Mighty Empire: The Origins of the American Revolution* (1988).

Sylvia Frey, *Water from the Rock: Black Resistance in a Revolutionary Age* (1991).

Woody Holton, *Forced Founders: Indians, Debtors, Slaves, and the Making of the American Revolution in Virginia* (1999).

Pauline Maier, *From Resistance to Rebellion: Colonial Radicals and the Development of American Opposition to Britain, 1765–1776* (1972).

Robert Middlekauff, *The Glorious Cause: The American Revolution, 1763–1789* (1982).

Mary Beth Norton, *Liberty's Daughters: The Revolutionary Experience of American Women, 1750–1800* (1980).

Charles Royster, *A Revolutionary People at War: The Continental Army and American Character, 1775–1783* (1996).

John Shy, *A People Numerous and Reflections on the Military Struggle for American Independence* (1990).

C H A P T E R
5

The Making of the Constitution

*In late May 1787, George Washington called to order a convention of fifty-five dele-
gates in Philadelphia. Throughout a hot, steamy summer, this group deliberated
and argued until it arrived at a plan to restructure the government of the United
States. The Constitution, as it was called, was a controversial reform, and it was
not ratified by the nine states necessary for it to take effect until the summer of 1788.
Yet the Constitution continues to be the framework of the United States, one of the
oldest frameworks of government still in place in the twenty-first century. Many
Americans at the time, however, were not convinced of the wisdom of the Constitution
or optimistic about its meaning for the future of the United States.*

*The Constitution was not the first framework of government for the country;
the Articles of Confederation, which offered a less centralized government than the
Constitution proposed, had been ratified in 1781. The central government under
the Articles had limited powers: it had no power to tax, it could not compel the
states to contribute to financing its operations, and it could not enforce a uniform
commercial policy. Its structure was weak as well. It had no executive branch and
no separate judiciary; instead, it relied on a legislature in which each state had
equal representation. Given the United States's recent experiences with a monarchy,
many Americans were satisfied with a decentralized government. And the Articles
period was not without its successes. Perhaps its most notable achievement was the
Northwest Ordinance, which laid the groundwork for the method by which new
states would enter the Union. Still many Americans soon concluded that the government was inadequate to meet the country's needs.*

*The shortcomings of the Articles were exacerbated by the crises that the new
nation encountered. An economic depression wracked the nation shortly after the
conclusion of war in 1781, and this was accompanied by a monetary crisis as
the value of paper money declined. The phrase "not worth a Continental" came into
usage, indicating the declining value of the new nation's currency. These difficulties
were compounded by diplomatic and commercial failures. The British continued to
occupy western forts on American territory, and Congress could not establish a national commercial policy because federal tariffs could be passed only if all the states
agreed to them. As the postwar depression worsened, Americans began to pressure
their government for relief. In western Massachusetts, farmers pleaded for lower
taxes and a larger supply of money. When the state government rejected all of their
requests in 1786, a group of farmers began forcibly closing down the courts in which
debtors were tried. Under the leadership of Daniel Shays, this rebellion spread*

throughout western Massachusetts, and it was ended only by calling out the state militia. Once Shays's Rebellion was put down, John Adams, who years before had led his own revolution, called these rebels "ignorant, restless, desperadoes, without conscience or principles." Many Americans concluded that the limited government under the Articles was a failure.

Given these concerns, the members of the Constitutional Convention sought to restructure the national government. Their deliberations resulted in a government with three branches, including an executive and a judiciary, as well as a legislature. The legislative branch was bicameral, with one house providing equal representation to all states and the other providing proportional representation based on population. The president was elected by the electoral college, in which the number of electors from each state was equal to the number of that state's senators and representatives. Perhaps most controversial was the three-fifths compromise, which included three-fifths of the slave population in a state's headcount; this increased the power of the states in which slavery existed.

The framers provided that the Constitution had to be ratified by nine of thirteen state conventions before it would become the law of the land. The national debate quickly divided the Federalists, who favored ratification, from the Antifederalists, who did not. The latter group argued that the Constitution was an exercise in elitism that would lead to rule by a wealthy, unrepresentative minority. They lauded the Revolution that had just been won and warned that the Constitution might lead to a return to "despotism" and "tyranny," pointing to the absence of a Bill of Rights to support their claim. In contrast, the Federalists, most brilliantly represented by Alexander Hamilton, James Madison, and John Jay in the Federalist Papers, *argued that the United States was in crisis and that the Constitution would preserve the republic and promote economic prosperity. When Jay and Hamilton pledged to support a Bill of Rights should the Constitution be ratified, they undercut much of the Antifederalist argument. By 1788, ratification was complete and the course of the United States changed yet again.*

QUESTIONS TO THINK ABOUT

Would the United States have survived as a nation if the Articles of Confederation had remained the framework of government? How would government and society have differed if the Articles had not been replaced by the Constitution? Was the framing and ratification of the Constitution "counterrevolutionary"? How important were slavery and differences between the states to the convention that wrote the Constitution?

DOCUMENTS

Pivotal questions, ranging from the place of religion in the republic to the status of slavery, had to be decided by the new nation, as the first four documents illustrate. Document 1 is a petition from Cato, "a poor negro," to the Pennsylvania Assembly, urging it to reject conservative attempts to repeal a law that set in motion an end to slavery. In Document 2, Hector St. John Crèvecoeur writes about life in two American locales. While he marvels at the "great American asylum" that exists in the North, he condemns the system of slavery that exists in Charleston, South Carolina. In contrast to the documents by Cato and Crèvecoeur, Document 3 is a petition from slaveholders in

Virginia urging the retention of slavery. Document 4 is a proposal authored by Thomas Jefferson that provides for the formal protection of religious freedom in Virginia. The next two documents consider the triumphs and dangers of the Articles of Confederation period. Document 5 is the Northwest Ordinance, which outlined the ways in which new states were to be created in the Northwest Territory. Note that this law outlaws slavery and guarantees freedom of religion and speech in this territory. In contrast, Document 6 describes the "unhappy time" of Shays's Rebellion in 1787, when the militia was called out to put down an uprising of farmers. The next three documents explore the debates surrounding the Constitution. Document 7 includes excerpts from *The Federalist Papers,* a series of eighty-five essays written by James Madison, Alexander Hamilton, and John Jay in 1787 and 1788 to explain and defend the Constitution. In contrast, in Document 8, Richard Henry Lee explains why an enlarged national government will be unrepresentative and despotic. Likewise, Patrick Henry, in Document 9, condemns the Constitution as creating a government that is too centralized. Finally, George Washington, in Document 10, commits his nation to religious freedom in his letter to a Jewish congregation in Rhode Island. This is the first public declaration that Jews in the United States would be guaranteed religious freedom.

1. Cato, an African American, Pleads for the Abolition of Slavery in Pennsylvania, 1781

Mr. PRINTER.

I AM a poor negro, who with myself and children have had the good fortune to get my freedom, by means of an act of assembly passed on the first of March 1780, and should now with my family be as happy a set of people as any on the face of the earth; but I am told the assembly are going to pass a law to send us all back to our masters. Why dear Mr. Printer, this would be the cruellest act that ever a sett of worthy good gentlemen could be guilty of. To make a law to hang us all, would be *merciful,* when compared with this law. . . . I have read the act which made me free, and I always read it with joy—and I always dwell with particular pleasure on the following words, spoken by the assembly in the top of the said law. "We esteem it a particular blessing granted to us, that we are enabled this day to add one more step to universal civilization, by removing as much as possible the sorrows of those, who have lived in *undeserved* bondage, and from which, by the assumed authority of the kings of Great-Britain, no effectual legal relief could be obtained" See it was the king of Great Britain that kept us in slavery before.—Now surely, after saying so, it cannot be possible for them to make slaves of us again—nobody, but the king of England can do it—and I sincerely pray, that he may never have it in his power. . . . [W]hat is most serious than all, what will our great father think of such doings? But I pray that he may be pleased to tern the hearts of the honourable assembly from this cruel law; and that he will be pleased to make us poor blacks deserving of his mercies.

CATO.

From collections of the Historical Society of Pennsylvania. Obtained from http://www.pbs.org/wgbh/ aia/part2/2h73t.html.

To the honourable the Representatives of the Freemen of the State of Pennsylvania . . .

. . . Whilst it pleased the great author of our beings to continue us in slavery, we submitted to our hard lot, and bore it with habitual patience; but rescued from our misery, and tasting the sweets of that liberty, for the defence of which this whole continent is now involved in war, we shall deem our selves the most wretched of the human race, if the proposed act should take place. Raised to the pinnacle of human happiness by a law unsought and unexpected by us, we find ourselves p[l]unged into all the horrors of hateful slavery; made doubly irksome by the small portion of freedom we have already enjoyed. . . . We fear we are too bold, but our all is a stake. The grand question of slavery or liberty, is too important for us to be silent—It is the momentous person of our lives; if we are silent this day, we may be silent for ever; returned into slavery we are deprived of even the right of petitioning; and this emboldens us to grasp the present moment, and to pray on behalf of ourselves and a number of our unhappy colour, that this house will not pass the bill. And we further pray that you may long possess that heart felt peace and joy, which will ever arise in the humane breast, when successfully employed in the relief of misery and distress.

2. Hector St. John Crèvecoeur Compares the Freedom in the North with Slavery in the South, 1782

LETTER III
WHAT IS AN AMERICAN?

I wish I could be acquainted with the feelings and thoughts which must agitate the heart and present themselves to the mind of an enlightened Englishman, when he first lands on this continent. . . . He is arrived on a new continent: a modern society offers itself to his contemplation, different from what he had hitherto seen. It is not composed, as in Europe, of great lords who possess every thing, and of a herd of people who have nothing. Here are no aristocratical families, no courts, no kings, no bishops, no ecclesiastical dominion, no invisible power giving to a few a very visible one, no great manufactures employing thousands, no great refinements of luxury. The rich and the poor are not so far removed from each other as they are in Europe. Some few towns excepted, we are all tillers of the earth, from Nova Scotia to West Florida. We are a people of cultivators, scattered over an immense territory, communicating with each other by means of good roads and navigable rivers, united by the silken bands of mild government, all respecting the laws, without dreading their power, because they are equitable. We are all animated with the spirit of an industry which is unfettered and unrestrained, because each person works for himself. . . .

In this great American asylum, the poor of Europe have by some means met together, and in consequence of various causes. . . . Every thing has tended to regenerate them. New laws, a new mode of living, a new social system. Here they are become men. In Europe they were as so many useless plants, wanting vegetative mould and refreshing showers. They withered; and were mowed down by want,

---

Letter III, "What Is an American?" and Letter IX, "Description of Charles-Town," in Hector Crèvecoeur, *Letters from an American Farmer* (London: Penguin Books, 1963), 40–45, 151–155.

hunger, and war; but now, by the power of transplantation, like all other plants, they have taken root and flourished! Formerly they were not numbered in any civil lists of their country, except in those of the poor: here they rank as citizens. By what invisible power hath this surprising metamorphosis been performed? By that of the laws and that of their industry. . . .

. . . What then is the American, this new man? He is neither an European, nor the descendent of an European: hence that strange mixture of blood, which you will find in no other country. I could point out to you a family, whose grandfather was an Englishman, whose wife was Dutch, whose son married a French woman, and whose present four sons have now four wives of different nations. He is an American, who, leaving behind him all his antient prejudices and manners, receives new ones from the new mode of life he has embraced, the new government he obeys, and the new rank he holds. He becomes an American by being received in the broad lap of our great *alma mater*. Here individuals of all nations are melted into a new race of men, whose labours and posterity will one day cause great changes in the world. Americans are the western pilgrims, who are carrying along with them that great mass of arts, sciences, vigour, and industry, which began long since in the east. They will finish the great circle. The Americans were once scattered all over Europe. Here they are incorporated into one of the finest systems of population which has ever appeared, and which will hereafter become distinct by the power of the different climates they inhabit. The American ought therefore to love this country much better than that wherein either he or his forefathers were born. Here the rewards of his industry follow, with equal steps, the progress of his labour. His labour is founded on the basis of nature, *self-interest:* can it want a stronger allurement? . . .

Men are like plants. The goodness and flavour of the fruit proceeds from the peculiar soil and exposition in which they grow. We are nothing but what we derive from the air we breathe, the climate we inhabit, the government we obey, the system of religion we profess, and the nature of our employment. . . .

LETTER IX
DESCRIPTION OF CHARLES-TOWN;
THOUGHTS ON SLAVERY; ON PHYSICAL EVIL;
A MELANCHOLY SCENE

Charles-Town is in the north what Lima is in the south; both are capitals of the richest provinces of their respective hemispheres. . . . The inhabitants are the gayest in America; it is called the center of our beau monde, and is always filled with the richest planters in the province, who resort hither in quest of health and pleasure. . . . An European at his first arrival must be greatly surprised when he sees the elegance of their houses, their sumptuous furniture, as well as the magnificence of their tables; can he imagine himself in a country, the establishment of which is so recent? . . .

While all is joy, festivity, and happiness, in Charles-Town, would you imagine that scenes of misery overspread in the country? Their ears, by habit, are become deaf, their hearts are hardened; they neither see, hear, nor feel for, the woes of their poor slaves, from whose painful labours all their wealth proceeds. Here the horrors of slavery, the hardship of incessant toils, are unseen; and no one thinks with compassion of those showers of sweat and of tears which from the bodies of Africans daily drop, and moisten the ground they till. The cracks of the whip, urging these miserable beings to excessive labour, are far too distant from the gay capital to be heard. . . . Strange order of things! O Nature, where art thou?—Are not these blacks thy children as well as we? . . .

. . . Thus planters get rich; so raw, so inexperienced, am I in this mode of life, that, were I to be possessed of a plantation, and my slaves treated as in general they are here, never could I rest in peace; my sleep would be perpetually disturbed by a retrospect of the frauds committed in Africa in order to entrap them; frauds, surpassing in enormity every thing which a common mind can possibly conceive. I should be thinking of the barbarous treatment they meet with on ship-board; of their anguish, of the despair necessarily inspired by their situation; when torn from their friends and relations: when delivered into the hands of a people, differently coloured, whom they cannot understand; carried in a strange machine over an ever-agitated element, which they had never seen before; and finally delivered over to the severities of the whippers and the excessive labours of the field. Can it be possible that the force of custom should ever make me deaf to all these reflections, and as insensible to the injustice of that trade, and to their miseries, as the rich inhabitants of this town seem to be?

3. Slaveholders in Virginia Argue Against the Abolition of Slavery, 1784–1785

Gentlemen,

When the British parliament usurped a Right to dispose of our Property without our consent we dissolved the Union with our parent country and established a . . . government of our own. We risked our Lives and Fortunes, and waded through Seas of Blood . . . we understand a very subtle and daring attempt is made to dispossess us of a very important Part of our Property . . . TO WREST US FROM OUR SLAVES, by an act of Legislature for general emancipation.

It is unsupported by Scripture. For we find in the Old Testament . . . slavery was permitted by the Deity himself. . . . It is also exceedingly impolitic. For it involves in it, and is productive of Want, Poverty, Distress, and Ruin to FREE citizens, Neglect, Famine and Death to the black Infant. . . . The Horrors of all Rapes, Murders, and Outrages which a vast multitude of unprincipled unpropertied, revengeful and remorseless Banditti are capable of perpetrating . . . sure and final Ruin to this now flourishing free and happy Country.

We solemnly adjure and humbly pray that you will discountenance and utterly reject every motion and proposal for emancipating our slaves. . . .

Some men of considerable weight to wrestle from us, by an Act of the legislature, the most valuable and indispensable Article of our Property, our SLAVES by general emancipation of them. . . . Such a scheme indeed consists very well with the principles and designs of the North, whose Finger is sufficiently visible in it. . . .

Petitions submitted in several Virginia counties in 1784 with almost 300 signatures and in Lundenburg County in 1785 with 161 signatures; from collections of the Library of Virginia. Obtained from http://www.pbs.org/wgbh/aia/part2/2h65.html.

No language can express our indignation, Contempt and Detestation of the apostate wretches. . . . It therefore cannot be admitted that any man had a right . . . to divest us of our known rights to property which are so clearly defined. . . . To an unequivocal Construction therefore of this Bill of rights we now appeal and claim the utmost benefits of . . . in whatever may tend . . . to preserve our rights . . . secure to us the Blessings of the free. . . .

And we shall ever Pray. . . .

4. Thomas Jefferson Proposes the Protection of Religious Freedom in Virginia, 1786

Whereas, Almighty God has created the mind free; that all attempts to influence it by temporal punishment, or burthens, or by civil incapacitations, tend only to beget habits of hypocrisy and meanness, and are a departure from the plan of the Holy Author of our religion, who, being Lord both of body and mind, yet chose not to propagate it by coercions on either, as was in his Almighty power to do; that the impious presumption of legislators and rulers, civil as well as ecclesiastical, who, being themselves but fallible and uninspired men, have assumed dominion over the faith of others, setting up their own opinions and modes of thinking as the only true and infallible and as such endeavoring to impose them on others, have established and maintained false religions over the greatest part of the world, and through all time; that to compel a man to furnish contributions of money for the propagation of opinions which he disbelieves, is sinful and tyrannical, and even the forcing him to support this or that teacher of his own religious persuasion, is depriving him of the comfortable liberty of giving his contributions to the particular pastor whose morals he would make his pattern, and whose powers he feels most persuasive to righteousness, and is withdrawing from the ministry those temporary rewards which, proceeding from an approbation of their personal conduct, are an additional incitement to earnest and unremitting labors, for the instruction of mankind; that our civil rights have no dependence on our religious opinions any more than our opinions in physics or geometry; that therefore the proscribing any citizen as unworthy of the public confidence by laying upon him an incapacity of being called to offices of trust and emolument, unless he profess or renounce this or that religious opinion, is depriving him injuriously of those privileges and advantages to which, in common with his fellow citizens, he has a natural right; that it tends only to corrupt the principles of that religion it is meant to encourage, by bribing, with a monopoly of worldly honors and emoluments, those who will externally profess and conform to it; that though indeed, those are criminal who do not withstand such temptation, yet, neither are those innocent who lay the bait in their way; that to suffer the civil magistrate to intrude his powers into the field of opinion, and to restrain the profession or propagation of principles on supposition of their ill tendency, is a dangerous fallacy, which at once destroys all religious liberty, because he, being of course judge of that tendency, will make his opinions the rules of judgment, and approve or condemn the sentiments of others only as they shall square with or differ from his

---

Thomas Jefferson, *The Virginia Statute for Religious Freedom* (1786).

own; that it is time enough for the rightful purposes of civil government, for its officers to interfere, when principles break out into overt acts against peace and good
order; and finally, that truth is great and will prevail, if left to herself; that she is the
proper and sufficient antagonist to error, and has nothing to fear from the conflict,
unless by human interposition disarmed of her natural weapons, free argument and
debate; errors ceasing to be dangerous when it is permitted freely to contradict them:

Be it enacted by the General Assembly, that no man shall be compelled to frequent or support any religious worship, place or ministry whatsoever, nor shall he
otherwise suffer on account of his religious opinions or belief; but that all men shall
be free to profess, and by argument to maintain, their opinions in matters of religion,
and that the same shall in no wise diminish, enlarge or affect their civil capacities.

And though we well know that this Assembly, elected by the people for the ordinary purposes of legislation only, have no power to restrain the acts of succeeding assemblies constituted with powers equal to our own, and that, therefore, to declare this
act to be irrevocable would be of no effect in law; yet we are free to declare, and do
declare, that the rights hereby asserted are of the natural rights of mankind; and that
if any act shall be hereafter passed to repeal the present, or to narrow its operation,
such act will be an infringement of natural right.

5. The Northwest Ordinance Lays Out the Method for New States Joining the Union, 1787

Section 1. Be it ordained by the United States in Congress assembled, That the said
territory, for the purposes of temporary government, be one district, subject, however, to be divided into two districts, as future circumstances may, in the opinion of
Congress, make it expedient. . . .

Sec. 3. Be it ordained by the authority aforesaid, That there shall be appointed,
from time to time, by Congress, a governor, whose commission shall continue in
force for the term of three years, unless sooner revoked by Congress; he shall reside
in the district, and have a freehold estate therein in one thousand acres of land, while
in the exercise of his office.

Sec. 4. . . . There shall also be appointed a court, to consist of three judges, any
two of whom to form a court, who shall have a common-law jurisdiction, and reside
in the district, and have each therein a freehold estate, in five hundred acres of land,
while in the exercise of their offices; and their commissions shall continue in force
during good behavior.

Sec. 5. The governor and judges, or a majority of them, shall adopt and publish
in the district such laws of the original States, criminal and civil, as may be necessary, and best suited to the circumstances of the district and report them to Congress
from time to time, which laws shall be in force in the district until the organization of
the general assembly therein, unless disapproved of by Congress; but afterwards the
legislature shall have authority to alter them as they shall think fit. . . .

Francis N. Thorpe, ed., *Federal and State Constitutions: Colonial Charters, and Other Organic Laws of the States, Territories, and Colonies, Now or Heretofore Forming the United States of America* (Washington, D.C.: U.S. Government Printing Office, 1909), 2:957–964.

Sec. 14. It is hereby ordained and declared, by the authority aforesaid, that the following articles shall be considered as articles of compact, between the original States and the people and States in the said territory, and forever remain unalterable, unless by common consent, to wit:

Article I

No person, demeaning himself in a peaceable and orderly manner, shall ever be molested on account of his mode of worship, or religious sentiments, in the said territories.

Article II

The inhabitants of the said territory shall always be entitled to the benefits of the writ of habeas corpus, and of the trial by jury; of a proportionate representation of the people in the legislature, and of judicial proceedings according to the course of common law. . . . And, in the just preservation of rights and property, it is understood and declared, that no law ought ever to be made or have force in the said territory, that shall, in any manner whatever, interfere with or affect private contracts, or engagements, bona fide, and without fraud previously formed.

Article III

Religion, morality, and knowledge being necessary to good government and the happiness of mankind, schools and the means of education shall forever be encouraged. The utmost good faith shall always be observed towards the Indians; their lands and property shall never be taken from them without their consent; and in their property, rights, and liberty they never shall be invaded or disturbed, unless in just and lawful wars authorized by Congress. . . .

Article IV

The said territory, and the States which may be formed therein, shall forever remain a part of this confederacy of the United States of America, subject to the Articles of Confederation, and to such alterations therein as shall be constitutionally made; and to all the acts and ordinances of the United States in Congress assembled, conformable thereto. . . .

Article V

There shall be formed in the said territory not less than three nor more than five States. . . . And whenever any of the said States shall have sixty thousand free inhabitants therein, such State shall be admitted, by its delegates, into the Congress of the United States, on an equal footing with the original States, in all respects whatever. . . .

Article VI

There shall be neither slavery nor involuntary servitude in the said territory, otherwise than in the punishment of crimes, whereof the party shall have been duly convicted: Provided always, That any person escaping into the same, from whom labor or service is lawfully claimed in any one of the original States, such fugitive may be lawfully reclaimed, and conveyed to the person claiming his or her labor or service as aforesaid.

6. Generals William Shepard and Benjamin Lincoln Regret the Disorder That Characterized Shays's Rebellion, 1787

General Shepard to Governor Bowdoin

Springfield

January 26, 1787

The unhappy time is come in which we have been obliged to shed blood. Shays, who was at the head of about twelve hundred men, marched yesterday afternoon about four o'clock, towards the public buildings in battle array. He marched his men in an open column by platoons. I sent several times by one of my aides, and two other gentlemen, Captains Buffington and Woodbridge, to him to know what he was after, or what he wanted. His reply was, he wanted barracks, and barracks he would have and stores. The answer returned was he must purchase them dear, if he had them.

He still proceeded on his march until he approached within two hundred and fifty yards of the arsenal. He then made a halt. I immediately sent Major Lyman, one of my aides, and Capt. Buffington to inform him not to march his troops any nearer the arsenal on his peril, as I was stationed here by order of your Excellency and the Secretary at War, for the defence of the public property; in case he did I should surely fire on him and his men. A Mr. Wheeler, who appeared to be one of Shays' aides, met Mr. Lyman, after he had delivered my orders in the most peremptory manner, and made answer, that was all he wanted. Mr. Lyman returned with his answer.

Shays immediately put his troops in motion, and marched on rapidly near one hundred yards. I then ordered Major Stephens, who commanded the artillery, to fire upon them. He accordingly did. The two first shots he endeavored to overshoot them, in hopes they would have taken warning without firing among them, but it had no effect on them. Major Stephens then directed his shot through the center of his column. The fourth or fifth shot put their whole column into the utmost confusion. . . .

Had I been disposed to destroy them, I might have charged upon their rear and flanks with my infantry and the two field pieces, and could have killed the greater part of his whole army within twenty-five minutes. . . .

I have received no reinforcement yet, and expect to be attacked this day by their whole force combined.

Letters of General William Shepard and Benjamin Lincoln to Governor James Bowdoin of Massachusetts (1787), reprinted from The Massachusetts Archives, 190, 317–320. Obtained from http://longman. awl.com/history/primarysource_6_4.html.

General Lincoln to Governor Bowdoin

Head Quarters, Springfield

January 28th, 1787

. . . On my arrival, I found that Shays had taken a post at a little village six miles north of this, with the whole force under his immediate command, and that Day had taken post in West Springfield, and that he had fixed a guard at the ferry house on the west side of the river, and that he had a guard at the bridge over Agawam river. By this disposition all communication from the north and west in the usual paths was cut off.

From a consideration of this insult on Government, that by an early move we should instantly convince the insurgents of its ability and determination speedily to disperse them; that we wanted the houses occupied by these men to cover our own troops; that General Patterson was on his march to join us, which to obstruct was an object with them; that a successful movement would give spirits to the troops; that it would be so was reduced to as great a certainty, as can be had in operations of this kind; from these considerations, Sir, with many others, I was induced to order the troops under arms at three o'clock in the afternoon, although the most of them had been so from one in the morning.

We moved about half after three. . . . They made a little show of force for a minute or two near the meeting house, and then retired in the utmost confusion and disorder. Our horse met them at the west end of the village, but the insurgents found means by crossing the fields and taking to the woods to escape them; some were taken who are aggravatedly guilty, but not the most so.

7. *The Federalist Papers* Illustrate the Advantages of Ratification of the Constitution, 1787–1788

Factions and Their Remedy (James Madison, No. 10)

To the People of the State of New York:

Among the numerous advantages promised by a well constructed Union, none deserves to be more accurately developed than its tendency to break and control the violence of faction. The friend of popular governments, never finds himself so much alarmed for their character and fate, as when he contemplates their propensity to this dangerous vice. . . .

By a faction I understand a number of citizens, whether amounting to a majority or minority of the whole, who are united and actuated by some common impulse of passion, or of interest, adverse to the rights of other citizens, or to the permanent and aggregate interests of the community. . . .

Alexander Hamilton, John Jay, and James Madison, *The Federalist* (New York: Random House, 1961), Nos. 10, 51, and 69.

The latent causes of faction are thus sown in the nature of man, and we see them every where brought into different degrees of activity, according to the different circumstances of civil society. A zeal for different opinions concerning religion, concerning Government and many other points, as well of speculation as of practice; an attachment to different leaders ambitiously contending for pre-eminence and power; or to persons of other descriptions whose fortunes have been interesting to the human passions, have in turn divided mankind into parties, inflamed them with mutual animosity, and rendered them much more disposed to vex and oppress each other, than to co-operate for their common good. So strong is this propensity of mankind to fall into mutual animosities, that where no substantial occasion presents itself, the most frivolous and fanciful distinctions have been sufficient to kindle their unfriendly passions, and excite their most violent conflicts. But the most common and durable source of factions, has been the various and unequal distribution of property. . . . The regulation of these various and interfering interests forms the principal task of modern Legislation, and involves the spirit of party and faction in the necessary and ordinary operations of Government. . . .

. . . [A] pure Democracy, by which I mean, a Society, consisting of a small number of citizens, who assemble and administer the Government in person, can admit of no cure for the mischiefs of faction. A common passion or interest will, in almost every case, be felt by a majority of the whole; a communication and concert results from the form of Government itself; and there is nothing to check the inducements to sacrifice the weaker party, or an obnoxious individual. . . .

A Republic, by which I mean a Government in which the scheme of representation takes place, opens a different prospect, and promises the cure for which we are seeking. . . .

The two great points of difference between a Democracy and a Republic are, first, the delegation of the Government, in the latter, to a small number of citizens elected by the rest: secondly, the greater number of citizens, and greater sphere of country, over which the latter may be extended.

The effect of the first difference is, on the one hand to refine and enlarge the public views, by passing them through the medium of a chosen body of citizens, whose wisdom may best discern the true interest of their country, and whose patriotism and love of justice, will be least likely to sacrifice it to temporary or partial considerations. . . .

. . . [T]he same advantage, which a Republic has over a Democracy, in controling the effects of faction, is enjoyed by a large over a small Republic—is enjoyed by the Union over the States composing it. Does this advantage consist in the substitution of Representatives, whose enlightened views and virtuous sentiments render them superior to local prejudices, and to schemes of injustice? It will not be denied, that the Representation of the Union will be most likely to possess these requisite endowments. Does it consist in the greater security afforded by a greater variety of parties, against the event of any one party being able to outnumber and oppress the rest? In an equal degree does the encreased variety of parties, comprised within the Union, encrease this security. Does it, in fine, consist in the greater obstacles opposed to the concert and accomplishment of the secret wishes of an unjust and interested majority? Here, again, the extent of the Union gives it the most palpable advantage. . . .

In the extent and proper structure of the Union, therefore, we behold a Republican remedy for the diseases most incident to Republican Government.

The System of Checks and Balances (Alexander Hamilton or James Madison, No. 51)

To the People of the State of New York:

To what expedient, then, shall we finally resort, for maintaining in practice the necessary partition of power among the several departments, as laid down in the Constitution? The only answer that can be given is, that as all these exterior provisions are found to be inadequate, the defect must be supplied, by so contriving the interior structure of the government as that its several constituent parts may, by their mutual relations, be the means of keeping each other in their proper places. . . .

. . . [T]he great security against a gradual concentration of the several powers in the same department, consists in giving to those who administer each department the necessary constitutional means and personal motives to resist encroachments of the others. The provision for defence must in this, as in all other cases, be made commensurate to the danger of attack. Ambition must be made to counteract ambition. The interest of the man must be connected with the constitutional rights of the place. It may be a reflection on human nature, that such devices should be necessary to control the abuses of government. But what is government itself, but the greatest of all reflections on human nature? If men were angels, no government would be necessary. If angels were to govern men, neither external nor internal controls on government would be necessary. . . .

But it is not possible to give to each department an equal power of self-defence. In republican government, the legislative authority necessarily predominates. The remedy for this inconveniency is to divide the legislature into different branches. . . . As the weight of the legislative authority requires that it should be thus divided, the weakness of the executive may require, on the other hand, that it should be fortified. . . .

A Defense of the Presidency (Alexander Hamilton, No. 69)

To the People of the State of New York:

I proceed now to trace the real characters of the proposed executive as they are marked out in the plan of the Convention. This will serve to place in a strong light the unfairness of the representations which have been made in regard to it. . . .

The President of the United States would be an officer elected by the people for *four* years. The King of Great-Britain is a perpetual and *hereditary* prince. The one would be amenable to personal punishment and disgrace: The person of the other is sacred and inviolable. The one would have a *qualified* negative upon the acts of the legislative body: The other has an *absolute* negative. The one would have a right to command the military and naval forces of the nation: The other in addition to this right, possesses that of *declaring* war, and of *raising* and *regulating* fleets and armies by his own authority. The one would have a concurrent power with a branch of the Legislature in the formation of treaties: The other is the *sole possessor* of the power of making treaties. The one would have a like concurrent authority in appointing to offices: The other is the sole author of all appointments. The one can infer no privileges whatever: The other can make denizens of aliens, noblemen of commoners, can erect corporations with all the rights incident to corporate bodies. The one can prescribe no rules concerning the commerce or currency of the nation: The other is in several respects the arbiter of commerce, and in this capacity can establish markets and fairs, can regulate weights and measures, can lay embargoes for a limited time, can coin money, can authorise or prohibit the circulation of foreign coin. The one has no particle of spiritual jurisdiction: The other is the supreme head and Governor of the national church!—What answer shall we give to those who would persuade us that things so unlike resemble each other?—The same that ought to be given to those who tell us, that a government, the whole power of which would be in the hands of the elective and periodical servants of the people, is an aristocracy, a monarchy, and a despotism.

8. Richard Henry Lee Opposes the Ratification of the Constitution, 1787

... [A] full and equal representation, is that which possesses the same interests, feelings, opinions, and views the people themselves would were they all assembled—a fair representation, therefore, should be so regulated, that every order of men in the community, according to the common course of elections, can have a share in it—in order to allow professional men, merchants, traders, farmers, mechanics, &c. to bring a just proportion of their best informed men respectively into the legislature, the representation must be considerably numerous—We have about 200 state senators in the United States, and a less number than that of federal representatives cannot, clearly, be a full representation of this people, in the affairs of internal taxation and police, were there but one legislature for the whole union. The representation cannot be equal, or the situation of the people proper for one government only—if the extreme parts of the society cannot be represented as fully as the central—It is apparently impracticable that this should be the case in this extensive country—it would be impossible to collect a representation of the parts of the country five, six, and seven hundred miles from the seat of government. ...

... [T]he laws of a free government rest on the confidence of the people, and operate gently—and never can extend the influence very far—if they are executed on free principles, about the centre, where the benefits of the government induce the people to support it voluntarily; yet they must be executed on the principles of fear and force in the extremes—This has been the case with every extensive republic of which we have any accurate account.

There are certain unalienable and fundamental rights, which in forming the social compact, ought to be explicitly ascertained and fixed. ... I do not pay much regard to the reasons given for not bottoming the new constitution on a better bill of rights. I still believe a complete federal bill of rights to be very practicable. ...

Richard Henry Lee, *Observations Leading to a Fair Examination of the System of Government Proposed by the Late Convention; and to Several Essential and Necessary Alterations in It. In a Number of Letters from the Federal Farmer to the Republican* (New York: Thomas Greenleaf, 1787), 202–205.

There is no reason to expect the numerous state governments, and their connections, will be very friendly to the execution of federal laws in those internal affairs, which hitherto have been under their own immediate management. There is more reason to believe, that the general government, far removed from the people, and none of its members elected oftener than once in two years, will be forgot or neglected, and its laws in many cases disregarded, unless a multitude of officers and military force be continually kept in view, and employed to enforce the execution of the laws, and to make the government feared and respected. . . . Neglected laws must first lead to anarchy and confusion; and a military execution of laws is only a shorter way to the same point—despotic government.

9. Patrick Henry Condemns the Centralization of Government if the Constitution Is Ratified, 1788

. . . I need not take much pains to show, that the principles of this system, are extremely pernicious, impolitic, and dangerous. Is this a Monarchy, like England—a compact between Prince and people; with checks on the former, to secure the liberty of the latter? Is this a Confederacy, like Holland—an association of a number of independent States, each of which retain its individual sovereignty? It is not a democracy, wherein the people retain all their rights securely. Had these principles been adhered to, we should not have been brought to this alarming transition, from a Confederacy to a consolidated Government. We have no detail of those great considerations which, in my opinion, ought to have abounded before we should recur to a government of this kind. Here is a revolution as radical as that which separated us from Great Britain. It is as radical, if in this transition our rights and privileges are endangered, and the sovereignty of the States be relinquished: And cannot we plainly see, that this is actually the case? The rights of conscience, trial by jury, liberty of the press, all your immunities and franchises, all pretensions to human rights and privileges, are rendered insecure, if not lost, by this change so loudly talked of by some, and inconsiderately by others. Is this same relinquishment of rights worthy of freemen? . . .

Gentlemen have told us within these walls, that the Union is gone—or, that the Union will be gone: Is not this trifling with the judgment of their fellow-citizens? Till they tell us the ground of their fears, I will consider them as imaginary: I rose to make inquiry where those dangers were; they could make no answer: I believe I never shall have that answer: Is there a disposition in the people of this country to revolt against the dominion of laws? Has there been a single tumult in Virginia? Have not the people of Virginia, when laboring under the severest pressure of accumulated distresses, manifested the most cordial acquiescence in the execution of the laws? What could be more awful than their unanimous acquiescence under general distresses? Is there any revolution in Virginia? Whither is the spirit of America gone? Whither is the genius of America fled? It was but yesterday, when our enemies marched in triumph through our country: Yet the people of this country could not be appalled by their pompous armaments: They stopped their career, and victoriously captured them: Where is the peril now compared to that? Some minds are agitated by

Patrick Henry, Speech to Virginia Ratifying Convention, 1788.

foreign alarms: Happily for us, there is no real danger from Europe: that country is engaged in more arduous business; from that quarter there is no cause of fear: You may sleep in safety forever for them. Where is the danger? If, Sir, there was any, I would recur to the American spirit to defend us;—that spirit which has enabled us to surmount the greatest difficulties: To that illustrious spirit I address my most fervent prayer, to prevent our adopting a system destructive to liberty. . . .

This Constitution is said to have beautiful features; but when I come to examine these features, Sir, they appear to me horridly frightful: Among other deformities, it has an awful squinting; it squints towards monarchy: And does not this raise indignation in the breast of every American? Your President may easily become King: Your Senate is so imperfectly constructed that your dearest rights may be sacrificed by what may be a small minority; and a very small minority may continue forever unchangeably this Government, although horridly defective: Where are your checks in the Government? Your strong holds will be in the hands of your enemies: It is on a supposition that our American Governors shall be honest, that all the good qualities of this Government are founded: But its defective, and imperfect construction, puts it in their power to perpetuate the worst of mischiefs, should they be bad men: And, Sir, would not all the world, from the Eastern to the Western hemisphere, blame our distracted folly in resting our rights upon the contingency of our rulers being good or bad.

10. George Washington Declares Freedom of Religion for Jewish People, 1790

Gentlemen.

While I receive, with much satisfaction, your Address replete with expressions of esteem; I rejoice in the opportunity of assuring you, that I shall always retain grateful remembrance of the cordial welcome I experienced on my visit to Newport, from all classes of citizens. . . .

The Citizens of the United States of America have a right to applaud Themselves for having given to mankind examples of an enlarged and liberal policy: a policy worthy of imitation. All possess alike liberty of conscience and immunities of citizenship. It is now no more that toleration is spoken of, as if it was by the indulgence of one class of people, that another enjoyed the exercise of their inherent natural rights. For happily the Government of the United States, which gives to bigotry no sanction, to persecution no assistance requires only that they who live under its protection should demean themselves as good citizens in giving it on all occasions their effectual support. . . .

May the Children of the Stock of Abraham, who dwell in this land, continue to merit and enjoy the good will of the other Inhabitants; while every one shall sit in safety under his own vine and figtree; and there shall be none to make him afraid. May the father of all mercies scatter light and not darkness in our paths, and make us all in our several vocations useful here, and in his own due time and way everlastingly happy.

George Washington, *Letter to Moses Seixas* (1790), in *The Papers of George Washington,* vol. 6, ed. Mark A. Mastromarino (Charlottesville: University of Virginia Press, 1996).

E S S A Y S

In 1913, Charles Beard argued that the framers of the Constitution were motivated first and foremost by a desire to protect their own economic interests. Beard's thesis initiated a debate that continues to the present over whether the Constitution was a necessary adjustment to the inadequate governmental structure provided by the Articles of Confederation or an overreaction—some might say counterrevolution—by the elite to popular government. The following two essays illustrate this argument. Alfred F. Young, who teaches at the University of Northern Illinois, takes a more critical stance toward the Constitutional Convention. He acknowledges that accommodations were made by the framers, but only because they were haunted by "ghosts," that is, by popular movements that were not represented at the Convention but surely figured in the framers' thinking. In contrast, Jack Rakove, professor of history at Stanford University, argues that the framers were actually led away from the notion that the Constitution ought to restrict entrance into public life. Rather than closing off opportunities for holding political office, they actually sought to enlarge political participation. Rakove contends that this path, in turn, created the problems of recruiting politicians who would remain in public office.

The Pressure of the People on the Framers of the Constitution

ALFRED F. YOUNG

On June 18, 1787, about three weeks into the Constitutional Convention at Philadelphia, Alexander Hamilton delivered a six-hour address that was easily the longest and most conservative the Convention would hear. Gouverneur Morris, a delegate from Pennsylvania, thought it was "the most able and impressive he had ever heard."

Beginning with the premise that "all communities divide themselves into the few and the many," "the wealthy well born" and "the people," Hamilton added the corollary that the "people are turbulent and changing; they seldom judge or determine right." Moving through history, the delegate from New York developed his ideal for a national government that would protect the few from "the imprudence of democracy" and guarantee "stability and permanence": a president and senate indirectly elected for life ("to serve during good behavior") to balance a house directly elected by a popular vote every three years. This "elective monarch" would have an absolute veto over laws passed by Congress. And the national government would appoint the governors of the states, who in turn would have the power to veto any laws by the state legislatures.

If others quickly saw a resemblance in all of this to the King, House of Lords and House of Commons of Great Britain, with the states reduced to colonies ruled by royal governors, they were not mistaken. The British constitution, in Hamilton's view, remained "the best model the world has ever produced."

Three days later a delegate reported that Hamilton's proposals "had been praised by everybody," but "he has been supported by none." Acknowledging that his plan

Alfred F. Young, "The Framers of the Constitution and the 'Genius' of the People," *In These Times,* September 9–15, 1987. Reprinted by permission of In These Times.

"went beyond the ideas of most members," Hamilton said he had brought it forward not "as a thing attainable by us, but as a model which we ought to approach as near as possible." When he signed the Constitution the framers finally agreed to on September 17, 1787, Hamilton could accurately say, "no plan was more remote from his own."

Why did the framers reject a plan so many admired? To ask this question is to go down a dark path into the heart of the Constitution few of its celebrants care to take. We have heard so much in our elementary and high school civics books about the "great compromises" within the Convention—between the large states and the small states, between the slaveholders and non-slaveholders, between North and South—that we have missed the much larger accommodation that was taking place between the delegates as a whole at the Convention and what they called "the people out of doors."

The Convention was unmistakably an elite body. The official exhibit for the bicentennial, "Miracle at Philadelphia," opens appropriately enough with a large oil portrait of Robert Morris, a delegate from Philadelphia, one of the richest merchants in America, and points out elsewhere that 11 out of 55 delegates were business associates of Morris'. The 55 were weighted with merchants, slaveholding planters and "monied men" who loaned money at interest. Among them were numerous lawyers and college graduates in a country where most men and only a few women had the rudiments of a formal education. They were far from a cross section of the four million or so Americans of that day, most of whom were farmers or artisans, fishermen or seamen, indentured servants or laborers, half of whom were women and about 600,000 of whom were African-American slaves.

I. The First Accommodation

Why did this elite reject Hamilton's plan that many of them praised? James Madison, the Constitution's chief architect, had the nub of the matter. The Constitution was "intended for the ages." To last it had to conform to the "genius" of the American people. "Genius" was a word eighteenth-century political thinkers used to mean spirit: we might say character or underlying values.

James Wilson, second only to Madison in his influence at Philadelphia, elaborated on the idea. "The British government cannot be our model. We have no materials for a similar one. Our manners, our law, the abolition of entail and primogeniture," which made for a more equal distribution of property among sons, "the whole genius of the people, are opposed to it."

This was long-range political philosophy. There was a short-range political problem that moved other realistic delegates in the same direction. Called together to revise the old Articles of Confederation, the delegates instead decided to scrap it and frame an entirely new constitution. It would have to be submitted to the people for ratification, most likely to conventions elected especially for the purpose. Repeatedly, conservatives recoiled from extreme proposals for which they knew they could not win popular support.

In response to a proposal to extend the federal judiciary into the states, Pierce Butler, a South Carolina planter, argued, "the people will not bear such innovations. The states will revolt at such encroachments." His assumption was "we must follow the example of Solomon, who gave the Athenians not the best government he could devise but the best they would receive."

The suffrage debate epitomized this line of thinking. Gouverneur Morris, Hamilton's admirer, proposed that the national government limit voting for the House to men who owned a freehold, i.e. a substantial farm, or its equivalent. "Give the vote to people who have no property and they will sell them to the rich who will be able to buy them," he said with some prescience. George Mason, author of Virginia's Bill of Rights, was aghast. "Eight or nine states have extended the right of suffrage beyond the freeholders. What will people there say if they should be disfranchised?"

Benjamin Franklin, the patriarch, speaking for one of the few times in the convention, paid tribute to "the lower class of freemen" who should not be disfranchised. James Wilson explained, "it would be very hard and disagreeable for the same person" who could vote for representatives for the state legislatures "to be excluded from a vote for this in the national legislature." Nathaniel Gorham, a Boston merchant, returned to the guiding principle: "the people will never allow" existing rights to suffrage to be abridged. "We must consult their rooted prejudices if we expect their concurrence in our propositions."

The result? Morris' proposal was defeated and the convention decided that whoever each state allowed to vote for its own assembly could vote for the House. It was a compromise that left the door open and in a matter of decades allowed states to introduce universal white male suffrage.

II. Ghosts of Years Past

Clearly there was a process of accommodation at work here. The popular movements of the Revolutionary Era were a presence at the Philadelphia Convention even if they were not present. The delegates, one might say, were haunted by ghosts, symbols of the broadly based movements elites had confronted in the making of the Revolution from 1765 to 1775, in waging the war from 1775 to 1781 and in the years since 1781 within their own states.

The first was the ghost of Thomas Paine, the most influential radical democrat of the Revolutionary Era. In 1776 Paine's pamphlet *Common Sense* (which sold at least 150,000 copies), in arguing for independence, rejected not only King George III but the principle of monarchy and the so-called checks and balances of the unwritten English constitution. In its place he offered a vision of a democratic government in which a single legislature would be supreme, the executive minimal, and representatives would be elected from small districts by a broad electorate for short terms so they could "return and mix again with the voters." John Adams considered *Common Sense* too "democratical," without even an attempt at "mixed government" that would balance "democracy" with "aristocracy."

The second ghost was that of Abraham Yates, a member of the state senate of New York typical of the new men who had risen to power in the 1780s in the state legislatures. We have forgotten him; Hamilton, who was very conscious of him, called him "an old Booby." He had begun as a shoemaker and was a self-taught lawyer and warm foe of the landlord aristocracy of the Hudson Valley which Hamilton had married into. As James Madison identified the "vices of the political system of the United States" in a memorandum in 1787, the Abraham Yateses were the number-one problem. The state legislatures had "an itch for paper money" laws, laws that prevented foreclosure on farm mortgages, and tax laws that soaked the rich. As Madison saw it, this meant that "debtors defrauded their creditors" and "the landed interest has borne hard on the mercantile interest." This, too, is what Hamilton had in mind when he spoke of the "depredations which the democratic spirit is apt to make on property" and what others meant by the "excess of democracy" in the states.

The third ghost was a very fresh one—Daniel Shays. In 1786 Shays, a captain in the Revolution, led a rebellion of debtor farmers in western Massachusetts which the state quelled with its own somewhat unreliable militia. There were "combustibles in every state," as George Washington put it, raising the specter of "Shaysism." This Madison enumerated among the "vices" of the system as "a want of guaranty to the states against internal violence." Worse still, Shaysites in many states were turning to the political system to elect their own kind. If they succeeded they would produce legal Shaysism, a danger for which the elites had no remedy.

The fourth ghost we can name [is] the ghost of Thomas Peters, although he had a thousand other names. In 1775, Peters, a Virginia slave, responded to a plea by the British to fight in their army and win their freedom. He served in an "Ethiopian Regiment," some of whose members bore the emblem "Liberty to Slaves" on their uniforms. After the war the British transported Peters and several thousand escaped slaves to Nova Scotia from whence Peters eventually led a group to return to Africa and the colony of Sierra Leone, a long odyssey to freedom. Eighteenth-century slaveholders, with no illusions about happy or contented slaves, were haunted by the specter of slaves in arms.

III. Elite Divisions

During the Revolutionary Era elites divided in response to these varied threats from below. One group, out of fear of "the mob" and then "the rabble in arms," embraced the British and became active Loyalists. After the war most of them went into exile. Another group who became patriots never lost their obsession with coercing popular movements.

"The mob begins to think and reason," Gouverneur Morris observed in 1774. "Poor reptiles, they bask in the sunshine and ere long they will bite." A snake had to be scotched. Other thought of the people as a horse that had to be whipped. This was coercion.

Far more important, however, were those patriot leaders who adopted a strategy of "swimming with a stream which it is impossible to stem." This was the metaphor of Robert R. Livingston, Jr., like Morris, a gentleman with a large tenanted estate in New York. Men of his class had to learn to "yield to the torrent if they hoped to direct its course."

Livingston and his group were able to shape New York's constitution, which some called a perfect blend of "aristocracy" and "democracy." John Hancock, the richest merchant in New England, had mastered this kind of politics and emerged as the most popular politician in Massachusetts. In Maryland Charles Carroll, a wealthy planter, instructed his anxious father about the need to "submit to partial losses" because "no great revolution can happen in a state without revolutions or mutations of private property. If we can save a third of our personal estate and all of our lands and Negroes, I shall think ourselves well off."

The major leaders at the Constitutional Convention in 1787 were heirs to both traditions: coercion and accommodation—Hamilton and Gouverneur Morris to the former, James Madison and James Wilson much more to the latter.

They all agreed on coercion to slay the ghosts of Daniel Shays and Thomas Peters. The Constitution gave the national government the power to "suppress insurrections" and protect the states from "domestic violence." There would be a national army under the command of the president, and authority to nationalize the state militias and suspend the right of habeas corpus in "cases of rebellion or invasion." In 1794 Hamilton, as secretary of the treasury, would exercise such powers fully (and needlessly) to suppress the Whiskey Rebellion in western Pennsylvania.

Southern slaveholders correctly interpreted the same powers as available to shackle the ghost of Thomas Peters. As it turned out, Virginia would not need a federal army to deal with Gabriel Prosser's insurrection in 1800 or Nat Turner's rebellion in 1830, but a federal army would capture John Brown after his raid at Harpers Ferry in 1859.

But how to deal with the ghosts of Thomas Paine and Abraham Yates? Here Madison and Wilson blended coercion with accommodation. They had three solutions to the threat of democratic majorities in the states.

Their first was clearly coercive. Like Hamilton, Madison wanted some kind of national veto over the state legislatures. He got several very specific curbs on the states written into fundamental law: no state could "emit" paper money or pass "laws impairing the obligation of contracts." Wilson was so overjoyed with these two clauses that he argued that if they alone "were inserted in the Constitution I think they would be worth our adoption."

But Madison considered the overall mechanism adopted to curb the states "short of the mark." The Constitution, laws and treaties were the "supreme law of the land" and ultimately a federal court could declare state laws unconstitutional. But this, Madison lamented, would only catch "mischiefs" after the fact. Thus they had clipped the wings of Abraham Yates but he could still fly.

The second solution to the problem of the states was decidedly democratic. They wanted to do an end-run around the state legislatures. The Articles of Confederation, said Madison, rested on "the pillars" of the state legislatures who elected delegates to Congress. The "great fabric to be raised would be more stable and durable if it should rest on the solid grounds of the people themselves"; hence, there would be popular elections to the House.

Wilson altered only the metaphor. He was for "raising the federal pyramid to a considerable altitude and for that reason wanted to give it as broad a base as possible." They would slay the ghost of Abraham Yates with the ghost of Thomas Paine.

This was risky business. They would reduce the risk by keeping the House of Representatives small. Under a ratio of one representative for every 30,000 people, the first house would have only 65 members; in 1776 Thomas Paine had suggested 390. But still, the House would be elected every two years, and with each state allowed to determine its own qualifications for voting, there was no telling who might end up in Congress.

There was also a risk in Madison's third solution to the problem of protecting propertied interests from democratic majorities: "extending the sphere" of government. Prevailing wisdom held that a republic could only succeed in a small geographic area; to rule an "extensive" country, some kind of despotism was considered inevitable.

Madison turned this idea on its head in his since famous *Federalist* essay No. 10. In a small republic, he argued, it was relatively easy for a majority to gang up on a particular "interest." "Extend the sphere," he wrote, and "you take in a greater variety of parties and interests." Then it would be more difficult for a majority "to discover their own strength and to act in unison with each other."

This was a prescription for a non-colonial empire that would expand across the continent, taking in new states as it dispossessed the Indians. The risk was there was no telling how far the "democratic" or "leveling" spirit might go in such likely would-be states as frontier Vermont, Kentucky and Tennessee.

IV. Democratic Divisions

In the spectrum of state constitutions adopted in the Revolutionary era, the federal Constitution of 1787 was, like New York's, somewhere between "aristocracy" and "democracy." It therefore should not surprise us—although it has eluded many modern critics of the Constitution—that in the contest over ratification in 1787–88, the democratic minded were divided.

Among agrarian democrats there was a gut feeling that the Constitution was the work of an old class enemy. "These lawyers and men of learning and monied men," argued Amos Singletary, a working farmer at the Massachusetts ratifying convention, "expect to be managers of this Constitution and get all the power and all the money into their own hands and then will swallow up all of us little folks . . . just as the whale swallowed up Jonah."

Democratic leaders like Melancton Smith of New York focused on the small size of the proposed House. Arguing from Paine's premise that the members of the legislature should "resemble those they represent," Smith feared that "a substantial yeoman of sense and discernment will hardly ever be chosen" and the government "will fall into the hands of the few and the great." Urban democrats, on the other hand, including a majority of the mechanics and tradesmen of the major cities who in the Revolution had been a bulwark of Paineite radicalism, were generally enthusiastic about the Constitution. They were impelled by their urgent stake in a stronger national government that would advance ocean-going commerce and protect American manufacturers from competition. But they would not have been as ardent about the new frame of government without its saving graces. It clearly preserved their rights to suffrage. And the process of ratification, like the Constitution itself, guaranteed them a voice. As early as 1776 the New York Committee of Mechanics held it as "a right which God has given them in common with all men to judge whether it be consistent with their interest to accept or reject a constitution."

Mechanics turned out en masse in the parades celebrating ratification, marching trade by trade. The slogans and symbols they carried expressed their political ideals. In New York the upholsterers had a float with an elegant "Federal Chair of State" flanked by the symbols of Liberty and Justice that they identified with the Constitution. In Philadelphia the bricklayers put on their banner "Both buildings and rulers are the work of our hands."

Democrats who were skeptical found it easier to come over because of the Constitution's redeeming features. Thomas Paine, off in Paris, considered the Constitution "a copy, though not quite as base as the original, of the form of the British government." He had always opposed a single executive and he objected to the "long duration of the Senate." But he was so convinced of "the absolute necessity" of a stronger federal government that "I would have voted for it myself had I been in America or even for a worse, rather than have none." It was crucial to Paine that there was an amending process, the means of "remedying its defects by the same appeal to the people by which it was to be established."

V. The Second Accommodation

In drafting the Constitution in 1787 the framers, self-styled Federalists, made their first accommodation with the "genius" of the people. In campaigning for its ratification in 1788 they made their second. At the outset, the conventions in the key states—Massachusetts, New York and Virginia—either had an anti-Federalist majority or were closely divided. To swing over a small group of "antis" in each state, Federalists had to promise that they would consider amendments. This was enough to secure ratification by narrow margins in Massachusetts, 187 to 168; in New York, 30 to 27; and in Virginia, 89 to 79.

What the anti-Federalists wanted were dozens of changes in the structure of the government that would cut back national power over the states, curb the powers of the presidency as well as protect individual liberties. What they got was far less. But in the first Congress in 1789, James Madison, true to his pledge, considered all the amendments and shepherded 12 amendments through both houses. The first two of these failed in the states; one would have enlarged the House. The 10 that were ratified by December 1791 were what we have since called the Bill of Rights, protecting freedom of expression and the rights of the accused before the law. Abraham Yates considered them "trivial and unimportant." But other democrats looked on them much more favorably. In time the limited meaning of freedom of speech in the First Amendment was broadened far beyond the framers' original intent. Later popular movements thought of the Bill of Rights as an essential part of the "constitutional" and "republican" rights that belonged to the people.

VI. The "Losers'" Role

There is a cautionary tale here that surely goes beyond the process of framing and adopting the Constitution and Bill of Rights from 1787 to 1791. The Constitution was as democratic as it was because of the influence of popular movements that were a presence, even if not present. The losers helped shape the results. We owe the Bill of Rights to the opponents of the Constitution, as we do many other features in the Constitution put in to anticipate opposition.

In American history popular movements often shaped elites, especially in times of crisis when elites were concerned with the "system." Elites have often divided in response to such threats and according to their perception of the "genius" of the people. Some have turned to coercion, others to accommodation. We run serious risk if we ignore this distinction. Would that we had fewer Gouverneur Morrises and Alexander Hamiltons and more James Madisons and James Wilsons to respond to the "genius" of the people.

The Concern of the Framers to Recruit Citizens to Enter Public Life

JACK N. RAKOVE

It has been some time since historians have displayed conspicuous interest in the actual drafting of the Constitution or the origins of particular clauses. Modern political controversies have drawn renewed attention to a few provisions—notably those involving war powers and impeachment. Yet more than seventy years after Charles Beard offered *An Economic Interpretation of the Constitution,* historians still seem preoccupied with identifying the political and social alignments that favored or opposed the creation of a stronger national government. Creditors and debtors have given way to cosmopolitans and localists and, more recently, to court and country. But the thrust of inquiry has changed less than one might suppose. . . . Just as the framers of the Constitution tend to be submerged within the larger Federalist movement, so the specific concerns that operated within the convention often seem less important than the arguments that were made for and against ratification.

And not without reason. The concerns of framers and ratifiers *had* diverged. The struggle between large and small states that had so dominated the internal politics of the convention did not remain a pivotal issue after September 1787. Similarly, the principal result of the ratification debates was the acceptance of an idea that the framers had not taken seriously: that a bill of rights could somehow provide a valuable check against the excesses of power. Moreover, the intensity of the struggle over ratification left a body of writings and speeches whose rich detail contrasts sharply with the spare words of the Constitution and the elliptical character of the convention's debates as evidence of the fundamental divisions with the American polity. Yet for all this, the Constitution should not be viewed solely through the lens of *The Federalist* and other ratification commentaries. For, once the passions of 1788 had faded and the polemical literature they produced had fallen into an obscurity from which only modern scholarship has rescued it, the language of the Constitution retained its force. That was where contemporaries turned when constitutional disputes arose, as they did as early as June 1789, and that is where historians ought to begin as well.

Was the Constitution consciously framed to promote a filtration of talent? No doubt many Federalists supported it because they believed it would enable a better

Jack N. Rakove, "The Structure of Politics at the Accession of George Washington," in Richard Beeman, Stephen Botein, and Edward C. Carter II, eds., *Beyond Confederation: Origins of the Constitution and American National Identity* (Williamsburg, Va.: Institute of Early American History and Culture), 266–272, 275–277, 279–281, 284–286. Copyright © 1987 by the University of North Carolina Press. Used by permission of the publisher.

class of leaders—or simply a better class—to recover political power. But it is difficult to demonstrate that this was what either the Constitution itself mandated or the framers intended. The *formal* criteria for membership in Congress were certainly not set high: the attainment of age twenty-five and seven years of citizenship for the House, age thirty and nine years of citizenship for the Senate; and the additional requirement that a member, "when elected, be an Inhabitant of that State in [for] which he shall be chosen" are all that Article I asks. Nor did the framers seek to restrict the size of the electorate, in the way, for example, that the Whig oligarchy of early Georgian England had managed to. Members of the House of Representatives were to be elected by the same voters who had been sending "demagogues" into the state legislatures.

Moreover, when one tracks the various provisions that would regulate the process of selection through the convention, it is apparent that the course of debate led the framers *away* from the idea that the Constitution ought to erect significant barriers against entrance into public life. Perhaps the best evidence of this can be found in the fate of efforts to establish property qualifications for appointment to office. As late as July 26, the convention had asked the Committee of Detail to draft a provision "requiring certain qualifications of landed property and citizenship in the United States for the Executive, the Judiciary, and the Members of both branches of the Legislature." In its report of August 6, however, the committee merely proposed that the legislature should be empowered "to establish such uniform Qualifications of the Members of each House, with Regard to Property, as to the said Legislature shall seem expedient." When this provision was taken up on August 10, Charles Pinckney pointedly noted that the committee had departed from its instructions. He moved instead to insert a clause requiring legislators "to swear that they were respectively possessed of a clear unencumbered Estate," with a suitably descending scale of property for the two houses.

The ensuing debate revealed that attempts to establish property qualifications were objectionable on both practical and theoretical grounds. Two committee members explained why their report had not met Pinckney's expectations. Fix the requirement too high, John Rutledge noted, and it would anger the people; fix it too low, and the qualifications would be made "nugatory." Moreover, Oliver Ellsworth added, it was impossible to establish a scale that would work equally well for different parts of the Union or for different periods in the history of the nation. These objections were so decisive that Pinckney's motion was rejected by a simple voice vote.

But that still left open the question whether the legislature ought to possess any discretionary power to establish conditions of membership. One problem was the difficulty of employing any criterion other than property. The more telling objection lay, however, against giving the legislature any discretion. As Hugh Williamson noted, such license could allow the lawyers who might well dominate the new congress to secure "future elections . . . to their own body." But if qualifications could not be fixed *constitutionally,* it seemed better to do away with them entirely. Otherwise, Madison warned, the legislature would be able "by degrees [to] subvert the Constitution." The entire clause was accordingly eliminated.

If the character of national legislators could not be regulated by imposing property requirements on the elected, could the same goal be achieved by limiting the suffrage? When the Committee of Detail proposed allowing the House of Representatives to be chosen by the same voters who elected the lower houses of the state legislatures, Gouverneur Morris and John Dickinson vigorously argued in favor of restricting the franchise to landed freeholders. But this proposal was also roundly rejected. The Constitution placed no restrictions on the right of suffrage.

Nor can it be said that the framers seriously considered just how elections for the House of Representatives were to be conducted. In agreeing to vest Congress with a residual power to determine the manner of electing congressmen, they were clearly concerned with the possibility that the state legislatures would manipulate the electoral process. But what is more striking is the latitude within which the states were to be allowed to act. As Madison himself noted,

> Whether the electors should vote by ballot or vivâ voce, should assemble at this place or that place; should be divided into districts or all meet at one place, sh[oul]d all vote for all the representatives; or all in a district vote for a number allotted to the district; these and many other points would depend on the Legislatures, and might materially affect the appointments.

Coming from one who presumably regarded the manner in which congressmen were to be elected as a critical element of the entire system—and who had once described voting by ballot as "the only radical cure for those arts of Electioneering which poison the very fountain of Liberty"—this was hardly a trivial concession. Indeed, nothing better illustrates the degree to which Madison's notion of the electoral virtues of the extended republic was simply a statement of faith. The indefinite character of his thinking on this subject was due in part to the greater priority he had been forced to place within the convention on the struggle to secure the principle of proportional representation; and it may also have reflected his disappointment that the Senate, the single branch of government on which he had originally fastened his deepest hopes, was to be elected by the state legislatures. In any event, there is no evidence that Madison had developed beyond generalities his notion of how representatives were to be elected. When in 1788 the states began adopting a variety of procedures for electing representatives—including not only district and statewide elections but also a hybrid in which electors voted statewide for members from particular districts—Madison informed Jefferson, "It is perhaps to be desired that various modes should be tried, as by that means only the best mode can be ascertained."

Decisions on other provisions also worked to remove formal barriers against election to the legislature. Instead of requiring a congressman to be "resident" in his state for a fixed period of years, the convention agreed that he need only be an "inhabitant" of the state at the time of election. When it came to deciding how legislators were to be paid, the convention did not presume that members of Congress would be independently wealthy. It authorized paying legislative salaries from the national treasury not merely to prevent the states from retaining undue influence over their representatives, but also from an expectation that newly admitted western states might balk at supporting an adequate representation if forced to defray legislative salaries from their own limited funds.

Finally, and perhaps most revealingly, the convention relaxed the prohibition against the appointment of legislators to other offices. Of all the provisions relating to conditions of membership, this was the most sharply controverted, and it was not resolved—and then only by the narrowest margin—until September 3. The report of the Committee of Detail would have prevented legislators from accepting any federal office during the term of their election, with senators further barred from "holding any such office for one year afterwards." Supporters of these restrictions argued the conventional whiggish view that, without such restraints, the legislature would attract, as George Mason noted with typical irony, "those generous and benevolent characters who will do justice to each other's merit, by carving out offices and rewards" for their own profit. But the majority, who eventually restricted the prohibition only to offices that had been either "created" or whose "emoluments [had been] increased" during a legislator's term, were apparently swayed by equally candid arguments in favor of promoting ambition. James Wilson put the key point bluntly when he declared that "he was far from thinking the ambition which aspired to Offices of dignity and trust, an ignoble or culpable one." Thus while the narrow margin with which the diluted version of this clause was approved indicates that the framers had not reached a consensus, they would nevertheless have agreed that the revision was intended to encourage men to enter legislative service in part from forthright calculations of personal ambition. Whether the ambitions to be unleashed belonged to corruptible "office-hunters" or to "those whose talents" would "give weight to the Govern[men]t" remained to be seen.

On balance, then, the principal concern of the framers was not to limit access to national office to those who were most conspicuously qualified to occupy it, but rather to open up the process of political recruitment in the hope that better men would be moved to enter public life and prove capable of achieving electoral success. For the new government to succeed in this respect, however, it would have to rely on the actual circumstances of political life rather than the formal requirements that the Constitution itself had failed to impose. Federalist desires could be realized only if the enlarged sphere of the extended republic worked to filter talent upward or if the simple prestige and power of the new government drew qualified men away from the privacy of their law offices, plantations, and countinghouses. Neither the formal provisions of the Constitution nor the heated debates of the ratification campaign could secure such results; they depended instead on other factors—personal as well as political—that no constitution could by itself legislate.

If the adoption of the Constitution was thus meant to release new ambitions, the preservation of its intricate system of checks and balances would also depend, Madison argued in *Federalist* No. 51, on directing those ambitions toward appropriate ends. "Ambition must be made to counteract ambition," he wrote. "The interest of the man must be connected with the constitutional rights of the place." Yet despite its apparent gritty realism, this celebrated statement was no less problematic than other early predictions about the likely operation of the Constitution.

For ambition could counteract ambition only if those elected made continuation in a particular office the object of their careers. The benefits of bringing more enlightened leaders into office would be lost if they chose not to stay in positions of responsibility. But if one thing is clear about the political system that the Constitution created, it is that it long failed to promote the stability of tenure that Federalists desired and anticipated. The evidence on this point is unambiguous. Well into the next century, the new system proved embarrassingly productive in its *recruitment* of aspirants to national office, but its record on *retention* was another matter entirely. The best that can be said for Congress is that its membership was marginally more stable than that of the state legislatures. Throughout the entire first century of its history, members entered and left Congress with a frequency that stands in sharp contrast with modern standards. During this period, the median term of service in the House of Representatives fluctuated between two and four years, and the proportion of members who served more than four terms never exceeded 10 percent. From 1790 to 1870, the median age of departure from the House remained steadily fixed in the mid-forties. And although the reasons why men left the House are often hard to come by, death, old age, and electoral defeat clearly played far less of a role in attrition before the late nineteenth century than they do today. . . .

The one group of congressmen whose ambitions can be described most easily are the ninety-odd members of the First Federal Congress of 1789–1790. Their experience in gaining and holding office marked the first test of the various predictions that had been vented while the Constitution was being adopted. The First Congress, of course, numbered fewer members than all but its immediate successor, and its ranks almost certainly included a higher proportion of prominent personalities than any later congress. To some extent, it is true, the likelihood that many of these first congressmen had taken major parts in both the Revolution and the debate over the Constitution would suggest that their motives did not accurately represent the range of ambitions that came into play once the age of the founding patriarchs gave way to the era of mass political parties. Yet even during the Revolution, decisions about the depth of political involvement—as opposed to simple allegiance—often reflected personal concerns, and by the late 1780s, recovery from the turmoil and dislocation of the war was well enough advanced to enable potential candidates to weigh the benefits and costs of office quite carefully according to the dictates of individual interest and ambition. Finally, although one cannot fault the framers of the Constitution for failing to anticipate how "change of circumstances, time, and a fuller population of our country" would affect the character of representation, the "moderate period of time" separating the drafting of the Constitution from the first elections allows us to ask how well the arguments of 1787–1788 corresponded to certain aspects of what might be called, with all due respect to Sir Lewis Namier, the structure of American politics at the accession of George Washington.

By any criterion, including those criteria that contemporaries would have applied, the victors in the first federal elections were a distinguished group. The roster of the First Congress included twenty members of the Federal Convention—among them Madison, Elbridge Gerry, Rufus King, Roger Sherman, William Samuel Johnson, Oliver Ellsworth, William Paterson, and Robert Morris—as well as a number of other men who had held prominent military or political positions during the war, such as Philip Schuyler, Elias Boudinot, Jeremiah Wadsworth, John Langdon, Richard Henry Lee, and Egbert Benson. Prestige alone offers no proof of legislative talent, but most members of the First Congress shared another trait that would have enabled contemporaries to agree that they possessed what Madison had called for in *Federalist* No. 10: "the most attractive merit, and the most diffusive and established characters." For in the milieu of the late 1780s, a notable record of involvement in the Revolution was itself the first and perhaps even sufficient test of political merit. In this respect, it is striking that fully half of the members of the First Congress were politically active before Independence, with no fewer than a third entering politics during the final crisis of 1774–1776, and an additional quarter first holding office during the remaining years of the war. . . .

Historians generally agree that the two Federalist movements of the 1780s and 1790s were committed to the preservation or restoration of traditional principles of deference and that their leadership (at least in the northern states) tended to be drawn from an established elite whose superiority was endangered by the democratizing impulses the Revolution had released. Yet among the "dual Federalists" who sat in the First Congress, it is striking to see how many fit the image of new men who had themselves struggled to gain—and not simply inherit—prestige and influence. Recognizing that their own rise to political power and higher social status had derived from participation in the Revolution, they were no less its products for resisting what they regarded as its excesses.

By way of example, consider the uncannily parallel paths that had led Oliver Ellsworth of Connecticut and William Paterson of New Jersey to the Senate in 1789. Both were born in 1745; both were graduates of the College of New Jersey; both served terms as state legal officers; both were delegates to the Federal Convention, where they collaborated on the making of the Great Compromise; and as the capstones of their political careers, both later accepted appointments to the Supreme Court, where they served together until Ellsworth's retirement in 1800. Both came from families with solidly middle-class credentials. Ellsworth's father was a respectable farmer, selectman, and militia captain who intended his second son for the ministry but saw him turn to law instead. Paterson emigrated with his family from Ireland in 1747; by 1750 his father was established in Princeton, where he prospered as a storekeeper and helped his eldest son take advantage of all the opportunities education could bestow.

The promise of education was one thing, however; success was another matter again. When war broke out in 1775, both men were still struggling to make a respectable career at law. Ellsworth had earned all of three pounds sterling during his first three years of practice; the one promising step he had taken was to marry a Wolcott and move to Hartford, where he could profit from his in-laws' connections and status. Paterson, too, had remained a poor country lawyer. Rather than take his chances in Philadelphia or even one of the larger neighboring towns, he pursued a thankless practice in rural New Jersey; most of his work involved protecting his father's debt-troubled property.

Perhaps native ability would have brought eventual success to these two future justices had the Revolution not intervened in their lives. Certainly they did not support the Revolution because they foresaw how their careers could benefit from Independence: neither had shown any ardent interest in politics before 1775 (though Ellsworth did serve a term in the Connecticut assembly in 1773). With Paterson and Ellsworth, as with so many of their colleagues, the events of the mid-1770s can be said, not so much to have furthered ambitions previously thwarted, but rather to have created ambitions which had hardly existed. Yet while their commitment to the whig cause enabled them to acquire substantial political influence within their states, in many ways professional prominence remained their deeper object. Paterson held no office at the time of his election to the Senate; he was busy instead pursuing a hefty legal practice that had expanded enormously upon the basis of his record as wartime attorney general. For his part, Ellsworth accepted election grudgingly, informing Governor Samuel Huntington that he would have preferred to retain his seat on the Connecticut Superior Court. "Considering, however, that in the present scituation of our publick affairs, it may be a duty, for a time, to waive personal considerations, I have concluded, by the leave of Providence, to attend the Congress at its first, and perhaps two or three of its first, sessions." Ellsworth went on to serve a full six-year term before replacing John Jay as chief justice; Paterson resigned even before the First Congress expired to accept election as governor of New Jersey.

Legislation and debate appealed little to Ellsworth and Paterson, but there were other attorneys who relished these activities to a degree that irked congressmen drawn from other occupations. Few, if any, members of the First Congress commanded greater respect in these areas than the two leading Federalist representatives from Massachusetts, Theodore Sedgwick and Fisher Ames. They, too, came from moderately respectable families that had struggled to maintain an estate and improve their social standing in the cramped and jealous world of a New England town. Having lost their fathers at an early age, both were forced to rely on a college education (Sedgwick at Yale, Ames at Harvard) and the diligent pursuit of legal studies to establish their own livelihoods. Like Paterson and Ellsworth, both had experienced the pangs of disappointment and idleness that were the dues of young attorneys, and like colleagues throughout America—including William Paterson— they knew the kind of resentment, not to say enmity, that their profession attracted. They naturally equated animosity against lawyers with aversion to the rule of law itself, and they viewed Shays's Rebellion of 1786 as proof of the need to restore a due sense of obedience to the restless citizenry of Massachusetts (a lost cause if ever there was one). Having relied upon their own talents and fortitude to make their way, with some success, in the world, they found it difficult to look sympathetically on the social jealousy and resentment of class that the Shaysite uprising embodied. For Sedgwick and Ames, as for so many other attorneys to come, election to Congress provided a welcome opportunity to escape the routine bickering of court appearances while continuing to practice the professional arts of draftsmanship and oratory. To his despondent and domestically overburdened wife—"a sufferer from chronic pregnancy and loneliness," his biographer has noted—Sedgwick wrote tender letters lamenting his confinement in Congress; but his correspondence with male friends reveals his pride in the legislative art. . . .

In certain ways, congressmen who did not feel too deeply attached to their constituencies could fit the original Madisonian ideal of representation better than those whose political loyalties never rose above their parochial roots. Yet to survey the diverse paths that brought the members of the First Congress to New York in 1789 is to realize how little relevance that ideal had to the actual recruitment and retention of national legislators. Even in 1789, when the existing political nation was still aroused over the character and fate of the Constitution and when the heady debates of the preceding months still resounded clearly, it is clear that men sought national office for various reasons, public and private, patriotic and self-interested. It is easy enough to explain why men so long committed to public life as Madison and Roger Sherman wished to attend Congress in 1789, nor is it much more difficult to gauge the balance of public and private concerns that brought Baldwin, Williamson, and the Philadelphia merchants (all members of the Federal Convention) there as well. But it is no less revealing to examine the motives of Benjamin Contee of Maryland, who may have hoped a seat in Congress would help him stave off his Philadelphia creditor, or Thomas Scott of Pennsylvania, who balked at taking his seat until he was assured that his son would inherit his position as prothonotary of Washington County. Rather than seek reelection to the Second Congress, Scott sought to retain his clerkship of the county court, but after Governor Thomas Mifflin removed him from this position, he ran successfully for the Third Congress and then, apparently, refused to run again.

In point of fact, of course, there was never a time when the political system operated solely as a filter of talent or when expedient calculations did not enter forthrightly into decisions to enter or leave Congress. Legislation was a tedious and often frustrating task that kept one away from family and business. Such appeal as it exerted in the early years of the new regime was probably felt most strongly either by those whose prior experience of the Revolution had already converted them to what John Jay called "the charms of liberty" or by those who (like Fisher Ames and William Branch Giles) were young enough to enter politics before finding themselves bound to another career. The great majority of congressmen acted on different calculations. If they sought election out of some sense of engagement with public issues, their commitment was far from permanent. And if, on the other hand, they hoped a term or two in Congress might redound to their personal advantage, the rewards they hoped to garner were more likely to come in the form of an appointment to the bench or, better yet, a customs collectorship—positions that were more secure and less demanding. Whatever the framers of 1787 may have intended, they could not alter the underlying character of political activity by constitutional fiat. At the close of the Revolution, politics remained more of an avocation than a profession. Over time, the emergence of the political party system provided a more reliable channel of recruitment than the powerful but erratic impulses of patriotism. But the persistence of high rates of turnover both in Congress and the state assemblies suggests that the dividends of legislative service were still found elsewhere, in a later appointment to a more comfortable sinecure. These were not quite the ambitions that the framers had hoped to evoke.

FURTHER READING

Charles Beard, *An Economic Interpretation of the Constitution of the United States* (1913).
Richard Beeman, et al., *Beyond Confederation: Origins of the Constitution and American National Identity* (1987).
Merrill Jensen, *The Articles of Confederation: An Interpretation of the Social-Constitutional History of the American Revolution* (1959).
Forrest McDonald, *Novus Ordo Seclorum: The Intellectual Origins of the Constitution* (1985).
Richard B. Morris, *Witness at the Creation: Hamilton, Madison, Jay, and the Constitution* (1985).
Jack Rakove, *Original Meanings: Politics and Ideas in the Making of the Constitution* (1996).
Gordon S. Wood, *The Creation of the American Republic, 1776–1787* (1969).

CHAPTER
6

Competing Visions of Empire in the Early National Period

The first president, by unanimous vote in the electoral college, was George Washington, war hero and patriot. Washington's inauguration, which evoked among the people a feeling of pride in the nation's revolutionary past and hope for its future, ushered in a brief period of political unity. This nationalist spirit was evident in the first session of Congress, which succeeded in passing a series of key measures. The Constitution had not defined the structure of the federal judiciary, but Congress acted quickly, passing the Judiciary Act of 1789, which established judicial procedures and lower federal courts. Next Congress imposed a tariff on imported goods to provide the federal government with revenue. Finally, as promised during the ratification debate, Congress passed the Bill of Rights: ten constitutional amendments that were sent to the states for ratification. Following ratification, Americans were guaranteed freedom of speech and religion and given rights to bear arms and avoid "cruel and unusual punishment."

Yet the unity was short-lived. Within a few years, the national government was divided into two political factions with different visions for the future of the United States. The principal expounders of these visions were Thomas Jefferson and Alexander Hamilton, both of whom served in Washington's cabinet. Hamilton dreamed of transforming the United States into a manufacturing giant like Britain. America, he was fond of saying, was "a Hercules in the cradle." Hamilton also was suspicious of the people—he considered the masses "turbulent and changing"—and believed the government would be strong if it won the favor of the financial elite. In contrast, Jefferson feared the growth of manufacturing because he sensed that it would decrease the citizenry's independence. His vision focused on a nation of commercial agriculture and independent farmers; virtue, he argued, was best maintained by those "who labor in the earth."

The divisions between Jefferson and Hamilton deepened when the United States was pulled into a European conflict in the 1790s. After the French Revolution, France declared war on Britain, Spain, and Holland. Whereas Jefferson and his followers saw the French Revolution as heir to the American war for independence, the people who shared Hamilton's views watched with horror as the revolution unraveled into unparalleled bloodshed. Out of these differences, political groups began *to coalesce. Those who were sympathetic to the French and fearful of Hamilton's vision formed Democratic-Republican societies. In response, another group, led by Hamilton, Washington, and John Adams, united under the Federalist banner. Acrimonious political battles and vitriolic debate became commonplace in the late 1790s. After John Adams was elected to succeed Washington, the divisions deepened as the United States became further embroiled in European conflicts and nearly went to war against France.*

Adams's failures as president almost guaranteed a Democratic-Republican victory in 1800, and Jefferson heralded his election as the "revolution of 1800." While this was undoubtedly an overstatement, his ascension to the presidency is noteworthy because the Federalists peacefully handed over their power to a hated rival. Jefferson hoped to set about realizing his vision of westward expansion, but the United States remained embroiled in European politics. Both British and French warships were harassing American ships, but the hostile posture of the British was particularly galling for many Americans. When Jefferson's successor, James Madison, assumed the White House, the United States was drifting toward a "second war of independence" with Britain. By 1812, the United States, led by a group of young and aggressive legislators known as "Warhawks," declared war on Britain. After a series of battles that put the future of the United States in danger—including the British attack on Washington and Baltimore—the war turned into a stalemate. Cooler heads prevailed and negotiations began, culminating in the Treaty of Ghent in 1815. Ironically, a war of ineptitude spawned a postwar wave of patriotism. It was during the siege of Baltimore, for example, that Francis Scott Key penned the words of what was to become the national anthem. As another example, Andrew Jackson led a motley American army to victory against the British in New Orleans. About two thousand British soldiers were killed or wounded in the battle, whereas only ten of Jackson's soldiers died. For many Americans, the victory was a stunning turn of events that summoned a huge expression of patriotic fervor. Nonetheless, the peace treaty had been signed two weeks before. Still, many Americans now felt they could turn their attention away from Europe and toward the American west.

◤ Q U E S T I O N S   T O   T H I N K   A B O U T

Whose vision of America's future, Jefferson's or Hamilton's, is most appealing to you? Whose vision was most fully realized? Why did issues of foreign policy plague the United States in the late eighteenth and early nineteenth centuries? How did the fears and hopes of those who belonged to the Federalists and to the Democratic-Republican party differ?

◤ D O C U M E N T S

In Document 1, Thomas Jefferson argues that the future of the United States is best left in the hands of the yeoman farmers, who will retain their virtue and industry. Document 2 is the first law enacted regarding naturalization. Note that it restricts citizenship to free white persons, and consider the impact that this definition might have in the years to come. In Document 3, Alexander Hamilton provides his vision of national development, which is in marked contrast to that of Jefferson. The next four documents illustrate the factional conflict that resulted from these very different visions of the direction of national development. In Document 4, Jefferson, in a letter to an Italian friend, writes of the "Anglican monarchical aristocratical party." Jefferson's friend ultimately made the letter public, and it was printed in American newspapers just as Jefferson was beginning his term as vice president in John Adams's administration. C. William Manning, a yeoman farmer and Jeffersonian, wrote Document 5 in 1798. Manning fears that the power of the few will enable them to subvert the government. Document 6 is a resolution secretly written by Jefferson for the state of Kentucky in response to a series of laws known as the Alien and Sedition Acts. In this resolution, Jefferson argues that the states have the right to say when Congress has exceeded its powers. This idea was destined to be used by other theorists, as we shall see in Chapters 8 and 14. In contrast, Document 7 is the ruling by Chief Justice John Marshall that states that the Constitution is paramount law. Finally, Document 8 illustrates the myth of the Americans and the United States that would develop in the early nineteenth century. Shortly after George Washington's death in 1799, his life was romanticized into one of mythic proportions.

1. Thomas Jefferson Celebrates the Virtue of the Yeoman Farmer, 1785

In Europe the lands are either cultivated, or locked up against the cultivator. Manufacture must therefore be resorted to of necessity not of choice, to support the surplus of their people. But we have an immensity of land courting the industry of the husbandman. Is it best then that all our citizens should be employed in its improvement, or that one half should be called off from that to exercise manufactures and handicraft arts for the other? Those who labor in the earth are the chosen people of God, if ever He had a chosen people, whose breasts He has made His peculiar deposit for substantial and genuine virtue. It is the focus in which he keeps alive that sacred fire, which otherwise might escape from the face of the earth. Corruption of morals in the mass of cultivators is a phenomenon of which no age nor nation has furnished an example. It is the mark set on those, who, not looking up to heaven, to their own soil and industry, as does the husbandman, for their subsistence, depend for it on casualties and caprice of customers. Dependence begets subservience and venality, suffocates the germ of virtue, and prepares fit tools for the designs of ambition. This, the natural progress and consequence of the arts, has sometimes perhaps been retarded by accidental circumstances; but, generally speaking, the proportion which the aggregate of the other classes of citizens bears in any State to that of its husbandmen, is the proportion of its unsound to its healthy parts, and is a good enough barometer whereby to measure its degree of corruption. While we have land to labor then, let us never wish to see our citizens occupied at a workbench, or twirling a distaff. Carpenters, masons, smiths, are wanting in husbandry; but, for the general operations of manufacture, let our workshops remain in Europe. It is better to carry provisions and materials to workmen there, than bring them to the provisions and materials, and with them their manners and principles. The loss by the transportation of commodities across the Atlantic will be made up in happiness and permanence of government. The mobs of great cities add just so much to the support of pure government, as sores do to the strength of the human body.

Thomas Jefferson, *Notes on the State of Virginia,* 1785, in *The Life and Selected Writings of Thomas Jefferson,* ed. Adrienne Koch and William Peden (New York: Library of America, 1984), 280.

2. Congress Establishes Its First Policy for Naturalization, 1790

SECTION 1. *Be it enacted by the Senate and House of Representatives of the United States of America in Congress assembled,* That any alien, being a free white person, who shall have resided within the limits and under the jurisdiction of the United States for the term of two years, may be admitted to become a citizen thereof, on application to any common law court of record, in any one of the states wherein he shall have resided for the term of one year at least, and making proof to the satisfaction of such court, that he is a person of good character, and taking the oath or affirmation prescribed by law, to support the constitution of the United States, which oath or affirmation such court shall administer; and the clerk of such court shall record such application, and the proceedings thereon; and thereupon such person shall be considered as a citizen of the United States. And the children of such persons so naturalized, dwelling within the United States, being under the age of twenty-one years at the time of such naturalization, shall also be considered as citizens of the United States. And the children of citizens of the United States, that may be born beyond sea, or out of the limits of the United States, shall be considered as natural born citizens: *Provided,* That the right of citizenship shall not descend to persons whose fathers have never been resident in the United States: *Provided also,* That no person heretofore proscribed by any state, shall be admitted a citizen as aforesaid, except by an act of the legislature of the state in which such person was proscribed.

APPROVED, March 26, 1790.

3. Alexander Hamilton Envisions a Developed American Economy, 1791

It is now proper to proceed a step further, and to enumerate the principal circumstances, from which it may be inferred—That manufacturing establishments not only occasion a positive augmentation of the Produce and Revenue of the Society, but that they contribute essentially to rendering them greater than they could possibly be, without such establishments. These circumstances are—

1. The division of Labour.
2. An extension of the use of Machinery.
3. Additional employment to classes of the community not ordinarily engaged in the business.
4. The promoting of emigration from foreign Countries.
5. The furnishing greater scope for the diversity of talents and dispositions which discriminate men from each other.

Naturalization Act of 1790, Statutes at Large of the United States of America 1789–1873, 1 (First Cong., 2d sess.), 103.

Alexander Hamilton, *Report on Manufactures* (1791), in Samuel McKee, Jr., ed., *Alexander Hamilton's Papers on Public Credit, Commerce and Finance* (New York: The Liberal Arts Press, 1934), 190–192, 195–199.

6. The affording a more ample and various field for enterprize.
7. The creating in some instances a new, and securing in all, a more certain and steady demand for the surplus produce of the soil.

Each of these circumstances has a considerable influence upon the total mass of industrious effort in a community. Together, they add to it a degree of energy and effect, which are not easily conceived. Some comments upon each of them, in the order in which they have been stated, may serve to explain their importance.

I. As to the Division of Labour.

It has justly been observed, that there is scarcely any thing of greater moment in the œconomy of a nation, than the proper division of labour. The separation of occupations causes each to be carried to a much greater perfection, than it could possible acquire, if they were blended. This arises principally from three circumstances.

1st—The greater skill and dexterity naturally resulting from a constant and undivided application to a single object. . . .

2nd. The œconomy of time—by avoiding the loss of it, incident to a frequent transition from one operation to another of a different nature. . . .

3rd. An extension of the use of Machinery. A man occupied on a single object will have it more in his power, and will be more naturally led to exert his imagination in devising methods to facilitate and abrige labour, than if he were perplexed by a variety of independent and dissimilar operations. . . .

And from these causes united, the mere separation of the occupation of the cultivator, from that of the Artificer, has the effect of augmenting the *productive powers* of labour, and with them, the total mass of the produce or revenue of a Country. In this single view of the subject, therefore, the utility of Artificers or Manufacturers, towards promoting an increase of productive industry, is apparent.

II. As to an extension of the use of Machinery a point which though partly anticipated requires to be placed in one or two additional lights.

The employment of Machinery forms an item of great importance in the general mass of national industry. 'Tis an artificial force brought in aid of the natural force of man; and, to all the purposes of labour, is an increase of hands; an accession of strength, *unincumbered too by the expence of maintaining the laborer.* May it not therefore be fairly inferred, that those occupations, which give greatest scope to the use of this auxiliary, contribute most to the general Stock of industrious effort, and, in consequence, to the general product of industry? . . .

If there be anything in a remark often to be met with—namely that there is, in the genius of the people of this country, a peculiar aptitude for mechanic improvements, it would operate as a forcible reason for giving opportunities to the exercise of that species of talent, by the propagation of manufactures.

VI. As to the affording a more ample and various field for enterprise.

. . . To cherish and stimulate the activity of the human mind, by multiplying the objects of enterprise, is not among the least considerable of the expedients, by which the wealth of a nation may be promoted. Even things in themselves not positively advantageous, sometimes become so, by their tendency to provoke exertion. Every new scene, which is opened to the busy nature of man to rouse and exert itself, is the addition of a new energy to the general stock of effort.

The spirit of enterprise, useful and prolific as it is, must necessarily be contracted or expanded in proportion to the simplicity or variety of the occupations and productions, which are to be found in a Society. It must be less in a nation of mere cultivators, than in a nation of cultivators and merchants; less in a nation of cultivators and merchants, than in a nation of cultivators, artificers and merchants.

VII. As to the creating, in some instances, a new, and securing in all a more certain and steady demand, for the surplus produce of the soil.

This is among the most important of the circumstances which have been indicated. It is a principal mean, by which the establishment of manufactures contributes to an augmentation of the produce or revenue of a country, and has an immediate and direct relation to the prosperity of Agriculture.

It is evident, that the exertions of the husbandman will be steady or fluctuating, vigorous or feeble, in proportion to the steadiness or fluctuation, adequateness, or inadequateness of the markets on which he must depend, for the vent of the surplus, which may be produced by his labour; and that such surplus in the ordinary course of things will be greater or less in the same proportion.

For the purpose of this vent, a domestic market is greatly to be preferred to a foreign one; because it is in the nature of things, far more to be relied upon.

It is a primary object of the policy of nations, to be able to supply themselves with subsistence from their own soils; and manufacturing nations, as far as circumstances permit, endeavor to procure, from the same source, the raw materials necessary for their own fabrics. This disposition, urged by the spirit of monopoly, is sometimes even carried to an injudicious extreme. It seems not always to be recollected, that nations, who have neither mines nor manufactures, can only obtain the manufactured articles, of which they stand in need, by an exchange of the products of their soils; and that, if those who can best furnish them with such articles are unwilling to give a due course to this exchange, they must of necessity make every possible effort to manufacture for themselves, the effect of which is that the manufacturing nations abrige the natural advantages of their situation, through an unwillingness to permit the Agricultural countries to enjoy the advantages of theirs, and sacrifice the interests of a mutually beneficial intercourse to the vain project of *selling every thing* and *buying nothing.*

But it is also a consequence of the policy, which has been noted, that the foreign demand for the products of Agricultural Countries, is, in a great degree, rather casual and occasional, than certain or constant. To what extent injurious interruptions of the demand for some of the staple commodities of the United States, may have been experienced, from that cause, must be referred to the judgment of those who are engaged in carrying on the commerce of the country; but it may be safely assumed, that such interruptions are at times very inconveniently felt, and that cases not unfrequently occur, in which markets are so confined and restricted, as to render the demand very unequal to the supply.

Independently likewise of the artificial impediments, which are created by the policy in question, there are natural causes tending to render the external demand for the surplus of Agricultural nations a precarious reliance. The differences of seasons, in the countries, which are the consumers make immense differences in the produce of their own soils, in different years; and consequently in the degrees of their necessity for foreign supply. Plentiful harvests with them, especially if similar ones occur at the same time in the countries, which are the furnishers, occasion of course a glut in the markets of the latter.

Considering how fast and how much the progress of new settlements in the United States must increase the surplus produce of the soil, and weighing seriously the tendency of the system, which prevails among most of the commercial nations of Europe; whatever dependence may be placed on the force of natural circumstances to counteract the effects of an artificial policy; there appear strong reasons to regard the foreign demand for that surplus as too uncertain a reliance, and to desire a substitute for it, in an extensive domestic market.

To secure such a market, there is no other expedient, than to promote manufacturing establishments. Manufacturers who constitute the most numerous class, after the Cultivators of land, are for that reason the principal consumers of the surplus of their labour.

This idea of an extensive domestic market for the surplus produce of the soil is of the first consequence. It is of all things, that which most effectually conduces to a flourishing state of Agriculture. If the effect of manufactories should be to detatch a portion of the hands, which would otherwise be engaged in Tillage, it might possibly cause a smaller quantity of lands to be under cultivation but by their tendency to procure a more certain demand for the surplus produce of the soil, they would, at the same time, cause the lands which were in cultivation to be better improved and more productive. And while, by their influence, the condition of each individual farmer would be meliorated, the total mass of Agricultural production would probably be increased. For this must evidently depend as much, if not more, upon the degree of improvement; than upon the number of acres under culture.

It merits particular observation, that the multiplication of manufactories not only furnishes a Market for those articles, which have been accustomed to be produced in abundance, in a country; but it likewise creates a demand for such as were either unknown or produced in inconsiderable quantities. The bowels as well as the surface of the earth are ransacked for articles which were before neglected. Animals, Plants and Minerals acquire an utility and value, which were before unexplored.

The foregoing considerations seem sufficient to establish, as general propositions, That it is the interest of nations to diversify the industrious pursuits of the individuals, who compose them—That the establishment of manufactures is calculated not only to increase the general stock of useful and productive labour; but even to improve the state of Agriculture in particular; certainly to advance the interests of those who are engaged in it.

4. Thomas Jefferson Berates the Federalists, 1796

Monticello, April 24, 1796

. . . The aspect of our politics has wonderfully changed since you left us. In place of that noble love of liberty and republican government which carried us triumphantly through the war, an Anglican monarchical aristocratical party has sprung up, whose avowed object is to draw over us the substance, as they have already done the forms,

Thomas Jefferson's Letter to Philip Mazzei (1796). Obtained from http://www.stockton.edu/~gilmorew/ Ocolhis/v1790-26.htm. This document is also available in *The Writings of Thomas Jefferson*, vol. 3 (Boston, Gray and Bower, 1830).

of the British government. The main body of our citizens, however, remain true to their republican principles; the whole landed interest is republican, and so is a great mass of talents. Against us are the Executive, the Judiciary, two out of three branches of the Legislature, all the officers of the government, all who want to be officers, all timid men who prefer the calm of despotism to the boisterous sea of liberty, British merchants and American trading on British capital, speculators and holders in the banks and public funds, a contrivance invented for the purposes of corruption, and for assimilating us in all things to the rotten as well as the sound parts of the British model. It would give you a fever were I to name to you the apostates who have gone over to these heresies, men who were Samsons in the field and Solomons in the council, but who have had their heads shorn by the harlot England. In short, we are likely to preserve the liberty we have obtained only by unremitting labors and perils. But we shall preserve it; and our mass of weight and wealth on the good side is so great, as to leave no danger that force will ever be attempted against us. We have only to awake and snap the Lilliputian cords [that bound Gulliver on Lilliput in Swift's *Gulliver's Travels*] with which they have been entangling us during the first sleep which succeeded our labors.

5. C. William Manning, a Republican, Fears for the Future of the Nation, 1798

In the sweat of thy face shalt thou get thy bread, until thou return to the ground, is the irreversible sentence of Heaven on man for his rebellion. To be sentenced to hard labor during life is very unpleasant to human nature. There is a great aversion to it perceivable in all men; yet it is absolutely necessary that a large majority of the world should labor, or we could not subsist. For labor is the sole parent of all property; the land yields nothing without it, and there is no . . . necessary of life but what costs labor and is generally esteemed valuable according to the labor it costs. Therefore, no person can possess property without laboring unless he gets it by force or craft, fraud or fortune, out of the earnings of others.

But from the great variety of capacities, strength, and abilities of men, there always was and always will be a very unequal distribution of property in the world. Many are so rich that they can live without labor—also the merchant, physician, lawyer, and divine, the philosopher and schoolmaster, the judicial and executive officers, and many others who could honestly get a living without bodily labors. As all these professions require a considerable expense of time and property to qualify themselves therefore, . . . so all these professions naturally unite in their schemes to make their callings as honorable and lucrative as possible.

Also, as ease and rest from labor are reasoned among the greatest pleasures of life, pursued by all with the greatest avidity, and when attained at once create a sense of superiority; and as pride and ostentation are natural to the human heart, these orders of men generally associate together and look down with too much contempt on those that labor.

C. William Manning, *The Key of Libberty* (1798). Obtained from http://www.stockton.edu/~gilmorew/ Ocolhis/v1790-26.htm.

As the interests and incomes of the few lie chiefly in money at interest, rents, salaries, and fees, that are fixed on the nominal value of money, they are interested in having money scarce and the price of labor and produce as low as possible. . . .

But the greatest danger the many are under in these money matters is from the judicial and executive officers, especially so as their incomes for a living are almost wholly gotten from the follies and distress of the many—they being governed by the same selfish principles as other men are. They are the most interested in the distresses of the many of any in the nation; the scarcer money is and the greater the distresses of the many are, the better for them. . . .

This is the reason why they ought to be kept entirely from the legislative body; . . . For in all these conceived differences of interests, it is the business and duty of the legislative body to determine what is justice, or what is right and wrong; and it is the duty of every individual in the nation to regulate his conduct according to their decisions. . . .

The reason why a free government has always failed is from the unreasonable demands and desires of the few. They cannot bear to be on a level with their fellow creatures, or submit to the determinations of a legislature where (as they call it) the swinish multitude is fairly represented, but sicken at the idea, and are ever hankering and striving after monarchy or aristocracy, where the people have nothing to do in matters of government but to support the few in luxury and idleness.

For these and many other reasons, a large majority of those that live without labor are ever opposed to the principles and operation of a free government; and though the whole of them do not amount to one-eighth part of the people, yet, by their combinations, arts, and schemes, have always made out to destroy it sooner or later.

6. Thomas Jefferson Advances the Power of the States, 1798

1. *Resolved,* That the several States composing, the United States of America, are not united on the principle of unlimited submission to their general government; but that, by a compact under the style and title of a Constitution for the United States, and of amendments thereto, they constituted a general government for special purposes— delegated to that government certain definite powers, reserving, each State to itself, the residuary mass of right to their own self-government; and that whensoever the general government assumes undelegated powers, its acts are unauthoritative, void, and of no force: that to this compact each State acceded as a State, and is an integral part, its co-States forming, as to itself, the other party: that the government created by this compact was not made the exclusive or final judge of the extent of the powers delegated to itself; since that would have made its discretion, and not the Constitution, the measure of its powers; but that, as in all other cases of compact among powers having no common judge, each party has an equal right to judge for itself, as well of infractions as of the mode and measure of redress.

Thomas Jefferson, *The Kentucky Resolutions of 1798.* Obtained from http://www.constitution.org/ cons/kent1798.htm. Also available in *The Virginia and Kentucky Resolutions, with the Alien Sedition and Other Acts, 1798–1799* (New York: A. Lovell, 1894).

2. *Resolved,* That the Constitution of the United States, having delegated to Congress a power to punish treason, counterfeiting the securities and current coin of the United States, piracies, and felonies committed on the high seas, and offenses against the law of nations, and no other crimes, whatsoever; and it being true as a general principle, and one of the amendments to the Constitution having also declared, that "the powers not delegated to the United States by the Constitution, not prohibited by it to the States, are reserved to the States respectively, or to the people," therefore the act of Congress, passed on the 14th day of July, 1798, and intituled "An Act in addition to the act intituled An Act for the punishment of certain crimes against the United States," as also the act passed by them on the — day of June, 1798, intituled "An Act to punish frauds committed on the bank of the United States," (and all their other acts which assume to create, define, or punish crimes, other than those so enumerated in the Constitution,) are altogether void, and of no force; and that the power to create, define, and punish such other crimes is reserved, and, of right, appertains solely and exclusively to the respective States, each within its own territory.

3. *Resolved,* That it is true as a general principle, and is also expressly declared by one of the amendments to the Constitution, that "the powers not delegated to the United States by the Constitution, nor prohibited by it to the States, are reserved to the States respectively, or to the people"; and that no power over the freedom of religion, freedom of speech, or freedom of the press being delegated to the United States by the Constitution, nor prohibited by it to the States, all lawful powers respecting the same did of right remain, and were reserved to the States or the people: that thus was manifested their determination to retain to themselves the right of judging how far the licentiousness of speech and of the press may be abridged without lessening their useful freedom, and how far those abuses which cannot be separated from their use should be tolerated, rather than the use be destroyed. And thus also they guarded against all abridgment by the United States of the freedom of religious opinions and exercises, and retained to themselves the right of protecting the same, as this State, by a law passed on the general demand of its citizens, had already protected them from all human restraint or interference. And that in addition to this general principle and express declaration, another and more special provision has been made by one of the amendments to the Constitution, which expressly declares, that "Congress shall make no law respecting an establishment of religion, or prohibiting the free exercise thereof, or abridging the freedom of speech or of the press": thereby guarding in the same sentence, and under the same words, the freedom of religion, of speech, and of the press: insomuch, that whatever violated either, throws down the sanctuary which covers the others, and that libels, falsehood, and defamation, equally with heresy and false religion, are withheld from the cognizance of federal tribunals. That, therefore, the act of Congress of the United States, passed on the 14th day of July, 1798, intituled "An Act in addition to the act intituled An Act for the punishment of certain crimes against the United States," which does abridge the freedom of the press, is not law, but is altogether void, and of no force.

4. *Resolved,* That alien friends are under the jurisdiction and protection of the laws of the State wherein they are: that no power over them has been delegated to the United States, nor prohibited to the individual States, distinct from their power over citizens. And it being true as a general principle, and one of the amendments to the Constitution having also declared, that "the powers not delegated to the

United States by the Constitution, nor prohibited by it to the States, are reserved to the States respectively, or to the people," the act of the Congress of the United States, passed on the — day of July, 1798, intituled "An Act concerning aliens," which assumes powers over alien friends, not delegated by the Constitution, is not law, but is altogether void, and of no force.

5. *Resolved,* That in addition to the general principle, as well as the express declaration, that powers not delegated are reserved, another and more special provision, inserted in the Constitution from abundant caution, has declared that "the migration or importation of such persons as any of the States now existing shall think proper to admit, shall not be prohibited by the Congress prior to the year 1808" that this commonwealth does admit the migration of alien friends, described as the subject of the said act concerning aliens: that a provision against prohibiting their migration, is a provision against all acts equivalent thereto, or it would be nugatory: that to remove them when migrated, is equivalent to a prohibition of their migration, and is, therefore, contrary to the said provision of the Constitution, and void.

6. *Resolved,* That the imprisonment of a person under the protection of the laws of this commonwealth, on his failure to obey the simple order of the President to depart out of the United States, as is undertaken by said act intituled "An Act concerning aliens" is contrary to the Constitution, one amendment to which has provided that "no person shalt be deprived of liberty without due progress of law"; and that another having provided that "in all criminal prosecutions the accused shall enjoy the right to public trial by an impartial jury, to be informed of the nature and cause of the accusation, to be confronted with the witnesses against him, to have compulsory process for obtaining witnesses in his favor, and to have the assistance of counsel for his defense;" the same act, undertaking to authorize the President to remove a person out of the United States, who is under the protection of the law, on his own suspicion, without accusation, without jury, without public trial, without confrontation of the witnesses against him, without hearing witnesses in his favor, without defense, without counsel, is contrary to the provision also of the Constitution, is therefore not law, but utterly void, and of no force. . . .

7. *Resolved,* That the construction applied by the General Government (as is evidenced by sundry of their proceedings) to those parts of the Constitution of the United States which delegate to Congress a power "to lay and collect taxes, duties, imports, and excises, to pay the debts, and provide for the common defense and general welfare of the United States," and "to make all laws which shall be necessary and proper for carrying into execution, the powers vested by the Constitution in the government of the United States, or in any department or officer thereof," goes to the destruction of all limits prescribed to their powers by the Constitution. . . .

8. *Resolved,* That a committee of conference and correspondence be appointed, who shall have in charge to communicate the preceding resolutions to the Legislatures of the several States: to assure them that this commonwealth continues in the same esteem of their friendship and union which it has manifested from that moment at which a common danger first suggested a common union: that it considers union, for specified national purposes, and particularly to those specified in their late federal compact, to be friendly, to the peace, happiness and prosperity of all the States: that faithful to that compact, according to the plain intent and meaning in which it was understood and acceded to by the several parties, it is sincerely anxious for its

preservation: that it does also believe, that to take from the States all the powers of self-government and transfer them to a general and consolidated government, without regard to the special delegations and reservations solemnly agreed to in that compact, is not for the peace, happiness or prosperity of these States; . . . that every State has a natural right in cases not within the compact, (*casus non fœderis*) to nullify of their own authority all assumptions of power by others within their limits: that without this right, they would be under the dominion, absolute and un-limited, of whosoever might exercise this right of judgment for them: that neverthe-less, this commonwealth, from motives of regard and respect for its co States, has wished to communicate with them on the subject: that with them alone it is proper to communicate, they alone being parties to the compact, and solely authorized to judge in the last resort of the powers exercised under it, Congress being not a party, but merely the creature of the compact, and subject as to its assumptions of power to the final judgment of those by whom, and for whose use itself and its powers were all created and modified; . . . free government is founded in jealousy, and not in confidence; it is jealousy and not confidence which prescribes limited constitutions, to bind down those whom we are obliged to trust with power: that our Constitution has accordingly fixed the limits to which, and no further, our confidence may go; and let the honest advocate of confidence read the Alien and Sedition acts, and say if the Constitution has not been wise in fixing limits to the government it created, and whether we should be wise in destroying those limits, Let him say what the government is, if it be not a tyranny, which the men of our choice have conferred on our President, and the President of our choice has assented to, and accepted over the friendly stranger to whom the mild spirit of our country and its law have pledged hospitality and protection: that the men of our choice have more respected the bare suspicion of the President, than the solid right of innocence, the claims of justification, the sacred force of truth, and the forms and substance of law and jus-tice. In questions of powers, then, let no more be heard of confidence in man, but bind him down from mischief by the chains of the Constitution. That this commonwealth does therefore call on its co-States for an expression of their sentiments on the acts concerning aliens and for the punishment of certain crimes herein before specified, plainly declaring whether these acts are or are not authorized by the federal compact. And it doubts not that their sense will be so announced as to prove their attachment unaltered to limited government, whether general or particular. And that the rights and liberties of their co-States will be exposed to no dangers by remaining embarked in a common bottom with their own. That they will concur with this commonwealth in considering the said acts as so palpably against the Constitution as to amount to an undisguised declaration that that compact is not meant to be the measure of the powers of the General Government, but that it will proceed in the exercise over these States, of all powers whatsoever: that they will view this as seizing the rights of the States, and consolidating them in the hands of the General Government, with a power assumed to bind the States (not merely as the cases made federal, casus fœderis but), in all cases whatsoever, by laws made, not with their consent, but by others against their consent: that this would be to surrender the form of government we have chosen, and live under one deriving its powers from its own will, and not from our authority; and that the co-States, recurring to their natural right in cases not made federal, will concur in declaring these acts void, and of no force, and will each take measures of its own for providing that neither these acts, nor any others of the General Government not plainly and intentionally authorized by the Constitution, shalt be exercised within their respective territories.

7. John Marshall Argues for the Primacy of the Federal Government, 1803

The question whether an act repugnant to the constitution can become the law of the land, is a question deeply interesting to the United States. . . . That the people have an original right to establish for their future government such principles as, in their opinion, shall most conduce to their own happiness, is the basis on which the whole American fabric has been erected. . . .

This original and supreme will organizes the government, and assigns to different departments their respective powers. It may either stop here or establish limits not to be transcended by those departments.

The government of the United States is of the latter description. The powers of the legislature are defined and limited; and that those limits may not be mistaken or forgotten, the constitution is written. . . . The distinction between a government with limited and unlimited powers is abolished if those limits do not confine the persons on whom they are imposed and if acts prohibited and acts allowed are of equal obligation. It is a proposition too plain to be contested, that the constitution controls any legislative act repugnant to it; or, that the legislature may alter the constitution by an ordinary act. Between these alternatives there is no middle ground. . . .

Certainly all those who have framed written constitutions contemplate them as forming the fundamental and paramount law of the nation, and consequently the theory of every such government must be that an act of the legislature repugnant to the Constitution is void.

This theory is essentially attached to a written constitution, and is consequently to be considered, by this court as one of the fundamental principles of our society. . . .

The Constitution is either a superior, paramount law, unchangeable by ordinary means, or it is on a level with ordinary legislative acts, and, like other acts, is alterable when the legislature shall please to alter it.

If the former part of the alternative be true, then a legislative act contrary to the Constitution is not law: if the latter part be true, then written Constitutions are absurd attempts, on the part of the people, to limit a power in its own nature illimitable. . . .

It is emphatically the province and duty of the judicial department to say what the law is. Those who apply the rule to particular cases, must of necessity expound and interpret that rule. If two laws conflict with each other, the courts must decide on the operation of each. . . .

If, then, the courts are to regard the Constitution, and the Constitution is superior to any ordinary act of the legislature, the Constitution, and not such ordinary act, must govern the case to which they both apply.

John Marshall, opinion in *Marbury v. Madison* (1803), in *United States Supreme Court Reporters,* vol. 5, p. 137.

8. Parson Weems Romanticizes the Life of George Washington, 1808

"When George," said she, "was about six years old, he was made the wealthy master of a *hatchet!* of which, like most little boys, he was immoderately fond, and was constantly going about chopping every thing that came in his way. One day, in the garden, where he often amused himself hacking his mother's pea-sticks, he unluckily tried the edge of his hatchet on the body of a beautiful young English cherry-tree, which he barked so terribly, that I don't believe the tree ever got the better of it. The next morning the old gentleman finding out what had befallen his tree, which, by the by, was a great favourite, came into the house, and with much warmth asked for the mischievous author, declaring at the same time, that he would not have taken five guineas for his tree. Nobody could tell him any thing about it. Presently George and his hatchet made their appearance. *George,* said his father, *do you know who killed that beautiful little cherry-tree yonder in the garden?* This was a *tough question;* and George staggered under it for a moment; but quickly recovered himself: and looking at his father, with the sweet face of youth brightened with the inexpressible charm of all-conquering truth, he bravely cried out, "*I can't tell a lie, Pa; you know I can't tell a lie. I did cut it with my hatchet.*"—*Run to my arms, you dearest boy*, cried his father in transports, *run to my arms; glad am I, George, that you killed my tree; for you have paid me for it a thousand fold. Such an act of heroism in my son, is more worth than a thousand trees, though blossomed with silver, and their fruits of purest gold.* . . .

To be happy in every situation is an argument of wisdom seldom attained by man. It proves that the heart is set on that which alone can ever completely satisfy it, i.e. the imitation of God in benevolent and useful life. This was the happy case with Washington. To establish in his country the golden reign of liberty was his grand wish. In the accomplishment of this he seeks his happiness. He abhors war; but, if war be necessary, to this end he bravely encounters it. His ruling passion must be obeyed. He beats his ploughshare into a sword, and exchanges the peace and pleasures of his farm for the din and dangers of the camp. Having won the great prize for which he contended, he returns to his plough. His military habits are laid by with the same ease as he would throw off an old coat. . . . Happy among his domestics, he does not regret the shining ranks, that, with ported arms used to pay him homage. The *useful citizen* is the high character he wishes to act—his sword turned into a ploughshare is his favourite instrument, and his beloved farm his stage. Agriculture had been always his delight. To breathe the *pure healthful* air of a *farm,* perfumed with odorous flowers, and enriched with golden harvests, and with numerous flocks and herds, appeared to him a life nearest connected with individual and national happiness. . . .

But, to a soul large and benevolent like his, to beautify his own farm, and to enrich his own family, seemed like doing nothing. To see the whole nation engaged in glorious toils, filling themselves with plenty, and inundating the sea-ports with food and raiment for the poor and needy of distant nations—this was his godlike ambition.

M[ason] L[ocke] Weems, *The Life of George Washington the Great: Enriched with a Number of Very Curious* . . . (Augusta, Ga.: Geo. P. Randolph, 1806), Early American Imprints, 2d ser., no. 11844.

But, knowing that his beloved countrymen could not long enjoy the honor and advantage of such glorious toils, unless they could easily convey their swelling harvests to their *own markets,* he hastened to rouse them to a proper sense of the infinite importance of forming canals and cuts between all the fine rivers that run through the United States. To give the greater weight to his counsel, he had first ascended the *sources* of those great rivers—ascertained the distance between them—the obstacles in the way of navigation—and the probable expense of removing them.

Agreeable to his wishes, two wealthy companies were soon formed to extend the navigation of James River and Potomac, the noblest rivers in Virginia. Struck with the exceeding benefit which both themselves and their country would speedily derive from a plan which he had not only suggested, but had taken such pains and expense to recommend, they pressed him to accept one hundred and fifty shares of the company's stock, amounting to near 40,000 dollars! But he instantly refused it, saying, "what will the world think if they should hear that I have taken 40,000 dollars for this affair? Will they not be apt to suspect, on my next proposition, that money is my motive? Thus, for the sake of money, which indeed I never coveted from my country, I may lose the power to do her some service, which may be worth more than all money!!"

But, while engaged in this goodly work, he was suddenly alarmed by the appearance of an evil, which threatened to put an end to all his well-meant labours for ever—this was, the *beginning dissolution* of the federal government!! The framers of that fair but flimsy fabric, having put it together according to the square and compass of equal rights and mutual interests, thought they had done enough. The good sense and virtue of the nation, it was supposed, would form a foundation of rock whereon it would safely rest, in spite of all commotions, foreign or domestic.

"But, alas!" said Washington, "experience has shown that men, unless constrained, will seldom do what is for their own good. . . . America is herself rushing into disorder and dissolution. We have powers sufficient for self-defence and glory: but those powers are not exerted. For fear congress should abuse it, the people will not trust their power with congress. Foreigners insult and injure us with impunity, for congress has no power to chastise them.—Ambitious men stir up factions; congress possesses no power to scourge them. Public creditors call for their money; congress has no power to collect it. In short, we cannot long subsist as a nation, without lodging somewhere a power that may command the full energies of the nation for defence from all its enemies, and for supply of all its wants. The people will soon be tired of such a government—they will sigh for a change—and many of them already begin to talk of *monarchy,* without horror!!"

In this, as in all cases of apprehended danger, his pen knew no rest. The leading characters of the nation were roused; and a CONVENTION was formed of deputies from the several states, to revise and amend the general government. Of this convention Washington was unanimously chosen president.—Their session commenced in Philadelphia, May, 1787, and ended in October. The fruit of their six months labour was the present excellent CONSTITUTION, which was no sooner adopted, than the eyes of the whole nation were fixed on him as the president.

Being now in his 57th year, and wedded to his farm and family, he had no wish to come forward again to the cares and dangers of public life. Ease was now become almost as necessary as dear to him. His reputation was already at the highest; and as to money, in the service of his country he had always refused it. These things considered, together with his acknowledged modesty and disinterestedness, we can hardly doubt the correctness of the declaration he made, when he said, that, *"the call to the magistracy was the most unwelcome he had ever heard."*

However, as soon as it was officially notified to him, in the spring of 1789, that he was unanimously elected president of the United States, and that congress, then sitting in New-York, was impatient to see him in the chair, he set out for that city. Then all along the roads where he passed, were seen the most charming proofs of that enthusiasm with which the hearts of all delighted to honour him. If it was only said, *"General Washington is coming,"* it was enough. The inhabitants all hastened from their houses to the highways, to get a sight of their great countryman.

E S S A Y S

It is difficult for us today to understand how fragile a republic the United States was in the late eighteenth and early nineteenth centuries. Political divisions and economic weaknesses plagued the new nation, and many European powers doubted whether the United States as a nation would survive. As American leaders grappled with the weaknesses that beset their nation, they differed on its most serious flaws. The following essays illustrate the leaders' differing perceptions of the dangers that the United States faced and their prescriptions for addressing these dangers. They focus less on the debates of modern historians than on the differences between those people in the early nineteenth century who created the first political party system. Linda Kerber, professor of history at the University of Iowa, describes the quandaries of the Federalists, a political party whose members feared that popular democracy might spin out of control. While they fostered economic development they were well aware that an urban proletariat would result. As a result, they sought a stability that would temper these developments. Drew McCoy, a historian who teaches at Clark University, explores the dilemmas of the Jeffersonian Republicans. Focusing on the ideas of Jefferson, McCoy illustrates how the Republicans, like their Federalist antagonists, perceived challenges for the future of the United States. Fearful of creating a dependent class, Jefferson set his sights westward, where he envisioned vast tracts of land being farmed by virtuous citizens of the young republic.

The Fears of the Federalists

LINDA K. KERBER

"Little whirlwinds of dry leaves and dirt portend a hurricane," warned Fisher Ames. The Federalist saw these little whirlwinds everywhere in America: in the ineffectuality of Jeffersonian foreign policy, in the willingness to embark on projects as unpredictable as the acquisition of Louisiana, in Jeffersonian expressions of confidence in the political amateur. As the Federalist read his current events, one after another of the sources of cultural stability was being undermined by Jeffersonian enthusiasms:

by the shift in the grounds and goals of scientific inquiry, by the rejection of the classical curriculum, and by what was believed to be a hostility to the institutions of social order, manifested by the revision of the judiciary system and the subsequent impeachment of judges.

The Jeffersonian approach to politics struck the articulate Federalists as dangerously naive. The optimism, the ready professions of faith in popular democracy, seemed to mask a failure to comprehend the ambivalence of the American social order. To these Federalists, American society, for all its surface stability and prosperity, was torn by internal contradiction. A population which had proved its capacity for revolutionary violence would not necessarily remain tranquil in the future. Moreover, even the early stages of industrialization and urban growth were providing the ingredients of a proletariat; there already existed a volatile class of permanently poor who, it was feared, might well be available for mob action. Finally, the expectation that the republic might deteriorate into demagogery and anarchy was given intellectual support by the widely accepted contemporary definitions of what popular democracy was and the conditions necessary to its stability. "I assure you," Jonathan Jackson told John Lowell, Jr., "that I feel quite satisfied in having had to pass through one Revolution. One is full enough for mortal man." It was a common Federalist fear that the Jeffersonians were insufficiently conscious of the precariousness of revolutionary accomplishments, and that this laxity might well prove disastrous. . . .

The expectation of violence and disintegration permeated Federalist political conversation in the opening years of the nineteenth century. "The power of the people, if uncontrolled, is . . . mobbish," remarked Fisher Ames in 1802. "It is a gov't by force without discipline." When Thomas Boylston Adams undertook to follow his brother John Quincy's advice and reread Xenophon, he expected no surprises: "The Athenians doubtless afford an excellent example of the *violence* to which a Democratic government necessarily leads a people." Josiah Quincy's Slaveslap Kiddnap proclaimed his vision of "the tempestuous sea of liberty":

> now tossing its proud waves to the skies, and hurling defiance toward the throne of the almighty; now sinking into its native abyss, and opening to view its unhallowed caverns, the dark abodes of filth and falsehood, and rapine and wretchedness. . . . From the top of Monticello, by the side of the great Jefferson, I have watched its wild uproar, while we philosophised together on its sublime horrors. There, safe from the surge . . . I have quaffed the high crowned cup to this exhilarating toast—TO YON TEMPESTUOUS SEA OF LIBERTY . . . MAY IT NEVER BE CALM.

H. L. Mencken once distinguished two varieties of democrats—those who see liberty primarily as the right of self-government, and those who see it primarily as the right to rebel against governors. American political theory usually denies the necessity to choose between the two options, but in the early years of the republic it was widely assumed that a choice had to be made. The former concept, of "positive" liberty, or the freedom to follow a "higher" pattern of behavior, has its analogues in Puritan thought, and is comparable to the elitist definition of the social order which many Americans, perhaps the majority, held in the half-century following 1770. The widespread assumption among Federalists that their opponents espoused the alternate concept of "negative" liberty, or individual immunity from restraint, was derived in part from some of the better-known Jeffersonian aphorisms, but it was also based on the Federalists' own experience. Primarily, it reflects their sense of the precariousness of the American social order. . . . All around them, the Federalists of the Old Republic saw familiar social habits decaying. The most obvious sign of changing social balances was the decline of deferential behavior. After the social dislocations of the 1770's and 1780's fewer people had a pedigree of gentility and fewer still were willing to recognize such pedigrees where they existed. Surely there had always been in America egalitarians who refused to defer to their social superiors: the Quakers, for example, or the unchurched men and women who had accompanied John Winthrop to Boston and had made it so difficult for him and his associates to establish the tightly structured community of which they had dreamed. The egalitarian current of the Revolutionary era turned exceptions to the rule into harbingers of a trend; by the first decade of the nineteenth century, gentlefolk all over the nation, except perhaps in the South, were complaining that they were treated with far less respect and awe than they were accustomed to. Men who saw sullen or, at best, bland countenances where formerly they had received broad smiles and a bow, took the sullenness as a personal affront. Their insistence that America possessed the social ingredients for a "mobocracy" may have been something of a rhetorical overstatement, but it was not mere fulmination: people who would not defer to anyone seemed unpredictable and capable of "mobbishness." . . .

The republic itself had been born in turbulence; that their nation had been created by rebellion and seccession was never far from the Federalist mind. Eighteenth-century America had been a society in which violence was endemic; as Howard Mumford Jones has recently reminded us, mob action was common during the revolutionary era. "American mobs were amenable to cunning leadership, sometimes disguised, sometimes demagogic; they pillaged, robbed, destroyed property, defied law, interfered with the normal course of justice, legislation, and administration, occasionally inflicted physical injuries." After the Revolution, similar violence was experienced in Boston, New Haven, Philadelphia, Charleston. It may well be that Shays' Rebellion was, in contemporary context, an anomaly; as one of the few episodes in which mob violence was forcibly resisted by a state legislature, Shays' Rebellion is merely better remembered than the numerous other occasions on which legislatures were more easily intimidated. Americans were not necessarily more temperate than their French contemporaries; since they met less resistance from constituted authority, they may simply have felt less need for extreme action.

The national government, only a dozen years old when Jefferson took office, was daily insulted, at home and abroad, by men who acted as though the republic were merely a temporary expedient. The Articles of Confederation, after all, had been in force for a dozen years before they had been abandoned; there was no guarantee in 1800 that the document which replaced the Articles would have a longer life. The federal government was insulted by the British, who had refused to honor all the terms of the Peace of 1783 until required to by the Jay Treaty; by the French, whose regular seizure of American shipping resulted in a "Quasi-War," and even by the Dey of Algiers, whose Barbary pirates exacted regular tribute. It was insulted at home by men who similarly refused to regard the new government as permanently established. Critics of national policies habitually spoke as though the Union did not deserve to survive; a threat of secession was a standard response of the frustrated politician. When William Blount thought he was being permitted to wield too little power in North Carolina, he attempted to arrange for the secession of the Western Territory; when Virginia objected to the Alien and Sedition Acts, she made sure her protests would be listened to by including a veiled threat of secession. Secession was the response of a group of New England Federalists to the prediction of Jefferson's re-election in 1804, of Aaron Burr to his isolated position after the Hamilton duel. And all through the early national period, the nation was insulted by men who seemed to cherish democracy primarily as a guarantee of their right of rebellion. The best known of these insults had been the violent demonstrations headed by the "whiskey rebels" and by John Fries, but there were many other occasions of riot in the early years of the republic. These riotous demonstrations generally accomplished little, but they are not unimportant; Federalists worried about them because they provided evidence that Americans had not lost the capacity for violence which they had demonstrated during the Revolution. "If there is no country possessed of more liberty than our own," the *Palladium* remarked, "there is probably none where there are more formidable indications of the error, prejudice and turbulence that will render it insecure." The nation had malcontents enough for Gouverneur Morris to conclude: "There is a moral tendency, and in some cases even a physical disposition, among the people of this country to overturn the Government. . . . The habits of monarchic government are not yet worn away among our native citizens, and therefore the opposition to lawful authority is frequently considered as a generous effort of patriotic virtue." The Whiskey Boys, Fries, the men who successively raised and tore down liberty poles in New England as late as 1798, made it impossible for Federalists to relax in Arcadia. They could not assume that the New World would escape the disastrous cycle of European history; they could not assume that the pastoral landscape of the Old Republic, settled by contented yeomen, would not be replaced by the congested landscape of the Old World, occupied by malcontented *canaille.*

There was reason to fear that the capacity of the American people for mobbishness was increasing. One analysis of the American scene which Federalists found almost disarmingly appropriate had been provided, ironically enough, by Thomas Jefferson as early as 1787. The passage appears in *Notes on Virginia,* and follows Jefferson's famous remark that "Those who labour in the earth are the chosen people of God, if ever he had a chosen people." Jefferson goes on to explain the contrast he had in mind and the reasons for his preference for the husbandman:

> Dependence begets subservience and venality, suffocates the germ of virtue, and prepares fit tools for the designs of ambition. . . . The mobs of great cities add just so much to the support of pure government, as sores do to the strength of the human body. It is the manners and spirit of a people which preserve a republic in vigour. A degeneracy in these is a canker which soon eats to the heart of its laws and constitution.

Jefferson could easily have found Federalists to agree with his statement, point by point. They would have changed the application from prediction to statement of fact, and they would not have limited their fear to "the mobs of great cities"; rather, mobbishness was a quality of which the Federalist feared all were capable. But they would have agreed that the urban poor were particularly restless, and they would have added that there seemed to be increasing numbers of poor people in America. Boston had slums by 1810; New York's seventh ward was swampy, stagnant and an unhealthy slum as early as the 1790's. Poor people were, by eighteenth-century definition, dependent on those who had jobs to offer and salaries to pay; the "manners and spirit" of the economically dependent, it was feared, could not possibly be as stalwart as those of the independent and self-sufficient yeoman. "You would never look at men and boys in workshops," said the Maryland Federalist Philip Barton Key, "for that virtue and spirit in defense [of the nation against an aggressor] that you would justly expect from the yeomanry of the country."

Now it is true enough that early America was an agricultural country; nine out of ten of her citizens still worked the land. But . . . [t]he noble husbandman [writes historian Leo Marx] is a mythical image, not a description of sociological reality: "He is the good shepherd of the old pastoral dressed in American homespun." Both shepherd and yeoman are models of beings who live in a [world] from which economic pressures are absent. The self-sufficient yeoman on the family-sized farm seeks not prosperity and wealth, but stability, "a virtual stasis that is a counterpart of the desired psychic balance or peace." Only in a world like his, free of economic tension, can the omission of a class structure seem believable. The image is mythical because it ignores economic fact; it draws life from the assumption that Americans could live independent of the international marketplace. Suppose one should deny the possibility; what then becomes of the image? "Let our workshops remain in Europe," Jefferson had counseled. "It is better to carry provisions and materials to workmen there, than bring them to the provisions and materials, and with them their manners and principles. The loss by the transportation of commodities across the Atlantic will be made up in happiness and permanence of government." But America's workshops were not to remain in Europe. The men who counseled agricultural self-sufficiency, Fisher Ames sneered, were themselves "clad in English broadcloth and Irish linen, . . . import their conveniences from England, and their politics from France. It is solemnly pronounced as the only wise policy for a country, where the children multiply faster than the sheep." Although the major boom in American industrialization is generally dated 1830–1865, it was rapidly becoming apparent in the early years of the nineteenth century—and to men like Tench Coxe and Alexander Hamilton and Oliver Wolcott much earlier—that the nation's destiny lay with the machine. It was inescapably obvious that with the machine would come further changes in the quality of American social life, changes in "manners and spirit."

Consciousness of the nation's industrial destiny may be said to have begun with Alexander Hamilton's great "Report on Manufactures" of 1791, the same year in which Samuel Slater began the operation of his spinning mill in Pawtucket. But American manufactures did not start with Slater; Hamilton's correspondence as he requested information for the Report reveals that manufacturing operations were already extensive. The social structure of the United States, however, seemed ill-suited to the development of an industrial society; available land, prosperous commerce, the heavy demand for handcrafted items meant that few men would be content to remain day laborers. How to industrialize without workers? To this question Hamilton offered three comments: first, the increased efficiency of machinery would enable it eventually to *replace* human hands, thus cutting the need for labor to a great extent; second, new hands could be encouraged to emigrate to America; and finally, more extensive use could be made of an as yet barely tapped source of labor. In England, Hamilton explained, "all the different processes for spinning cotton, are performed by . . . machines, which are put in motion by water, and attended chiefly by women and children."

Hamilton was not the progenitor of child labor in America; he was endorsing a trend, not initiating one. To get the information on which the Report was based, he had instructed Treasury agents throughout the country to report to him on the state of manufactures in their area; they, in turn, polled local businessmen and sent their letters on to the Secretary of the Treasury. The information thus collected showed that child labor was already extensive in certain segments of the economy: in yarn manufacture, in cotton and woolcarding, and in the making of nails. By 1803, Oliver Wolcott was finding it difficult to recruit boys to work in his cousin's nail factory, not because children were not working, but the contrary: "Children who have health and are not utterly depraved in their morals," he explained, "are worth money and can easily find employment." Samuel Slater's factory opened with nine workers—seven boys and two girls, none older than twelve years; the youngest was seven. When, in 1801, Josiah Quincy visited one of Slater's mills, he found that the machinery was tended by over a hundred children from four to ten years old, under a single supervisor, who were paid from 12 to 25 cents a day. "Our attendant was very eloquent," Quincy remarked in his diary, "on the usefulness of the manufacture, and the employment it supplied for so many poor children. But an eloquence was exerted on the other side of the question more commanding than his, which called us to pity these little creatures, plying in a contracted room, among flyers and cogs, at an age when nature requires for them air, space, and sports. There was a dull dejection in the countenances of all of them." The children who worked in the mills did not have air, space, and sports as an option; if they were not in the textile factories they joined the "abundance of poor children" which Noah Webster reported to be wandering about the streets, "clothed in dirty rags, illy educated in every respect." By 1809, the nation's cotton mills employed four thousand workers, of whom thirty-five hundred were women and children under age sixteen. Labor statistics, and especially statistics of child labor for the years before 1820, are very scattered, vague, and impressionistic. But they do indicate that child labor, especially in the textile regions, continued and increased. Typically whole families worked in the mills; the men were paid something less than a living wage, and families made ends meet by adding the labor of wives and children, much as Hamilton had predicted.

The prevalence of woman and child labor in early American industry is generally assessed in the context in which Hamilton had placed it. It is taken as an indication of scarcity of labor, as evidence of an expanding economy which offered most men something better to do than to work as factory operatives. Treated in this manner, child labor is seen almost as an index of American prosperity. All this may be true. But we should not ignore the other social conditions of which child labor may be an index; we should not ignore what it tells us about the men who *were* common laborers, and whose dollar a day salary, which made them the best paid common laborers in the West, did not provide for a family sufficiently so that it did not have to send its children into the mills. An American working class was being formed in the early national period, and while class lines were far more flexible, and living conditions were far better than those prevalent in Europe, they were severe enough. The number of people in the early republic who might be labeled members of a proletariat was relatively small, but the conditions of their lives were grim, for all the open-endedness and social mobility of American life. Men do not live by comparisons, but by the conditions of their own lives.

"The time is not distant when this Country will abound with mechanics & manufacturers who will receive their bread from their employers," Gouverneur Morris had predicted in the Constitutional Convention. Two decades later Morris was sounding like Montesquieu: "The strongest aristocratic Feature in our political organization is that which Democrats are more attached to, the Right of universal Suffrage." Montesquieu had suggested that universal suffrage worked to strengthen the power of the rich because the employer or landowner could command the votes of those who were economically dependent on him; Thomas Jefferson himself had warned that "Dependence begets subservience and venality." Would America be transformed when her working population became a salaried one? Would there be an American proletariat? And if there were, would it behave any differently from the European? The pastoral idea was predicated on the continued *absence* of certain things: factories, urban concentrations of population, the presence of the extremely poor. If these things were not absent, pastoral America could not exist; and wherever the northern Federalist leader looked, it seemed more and more apparent that these conditions would not be absent much longer.

The Federalist anticipated violence, in short, because his countrymen had demonstrated their capacity for it during the Revolution, and because he saw developing a class of poor and unskilled laborers who might easily be encouraged to indulge what the Federalist knew to be a general human capacity for turmoil. Over and over, Federalist spokesmen identified their greatest fear: the experimental republic would be destroyed, as the French republic had been, by the "turbulence" and "mobbishness" of which the public was capable. To curb this tendency to "mobbishness," then, was to save the republic, and an act of patriotism. "Every friend of liberty," explained one editorial writer, "would be shocked if the people were deprived of all political power. . . . But . . . if the people will not erect any barriers against their own intemperance and giddiness, or will not respect and sustain them after they are erected, their power will be soon snatched out of their hands, and their own heads broken with it—as in *France*." . . .

A republican democracy was assumed to be a contradiction in terms; Democratic-Republican as a party label a non sequitur. It was Federalism and Republicanism, they insisted, which went together; both defined a version of popular government characterized by the built-in, self-limiting features which popular government required if it was to endure. In categorizing Americans as "all Federalists, all Republicans" Jefferson was seen either to be making an unexpected and complete capitulation or, what was more likely, deliberately befogging the issues. The former alternative did not seem inconceivable to Federalists, who still regarded the two-party arrangement as novel. The first party to be in power had the firmly established habit of identifying itself with the government, its personnel with the national administration, and its members with the heroes of the American Revolution. Opposition to party was easily equated with a near-treasonable opposition to the government, and the development of an opposition party was often viewed as the cause, rather than the reflection, of "political rancour & malevolence." . . .

. . . Americans of both parties were aware that theirs was the only republic of the time, and that it was an extremely perilous experiment. In his examination of the causes of the War of 1812, Roger H. Brown has pointed to the American's fear that there may have been "some fatal weakness inherent in the republican form of government that accounted for its rare and fleeting occurrence." Both parties were intensely concerned for the continuation and security of their holy experiment, but their jealous protectiveness of that experiment was displayed in varying fashion. The early years of the republic were years of great accomplishment and also of tremendous frustration. It seems to have been habitual among Republicans to place the blame for that frustration on foreign nations and the conduct of foreign affairs, a way of thinking which, Brown suggests, eventually led them to justify the War of 1812. But one may also speculate that one of the sources of Federalist resistance to that war was a well-established habit of thought which tended to place blame for political failure, even in foreign affairs, on the nation's own internal weaknesses.

Repeatedly the Federalists insisted that Americans interpret the French Revolution as a cautionary tale. Democracy was never static; constant vigilance was required to keep popular government stable. And many Federalists had come to fear that Americans lacked that vigilance. . . .

Americans of both parties were fond of the notion that the virtue of the citizen and the stability of the republic were linked. "Virtue . . . is the foundation of Republics," explained a contributor to the *Gazette of the United States* who signed himself "Serranus." "In these, all Power emanating from the people, when they become corrupt, it is in vain to look for purity or disinterestedness, in the administration of their affairs. A polluted fountain must necessarily pour forth a foul and turbid stream. Hence, Morals [,] of great importance in every scheme of government, are of indispensable necessity in a free Commonwealth." Sustenance for this point of view might be found by reading Montesquieu, who taught that whereas what makes the laws effective in a despotism was fear, a republic must depend on the virtue of its citizens. "There is no great share of probity necessary to support a monarchical or despotic government; the force of the laws in one, and the Prince's arm in the other, are sufficient to direct and maintain the whole. But in a popular state one spring more is necessary, namely, virtue." The debaters in the Constitutional Convention had cited Montesquieu more often than Locke, and he continued to be quoted—and misquoted—in the popular press. During the Convention, his arguments in favor of the separation and balance of powers had proved most useful; after the form of government was settled, emphasis shifted to his insight that only a virtuous and moral citizenry could make a republic viable.

If one is willing to assume that men are naturally virtuous, then the foundations of a healthy republic were already present in American society and could be counted on to persist. But few Federalists were able to share this cheerful Jeffersonian assumption. Their attitude stemmed partly from the old Puritan awareness of man's natural depravity, but even more it stemmed from an understanding of the extreme fragility of their experiment in democracy and an awareness of the substantial demands for self-restraint and individual responsibility that republican government places on its citizens. Theirs was a style of consciousness that had been characteristic of the members of the Constitutional Convention, who had been frank in their acknowledgement—even insistence—that the sort of government they had devised depended for its continued existence on a public superior in its political sophistication to any other public, anywhere on the globe. There were to be checks and balances to restrain the corrupting influence of power, but in the last analysis it was citizens, not devices, who would have to guard the republic. The Founders were equally frank in their acknowledgement that the average American might not be able to sustain the burdens placed on him. Because the American public was better educated, more endowed with landed property than any other, the risk seemed worth taking. Americans had shown in their state governments that they were capable of self-rule, but they were also capable of riot. He had taken democracy, Gouverneur Morris said, "not only . . . as a Man does his Wife for better or worse, but what few Men do with their Wives, . . . knowing all its bad Qualities." . . .

Only a virtuous citizenry would sustain a republic and, in a sinful world, a virtuous citizenry was made, not born. Could the Jeffersonians, who seemed so ready to ignore the issue altogether, be trusted to educate the people to virtue and enlightenment? Federalists had their doubts; for their part, the press and the pulpit seemed the most promising means of reinforcing what tendency to virtue and morality already existed. It was through the press, Thomas Green Fessenden thought, that the French had been persuaded to endorse the Revolution and the English persuaded to eschew it. "LITERATURE, well or ill-conducted . . . is the great engine, by which . . . all civilized States must ultimately be supported or overthrown," he asserted. Federalists treated the triumph of Thomas Jefferson, David H. Fischer has remarked, as "an object lesson in the power of the printed word," and bent their energies to establishing newspapers and increasing their circulation in an attempt to ensure that as many printed words as possible were of Federalist origin. In this they perhaps overestimated the Word, a tendency not unusual among men who believed that "words are things," who measured the success of a republic by the excellence of its literature and oratory, and who defined their opponents as anti-intellectuals. But the effort also suggested the variant of democracy that was Federalism. Federalists insisted that they would have retained their office had the American people not been deceived. The fault lay not with republican government, but with the capacity of the opposition for deceptive techniques, and with the understandable human propensity to listen to those who spoke of happiness rather than of stern duty or of rectitude.

"I am willing you should call this the Age of Frivolity as you do; and would not object if you had named it the Age of Folly, Vice, Frenzy, Fury, Brutality, Daemons, Buonaparte, Tom Paine, or the Age of the burning Brand from the bottomless Pitt: or any thing but the Age of Reason," John Adams told a friend. In an age of unreason, something more than newspapers was required to sustain the virtue that alone could sustain the republic; something more than a liberal education was required to counteract the disorderly passions that threatened to disrupt the state. William Crafts typically warned that a nation "subject to its passions" could not possibly be virtuous; "Passion, so far as it prevails, destroys reason," counseled Tapping Reeve, "and when it gains an entire ascendancy over men, it renders them bedlamites."

In this context, Faith had a political as well as a supernatural function; the God of the Federalists often appears to behave like a fourth branch of Government. "Where is the security for property, for reputation, for life, if the sense of religious obligation desert the oaths which are the instruments of investigation in courts of justice?" George Washington had asked in the Farewell Address. "Give religion to the winds," wrote Abigail Adams, "and what tye is found strong enough to bind man to his duty, to restrain his inordinate passions? Honour is phantom. Moral principal [*sic*] feeble and unstable—nothing but a firm belief and well grounded assurance that man is an accountable being, and that he is to render that account to a Being who will not be mocked, and cannot be deceived, will prove a sufficient Barrier, or stem the torrent of unruly passions and appetites."

Religious obligation would reinforce moral obligation; moral obligation would make popular government orderly and stable. This paradoxical insistence that religious faith was a necessary ingredient in a social order which forbade the establishment of religion was both widespread and persistent. . . .

The Jeffersonians were dangerous, Simeon Baldwin explained, because their influence was used to break down the "barrier of habitual morality . . . both as it respects our civil & our religious institutions . . . if the restraints of Law, of education, of habit & [of what the opposition was pleased to call] superstitions and prejudice [i.e., religion] shall be entirely removed, I am confident we shall have more *positive* vice, than is even now exhibited at the South. The human propensities when released from those restraints will like the pendulum vibrate & when urged by precept & allowed by Example they will vibrate to an extreme." They were vibrating, even then, in the camp meetings of the Great Revival. Cane Ridge, Kentucky, in the summer of 1801 set the pattern for subsequent revivals, at which salvation was demonstrated by ranting, twitching, fainting and other behavior closely resembling the cataleptic fit. The revivalists were not only saving themselves, they explained, they were redeeming the entire nation. But some people could not be comfortable in a nation so redeemed. The revival encouraged the free play of passions quite as much as militant deism did; like so many other disturbing trends in American life, it came out of a western wilderness which had voted for Jefferson and which the purchase of Louisiana had done much to enlarge. Religious liberty should mean that men were free to choose the institutional form of their faith, Federalists thought, but they feared if it were also construed to encourage the growth of deism on the one hand or of noninstitutional evangelicalism on the other, then not only the churches, but the entire national establishment would be threatened.

In the years after the Revolution, the American walked a strange tightrope between optimism and pessimism. The Revolution had been both a radical break with the past and a conservative affirmation of it; that ambivalence persisted through the early years of the national experience. The Federalist characteristically searched the American social order to find the stability that would justify the Revolution; for the same purpose the Democrat searched it to find flexibility. The Jeffersonian, at least in theory, endorsed flexibility, unpredictability, open-endedness; he led the Federalist to wonder how a society so characterized could endure. The Virginia democrat lived in one of the least flexible of American social arrangements; when the Federalist found him endorsing unpredictability he logically concluded that the Virginian was a hypocrite. Men long for what they do not have; the Federalist's glorification of social stability—his castigation of the decline of deferential behavior, his objection to the annexation of the "howling wilderness" of Louisiana, his jealous maintenance of an extensive federal judiciary, his concern for the advancement of intellectuality, virtue, and traditional religious observance—may well have come out of his appreciation of the forces that were operating to increase the anxieties of American life.

The Fears of the Jeffersonian Republicans

DREW R. MCCOY

Sometime during the summer or early fall of 1780, as the war for independence approached its most critical juncture and Americans faced an increasingly problematic future, the secretary of the French legation in Philadelphia, François Marbois, initiated a chain of events that would produce an intellectual and literary landmark of the Revolutionary age. As part of the French government's effort to secure useful information about its new and largely unknown ally, Marbois circulated a detailed questionnaire among influential members of the Continental Congress. When a copy of the questionnaire found its way to Thomas Jefferson, then the besieged governor of Virginia, he seized the opportunity to organize his wide-ranging reflections on the conditions and prospects of his native country. Many revisions and several years later, when the *Notes on the State of Virginia* publicly appeared, they included what was to become Jefferson's best-known commentary on political economy. His celebration of "those who labour in the earth" as "the chosen people of God" has become a centerpiece of the republic's cultural heritage, a quintessential expression of its impassioned concern for the natural, earthbound virtue of a simple and uncorrupted people.

Jefferson's classic statement is so familiar that it might, at first glance, seem to require neither explanation nor analytical elaboration. But lurking beneath his deceptively simple paean to an agricultural way of life was a more sophisticated perception of how societies normally changed through time as well as an acute understanding of the moral and political implications of a social process that he assumed was inevitable. His memorable observations on the comparative merits of agriculture and manufactures were directly informed by a characteristically eighteenth-century conception of social change.

Jefferson was responding in the *Notes* to Marbois's inquiry about the present state of commerce and manufactures in Virginia. Making a distinction customary of the times, Jefferson reported that the Revolution had encouraged the prolific production of very coarse clothing "within our families," but for the "finer" manufactures Virginians desired, he continued, they would undoubtedly continue to rely on importations from abroad. Recognizing that such a pattern would be considered unfortunate by "the political economists of Europe," who had established the principle "that every state should endeavour to manufacture for itself," Jefferson contended that it was instead a wise and necessary response to peculiar American conditions and to the lessons of history. In Europe, where the land was either fully cultivated or "locked up against the cultivator" by the bars of aristocratic tradition, manufacturing was "resorted to of necessity not of choice." New forms of employment had to be created, in other words, for those people who could not find occupations on the land. In America, by contrast, where "an immensity of land" courted the industry of even a rapidly expanding population, an alternative form of political economy that would not force men into manufacturing was both feasible and eminently desirable. Citing

Drew R. McCoy, *The Elusive Republic: Political Economy in Jeffersonian America* (published for the Institute of Early American History and Culture, Williamsburg, Virginia, by the University of North Carolina Press, Chapel Hill), 13–15, 185–199, 204–205. Copyright © 1981 by the University of North Carolina Press. Used by permission of the publisher.

the "happiness and permanence of government" in a society of independent and virtuous husbandmen, Jefferson emphasized the moral and political advantages of America's social opportunity that far outweighed narrowly economic considerations. If his countrymen foolishly and prematurely embraced manufacturing, he predicted, a consequent and inevitable corruption of morals would necessarily endanger the fabric of republican government. Once large numbers of Americans abandoned secure employment on the land to labor in workshops, they would become dependent on "the casualties and caprice of customers" for their subsistence, and such dependence had historically bred a "subservience and venality" that suffocated "the germ of virtue" and prepared "fit tools for the designs of ambition." "It is the manners and spirit of a people which preserve a republic in vigour," Jefferson cautioned his readers, since "a degeneracy in these is a canker which soon eats to the heart of its laws and constitution."

Jefferson's effusive optimism about his country's peculiar social potential could not obscure some nagging fears. He worried, on the one hand, that his contemporaries might blindly follow the maxims of European political economists, ignore his wisdom, and plunge into manufacturing. Education and a commitment to republican principles might defuse this particular danger, but a larger and less tractable problem loomed on the horizon. Jefferson recognized that the loathsome dependence, subservience, venality, and corruption that he so much dreaded—everything, in short, that he associated with European political economy—were in large part the unavoidable outgrowth of what he referred to as "the natural progress and consequence of the arts." He alluded here to a universal process that eighteenth-century social thinkers often described, a process whose repercussions might "sometimes perhaps" be "retarded by accidental circumstances," as Jefferson put it, but which inevitably had to be felt. Like most enlightened thinkers of his age, Jefferson conceived of natural laws of social and cultural development that applied to America as much as to Europe. Vast resources of land might forestall the unfavorable consequences of this "natural progress" of the arts, but he never doubted that eventually America would be swept up in an inexorable logic of social change. Jefferson's plea in the *Notes on Virginia,* a plea that he would make throughout his public life, was that his countrymen not abuse or disregard the natural advantages that could postpone, but never prevent, a familiar and politically dangerous course of social development. . . .

Many years after his first election to the presidency, Thomas Jefferson commented that "the revolution of 1800" was "as real a revolution in the principles of our government as that of 1776 was in its form." Jefferson was undoubtedly using the term "revolution" not in the modern sense of a radical creation of a new order, but in the traditional sense of a return to first principles, of a restoration of original values and ideals that had been overturned or repudiated. For him, the election of 1800 was a revolution because it marked a turning back to the true republican spirit of 1776. Jefferson was excited by the prospect of the first implementation of the principles of America's republican revolution in the national government created by the Constitution of 1787, since in his eyes a minority faction consisting of an American Walpole and his corrupt minions had captured control of that government almost immediately after its establishment. From Jefferson's perspective, indeed, the Federalists had done more than threaten to corrupt American government by mimicking the English "court" model. Just as frightening was their apparent desire to mold the young republic's political economy along English lines, a desire reflected both in their call for the extensive development of government-subsidized manufacturing enterprises and in their attempt to stimulate a highly commercialized economy anchored to such premature and speculative ventures as an overextended carrying trade. Jefferson's fundamental goal in 1801 was to end this threatened "Anglicization" of both American government and society. In so doing he would restore the basis for the development of a truly republican political economy, one that would be patterned after Benjamin Franklin's vision of a predominantly agricultural empire that would expand across space, rather than develop through time.

Within the Jeffersonian framework of assumptions and beliefs, three essential conditions were necessary to create and sustain such a republican political economy: a national government free from any taint of corruption, an unobstructed access to an ample supply of open land, and a relatively liberal international commercial order that would offer adequate foreign markets for America's flourishing agricultural surplus. The history of the 1790s had demonstrated all too well to the Jeffersonians the predominant danger to a republican political economy of corruption emanating from the federal government. They were especially troubled by the deleterious political, social, and moral repercussions of the Federalists' financial system, which they regarded as the primary vehicle of corruption both in the political system and in the country at large. Although Jefferson concluded rather soon after his election that his administration could not safely dismantle Hamilton's entire system with a few swift strokes, he was committed to doing everything possible to control that system's effects and gradually reduce its pernicious influence. Extinguishing the national debt as rapidly as possible, reducing government expenditures (especially on the military), and repealing the Federalist battery of direct and excise taxes became primary goals of the Jeffersonians in power, who sought by such means to purge the national government of Hamiltonian fiscalism in accordance with their cherished "country" principles.

In itself, the electoral revolution of 1800 promised to remove the primary threat to a republican political economy posed by the machinations of a corrupt administration. But the Jeffersonians also had to secure the other necessary guarantors of republicanism: landed and commercial expansion. Although the pressure of population growth on the supply of land in the United States had never been a problem of the same immediate magnitude as political corruption, the social and economic dislocations of the 1780s had prompted some concern with this matter. Through the Louisiana Purchase of 1803, undoubtedly the greatest achievement of his presidency, Jefferson appeared to eliminate this problem for generations, if not for centuries, to come. But the third and thorniest problem, in the form of long-standing restrictions on American commerce, proved far more frustrating and intractable. Through an embargo and finally a war the Jeffersonians consistently tried but failed to remove this nagging impediment to the fulfillment of their republican vision.

The presidential administrations from 1801 to 1817 appear more consistent when viewed from this perspective—that is, as a sustained Jeffersonian attempt to secure the requisite conditions for a republican political economy. Securing such a political economy, as the Jeffersonians conceived of it, required more than merely capturing control of the government from a corrupt minority faction; it also required the elimination of specific dangers and the maintenance of certain conditions, and these concerns largely shaped the Jeffersonian approach to both domestic and foreign policy. There was never any question that positive, concrete measures would have to be taken to forestall the development of social conditions that were considered antithetical to republicanism. Hamilton and the Federalists had threatened to make American society old and corrupt long before its time. Now the Jeffersonians set out to reverse the direction of Federalist policy in order to maintain the country at a relatively youthful stage of development. Hoping to avoid the social evils both of barbarous simplicity and of overrefined, decadent maturity, the Jeffersonians proposed to escape the burden of an economically sophisticated society without sacrificing a necessary degree of republican civilization. Their aspiration to evade social corruption and the ravages of time was a fragile and demanding dream, and the quest to fulfill it was not without its ironies.

On the one hand, the Republican party attracted political support from scores of Americans whose outlook can properly be termed entrepreneurial. Opposition to the Federalist system was never limited to agrarian-minded ideologues who unequivocally opposed a dynamic commercial economy. Many Jeffersonians were anxious to participate in the creation of an expansive economy and to reap its many rewards. Frustrated by the failure of Federalist policies to serve their immediate needs, ambitious men-on-the-make, engaged in a variety of economic pursuits, enlisted under the banner of Jeffersonianism in a crusade to secure the advantages and opportunities they desired. Perhaps some of them saw no contradiction between their personal material ambitions and the traditional vision of a simple, bucolic republic articulated by the leader of their party. Assessing the economic psychology of many of these enterprising Jeffersonians, one scholar has suggested the complex paradox "of capitalists of all occupations denying the spirit of their occupations," adding that "it appears that many Republicans wanted what the Federalists were offering, but they wanted it faster, and they did not want to admit that they wanted it at all." Such a characterization cannot be applied, however, to Jefferson and Madison, and in their case we observe a more poignant irony. As their experience as policymakers soon demonstrated, the Jeffersonian endeavor to secure a peaceful, predominantly agricultural republic demanded a tenaciously expansive foreign policy—a foreign policy that ultimately endangered both the peace and the agricultural character of the young republic.

In developing his analysis of Britain's mercantilist political economy during the 1760s and 1770s, Benjamin Franklin had recognized that corruption could result from both natural and artificial causes. A high population density brought about by the biological pressure of population growth on a limited supply of land was one route to social decay. But as Franklin and many other eighteenth-century writers so often noted, decay also resulted from a corrupt political system that deviously induced extreme social inequality, depopulation of the countryside, urban squalor, luxury manufacturing, and the like. Both routes to corruption had devastating consequences; the difference was that while one was natural and seemingly inevitable, the other was not. During the 1780s James Madison had pondered this distinction, most notably in his correspondence with Jefferson, and had reached the rather pessimistic conclusion that even in the absence of a corrupt political system "a certain degree of misery seems inseparable from a high degree of populousness." Ultimately, he suggested, republican America would offer no exception to this rule. Although

Jefferson agreed that the United States would remain virtuous only "as long as there shall be vacant lands in any part of America" and people were not "piled upon one another in large cities, as in Europe," he was confident that such a crisis would not arise "for many centuries." If social decay was to afflict the young republic, Jefferson believed that threat stemmed more from artificial than from natural causes, from a corrupt political system rather than from the inevitable pressure of population growth on the American supply of land. Nevertheless, Jefferson was not totally unconcerned with the problem of land, especially in the realm of theory and speculation. His confidence about the American future betrayed his assumption that America's western (and perhaps northern and southern) boundaries would be regularly extended, always bringing in a fresh supply of virgin land. Should that assumption be challenged, especially by a formidable foreign power, however, a theoretical problem might indeed become a more immediate and practical one.

It is interesting, in this regard, to observe Jefferson's reactions to the writings of Thomas R. Malthus, the British parson and political economist who popularized the theory of population pressure on subsistence, especially since Jefferson gave Malthus's writings particularly close attention near the end of his first presidential administration. Malthus had first presented his views on population in an anonymous pamphlet published in 1798, and his basic thesis was straightforward. Reacting against the optimistic forecasts of social improvement that were common in the late eighteenth century . . . , Malthus argued that given the biological facts of population and subsistence, such visions of perfectibility for the mass of mankind were chimerical. Instead, the widespread vice, misery, and poverty that so appalled these "speculative philosophers" were the inevitable lot of humanity. The problem, simply stated, was that "the power of population is indefinitely greater than the power in the earth to produce subsistence for man." The irrepressible passion between the sexes, when unchecked, resulted in a geometrical rate of population growth, whereas the supply of food and available means of nourishment could increase only arithmetically at best. This "perpetual tendency in the race of man to increase beyond the means of subsistence," Malthus explained, "is one of the general laws of animated nature, which we can have no reason to expect will change."

Malthus suggested, in short, that all societies were destined to proceed rapidly through the familiar stages of social development toward a state of overpopulation, corruption, and old age. Old age might be postponed, especially in a society with an abundance of land, but not forever. In discussing population growth in America, Malthus emphasized the point that there was no final escape from the predicament he described, for not even a vast reservoir of fertile land could repeal the natural laws of population and subsistence. "Perpetual youth" for a nation was impossible; anyone who expected the United States to remain a land with relatively little poverty and misery forever, he commented, "might as reasonably expect to prevent a wife or mistress from growing old by never exposing her to the sun and air." "It is, undoubtedly, a most disheartening reflection," he grimly concluded, "that the great obstacle in the way to any extraordinary improvement in society, is of a nature that we can never hope to overcome."

Malthus's arguments should have been especially discouraging to Americans, since he contended that the necessary social basis for republicanism was precariously ephemeral. Extreme inequality, widespread poverty, extensive landless dependency—

indeed, everything Americans considered antithetical to republicanism—were, according to Malthus, biologically inevitable. American readers could take solace only in the English parson's concession that there were "many modes of treatment in the political, as well as animal body, that contribute to accelerate or retard the approaches of age." . . .

President Thomas Jefferson was one such reader. By early 1804 he was perusing a borrowed copy of "the new work of Malthus on population," and he pronounced it "one of the ablest I have ever seen." . . .

. . . Ironically, what Jefferson found least useful and convincing in Malthus was the population theory that the parson was best known for; the president's general praise for the essay appears to have been prompted by its restatement of laissez-faire, anti-mercantilist doctrine. Jefferson particularly chastised Malthus for failing to recognize the irrelevance of his population theory to the American experience. "From the singular circumstance of the immense extent of rich and uncultivated lands in this country, furnishing an increase of food in the same ratio with that of population," Jefferson noted, "the greater part of his book is inapplicable to us, but as a matter of speculation." Population pressure on subsistence would never be an immediate problem in America because "the resource of emigration" to virgin territory was always available. Discussing Malthus's theory with the French economist Say, Jefferson expanded this observation into a more general statement. "The differences of circumstance between this and the old countries of Europe," he wrote, "furnish differences of fact whereon to reason, in questions of political economy, and will consequently produce sometimes a difference of result." Echoing Franklin's observations of fifty years earlier, Jefferson continued: "There, for instance, the quantity of food is fixed, or increasing in a slow and only arithmetical ratio, and the proportion is limited by the same ratio. Supernumerary births consequently add only to your mortality. Here the immense extent of uncultivated and fertile lands enables every one who will labor, to marry young, and to raise a family of any size. Our food, then, may increase geometrically with our laborers, and our births, however multiplied, become effective." Jefferson went on to argue, in this regard, that America provided a further exception to the European rule of balanced economies and national self-sufficiency:

> Again, there the best distribution of labor is supposed to be that which places the manufacturing hands along side the agricultural; so that the one part shall feed both, and the other part furnish both with clothes and other comforts. Would that be best here? Egoism and first appearances say yes. Or would it be better that all our laborers should be employed in agriculture? In this case a double or treble portion of fertile lands would be brought into culture; a double or treble creation of food be produced, and its surplus go to nourish the now perishing births of Europe, who in return would manufacture and send us in exchange our clothes and other comforts. Morality listens to this, and so invariably do the laws of nature create our duties and interests, that when they seem to be at variance, we ought to suspect some fallacy in our reasonings. In solving this question, too, we should allow its just weight to the moral and physical preference of the agricultural, over the manufacturing, man.

This statement was a striking reaffirmation of Jefferson's fundamental beliefs on the subject of political economy, a statement that differed very little from his well-known observations in the *Notes on Virginia* of twenty years earlier. Jefferson's encounter with Malthus thus served, in the end, to reconfirm his basic vision of a predominantly agricultural America that would continue to export its bountiful surpluses of food abroad. Such a republic, he believed, would best serve not only its own citizens, by permitting them to pursue a virtuous way of life, but also the European victims of a Malthusian fate, by providing them with the subsistence they desperately needed. It seems clear, above all, that Jefferson's brimming confidence during this period—expressed both in his response to Malthus and in his restatement of agrarian beliefs—must be viewed in the context of the Louisiana Purchase. With the Federalists properly and, Republicans hoped, permanently displaced from power in the national government, there was no need to worry about the dangers to a republican political economy from political corruption. With Louisiana safely added to the Union, there was also no need to worry about the danger of foreign powers choking off the American supply of land. The acquisition of Louisiana probably removed any Mathusian doubts Jefferson might have had about the long-range viability of republicanism in America. Indeed, the Louisiana question touched on so many aspects of the Jeffersonian vision of a republican political economy that it deserves much closer investigation.

The Mississippi crisis of 1801–1803, which culminated in the Louisiana Purchase, affected crucial and long-standing American concerns. Since the 1780s most Americans had regarded free navigation of the Mississippi River and the right of deposit at New Orleans as essential to the national interest. Without the access to market that these conditions permitted, westward expansion would be stalled, because settlers in the trans-Appalachian regions necessarily depended on the Mississippi and its tributaries to sustain them as active and prosperous republican farmers. . . .

. . . [C]ontrol of the Mississippi permitted westerners to engage in a secure and dynamically expanding foreign commerce and, as always, Americans saw the significance of commerce in very broad social and moral terms. It was repeatedly asserted that an active commerce that provided a secure and dependable access to foreign markets was absolutely necessary to establish and maintain the republican character of western society. . . .

By rectifying the chronic problem of an uncertain, rapidly fluctuating demand for western agricultural surpluses, the Purchase thus served an important social and moral purpose. "No ruinous fluctuations in commerce need now be apprehended," noted another western commentator, for "agriculture may depend upon those steady markets which trade shall open to industry." There could be no doubt that a "want of markets for the produce of the soil" always had disastrous consequences, for "it saps the foundations of our prosperity; subverts the end of society, and literally tends to keep us in that rude, uncultivated state, which has excited the derision and contempt of other communities." "As long as this is the state of our country," the same observer queried in familiar fashion, "what encouragement is there for the mind to throw off its native ferocity?" By permanently securing control of the Mississippi River and the promise of boundless foreign markets beyond, the Louisiana Purchase did more than pave the way for economic prosperity. By providing the incentive to industry that shaped a republican people, it laid the necessary basis for the westward expansion of republican civilization itself. . . .

Jefferson's notion of a continuously expanding "empire of liberty" in the Western Hemisphere was a bold intellectual stroke, because it flew in the face of the traditional republican association of expansion and empire with luxury, corruption, and especially despotism. The familiar bugbear of the Roman Empire and its decline through imperial expansion was the most common source of this association. According to Jefferson and most American republicans, expansion would preserve, rather than undermine, the republican character of America. In addition to forestalling development through time and diffusing the spirit of faction, expansion was crucial to American security in its broadest sense. Removing the French from Louisiana also removed the need for a dangerous military establishment in the face of a contiguous foreign threat. It greatly reduced, too, the likelihood of American involvement in a ruinous war that would impose on the young republic the vicious Old World system of national debts, armies, navies, taxation, and the like. For a plethora of reasons, in short, peaceful expansion was sustaining the Jeffersonian republic.

But if the Louisiana Purchase removed some serious obstacles to the realization of Jefferson's republican empire, it also exposed some of the tensions and contradictions within that vision. Since the proper functioning of the empire required both westward and commercial expansion, an assertive, even aggressive, foreign policy would often be necessary to secure the republic. The Jeffersonians frequently boasted of the isolation and independence of the United States; curiously, this claim obscured the fact that American republicanism demanded both an open international commercial order and the absence of any competing presence on the North American continent. The United States could isolate itself from foreign affairs and the potential for conflict only if it was willing to resign its tenacious commitment to westward expansion and free trade. To do this, however, would be to abandon the two most important pillars of the Jeffersonian vision of a republican political economy. Indeed, given the commitment to that vision, the national independence and isolated self-sufficiency boasted of by the Jeffersonians were illusory.

FURTHER READING

Joyce Oldham Appleby, *Inheriting the Revolution: The First Generation of Americans* (2000).

Lance Banning, *The Jeffersonian Persuasion: Evolution of a Party Ideology* (1978).

Stanley Elkins and Eric McKitrick, *The Age of Federalism, 1788–1800* (1993).

Richard Hofstadter, *The Idea of a Party System: The Rise of Legitimate Opposition in the United States, 1780–1840* (1970).

Linda K. Kerber, *Women of the Republic: Intellect and Ideology in Republican America* (1980).

James Roger Sharp, *American Politics in the Early Republic: The New Nation in Crisis* (1993).

David Waldstreicher, *In the Midst of Perpetual Fetes: The Making of American Nationalism, 1776–1820* (1997).

CHAPTER
7

Westward Movement,
the Market Revolution,
and Indian Removal

When Congress authorized the Louisiana Purchase in 1803, it made the United States one of the largest nations in the world, doubling its size with the stroke of a pen. The United States paid France $15 million for over 600 million acres of land; this worked out to less than 3 cents an acre. Many Americans saw this land as open for development. In the decades following the Louisiana Purchase, Americans moved westward, building farms and planting crops, and creating an economy that knit the nation together. Indians, however, were not a part of the negotiations between France and the United States that resulted in the Louisiana Purchase. And most of them viewed the economic development and westward migration of American citizens with dread.

In the years following the War of 1812, a group of American statesmen envisioned a national economic policy that would foster economic development. Known as the "American System," this plan called for a national bank, protective tariffs, and improved transportation and communication. The American System would not be enacted in its entirety, but building on the foundation that had been created by the Wilderness Road in 1795, some four thousand miles of turnpikes were constructed by 1821. Innovations in transportation—including canal boats, steamboats, and railroads—led to what historians call a "transportation revolution"; the costs of transporting bulky goods fell 95 percent between 1825 and 1855, while the speed of transport increased fivefold. During this period, the Supreme Court issued a series of decisions that aided business and fostered economic development. Contracts, the Court held, were secure from the meddling of state and local officials, and Congress was supreme in dealing with interstate commerce.

Taken together, these changes laid the foundation for the market revolution. Whereas before this time, individuals had themselves produced much of what they ate and wore and built the places in which they lived, they now increasingly produced commodities for sale and used the income they earned to purchase goods produced by others. Because certain regions of the nation had natural advantages, a national market economy developed. People in the South specialized in producing crops for *export; those in the northwest produced food to feed those people in the East and the South who were specializing in export agriculture, commerce, or manufacturing. These changes brought opportunities and challenges for all Americans—factory workers and farmers, living in both the North and South—that will be addressed in later chapters.*

The challenges for Indian people stemming from this westward migration and the market revolution were even greater than those faced by white and black Americans. As Americans moved westward, they inevitably came into contact with native people. Indian-white interaction had existed for centuries, and native people had accepted some aspects of Euro-American society and rejected others. The increase in these interactions in the early nineteenth century, however, made the Indian response more urgent. Some Indians fostered movements of revitalization that attempted to reclaim aspects of culture that had been lost as a result of interaction with whites. Some of these revitalization movements were powerful forces stimulating efforts by Indians to band together and contest white society. The most notable movement began in 1805 when a Shawnee man named Lalawathika seemingly returned from death. He told of meeting the Master of Life, who showed him the way to lead his people out of degradation. Known to Americans as the Prophet, he adopted the name Tenskwatawa and began to preach a message advocating a return to a traditional lifestyle. By 1807, he began to suggest that Indian groups unite to resist white expansion. Just prior to the War of 1812, Tenskwatawa and his brother Tecumseh built a confederacy of Indian nations to challenge American military aims in present-day Indiana. The movement ended in bloody conflict, the most notable battle being the Battle of Tippecanoe, in which the American army aided by frontiersmen defeated the Indian coalition. Yet other efforts would be made by Indians to resist the westward migration in the decades to follow.

Some Indians sought to accept such innovations. In particular, people from the Creek and Cherokee nations were active in embracing such aspects of white society as written language, farming, and even slavery. By 1827, the Cherokees had drafted and ratified a constitution; one year later they began publishing their own newspaper. Unfortunately for them, the state of Georgia dismissed these changes. In 1828, the Cherokee constitution was annulled by the Georgia legislature. Despite—or perhaps because of—legal appeals to the U.S. Supreme Court, the hostility toward the Cherokees increased. Between 1830 and 1835, Indian nations in the southeastern United States, Cherokees and Creeks included, were forced to remove to "Indian territory" in present-day Oklahoma.

◤ Q U E S T I O N S   T O   T H I N K   A B O U T

In what ways did the transportation and market revolutions change the everyday lives of Americans? How could white-Indian interaction reflect a combination of cooperation and savagery? Which strategy used by Indians—resistance or acculturation—was more successful in grappling with the westward migration of white Americans?

◤ D O C U M E N T S

In Document 1, Joseph Brant, a member of the Mohawk nation, provides a scathing critique of the hypocrisies of white society. Document 2 is an address by Sagoyewatha, also known as Red Jacket, to a Massachusetts missionary. Note how Sagoyewatha, who was a member of the Seneca nation, chides the missionary for his attempt to convert the Indians to Christianity. One significant purpose of the journey of Lewis and Clark to the Pacific Ocean was to engage in diplomacy with native peoples. In Document 3, we see a letter written in 1806 by William Clark to a white man who has offered assistance in dealing with the Indians and a speech that Clark delivered to the Yellowstone Indians. The next three documents illustrate the conflicts between Indians and the U.S. government that developed around the time of the War of 1812. In Document 4, Tecumseh, in a speech delivered to Governor William H. Harrison in 1810, recounts the misdeeds of whites and expresses his belief that the only way to stop "this evil" is for all Indians to unite. In Document 5, Tecumseh's brother, Tenskwatawa, recounts his vision of going to the World Above and the knowledge he gained from the journey with regard to revitalizing Indian culture. In contrast, Document 6 is a speech in Congress by Felix Grundy in 1811 that advocates war with Britain because of the dangers in the West posed by Indians in league with the British. The next three documents illustrate developments following the War of 1812: Americans looked westward, government and private agencies fostered economic development, and diplomats attempted to gain international harmony. In Document 7, *McCulloch* v. *Maryland* (1819), which considered whether the state of Maryland could tax the national bank, Chief Justice John Marshall held both that Congress had more powers than were specifically given it in the Constitution and that federal laws were superior to state laws. This ruling fostered economic development and national centralization. Document 8 is the Monroe Doctrine, which declares that the Western Hemisphere is closed to further European colonization. In Document 9, President John Quincy Adams, in his first annual message to Congress in 1825, urges a group of internal improvement projects, including exploring the West and fostering scientific research. As these efforts to foster economic growth were taking place, the condition of Indians was deteriorating. Document 10 is an appeal by the Cherokee nation against removal from Georgia in 1830. Their pleas ultimately went unheard.

1. Joseph Brant Compares Indian and White Civilizations, 1789

I was, sir, born of Indian parents, and lived while a child, among those you are pleased to call savages; I was afterwards sent to live among the white people, and educated at one of your schools; since which period, I have been honoured, much beyond my deserts, by an acquaintance with a number of principal characters both in Europe and America. After all this experience, and after every exertion to divest myself of prejudice, I am obliged to give my opinion in favour of my own people. . . . I will not enlarge on an idea so singular in civilized life, and perhaps disagreeable to you; and will only observe, that among us, we have no law but that written on the heart of every rational creature by the immediate finger of the great Spirit of the universe himself. We have no prisons—we have no pompous parade of courts; and yet judges are as highly esteemed among us, as they are among you, and their decisions as highly revered; property, to say the least, is as well guarded, and crimes are as impartially punished. We have among us no splendid villains, above the controul of that law, which influences our decisions; in a word, we have no robbery under

American Museum 6 (September 1789): 226–227, quoted in Isabel Thompson Kelsay, *Joseph Brant* (Syracuse, N.Y.: Syracuse University Press, 1984).

the colour of law—daring wickedness here is never suffered to triumph over helpless innocence—the estates of widows and orphans are never devoured by enterprising sharpers. Our sachems, and our warriors, eat their own bread, and not the bread of wretchedness. No person, among us, desires any other reward for performing a brave and worthy action, than the consciousness of serving his nation. Our wise men are called fathers—they are truly deserving the character; they are always accessible—I will not say to the meanest of our people—for we have none mean, but such as render themselves so by their vices.

. . . We do not hunger and thirst after those superfluities of life, that are the ruin of thousands of families among you. Our ornaments, in general, are simple, and easily obtained. Envy and covetousness, those worms that destroy the fair flower of human happiness, are unknown in this climate.

The palaces and prisons among you, form a most dreadful contrast. Go to the former places, and you will see, perhaps, a deformed piece of earth swelled with pride, and assuming airs, that become none but the Spirit above. Go to one of your prisons—here description utterly fails!—certainly the sight of an Indian torture, is not half so painful to a well informed mind. Kill them [the prisoners], if you please—kill them, too, by torture; but let the torture last no longer than a day. . . . Those you call savages, relent—the most furious of our tormentors exhausts his rage in a few hours, and dispatches the unhappy victim with a sudden stroke.

But for what are many of your prisoners confined? For debt! Astonishing! and will you ever again call the Indian nations cruel?—Liberty, to a rational creature, as much exceeds property, as the light of the sun does that of the most twinkling star: but you put them on a level, to the everlasting disgrace of civilization. . . . And I seriously declare, that I had rather die by the most severe tortures ever inflicted by any savage nation on the continent, than languish in one of your prisons for a single year. Great Maker of the world! and do you call yourselves christians? . . . Does then the religion of him whom you call your Saviour, inspire this conduct, and lead to this practice? Surely no. It was a sentence that once struck my mind with some force, that "a bruised reed he never broke." Cease then, while these practices continue among you, to call yourselves christians, lest you publish to the world your hypocrisy. Cease to call other nations savage, when you are tenfold more the children of cruelty, than they.

2. Iroquois Chief Red Jacket Decries the Day When Whites Arrived, 1805

"Brother; Listen to what we say.

"There was a time when our forefathers owned this great island. Their seats extended from the rising to the setting sun. The Great Spirit had made it for the use of Indians. He had created the buffalo, the deer, and other animals for food. He had made the bear and the beaver. Their skins served us for clothing. He had scattered them over the country, and taught us how to take them. He had caused the earth to

Red Jacket's Reply to Reverend Cram (1805), first published in *Monthly Anthology and Boston Review* 6 (April 1809): 221–224. This document can also be found in Christopher Densmore, *Red Jacket: Iroquois Diplomat and Orator* (Syracuse, N.Y.: Syracuse University Press, 1999), 135–140.

produce corn for bread. All this He had done for his red children, because He loved them. If we had some disputes about our hunting ground, they were generally settled without the shedding of much blood. But an evil day came upon us. Your forefathers crossed the great water, and landed on this island. Their numbers were small. They found friends and not enemies. They told us they had fled from their own country for fear of wicked men, and had come here to enjoy their religion. They asked for a small seat. We took pity on them, granted their request: and they sat down amongst us. We gave them corn and meat, they gave us poison (alluding, it is supposed, to ardent spirits) in return.

"The white people had now found our country. Tidings were carried back, and more came amongst us. Yet we did not fear them. We took them to be friends. They called us brothers. We believed them, and gave them a larger seat. At length their numbers had greatly increased. They wanted more land: they wanted our country. Our eyes were opened, and our minds became uneasy. Wars took place, Indians were hired to fight against Indians, and many of our people were destroyed. They also brought strong liquor amongst us. It was strong and powerful, and has slain thousands.

"Brother; Our seats were once large and yours were small. You have now become a great people, and we have scarcely a place left to spread our blankets. You have got our country, but are not satisfied; you want to force your religion upon us.

"Brother; Continue to listen.

"You say that you are sent to instruct us how to worship the Great Spirit agreeably to his mind, and, if we do not take hold of the religion which you white people teach, we shall be unhappy hereafter. You say that you are right and we are lost. How do we know this to be true? We understand that your religion is written in a book. If it was intended for us as well as you, why has not the Great Spirit given to us, and not only to us, but why did he not give to our forefathers the knowledge of that book, with the means of understanding it rightly? We only know what you tell us about it. How shall we know when to believe, being so often deceived by the white people?

"Brother; You say there is but one way to worship and serve the Great Spirit. If there is but one religion; why do you white people differ so much about it? Why not all agreed, as you can all read the book?

"Brother; We do not understand these things.

"We are told that your religion was given to your forefathers, and has been handed down from father to son. We also have a religion, which was given to our forefathers, and has been handed down to us their children. We worship in that way. It teaches us to be thankful for all the favors we receive; to love each other, and to be united. We never quarrel about religion.

"Brother; The Great Spirit has made us all, but he has made a great difference between his white and red children. He has given us different complexions and different customs. To you He has given the arts. To these He has not opened our eyes. We know these things to be true. Since He has made so great a difference between us in other things; why may we not conclude that He has given us a different religion according to our understanding? The Great Spirit does right. He knows what is best for his children; we are satisfied.

"Brother; We do not wish to destroy your religion or take it from you. We only want to enjoy our own.

"Brother; We are told that you have been preaching to white people in this place. These people are our neighbors. We are acquainted with them. We will wait a little while, and see what effect your preaching has upon them. If we find it does them good, makes them honest, and less disposed to cheat Indians; we will then consider again of what you have said.

"Brother; You have now heard our answer to your talk, and this is all we have to say at present.

"As we are going to part, we will come and take you by the hand, and hope the Great Spirit will protect you on your journey, and return you safe to your friends."

As the Indians began to approach the missionary, he rose hastily from his seat and replied, that he could not take them by the hand; that there was no fellowship between the religion of God and the works of the devil.

This being interpreted to the Indians, they smiled, and retired in a peaceable manner.

It being afterwards suggested to the missionary that his reply to the Indians was rather indiscreet; he observed, that he supposed the ceremony of shaking hands would be received by them as a token that he assented to what was said. Being otherwise informed, he said he was very sorry for the expressions.

3. William Clark Enters into Diplomacy with Native People, 1806

SIR   In the winter of 1805, you were so obliging as to express a disposition to assist us in the execution of any measure relative to the Savages with whome you were conversant, or that you would lend your aid in furthering the friendly views of our government in relation to the Same. no object as we then informed you did at that time present itself to our view, which we conceived worthy of your attention. at present we have a commission to charge you with, which if executed, we have no doubt will tend to advance your private interest, while it will also promote those of the U. States in relation to the intercourse of her citizens with the Indian nations in the interior of North America. It is that of provailing on some of the most influensial Chiefs of those bands of Sioux who usially resort the borders of the Missouri to visit the Seat of our Government, and to accompany them there yourself with us. The Tetons of the burnt woods, Teton Ockandandas, and other bands of Tetons, Cisitons, and yanktons of the Plains are the Objects of our attention on this occasion, Particularly the Bands of Tetons; those untill some effectual measures be taken to render them pacific, will always prove a serious source of inconveniance to the free navigation of the Missouri, or at least to it's upper branches, from whence the richest portion of it's fur trade is to be derived.

The ardent wish of our government has ever been to conciliate the esteem and secure the friendship of all the Savage nations within their territory by the exercise of every consistent and pacific measure in her power, applying those of coercion only in the last resort; certain we are that her disposition towards the native inhabitants of her newly acquired Territory of Louisiana is not less friendly; but we are also positive that she will not long suffer her citizens to be deprived of the free navigation of the Missouri by a fiew comparitively feeble bands of Savages who may be so illy advised

Letter to Hugh Henney and speech prepared for Yellowstone Indians, in Meriwether Lewis and William Clark, *The Journals of Lewis and Clark*, vol. 5 (1806), in *Original Journals of the Lewis and Clark Expedition, 1804–1806*, ed. Reuben Gold Thwaites (New York: Dodd, Mead, 1905), 282–283, 285–286, 299–301.

as to refuse her proffered friendship and continue their depridation on her citizens who may in future assend or decend that river.

We believe that the sureest guarantee of savage fidility to any nation is a thorough conviction on their minds that their government possesses the power of punishing promptly every act of aggression committed on their part against the person or property of their citizens; to produce this conviction without the use of violence, is the wish of our government; and to effect it, we cannot devise a more expedient method than that of takeing some of the best informed and most influential Chiefs with us to the U. States, where they will have an ample view of our population and resources, become convinced themselves, and on their return convince their nations of the futility of an attempt to oppose the Will of our government, particularly when they shall find, that their acquiescence will be productive of greater advantages to their nation than their most sanguine hopes could lead them to expect from oppersition.

We have before mentioned to you the intentions of our government to form tradeing establishments on the Missouri with a view to secure the attatchments of the nativs and emeliorate their sufferings by furnishing them with such articles as are necessary for their comfort on the most moderate terms in exchange for their peltries and furs. . . . an Indian *Agent* will of course be necessary at that post. your long acquaintance and influence with those people necessary places your protentions to that appointment on the fairest Ground, and should you think proper to under take the commission now proposed, it will still further advance those pretentions. . . .

In your communication with the *Sioux,* in addition to other considerations which may suggest themselves to your mind, you will be pleased to assure them of the friendly views of our government towards them, their power and resources, their intention of establishing trading houses in their neighborhood and the objects of those establishments. inform them that the mouth of all the rivers through [which] traders convey Merchindize to their country are now in possession of the United States, who can at pleasure cut off all communication between themselves and their accustomed traders, and consequently the interest they have in cultivateing our friendship. You may also promis them in the event of their going on with us, that they shall receive from our government a considerable preasent in Merchindize, which will be conveyed at the public expence with them to their nation on their return. urge them also to go imediately, on the ground, that their doing so will haisten the establishment of the tradeing house in contemplation.

[Speech prepared for Yellowstone Indians]

Children   The Great Spirit has given a fair and bright day for us to meet together in his View that he may inspect us in this all we say and do.

Children   I take you all by the hand as the children of your Great father the President of the U. States of America who is the great chief of all the white people towards the riseing sun.

Children   This Great Chief who is Benevolent, just, wise & bountifull has sent me and one other of his chiefs (who is at this time in the country of the Blackfoot Indians) to all his read children on the Missourei and its waters quite to the great lake of the West where the land ends and the [sun] sets on the face of the great water, to know their wants and inform him of them on our return. . . .

Children   The object of my comeing to see you is not to do you injurey but to do you good   the Great Chief of all the white people who has more goods at his command than could be piled up in the circle of your camp, wishing that all his read children should be happy has sent me here to know your wants that he may supply them.

Children   Your great father the Chief of the white people intends to build a house and fill it with such things as you may want and exchange with you for your skins & furs at a very low price. & has derected me [to] enquire of you, at what place would be most convenient for to build this house. and what articles you are in want of that he might send them imediately on my return

Children   The people in my country is like the grass in your plains noumerous they are also rich and bountifull. and love their read brethren who inhabit the waters of the Missoure

Children   I have been out from my country two winters, I am pore necked and nothing to keep of[f] the rain.   when I set out from my country I had a plenty but have given it all to my read children whome I have seen on my way to the Great Lake of the West. and have now nothing. . . .

Children   The red children of your great father who live near him and have opened their ears to his counsels are rich and hapy have plenty of horses cows & Hogs fowls bread &c. &c. live in good houses, and sleep sound. and all those of his red children who inhabit the waters of the Missouri who open their ears to what I say and follow the counsels of their great father the President of the United States, will in a fiew years be a[s] hapy as those mentioned &c.

Children   It is the wish of your Great father the Chief of all the white people that some 2 of the principal Chiefs of this [blank space in MS.] Nation should Visit him at his great city and receive from his own mouth. his good counsels, and from his own hands his abundant gifts,   Those of his red children who visit him do not return with empty hands, he [will] send them to their nation loaded with presents

Children   If any one two or 3 of your great chiefs wishes to visit your great father and will go with me, he will send you back next Summer loaded with presents and some goods for the nation. You will then see with your own eyes and here with your own years what the white people can do for you. they do not speak with two tongues nor promis what they can't perform

Children   Consult together and give me an answer as soon as possible   your great father is anxious to here from (& see his red children who wish to visit him)   I cannot stay but must proceed on & inform him &c.

4. Shawnee Chief Tecumseh Recounts the Misdeeds of Whites and Calls for Indian Unity, 1810

Brother, I wish you to give me close attention, because I think you do not clearly understand. I want to speak to you about promises that the Americans have made.

You recall the time when the Jesus Indians of the Delawares lived near the Americans, and had confidence in their promises of friendship, and thought they

Speech to William Harrison, governor of the Indian Territory, August 11, 1810. Obtained from http://www.ilhawaii.net/~stony/shawnee.html.

were secure, yet the Americans murdered all the men, women, and children, even as they prayed to Jesus?

The same promises were given to the Shawnee one time. It was at Fort Finney, where some of my people were forced to make a treaty. Flags were given to my people, and they were told they were now the children of the Americans. We were told, if any white people mean to harm you, hold up these flags and you will then be safe from all danger. We did this in good faith. But what happened? Our beloved chief Moluntha stood with the American flag in front of him and that very peace treaty in his hand, but his head was chopped by an American officer, and that American officer was never punished.

Brother, after such bitter events, can you blame me for placing little confidence in the promises of Americans? . . .

It is you, the Americans, by such bad deeds, who push the red men to do mischief. You do not want unity among the tribes, and you destroy it. You try to make differences between them. We, their leaders, wish them to unite and consider their land the common property of all, but you try to keep them from this. You separate the tribes and deal with them that way, one by one, and advise them not to come into this union. Your states have set an example of forming a union among all the Fires, why should you censure the Indians for following that example?

But, brother, I mean to bring all the tribes together, in spite of you, and until I have finished, I will not go to visit your president. Maybe I will when I have finished, maybe. The reason I tell you this, you want, by making your distinctions of Indian tribes and allotting to each a particular tract of land, to set them against each other, and thus to weaken us. . . .

The only way to stop this evil is for all the red men to unite in claiming an equal right in the land. That is how it was at first, and should be still, for the land never was divided, but was for the use of everyone. Any tribe could go to an empty land and make a home there. And if they left, another tribe could come there and make a home. No groups among us have a right to sell, even to one another, and surely not to outsiders who want all, and will not do with less.

Sell a country! Why not sell the air, the clouds, and the Great Sea, as well as the earth? Did not the Great Good Spirit make them all for the use of his children?

Brother, I was glad to hear what you told us. you said that if we could prove that the land was sold by people who had no right to sell it, you would restore it. I will prove that those who did sell did not own it. Did they have a deed? A title? No! You say those prove someone owns land. Those chiefs only spoke a claim, and so you pretended to believe their claim, only because you wanted the land. But the many tribes with me will not agree with those claims. They have never had a title to sell, and we agree this proves you could not buy it from them. If the land is not given back to us, you will see, when we return to our homes from here, how it will be settled. It will be like this:

We shall have a great council, at which all tribes will be present. We shall show to those who sold that they had no rights to the claim they set up, and we shall see what will be done to those chiefs who did sell the land to you. I am not alone in this determination, it is the determination of all the warriors and red people who listen to me. Brother, I now wish you to listen to me. If you do not wipe out that treaty, it will seem that you wish me to kill all the chiefs who sold the land! I tell you so because

I am authorized by all tribes to do so! I am the head of them all! All my warriors will meet together with me in two or three moons from now. Then I will call for those chiefs who sold you this land, and we shall know what to do with them. If you do not restore the land, you will have had a hand in killing them!

I am Shawnee! I am a warrior! My forefathers were warriors. From them I took only my birth into this world. From my tribe I take nothing. I am the maker of my own destiny! And of that I might make the destiny of my red people, of our nation, as great as I conceive to in my mind, when I think of Weshemoneto, who rules this universe! I would not then have to come to Governor Harrison and ask him to tear up this treaty and wipe away the marks upon the land. No! I would say to him, "Sir, you may return to your own country!" The being within me hears the voice of the ages, which tells me that once, always, and until lately, there were no white men on all this island, that it then belonged to the red men, children of the same parents, placed on it by the Great Good Spirit who made them, to keep it, to traverse it, to enjoy its yield, and to people it with the same race. Once they were a happy race! Now they are made miserable by the white people, who are never contented but are always coming in! You do this always, after promising not to anyone, yet you ask us to have confidence in your promises. How can we have confidence in the white people? When Jesus Christ came upon the earth, you killed him, the son of your own God, you nailed him up! You thought he was dead, but you were mistaken. And only after you thought you killed him did you worship him, and start killing those who would not worship him. What kind of a people is this for us to trust?

Now, Brother, everything I have said to you is the truth, as Weshemoneto has inspired me to speak only truth to you. I have declared myself freely to you about my intentions. And I want to know your intentions. I want to know what you are going to do about the taking of our land. I want to hear you say that you understand now, and will wipe out that pretended treaty, so that the tribes can be at peace with each other, as you pretend you want them to be. Tell me, brother. I want to know now.

5. Tenskwatawa (the Shawnee Prophet) Relates His Journey to the World Above, 1810

I died and went to the World Above, and saw it.

The punishments I saw terrify you! But listen, those punishments will be upon you unless you follow me through the door that I am opening for you!

Our Creator put us on this wide, rich land, and told us we were free to go where the game was, where the soil was good for planting. That was our state of true happiness. We did not have to beg for anything. Our Creator had taught us how to find and make everything we needed, from trees and plants and animals and stone. We lived in bark, and we wore only the skins of animals.

Thus were we created. Thus we lived for a long time, proud and happy. We had never eaten pig meat, nor tasted the poison called whiskey, nor worn wool from sheep, nor struck fire or dug earth with steel, nor cooked in iron, nor hunted and

---

Message of the Shawnee Prophet Tenskwatawa, "he who opens the door." Obtained from http://courses. smsu.edu/ftm922f/Documents/Prophet&Tecumseh.htm.

fought with loud guns, nor ever had diseases which soured our blood or rotted our organs. We were pure, so we were strong and happy.

For many years we traded furs to the English or the French, for wool blankets and guns and iron things, for steel awls and needles and axes, for mirrors, for pretty things made of beads and silver. And for liquor. This was foolish, but we did not know it. We shut our ears to the Great Good Spirit. We did not want to hear that we were being foolish.

But now those things of the white men have corrupted us, and made us weak and needful. Our men forgot how to hunt without noisy guns. Our women don't want to make fire without steel, or cook without iron, or sew without metal awls and needles, or fish without steel hooks. Some look in those mirrors all the time, and no longer teach their daughters to make leather or render bear oil. We learned to need the white men's goods, and so now a People who never had to beg for anything must beg for everything!

Some of our women married white men, and made half-breeds. Many of us now crave liquor. He whose filthy name I will not speak, he who was I before, was one of the worst of those drunkards. There are drunkards in almost every family. You know how bad this is.

And so you see what has happened to us. We were fools to take all these things that weakened us. We did not need them then, but we believe we need them now. We turned our backs on the old ways. Instead of thanking the Great Spirit for all we used to have, we turned to the white man and asked them for more. So now we depend upon the very people who destroy us! This is our weakness! Our corruption! Our Creator scolded me, "If you had lived the way I taught you, the white men could never have got you under their foot!"

And that is why Our Creator purified me and sent me down to you full of the shinning power, to make you what you were before!

No red man must ever drink liquor, or he will go and have the hot lead poured in his mouth!

No red man shall take more than one wife in the future. No red man shall run after women. If he is single, let him take a wife, and lie only with her.

Any red woman who is living with a white man must return to her people, and must leave her children with the husband, so that all nations will be pure in their blood.

Now hear what I was told about dealing with white men! These things we must do, to cleanse ourselves of their corruption!

Do not eat any food that is raised or cooked by a white person. It is not good for us. Eat not their bread made of wheat, for Our Creator gave us corn for our bread. Eat not the meat of their filthy swine, nor of their chicken fowls, nor the beef of their cattle, which are tame and thus have no spirit in them. Their foods will seem to fill your empty belly, but this deceives you for food without spirit does not nourish you.

There are two kinds of white men. There are the Americans, and there are the others. You may give your hand in friendship to the French, or the Spaniards, or the British. But the Americans are not like those. The Americans come from the slime of the sea, with mud and weeds in their claws, and they are a kind of crayfish serpent whose claws grab in our earth and take it from us. . . .

. . . Remember it is the wish of the Great Good Spirit that we have no more commerce with white men!

We may keep our guns, and if we need to defend ourselves against American white men, the guns will kill them because they are a white man's weapon. But arrows will kill American intruders, too! You must go to the grandfathers and have them teach you to make good bows and shape arrowheads, and you must recover the old hunting skills. . . .

We will no longer do the frolic dances that excite lust. The Great Good Spirit will teach me the old dances we did before the corruption, and from these dances we will receive strength and happiness!

6. Congressman Felix Grundy
Advocates War with Britain, 1811

My mind is irresistibly drawn to the West.

Although others may not strongly feel the bearing which the late transactions in that quarter have on this subject, upon my mind they have great influence. It cannot be believed by any man who will reflect, that the savage tribes, uninfluenced by other Powers, would think of making war on the United States. They understand too well their own weakness, and our strength. They have already felt the weight of our arms; they know they hold the very soil on which they live as tenants at sufferance. How, then, sir are we to account for their late conduct? In one way only; some powerful nation must have intrigued with them, and turned their peaceful disposition towards us into hostilities. Great Britain alone has intercourse with those Northern tribes; I therefore infer, that if British gold has not been employed, their baubles and trinkets, and the promise of support and a place of refuge if necessary, have had their effect.

If I am right in this conjecture, war is not to commence by sea or land, it is already begun; and some of the richest blood of our country has already been shed.

7. John Marshall Advances a Broad
Construction of the Constitution, 1819

The government of the Union, then (whatever may be the influence of this fact on the case), is, emphatically and truly, a government of the people. In form, and in substance, it emanates from them. Its powers are granted by them, and are to be exercised directly on them, and for their benefit. . . .

If any one proposition could command the universal assent of mankind, we might expect it would be this—that the government of the Union, though limited in its powers, is supreme within its sphere of action. This would seem to result, necessarily from its nature. It is the government of all; its powers are delegated by all; it represents all, and acts for all. Though any one state may be willing to control its operations, no state is willing to allow others to control them. The nation, on those

Speech in Congress, December 1811, in *The Debates and Proceedings in the Congress of the United States,* 12th Cong., 1st sess. (Washington: Gales and Seaton, 1853), 425.

John Marshall, opinion in *McCulloch v. Maryland* (1819), in *United States Supreme Court Reporters,* vol. 17, p. 316.

subjects on which it can act, must necessarily bind its component parts. But this question is not left to mere reason: the people have, in express terms, decided it . . . "this constitution, and the laws of the United States, which shall be made in pursuance thereof, shall be the supreme law of the land," and by requiring that the members of the state legislatures, and the officers of the executive and judicial departments of the states, shall take the oath of fidelity to it. The government of the United States, then, though limited in its powers, is supreme; and its laws, when made in pursuance of the constitution, form the supreme law of the land, "anything in the constitution or laws of any state to the contrary notwithstanding."

8. James Monroe Declares That European Powers May Not Interfere in the Americas, 1823

. . . [A]s a principle in which the rights and interests of the United States are involved, that the American continents, by the free and independent condition which they have assumed and maintain, are henceforth not to be considered as subjects for future colonization by any European powers.

. . . Of events in that quarter of the globe, with which we have so much intercourse, and from which we derive our origin, we have always been anxious and interested spectators. The citizens of the United States cherish sentiments the most friendly, in favor of the liberty and happiness of their fellow men on that side of the Atlantic. In the wars of the European powers, in matters relating to themselves, we have never taken any part, nor does it comport with our policy so to do. It is only when our rights are invaded, or seriously menaced, that we resent injuries, or make preparation for our defense. With the movements in this hemisphere, we are, of necessity, more immediately connected, and by causes which must be obvious to all enlightened and impartial observers. The political system of the allied powers is essentially different, in this respect, from that of America. This difference proceeds from that which exists in their respective governments. And to the defence of our own, which has been achieved by the loss of so much blood and treasure, and matured by the wisdom of their most enlightened citizens, and under which we have enjoyed unexampled felicity, this whole nation is devoted. We owe it, therefore, to candor, and to the amicable relations existing between the United States and those powers, to declare, that we should consider any attempt on their part to extend their system to any portion of this hemisphere, as dangerous to our peace and safety. With the existing colonies or dependencies of any European power, we have not interfered, and shall not interfere. But, with the governments who have declared their independence and maintained it, and whose independence we have, on great consideration and on just principles, acknowledged, we could not view any interposition for the purpose of oppressing them, or controlling, in any other manner, their destiny, by any European power, in any other light than as the manifestation of an unfriendly disposition towards the United States. In the war between these new governments and Spain, we declared our neutrality at the time of their recognition, and to this we have adhered, and shall continue to adhere, provided no change shall occur, which,

James Monroe, *The Monroe Doctrine* (1823).

in the judgment of the competent authorities of this government, shall make a corresponding change, on the part of the United States, indispensable to their security.

. . . Our policy, in regard to Europe, which was adopted at an early stage of the wars which have so long agitated that quarter of the globe, nevertheless remains the same, which is, not to interfere in the internal concerns of any of its powers; to consider the government de facto as the legitimate government for us; to cultivate friendly relations with it, and to preserve those relations by a frank, firm, and manly policy, meeting, in all instances, the just claims of every power; submitting to injuries from none. But, in regard to those continents, circumstances are eminently and conspicuously different.

It is impossible that the allied powers should extend their political system to any portion of either continent, without endangering our peace and happiness; nor can any one believe that our Southern Brethren, if left to themselves, would adopt it of their own accord. It is equally impossible, therefore, that we should behold such interposition, in any form, with indifference. If we look to the comparative strength and resources of Spain and those new governments, and their distance from each other, it must be obvious that she can never subdue them. It is still the true policy of the United States, to leave the parties to themselves, in the hope that other powers will pursue the same course.

9. John Quincy Adams Urges Internal Improvements, 1825

In assuming her station among the civilized nations of the earth it would seem that our country had contracted the engagement to contribute her share of mind, of labor, and of expense to the improvement of those and of expense to the improvement of those parts of knowledge which lie beyond the reach of individual acquisition, and particularly to geographical and astronomical science. Looking back to the history only of the half century since the declaration of our independence, and observing the generous emulation with which the Governments of France, Great Britain, and Russia have devoted the genius, the intelligence, the treasures of their respective nations to the common improvement of the species in these branches of science, is it not incumbent upon us to inquire whether we are not bound by obligations of a high and honorable character to contribute our portion of energy and exertion to the common stock? The voyages of discovery prosecuted in the course of that time at the expense of those nations have not only redounded to their glory, but to the improvement of human knowledge. We have been partakers of that improvement and owe for it a sacred debt, not only of gratitude, but of equal or proportional exertion in the same common cause. . . .

In inviting the attention of Congress to the subject of internal improvements upon a view thus enlarged it is not my design to recommend the equipment of an expedition for circumnavigating the globe for purposes of scientific research and inquiry. We have objects of useful investigation nearer home, and to which our cares

John Quincy Adams, *Annual Message to Congress* (1825), in *The Selected Writings of John and John Quincy Adams,* ed. Adrienne Koch and William Peden (New York: Alfred A. Knopf, 1946), 361–364.

may be more beneficially applied. The interior of our own territories has been imperfectly explored. Our coasts along many degrees of latitude upon the shores of the Pacific ocean, though much frequented by our spirited commercial navigators, have been barely visited by our public ships. The River of the West, first fully discovered and navigated by a countryman of our own, still bears the name of the ship in which he ascended its waters, and claims the protection of our armed national flag at its mouth. With the establishment of a military post there or at some other point of that coast, recommended by my predecessor and already matured in the deliberations of the last Congress, I would suggest the expediency of connecting the equipment of a public ship for the exploration of the whole northwest coast of this continent.

The establishment of an uniform standard of weights and measures was one of the specific objects contemplated in the formation of our Constitution, and to fix that standard was one of the powers delegated by express terms in that instrument to Congress. . . .

Connected with the establishment of an university, or separate from it, might be undertaken the erection of an astronomical observatory, with provision for the support of an astronomer, to be in constant attendance of observation upon the phenomena of the heavens, and for the periodical publication of his observations. . . .

And while scarcely a year passes over our heads without bringing some new astronomical discovery to light, which we must fain receive at second hand from Europe, are we not cutting ourselves off from the means of returning light for light while we have neither observatory nor observer upon our half of the globe and the earth revolves in perpetual darkness to our unsearching eyes?

10. The Cherokee Nation Pleads to Remain "on the Land of Our Fathers," 1830

We are aware, that some persons suppose it will be for our advantage to remove beyond the Mississippi. We think otherwise. Our people universally think otherwise. Thinking that it would be fatal to their interests, they have almost to a man sent their memorial to congress, deprecating the necessity of a removal. This question was distinctly before their minds when they signed their memorial. Not an adult person can be found, who has not an opinion on the subject, and if the people were to understand distinctly, that they could be protected against the laws of the neighboring states, there is probably not an adult person in the nation, who would think it best to remove; though possibly a few might emigrate individually. There are doubtless many, who would flee to an unknown country, however beset with dangers, privations and sufferings, rather than be sentenced to spend six years in a Georgia prison for advising one of their neighbors not to betray his country. And there are others who could not think of living as outlaws in their native land, exposed to numberless vexations, and excluded from being parties or witnesses in a court of justice. It is incredible that Georgia should ever have enacted the oppressive laws to which reference is here made, unless she had supposed that something extremely terrific in its character was necessary in order to make the Cherokees

"Memorial of the Cherokee Nation," *Niles Weekly Register,* 38 (August 21, 1830): 454–457.

willing to remove. We are not willing to remove; and if we could be brought to this extremity, it would be not by argument, not because our judgment was satisfied, not because our condition will be improved; but only because we cannot endure to be deprived of our national and individual rights and subjected to a process of intolerable oppression.

We wish to remain on the land of our fathers. We have a perfect and original right to remain without interruption or molestation. The treaties with us, and laws of the United States made in pursuance of treaties, guarantee our residence and our privileges, and secure us against intruders. Our only request is, that these treaties may be fulfilled, and these laws executed. . . .

The removal of families to a new country, even under the most favorable auspices, and when the spirits are sustained by pleasing visions of the future, is attended with much depression of mind and sinking of heart. This is the case, when the removal is a matter of decided preference, and when the persons concerned are in early youth or vigorous manhood. Judge, then, what must be the circumstances of a removal, when a whole community, embracing persons of all classes and every description, from the infant to the man of extreme old age, the sick, the blind, the lame, the improvident, the reckless, the desperate, as well as the prudent, the considerate, the industrious, are compelled to remove by odious and intolerable vexations and persecutions, brought upon them in the forms of law, when all will agree only in this, that they have been cruelly robbed of their country, in violation of the most solemn compacts, which it is possible for communities to form with each other; and that, if they should make themselves comfortable in their new residence, they have nothing to expect hereafter but to be the victims of a future legalized robbery!

Such we deem, and are absolutely certain, will be the feelings of the whole Cherokee people, if they are forcibly compelled, by the laws of Georgia, to remove; and with these feelings, how is it possible that we should pursue our present course of improvement, or avoid sinking into utter despondency? We have been called a poor, ignorant, and degraded people. We certainly are not rich; nor have we ever boasted of our knowledge, or our moral or intellectual elevation. But there is not a man within our limits so ignorant as not to know that he has a right to live on the land of his fathers, in the possession of his immemorial privileges, and that this right has been acknowledged and guaranteed by the United States; nor is there a man so degraded as not to feel a keen sense of injury, on being deprived of this right and driven into exile.

ESSAYS

The market revolution and the westward movement of Americans had a profound and often a devastating impact on the Indians. As indigenous people faced increasing pressure in the early decades of the nineteenth century, their responses varied. Some used Christian teachings to oppose white expansion westward. Others attempted to inculcate specific aspects of American culture into their society. The following two essays illustrate two very different answers to the Indians' dilemma. Gregory Evans Dowd, a historian at the University of Notre Dame, focuses on attempts led by Tecumseh and his brother Tenskwatawa (also known as the Prophet) to unite Indian nations and oppose the white invasion. Note how Tenskwatawa used visions and prophecy to foster his political aims.

In contrast, Theda Perdue, a member of the department of history at the University of North Carolina at Chapel Hill, analyzes the Cherokees, who embraced the "civilization" efforts of the American government as their best hope for avoiding forced removal from their homes. These struggles with civilization, Professor Perdue argues, affected Cherokee women and men in different ways.

Indians Utilizing a Strategy of Armed Resistance

GREGORY EVANS DOWD

A new order emerged in the trans-Appalachian borderlands following the defeat of pan-Indianism in the mid-1790s. Through Jay's Treaty (1794) with Britain, which like other European-American treaties ignored Indian possessions, the United States secured the military posts within its territorial claims. In the Treaty of San Lorenzo (1795), Spain recognized the American claim to lands at the core of the Creek confederacy. The influence of Britain and Spain in North America, visibly in retreat at these treaty tables, receded still farther as truly devastating wars deranged Europe. As European power in Indian country ebbed through diplomatic channels, American power flowed aggressively to replace it. It flowed directly into Indian councils, where it found considerable Native American tolerance, if not support.

Indians believing in the need for the conscious adaptation of European ways, many of whom had been once, when armed from Europe, willing to league with nativists against the United States, now sought to come to terms with the republic. American agents, paid by the federal government, worked closely with these Indian leaders. Their combined efforts promoted a mission of "civilization." Rapidly among the Cherokees but with less success among the Creeks, Shawnees, and Delawares, the "plan of civilization," supported by the federal government and by several churches, became rooted in tribal government.

Among all the involved peoples, however, including the republic's citizens, the civilizing mission met a thicket of difficulties. The Anglo-American brambles grew not only from the opposition of citizens interested in Indian lands, but also out of an intellectual seedbed sown with incompatible crops, as many scholars have shown. An essential motivation of the mission, the assumed superiority of Anglo-American culture, entangled it from the start, for the missionaries' conviction of their religious and cultural superiority alienated the targeted peoples. This was as true of nonreligious agents as it was of the religious missionaries.

The secular employees of the mission, moreover, underestimated the obstacles that spread across their path, a failing that led them into tactical contradictions. Once they undertook the mission, they never adequately reconciled their aims with their methods. In what one scholar calls a "lapse in logic," these Americans sought to make good citizens out of the Indians, but employed coercion, cajolery, and deception to do so. The agents were under great pressure from American governments—territorial, state, and federal—to accomplish their task, with the understanding that it would increase the land available to the republic. Governments and missionaries alike claimed that if Indian men abandoned hunting and took up the plow, they could live well, and on less land. The surplus lands would then come up for grabs. In practice the process inverted. Pressured by their land-hungry countrymen, American agents among the Indians obtained land cessions from impoverished Indians even before the successful conversion of Indian men into yeomen farmers. To justify the inversion, the mission's proponents came to argue that by restricting Indian land they restricted Indian hunting and thereby compelled Indian men to farm. The American acquisition of Indian land perversely took on a philanthropic guise; taking became giving.

As early a professional historian of the era as Henry Adams noticed the moral contradictions within the civilizing mission. Adams discovered that although President Thomas Jefferson had advocated the establishment of an Indian farming class, he had sought to do so through the manipulation of Indian debt. In Adams's words, Jefferson "deliberately ordered his Indian agents to tempt the tribal chiefs into debt in order to oblige them to sell the tribal lands, which did not belong to them, but to their tribes." Jefferson, that indebted foe of debt, attempted to create an independent Indian yeomanry by driving Indian leaders into the red. This contradiction, between Federal efforts to "improve" Indian economies on the one hand, while both increasing Indian indebtedness and decreasing Indian landholding on the other, placed the civilizing mission precariously upon a badly fissured foundation. The contradiction, with the others, had to be sustained; the federal government had to meet world opinion with a policy of benevolence while also meeting its citizens' desire for land.

The dense undergrowth of the Indians' recent history [laid] violent hazards in the way of the "plan of civilization," and the most vital and stubborn of the strands took the form of prophetic nativism. Between 1795 and 1815, individual prophets and groups of Indians claiming supernatural inspiration posed direct challenges to those leaders who advocated political and even cultural accommodation to the power of the United States. Insurgent nativists drew upon their histories of intertribal cooperation. They looked to their shared beliefs in the ritual demands of power. Turning to the spirits as well as to their intertribal comrades, they attempted to rally support against those tribal leaders who ceded land to the Americans. Prophetic parties of Shawnees, Delawares, Creeks, and many others actually broke with their accommodating countrymen to prepare an intertribal, Indian union against the expansion of the United States, an effort that eventually merged with the War of 1812. . . .

The apocalyptic teachings of the early nineteenth-century prophets bore the two faces of doom and glory. A Delaware woman who had visions in 1806 warned that if the Big House Ceremony were not celebrated with care, a whirlwind would soon wipe out the people completely. The Trout thought the world "broken," that it "declines." The Indians to the west of the Ottawas would soon all "fall off and die," unless they sent deputies to be instructed in ritual. Handsome Lake warned of a "visitation of Sickness" if his teachings were neglected. But the fear induced by such threats was offset by the hope that came with prophetic promises. The Trout believed that, through the power of a war-club dance, the Ottawas and Chippewas would "distroy every white man in america." Tenskwatawa's first visions also contained such notions, shaped in traditional myth. He encountered a crab, a common "earth diver" in Native American creation stories, a being that brought up the muck from which the earth was made. The Great Spirit promised the Shawnee Prophet that if the Indians abided by his teachings, the crab would "turn over the land so that the white people are covered." Later Tenskwatawa indicated that Anglo-Americans were not in danger as long as they left the prophet's town at Greenville, Ohio, alone. But if the United States attempted to meet his prophecy with force, "if the white people would go to war, they would be destroyed by a day of judgement," or, according to another source, "there will be an End to the World."

On the eve of the War of 1812, prophecy in the North, despite its innovations, belonged to a developing tradition as old as the peoples' elders. Nativists had previously expressed that tradition most vigorously between 1745 and 1775, especially after 1760. They had continued to invoke it, though often in the shadow of cooperation with Great Britain, during the long wars of the 1770s through 1790s. They did so as participants in a broad movement: challenging tribal boundaries, altering Indian identity, inventing a strategy of resistance against Anglo-American expansion. . . .

In 1809, the annuity chiefs unwittingly and negligently galvanized the nativists with another land cession. The affair began in the summer of 1809, when the secretary of war wrote Harrison that he could proceed with his desire to purchase more lands along the Wabash, but only if the governor was certain that the undertaking "will excite no disagreeable apprehension and produce no undesirable effects before It shall be made." Harrison proceeded to negotiate with the Delaware, Potowatomi, Miami, and Eel River Indians, making separate treaties with the Weas and Kickapoos later that year. The main text agreed to, the Treaty of Fort Wayne, ceded over two and one half million acres to the United States, for about two cents an acre—a high price in Indian treaties, but still a massively unequal exchange.

The Treaty of Fort Wayne has long been recognized as a milestone on the road to the battle of Tippecanoe. From this period forward in histories of the West on the eve of the War of 1812, Tenskwatawa's brother, Tecumseh, fashions and leads the pan-Indian movement. . . .

The prophet, however, lost no power following the treaty; he still led the nativists from his headquarters at Tippecanoe. His preaching . . . had always exhibited both the political overtones and material concerns that political and social historians seek to grasp and find worth grasping. Like Tecumseh, Tenskwatawa spoke out vigorously against both the Fort Wayne cession and the Indians who had agreed to it. In the spring and summer of 1810, half a year after the signing of the treaty, the Prophet informed a discovered American spy that his people were "much exasperated at the cession of Lands made last winter" and that they had "agreed that the Tract on the N. west side of the Wabash should not be surveyed." His disciples followed up this declaration by successfully opposing a surveying party in September.

Tecumseh, meanwhile, spoke out against the government chiefs long targeted by Tenskwatawa. In August 1810 Tecumseh informed Harrison that he intended "to level all distinctions to destroy the village chiefs by whom all mischief is done; it is they who sell our land to the Americans." He asked Harrison to repudiate the Fort Wayne treaty, for the annuity chiefs "had no right" to sell the claim. He did not threaten Harrison with war; rather he threatened "to kill all the chiefs who sold you this land." By retaining the American claim, Tecumseh warned, "you will have a hand in killing them." Tecumseh, like the prophet, was still less openly hostile to the United States than he was to its allies among Indian leaders. . . .

It is on the subject of Indian unity that scholars and tale-spinners alike have most emphasized the particular wisdom of Tecumseh. Even here, although he was an energetic ambassador and a man of martial distinction, Tecumseh, like his brother, was more participant in than progenitor of the movement we associate with his name. Tecumseh drew on both the nativist vision of his brother and the broader dreams and practical legacies of two generations of militants.

In his speech to Harrison that August, Tecumseh argued, as had Ohioan and Great Lakes Country militants for at least three decades, that "all the lands in the western country was the common property of all the tribes." No land could be sold without the consent of all. To establish the principle, he intended, as had others, to unite the tribes in a movement against American expansion. The prophet also argued that "no sale was good unless made by all the Tribes," and he welcomed Indians of all tribes to join in his spiritual revival, his rebellion against the authority of annuity chiefs, his rejection of Christianity, and his defense of Indian lands.

To support his intertribal call, the Shawnee Prophet had at his disposal a concept of Indian identity that had been developing since at least the middle of the eighteenth century, a concept embodied in the notion of the separate creation of whites and Indians. The notion did not lead directly to nativism; it was so widespread that even such federally recognized chiefs as Black Hoof and the Wyandot Tahre expressed the view at the turn of the nineteenth century. But government chiefs could never turn it to their advantage with the dexterity of the nativists, for in its logical conclusion, the doctrine meant an Indian rejection of American control.

In 1805 the Presbyterian missionary, James Hughes, found the Wyandots divided over their concept of the creation. Some believed in a single Great Spirit, others held "that there are two Gods, one the creator of the white people, and the other of the Indians, whom they call the Warrior." The Shawnee Prophet believed something akin to the latter notion, as he told C. C. Trowbridge in 1824. He recalled that at the creation "The Great Spirit then opened a door, and looking down they saw a white man seated upon the ground. . . . The Great Spirit told them that this white man was not made by himself but by another spirit who made & governed the whites & over whom he had no controul." The Trout, the Ottawa spokesman for the nativist movement, further defined the Americans (he distinguished, as had the Ottawa Pontiac before him, between the Anglo-Americans whose seaboard polities thrust aggressively westward and the less expansionist Canadians) as creatures of the "Evil Spirit" from "Scum of the great water."

The separate, even evil, nature of American citizens emerged also in Indian interpretations of Christianity. As in the mid-eighteenth century, some Indians turned Christianity against Christians to demonstrate the depth of the missionaries' abomination. In crucifying Jesus, these argued, Europeans had killed their own God. During the first, more militantly anti-Christian phase of Handsome Lake's mission, his half-brother Cornplanter, who "liked some ways of the white people," told the Quaker missionary Henry Simmons, "it was the white people who kill'd our Saviour." Simmons countered, "it was the Jews," and then tried to drive the point home by dragging out the already hackneyed argument that Indians were members of the lost tribes of Israel: "Indians were their descendants, for many of their habits were Similar to the Jews, in former days." We don't know what Cornplanter made of that contention— perhaps he was simply at a loss for words—but twentieth-century practitioners of the

Handsome Lake Religion have made no mention of it and consider the crucifixion a deed performed by whites. They have learned that the Seneca Prophet, in his early visions, met Jesus, who described himself as "a man upon the earth who was slain by his own people." Jesus had ordered Handsome Lake to "tell your people that they will become lost when they follow the ways of the white people."

Nativistic northwesterners leaned more heavily on the argument. Responding to a Moravian missionary in 1806, one of Tenskwatawa's followers said of the crucifixion, "Granted that what you say is true, He did not die in Indian land but among the white people." In 1810 Tecumseh himself, revealing his own concerns for things spiritual, asked Harrison in the same pointed terms, "How can we have confidence in the white people[?] when Jesus Christ came upon the earth you kill'd and nail'd him on a cross." Given the Shawnee's nativistic assumptions, it was a logical question.

If, as the Shawnee Prophet said, Americans were unchangeably inimical to Indians, if "the Great Spirit did not mean that the white and red people should live near each other" because whites "poison'd the land," and if all Indians came from a common creation different from that of others, then it only made sense that Indians should unite against the American threat. In emphasizing their separation, Indians gave spiritual sanction to Native American unity.

Intertribal, Prophetic Nativism

Tecumseh has captured a more prominent place in American history than any Indian of his day, arguably of any day. . . .

Tecumseh did *not,* however, significantly differ from his followers in culture or in vision; nor was it tribalism that blocked his success. He certainly stood out as an expert organizer, warrior, and an indefatigable traveler, although many others from the revolutionary era and the two decades that followed it could rival him even in those talents. In his hopes and in his vision, moreover, he stood with, not beyond or outside of, the militant nativists of the Eastern Woodlands. His most recent biographer, Bil Gilbert, credits Tecumseh with having "conceived of a plan for uniting the red people," but Tecumseh was not the plan's sole creator; he drew upon traditions of nativism and networks of intertribal relations that had been vibrant throughout the trans-Appalachian borderlands, reaching back into the past beyond the time of Neolin and Pontiac. With Tecumseh, also drawing from this legacy, stood the prophets.

The major northern religious leaders urged forms of intertribal unity between 1805 and 1812. Even Handsome Lake, whose Senecas were entirely surrounded by U.S. citizens, who had little direct contact with other militants, and who prudently drew back from military alliance as the War of 1812 erupted, nonetheless showed a certain solidarity with the more western Indians by demanding that his followers refuse to support the United States. Nor did Handsome Lake ignore other peoples; he sent his word to Sandusky in 1804 and visited the region in 1806. But his influence remained largely confined to the reservations east of Lake Erie.

Tenskwatawa promoted pan-Indianism not with words alone, or only with the elaboration of separation theology, but with the time-honored if paradoxical political device of secession. Like the Susquehanna Delawares and Shawnees who had fled Anglo-Iroquois authority by both removing to Ohio and settling in polyglot villages in the early eighteenth century, like the Chickamaugas who had broken with the

Cherokees to settle the Tennessee with their militant Shawnee allies during the American Revolution, Tenskwatawa broke from his hosts, invited Indians of all nations to join him, and settled new towns. He did so first at Greenville (1806–8), in symbolic defiance of the Treaty of Greenville, and later at Tippecanoe (1808–12), in outright defiance of Little Turtle's claim to authority over that land. The prophet warned Little Turtle that plans for the Tippecanoe settlement had been "layed by all the Indians in America and had been sanctioned by the Great Spirit." He then informed the Miami leader that Indian unity alone would end Indian poverty and defend Indian land.

One band of Wyandots, joining the prophet in 1810, bound the movement of earlier decades by bringing with them "the Great Belt which was the Symbol of Union between the Tribes in their late war with the United States." Consciously reviving the pan-Indianism of their recent past, these Wyandots, in the prophet's words, could not "sit still and see the property of all the Indians usurped."

Drawing upon the same tradition of resistance and adhering to Tenskwatawa, the Trout also advocated Indian unity. In the spring of 1807, before Tecumseh gained notice, this Ottawa addressed Ottawas and Chippewas, requesting that each of their villages send at least two deputies to his village, L'arbre Croche, to carry out the will of the Great Spirit. And he specifically demanded, in the voice of the Great Spirit, an end to intertribal hostilities: "You are, however, never to go to War against each other. But to cultivate peace between your different Tribes, that they may become one great people." The following spring, in the turbulent wake of a large land sale by Ottawas, Chippewas, Wyandots, and Potawatomis to the United States, militants of all four tribes declared it "a crime punishable by Death for any Indian to put his name on paper for the perpose of parting with any of their lands."

The third prophet, Main Poc of the Potawatomis, stood for northern Indian solidarity, but limited his vision to what Americans would call the Old Northwest. He waged sporadic war on the trans-Mississippi Osage Indians, a war fought also by northern refugees who had already fled across that great river. Main Poc deviated in other ways: even after donning the prophetic mantle, he accepted a bribe from Wells, though it does not seem to have changed his behavior. Further, he continued to drink, advocating only temperance, while other nativists, as a rule, advocated abstinence. But Main Poc did think beyond the boundaries of his "tribe." This Potawatomi, in fact, recommended Tippecanoe to Tenskwatawa as a good site for a town. As hostilities neared in the fall of 1811, Main Poc actively sought recruits beyond his people, among the Ottawas and Chippewas. . . .

. . . [T]he military and diplomatic accomplishments of the nativists who bore arms in the War of 1812 would not approach those of their militant predecessors in the revolutionary era. The odds against pan-Indian success had increased sharply since the early 1790s. By 1812 American citizens outnumbered Indians in the region between the Appalachians and the Mississippi by a margin of seven-to-one. The new states of Kentucky, Tennessee, and Ohio formed a pounding wedge that split the Indian quest for unity, already rotten with civil conflict, into two deteriorating blocs. Meanwhile Louisiana, admitted to statehood in 1812, and Missouri, established as a territory that same year, applied additional pressure from the west, disrupting Indian travel on the Mississippi River. The lower portion of the Ohio River had become similarly dominated not only by Kentucky but by the organized territories of Indiana and Illinois. The Upper Ohio, of course, had been finally lost by the independent peoples in 1795. This weighty American presence, combined with the loss of Cherokees as military allies, meant that the pan-Indian effort associated with Tecumseh would be more a severe aftershock than a seismic rift, a mere reminder of greater deeds done long ago. . . .

The increasing regionalization was serious enough, but further weakening pan-Indianism in this period was the failure of the militant nativists to come to terms with those, among each of their own peoples, who now cooperated with the United States, those who were now—more than ever—enemies at home. . . .

This all meant that in 1812, accommodating Indians in the North as well as in the South would stick with the United States, even to the point, for some, of firing upon their nativistic relatives. The age of Tecumseh created little room for a joint alliance of nativist and accommodationist with Britain. Not only, then, did the War of 1812 bring an end to any serious military cooperation between northern and southern Indians, it also thrust peoples of both regions into the maelstrom of civil war.

In a narrow sense, however paradoxically, these years of devastating internal conflict and pan-Indian failure saw nativism's greatest triumph, for what unity was achieved owed itself, in the largest measure, to the spread of emphatically religious nativist thought along the networks that had for years brought warriors together from across the wide trans-Appalachian borderlands. While in the late eighteenth century multiple readings of opportunities brought into the same camp Indians of various persuasions—accommodationists who saw chances for Spanish or British alliance and nativists who sought to fight the Americans at all costs—in the first decades of the nineteenth century the United States fought against groups often wholly influenced by nativism. But however much the period saw nativism's greatest success among the Indians who bordered the states, it was not pan-Indianism's greatest triumph, as it is often portrayed in studies of Tecumseh. Instead, the War of 1812 stands as pan-Indianism's most thorough failure, its crushing defeat, its disappointing anticlimax. . . .

The nativists failed. Measured by their own goals, the failure was complete. The union of all Indians, the rescue by sacred power, and the demise of containment of the Anglo-Americans did not come about. We might expect the failure to have led to repudiation; instead the ideas continued to animate isolated groups of believers on both sides of the Mississippi. Notions of Indian unity, of separation from Americans, and of the possible rescue by the sacred powers inspired resisters of removal under Black Hawk in Illinois as well as the far more powerful Seminoles of Florida, but the notions also lived on in the memory of people who would never again bear arms against the United States. As nativistic notions persisted, so did their Native American antitheses.

Nativism lived on in large measure because its opposition had failed just as bitterly. Within a generation of the murder of Francis and the battle death of Tecumseh, the United States had driven most of its Indian allies as well as its Indian enemies west of the Mississippi. There, and in scattered hollows throughout the East, the debates of the ages of Pontiac and Tecumseh found resonance: some continued to seek an accommodation with the United States, others argued for the irreconcilable differences separating all Indians, whatever their particular people, from the nation that stole their lands. . . .

Tenskwatawa himself, the symbol of religious nativism in the Northwest, weathered the War of 1812 and lived out his natural life. Had nativism depended solely upon this prophet it would have had a slim chance for survival, for in his later years, richly narrated by historian R. David Edmunds, Tenskwatawa did little to honor his own memory. He gave up the armed struggle with the end of the war, and he lost most of his followers, living first as a dependent of the British and later of the Americans. But he had not lost all authority with the escape of victory. He headed a small camp of Shawnee, Kickapoo, Sauk, and Fox refugees in Ontario until about 1825, when he returned to Black Hoof's town in Ohio. There his influence increased briefly; he may even have played a leading role in a Shawnee witch scare. But in contrast to his earlier years as a defender of the northern Indians against American expansion, he collaborated in these years in American plans for removal; he turned accommodationist. He led a large Shawnee contingent on a poorly supplied, starvation-ridden, two-year migration to Kansas between 1826 and 1828. Having given up the fight, Tenskwatawa gradually lost his remaining sway among the Shawnees. He managed to display in the West some vestigial religious authority, establishing a "Prophetstown" in his new Kansan land, but with few followers to inhabit the village, it could only have stood as a humiliating reminder of his earlier triumphs and failures.

Tenskwatawa, however, had never been the single font from which all nativism had sprung. A player in a crowded field, his end was obscure and unknown to most. Among Indians throughout the era of removal, the memory of militant nativism ran a course that diverged from the downward personal trajectory of the Shawnee Prophet's career. Militant nativism survived, occasionally gaining strength, but always turning its main energies against its Indian opposition. . . .

. . . In the nativists' view, their failure was not one of their prophets' misunderstandings, but of the Indians' seduction by the Anglo-Americans. The nativists could see that they had not been rescued by the sacred powers, but they could also maintain that the ways of their Indian opponents had proved no more effective in preserving their lands and people. The United States, by driving its friends as well as its enemies across the Mississippi, gave force to nativistic arguments that Indians would never be welcome either in the neighborhood of whites or in the Christian heaven. It is not surprising, therefore, that Shawnees west of the Mississippi, despite the disastrous failure of their forebears' nativism, continued to speak of separate heavens for Indians and whites. It is not surprising that they spoke of an "anti-christian sage," unnamed in our record, who had just a "few years" before Josiah Gregg took his notes in the 1830s opposed the work of missionaries.

In the manner of the earlier prophets, the sage had collapsed with all the appearance of death, "and became stiff and cold, except a spot upon his breast, which still retained the heat of life." Awakening, he told his friends and family that he "had ascended to the Indian's heaven." There his grandfather gave him a warning, a warning flushed with the memory of numerous Shawnee "removals." As Anglo-America had forced them repeatedly from their homes and had failed to honor promises made even to its Indian allies, so, the grandfather warned the new prophet, would Christian promises yield no salvation, no heavenly mansion: "Beware of the religion of the white man: . . . every Indian who embraces it is obliged to take the road to the white man's heaven; and yet no red man is permitted to enter there, but will have to wander about forever without a resting place."

Indians Utilizing a Strategy of Accommodation

THEDA PERDUE

War and trade dominated Cherokee society in the eighteenth century, but by the end of the century, neither seemed to have much of a future. Overhunting contributed to a decline in deer, encroaching white settlements and roaming livestock destroyed the deer's habitat, and other commodities replaced deerskins in trans-Atlantic commerce. The colonial wars that had claimed thousands of lives and had destroyed orchards, fields, homes, and towns, too, seemed to be at an end. Europeans settled their differences or moved to another theater, and British colonists won their independence. The Cherokees, who had participated in European colonial expansion as allies and trading partners, found themselves with an economy geared to trade and a government shaped by warriors. The United States, invigorated by its political reorganization in 1789, had little use for such anachronistic Native societies, and it embarked on an Indian policy designed to accommodate the land needs of its expanding population and the moral imperatives of its republican ideology. The federal government took on the task of "civilizing" the Indians, that is, converting them culturally into Anglo-Americans. Although eighteenth-century changes threatened the marginalization of women politically and economically, "civilization" implied a far more dramatic transformation. Guided by an idealized view of men and women in their own society, reformers sought to turn men into industrious, republican farmers and women into chaste, orderly housewives. . . .

The civilization program became an official part of Cherokee relations with the federal government in 1791 when the Cherokees signed the Treaty of Holston. The treaty provided that the federal government furnish the Cherokees with "implements of husbandry" and send residential agents to give instruction in their use. As a result of this aid, "the Cherokee nation may be led to a greater degree of civilization, and to become herdsmen and cultivators, instead of remaining in a state of hunters." In 1793 the Indian Trade and Intercourse Act committed the United States to providing agricultural implements and draft animals to all Indians and to appointing agents to instruct Native people in their use. The Cherokees, devastated by invasion and impoverished by the decline of the deerskin trade, welcomed assistance. Yet they must have been somewhat bemused by the proffered lessons in agriculture. Not only had Cherokee women been farming for centuries, but many of the crops and techniques used by Euro-Americans came from Native peoples.

In 1796 George Washington outlined the key provisions of the civilization program in a letter addressed to "Beloved Cherokees." In it, he pointed out that "you now see that the game with which your woods once abounded, are growing scarce, and you know that when you cannot find a deer or other game to kill, you must remain hungry." Washington noted that "some of you already experience the advantage of keeping cattle and hogs." He urged other Cherokees to follow their example: "Let all keep them and increase their numbers, and you will have plenty of meat. To these add

Theda Perdue, *Cherokee Women: Gender and Culture Change, 1700–1835* (Lincoln: University of Nebraska Press, 1998), 109–113, 115–116, 118–120, 125–126, 128–129, 133–134. Copyright © 1998 University of Nebraska Press. Reprinted by permission of the University of Nebraska Press.

sheep, and they will give you clothing as well as food." Washington also encouraged commercial agriculture: "Your lands are good and of great extent. By proper management you can raise live stock not only for your own wants, but to sell to the White people." The president recommended the use of the plow to increase production and the adoption of wheat, which he claimed "makes the best bread." To this point, the president's letter is ungendered—it appears to address all Cherokees—but then he turned to the cultivation of fiber crops: "You will easily add flax and cotton which you may dispose of to the White people; or have it made up by your own women into clothing for yourselves. Your wives and daughters can soon learn to spin and weave."

Washington's instructions did not bode well for Cherokee women. Directly addressing Cherokee men, the president implied that animal husbandry and farming were male responsibilities in a "civilized" society. Spinning, weaving, and sewing were women's work. Such expectations threatened the traditional division of labor in Cherokee society and whatever remnants of female autonomy remained. The president assumed that Cherokee men would take up the tasks and adopt the work habits common in the United States while women would become helpmates, mere auxiliaries. In order to convert men from hunters into farmers, "civilizers" had to transform Cherokee conceptions of gender.

Beyond Washington's economic message, however, was an even more ominous signal to Cherokee women: in a "civilized" society women belonged to men, who both headed households and governed the nation. The president addressed Cherokee women only through men: "*your own* women"; "*your* wives and daughters." Washington also hoped to accelerate the political centralization already under way in the Cherokee Nation. He suggested that the Cherokees send representatives to an annual meeting, the forerunner of the Cherokees' National Council, where they could meet with United States agents and "talk together on the affairs of your nation." The president probably did not expect these representatives to include women.

The government's program to "civilize" Indians rested on an image of Indians as hunters who derived their livelihood from vast game preserves. These hunting grounds presented both an obstacle to "civilization" and a boon to those who succeeded in "civilizing" their proprietors. Native people who became farmers presumably would no longer need their excess lands and would willingly cede them for additional aid to improve their farms. Therefore, land cession supposedly benefitted both Native people and white pioneers.

Total expulsion of Native peoples from the eastern United States was an idea that dated back to the purchase of Louisiana in 1803. Thomas Jefferson suggested an exchange of lands in the East for tracts in the West, and he specifically proposed such a scheme to the Cherokees and Choctaws. Jefferson, however, did not press the issue, because he believed that Native peoples would become "civilized," live contentedly on reduced acreage, and blend into American society. Land cessions negotiated during Jefferson's administration provoked intense factionalism as well as creating population displacement, and so some Cherokees expressed interest in moving west, and the federal government encouraged individual families to migrate to what is today Arkansas. Treaties negotiated in 1817 and 1819 provided not only for land cessions but also for voluntary removal to the West. By the 1820s, two to three thousand Cherokees lived west of the Mississippi while approximately sixteen thousand remained in their homeland in the East.

Some Cherokees believed that "civilization" was their best protection against forced removal. Consequently, they spoke English, sent their children to school, and converted to Christianity. They established a Cherokee republic with written laws, a court system, and a national police force. They also tried to conform to Anglo-American notions about appropriate behavior for men and women. Trade and warfare had accentuated traditional roles for men and women, but "civilization" threatened to usher in new roles by making men farmers and women housewives.

The Cherokees who are most visible in the historical record succeeded in this transformation. They reacted to the crisis of the late eighteenth and early nineteenth centuries by trying to re-create Cherokee culture and society in ways that accommodated "civilization." As a result, Cherokees laid claim to the title of "most civilized Indian tribe" in America. Although they comprised a minority, the Cherokees who enthusiastically embraced "civilization" dominated Cherokee economic and political life as well as Cherokee history. Not surprisingly, men—particularly wealthy and powerful men—play the lead roles in this history. The documents recording their actions and beliefs usually mentioned women only incidentally. Whereas the history of these men forms a compelling narrative of Cherokee "civilization," ferreting out the experiences of women and using them to create an alternative narrative forces reconsideration of Cherokee culture change, even in a period when it seemed so dramatic.

An Indian policy developed in Washington faced an uncertain future among the people for whom it was designed. The Cherokees, like most other Native people, did not reject the civilization program, nor did they embrace it wholeheartedly. They simply adopted those aspects of the policy that seemed to address their particular set of problems. The result was not always what policy makers had intended. The Cherokees accepted many of the technological innovations offered by government agents, and Cherokee homesteads began to resemble those that dotted the rural landscape of the United States. Where gender was concerned, however, the transformation proved far less successful. Male hunters and female farmers were anathema to "civilization," and since hunting was no longer a viable enterprise, "civilizers" expected men to replace women as farmers. These expectations, however, failed to take into account the durability of gender conventions and the adaptability of Cherokee culture.

Benjamin Hawkins, who resided permanently with the Creeks, was also responsible for implementing the civilization program among the Cherokees. When he visited the Cherokees in the fall of 1796, the men were absent, and so Hawkins spent his time primarily with women. One of his hostesses, a Mrs. Gagg, invited a group of women over to meet him: "They informed me that the men were all in the woods hunting, that they alone were at home to receive me, that they rejoiced much at what they had heard and hoped it would prove true, that they had made some cotton, and would make more and follow the instruction of the agent and the advise of the President." Because "civilization" rested on agriculture and domestic manufactures, tasks women traditionally performed, the women believed that the civilization program validated what they did and promised to help them do their work more successfully on their homesteads.

Women's level of production became apparent to Hawkins when he visited women in the town of Etowah: "They informed me they performed most of the labour, the men assisted but little and that in the corn. They generally made a plenty of corn and sweet potatoes and pumpkins. They made beans, ground peas, cymblins, gourds, watermelons, collards and onions." Furthermore, these women kept livestock. One group of women told Hawkins that they raised "hogs, some cattle, and a great many poultry," and he encountered other women driving cattle to market. Women also had primary responsibility for domestic manufactures. They told Hawkins that "they made sugar, had raised some cotton, and manufactured their baskets, sifters, pots and earthen pans." Again and again they indicated to him their support for "the plan contemplated by the government for the bettering of the condition of the Red people," because they understood the concrete ways in which support for agriculture, animal husbandry, and domestic manufactures could improve their lives.

Women envisioned "civilization" bringing improvement, not profound change. The matters Hawkins discussed with them were perfectly comprehensible because farming, tending livestock, and making utilitarian items had long been part of their world. In some ways, surprisingly little had changed during the preceding century: they continued to farm as their ancestors had for centuries. Metal hoes made the job easier, but the work remained the same. Agricultural production had expanded to include a number of crops introduced by Europeans and Africans. These included watermelons, onions, collards, fruit trees, and even a little cotton. But farming remained women's work. . . .

The prosperous farms and industrious work habits . . . , according to "civilizers," represented the Cherokees' hope for the future, while hunting deer and trading skins reflected the past. Hawkins described the poverty reliance on hunting had brought: "Their men hunted in their proper season and aided them with the skins in providing cloaths and blankets, such as I saw, but this was not sufficient to make them comfortable and the poor old men, women and children were under the necessity of sleeping as I saw them in their town house." Nevertheless, many men persisted in their hunting economy. When agent Return J. Meigs arrived in 1801, he had to settle a hunting party's claim for 123 deerskins, 40 bearskins, 5 small furs, and a buffalo skin that its eight members had left in the hunting grounds the previous year when a group of whites threatened them. Like Hawkins, Meigs discovered that by November the chiefs had "gone to their hunting grounds & will not return for two or three months." Yet hunting days were numbered. By 1808 losses from hunting camps were more likely to be half a bear and some deermeat than a substantial pile of skins. Hunting, however, was one of the things that defined masculinity, and few Cherokee men were willing to forgo it. When a twenty-four-year-old man applied for admission to the school at Brainerd, he requested permission to hunt to clothe himself: he received instead a job on the farm.

The persistence of hunting and the Cherokees' attachment to hunting grounds troubled "civilizers." Thomas Jefferson instructed Hawkins in 1803 "to promote among the Indians a sense of the superior value of a little land, well cultivated, over a great deal, unimproved." Eventually, he hoped, their hunting grounds "will be found useless, and even disadvantageous." When Cherokee men's devotion to the chase momentarily thwarted Meigs's attempt to secure a cession of the Cumberland Mountain region in 1805, he complained: "That land is of no use to them. There is not a single family on it, & the hunting is very poor. Yet those of idle dispositions spend much time in rambling there & often return with a stolen horse which they have afterwards to pay for. In fact it is only a nursery of savage habits and operates against civilization which is much impeded by their holding such immense tracts of wilderness." Meigs summarized the civilizers' major concerns. First of all, hunting promoted idleness rather than the industriousness on which civilization was based. Second, the common ground encouraged a disregard for private property. And finally, "wilderness" stood in direct opposition to "civilized" towns, pastures, and fields. Meigs, Hawkins, Jefferson, and other "civilizers" linked the cession of hunting grounds with the civilizing process. Herdsmen and farmers presumably no longer needed vast forests, and so the United States looked forward to the acquisition of the Indians' "surplus & waste lands."

The hunting grounds were not the only target. When the United States acquired Louisiana in 1803, Jefferson suggested that the land be used to resettle Native peoples from east of the Mississippi. Meigs actively promoted the exchange of the Cherokee homeland for a new country in the west, but most Cherokees opposed the measure. In order to achieve an exchange, the United States had to alter Cherokees' conception of the land. "The Mother Earth has been divided," the Cherokee council asserted in 1801, "one part [to the] whites and the other is [to] the red people where the present have been rais^d from their infancy to the years of manhood." For them, their country was more than a commodity to be bought and sold.

Land was not a part of the Cherokees' nascent market economy. They held land in common, and any Cherokee could use unoccupied land as long as it did not infringe on the rights of neighbors. The common ownership of realty enabled the Cherokees to invest in other forms of property, including improvements to realty such as fences and houses, which they did sell to one another. But no Cherokee sold improvements on their part of "Mother Earth" to those on the other part: they strictly curtailed property rights in realty. Ultimately, Hawkins believed "the acquirement of individual property by agricultural improvements, by raising stock, and by domestic manufactures . . . will prepare them to accommodate their white neighbours with lands on reasonable terms." That is, individual ownership of other kinds of property not only "civilized" Indians, but it eventually made them more receptive to the notion that land—like deerskins, fabric, or livestock—was a commodity to be sold. The linkage between land cessions and "civilization" became increasingly apparent as Cherokees committed themselves to the program.

Most Cherokee men, long familiar with the machinations of Euro-Americans, viewed "civilization" with suspicion from the very start. One Cherokee man revealed to John Norton that upon hearing the president's plan, "many of us thought it was only some refined scheme calculated to gain an influence over us, rather than ameliorate our situation; and slighted his advice and proposals." The fact that the president of the United States, who normally sent messages about war and trade, now wanted to talk about farming was enough to make the most gullible Cherokee man suspicious. Consequently, Cherokee men at first chose to ignore the civilization program. As a result, men suffered by comparison to women. John McDonald, an intermarried white man, told Norton that "the females have however made much greater advances in industry than the males, they now manufacture a great quantity of cloth; but the latter have not made proportionate progress in Agriculture." The men's initial lack of enthusiasm and relative failure may well have derived from their assumption that because farming was women's work, "civilization" had little to do with them. For the civilization program to succeed among men, they had to adapt it to Cherokee culture. . . .

Men found ways to contribute to agricultural productivity and compensate for the women's labor lost to spinning and weaving without actually farming themselves. In the first decade of the nineteenth century, many of them began to lease or rent land to white families on shares. The council had grave misgivings about the practice since it brought large numbers of white people into the Nation, and expelling them at the end of the year was difficult. In 1808 the council considered banning the practice, but Agent Meigs protested: "I wish you to weigh this matter well before you act because I think you will find that you will again want the help of poor [white] people to raise corn & do other work for you & in a year or two you will do it. All People that ever I know hire poor people to work for them. Some families dont want to hire because they have help enough of their own; but other families have not hands of their own & they ought not to be deprived of having help when they can find it." Meigs clearly saw sharecropping as a way for Cherokees to increase agricultural productivity, but by 1811 he had changed his mind. Instead, sharecropping was a way for Cherokee men to avoid work: "They have no need for white men as croppers because it encourages idleness in Indians." As concern over intruders grew, the practice of cropping declined.

Cherokees found another form of labor in African slaves. Traders had brought their own slaves into the Cherokee country in the eighteenth century, and Cherokee warriors had participated in a frontier slave trade. Like horse stealing, the theft of slaves presented men with an opportunity to remain warriors, and so an illicit traffic in slaves continued well into the nineteenth century. By the early nineteenth century, however, Cherokees also were acquiring slaves for their own use. The transition to slave labor, like that to livestock herding, seems to have been one in which Cherokees invested little thought. When Young Wolf wrote his will in 1814, he explained how he managed to accumulate his estate: "From herding my brother's cattle I recevd one calf which I took my start from, except my own industry, & with cow & calf which I sold, I bought two sows & thirteen piggs sometime after I was abel to purchase three mares & the increase of them since is amounted to thirty more or less & from that start I gathered money enough to purchase a negro woman named Tabb, also a negro man named Ceasar." By 1809 slaves in the Cherokee Nation numbered 583. Although some of these probably belonged to whites employed by or married to Cherokees, most belonged to Indians. According to a census taken in 1825, the number had increased to 1,277, and by 1835 it had reached nearly 1,600. Instead of becoming the yeoman farmers so admired by Washington and Jefferson, most Cherokee men (like Washington and Jefferson) seemed more inclined to adopt the aristocratic planter as a role model. Only a very few ever achieved this goal, but those who did dominated Cherokee economic and political life.

The introduction of slave labor into the economy had a profound effect on Cherokee women and men. Cherokees were in the process of acquiring the racial attitudes of white southerners, and the use of this subject race in agriculture demeaned the traditional labor of women. The fact that slaves cultivated the fields of upper-class Cherokees made all Cherokee men less likely to embrace farming since one risked ignominy by agricultural labor. The use of slaves in farming also challenged women's view of themselves. If growing corn contributed to the gender identity of women, what happened when black men joined or replaced them in the fields? Gradually they saw their traditional role as women compromised. . . .

On the surface, the civilization program seems to have reversed the eighteenth-century trend that concentrated economic power in the hands of men at the expense of women. Nineteenth-century observers agreed that men lagged behind women in adapting to the new economic order. But a market economy underlay the civilization program as surely as it had the deerskin trade. The Cherokees were never going to be able to create the agrarian republic of yeomen farmers envisioned, but not practiced, by Jeffersonians. The economic expansion of the United States drew the Cherokees into a maelstrom from which they could not have escaped even had they been so inclined. As it was, the Cherokees had long ago adapted their political and economic institutions to the demands of an international market. The vast majority of Cherokee men and women had little desire to withdraw. . . .

. . . [N]ot all Cherokees shared equally in the spoils of economic expansion. In 1809 Meigs wrote to the secretary of war: "A spirit of industry does by no means pervade the general population. The greatest number are extremely poor from want of industry. The hunting life is here at an end: but a predilection for the hunter state pervades a great part of the Cherokees." These Cherokees, he believed, should move west of the Mississippi. Meigs defined "want of industry" as the refusal of "the men to labour in the Fields with their own hands." But even wealthy Cherokee men did not "labour." They merely had the capital, inherited from white fathers or acquired through trade, horse stealing, or official position, to invest in other kinds of labor. As town chiefs and members of the National Council, prominent men had the power to award themselves contracts and permits or to receive gifts, bribes, and private reservations from the federal government. These men adroitly used their capital and political positions to increase wealth and the symbol of success, individual property.

The statistical table Agent Meigs sent to the secretary of war in 1809 indicated a remarkable change in Cherokee material culture. "The Cherokees," he asserted, "[have] prospered by the pastoral life and by domestic manufactures." Livestock abounded and spinning wheels whirred throughout the Nation. In more fundamental ways, however, Cherokee lives remained remarkably untouched: the Cherokees had adapted "civilization" to their own expectations of men and women. Cherokee women used the civilization program to embellish their culture, but they did not transform it. Certainly, women added new crops, cotton in particular, and new skills such as spinning and weaving, but they continued to farm, keep house, and tend children just as they always had done. Similarly, men's culture retained the basic ethic of eighteenth-century hunting and warring. Aggression and competition, however, found expression in the rapidly expanding market economy. The deerskin trade had educated men far more than women in European economic practices and values, and the industrial and market revolutions and the civilization program made that knowledge increasingly valuable. Unlike the deerskin trade of the eighteenth century, the emerging "civilized" economy generated substantial Native wealth, considerable internal inequality, and a host of problems that the Cherokees had never before had to confront. As the first decade of the nineteenth century drew to a close, Cherokees had to resolve complex issues involving the individual ownership, state protection, legitimate enhancement, and just inheritance of property. Men and women shared many of the same concerns about both real and chattel property, but their property interests were rooted in different gender conventions: individual property reflected male culture while common ownership of realty formed the basis of women's culture. The Cherokees' attempt to reconcile the corporate ethic of farmers and the competitive ethic of entrepreneurs gave rise to the Cherokee republic.

FURTHER READING

Stephen E. Ambrose, *Undaunted Courage: Meriwether Lewis, Thomas Jefferson, and the Opening of the American West* (1997).

Stephen Aron, *How the West Was Lost: The Transformation of Kentucky from Daniel Boone to Henry Clay* (1996).

Andrew Cayton, *The Frontier Republic: Ideology and Politics in the Ohio Country, 1789–1812* (1986).

John Mack Farragher, *Daniel Boone: The Life and Legend of an American Pioneer* (1992).

Francis Paul Prucha, *American Indian Policy in the Formative Years: The Indian Trade and Intercourse Acts, 1790–1834* (1962).

George R. Taylor, *The Transportation Revolution, 1815–1860* (1951).

Anthony F. C. Wallace, *The Death and Rebirth of the Seneca* (1969).

CHAPTER
8

Nationalism, Sectionalism, and Expansionism in the Age of Jackson

When a Frenchman visiting the United States witnessed a parade in New York City in 1834, he was dazzled: It was a mile-long procession lit by hundreds of torches, and it included banners, portraits of political leaders, and even a live eagle mounted on a pole (see Document 7 in this chapter). "These scenes belong to history," he later wrote. "They are the episodes of a wondrous epic which will bequeath a lasting memory to posterity, that of the coming of democracy." For this visitor, the political world in the United States differed radically from that in his European home. Americans were enjoying the burgeoning of a democracy that was likely to reverberate throughout the world. Historians have found reason to substantiate these claims. In the early nineteenth century, ballot restrictions were eased so that all white men, even those who owned no property, could vote. By 1840, those Americans who could vote were voting in record numbers. Politics became a pageant, filling the streets with demonstrations and parades. Andrew Jackson, elected in 1828, was heralded by his supporters as a man of the people.

However, other historians have considered these developments in a different light. Not only was universal suffrage restricted to white men, but free black men were losing their voting rights in a number of states during this period. In this purported era of democracy, Indian removal, as we saw in the last chapter, was accelerating. The United States, many historians argue, was not a paragon of democracy, but rather "a white man's republic." Still other historians contend that the level of democracy even among white voters is overstated. Politics might have appeared as pageantry, but this was really a façade. Elections decided less than voters believed.

Whether politics represented the flowering of democracy or was a sham, political organization and behavior changed beginning in 1824. The second party system, as it is called, developed in large part in reaction to the political career of Andrew Jackson. Defeated by John Quincy Adams in 1824, Jackson vowed revenge in the next presidential election. Following his resounding victory in 1828 as leader of the Democratic Party, he set about creating a federal bureaucracy that would be loyal

*to him and his party. The adage "to the victor belong the spoils" was cited to defend
the appointment of loyal Democrats to government jobs. A series of divisive political
battles over such issues as a national bank followed. By 1834, a group of politicians
who opposed Jackson's initiatives formed an alternative party, which they called the
Whigs, in opposition to "King Andrew." For the next twenty years, national elections
were closely contested, eligible voters participated in large numbers, and professional
politicians vied for votes and rewarded their followers with patronage if they were
victorious. Whereas politicians at one time had disdained campaigning for office, the
second party system fostered raucous campaigns and ambitious politicians.*

*In this new political environment, politicians addressed issues that would con-
tinue to plague the United States in the years to come. Perhaps the most ominous was
the question of states' rights and national power. In 1832, Congress passed a tariff
that seemed excessive to southern political leaders. Because the southern economy continued to be based on agriculture, the South benefited less from tariffs than did the
North. Senator John C. Calhoun from South Carolina responded to this "tariff of
abominations" by arguing that a state had the right to "nullify" laws with which
it disagreed. Jackson responded as a nationalist and declared nullification illegal.
Ultimately a compromise was reached, but certainly there were aspects of the debate
that were not settled. Historians have considered this crisis a prelude to the Civil War.*

*One area in which most politicians and voters could agree, however, was the
urgency of expanding westward. Westward migration, so the argument went, would
not only increase national power but also bring benefits to those who were conquered.
By 1845, this impulse was encoded in an ideology known as "manifest destiny."
According to journalist John L. O'Sullivan, it was "the fulfillment of our manifest
destiny to overspread the continent." Armed with a rhetoric that knit westward
expansion with national fulfillment, Americans in the 1840s pushed for annexation
of western lands. The United States annexed Texas in 1845, gained Oregon in a
treaty with Great Britain, and conquered regions of Mexico following the Mexican-
American War, which began in 1846. As of 1848, the United States, which now
comprised nearly three million square miles, had tripled in size in seventy-some years.
This "white man's republic" seemingly had fulfilled its destiny. Yet storm clouds were
on the horizon, as we shall see, precisely because of the territories in the West.*

QUESTIONS TO THINK ABOUT

To what degree was this a period of increasing democracy? How were notions about "the
people" or "the common man" used to celebrate the potential of the United States? How
were these celebrations linked to expansion and "manifest destiny"? Can you envision
how the question of nullification was ominous for American nationalists?

DOCUMENTS

The first three documents illustrate the issues of nationalism and sectionalism during
the presidency of Andrew Jackson. In Document 1, Senator John C. Calhoun of South
Carolina argues against the "tariff of abominations" and for an open market. In contrast,
in Document 2, Senator Daniel Webster of Massachusetts argues that the people have
ratified a Constitution that has made the national government the supreme law of the
land. President Andrew Jackson, in Document 3, is responding to the action of South

Carolina in calling for the nullification of a federal law. Jackson agrees with Webster, arguing that no state can declare a law void because the Constitution has formed a government in which all the people are represented. In Document 4, George Bancroft illustrates commonly held ideas that both celebrate democracy and express a faith that the people are supreme in their wisdom. Document 5 gives us a view of the battle at the Alamo in 1836 from the point of view of a Mexican colonel. The next two documents echo the beliefs of Bancroft. In Document 6, Democratic newspaper editor John L. O'Sullivan argues that free and unbridled democracy is the cause of humanity. Michel Chevelier in Document 7 marvels at a procession of Democrats in New York City in 1839. The final four documents grapple with the issue of expansion in the 1840s. Document 8 is another view from O'Sullivan, the man who coined the term "manifest destiny." In this selection, O'Sullivan anticipates the march westward of Americans into California. In Documents 9 and 10, two U.S. senators justify expansion. In Document 9, Senator Thomas Hart Benton links the westward movement with the migration of white people through Asia and Europe for millennia. Senator John Dix, in Document 10, argues that the people living in the western regions must give way to what he calls the advancing wave of civilization. Document 11 provides a colorful portrait by Walter Colton of the rush to the California gold fields. Note the cultural diversity of the people who are at work in the mines.

1. John C. Calhoun Argues for Rights of States, 1828

The Committee do not propose to enter into an elaborate, or refined argument on the question of the Constitutionality of the Tariff System. The Gen[era]l Government is one of specifick powers, and it can rightfully exercise only the powers expressly granted, and those that may be necessary and proper to carry them into effect, all others being reserved expressly to the States, or the people. It results necessarily, that those who claim to exercise power under the Constitution, are bound to show, that it is expressly granted, or that it is necessary and proper as a means to some of the granted powers. The advocates of the Tariff have offered no such proof. . . .

So partial are the effects of the system, that its burdens are exclusively on one side, and the benefits on the other. It imposes on the agricultural interest of the south, including the South west, with that portion of our commerce and navigation engaged in foreign trade, the burden not only of sustaining the system itself, but that also of the Government. . . .

That the manufacturing States, even in their own opinion, bear no share of the burden of the Tariff in reality, we may infer with the greatest certainty from their conduct. The fact that they urgently demand an increase, and consider any addition as a blessing, and a failure to obtain one, a curse, is the strongest confession, that whatever burden it imposes in reality, falls, not on them but on others. Men ask not for burdens, but benefits. The tax paid by the duties on impost [*sic*] by which, with the exception of the receipts in the sale of publick land and a few incidental items, the Government is wholly supported, and which in its gross amount annually equals about $23,000,000 is then in truth no tax on them. Whatever portion of it they advance, as consumers of the articles on which it is imposed, returns to

The Papers of John C. Calhoun, ed. Clyde N. Wilson and W. Edwin Hemphill, vol. 10 (Columbia, S.C.: University of South Carolina Press, 1959), 444–532.

them . . . with usurious interest through an artfully contrived system. That such are the facts, the Committee will proceed to demonstrate by other arguments, besides the confession of the party interested through their acts, as conclusive as that ought to be considered. . . .

We cultivate certain great staples for the supply of the general market of the world; they manufacture almost exclusively for the home market. Their object in the Tariff is to keep down foreign competition, in order to obtain a monopoly of the domestick market. The effect on us is to compel us to purchase at a higher price, both what we purchase from them and from others, without receiving a correspondent increase in the price, of what we sell. . . .

We are told by those who pretend to understand our interest better than we do, that the excess of production, and not the Tariff, is the evil which afflicts us, and that our true remedy is a reduction of the quantity of cotton, rice and tobacco which we raise, and not a repeal of the Tariff. They assert that low prices are the necessary consequence of excess of supply, and that the only proper correction is in diminishing the quantity. . . . Our market is the world, and as we cannot imitate their example by enlarging it for our products through the exclusion of others, we must decline to their advice, which instead of alleviating would increase our embarrassment. We have no monopoly in the supply of our products. One half of the globe may produce them. Should we reduce our production, others stand ready by increasing theirs to take our place, and instead of raising prices, we would only diminish our share of the supply. We are thus compelled to produce on the penalty of loosing our hold on the general market. Once lost it may be lost forever; and lose it we must, if we continue to be compelled as we now are, on the one hand by general competition of the world to sell low, and on the other by the Tariff to buy high. We cannot withstand this double action. Our ruin must follow. In fact our only permanent and safe remedy is not the rise in the price of what we sell in which we can receive but little aid from our Government, but a reduction in that which we buy which is prevented by the interference of the Government. Give us a free and open competition in our own market, and we fear not to encounter like competition in the general market of the world. If under all of our discouragement by the acts of our Government, we are still able to contend there against the world, can it be doubted, if this impediment were removed, we would force out all competitors; and thus also enlarge our market, not by the oppression of our fellow citizens of other States, but by our industry, enterprize [*sic*] and natural advantages.

2. Daniel Webster Lays Out His Nationalist Vision, 1830

Sir, let me recur to pleasing recollections; let me indulge in refreshing remembrance of the past; let me remind you that, in early times, no States cherished greater harmony, both of principle and feeling, than Massachusetts and South Carolina. Would to God that harmony might again return! . . .

Second Reply to Hayne, January 26–27, 1830, in Daniel Webster, *Speeches and Formal Writings,* 1: 285–348, as reprinted in Kenneth E. Shewmaker, ed., *Daniel Webster: The Completest Man* (Hanover, N.H.: University Press of New England, 1990), 113–120.

I understand the honorable gentleman from South Carolina to maintain, that it is a right of the State legislatures to interfere, whenever, in their judgment, this government transcends its constitutional limits, and to arrest the operation of its laws.

I understand him to maintain this right, as a right existing *under* the Constitution, not as a right to overthrow it on the ground of extreme necessity, such as would justify violent revolution.

I understand him to maintain an authority, on the part of the States, thus to interfere, for the purpose of correcting the exercise of power by the general government, of checking it, and of compelling it to conform to their opinion of the extent of its powers.

I understand him to maintain, that the ultimate power of judging of the constitutional extent of its own authority is not lodged exclusively in the general government, or any branch of it: but that, on the contrary, the States may lawfully decide for themselves, and each State for itself, whether, in a given case, the act of the general government transcends its power.

I understand him to insist, that, if the exigency of the case, in the opinion of any State government, require it, such State government may, by its own sovereign authority, annul an act of the general government which it deems plainly and palpably unconstitutional.

This is the sum of what I understand from him to be the South Carolina doctrine, and the doctrine which he maintains. I propose to consider it, and compare it with the Constitution. . . .

This leads us to inquire into the origin of this government and the source of its power. Whose agent is it? Is it the creature of the State legislatures, or the creature of the people? If the government of the United States be the agent of the State governments, then they may control it, provided they can agree in the manner of controlling it; if it be the agent of the people, then the people alone can control it, restrain it, modify, or reform it. It is observable enough, that the doctrine for which the honorable gentleman contends leads him to the necessity of maintaining, not only that this general government is the creature of the States, but that it is the creature of each of the States severally, so that each may assert the power for itself of determining whether it acts within the limits of its authority. It is the servant of four-and-twenty masters of different wills and different purposes and yet bound to obey all. This absurdity (for it seems no less) arises from a misconception as to the origin of this government and its true character. It is, Sir, the people's Constitution, the people's government, made for the people, made by the people, and answerable to the people. The people of the United States have declared that the Constitution shall be the supreme law. We must either admit the proposition, or dispute their authority. The States are, unquestionably, sovereign, so far as their sovereignty is not affected by this supreme law. But the State legislatures, as political bodies, however sovereign, are yet not sovereign over the people. So far as the people have given power to the general government, so far the grant is unquestionably good, and the government holds of the people, and not of the State governments. We are all agents of the same supreme power, the people. The general government and the State governments derive their authority from the same source. Neither can, in relation to the other, be called primary, though one is definite and restricted, and the other general and residuary. The national government possesses those powers which it can be shown the people have conferred on it, and no more. All the rest belongs to the State governments, or to the people themselves. So far as the people have restrained State sovereignty, by the expression of their will, in the Constitution of the United States, so far, it must be admitted, State sovereignty is effectually controlled. I do not contend that it is, or ought to be, controlled farther. The sentiment to which I have referred propounds that State sovereignty is only to be controlled by its own "feeling of justice": that is to say, it is not to be controlled at all, for one who is to follow his own feelings is under no legal control. Now, however men may think this ought to be, the fact is, that the people of the United States have chosen to impose control on State sovereignties. There are those, doubtless, who wish they had been left without restraint; but the Constitution has ordered the matter differently. To make war, for instance, is an exercise of sovereignty; but the Constitution declares that no State shall make war. To coin money is another exercise of sovereign power, but no State is at liberty to coin money. Again, the Constitution says that no sovereign State shall be so sovereign as to make a treaty. These prohibitions, it must be confessed, are a control on the State sovereignty of South Carolina, as well as of the other States, which does not arise "from her own feelings of honorable justice." The opinion referred to, therefore, is in defiance of the plainest provisions of the Constitution. . . .

. . . I hold [this government] to be a popular government, erected by the people; those who administer it, responsible to the people; and itself capable of being amended and modified, just as the people may choose it should be. It is as popular, just as truly emanating from the people, as the State governments. It is created for one purpose; the State governments for another. It has its own powers; they have theirs. There is no more authority with them to arrest the operation of a law of Congress, than with Congress to arrest the operation of their laws. . . . The States cannot now make war; they cannot contract alliances; they cannot make, each for itself, separate regulations of commerce; they cannot lay imposts; they cannot coin money. If this Constitution, Sir, be the creature of State legislatures, it must be admitted that it has obtained a strange control over the volitions of its creators. . . .

. . . Sir, the people have wisely provided, in the Constitution itself, a proper, suitable mode and tribunal for settling questions of constitutional law. There are in the Constitution grants of powers to Congress, and restrictions on these powers. There are, also, prohibitions on the States. Some authority must, therefore, necessarily exist, having the ultimate jurisdiction to fix and ascertain the interpretation of these grants, restrictions, and prohibitions. The Constitution has itself pointed out, ordained, and established that authority. How has it accomplished this great and essential end? By declaring, Sir, that *the Constitution, and the laws of the United States made in pursuance thereof, shall be the supreme law of the land, any thing in the constitution or laws of any State to the contrary notwithstanding.*

This, Sir, was the first great step. By this the supremacy of the Constitution and laws of the United States is declared. The people so will it. No State law is to be valid which comes in conflict with the Constitution, or any law of the United States passed in pursuance of it. But who shall decide this question of interference? To whom lies the last appeal? This, Sir, the Constitution itself decides also, by declaring, *that the judicial power shall extend to all cases arising under the Constitution and laws of the United States.* These two provisions cover the whole ground. They are, in truth, the keystone of the arch! With these it is a government; without them it is a confederation. . . . Congress established, at its very first session, in the judicial act, a mode for carrying them into full effect, and for bringing all questions of constitutional power to the final decision of the Supreme Court. It then, Sir, became a government. It then had the means of self-protection; and but for this, it would, in all probability, have been now among things which are past. Having constituted the government, and declared its powers, the people have further said, that, since somebody must decide on the extent of these powers, the government shall itself decide; subject, always, like other popular governments, to its responsibility to the people.

—Liberty *and* Union, now and for ever, one and inseparable!

3. Andrew Jackson Condemns the Rights of "Nullification" and Secession, 1832

To preserve this bond of our political existence from destruction, to maintain inviolate this state of national honor and prosperity, and to justify the confidence my fellow-citizens have reposed in me, I, Andrew Jackson, President of the United States, have thought proper to issue this my proclamation, stating my views of the Constitution and laws applicable to the measures adopted by the convention of South Carolina and to the reasons they have put forth to sustain them, declaring the course which duty will require me to pursue, and, appealing to the understanding and patriotism of the people, warn them of the consequences that must inevitably result from an observance of the dictates of the convention.

The ordinance is founded, not on the indefeasible right of resisting acts which are plainly unconstitutional and too oppressive to be endured, but on the strange position that any one State may not only declare an act of Congress void, but prohibit its execution; that they may do this consistently with the Constitution; that the true construction of that instrument permits a State to retain its place in the Union and yet be bound by no other of its laws than those it may choose to consider as constitutional. It is true, they add, that to justify this abrogation of a law it must be palpably contrary to the Constitution; but it is evident that to give the right of resisting laws of that description, coupled with the uncontrolled right to decide what laws deserve that character, is to give the power of resisting all laws; for as by the theory there is no appeal, the reasons alleged by the State, good or bad, must prevail. . . .

This right to secede is deduced from the nature of the Constitution, which, they say, is a compact between sovereign States who have preserved their whole sovereignty and therefore are subject to no superior; that because they made the compact they can break it when in their opinion it has been departed from by the other States. Fallacious as this course of reasoning is, it enlists State pride and finds advocates in the honest prejudices of those who have not studied the nature of our Government sufficiently to see the radical error on which it rests.

The people of the United States formed the Constitution, acting through the State legislatures in making the compact, to meet and discuss its provisions, and acting in separate conventions when they ratified those provisions; but the terms

---

Andrew Jackson, "Proclamation to the People of South Carolina, December 10, 1832."

used in its construction show it to be a Government in which the people of all the States, collectively, are represented. We are *one people* in the choice of President and Vice-President. Here the States have no other agency than to direct the mode in which the votes shall be given. The candidates having the majority of all the votes are chosen. The electors of a majority of States may have given their votes for one candidate, and yet another may be chosen. The people, then, and not the States, are represented in the executive branch.

In the House of Representatives there is this difference, that the people of one State do not, as in the case of President and Vice-President, all vote for the same officers. The people of all the States do not vote for all the members, each State electing only its own representatives. But this creates no material distinction. When chosen, they are all representatives of the United States, not representatives of the particular State from which they come. They are paid by the United States, not by the State; nor are they accountable to it for any act done in the performance of their legislative functions; and however they may in practice, as it is their duty to do, consult and prefer the interests of their particular constituents when they come in conflict with any other partial or local interest, yet it is their first and highest duty, as representatives of the United States, to promote the general good.

The Constitution of the United States . . . forms a *government,* not a league; and whether it be formed by compact between the States or in any other manner, its character is the same. It is a Government in which all the people are represented, which operates directly on the people individually, not upon the States; they retained all the power they did not grant. But each State, having expressly parted with so many powers as to constitute, jointly with the other States, a single nation, can not, from that period, possess any right to secede, because such secession does not break a league, but destroys the unity of a nation. . . .

Fellow-citizens of my native State, let me not only admonish you, as the First Magistrate of our common country, not to incur the penalty of its laws, but use the influence that a father would over his children whom he saw rushing to certain ruin. In that paternal language, with that paternal feeling, let me tell you, my countrymen, that you are deluded by men who are either deceived themselves or wish to deceive you. . . . They are not champions of liberty, emulating the fame of our Revolutionary fathers, nor are you an oppressed people, contending, as they repeat to you, against worse than colonial vassalage. You are free members of a flourishing and happy Union. There is no settled design to oppress you.

4. Historian George Bancroft Asserts His Faith in the Wisdom of the People, 1835

The best government rests on the people and not on the few, on persons and not on property, on the free development of public opinion and not on authority; because the munificent Author of our being has conferred the gifts of mind upon every member of the human race without distinction of outward circumstances. Whatever of other possessions may be engrossed, mind asserts its own independence. Lands,

---

George Bancroft, address at Williams College, 1835.

estates, the produce of mines, the prolific abundance of the seas, may be usurped by a privileged class. Avarice, assuming the form of ambitious power, may grasp realm after realm, subdue continents, compass the earth in its schemes of aggrandizement, and sigh after other worlds; but mind eludes the power of appropriation; it exists only in its own individuality; it is a property which cannot be confiscated and cannot be torn away; it laughs at chains; it bursts from imprisonment; it defies monopoly. A government of equal rights must, therefore, rest upon mind; not wealth, not brute force, the sum of the moral intelligence of the community should rule the State. . . .

The public happiness is the true object of legislation, and can be secured only by the masses of mankind themselves awakening to the knowledge and the care of their own interests. Our free institutions have reversed the false and ignoble distinctions between men; and refusing to gratify the pride of caste, have acknowledged the common mind to be the true material for a commonwealth. Every thing has hitherto been done for the happy few. It is not possible to endow an aristocracy with greater benefits than they have already enjoyed; there is no room to hope that individuals will be more highly gifted or more fully developed than the greatest sages of past times. The world can advance only through the culture of the moral and intellectual powers of the people. To accomplish this end by means of the people themselves is the highest purpose of government. If it be the duty of the individual to strive after a perfection like the perfection of God, how much more ought a nation to be the image of Deity. The common mind is the true Parian marble, fit to be wrought into likeness to a God. The duty of America is to secure the culture and the happiness of the masses by their reliance on themselves.

The absence of the prejudices of the old world leaves us here the opportunity of consulting independent truth; and man is left to apply the instinct of freedom to every social relation and public interest. . . .

. . . There may be those who scoff at the suggestion, that the decision of the whole is to be preferred to the judgment of the enlightened few. They say in their hearts that the masses are ignorant; that farmers know nothing of legislation; that mechanics should not quit their workshops to join in forming public opinion. But true political science does indeed venerate the masses. It maintains, not as has been perversely asserted, that "the people can make right," but that the people can DISCERN right. Individuals are but shadows, too often engrossed by the pursuit of shadows; the race is immortal: individuals are of limited sagacity; the common mind is infinite in its experience: individuals are languid and blind; the many are ever wakeful: individuals are corrupt; the race has been redeemed: individuals are time-serving; the masses are fearless: individuals may be false, the masses are ingenuous and sincere: individuals claim the divine sanction of truth for the deceitful conceptions of their own fancies; the Spirit of God breathes through the combined intelligence of the people. Truth is not to be ascertained by the impulses of an individual; it emerges from the contradictions of personal opinions; it raises itself in majestic serenity above the strifes of parties and the conflict of sects; it acknowledges neither the solitary mind, nor the separate faction as its oracle; but owns as its only faithful interpreter the dictates of pure reason itself, proclaimed by the general voice of mankind. The decrees of the universal conscience are the nearest approach to the presence of God in the soul of man.

. . . "ALL THE GREAT AND NOBLE INSTITUTIONS OF THE WORLD HAVE COME FROM POPULAR EFFORTS."

5. Lieutenant-Colonel José Enrique de la Peña Defends Mexico's Actions Against the Texans, 1836

The insults lavished upon the nation as represented by the customs officials and commanders of military detachments, the disregard for laws, and the attitudes with which the colonists looked upon those who had given them a country were more than sufficient causes to justify war on our part. They were the aggressors and we the attacked, they the ingrates, we the benefactors. When they were in want we had given them sustenance, yet as soon as they gained strength they used it to destroy us.

The neglect, the apathy, or, even more, the criminal indifference with which all [Mexican] governments without exception have watched over the national interests; the failure to enforce the colonization laws; the lack of sympathy with which the colonists had been regarded and the loyalty that these still had for their native country; these things led us into these circumstances. Because of all this, war was inevitable, for between war and dishonor there was no doubt as to the choice. . . .

On the 17th of February the commander in chief had proclaimed to the army: "Comrades in arms," he said, "our most sacred duties have brought us to these uninhabited lands and demand our engaging in combat against a rabble of wretched adventurers to whom our authorities have unwisely given benefits that even Mexicans did not enjoy, and who have taken possession of this vast and fertile area, convinced that our own unfortunate internal divisions have rendered us incapable of defending our soil. Wretches! Soon will they become aware of their folly! Soldiers, our comrades have been shamefully sacrificed at Anáhuac, Goliad, and Béjar, and you are those destined to punish these murderers. My friends: we will march as long as the interests of the nation that we serve demand. The claimants to the acres of Texas land will soon know to their sorrow that their reinforcements from New Orleans, Mobile, Boston, New York, and other points north, whence they should never have come, are insignificant, and that Mexicans, generous by nature, will not leave unpunished affronts resulting in injury or discredit to their country, regardless of who the aggressors may be."

This address was received enthusiastically, but the army needed no incitement; knowing that it was about to engage in the defense of the country and to avenge less fortunate comrades was enough for its ardor to become as great as the noble and just cause it was about to defend. . . . For their part, the enemy leaders had addressed their own men in terms not unlike those of our commander. They said that we were a bunch of mercenaries, blind instruments of tyranny; that without any right we were about to invade their territory; that we would bring desolation and death to their peaceful homes and would seize their possessions; that we were savage men who would rape their women, decapitate their children, destroy everything, and render into ashes the fruits of their industry and their efforts. Unfortunately they did partially foresee what would happen, but they also committed atrocities that we did not commit, and in this rivalry of evil and extermination, I do not dare to venture who had the ignominious advantage, they or we! . . .

José Enrique de la Peña, *With Santa Anna in Texas: A Personal Narrative of the Revolution,* trans. Carmen Perry (College Station: Texas A&M University Press, 1975), 4–5, 40–52. Published by Texas A&M University Press.

When our commander in chief haughtily rejected the agreement that the enemy had proposed, [the Alamo's Commander, William B.] Travis became infuriated at the contemptible manner in which he had been treated and, expecting no honorable way of salvation, chose the path that strong souls choose in crisis, that of dying with honor, and selected the Alamo for his grave. . . .

Our commander became more furious when he saw that the enemy resisted the idea of surrender. He believed as others did that the fame and honor of the army were compromised the longer the enemy lived. . . . In fact, it was necessary only to await the artillery's arrival at Béjar for these to surrender; undoubtedly they could not have resisted for many hours the destruction and imposing fire from twenty cannon. . . .

Among the defenders there were thirty or more colonists; the rest were pirates, used to defying danger and to disdaining death, and who for that reason fought courageously; their courage, to my way of thinking, merited them the mercy for which, toward the last, some of them pleaded; others not knowing the language, were unable to do so. . . . The order had been given to spare no one but the women and this was carried out, but such carnage was useless and had we prevented it, we would have saved much blood on our part. . . .

This scene of extermination went on for an hour before the curtain of death covered and ended it: shortly after six in the morning it was all finished.

6. John L. O'Sullivan, a Democratic Newspaperman, Venerates Democracy and the "Democratic Principle," 1837

We believe, then, in the principle of *democratic republicanism,* in its strongest and purest sense. We have an abiding confidence in the virtue, intelligence, and full capacity for self-government of the great mass of our people—our industrious, honest, manly, intelligent millions of freemen.

We are opposed to all self-styled "wholesome restraints" on the free action of the popular opinion and will, other than those which have for their sole object the prevention of precipitate legislation. . . .

In the first place, the greatest number are *more likely,* at least as a general rule, to understand and follow their own greatest good than is the minority.

In the second, a minority is much more likely to abuse power for the promotion of its own selfish interests, at the expense of the majority of numbers—the substantial and producing mass of the nation—than the latter is to oppress unjustly the former. The social evil is also, in that case, proportionately greater. This is abundantly proved by the history of all aristocratic interests that have existed, in various degrees and modifications, in the world. . . .

In the third place, there does not naturally exist any such original superiority of a minority class above the great mass of a community in intelligence and competence for the duties of government. . . .

John L. O'Sullivan, "The Democratic Principle," *United States Magazine and Democratic Review* (October 1837).

. . . [D]emocracy is the cause of humanity. It has faith in human nature. It believes in its essential equality and fundamental goodness. It respects, with a solemn reverence to which the proudest artificial institutions and distinctions of society have no claim, the human soul. It is the cause of philanthropy. Its object is to emancipate the mind of the mass of men from the degrading and disheartening fetters of social distinctions and advantages; to bid it walk abroad through the free creation "in its own majesty"; to war against all fraud, oppression, and violence; by striking at their root, to reform all the infinitely varied human misery which has grown out of the old and false ideas by which the world has been so long misgoverned.

7. Michel Chevelier, a French Visitor, Marvels at the Pageantry of Politics, 1839

But this entry of the hickory [that is, the entrance of Andrew Jackson] was but a by-matter compared with the procession I witnessed in New York. It was in the night after the closing of the polls, when victory had pronounced in favour of the democratic party. . . . The procession was nearly a mile long; the democrats marched in good order to the glare of torches; the banners were more numerous than I had ever seen them in any religious festival; all were in transparency, on account of the darkness. On some were inscribed the names of the democratic societies or sections; *Democratic young men of the ninth* or *eleventh ward;* others bore imprecations against the Bank of the United States; *Nick Biddle* and *Old Nick* here figured largely, and formed the pendant of our *libera nos a malo.* Then came portraits of General Jackson afoot and on horseback; there was one in the uniform of a general, and another in the person of the Tennessee farmer, with the famous hickory cane in his hand. Those of Washington and Jefferson, surrounded with democratic mottoes, were mingled with emblems in all tastes and of all colours. Among these figured an eagle, not a painting, but a real live eagle, tied by the legs, surrounded by a wreath of leaves, and hoisted upon a pole, after the manner of the Roman standards. The imperial bird was carried by a stout sailor, more pleased than ever was a sergeant permitted to hold one of the strings of the canopy, in a catholic ceremony. From further than the eye could reach, came marching on the democrats. I was struck with the resemblance of their air to the train that escorts the *viaticum* in Mexico or Puebla. The American standard-bearers were as grave as the Mexican Indians who bore the sacred tapers. The democratic procession, also, like the Catholic procession, had its halting places; it stopped before the houses of the Jackson men to fill the air with cheers, and halted at the doors of the leaders of the Opposition, to give three, six, or nine groans. If these scenes were to find a painter, they would be admired at a distance, not less than the triumphs and sacrificial pomps, which the ancients have left us delineated in marble and brass; for they are not mere grotesques after the manner of Rembrandt, they belong to history, they partake of the grand; they are the episodes of a wondrous epic which will bequeath a lasting memory to posterity; that of the coming of democracy.

Michel Chevelier, *Society, Manners, and Politics in the United States* (Boston: Weeks, Jordan and Company, 1839), 318–319.

8. John L. O'Sullivan Defines "Manifest Destiny," 1845

Texas is now ours. Already, before these words are written, her Convention has undoubtedly ratified the acceptance, by her Congress, of our proffered invitation into the Union; and made the requisite changes in her already republican form of constitution to adapt it to its future federal relations. Her star and her stripe may already be said to have taken their place in the glorious blazon of our common nationality; and the sweep of our eagle's wing already includes within its circuit the wide extent of her fair and fertile land. . . .

Why, were other reasoning wanting, in favor of now elevating this question of the reception of Texas into the Union, out of the lower region of our past party dissensions, up to its proper level of a high and broad nationality, it surely is to be found, found abundantly, in the manner in which other nations have undertaken to intrude themselves into it, between us and the proper parties to the case, in a spirit of hostile interference against us, for the avowed object of thwarting our policy and hampering our power, limiting our greatness and checking the fulfilment of our manifest destiny to overspread the continent allotted by Providence for the free development of our yearly multiplying millions. This we have seen done by England, our old rival and enemy; and by France, strangely coupled with her against us. . . .

It is wholly untrue, and unjust to ourselves, the pretence that the Annexation has been a measure of spoliation, unrightful and unrighteous—of military conquest under forms of peace and law—of territorial aggrandizement at the expense of justice, and justice due by a double sanctity to the weak. . . . If Texas became peopled with an American population, it was by no contrivance of our government, but on the express invitation of that of Mexico herself; accompanied with such guaranties of State independence, and the maintenance of a federal system analogous to our own, as constituted a compact fully justifying the strongest measures of redress on the part of those afterwards deceived in this guaranty, and sought to be enslaved under the yoke imposed by its violation. She was released, rightfully and absolutely released, from all Mexican allegiance, or duty of cohesion to the Mexican political body, by the acts and fault of Mexico herself, and Mexico alone. There never was a clearer case. It was not revolution; it was resistance to revolution. . . .

Nor is there any just foundation for the charge that Annexation is a great pro-slavery measure—calculated to increase and perpetuate that institution. Slavery had nothing to do with it. Opinions were and are greatly divided, both at the North and South, as to the influence to be exerted by it on Slavery and the Slave States. . . .

California will, probably, next fall away from the loose adhesion which, in such a country as Mexico, holds a remote province in a slight equivocal kind of dependence on the metropolis. Imbecile and distracted, Mexico never can exert any real governmental authority over such a country. . . . Already the advance guard of the irresistible army of Anglo-Saxon emigration has begun to pour down upon it, armed with the plough and the rifle, and marking its trail with schools and colleges,

---

John L. O'Sullivan, Editorial on Manifest Destiny and Texas Annexation, *United States Magazine and Democratic Review* (October 1837).

courts and representative halls, mills and meeting-houses. A population will soon be in actual occupation of California, over which it will be idle for Mexico to dream of dominion. They will necessarily become independent. All this without agency of our government, without responsibility of our people—in the natural flow of events, the spontaneous working of principles, and the adaptation of the tendencies and wants of the human race to the elemental circumstances in the midst of which they find themselves placed.

9. Senator Thomas Hart Benton Justifies White Supremacy, 1846

It would seem that the White race alone received the divine command, to subdue and replenish the earth! for it is the only race that has obeyed it—the only one that hunts out new and distant lands, and even a New World, to subdue and replenish. Starting from western Asia, taking Europe for their field, and the Sun for their guide, and leaving the Mongolians behind, they arrived, after many ages, on the shores of the Atlantic, which they lit up with the lights of science and religion, and adorned with the useful and the elegant arts. Three and a half centuries ago, this race, in obedience to the great command, arrived in the New World, and found new lands to subdue and replenish. . . . The van of the Caucasian race now top the Rocky Mountains, and spread down to the shores of the Pacific. In a few years a great population will grow up there, luminous with the accumulated lights of European and American civilization. Their presence in such a position cannot be without its influence upon eastern Asia. . . . Civilization, or extinction, has been the fate of all people who have found themselves in the track of the advancing Whites, and civilization, always the preference of the Whites, has been pressed as an object, while extinction has followed as a consequence of its resistance. The Black and the Red races have often felt their ameliorating influence.

10. Senator John Dix Advocates Expansion into Mexico, 1848

Sir, no one who has paid a moderate degree of attention to the laws and elements of our increase, can doubt that our population is destined to spread itself across the American continent, filling up, with more or less completeness, according to attractions of soil and climate, the space that intervenes between the Atlantic and Pacific oceans. This eventual, and, perhaps, in the order of time, this not very distant extension of our settlements over a tract of country, with a diameter, as we go westward, greatly disproportioned to its length, becomes a subject of the highest interest to us. On the whole extent of our northern flank, from New Brunswick to the point where the northern boundary of Oregon touches the Pacific, we are in contact with British colonists, having, for the most part, the same common origin with ourselves,

Thomas Hart Benton, speech before the U.S. Senate, *Congressional Globe*, May 28, 1846.

Congressional Globe, January 26, 1848, 181–182.

but controlled and moulded by political influences from the Eastern hemisphere, if not adverse, certainly not decidedly friendly to us. . . .

From our northern boundary, we turn to our southern. What races are to border on us here, what is to be their social and political character, and what their means of annoyance? Are our two frontiers, only seven parallels of latitude apart when we pass Texas, to be flanked by settlements having no common bond of union with ours? Our whole southern line is conterminous, throughout its whole extent, with the territories of Mexico, a large portion of which is nearly unpopulated. . . . The aboriginal races, which occupy and overrun a portion of California and New Mexico, must there, as everywhere else, give way before the advancing wave of civilization, either to be overwhelmed by it, or to be driven upon perpetually contracting areas, where, from a diminution of their accustomed sources of subsistence, they must ultimately become extinct by force of an invincible law. We see the operation of this law in every portion of this continent. We have no power to control it, if we would. It is the behest of Providence that idleness, and ignorance, and barbarism, shall give place to industry, and knowledge, and civilization. The European and mixed races, which possess Mexico, are not likely, either from moral or physical energy, to become formidable rivals or enemies. The bold and courageous enterprise which overran and conquered Mexico, appears not to have descended to the present possessors of the soil. Either from the influence of climate or the admixture of races—the fusion of castes, to use the technical phrase—the conquerors have, in turn, become the conquered. The ancient Castilian energy is, in a great degree, subdued; and it has given place, with many other noble traits of the Spanish character, to a peculiarity which seems to have marked the race in that country, under whatever combinations it is found—a proneness to civil discord, and a suicidal waste of its own strength.

With such a territory and such a people on our southern border, what is to be the inevitable course of empire? It needs no powers of prophecy to foretell. Sir, I desire to speak plainly: why should we not, when we are discussing the operation of moral and physical laws, which are beyond our control? As our population moves westward on our own territory, portions will cross our southern boundary. Settlements will be formed within the unoccupied and sparsely-peopled territory of Mexico. Uncongenial habits and tastes, differences of political opinion and principle, and numberless other elements of diversity will lead to a separation of these newly-formed societies from the inefficient government of Mexico. They will not endure to be held in subjection to a system, which neither yields them protection nor offers any incentive to their proper development and growth. They will form independent States on the basis of constitutions identical in all their leading features with our own; and they will naturally seek to unite their fortunes to ours. The fate of California is already sealed: it can never be reunited to Mexico. The operation of the great causes, to which I have alluded, must, at no distant day, detach the whole of northern Mexico from the southern portion of that republic. It is for the very reason that she is incapable of defending her possessions against the elements of disorder within and the progress of better influences from without, that I desire to see the inevitable political change which is to be wrought in the condition of her northern departments, brought about without any improper interference on our part.

11. Walter Colton, a Californian, Describes the Excitement of the Gold Rush, 1848

Tuesday, June 20. [1848]   My messenger sent to the mines, has returned with specimens of the gold; he dismounted in a sea of upturned faces. As he drew forth the yellow lumps from his pockets, and passed them around among the eager crowd, the doubts, which had lingered till now, fled. . . . All were off for the mines, some on horses, some on carts, and some on crutches, and one went in a litter. An American woman, who had recently established a boarding-house here, pulled up stakes, and was off before her lodgers had even time to pay their bills. Debtors ran, of course. I have only a community of women left, and a gang of prisoners, with here and there a soldier, who will give his captain the slip at the first chance. I don't blame the fellow a whit; seven dollars a month, while others are making two or three hundred a day! that is too much for human nature to stand. . . .

Tuesday, July 18.   Another bag of gold from the mines, and another spasm in the community. It was brought down by a sailor from Yuba river, and contains a hundred and thirty-six ounces. It is the most beautiful gold that has appeared in the market; it looks like the yellow scales of the dolphin, passing through his rainbow hues at death. My carpenters, at work on the school-house, on seeing it, threw down their saws and planes, shouldered their picks and are off for the Yuba. Three seamen ran from the Warren, forfeiting their four years' pay; and a whole platoon of soldiers from the fort left only their colors behind. One old woman declared she would never again break an egg or kill a chicken, without examining yolk and gizzard. . . .

Thursday, Aug. 16.   Four citizens of Monterey are just in from the gold mines on Feather River, where they worked in company with three others. They employed about thirty wild Indians, who are attached to the rancho owned by one of the party. They worked precisely seven weeks and three days, and have divided seventy-six thousand eight hundred and forty-four dollars,—nearly eleven thousand dollars to each. Make a dot there, and let me introduce a man, well known to me, who has worked on the Yuba river sixty-four days, and brought back, as the result of his in-dividual labor, five thousand three hundred and fifty-six dollars. . . . Make another dot there, and let me introduce a woman, of Sonoranian birth, who has worked in the dry diggings forty-six days, and brought back two thousand one hundred and twenty-five dollars. Is not this enough to make a man throw down his leger and shoulder a pick? . . .

Tuesday, Aug. 28.   The gold mines have upset all social and domestic arrangements in Monterey; the master has become his own servant, and the servant his own lord. The millionaire is obliged to groom his own horse, and roll his wheelbarrow; and the hidalgo—in whose veins flow the blood of all the Cortes—to clean his own boots! Here is lady L——, who has lived here seventeen years, the pride and ornament of the place, with a broomstick in her jewelled hand!

Walter Colton, *Three Years in California* (New York: A. S. Barnes and Co., 1850; reprint, Stanford, Calif.: Stanford University Press, 1949), 246–249, 252–253.

E S S A Y S

Historians have long wondered what the celebrations of the "common man" and "democracy," the revelry in public parades and political campaigns, and the high rates of voter turnout in elections really meant to American society and politics. Whereas some scholars have argued that these facts illustrate a first step in the development of a civic democracy, others focus on the less appealing aspects. Historical arguments in the second group are wide-ranging, from a condemnation of politics in this period as a democracy for white men only to a focus on the excesses of the raucous celebrations in the period. The following two essays touch on this last argument. Although Mary P. Ryan, a historian at the University of California, Berkeley, remains mindful of the inequalities of the period, she focuses on the democracy in the streets, which was as chaotic as it was colorful. But these celebrations, she contends, represent a public democracy that we rarely see today. In contrast, Glenn C. Altschuler and Stuart M. Blumin, both of whom teach at Cornell University, consider antebellum politics to be an expression of a "rude republic." Many Americans, they contend, were turned off by politics *because* of its boisterousness. While they might honor the American republic, these historians conclude, people in the United States in this period did not honor American politics.

Antebellum Politics as Raucous Democracy

MARY P. RYAN

In April 1834 a crowd gathered at Castle Garden in New York for "a day of general rejoicing." This festival, which brought an estimated 24,000 New Yorkers to a civic landmark on the tip of Manhattan Island, was the culmination of three days of boisterous activity on the city streets. The day before, two competing parades had clogged the downtown thoroughfares. The first formed when an open meeting of 20,000 adjourned into a procession and "rigged up a beautiful little frigate in complete order and named it the *Constitution.* As this moveable political symbol passed down Wall Street it met up with a second procession and engaged in a mock naval battle with a vessel called *Veto.* A special kind of public ritual was in process. These were partisan processions staged by Whigs and Jacksonians in the course of an electoral campaign. The meetings, processions, and drama continued until about 10 P.M. on the third day of the voting, when some 15,000 souls gathered on Wall Street to learn the final tally of votes."

. . . Much of what is known as Jacksonian democracy was acted out on the same principles as the everyday sociability and holiday conviviality of the city. The meeting of October 1835 that launched the radical democratic politics of the Loco-Foco wing of the Jacksonian movement was recorded in the press as follows: "After the adoption of the resolutions a motion was carried that the meeting adjourn to the street in front of the Hall and form a procession with their antimonopoly Banners, Flags, etc., which was accordingly carried—and some thousands of the meeting bearing

Mary P. Ryan, *Civic Wars: Democracy and Public Life in the American City During the Nineteenth Century* (Berkeley: University of California Press, 1997), 94–96, 108–110, 112–117, 119–121, 124, 129–131. Reprinted by permission of The Regents of the University of California.

torches, candles, etc., marched up the Bowery cheering their Democratic citizens on the way." By the end of the 1840s the enthusiasm had spread across the land. Whigs and Jacksonians locked horns in New Orleans as early as 1837, and in the 1849 municipal election the Democrats marched "through some of the principle [*sic*] streets with a profusion of June torches, making a splendid display. The principle feature of the procession was an artificial chicken cock of gigantic dimensions, triumphantly born aloft, and which attracted universal attention." When San Franciscans elected their first mayor in 1850, their festivities included a band stationed on the balcony above the Plaza and a parade of carts pulled by teams of horses, adorned with flags and banners, and carrying voters to the polls. And this was just a primary election. The final polling featured a dashing equestrian display in the Plaza by one Captain Bryant, who carried off the office of sheriff. The Democrats also pitched a tent in the Plaza and named it "Tammany Hall." One of the first things that the forty-niners hastily unpacked on arrival in California were these rites of representation: ward meetings, parades, partisan loyalties.

Such public displays indicate that city people defined themselves not just according to . . . social groupings . . . but by the political status of citizen and by a range of partisan affiliations. Political campaigns were yet another example of the immense potential for associated activity in urban public space: They were staged, like civic ceremonies, in places such as Wall Street, the Plaza, "the principle streets of the city." But there was more at stake in these partisan gatherings than in [other] aspects of civic culture. . . . First of all, these partisan public events were a direct exercise of political citizenship and brought into play the doctrine of popular sovereignty, a title to rights, and a token of power. With his treasured (exclusively male) franchise, the citizen became an actual participant in self-government. Second, when sovereign citizens came together for expressly political reasons, they did something more than display their cultural differences; they acknowledged and acted on their interdependency and agreed implicitly to work together to achieve some things, however, circumscribed, that could not be trusted to chance, the market, or individual effort. Third, [this] political culture . . . put urban heterogeneity to an extreme and decisive test. A partisan election placed different opinions in open competition: It was a declaration of civic war. A participant at the founding meeting of the Loco-Focos proudly described the event as "a struggle of gladiators on the platform around the chair;—the loudest vociferations are heard, and Tammany trembles with intestine war."

The contentious urban politics of the Jacksonian era was also, as Tocqueville had divined, a major stimulant to the frenetic formation of voluntary associations during the antebellum period. "In all the countries where political associations are prohibited, civil associations are rare. It is hardly probable that this is the result of accident; but the inference should rather be, that there is a natural and perhaps a necessary connection between these two kinds of association." Political events in New York, New Orleans, and San Francisco between 1825 and 1850 lend support to Tocqueville's inference. In fact the precise distinctions between politics, government, and more general urban associations are often difficult to determine. Antebellum citizenship was most always exercised in association with one's fellows: To the pioneers of antebellum democracy, the sacred civic act was not a private exercise of conscience or the individual practice of intellect but, in the words of the Loco-Focos, "speechifying and resolutions at political meetings." . . .

Democratizing the Public

Public meetings were part cause and part effect of a major campaign to dissolve the bonds of deference that wove through republican institutions and to build democratic procedures. As of 1820 democracy was a relatively limited component of municipal government. The municipal charter of New York, for example, entrusted the public good to a common council that was composed of and elected by propertied citizens. Elected council members in turn rarely consulted with the citizenry, before or after they entered office. The passage from deferential republicanism to "pure democracy" was gradual but ultimately decisive. In 1821 the city of New York removed most all property restrictions on the franchise (making a pointed exception for those of African descent). The same reform was accomplished in New Orleans when a statewide constitutional convention met in 1845. City charters and state constitutions alike were rewritten to bind legislators closer to the electorate. . . .

The purport of these reforms was to invest governmental legitimacy in representative procedures, whose advances in the 1830s and 1840s tell a familiar story: Elections became the critical act of a republican polity; the Jacksonians masterminded techniques of persuading voters; and electoral contests became a standoff between two principal party organizations. But neither the institution of representative government nor the creation of two parties was sufficient to create what the Loco-Focos would call pure democracy. That political ideal also reordered the relationships between voters and office holders, and among fellow citizens. Deference gave way to participation and converted harmony into opposition, which was the trademark of a public meeting.

Face-to-face congregations in public space were the most caustic solvents of the barrier between electors and office holders. As early as 1827, when the press had just begun addressing local issues, some public assemblages were defying the etiquette of deference. The *New York Evening Post* embraced direct democracy along with the party of Jackson in this account of a November rally: "The number who attended the late Jackson meeting in the park were so numerous and unprecedented. . . . Jackson is the favorite of the people." A Democratic meeting on March 28, 1834, illustrates the forward momentum of popular politics: It was called "The Great Meeting of the People—Triumphant Expression of Public Opinions." At about the same time the democratization of political institutions became a matter of debate in the Louisiana constitutional convention and moved candidates for office in New Orleans to announce themselves forthrightly as "Friendly to Popular Rights." Already in 1834 the *Bee* extolled the spirit that animated the Democratic public meetings of that era as "the power of the People when they declare their will." . . .

It was through the circuit of the public meetings, furthermore, that the spirit of democracy was thrust into the annals of the American political tradition. Perhaps the most memorable public meeting of the era was that "Great Democratick Republican County Meeting" that took place in New York on October 30, 1835. Its claim to fame is the formulation of the major planks of the Democratic Party platform for well into the future—opposition to the national bank, tariffs, monopolies, and paper money. It is also justly famed for the flair of its democratic expression. This meeting made its historical mark after some party leaders, expecting a popular defeat, tried to terminate a nominating meeting by extinguishing the lights in the public hall. Then, as the story goes, "Total darkness, for a moment, prevailed; but in a twinkling of an eye hundreds of candles were pulled from the pockets of the people, which by the aid of Loco-Foco matches were immediately lighted and old Tammany, amid the cheers of the democracy blazed in her premature and resplendent glory."

The "cheers of the Democracy" that went up from the public hall in 1835 thrust the name "Loco-Foco" into the American historical record and have rightfully captured the attention of historians. Other principles, proclaimed in a more reserved manner at that meeting, also merit comment. The single largest concern of the twenty-four resolutions passed that evening in October was the rights and procedures of the public meeting. Resolution 6 put it this way: "the people have the right and duty at all times . . . to assemble together to consult for the common good." References to an older construction of the public, as some larger good that stood above and apart from the mixed and mundane interests of the citizenry, were overshadowed by appeals to the "people" as they "assembled together." The members of a public meeting were obliged to "Give utterances to their sentiments, give instruction to their representatives, and to apply to the legislature for redress of wrong and grievances, by address, petitions and remonstrances." Subsequent resolutions went on to spell out the procedures of popular expression, free assembly, direct elections, reduced terms in office, and majority rule. Two weeks later the *Evening Post* put this vernacular political theory forthrightly: "to carry on to the fullest extent the principles of pure democracy." . . .

Many antebellum politicians harbored a deep antipathy to the democracy of the public meeting. To James Brooks such political associations were hardly better than barnyard gatherings: "Men must be herded as cattle are herded. All classes, all parties, all occupations make use of societies for all purposes. . . . The societies of the day—not the thinking individual men who make them up—are the winds that often form the gale of public opinion." Others were still plotting to maintain suffrage as a privilege of the propertied and to install presidential authority behind the fortress of a ten-year term. But such antidemocratic sentiments were rarely spoken in a loud public voice after 1840. In the words of one historian the rivals of the Jacksonians maintained "An almost deafening silence on the entire subject of political democracy." When the political faction that opposed Andrew Jackson's attack on the Bank of the United States found its name, "The Whig Party," during the New York City municipal election of 1834, it entered the partisan fray on terms set by radical democrats. By organizing publicly in order to object to the policies of an administration sitting in Washington, they provided the final solidification of a democracy of difference: They practiced and legitimized open, institutionalized, popular opposition.

Well before the presidential election of 1840, which heralded the second party system at the national electoral level, the Whigs had gone public in New York and New Orleans. In New Orleans in 1837 they claimed "The Whig Party is actually the Democratic Party." And in New York they adopted the official title "Democratic Whigs." Soon the opposition employed the nominating procedures of the Loco-Focos, complete with ward-level public meetings and primary elections. They had installed a decisive, quite close, and cogent bipartisan political rivalry that would endure for fifteen years. As a number of historians have demonstrated, the Whigs and Jacksonians placed before the American people a clear set of ideological and programmatic choices on everything from finance to public investment, the judiciary, and the corporations. By the late 1840s the Whigs had capitulated to popular procedure and created a foundation for democratic contestation in each city. The *New Orleans Picayune* geared up for a "struggle" on election day; in San Francisco the *Alta Californian* endorsed a system of representation in which "everyone will have the opportunity to express his wishes"; and the *New York Tribune* published calls to meetings of "The Democratic Whig Party" in every ward of the city.

As the principles of democratic opposition spread from the Jacksonians to the Whigs and from the Northeast to the South and West, its physical setting became more picturesque. In New Orleans in the 1840s the haughty Whigs met at the St. Louis Hotel or the Exchange, while the more populist Democrats assembled in the open air along Canal Street. The first American-style election in San Francisco in the spring of 1850 revealed the range of spatial possibilities that had become available for electioneering purposes at midcentury. The Whigs called the faithful to deposit their ballots in a "Primary election" to take place "At the house on Clay Street, three doors below Elleard's." The Democrats chose their candidate at a primary election held in Portsmouth Square from 7 A.M. to 7 P.M. and then ratified the nomination with a mass meeting in the same central location, where they called for yet another public meeting a few days later. This announcement—"The rights of the people will Not be Sold. Independent Mass meeting to rally the nomination of the Independent Washington Club"—includes a special invitation to "mechanics, workingmen, and all who are opposed to private clichés and hackneyed politicians." Democratic procedures of nominating representatives had become habitual by 1850: They were transmitted across the continent, available to third parties, and already associated with "hackneyed politicians."

This aggressive public spirit was maintained through election day itself. The actual casting of votes . . . reassembled the same people for a more prolonged, festive, and decisive public meeting. Ward meetings orchestrated this transition by appointing as many as 200 of their number to act as a "vigilance committee," pledged to stand watch over the polls for the duration of the balloting. At a time when municipalities restricted efforts to create a registry of voters as antidemocratic, the election was still a quite open convocation. The ward assemblies, nominating conventions, and elections were transfer points in a relay of authority, a direct passing of the baton of power unto another representation of the people. Meeting-place democracy shared in the public character of the civic parade: It transpired in open urban space and was diffused through segments such as wards, centered in times and spaces such as election day, and invested with a festive and contentious sociability. In scarcely two decades the sedate and constricted republican form . . . had been stormed and supplanted by the boisterous politics of the public meeting. . . .

The Political Definition of the People

The rhetoric of democracy seemed forthright: It proclaimed the rights of all the people to participate in the process of representation. But democracy as an actual political practice was something else again: It almost always came with strings attached and with specific provisos as to which people counted at any particular time and place. Of the cities of New York, New Orleans, and San Francisco between 1825 and 1850, at least this much can be said: The ranks of "the people who counted" had expanded significantly. In fact one of the major consequences of the culture of public meetings was to beg the question of who were, exactly, the people.

The Loco-Foco meeting answered this provocative question in the expansive language of "Equal Rights," ostensibly welcoming everyone into the democratic public. The first of the Loco-Foco's fabled resolutions proclaimed that "'all men are created equal'—that these United States are a nation—and that the national rights of every citizen are equal and indivisible." The third resolution elaborated, "That in a free state all distinctions but those of merit are odious and offensive and to be discouraged by a people jealous of their liberties." The principle was underscored again in resolution 4, which characterized all laws that would thwart "equal rights and privileges by the great body of the people [as] odious, unjust and unconstitutional." This notion of equal citizenship did not appear out of nowhere, however, or descend from high-minded universalistic principles of republicanism. It was championed by select social groups who had found in the public meeting a place to mobilize to claim their equal rights.

The notion of equal rights was the cutting edge (hardly the culmination) of a movement to expand access to democratic citizenship. In the early nineteenth century it was a political tool wielded most effectively by white males of the middling and lower social ranks. By the mid-1820s propertyless white men had secured the franchise, won the right to hold public office, and found a niche in the Democratic Republican Party. Soon this party of the "people" had booted the federalist "aristocracy" out of power across the nation. By the 1830s the ward-level meetings of Jacksonians styled their party the champions of the people against "the arts of the aristocracy" as practiced by the Whigs. The first mayor "ever elevated to that office by the suffrage of the people" was hailed in the *Evening Post* as a conqueror of "Besotted bank merchants" and champion of "the poor laborer who will not kneel at their footstool, who will not lay down his inestimable rights of equal political freedom, and consent to be their abject slave." By that raucous spring election of 1835 this rhetorical division of the people, between aristocrats and common men, had become a matter of electoral strategy. The Jacksonian press noted, for example, that although the fifteenth ward "is considered [in] an especial manner as the quarter of the aristocracy, yet there are enough democrats residing within it to secure the success of the democratic ticket if they will but exert themselves with spirit." In that year the Jacksonians lost the fifteenth ward, but by only a small margin. . . .

This is not to say that the political hospitality to difference was without its clear limits as of 1850. Some barriers to being counted among the people were left intact, and others were even fortified during the age of Jackson. The political public, the whole representative circuit from the ballot box and its contiguous spaces—the parade, the nominating conventions, the rowdy congregation at the polling places—to public offices and legislative assemblies, was a pristinely white and decisively male universe. The political invisibility of both women and nonwhites coexisted with their often vivid representation in civic culture and their relatively easy access to public space. This contradiction suggests that participation in formal politics, the right to act as a citizen, was by no means an automatic translation from social and cultural publicness. This quandary requires attention.

The barrier to participation in the political public was particularly effective against women. The demand for women's suffrage raised at Seneca Falls in 1848 was seldom heard downstate, where women were seldom given even a symbolic role in partisan activities. The notice that a place for the ladies had been reserved among the Whigs gathered at New Orleans's St. Louis Hotel in 1849 was a novel appearance of women anywhere near the sites of party politics. Likewise, women seldom formed truly *public* meetings. . . .

The status of nonwhites in the democratic public was equally anomalous and foreboding. But in this case, exclusion from citizenship was, on occasion, posed as a public and political question. In New Orleans the slave system placed the political status of all those of African American descent beyond the pale of citizenship. But once slavery was abolished in New York, democrats had to consider the meaning of citizenship for nonwhites. The constitution of 1821, the same document that removed property qualification for whites, severely restricted African American suffrage. It stipulated that only those New Yorkers of African ancestry who possessed $250 of property were entitled to vote. By this standard only 298 of almost 30,000 African Americans were granted the right. Yet this small group of enfranchised citizens pushed the democratic possibilities to their maximum. In 1837 they organized to end the property restrictions and succeeded (along with their white abolitionist allies in the Liberty Party) in placing their demands before the electorate. That referendum that demanded simply "Equal suffrage for Colored Persons" went down to a crushing defeat, by a margin of 2.6 to 1.

This mandate of the people made the hostilities to African Americans harbored by so many antebellum Americans a public matter. The Democratic Party was particularly quick to exploit these prejudices, saying, for example, that "Negroes are among but not of us" and vowing to "uphold our own race and kindred." The hostility broke out in vicious attacks on both African American neighborhoods and abolitionist conventions in New York in the 1830s. . . .

As of 1849 the history of democratic political institutions seemed to be still advancing by precarious steps while dodging roadblocks such as race and gender. Perhaps Tocqueville's prediction of 1831 would prove right: "The further electoral rights are extended, the greater is the need of extending them: for after each concession the strength of democracy increases, and its demands increase with its strength." At the middle of the nineteenth century the progress of enfranchisement seemed to be moving onward and outward: It had leapt over distinctions of property, had beat back attempts to restrict the citizenship of the foreign born and Catholics, and had sidestepped the absolute racial standards of exclusion. Only the difference of gender seemed a categorical bar to full rights of citizenship. As of 1850 there was still a long way to go in establishing equality of citizenship, but the democratic project was set on a forward course. . . .

The course of the democratic public through the 1830s and 1840s also ran roughshod over any refined notion of political protocol or decorum. The sheer number of what were called mobs or riots, disorderly expressions of public opinions on a panoply of issues, was higher than at any other time in American urban history. These minor civic wars were a fixture of antebellum democracy, and a goodly portion of them actually coincided with election campaigns. During the 1830s an election combined politics, ceremony, and donnybrook into one urban pageant and brought all sorts of civic differences jostling together in the streets. The processions through lower Manhattan described at the outset of this chapter and the ensuing battle between *Constitution* and *Veto* were classified as a riot in the great compendium of urban disorder collected by police chief J. T. Headley in 1873. The event, which Headley saw as "savage onslaughts" of the "mob" and filled the city presses with "rumors of bloody wars," was serious enough to bring out the forces of law and order for the first time in the rowdy history of New York elections. The mayor called up a special force of constables "to preserve the public peace." In the heat of the skirmish between Whigs and Democrats the mayor himself could be found "mounting the steps. He held up his staff of office and commanded the peace. But the half-drunken mob had now got beyond the fear of the mere symbol of authority and answered him with a shower of stones, and then charged on the force that surrounded him. A fierce and bloody fight followed."

At the time, however, outbreaks such as this were taken more in stride, even reported in a jocular fashion. One contemporary observer of the rancorous election of 1834 reported that "A good temper prevailed" and provoked "nothing more serious as a black eye." Routine ethnic rivalries were often dismissed as "Irish shillelagh frolic" or "a furious fight . . . which resulted in sundry broken heads and bloody noses." Indeed, although riots were regular occurrences in antebellum cities, they caused few fatalities. (A total of two lives were lost in scores of riots that plagued New York in the 1830s and early 1840s.) The raucous election scene in New Orleans in 1847 was reported with the same equanimity: "municipal election yesterday passed off with little disturbance . . . some little squabbling" in the second municipality. Through most of the period this routine "high spirit" fell within the capacious range of civic tolerance. Not until 1845 in New York did rioting provoke a concerted attempt to establish a professional police department, and this initiative of a short-lived reform government resulted in only a minor buttressing of the old public-watch system. A mayor could take a blow to the face without taking undue offense. The pugnacious style of politics could even be excused when the perpetrators were recent citizens and ethnic and religious minorities. The *Evening Post* excused the aggressive political behavior of the Irish, saying, "they were quick, irritable and generous . . . and not particularly disinclined to a row . . . impatient of insult and coercion . . . no rational man would provoke them." This commentator reserved his apprehension not for the mob but for the specter of "armed soldiers" should they be called up to keep order. In general antebellum citizens treasured public assembly at least as much as public order. One anonymous source put the stakes of public democracy this way during the election of 1834: "has it come to this. Has a democrat no right to speak his honest opinion in the public street." In 1834, and late into the next decade, the streets of cities such as New York remained open and hospitable to democratic speech even when it got a little raucous.

In fact a riot was not so much a breakdown of democratic process as its conduct by another means. The electoral contests that were the life of a democracy were from the first washed in the rhetoric of warfare. The Loco-Focos' offensive in New York in 1835 was heralded as a "struggle of gladiators," and the whole Democratic cause was one of "Warring not against individuals but against a system of wrong and oppression." When the Whigs joined in open democratic contention, their war cries, especially in the belligerent words of James Watson Webb of the *New York Courier and Enquirer,* were even more incendiary: calls to "armour, . . . fire and sword" against the "enemy." In other words the election "riots" condensed and gave a sometimes violent physical dimension to the conflict that was intrinsic to popular democracy. Any public meeting could cross over the border into a mob. . . . In sum, a riot was a species of political action not entirely unlike a public meeting. It was a congregation in open space to publish the collective opinion of a distinctive group. It was, like a partisan election, an act of civic warfare and an intrinsic part of what the *Evening Post* called "The great experiment we are making in popular government." Late in the 1840s this forceful expression of civic differences was still within the bonds of urban civility.

Antebellum Politics as Political Manipulation

GLENN C. ALTSCHULER AND STUART M. BLUMIN

The political procession that one day disturbed the customary quiet of the House of the Seven Gables touched a "powerful impulse" in Nathaniel Hawthorne's mysterious recluse, Clifford Pyncheon, to look out upon the "rush and roar of the human tide." The view was, however, a disappointing one, as the partisans, with their "hundreds of flaunting banners, and drums, fifes, clarions, and cymbals, reverberating between the rows of buildings," marched down too narrow a street and too close to Clifford's window. "The spectator feels it to be fool's play," Hawthorne explains, "when he can distinguish the tedious commonplace of each man's visage, with the perspiration and weary self-importance on it, and the very cut of his pantaloons, and the stiffness or laxity of his shirt-collar, and the dust on the back of his black coat." To be majestic, the procession must be seen from a more distant vantage point, "for then, by its remoteness, it melts all the petty personalities, of which it has been made up, into one broad mass of existence,—one great life,—one collected body of mankind, with a vast, homogeneous spirit animating it." Proximity might actually add to the effect on an "impressible person," but only should he, "standing alone over the brink of one of these processions, . . . behold it, not in its atoms, but in its aggregate,—as a mighty river of life, massive in its tide, and black with mystery, and, out of its depths, calling to the kindred depth within him."

As with the parade, so too, we would argue, with the more varied and complex processes of American electoral democracy—all can be seen from up close and from afar, by more and less "impressible" observers, absorbed in the animating spirit or attentive to the "tedious commonplace of each man's visage," beholding the "atoms" as well as the "aggregate." Historians of the United States, observing closely or from a distance, have been impressed for a very long time with the animating spirit of the nineteenth-century political spectacle, and have developed a nearly consensual view of post-Jacksonian American politics as a genuinely massive activity in which the vast majority of ordinary Americans—white, voting males, most evidently—

Glenn C. Altschuler and Stuart M. Blumin, *Rude Republic: Americans and Their Politics in the Nineteenth Century* (Princeton, N.J.: Princeton University Press, 2000), 3–11. Copyright © 2000 by Princeton University Press. Reprinted by permission of Princeton University Press.

participated with an effectiveness born of enthusiasm for and deep commitment to their political party, to specific programs and leaders, and to the idea and practice of democracy itself. "There is considerable evidence," observes Jean H. Baker, "that nineteenth-century Americans gave closer attention to politics than is the case today, thereby guaranteeing a broader, deeper understanding of issues. . . . [P]arty rallies were better attended than Sunday services or even meetings of itinerant preachers," and elections "became secular holy days." This is an assessment with which more than one generation of historians would agree. Most historians would agree also that politics, and partisan commitment especially, colored many other aspects of American life. "Politics seem to enter into everything," complained a nonpartisan editor during the heat of the 1860 campaign, and William E. Gienapp has made of this the defining phrase of the penetration of politics into the lives of Clifford Pyncheon's younger and more active fellow citizens: "More than in any subsequent era," he explains, "political life formed the very essence of the pre–Civil War generation's experience." Disagreeing only with the temporal specificity of this claim, Michael E. McGerr restates it with a compelling metaphor, suggestive, again, of point of view. Both before and after the Civil War, he argues, the political party was not merely an institution for formulating public policy and organizing election campaigns, but "a natural lens through which to view the world."

The campaign spectacle of parades and mass rallies, and the high energy of election days in which very large proportions of eligible voters cast ballots, were only part of the process of political engagement. Prior to these events on the political calendar were the local party caucuses open to all the party's adherents, and the various nominating conventions to which these meetings of ordinary citizens sent delegates to represent them. At its grass roots, according to Robert H. Wiebe, America's parties functioned as a "lodge democracy," in which "leaders were made and unmade by their brothers, and all parties in the process assumed an underlying equality." More than that, the process was open to all who cared to participate: "All one needed to get into politics," Wiebe insists, "was to get into it." Fueling both the desire to join and the ongoing political battle, moreover, were partisan newspapers, maintained in cities and small towns throughout the nation, and functioning not only as local party mobilizing agencies and bulletin boards, but also as educators of the public, discussing political issues and providing summaries or transcripts of legislative proceedings and presidential and gubernatorial messages even during periods of political quiescence. "The pages of the press," McGerr asserts, "made partisanship seem essential to men's identity." Finally, the frequency of elections assured that these periods of quiescence would not last long. The election cycle varied from place to place, but everywhere in America there were annual local elections, usually in the late winter or spring, and everywhere there was some kind of partisan election—state, congressional, presidential—each year in the late summer or fall. Frequent elections meant that Americans were "perpetually acting" in a ritual of democratic reaffirmation. The political calendar, concludes Joel H. Silbey, "ensured that Americans were caught up in semipermanent and unstinting partisan warfare somewhere throughout the year every year."

This is an attractive perspective on a young and vibrant democracy, evoking the image of a political "golden age" (a phrase used from time to time to describe this era), and affirming the study of politics as a relatively unmediated manifestation of democratic American culture. The view from Clifford's window is a little more un-settling. The different expressions and postures it reveals call upon us to recognize a much more variable set of political attitudes and relations, including those less likely to affirm either the democratic responsiveness or the centrality to American life and culture of the partisan political system. Some historians have gained this view . . . by recognizing the direction and manipulation of nominations and cam-paigns by political leaders, the persisting deference by ordinary citizens to these leaders well into the era of "lodge democracy," and the essential role played by party organizers in stimulating broad participation in campaigns and elections. What is largely missing from the historical literature, however, is any sustained analysis of the nature and depth of popular political engagement, and of the possi-bility, even during this period of high voter turnout, spectacular campaigns, fre-quent elections, and a pervasive political press, of *variable* relations to political affairs on the part of those who cannot be recognized as political leaders. It is our contention that the political engagement of nineteenth-century Americans did vary significantly, over time and among ordinary citizens at any given time, and that the recognition of these variations leads to fundamental questions about Americans and their politics. . . .

Political engagement is in many respects a behavioral phenomenon, consisting of participation of various sorts in the more and less institutionalized aspects of the political process. Men (and during the nineteenth century, only men) could be public officeholders, editors of political newspapers, officers and members of party central committees, convention delegates, and behind-the-scenes manipulators of political affairs. Or, they could attend caucuses, join campaign clubs, work at the polls, and vote; while both women and men could appear at campaign rallies, listen to speeches, read editorials in the partisan press, sign petitions, and argue politics with their friends and family. That they could also neglect to do these things—to absent themselves from a convention or rally, to read a book rather than a political newspaper, to discuss the weather rather than politics—requires us to relate political participation to the whole range of activities that constitutes a given social world, and in some fashion to measure its significance within that world. . . . And just as political participation can vary, so too can political attitude—from enthusiasm to indifference, from belief to skepticism, from appreciation to hostility. This, too, must be measured in some way, and related to political action as something to isolate within, but not from, American life.

The political action to which we refer was, from the 1830s through the end of the century and beyond, mostly partisan in nature. There were, to be sure, important elements of public life in American communities that the political parties often could not and did not reach: more and less official and regular "town meetings" of local cit-izens; local elections of certain kinds (and of all kinds in some places); religious, benevolent, and reform activities of high-minded women and men; and extralegal vigilante committees in areas where public institutions were not, or not yet, well established. Particularly in the years before the establishment of strong party insti-tutions, there were lines of political influence and loyalty that were personal rather than partisan. But if Americans experienced for a time the pre-party "meeting-place democracy" that Mary P. Ryan has recently described, and if established local leaders continued to exercise a considerable personal influence, the reach of the institutionalized parties was clearly expanding across all of these domains. More ritualized and celebratory public events, such as Fourth of July parades and local agricultural fairs, retained their nonpartisan character through nearly all these years (though the passions of the Civil War years challenged some of them), and, as Jean Baker has convincingly argued, continued to contribute in a quite different way to the sense and meaning of civic life. But the parties, as we will discuss, quickly assumed the organization of what virtually everyone in the nineteenth century referred to when they used the term "politics." It is to this customary and popular understanding of the term that we will subscribe, relating a narrowly defined partisan politics to other forms of influence and civic life when these shared or competed for a presence on the public stage.

Several reasons for positing a more complex and conflicted relation to political affairs among Americans emerge from even a preliminary consideration of politics (understood narrowly or even broadly) as one of a number of influences, interests, and venues within the larger society and culture. Perhaps the most important of these is religion, and the fact that political democratization was paralleled in nineteenth-century America, and particularly in the antebellum era, by an increasing commitment on the part of large numbers of Americans to the beliefs and behavioral dictates of evangelical Christianity. Political historians have recognized this parallel development and have probed in considerable detail not only the ethnoreligious foundations of partisan affiliation, but also the religious roots of reform movements, such as temperance and abolition, that entered the political arena. Perhaps because of these connections, however, they have not stressed sufficiently the power of religious sensibilities to subordinate politics to what many believed were more important activities and preoccupations, and have not recognized the degree to which politics and religion could be placed by some in an adversarial relation. Richard Carwardine, for example, acknowledges that evangelicals in the 1840s railed against the new public maxim that "all is fair in politics," lamented the decline of moral standards under the rule of "maddened, wine-heated politicians," and lambasted hickory-pole and cider-barrel electioneering as a "reckless waste in useless trappings." He notes that some religious men eschewed politics entirely: "I am myself a candidate, but it is for eternal life." But these sentiments quickly fade from his narrative when Carwardine turns to the realization by evangelicals that they could not pursue their crusades against alcohol, slavery, and Catholicism by "swimming against the tide of American popular culture." Thereafter, he argues, religion and politics became parts of an "organic seamless whole."

We believe, however, that what Mark Y. Hanley has called "the Protestant quarrel with the American republic" was more enduring among a broad group of conservative Christians. Hanley describes the efforts of Ezra Stiles, Francis Wayland, Charles Hodge, Horace Bushnell, and a number of lesser-known clergy to assure that a transcendent and redemptive Christianity remain uncorrupted by the new American "liberal order." What troubled these divines was an illusory "new freedom beyond faith" that included an absorption of the mind and spirit in political affairs and an arrogant conflation of political with spiritual progress: "When did [Christ] condescend to tell us that ours is the true form of government?" asked Bushnell. "When lend himself to any such mischievous flattery as this?" Bushnell raised these questions in the context of the fervent presidential campaign of 1840, but evangelicals and other Protestants continued to insist throughout the antebellum era, and later, that politics be kept out of the pulpit and the religious press, and that men and women go beyond and beneath matters of state to examine the state of their souls. What effects did these exhortations have on the political commitment of ordinary Christians? Did some churchgoers vote in secular elections but also contain or compartmentalize their political enthusiasm? Did others withdraw from political affairs? Might not the borrowing of religious rhetoric by nineteenth-century politicians have been a device for attracting those whose deeper instincts were to protect themselves from political dangers?

A second reason for questioning the pervasiveness of political engagement is the tension, obvious in so many ways, between political activism and the pursuit of upper- and middle-class respectability. Just as evangelical Christianity and political democracy developed simultaneously in a partly conflicted relation, so too did the emergence of new forms and a heightened pursuit of social respectability coincide with the development of political practices that were widely perceived as disreputable. European visitors commented frequently on the coarseness of the new American politics—on the need to shake "one hard greasy paw" after another, on the "uncouth mosaic of expectoration and nutshells" (Mrs. Trollope's name for the characteristic American citizen was George Washington Spitchew)—and Robert Wiebe contends that some Americans eagerly translated this problem into the solution, indeed the defining virtue, of American politics in the Age of the Common Man. Without apology they created an egalitarian politics appropriate to what we call here a rude republic—a political nation just taking shape, and one that prided itself on its challenge to deference and its disdain for the formalities of polite address. This rude republic, we believe, was formed across the nineteenth century in ways that unsettled not only visiting Europeans but also many respectable Americans. Blatant office-seeking and behind-the-scenes maneuvering, the cultivation of political loyalty among newly enfranchised workers and recently arrived immigrants, the inclusion in political organizations of saloonkeepers, street toughs, and other unsavory characters, the employment of manipulative techniques of mass appeal, and the equation of these techniques with other forms of crude humbuggery, imparted an unseemliness to politics that considerably complicated the simultaneous pursuit of respectability and an active political life. William Gienapp cites one elite Philadelphian who complained of "'the mere chicanery of politics,' which made the pursuit of office 'attended by a degradation of character & sacrifice of principle startling enough to drive every man of taste & feeling into deeper shades of private life,'" and it is clear that many social elites did find it more difficult to participate in a rude republic of voting masses and saloon-based precinct captains, of torchlight parades and vulgar oratory. By no means all withdrew into "deeper shades of private life," but those elites who remained active in the party period were compelled to adjust to new and uncomfortably disreputable associations and activities.

These concerns pertain as well to those more modestly positioned individuals and families who made new claims of social respectability as part of an emerging middle class. The most complex patterns of middle-class formation were to be found in the largest cities, where politics were also perceived as being especially unseemly and corrupt. In the cities, middle-class respectability was grounded in a variety of new social environments and experiences: enlarged and refined, parlor-centered homes;

similarly embellished commercial, managerial, and professional workplaces; increasingly homogeneous residential neighborhoods and business districts; a variety
of new commercial and voluntary institutions providing respectable entertainment
and sociability. The essence of all of these was class segregation, and in particular the
insulation of middle-class individuals and families from the rough world of the native
and immigrant working class. Political activities of various kinds could threaten
that insulation and the sense of social well-being that went with it. Indeed, at a time
when theaters, retail shopping districts, and even church congregations were increasingly segregated by class, political gatherings remained among the most socially
promiscuous of the city's affairs. Was this in fact a source of political disengagement
among the urban middle class? And what about the far larger number of middling
folk who lived in smaller towns and in the countryside, where politics was less (or
less famously) corrupt and social promiscuity less (or less obviously) problematic?
Richard Bushman has demonstrated the appeal of city-bred social styles in rural
and small-town America, but if rustic Americans pursued a "vernacular gentility"
to confirm their middle-class status, does it follow that they faced the same compli-
cations of political engagement that we have posited for their urban counterparts?
What, indeed, were the social implications of political engagement—and the effects
on political engagement of upper- and middle-class social sensibilities—in both
the city and the country?

In defining vernacular gentility, Bushman describes a rural middle class, "without pretensions to public office," that failed to develop the sense of public duty and
privilege that had once been an important part of the aristocratic package of values
and behavior. "The realm of the middling people was the family rather than town
or county." This selective importation of genteel qualities is suggestive of what historians frequently have labeled "liberalism," that political theory or sensibility emphasizing individual rights over corporate responsibilities and asserting the superiority
of the free market over public activity and control. Historians ordinarily discuss liberalism as a well-reasoned article of conviction, and as a mode of political action
that would use politics to limit the prerogatives of the state and to enlarge individual freedoms. There is not necessarily a paradox in this, and it is surely the case
that many Americans have engaged fervently in politics with just such ends in
mind. But we believe it is possible to identify another kind of liberalism that did
little to nurture, and much to discourage, political participation. Less theoretical or
even thoughtful, more humdrum even in its description—following Bushman, we
call it "vernacular liberalism"—it is no more than an unreflective absorption in the
daily routines of work, family, and social life, those private and communal domains
that the small governments of the era hardly touched. To be sure, there is nothing in
the "realm of the family" that would have prevented its male members from an active
engagement or its female members from an active interest in the larger realms of
politics and the state in nineteenth-century America. But we suspect that the radical
disconnectedness and "privatism" observed in America by Tocqueville and other
European visitors in this period translated in many instances into a primacy of self
and family that confined politics to a lower order of personal commitment than is
generally recognized. Tocqueville himself argued that Americans were passionately
interested in politics, but he would not have seen much or many of those people to
whom we refer. Neither have many historians ferreted them out from their chimney

corners and workbenches. Most Americans did vote, and for many historians that has been enough. We would look more closely at "liberalism," not merely as a political theory, but also, for some, as an apolitical way of life.

The republicanism that historians so frequently place in opposition to liberalism as a source or summation of American values was itself capable of complicating and even limiting political engagement. Most importantly, it fueled the antipartyism that historians have found during the earliest years of the second party system, and that, we believe, continued as a significant element of American political culture long after the more reluctantly partisan Whigs adopted the structures and campaign techniques pioneered by Democrats. Indeed, the feeling that parties were corrupting the political process may have strengthened as the two major parties came to resemble each other in structure and technique, and as the party system came to dominate, seemingly permanently, the republican political process. It was in this context of party hegemony and a wary public that the cult of George Washington served to express antipartyism (the Farewell Address was this movement's basic text, and was read aloud at many public gatherings), and to offer military heroism and sacrifice as a sounder basis of patriotism and republican virtue. The parties themselves understood the potentially alienating effects of this popular contrast between the politician and the military hero. They frequently offered their presidential nominations to former military commanders with otherwise minimal political credentials, and introduced military motifs into their campaigns even when no general could be found to head the ticket (rarely a problem in the post–Civil War era). Campaign biographers, as William Burlie Brown has shown, were increasingly inclined to disavow any kind of political apprenticeship for their subjects, whether or not they had been military men, and to claim that only their opponents were politicians by trade. "The conclusion is inescapable," writes Brown, "that the basic assumptions of the biographers are that their audience believes the politician is evil and party politics is evil twice compounded." And yet, inevitably, it was the party that offered military heroes and other disinterested amateurs to the voting public. No significant candidacies were mounted by such paragons of republicanism outside the party's structures and campaign machinery. Those who loathed the party and its professional politicians, therefore, had to reconcile some significantly discordant elements of the candidacy of any latter-day George Washington.

The great public-school reforms of the 1840s and beyond offer insights into this tension between party politics and a republicanism grounded in military service. School reformers developed curricula and purchased textbooks that underscored the military origins of republican virtue while making no concessions to partisan institutions. Jean Baker has argued that the experience of schooling in the antebellum era "trained young white males in their public roles of delegating power, rotating leadership, limiting power, and supporting the government." None of this entered the formal curriculum, however, and the "training" Baker alludes to consisted mainly of the manner in which restive school children resisted the tyrannies of their overbearing teachers. Against this problematic inference we would place Baker's own observation that the schools "did not introduce their students to public issues or political parties, as twentieth-century civics courses would." Remarkably, American school children of the antebellum era were given no political history of their nation. American history texts culminated in the Revolutionary War, and the message of this climactic event was the patriotic virtue of Washington and his men-at-arms. It is curricular decisions of this sort, made by men who were as convinced as Horace Bushnell was about the significance of early childhood nurturance in the shaping of enduring values, that seem to us most important in conveying the intended and actual effects of public schooling upon republican civic consciousness. Americans were taught to honor the American republic, but not American politics. For how many did this kind of republicanism remain a cultural resource for resisting engagement in the "affairs of party"?

F U R T H E R   R E A D I N G

John M. Belohlavek, *"Let the Eagle Soar!": The Foreign Policy of Andrew Jackson* (1985).

William W. Freehling, *Prelude to Civil War: The Nullification Controversy in South Carolina* (1966).

Reginald Horsman, *Race and Manifest Destiny* (1981).

Daniel Walker Howe, *The Political Culture of the American Whigs* (1979).

Richard P. McCormick, *The Second Party System: Party Formation in the Jacksonian Era* (1966).

Charles Sellers, *The Market Revolution: Jacksonian America, 1815–1846* (1991).

Harry L. Watson, *Liberty and Power: The Politics of Jacksonian America* (1990).

CHAPTER
9

Reform and the Great Awakening in the Early Nineteenth Century

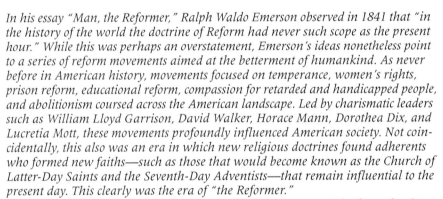

In his essay "Man, the Reformer," Ralph Waldo Emerson observed in 1841 that "in the history of the world the doctrine of Reform had never such scope as the present hour." While this was perhaps an overstatement, Emerson's ideas nonetheless point to a series of reform movements aimed at the betterment of humankind. As never before in American history, movements focused on temperance, women's rights, prison reform, educational reform, compassion for retarded and handicapped people, and abolitionism coursed across the American landscape. Led by charismatic leaders such as William Lloyd Garrison, David Walker, Horace Mann, Dorothea Dix, and Lucretia Mott, these movements profoundly influenced American society. Not coincidentally, this also was an era in which new religious doctrines found adherents who formed new faiths—such as those that would become known as the Church of Latter-Day Saints and the Seventh-Day Adventists—that remain influential to the present day. This clearly was the era of "the Reformer."

We can attempt to explain the growth of reform movements in the early nineteenth century by considering four interlocking factors. First, this was a period of great societal change. Americans not only puzzled over changes in society, but questioned how old patterns of social organization might be reestablished in new forms. Religious belief and social reform were often cited as forces that might either recapture the old order or point to ways in which a new order could be created. Second, the early nineteenth century saw the growth of intellectual movements that rejected the rationalism of an earlier age. Americans were now fascinated with the gothic, with the sense of mystery, with romanticism and sentimentality. These ideas, which permeated society, are important for the purposes of this chapter because sentimentality could encourage the development of empathy for others. If Americans could "feel" the human costs of alcohol abuse or of slavery, for example, they could empathize with the victims and work to eradicate such evils. Third, many Americans continued to be imbued with a belief in progress. They continued to see the United States as a place of destiny, a nation with a mission of greatness. If conditions could improve, it followed that people should play an active role in bringing that improvement about.

Related to notions of progress and perfectibility is the fourth and perhaps the most important underlying factor: religious change. Between roughly 1795 and 1837, many Americans were roused by religious revivals that changed their views of the possibilities of the world. Known as the Second Great Awakening, this religious movement fostered the growth of Christian belief, particularly among those in denominations, such as the Methodists and the Baptists, that saw humans as having a greater role in their own salvation. If individuals could be saved, it followed that if all were delivered, the result might be a perfect society. If individuals could choose good over evil, they could eradicate sin from the world. Underlying these reform movements, then, was "millennialism," the belief that a thousand-year era of peace, harmony, and Christian brotherhood on earth would precede the Second Coming of Christ. Given Americans' tendency to see their nation as having a role in momentous events, it was not surprising that they saw the millennium as being set in the United States.

QUESTIONS TO THINK ABOUT

In this era, religious movements developed that underscored the possibility that everyone in society could achieve perfection and salvation. This differed from the belief in earlier eras that salvation was limited to a few people who were saved by a gracious God. How might these changing views be linked to reform movements? Were reformers concerned more about improving society or about controlling it? How might people in reform movements, such as abolitionism, view the government? Was it a positive or negative force?

DOCUMENTS

The first two documents depict the emotional religious experiences that many Americans underwent in the early nineteenth century. In Document 1, Peter Cartwright, a Methodist evangelist, describes his conversion in 1801. He then recounts the revivals that began in Cane Ridge, Kentucky, in 1801 and spread throughout the West. In contrast, Frances Trollope, a visitor from Europe, penned an acerbic portrait of a camp revival meeting in 1829. Note how women who underwent conversion experiences particularly bother her. The remaining documents focus on reform movements. Document 3 is an appeal written in 1829 in Boston by David Walker, an African American, focusing on the evils of slavery. In Document 4, William Lloyd Garrison, who was profoundly influenced by Walker, introduces his newspaper *The Liberator* with a call for immediate abolition. Thomas S. Grimké, in Document 5, makes an appeal for temperance by arguing that people who object to the use of alcohol are both patriotic and Christian. Document 6 is a segment of Ralph Waldo Emerson's essay on reform, written in 1841, that stresses "the new spirit" of reform in the United States. Some reformers attempted to create communities that were perfect, as Document 7 illustrates. Elizabeth Peabody was active in planning the Brook Farm community because she believed that one must "come out . . . from the world" in order to live a moral life. Reformers were active in a variety of causes, as shown by the final two documents. Dorothea Dix's letter to the Massachusetts legislature in Document 8 is a chilling depiction of the treatment endured by the mentally ill in jails and almshouses. In Document 9, Horace Mann stresses the importance of the public school because it can reform children and address many of the evils of society.

1. Peter Cartwright, a Methodist Itinerant Preacher, Marvels at the Power of Religious Revivals, 1801

In 1801, when I was in my sixteenth year, my father, my eldest half brother, and myself, attended a wedding about five miles from home, where there was a great deal of drinking and dancing, which was very common at marriages in those days. I drank little or nothing; my delight was in dancing. After a late hour in the night, we mounted our horses and started for home. I was riding my race-horse.

A few minutes after we had put up the horses, and were sitting by the fire, I began to reflect on the manner in which I had spent the day and evening. I felt guilty and condemned. I rose and walked the floor. My mother was in bed. It seemed to me, all of a sudden, my blood rushed to my head, my heart palpitated, in a few minutes I turned blind; an awful impression rested on my mind that death had come and I was unprepared to die. I fell on my knees and began to ask God to have mercy on me.

My mother sprang from her bed, and was soon on her knees by my side, praying for me, and exhorting me to look to Christ for mercy, and then and there I promised the Lord that if he would spare me, I would seek and serve him; and I never fully broke that promise. My mother prayed for me a long time. At length we lay down, but there was little sleep for me. Next morning I rose, feeling wretched beyond expression. I tried to read in the Testament, and retired many times to secret prayer through the day, but found no relief. I gave up my racehorse to my father, and requested him to sell him. I went and brought my pack of cards, and gave them to mother, who threw them into the fire, and they were consumed. I fasted, watched, and prayed, and engaged in regular reading of the Testament. I was so distressed and miserable, that I was incapable of any regular business.

My father was greatly distressed on my account, thinking I must die, and he would lose his only son. He bade me retire altogether from business, and take care of myself. . . .

There were no camp-meetings in regular form at this time, but as there was a great waking up among the Churches, from the revival that had broken out at Cane Ridge, before mentioned, many flocked to those sacramental meetings. The church would not hold the tenth part of the congregation. Accordingly, the officers of the Church erected a stand in a contiguous shady grove, and prepared seats for a large congregation.

The people crowded to this meeting from far and near. They came in their large wagons, with victuals mostly prepared. The women slept in the wagons, and the men under them. Many stayed on the ground night and day for a number of nights and days together. Others were provided for among the neighbors around. The power of God was wonderfully displayed; scores of sinners fell under the preaching, like men slain in mighty battle; Christians shouted aloud for joy.

To this meeting I repaired, a guilty, wretched sinner. On the Saturday evening of said meeting, I went, with weeping multitudes, and bowed before the stand, and earnestly prayed for mercy. In the midst of a solemn struggle of soul, an impression

Peter Cartwright, *Autobiography of Peter Cartwright, the Backwoods Preacher,* ed. W. P. Strickland (New York: Phillips and Hunt, 1856), 34–35, 37–38, 45, 48–49.

was made on my mind, as though a voice said to me, "Thy sins are all forgiven thee." Divine light flashed all round me, unspeakable joy sprung up in my soul. I rose to my feet, opened my eyes, and it really seemed as if I was in heaven; the trees, the leaves on them, and everything seemed, and I really thought were, praising God. My mother raised the shout, my Christian friends crowded around me and joined me in praising God; and though I have been since then, in many instances, unfaithful, yet I have never, for one moment, doubted that the Lord did, then and there, forgive my sins and give me religion. . . .

From 1801 for years a blessed revival of religion spread through almost the entire inhabited parts of the West, Kentucky, Tennessee, the Carolinas, and many other parts, especially through the Cumberland country, which was so called from the Cumberland River, which headed and mouthed in Kentucky, but in its great bend circled south through Tennessee, near Nashville. The Presbyterians and Methodists in a great measure united in this work, met together, prayed together, and preached together.

In this revival originated our camp-meetings, and in both these denominations they were held every year, and, indeed, have been ever since, more or less. They would erect their camps with logs or frame them, and cover them with clapboards or shingles. They would also erect a shed, sufficiently large to protect five thousand people from wind and rain, and cover it with boards or shingles; build a large stand, seat the shed, and here they would collect together from forty to fifty miles around, sometimes further than that. Ten, twenty, and sometimes thirty ministers, of different denominations, would come together and preach night and day, four or five days together; and, indeed, I have known these camp-meetings to last three or four weeks, and great good resulted from them. I have seen more than a hundred sinners fall like dead men under one powerful sermon, and I have seen and heard more than five hundred Christians all shouting aloud the high praises of God at once; and I will venture to assert that many happy thousands were awakened and converted to God at these camp-meetings. Some sinners mocked, some of the old dry professors opposed, some of the old starched Presbyterian preachers preached against these exercises, but still the work went on and spread almost in every direction, gathering additional force, until our country seemed all coming home to God. . . .

[A] new exercise broke out among us, called the *jerks,* which was overwhelming in its effects upon the bodies and minds of the people. No matter whether they were saints or sinners, they would be taken under a warm song or sermon, and seized with a convulsive jerking all over, which they could not by any possibility avoid, and the more they resisted the more they jerked. If they would not strive against it and pray in good earnest, the jerking would usually abate. I have seen more than five hundred persons jerking at one time in my large congregations. Most usually persons taken with the jerks, to obtain relief, as they said, would rise up and dance. Some would run, but could not get away. Some would resist; on such the jerks were generally very severe.

To see those proud young gentlemen and young ladies, dressed in their silks, jewelry, and prunella, from top to toe, take the *jerks* would often excite my risibilities. The first jerk or so, you would see their fine bonnets, caps, and combs fly; and so sudden would be the jerking of the head that their long loose hair would crack almost as loud as a wagoners whip.

2. Frances Trollope, an Englishwoman, Views a Religious Meeting in Indiana, 1829

It was in the course of this summer that I found the opportunity I had long wished for, of attending a camp-meeting. . . .

The prospect of passing a night in the back woods of Indiana was by no means agreeable, but I screwed my courage to the proper pitch, and set forth determined to see with my own eyes, and hear with my own ears, what a camp-meeting really was. . . .

We reached the ground about an hour before midnight, and the approach to it was highly picturesque. The spot chosen was the verge of an unbroken forest, where a space of about twenty acres appeared to have been partially cleared for the purpose. Tents of different sizes were pitched very near together in a circle round the cleared space; behind them were ranged an exterior circle of carriages of every description, and at the back of each were fastened the horses which had drawn them thither. Through this triple circle of defence we distinguished numerous fires burning brightly within it; and still more numerous lights flickering from the trees that were left in the enclosure. The moon was in meridian splendour above our heads.

. . . Four high frames, constructed in the form of altars, were placed at the four corners of the enclosure; on these were supported layers of earth and sod, on which burned immense fires of blazing pinewood. On one side a rude platform was erected to accommodate the preachers, fifteen of whom attended this meeting, and with very short intervals for necessary refreshment and private devotion, preached in rotation, day and night, from Tuesday to Saturday.

When we arrived the preachers were silent; but we heard issuing from nearly every tent mingled sounds of praying, preaching, singing, and lamentation. The curtains in front of each tent were dropped, and the faint light that gleamed through the white drapery, backed as it was by the dark forest, had a beautiful and mysterious effect, that set the imagination at work; and had the sounds which vibrated around us been less discordant, harsh, and unnatural, I should have enjoyed it. . . .

Great numbers of persons were walking about the ground, who appeared like ourselves to be present only as spectators; some of these very unceremoniously contrived to raise the drapery of [one] tent, at one corner, so as to afford us a perfect view of the interior.

The floor was covered with straw, which round the sides was heaped in masses, that might serve as seats, but which at that moment were used to support the heads and the arms of the close-packed circle of men and women who kneeled on the floor.

Out of about thirty persons thus placed, perhaps half a dozen were men. One of these, a handsome looking youth of eighteen or twenty, kneeled just below the opening through which I looked. His arm was encircling the neck of a young girl who knelt beside him, with her hair hanging dishevelled upon her shoulders, and her features working with the most violent agitation; soon after they both fell forward on the straw, as if unable to endure in any other attitude the burning eloquence of a tall grim figure in black, who, standing erect in the centre, was uttering with incredible

---

Frances Trollope, *Domestic Manners of the Americans* (London: Whittaker, Treacher, 1830), 137–138, 140–143.

vehemence an oration that seemed to hover between praying and preaching; his arms hung stiff and immovable by his side, and he looked like an ill-constructed machine, set in action by a movement so violent, as to threaten its own destruction, so jerkingly, painfully, yet rapidly, did his words tumble out; the kneeling circle ceased not to call, in every variety of tone, on the name of Jesus; accompanied with sobs, groans, and a sort of low howling inexpressibly painful to listen to. . . .

We made the circuit of the tents, pausing where attention was particularly excited by sounds more vehement than ordinary. We contrived to look into many; all were strewed with straw, and the distorted figures that we saw kneeling, sitting, and lying amongst it, joined to the woful and convulsive cries, gave to each the air of a cell in Bedlam.

One tent was occupied exclusively by negroes. They were all full-dressed, and looked exactly as if they were performing a scene on the stage. One woman wore a dress of pink gauze trimmed with silver lace; another was dressed in pale yellow silk; one or two had splendid turbans; and all wore a profusion of ornaments. The men were in snow white pantaloons, with gay coloured linen jackets. One of these, a youth of coal-black comeliness, was preaching with the most violent gesticulations, frequently springing high from the ground, and clapping his hands over his head. Could our missionary societies have heard the trash he uttered, by way of an address to the Deity, they might perhaps have doubted whether his conversion had much enlightened his mind.

At midnight a horn sounded through the camp, which, we were told, was to call the people from private to public worship; and we presently saw them flocking from all sides to the front of the preachers' stand. . . . There were about two thousand persons assembled.

One of the preachers began in a low nasal tone, and, like all other Methodist preachers, assured us of the enormous depravity of man as he comes from the hands of his Maker, and of his perfect sanctification after he had wrestled sufficiently with the Lord to get hold of him, *et cetera.* . . . The preacher told them [the crowd] that "this night was the time fixed upon for anxious sinners to wrestle with the Lord"; that he and his brethren "were at hand to help them"; and that such as needed their help were to come forward into "the pen." . . . "The pen" was the space immediately below the preacher's stand; we were therefore placed on the edge of it, and were enabled to see and hear all that took place in the very centre of this extraordinary exhibition.

The crowd fell back at the mention of the *pen,* and for some minutes there was a vacant space before us. The preachers came down from their stand, and placed themselves in the midst of it, beginning to sing a hymn, calling upon the penitents to come forth. As they sang they kept turning themselves round to every part of the crowd, and, by degrees, the voices of the whole multitude joined in chorus. This was the only moment at which I perceived any thing like the solemn and beautiful effect which I had heard ascribed to this woodland worship. . . . But ere I had well enjoyed it, the scene changed, and sublimity gave place to horror and disgust.

. . . Above a hundred persons, nearly all females, came forward, uttering howlings and groans so terrible that I shall never cease to shudder when I recall them. They appeared to drag each other forward, and, on the word being given "Let us pray," they all fell on their knees; but this posture was soon changed for others that permitted greater scope for the convulsive movements of their limbs; and they were soon all lying on the ground in an indescribable confusion of heads and legs. They threw about their limbs with such incessant and violent motion, that I was every instant expecting some serious accident to occur.

. . . Hysterical sobbings, convulsive groans, shrieks and screams the most appalling, burst forth on all sides. I felt sick with horror. . . .

Many of these wretched creatures were beautiful young females. The preachers moved about among them, at once exciting and soothing their agonies. I heard the muttered "Sister! dear sister!" I saw the insidious lips approach the cheeks of the unhappy girls; I heard the murmured confessions of the poor victims, and I watched their tormentors, breathing into their ears consolations that tinged the pale cheek with red. Had I been a man, I am sure I should have been guilty of some rash act of interference; nor do I believe that such a scene could have been acted in the presence of Englishmen without instant punishment being inflicted; not to mention the salutary discipline of the treadmill, which, beyond all question, would, in England, have been applied to check so turbulent and so vicious a scene.

3. African American Abolitionist David Walker Castigates the United States for Its Slave System, 1829

[W]e, (coloured people of these United States of America) are the *most wretched, degraded* and *abject* set of beings that *ever lived* since the world began; and that the white Americans having reduced us to the wretched state of *slavery,* treat us in that condition *more cruel* (they being an enlighted and Christian people,) than any heathen nation did any people whom it had reduced to our condition. These affirmations are so well confirmed in the minds of all unprejudiced men, who have taken the trouble to read histories, that they need no elucidation from me. . . . [T]hose enemies who have for hundreds of years stolen our *rights,* and kept us ignorant of Him and His divine worship, he will remove. Millions of whom, are this day, so ignorant and avaricious, that they cannot conceive how God can have an attribute of justice, and show mercy to us because it pleased Him to make us black—which colour, Mr. Jefferson calls unfortunate!!!!!! As though we are not as thankful to our God, for having made us as it pleased himself, as they (the whites,) are for having made them white. They think because they hold us in their infernal chains of slavery, that we wish to be white, or of their color—but they are dreadfully deceived—we wish to be just as it pleased our Creator to have made us, and no avaricious and unmerciful wretches, have any business to make slaves of, or hold us in slavery. How would they like for us to make slaves of, and hold them in cruel slavery, and murder them as they do us?—But is Mr. Jefferson's assertions true? viz. "that it is unfortunate for us that our Creator has been pleased to make us *black.*" We will not take his say so, for the fact. The world will have an opportunity to see whether it is unfortunate for us, that our Creator *has made us* darker than the *whites.* . . .

We, and the world wish to see the charges of Mr. Jefferson refuted by the blacks *themselves,* according to their chance; for we must remember that what the whites have written respecting this subject, is other men's labours, and did not emanate from the blacks. I know well, that there are some talents and learning among the

---

David Walker, *Walker's Appeal* (1829).

coloured people of this country, which we have not a chance to develop, in consequence of oppression; but our oppression ought not to hinder us from acquiring all we can. For we will have a chance to develop them by and by. God will not suffer us, always to be oppressed. Our sufferings will come to an *end,* in spite of all the Americans this side of *eternity.* Then we will want all the learning and talents among ourselves, and perhaps more, to govern ourselves.—"Every dog must have its day," the American's is coming to an end. . . .

Are we MEN!!—I ask you, O my brethren! are we MEN? Did our Creator make us to be slaves to dust and ashes like ourselves? Are they not dying worms as well as we? Have they not to make their appearance before the tribunal of Heaven, to answer for the deeds done in the body, as well as we? Have we any other Master but Jesus Christ alone? Is he not their Master as well as ours?—What right then, have we to obey and call any other Master, but Himself? How we could be so *submissive* to a gang of men, whom we cannot tell whether they are *as good* as ourselves or not, I never could conceive. However, this is shut up with the Lord, and we cannot precisely tell—but I declare, we judge men by their works. . . .

. . . Remember Americans, that we must and shall be free and enlightened as you are, will you wait until we shall, under God, obtain our liberty by the crushing arm of power? Will it not be dreadful for you? I speak Americans for your good. We must and shall be free I say, in spite of you. You may do your best to keep us in wretchedness and misery, to enrich you and your children, but God will deliver us from under you. And wo, wo, will be to you if we have to obtain our freedom by fighting. Throw away your fears and prejudices then, and enlighten us and treat us like men, and we will like you more than we do now hate you, and tell us now no more about colonization, for America is as much our country, as it is yours.—

Treat us like men, and there is no danger but we will all live in peace and happiness together. For we are not like you, hard hearted, unmerciful, and unforgiving. . . .

If any are anxious to ascertain who I am, know the world, that I am one of the oppressed, degraded and wretched sons of Africa, rendered so by the avaricious and unmerciful, among the whites.—If any wish to plunge me into the wretched incapacity of a slave, or murder me for the truth, know ye, that I am in the hand of God, and at your disposal. I count my life not dear unto me, but I am ready to be offered at any moment. For what is the use of living, when in fact I am dead. But remember, Americans, that as miserable, wretched, degraded and abject as you have made us in preceding, and in this generation, to support you and your families, that some of you, (whites) on the continent of America, will yet curse the day that you ever were born. You want slaves, and want us for your slaves!!! My colour will yet, root some of you out of the very face of the earth!!!!!! . . .

See your Declaration Americans!!! Do you understand your own language? Hear your language, proclaimed to the world, July 4th, 1776—

> We hold these truths to be self evident—that ALL men are created EQUAL!! that they *are endowed by their creator with certain unalienable rights;* that among these are life, *liberty,* and the pursuit of happiness!!

Compare your own language above, extracted from your Declaration of Independence, with your cruelties and murders inflicted by your cruel and unmerciful fathers and yourselves on our fathers and on us—men who have never given your fathers or you the least provocation!!!!!!

Hear your language further! . . .

But when a long train of abuses and usurpation, pursuing invariably the same object, evinces a design to reduce them under absolute despotism, it is their *right,* it is their *duty,* to throw off such government, and to provide new guards for their future security.

Now, Americans! I ask you candidly, was your sufferings under Great Britain, one hundredth part as cruel and tyrannical as you have rendered ours under you?

4. William Lloyd Garrison Calls for Immediate Abolition, 1831

To the Public

During my recent tour for the purpose of exciting the minds of the people by a series of discourses on the subject of slavery, every place that I visited gave fresh evidence of the fact, that a greater revolution in public sentiment was to be effected in the free States—*and particularly in New-England*—than at the South. I found contempt more bitter, opposition more active, detraction more relentless, prejudice more stubborn, and apathy more frozen, than among slave-owners themselves. Of course, there were individual exceptions to the contrary. This state of things afflicted, but did not dishearten me. I determined, at every hazard, to lift up the standard of emancipation in the eyes of the nation, *within sight of Bunker Hill and in the birthplace of liberty.* That standard is now unfurled; and long may it float, unhurt by the spoliations of time or the missiles of a desperate foe—yea, till every chain be broken, and every bondman set free! Let Southern oppressors tremble—let their secret abettors tremble—let their Northern apologists tremble—let all the enemies of the persecuted blacks tremble. . . .

Assenting to the "self-evident truth" maintained in the American Declaration of Independence, "that all men are created equal, and endowed by their Creator with certain inalienable rights—among which are life, liberty and the pursuit of happiness," I shall strenuously contend for the immediate enfranchisement of our slave population. In Park-Street Church, on the Fourth of July, 1829, in an address on slavery, I unreflectingly assented to the popular but pernicious doctrine of *gradual* abolition. I seize this opportunity to make a full and unequivocal recantation, and thus publicly to ask pardon of my God, of my country, and of my brethren the poor slaves, for having uttered a sentiment so full of timidity, injustice, and absurdity. A similar recantation, from my pen, was published in the *Genius of Universal Emancipation* at Baltimore, in September, 1829. My conscience is now satisfied.

I am aware that many object to the severity of my language; but is there not cause for severity? I *will be* as harsh as truth, and as uncompromising as justice. On this subject, I do not wish to think, or speak, or write, with moderation. No! no! Tell a man whose house is on fire to give a moderate alarm; tell him to moderately rescue his wife from the hands of the ravisher; tell the mother to gradually extricate her babe from the fire into which it has fallen;—but urge me not to use moderation in a cause like the present. I am in earnest—I will not equivocate—I will not excuse—I will not retreat a single inch—AND I WILL BE HEARD. . . .

William Lloyd Garrison, Editorial, *The Liberator,* January 1, 1831.

An attempt has been made—it is still making—we regret to say, with considerable success—to inflame the minds of our working classes against the more opulent, and to persuade men that they are contemned and oppressed by a wealthy aristocracy. That public grievances exist, is unquestionably true; but they are not confined to any one class of society. Every profession is interested in their removal—the rich as well as the poor. . . .

Walker's Pamphlet

The Legislature of North Carolina has lately been sitting with closed doors, in consequence of a message from the Governor relative to the above pamphlet [see Document 3, David Walker's appeal]. The south may reasonably be alarmed at the circulation of Mr Walker's Appeal; for a better promoter of insurrection was never sent forth to an oppressed people. In a future number, we propose to examine it, as also various editorial comments thereon—it being one of the most remarkable productions of the age. We have already publicly deprecated its spirit.

5. Thomas Grimké, a Southerner, Advocates Temperance as a Form of Patriotism, 1833

The Temperance Reformation is peculiarly Christian, American. The great characteristics of Christianism, and of the political institutions of our country, are stamped upon its face. It appeals to the sense of duty and the spirit of usefulness. Its arguments, as in the inductive philosophy, are gathered from facts. Observation and experience are its tests; while health, order, industry and happiness, in a word, the good of the people, are the object of its labors, and the reward of its victory. . . .

. . . I speak of a patriotism, which is *the very sunlight of society,* cheerful, diffusive, invigorative: and of a patriot, who like the sunbeam, is benevolent and useful, tho' scarcely ever noticed. . . . I shall speak then, of the patriotism of the people in private life, not of the patriotism of their rulers in public. . . .

To provide for the *health* of the community, is one of the duties of patriotism. And is not the Temperance Reformation one of the most simple yet powerful agents in the establishment and preservation of health? . . .

In a word, the vice of intemperance is the prolific parent of disease in every age and condition of life, and in every state of society, whether civilized or barbarous. And is not the Temperance Reformation the cause of GENUINE PATRIOTISM; since its object is to deliver every community from so vast an amount of loathsome, excruciating and obstinate disease, and to transmit to children, and to children's children, a sound constitution?

The preservation of *property* and *life* is among the most important duties of a good government. Almost all the civil and political institutions of society embrace these, directly or indirectly, as primary objects. They are inseparable from the chief ends of society; because, without security to them, society cannot exist. We shall

Thomas S. Grimké, *Address on the Patriot Character of the Temperance Reformation* (Charleston: Observor Office Press, 1833), 5, 7–11.

hereafter speak of the great value of temperance in promoting the spirit of industry and frugality, in relation to the individual and his family: and we cannot doubt its vast importance, when we consider to what an extent we ourselves and our property are either in the power, or are actually entrusted to the care of others. . . .

How often life has been endangered or lost, or property either ruined or impaired in value, from the intemperance of others, needs neither argument to convince us, nor facts to illustrate and corroborate the position. The records of our criminal courts, are of themselves the highest evidence of the melancholy truth. . . .

It is equally the duty of patriotism to cultivate among the people the spirit of *industry* and *economy*. But what can be a more formidable enemy to them than the immoderate use of spirituous liquors? Experience has set beyond all controversy this truth, as a rule, little less than universal, that intemperance is the mother of irregular habits in business of every description. . . . How many of the young have traced the ruin of their prospects to the sin of intemperance! How many of the middle aged have beheld in this, the loss of property and credit! How many of the old have looked back from the pallet of straw and the hovel of wretchedness, to the comforts of competency or the enjoyments of wealth, and have found the cause of their misery in the inebriating cup! What multitudes have been crowded into our pauper establishments, and hospitals, and lunatic asylums, from their indulgence in this vice. . . . And is it not the office of enlightened patriotism, to relieve the individual and society from the countless variety of evils that flow from intemperance, thro' idleness and prodigality? . . . What, then, shall we say of the patriotism, which saves not merely one man, but thousands and tens of thousands, from the public receptacles of the sick, the maniac and the pauper? Which purifies the atmosphere of public and private business, and establishes on sure foundations, the habits of industry and economy? Shall we not say, that, such patriotism is full of benevolence and wisdom? *And what is the* TEMPERANCE *cause but such* PATRIOTISM?

6. Ralph Waldo Emerson Considers the United States as a Center of Reform, 1841

In the history of the world the doctrine of Reform had never such scope as the present hour. . . . All things . . . hear the trumpet, and must rush to judgment, Christianity, the laws, commerce, schools, the farm, the laboratory; and not a kingdom, town, statute, rite, calling, man, or woman, but is threatened by the new spirit. . . .

It cannot be wondered at that this general inquest into abuses should arise in the bosom of society, when one considers the practical impediments that stand in the way of virtuous young men. The young man, on entering life, finds the way to lucrative employments blocked with abuses. The ways of trade are grown selfish to the borders of theft, and supple to the borders (if not beyond the borders) of fraud. The employments of commerce are not intrinsically unfit for a man, or less genial to his faculties; but these are now in their general course so vitiated by derelictions and abuses at which all connive that it requires more vigor and resources than can be

Ralph Waldo Emerson, "Man the Reformer" (1841). This document can also be found in Erik Bruun and Jay Crosby, *Our Nation's Archive* (New York: Black Dog and Leventhal Publishers, 1999), 261–262.

expected of every young man to right himself in them; he is lost in them; he cannot move hand or foot in them. Has he genius and virtue? the less does he find them fit for him to grow in, and if he would thrive in them, he must sacrifice all the brilliant dreams of boyhood and youth as dreams; he must forget the prayers of his childhood and must take on him the harness of routine and obsequiousness. If not so minded, nothing is left him but to begin the world anew, as he does who puts the spade into the ground for food. We are all implicated of course in this charge; it is only necessary to ask a few questions as to the progress of the articles of commerce from the fields where they grew, to our houses, to become aware that we eat and drink and wear perjury and fraud in a hundred commodities. . . .

. . . We are to revise the whole of our social structure, the State, the school, religion, marriage, trade, science, and explore their foundations in our own nature; we are to see that the world not only fitted the former men, but fits us, and to clear ourselves of every usage which has not its roots in our own mind. What is a man born for but to be a Reformer, a Remaker of what man has made; a renouncer of lies; a restorer of truth and good, imitating that great Nature which embosoms us all, and which sleeps no moment on an old past, but every hour repairs herself, yielding us every morning a new day, and with every pulsation a new life? Let him renounce everything which is not true to him, and put all his practices back on their first thoughts, and do nothing for which he has not the whole world for his reason. . . .

. . . The State must consider the poor man, and all voices must speak for him. Every child that is born must have a just chance for his bread. Let the amelioration in our laws of property proceed from the concession of the rich, not from the grasping of the poor. Let us begin by habitual imparting. Let us understand that the equitable rule is that no one should take more than his share, let him be ever so rich. Let me feel that I am to be a lover. I am to see to it that the world is the better for me, and to find my reward in the act. Love would put a new face on this weary old world in which we dwell as pagans and enemies too long, and it would warm the heart to see how fast the vain diplomacy of statesmen, the impotence of armies, and navies, and lines of defence, would be superseded by this unarmed child. . . . This great, overgrown, dead Christendom of ours still keeps alive at least the name of a lover of mankind. But one day all men will be lovers; and every calamity will be dissolved in the universal Sunshine.

7. Elizabeth Peabody Explains the Benefits of Brook Farm, 1843

In order to live a religious and moral life worthy the name, they feel it is necessary to come out in some degree from the world, and to form themselves into a community of property, so far as to exclude competition and the ordinary rules of trade; while they reserve sufficient private property or the means of obtaining it, for all purposes of independence, and isolation at will. They have bought a farm, in order to make agriculture the basis of their life, it being the most direct and simple in relation to nature. . . .

Elizabeth Peabody, "Individual Accumulation Will Be Seen in Its Naked Selfishness" (1843). This document can also be found in Erik Bruun and Jay Crosby, *Our Nation's Archive* (New York: Black Dog and Leventhal Publishers, 1999), 264–266.

The plan of the Community, as an economy, is in brief this: for all who have property to take stock, and receive a fixed interest thereon: then to keep house or board in commons, as they shall severally desire, at the cost of provisions purchased at wholesale, or raised on the farm; and for all to labor in community, and be paid at a certain rate an hour, choosing their own number of hours, and their own kind of work. With the results of this labor and their interest, they are to pay their board, and also purchase whatever else they require at cost, at the warehouses of the Community, which are to be filled by the Community as such. To perfect this economy, in the course of time they must have all trades and all modes of business carried on among themselves, from the lowest mechanical trade, which contributes to the health and comfort of life, to the finest art, which adorns it with food and drapery for the mind.

All labor, whether bodily or intellectual, is to be paid at the same rate of wages; on the principle that as the labor becomes merely bodily, it is a greater sacrifice to the individual laborer to give his time to it; because time is desirable for the cultivation of the intellectual, in exact proportion to ignorance. Besides, intellectual labor involves in itself higher pleasures, and is more its own reward, than bodily labor.

After becoming members of this Community, none will be engaged merely in bodily labor. The hours of labor for the Association will be limited by a general law, and can be curtailed at the will of the individual still more; and means will be given to all for intellectual improvement and for social intercourse, calculated to refine and expand. The hours redeemed from labor by community, will not be re-applied to the acquisition of wealth, but to the production of intellectual goods. . . . As a Community, [this Community] will traffic with the world at large, in the products of agricultural labor; and it will sell education to as many young persons as can be domesticated in the families, and enter into the common life with their own children. In the end it hopes to be enabled to provide, not only all the necessaries, but all the elegances desirable for bodily and for spiritual health: books, apparatus, collections for science, works of art, means of beautiful amusement. These things are to be common to all; and thus that object, which alone gilds and refines the passion for individual accumulation, will no longer exist for desire, and whenever the sordid passion appears, it will be seen in its naked selfishness. In its ultimate success, the Community will realize all the ends which selfishness seeks, but involved in spiritual blessings, which only greatness of soul can aspire after.

. . . Everything can be said of it, in a degree, which Christ said of his kingdom, and therefore it is believed that in some measure it does embody his idea. For its gate of entrance is strait and narrow. It is literally a pearl hidden in a field. Those only who are willing to lose their life for its sake shall find it.

8. Dorothea Dix Depicts the Horrible Conditions Endured by the Mentally Ill, 1843

Gentlemen,—I respectfully ask to present this Memorial, believing that the cause, which actuates to and sanctions so unusual a movement, presents no equivocal claim to public consideration and sympathy. Surrendering to calm and deep convictions

Dorothea Dix, petition of the Massachusetts Legislature (1843). This document can also be found in Erik Bruun and Jay Crosby, *Our Nation's Archive* (New York: Black Dog and Leventhal Publishers, 1999), 266–268.

of duty my habitual views of what is womanly and becoming, I proceed briefly to explain what has conducted me before you unsolicited and unsustained, trusting, while I do so, that the memorialist will be speedily forgotten in the memorial. . . .

. . . I come to place before the Legislature of Massachusetts the condition of the miserable, the desolate, the outcast. I come as the advocate of helpless, forgotten, insane, and idiotic men and women; of beings sunk to a condition from which the most unconcerned would start with real horror; of beings wretched in our prisons, and more wretched in our almshouses. . . .

As I state cold, severe facts, I feel obliged to refer to persons, and definitely to indicate localities. But it is upon my subject, not upon localities or individuals, I desire to fix attention; and I would speak as kindly as possible of all wardens, keepers, and other responsible officers, believing that most of these have erred not through hardness of heart and wilful cruelty so much as want of skill and knowledge, and want of consideration. . . . Prisons are not constructed in view of being converted into county hospitals, and almshouses are not founded as receptacles for the insane. And yet, in the face of justice and common sense, wardens are by law compelled to receive, and the masters of almshouses not to refuse, insane and idiotic subjects in all stages of mental disease and privation.

It is the Commonwealth, not its integral parts, that is accountable for most of the abuses which have lately and do still exist. I repeat it, it is defective legislation which perpetuates and multiplies these abuses. . . .

. . . I have seen many who, part of the year, are chained or caged. The use of cages all but universal. . . . [C]hains are less common; negligences frequent, wilful abuse less frequent than sufferings proceeding from ignorance, or want of consideration. I encountered during the last three months many poor creatures wandering reckless and unprotected through the country. . . . I have heard that responsible persons, controlling the almshouses, have not thought themselves culpable in sending away from their shelter, to cast upon the chances of remote relief, insane men and women. These, left on the highways, unfriended and incompetent to control or direct their own movements, sometimes have found refuge in the hospital, and others have not been traced. But I cannot particularize. In traversing the State, I have found hundreds of insane persons in every variety of circumstance and condition, many whose situation could not and need not be improved; a less number, but that very large, whose lives are the saddest pictures of human suffering and degradation. . . .

DANVERS. November. Visited the almshouse. A large building, much out of repair. . . .

Long before reaching the house, wild shouts, snatches of rude songs, imprecations and obscene language, fell upon the ear, proceeding from the occupant of a low building, rather remote from the principal building to which my course was directed. Found the mistress, and was conducted to the place which was called "the home" of the forlorn maniac, a young woman, exhibiting a condition of neglect and misery blotting out the faintest idea of comfort, and outraging every sentiment of decency. She had been, I learnt, a respectable person, industrious and worthy. Disappointments and trials shook her mind, and, finally, laid prostrate reason and self-control. . . . She had passed from one degree of violence to another, in swift progress. There she stood, clinging to or beating upon the bars of her caged apartment, the contracted size of which afforded space only for increasing accumulations of filth, a loud spectacle. There she stood with naked arms and dishevelled hair, the unwashed frame invested with fragments of unclean garments, the air so extremely offensive, though ventilation was afforded on all sides save one, that it was not possible to remain beyond a few moments without retreating for recovery to the outward air. Irritation of body, produced by utter filth and exposure, incited her to the horrid process of tearing off her skin by inches. Her face, neck, and person were thus disfigured to hideousness. She held up a fragment just rent off. To my exclamation of horror, the mistress replied: "Oh, we can't help it. Half the skin is off sometimes. We can do nothing with her; and it makes no difference what she eats, for she consumes her own filth as readily as the food which is brought her." . . .

Men of Massachusetts, I beg, I implore, I demand pity and protection for these of my suffering, outraged sex. Fathers, husbands, brothers, I would supplicate you for this boon; but what do I say. . . . Here you will put away the cold, calculating spirit of selfishness and self-seeking; lay off the armor of local strife and political opposition; here and now, for once, forgetful of the earthly and perishable, come up to these halls and consecrate them with one heart and one mind to works of righteousness and just judgment. Become the benefactors of your race, the just guardians of the solemn rights you hold in trust. . . .

Gentlemen, I commit to you this sacred cause. Your action upon this subject will affect the present and future condition of hundreds and of thousands.

9. Horace Mann Explains the Significance of the Public School, 1849

Under the Providence of God, our means of education are the grand machinery by which the "raw material" of human nature can be worked up into inventors and discoverers, into skilled artisans and scientific farmers, into scholars and jurists, into the founders of benevolent institutions, and the great expounders of ethical and theological science. By means of early education, those embryos of talent may be quickened, which will solve the difficult problems of political and economical law; and by them, too, the genius may be kindled which will blaze forth in the Poets of Humanity. Our schools, far more than they have done, may supply the Presidents and Professors of Colleges, and Superintendents of Public Instruction, all over the land; and send, not only into our sister states, but across the Atlantic, the men of practical science, to superintend the construction of the great works of art. Here, too, may those judicial powers be developed and invigorated, which will make legal principles so clear and convincing as to prevent appeals to force; and, should the clouds of war ever lower over our country, some hero may be found,—the nursling of our schools, and ready to become the leader of our armies,—that best of all heroes, who will secure the glories of a peace, unstained by the magnificent murders of the battle-field. . . .

Without undervaluing any other human agency, it may be safely affirmed that the Common School, improved and energized, as it can easily be, may become the most effective and benignant of all the forces of civilization. Two reasons sustain this position. In the first place, there is a universality in its operation, which can be affirmed of no other institution whatever. If administered in the spirit of justice and

Horace Mann, Massachusetts Board of Education, *Twelfth Annual Report of . . . the Secretary of the Board* (Boston, 1849), 32, 37.

conciliation, all the rising generation may be brought within the circle of its reformatory and elevating influences. And, in the second place, the materials upon which it operates are so pliant and ductile as to be susceptible of assuming a greater variety of forms than any other earthly work of the Creator. The inflexibility and ruggedness of the oak, when compared with the lithe sapling or the tender germ, are but feeble emblems to typify the docility of childhood, when contrasted with the obduracy and intractableness of man. It is these inherent advantages of the Common School, which, in our own State, have produced results so striking, from a system so imperfect, and an administration so feeble. In teaching the blind, and the deaf and dumb, in kindling the latent spark of intelligence that lurks in an idiot's mind, and in the more holy work of reforming abandoned and outcast children, education has proved what it can do, by glorious experiments. These wonders, it has done in its infancy, and with the lights of a limited experience; but, when its faculties shall be fully developed, when it shall be trained to wield its mighty energies for the protection of society against the giant vices which now invade and torment it;—against intemperance, avarice, war, slavery, bigotry, the woes of want and the wickedness of waste,—then, there will not be a height to which these enemies of the race can escape, which it will not scale, nor a Titan among them all, whom it will not slay.

📑 E S S A Y S

Religious revivalism was a vital factor underlying the reform movements of the antebellum era. Religious change, moreover, was significant in and of itself. It altered the way in which people interacted with one another and with their government and society. Historians, however, disagree over what motivated Americans to embrace religious belief and what religious change meant for the larger American society. The following two essays illustrate that disagreement. Paul E. Johnson, a historian at the University of South Carolina, focuses on the religious revivals that swept through Rochester, New York, in the 1830s. He shows how the revivals stressed not only that people were moral free agents, but that they had a responsibility to reach out to others. The result was attempts to foster morality within society that resulted in movements of social control aimed at the working classes. In contrast, Nathan O. Hatch, professor of history at the University of Notre Dame, concentrates on the democratization that resulted from religious revivalism. Professor Hatch argues that religious change was a powerful force that not only fostered the democratization of American society, but also fostered populist currents within American Protestantism that created challenges for the denominations themselves.

Religious Reform as a Form of Social Control

PAUL E. JOHNSON

Charles Finney's revival enlarged every Protestant church, broke down sectarian boundaries, and mobilized a religious community that had at its disposal enormous economic power. Motives which determined the use of that power derived from the revival, and they were frankly millenarian.

Excerpt from chapter 5, "Pentecost," and chapter 6, "Christian Soldiers," from Paul E. Johnson, *A Shopkeeper's Millennium: Society and Revivals in Rochester, New York, 1815–1837*, pp. 109–128. Copyright 1979 by Paul E. Johnson. Reprinted by permission of Hill and Wang, a division of Farrar, Straus and Giroux, LLC.

As Rochester Protestants looked beyond their community in 1831, they saw something awesome. For news of Finney's revival had helped touch off a wave of religious enthusiasm throughout much of the northern United States. The revival moved west into Ohio and Michigan, east into Utica, Albany, and the market towns of inland New England. Even Philadelphia and New York City felt its power. Vermont's congregational churches grew by 29 percent in 1831. During the same twelve months the churches of Connecticut swelled by over a third. After scanning reports from western New York, the Presbyterian General Assembly announced in wonder that "the work has been so general and thorough, that the whole customs of society have changed." Never before had so many Americans experienced religion in so short a time. Lyman Beecher, who watched the excitement from Boston, declared that the revival of 1831 was the greatest revival of religion that the world had ever seen.

Rochester Protestants saw conversions multiply and heard of powerful revivals throughout Yankee Christendom. They saw divisions among themselves melt away, and they began to sense that the pre-millennial unanimity was at hand—and that they and people like them were bringing it about. They had converted their families and neighbors through prayer. Through ceaseless effort they could use the same power to convert the world. It was Finney himself who told them that "if they were united all over the world the Millennium might be brought about in three months." He did not mean that Christ was coming to Rochester. The immediate and gory millennium predicted in Revelation had no place in evangelical thinking. Utopia would be realized on earth, and it would be made by God with the active and united collaboration of His people. It was not the physical reign of Christ that Finney predicted but the reign of Christianity. The millennium would be accomplished when sober, godly men—men whose every step was guided by a living faith in Jesus—exercised power in this world. Clearly, the revival of 1831 was a turning point in the long struggle to establish that state of affairs. American Protestants knew that, and John Humphrey Noyes later recalled that "in 1831, the whole orthodox church was in a state of ebullition in regard to the Millennium." Rochester evangelicals stood at the center of that excitement.

After 1831 the goal of revivals was the christianization of the world. With that at stake, membership in a Protestant church entailed new kinds of personal commitment. Newcomers to Brick Presbyterian Church in the 1820s had agreed to obey the laws of God and of the church, to treat fellow members as brothers, and "to live as an humble Christian." Each new convert was told that "renouncing all ungodliness and every worldly lust, you give up your all, soul and body, to be the Lord's, promising to walk before him in holiness and love all the days of your life." Not easy requirements, certainly, but in essence personal and passive. With the Finney revival, the in-grown piety of the 1820s turned outward and aggressive. In 1831 Brick Church rewrote its covenant, and every member signed this evangelical manifesto:

> We [note that the singular "you" has disappeared] do now, in the presence of the Eternal God, and these witnesses, covenant to be the Lord's. *We promise to renounce all the ways of sin, and to make it the business of our life to do good and promote the declarative glory of our heavenly Father.* We promise steadily and devoutly to attend upon the institutions and ordinances of Christ as administered in this church, and to submit ourselves to its direction and discipline, until our present relation shall be regularly dissolved. We promise to be kind and affectionate to all the members of this church, to be tender of their

character, and to endeavor to the utmost of our ability, to promote their growth in grace. *We promise to make it the great business of our life to glorify God and build up the Redeemer's Kingdom in this fallen world,* and constantly to endeavor to present our bodies a living sacrifice, holy and acceptable to Him.

In that final passage, the congregation affirmed that its actions—both individually and in concert—were finally meaningful only in relation to the Coming Kingdom. Everything they did tended either to bring it closer or push it farther away.

Guiding the new activism was a revolution in ideas about human ability. The Reverend William James of Brick Church had insisted in 1828 that most men were innately sinful. Christians could not change them, but only govern their excesses through *"a system of moral regulations, founded upon the natural relations between moral beings, and having for its immediate end the happiness of the community."* We have seen, however, that certain of those "natural relations" were in disarray, and that the businessmen and master workmen who were expected to govern within them were the most active participants in the revival. Evangelical theology absolved them of responsibility by teaching that virtue and order were products not of external authority but of choices made by morally responsible individuals. Nowhere, perhaps, was this put more simply than in the Sunday schools. In the 1820s children had been taught to read and then forced to memorize huge parts of the Bible. (Thirteen-year-old Jane Wilson won a prize in 1823 when she committed a numbing 1,650 verses to memory.) After 1831 Sunday-school scholars stopped memorizing the Bible. The object now was to have them study a few verses a week and to come to an understanding of them, and thus to prepare themselves for conversion and for "an active and useful Christian life." Unregenerate persons were no longer to be disciplined by immutable authority and through fixed social relationships. They were free and redeemable moral agents, accountable for their actions, capable of accepting or rejecting God's promise. It was the duty of Christian gentlemen not to govern them and accept responsibility for their actions but to educate them and change their hearts.

William Wisner, pastor at Brick Church during these years, catalogued developments that were "indispensably necessary to the bringing of millennial glory." First, of course, was more revivals. Second, and tied directly to the first, was the return of God's people to the uncompromising personal standards of the primitive Christians and Protestant martyrs. For the public and private behavior of converts advertised what God had done for them. If a Christian drank or broke the Sabbath or cheated his customers or engaged in frivolous conversation, he weakened not only his own reputation but the awesome cause he represented. While Christian women were admonished to discourage flattery and idle talk and to bring every conversation onto the great subject, troubled businessmen were actually seen returning money to families they had cheated. Isaac Lyon, half-owner of the Rochester Woolen Mills, was seen riding a canal boat on Sunday in the fall of 1833. Immediately he was before the trustees of his church. Lyon was pardoned after writing a confession into the minutes and reading it to the full congregation. He confessed that he had broken the eighth commandment. But more serious, he admitted, was that his sin was witnessed by others who knew his standing in the church and in the community, and for whom the behavior of Isaac Lyon reflected directly on the evangelical cause. He had shamed Christ in public and given His enemies cause to celebrate.

Finney's revival had, however, centered among persons whose honesty and personal morals were beyond question before they converted. Personal piety and circumspect public behavior were at bottom means toward the furtherance of revivals. At the moment of rebirth, the question came to each of them: "Lord, what wilt thou have me do?" The answer was obvious: unite with other Christians and convert the world. The world, however, contained bad habits, people, and institutions that inhibited revivals and whose removal must precede the millennium. Among church members who had lived in Rochester in the late 1820s, the right course of action was clear. With one hand they evangelized among their own unchurched poor. With the other they waged an absolutist and savage war on strong drink.

On New Year's Eve of the revival winter, Finney's co-worker Theodore Weld delivered a four-hour temperance lecture at First Presbyterian Church. Weld began by describing a huge open pit at his right hand, and thousands of the victims of drink at his left. First he isolated the most hopeless—the runaway fathers, paupers, criminals, and maniacs—and marched them into the grave. He moved higher and higher into society, until only a few well-dressed tipplers remained outside the grave. Not even these were spared. While the audience rose to its feet the most temperate drinkers, along with their wives and helpless children, were swallowed up and lost. Weld turned to the crowd and demanded that they not only abstain from drinking and encourage the reform of others but that they unite to stamp it out. They must not drink or sell liquor, rent to a grogshop, sell grain to distillers, or patronize merchants who continued to trade in ardent spirits. They must, in short, utterly disengage from the traffic in liquor and use whatever power they had to make others do the same. A packed house stood silent.

The Reverend Penney rose from his seat beside the Methodist and Baptist preachers and demanded that vendors in the audience stop selling liquor immediately. Eight or ten did so on the spot, and the wholesale grocers retired to hold a meeting of their own. The next day Elijah and Albert Smith, Baptists who owned the largest grocery and provisions warehouse in the city, rolled their stock of whiskey out onto the sidewalk. While cheering Christians and awestruck sinners looked on, they smashed the barrels and let thousands of gallons of liquid poison run out onto Exchange Street.

Within a week, Everard Peck wrote home that "the principal merchants who have traded largely in ardent spirits are about abandoning this unholy traffic & we almost hope to see this deadly poison expelled from our village." The performance of the Smith brothers was being repeated throughout Rochester. Sometimes wealthy converts walked into groceries, bought up all the liquor, and threw it away. A few grocers with a fine taste for symbolism poured their whiskey into the Canal. Even grocers who stayed outside the churches found that whiskey on their shelves was bad for business. The firm of Rossiter and Knox announced that it was discontinuing the sale of whiskey, but "not thinking it a duty to 'feed the Erie Canal' with their property, offer to sell at cost their whole stock of liquors. . . ." Those who resisted were refused advertising space in some newspapers, and in denying the power of a united evangelical community they toyed with economic ruin. S. P. Needham held out for three years, but in 1834 he announced that he planned to liquidate his stock of groceries, provisions, and liquors and leave Rochester. "Church Dominancy," he explained, "has such influence over this community that no honest man can do his own business in his own way. . . ."

Almost immediately, Weld's absolutist temperance pledge became a condition of conversion—the most visible symbol of individual rebirth. The teetotal pledge was only the most forceful indication of church members' willingness to use whatever power they had to coerce others into being good, or at least to deny them the means of being bad. While whiskey ran into the gutters, two other symbols of the riotous twenties disappeared. John and Joseph Christopher, both of them new Episcopalians, bought the theater next door to their hotel, closed it, and had it reopened as a livery stable. The Presbyterian Sprague brothers bought the circus building and turned it into a soap factory. Increasingly, the wicked had no place to go.

These were open and forceful attacks on the leisure activities of the new working class, something very much like class violence. But Christians waged war on sin, not workingmen. Alcohol, the circus, the theater, and other workingmen's entertainments were evil because they wasted men's time and clouded their minds and thus blocked the millennium. Evangelicals fought these evils in order to prepare society for new revivals. It was missionary work, little more. And in the winter following Finney's departure, it began to bear fruit.

With one arm evangelicals attacked the bad habits and tawdry amusements of unregenerate workingmen. With the other they offered redemption. They invited humbler men into their churches. They poured money into poor congregations, financed the establishment of new churches in working-class neighborhoods, and used their wealth and social position to help poor but deserving brethren. By the middle 1830s hundreds of workingmen were in the churches and participating in middle-class crusades.

While Finney was still in town, rich evangelicals met to organize a church for canal workers, transients, and Rochester's unchurched poor. The committee was headed by Jonothan Child, the most active Episcopal layman in Rochester, and it included rich men from every church. The new congregation was to be a "free" church which abolished pew rents in an attempt to erase class distinctions among the membership. Organized in 1832 as Free Presbyterian Church, this mission was an enormous success. The founding congregation numbered only 45 persons, most of them wealthy members from older Presbyterian churches. At the end of one year, the membership had swelled to 237. Inspired by this success, members of old churches founded Second Baptist and Bethel Presbyterian as free congregations in the mid-1830s. In these churches some of the wealthiest men in Rochester brought their families to worship in fellowship with newly pious day laborers, boatmen, and journeyman craftsmen.

At the same time Finney's converts assisted the older working-class churches in every way they could. First Methodist—made up overwhelmingly of workingmen and their families—was the largest congregation in Rochester by 1834, and much of that growth was made possible by the benevolence of wealthy evangelicals. Twice in the 1830s that unlucky congregation saw its church burn to the ground. After the fire of 1832, the Methodists obtained a loan from the bank at Hartford, recommended and countersigned by rich Presbyterians. When the church caught fire in 1834, Methodists held an open meeting in the courthouse square, attended by ministers and laymen of every denomination. They passed the hat and received enough money to build another new church. The little knot of Freewill Baptists who began meeting at the courthouse in 1836 also enjoyed revival-induced benevolence.

While dividing Sundays between his congregation and the inmates of the county jail, the minister remarked, "We are treated with much kindness by all classes, and especially by all evangelical Christians." His remarks took on weight two months later, when a member of Third Presbyterian Church gave him a thousand dollars to build a meetinghouse.

Even the smallest and most despised congregations could look to Finney's converts for help. The African Methodist Church had been built in 1827 with donations from white church members, but in the 1830s that church was financially troubled. The leading trustee and the man most frequently chosen as spokesman for the Rochester black community was Austin Steward, a Main Street grocer. Steward spent his profits on the church and on the unsuccessful Wilberforce Colony in Canada. By the middle 1830s both he and his congregation were bankrupt. But Steward had been in Rochester since 1817, and he had old friends among white evangelicals. He had also been among the first of the smaller grocers to stop selling liquor. Wealthy Presbyterians organized and provided him with interest-free loans, free legal advice, and promises of exclusive patronage. And when the temperance society organized a huge non-alcoholic Fourth of July picnic in 1837, it was Austin Steward who received the catering contract. Within a year, both Steward and the African Methodists were back on their feet.

Simultaneously, evangelicals established institutions to encourage workingmen to reform themselves and to sustain those who reformed. In 1831 rich church members founded the Rochester Savings Bank to encourage working-class thrift and personal discipline, and served without pay on its board of directors. At the same time the congregations at First Presbyterian, St. Luke's Episcopal, and Free Presbyterian Churches organized schools to teach reading, writing, and proper thoughts to poor children, and to keep them away from "the highways and resorts of dissipation." The parents of these children had to contend with the wealthy women who organized the Female Charitable Society, and who went door-to-door in poor neighborhoods determining which families needed help and which deserved it. Work was scarce during the winter months, and unpredictable even during busy times. With the exceptions of the dreaded almshouse and, of course, the churches themselves, this society of Christian women was the only relief organization in Rochester.

Evangelicals encouraged working-class churches and churchmembers not out of pity or as an attempt to bribe workingmen but to build up the Kingdom of Christ in Rochester. They were enormously successful. In 1832 trustees at Second Presbyterian invited the evangelist Jedediah Burchard into their church. Burchard was a crude, half-educated man and a powerful preacher, and he drew a new kind of audience. Word moved quickly, and the revival spread again to every church. Baptist, Methodist, Presbyterian, and Episcopal ministers preached from the same pulpit, and the place of meeting shifted indiscriminately between churches. In the following year and again in 1836, Rochester ministers repeated the performance without outside help. These were powerful revivals. In many congregations—First Methodist, Second Presbyterian, and a growing number of new churches—the revivals of the middle 1830s dwarfed Finney's earlier triumph. "It begins," stated one of Finney's busy converts, "to look like the millennium. . . ."

Enthusiasm generated in 1831 was moving into new places. For while businessmen and master craftsmen and their families continued to join churches in the 1830s, they did so in the company of large numbers of wage earners. In 1830–31 journeyman craftsmen had accounted for only 22 percent of male converts—half their proportion of the male work force. Burchard wakened the workingmen, and in subsequent years middle-class missionaries converted hundreds of wage-earning Rochesterians. A full 42 percent of the men who joined churches between 1832 and 1837 were journeyman craftsmen. The workingman's revival was in fact much larger than can be demonstrated systematically, for available evidence seriously underestimates the number of working-class converts. The records of some poor churches—First Methodist and Free Presbyterian in particular—are incomplete. And city directories excluded the most transient and thus generally the youngest and poorest men. These sources identify one in seven journeymen in 1837 as Protestant church members. Were records complete, it is likely that the figure would rise to one in four.

The revivals of 1832–36 were results of middle-class missions, and the churches that benefited from them were without exception middle-class organizations. We are thus left with the question why hundreds of wage earners allied themselves with bourgeois evangelism in the 1830s. Missionaries thought they knew the answer: revivals, they claimed, separated workingmen who were capable of discipline and self-restraint from those who were not.

They were, of course, mistaken. Many wage earners rejected strong drink and riotous amusements as vehemently as they rejected the middle class and its religion. The best bootmakers in Rochester were tramping journeymen from New York City. These independent craftsmen read widely and debated skillfully and defiantly— often on religious subjects—and they avoided excessive drinking and discouraged it in others. Among workingmen who stayed in Rochester, there is ample evidence that individual and group discipline could sustain resistance as well as pious docility. In 1833 journeyman carpenters struck for a ten-hour day, and they protected their strike by telling newcomers to come to them rather than to masters in search of jobs. They met with some success, for at one point all but two contractors agreed to their terms. The carpenters fought the same battle annually until 1836, and there were similar organizations among stonemasons, boat builders, coopers, and calkers. These were orderly, sustained, and well-planned contests with employers, and it is doubtful that they could have been conducted by a working class made up of drunkards and degenerates.

Thus the division between "rough" and "respectable" workingmen did not simply separate those who went to church from those who did not. Of nine leaders of journeymen's societies whose names are known, none belonged to a Protestant church. Indeed many workmen, drawing on traditions of republican skepticism that stretched back to the Revolution, openly opposed the churches. Celebrations of Thomas Paine's birthday were working-class festivals in the middle 1830s, and Rochester was among the few cities outside the old seaports that supported free-thought newspapers. Along with anti-evangelical diatribes and formal disproofs of the existence of God, the free-thought editors printed essays in support of strikes and suggestions that workingmen needed education and self-respect, not middle-class temperance sermons. Paine himself, we may recall, had combined irreligion with calls for education, and with active opposition to violent sports and heavy drinking. There was more than one road to self-improvement in the 1830s.

Why, then, did so many wage earners take the road pointed out by their masters? Some—perhaps most—were already tied to the business community. Many were sons and younger brothers of Finney's middle-class converts, and no doubt many others were trusty employees who followed their masters into church. Still others may have been drawn to evangelists who proclaimed a spiritual rather than a worldly aristocracy among men, and who directed some of their assaults upon the rich and powerful. But with all of this said, the most powerful source of the workingman's revival was the simple, coercive fact that wage earners worked for men who insisted on seeing them in church. In 1836 a free-thought editor announced that clerks were being forced to attend revival meetings. He quoted one of them: "I don't give a d——n. I get five dollars more in a month than before I got religion." We shall see that he was not alone.

"We hope," wrote a Baptist editor in 1834, "the time will come when men will have done employing intemperate mechanics, and when ardent spirits will cease to distract, disturb, and ruin." His hopes were based on the new willingness of Christian employers to demand not only hard work but personal piety of their employees. In the spring of 1831, William Howell completed work on one of the largest and most elegant packet boats ever put on the canal. The job employed thirty boat builders, and Howell announced with satisfaction that it was completed "without the stimulus of ardent spirits or liquid poison." Lewis Selye, a young convert who began manufacturing fire engines in 1833, advertised work for machinists, but noted that "none need apply except those of moral habits and the best of workmen." Applicants at the Rochester Woolen Mills (which hired one of the largest work forces in town) were told that they "must be of moral and temperate habits. . . ." The iron founders Thomas Kempshall and John Bush owned another establishment that hired large numbers of men. They commented on their position for a machinist and pattern-maker that "a man of steady habits will find it a pleasant situation," and added that "none but temperate men need apply."

In the 1830s Christian employers announced that only sober, God-fearing applicants need knock at their doors. The effect of that attempt to impose religious standards on the labor market can be measured partially and indirectly through analysis of population mobility. For if a workman established a fixed home in Rochester, his rootedness may have meant many things. But first of all it meant that he had found steady work. An analysis of residential stability among churchgoing and non-churchgoing wage earners between 1834 and 1838 suggests strongly that working-men who did not join churches had trouble finding jobs. Churchgoing clerks were twice as stable as non-churchgoers in the same occupation. Among journeymen and laborers, churchgoers were three-and-one-half times as likely to stay in town as were non-church members. These relationships persist, it should be noted, when they are controlled for age, property holdings, and length of prior residence. Workmen who went to church became settled residents of Rochester *because* they went to church. Their non-churchgoing workmates stayed a few months or years and then moved on to other, perhaps friendlier, towns.

Church membership played an equally powerful role in selecting those wage earners who rose to the ownership of their own stores and workshops. Opportunities for journeymen shrank during these years. In 1827, 16 percent of all men in skilled blue-collar occupations owned workshops. Within the next ten years that figure dropped to 11 percent. Simple arithmetic told journeymen that few of them could hope to become master craftsmen. Yet over half the churchgoing journeymen completed that step. Among their non-churchgoing workmates, the comparable figure was less than one in five—and this among the tiny minority who stayed in Rochester. There was a similar pattern among laborers. By 1837 one man in three possessed little or no skill and depended for his livelihood upon casual, scarce, and low-paying work. For those who wished to move up, the most sensible step was to acquire skills and thus move into better-paying and more secure employment. Two-thirds of the laborers who joined churches made that step between 1827 and 1837. Non-church members in the same occupation moved out of Rochester three times as often, and those who stayed rose at about half the rate attained by church members.

The pattern was identical among clerks. In the 1830s a position as clerk was no longer a stepping-stone to the ownership of a substantial business. More and more had to settle for a small store or for permanent wage-earning status. Few completed the step from clerk to merchant. Most of those who did belonged to Protestant churches. Of the clerks who joined churches during the revivals and who remained in Rochester in 1837, 72 percent became merchants, professionals, or shopkeepers. Most non-churchgoing clerks left Rochester. Of those who stayed, half skidded into blue-collar jobs.

While it varied between occupations, the relation between occupational advancement and membership in a church was strong throughout the wage-earning population. A full 63 percent of churchgoing wage earners who stayed in Rochester between 1827 and 1837 improved their occupational standing. Only 2 percent (one man) declined. Most of the non-church members who worked beside them in 1827 did not stay long enough to have their occupations measured twice. The few who did advanced about half as often as did church members, and they were six times as likely to decline.

The most stable and successful workmen in Rochester were those who went to church. That much can be demonstrated in a systematic way. But the reasons why church members prospered while non-church members moved away or stagnated are not so easily counted. The most obvious explanation is that membership in a church induced habits and attitudes that fit comfortably with a market economy and a disciplined work environment. It is likely that churchgoers were objectively better workers than others, that they worked hard and saved their money, and that they came to the shop sober and on time. No doubt those qualities were crucial to their success. But they were useless until other men decided to reward them. In Rochester no man made his way alone. Whether his career prospered or went sour depended on decisions made by others: decisions to hire him, to promote him, to enter into partnership with him, and to recommend him to neighbors and friends. Social mobility was a social product, and patterns of mobility cannot be explained apart from the means by which individual successes and failures were brought about. Here it will be helpful to trace the entry of individual converts into the business community in the 1830s. We shall find—and it should come as no surprise—that their mobility was directly sponsored by the churchgoing elite.

The carpenter Lauren Parsons took the simplest route. He joined his employer's church in 1831, and went into partnership with him the following year. There were others who did the same. Of the thirty-one wage-earning converts who went into business in the 1830s, sixteen did so in partnership with others. Only four joined with relatives, suggesting that, like Lauren Parsons, they were indeed recruited from outside the old business-owning families. Ten of the sixteen, however, entered business in partnership with other church members—eight of them with members of their own congregations. Here was the most direct kind of sponsorship.

But the career of Lewis Selye suggests that aid to aspiring converts went far beyond formal partnerships. In 1827 Selye was a propertyless journeyman blacksmith. Ten years later he was sole proprietor of a machine shop and fire-engine factory, and one of the richest men in Rochester. An editor described Selye's factory as "a compliment to the ingenuity and enterprise of our townsman . . . who has established this and other branches of business through the force of his own skill and perseverence, unaided by any stock companies or capitalists." True, Selye never formed a partnership. But he had help nonetheless. Decisions that paved the way for Lewis Selye's success were made by the town fathers themselves. He built his first fire engine in 1833 at the request of the village trustees—four months after he joined Brick Presbyterian Church. The same city officials, all of them rich church members, lent their prestigious endorsements to his advertisements.

Despite this assistance, the road was not always smooth for Lewis Selye. In 1837 a sharp decline in orders forced him to close the shop. He sold the business to Martin Briggs, a member of his church and an in-law of the powerful Scrantom family. But the transaction was never put on paper. Lewis Selye appeared as an engine builder in the directory compiled months later, and he continued throughout the 1840s as a successful manufacturer and Whig politician, and as a trustee of Brick Church. It appears that Martin Briggs had not bought him out in 1837. He had bailed him out.

Alvah Strong was another young man who reaped material as well as spiritual rewards from his association with the churches. Strong's father was a doctor and boardinghouse keeper whose clientele consisted first of laborers who dug the canal, then of Rochester workingmen. His brother owned a small candy and fruit store on Exchange Street. The Strongs were not a rich family, but their early and continuous residence in Rochester and their prominence within the Baptist Church (the father was one of the oldest members, the brother was superintendent of the Sunday school) gained them entry into the town's church-bounded community of respectability. Alvah Strong wanted to be a newspaperman. He served an apprenticeship on one Rochester weekly and worked as foreman on another in the 1820s. Then he traveled through the state working as a journeyman. In 1831 Erastus Shepard, a former employer, moved to Rochester and bought the *Anti-Masonic Enquirer.* He offered Alvah Strong a partnership, largely because Strong's "knowledge of the place, and familiarity with the people would strengthen the concern." Strong and Shepard both converted during the Finney revival. Neither had much money, and for the first few years they operated the paper on credit. "Our good name and our industry," Strong explained, "were our capital, so that we commanded credit when it was needed." Most of the money came from wealthy evangelicals who, in 1834, financed the *Enquirer*'s transition into a Whig daily.

Alvah Strong and Lewis Selye earned the friendship of rich evangelicals not only by joining their churches but by living up to Christian standards and enforcing them on others. Selye became a leading layman at Brick Church, and he demanded total abstinence of the men who worked for him. And there were no more consistent temperance editorializers than Alvah Strong and Erastus Shepard. Here, obviously, were men upon whom Christian money was well spent.

There were, of course, converts who began new lives and then slid backward. These found that the churches could dispense punishments as well as rewards. John Denio was a young printer who moved to Rochester in 1833, joined Brick Presbyterian Church, and bought the *Rochester Gem* from his fellow communicant Edwin Scrantom. During the following summer, he was seen in a hotel bar joking and drinking wine with a group of traveling salesmen. When called before the trustees of his church (yes, Lewis Selye was among them), Denio angrily denied that he had done anything wrong. He was excommunicated on the spot. Within a year, the *Gem* had been taken over by Shepard and Strong, and its ruined editor had disappeared from Rochester. Ela Burnap, an old resident of the town, experienced a similar fall from grace. In 1830 he was a master silversmith and the owner of a house on North Fitzhugh, the most uniformly wealthy block in the city. But two years later, another church member saw him drunk. He was suspended from his church. Unlike John Denio, Burnap stayed in Rochester. In 1837 the tax assessor found him working as a watchmaker and living in a rented house on the outskirts of town.

Charles Finney's revival mobilized economic power in Rochester and injected religious motives into its use. The careers of Lewis Selye, Alvah Strong, John Denio, and Ela Burnap reflect that fact. In the 1830s men seeking jobs and credit knocked at the doors of businessmen pushed by their changed souls and by enormous social pressure to prepare Rochester for the millennium. By dispensing and withholding patronage, Christian entrepreneurs regulated the membership of their own class, and to a large extent of the community as a whole. Conversion and abstinence from strong drink became crucial economic credentials. For membership in a church and participation in its crusades put a man into the community in which economic decisions were made, and at a time when religious criteria dominated those choices. By the middle 1830s there were two working classes in Rochester: a church-going minority tied closely to the sources of steady work and advancement, and a floating majority that faced insecure employment and stifled opportunities.

In the late 1820s Rochester had divided bitterly along ideological and class lines. Charles Finney's revival melted the first of those divisions, and subsequent enthusiasms transformed the second. Now society split starkly between those who loved Jesus and those who did not. In 1833 a Presbyterian woman walked through a poor neighborhood with her maid, an Irish girl who had quit the Catholic Church and joined with the Presbyterians. Apparently they were insulted in the street. The woman went home and wrote, "The work of the Lord among Christians deepens in some & others grow bolder in opposition. There will soon be two parties. . . ."

Religious Revivalism as a Form of Democratization

NATHAN O. HATCH

. . . [T]he theme of democratization is central to understanding the development of American Christianity, and . . . the years of the early republic are the most crucial in revealing that process. The wave of popular religious movements that broke

Nathan O. Hatch, *The Democratization of American Christianity* (New Haven, Conn.: Yale University Press, 1989), 3–11, 13–16. Copyright © 1989. Reprinted by permission of Yale University Press.

upon the United States in the half century after independence did more to Christianize American society than anything before or since. Nothing makes that point more clearly than the growth of Methodist and Baptist movements among white and black Americans. Starting from scratch just prior to the Revolution, Methodism in America grew at a rate that terrified other more established denominations. By 1820 Methodist membership numbered a quarter million; by 1830 it was twice that number. Baptist membership multiplied tenfold in the three decades after the Revolution; the number of churches increased from five hundred to over twenty-five hundred. The black church in America was born amidst the crusading vigor of these movements and quickly assumed its own distinct character and broad appeal. By the middle of the nineteenth century, Methodist and Baptist churches had splintered into a score of separate denominations, white and black. In total these movements eventually constituted two-thirds of the Protestant ministers and church members in the United States.

Between the American Revolution and 1845, the population of the United States grew at a staggering rate: two and a half million became twenty million in seventy years. . . .

Amidst this population boom, American Christianity became a mass enterprise. The eighteen hundred Christian ministers serving in 1775 swelled to nearly forty thousand by 1845. The number of preachers per capita more than tripled; the colonial legacy of one minister per fifteen hundred inhabitants became one per five hundred. This greater preaching density was remarkable given the spiraling population and the restless movement of peoples to occupy land beyond the reach of any church organization. The sheer number of new preachers in the young republic was not a predictable outgrowth of religious conditions in the British colonies. Rather, their sudden growth indicated a profound religious upsurge and resulted in a vastly altered religious landscape. Twice the number of denominations competed for adherents, and insurgent groups enjoyed the upper hand. For example, an upstart church such as the Freewill Baptists had almost as many preachers in the early republic as did the Episcopalians. Antimission Baptist preachers far outnumbered both Roman Catholic priests and Lutheran pastors. One new denominational cluster, the Christians and the Disciples of Christ, had an estimated four thousand preachers, equalling the number of clergy serving Presbyterian denominations. The Congregationalists, which had twice the clergy of any other American church in 1775, could not muster one-tenth the preaching force of the Methodists in 1845. . . .

Abstractions and generalities about the Second Great Awakening as a conservative force have obscured the egalitarianism powerfully at work in the new nation. As common people became significant actors on the religious scene, there was increasing confusion and angry debate over the purpose and function of the church. A style of religious leadership that the public deemed "untutored" and "irregular" as late as the First Great Awakening became overwhelmingly successful, even normative, in the first decades of the republic. Ministers from different classes vied with each other to serve as divine spokesmen. Democratic or populist leaders associated virtue with ordinary people and exalted the vernacular in word, print, and song.

The canon of American religious history grows out of traditions that are intellectually respectable and institutionally cohesive. Yet American Protestantism has been skewed away from central ecclesiastical institutions and high culture; it has been pushed and pulled into its present shape by a democratic or populist orientation. At the very time that British clergy were confounded by their own gentility in trying to influence working-class culture, America exalted religious leaders short on social graces, family connections, and literary education. These religious activists pitched their messages to the unschooled and unsophisticated. Their movements offered the humble a marvelous sense of individual potential and of collective aspiration.

Religious populism has been a residual agent of change in America over the last two centuries, an inhibitor of genteel tradition and a recurring source of new religious movements. Deep and powerful undercurrents of democratic Christianity distinguish the United States from other modern industrial democracies. These currents insure that churches in this land do not withhold faith from the rank and file. Instead, religious leaders have pursued people wherever they could be found; embraced them without regard to social standing; and challenged them to think, to interpret Scripture, and to organize the church for themselves. Religious populism, reflecting the passions of ordinary people and the charisma of democratic movement-builders, remains among the oldest and deepest impulses in American life.

The American Revolution is the most crucial event in American history. The generation overshadowed by it and its counterpart in France stands at the fault line that separates an older world, premised on standards of deference, patronage, and ordered succession, from a newer one that continues to shape our values. The American Revolution and the beliefs flowing from it created a cultural ferment over the meaning of freedom. Turmoil swirled around the crucial issues of authority, organization, and leadership.

Above all, the Revolution dramatically expanded the circle of people who considered themselves capable of thinking for themselves about issues of freedom, equality, sovereignty, and representation. Respect for authority, tradition, station, and education eroded. Ordinary people moved toward these new horizons aided by a powerful new vocabulary, a rhetoric of liberty that would not have occurred to them were it not for the Revolution. In time, the issue of the well-being of ordinary people became central to the definition of being American, public opinion came to assume normative significance, and leaders could not survive who would not, to use Patrick Henry's phrase, "bow with utmost deference to the majesty of the people." The correct solution to any important problem, political, legal, or religious, would have to appear to be the people's choice. "In the early nineteenth century," Sean Wilentz has written, "to be an American citizen was by definition to be a republican, the inheritor of a revolutionary legacy in a world ruled by aristocrats and kings."

This [essay] argues that the transitional period between 1780 and 1830 left as indelible an imprint upon the structures of American Christianity as it did upon those of American political life. Only land, Robert Wiebe has noted, could compete with Christianity as the pulse of a new democratic society. The age of the democratic revolutions unfolded with awesome moment for people of every social rank. Not since the English Civil War had such swift and unpredictable currents threatened the traditions of Western society. It was not merely the winning of battles and the writing of constitutions that excited apocalyptic visions in the minds of ordinary people but the realization that the very structures of society were undergoing a democratic winnowing. Political convulsions seemed cataclysmic; the cement of an ordered society seemed to be dissolving. People confronted new kinds of issues: common folk not respecting their betters, organized factions speaking and writing against civil authority, the uncoupling of church and state, and the abandonment of settled communities in droves by people seeking a stake in the back country. These events seemed so far outside the range of ordinary experience that people rushed to biblical prophecy for help in understanding the troubled times that were upon them.

Amidst such acute uncertainty, many humble Christians in America began to redeem a dual legacy. They yoked strenuous demands for revivals, in the name of George Whitefield, with calls for the expansion of popular sovereignty, in the name of the Revolution. Linking these equally potent traditions sent American Christianity cascading in many creative directions in the early republic. Church authorities had few resources to restrain this surge of movements fueled by the passions of ordinary people. Nothing illustrates this better than the way in which American Methodism veered sharply away from the course of British Methodism during these years. The heavy, centralizing hand of Jabez Bunting kept British Methodism firmly grounded in traditional notions of authority and leadership. It was unthinkable to British church leaders that a radical and eccentric revivalist like the American itinerant Lorenzo Dow should be allowed to influence their congregations, and after 1800 the British leadership successfully barred Dow from their meetings. This sort of control was impossible in America. Despite the misgivings of American bishops and elders, Dow took the camp-meeting circuit by storm. His popular support prevented them from mounting a direct challenge to his authority.

A diverse array of evangelical firebrands went about the task of movement-building in the generation after the Revolution. Intent on bringing evangelical conversion to the mass of ordinary Americans, they could rarely divorce that message from contagious new democratic vocabularies and impulses that swept through American popular cultures. Class structure was viewed as society's fundamental problem. There was widespread disdain for the supposed lessons of history and tradition, and a call for reform using the rhetoric of the Revolution. The press swiftly became a sword of democracy, fueling ardent faith in the future of the American republic.

At the same time, Americans who espoused evangelical and egalitarian convictions, in whatever combination, were free to experiment with new forms of organization and belief. Within a few years of Jefferson's election in 1800, it became anachronistic to speak of dissent in America—as if there were still a commonly recognized center against which new or emerging groups defined themselves. There was little to restrain a variety of new groups from vying to establish their identity as a counterestablishment. The Christian movement, the Methodists, and the Mormons all commonly referred to all other Protestant denominations as "sectarians."

The fundamental history of this period may be, as Roland Berthoff suggests, a story of things left out. Churches and religious movements after 1800 operated in a climate of withering ecclesiastical establishments. The federal government, a "midget institution in a giant land," had almost no internal functions. And a rampant migration of people continued to snap old networks of personal authority. American churches did not face the kind of external social and political pressures that in Great Britain often forced Christianity and liberty to march in opposite directions. Such isolation made it possible for religious outsiders to see their own destiny as part and parcel of the meaning of America itself. If the earth did belong to the living, as President Jefferson claimed, why should the successful newcomer defer to the claims of education, status, and longevity? . . .

. . . Francis Asbury claimed it was his duty to condescend to people of low estate, and Peter Cartwright, dispensing with the trappings of respectability, recast the gospel in a familiar idiom. Most important, they welcomed hundreds of common people into the ministry, creating a cadre of preachers who felt and articulated the interests of ordinary people. In America, established religious institutions linked to the upper classes remained too weak to make a whole society accept their language and analysis. The field remained open for the repeated onslaughts of religious populists.

A Passion for Equality

America's nonrestrictive environment permitted an unexpected and often explosive conjunction of evangelical fervor and popular sovereignty. It was this engine that accelerated the process of Christianization within American popular culture, allowing indigenous expressions of faith to take hold among ordinary people, white and black. This expansion of evangelical Christianity did not proceed primarily from the nimble response of religious elites meeting the challenge before them. Rather, Christianity was effectively reshaped by common people who molded it in their own image and who threw themselves into expanding its influence. Increasingly assertive common people wanted their leaders unpretentious, their doctrines self-evident and down-to-earth, their music lively and singable, and their churches in local hands. It was this upsurge of democratic hope that characterized so many religious cultures in the early republic and brought Baptists, Methodists, Disciples of Christ, and a host of other insurgent groups to the fore. The rise of evangelical Christianity in the early republic is, in some measure, a story of the success of common people in shaping the culture after their own priorities rather than the priorities outlined by gentlemen such as the framers of the Constitution.

It is easy to miss the democratic character of the early republic's insurgent religious movements. The Methodists, after all, retained power in a structured hierarchy under the control of bishops. The Mormons reverted to rule by a single religious prophet and revelator. And groups such as the Disciples of Christ, despite professed democratic structures, were eventually controlled by such powerful individuals as Alexander Campbell, who had little patience with dissent. As ecclesiastical structures, these movements often turned out to be less democratic than the congregational structure of the New England Standing Order. The rise of popular sovereignty, as Edmund S. Morgan suggests, often has involved insurgent leaders glorifying the many as a way to legitimate their own authority.

The democratization of Christianity, then, has less to do with the specifics of polity and governance and more with the incarnation of the church into popular culture. In at least three respects the popular religious movements of the early republic articulated a profoundly democratic spirit. First, they denied the age-old distinction that set the clergy apart as a separate order of men, and they refused to defer to learned theologians and traditional orthodoxies. All were democratic or populist in the way they instinctively associated virtue with ordinary people rather than with elites, exalted the vernacular in word and song as the hallowed channel for communicating with and about God, and freely turned over the reigns of power. These groups also shared with the Jeffersonian Republicans an overt rejection of the past as a repository of wisdom. By redefining leadership itself, these movements reconstructed the foundations of religion in keeping with the values and priorities of ordinary people.

Second, these movements empowered ordinary people by taking their deepest spiritual impulses at face value rather than subjecting them to the scrutiny of ortho-dox doctrine and the frowns of respectable clergymen. In the last two decades of the century, preachers from a wide range of new religious movements openly fanned the flames of religious ecstasy. Rejecting the Yankee Calvinism of his youth in 1775, Henry Alline found that his soul was transported with divine love, "ravished with a divine ecstacy beyond any doubts or fears, or thoughts of being then de-ceived." What had been defined as "enthusiasm" was increasingly advocated from the pulpit as an essential part of Christianity. Such a shift in emphasis, accompa-nied by rousing gospel singing rather than formal church music reflected the com-mon people's success in defining the nature of faith for themselves. In addition, an unprecedented wave of religious leaders in the last quarter of the eighteenth century expressed their openness to a variety of signs and wonders, in short, an admission of increased supernatural involvement in everyday life. Scores of preachers' jour-nals, from Methodists and Baptists, from north and south, from white and black, indicated a ready acceptance to consider dreams and visions as inspired by God, normal manifestations of divine guidance and instruction. "I know the word of God is our infallible guide, and by it we are to try all our dreams and feelings," conceded the Methodist stalwart Freeborn Garrettson. But he added, "I also know, that both sleeping and waking, things of a divine nature have been revealed to me." Volatile aspects of popular religion, long held in check by the church, were recog-nized and encouraged from the pulpit. It is no wonder that a dismayed writer in the *Connecticut Evangelical Magazine* countered in 1805: "No person is warranted from the word of God to publish to the world the discoveries of heaven or hell which he supposes he has had in a dream, or trance, or vision."

The early republic was also a democratic movement in a third sense. Religious outsiders, flushed with confidence about their prospects, had little sense of their limitations. They dreamed that a new age of religious and social harmony would naturally spring up out of their efforts to overthrow coercive and authoritarian structures. This upsurge of democratic hope, this passion for equality, led to a welter of diverse and competing forms, many of them structured in highly undemocratic ways. The Methodists under Francis Asbury, for instance, used authoritarian means to build a church that would not be a respecter of persons. This church faced the curious paradox of gaining phenomenal influence among laypersons with whom it would not share ecclesiastical authority. Similarly, the Mormons used a virtual re-ligious dictatorship as the means to return power to illiterate men. Yet despite these authoritarian structures, the fundamental impetus of these movements was to make Christianity a liberating force; people were given the right to think and act for themselves rather than depending upon the mediations of an educated elite. The most fascinating religious story of the early republic is the signal achievements of these and other populist religious leaders—outsiders who used democratic persuasions to reconstruct the foundations of religious authority. . . .

. . . . The most unusual feature of Christianity in this era is its remarkable set of popular leaders. Not since the crusading vigor of the early Puritans or of first-generation Methodists had an English-speaking culture produced a generation of so many rootless, visionary young preachers. Alienated from conventional religious forms, these bold intruders pursued their divergent courses with remarkably similar dispositions. Their faces set like flint, they proclaimed the gospel with an amazing energy, self-sacrifice, and missionary zeal. Henry Alline, for instance, a farmer and tanner from Rhode Island, unleashed his fiery evangelism upon the whole of Nova Scotia on the eve of the American Revolution. He died in 1784 at the age of thirty-five after less than a decade of relentless labor and driving asceticism. Recalling his experience in the Kentucky Revival at the turn of the century, Richard McNemar, a Methodist-turned-Presbyterian-turned-Christian-turned-Shaker, captured his generation's fervor:

> As full of zeal and pure desire
> As e're a coal was full of fire
> I flash'd & blazed by day and night
> a burning & a shining light.

Leaders without formal training (Barton Stone, the Christian; William Miller, the Adventist; Francis Asbury, the Methodist; John Leland, the Baptist; Richard Allen, the African Methodist Episcopal; and Joseph Smith, the Latter-Day Saint) went outside normal denominational frameworks to develop large followings by the democratic art of persuasion. These are inherently interesting personalities, un-branded individualists, who chose to storm heaven by the back door. Widely diverse in religious convictions, they were alike in their ability to portray, in compelling terms, the deepest hopes and aspirations of popular constituencies. It was said that Joseph Smith had "his own original eloquence, peculiar to himself, not polished, not studied, not smoothed and softened by education and refined by art." A New England clergyman, who resented uneducated and unrefined greenhorns presuming to speak in the Lord's name, put it this way: "They measure the progress of religion by the numbers who flock to their standards, not by the prevalence of faith and piety, justice and charity and the public virtues in society in general." This new style of gospel minister, remarkably attuned to popular sentiment, amazed Tocqueville. "Where I expect to find a priest," he said, "I find a politician."

These individuals were reacting to deep cultural shifts transforming the relationship between leaders and people; focusing on the issue of leadership allows a clear view of this process. Most important, it shows that the fundamental religious debates in the early republic were not merely a clash of intellectual and theological differences but also a passionate social struggle with power and authority. Deep-seated class antagonism separated clergy from clergy. The learned and orthodox disdained early Methodism's new revival measures, notions of free will, and perfectionism. But they despaired that the wrong sort of people had joined Methodism—people who rejected social authority's claim to religious power. While the eighteenth century had seen a steady growth of authority based on popular appeal, particularly in various forms of religious dissent, the Revolution quickened the pace. Those who defended clerical authority as the right of a gentry minority were pitted against rough-hewn leaders who denied the right of any one class of people to speak for another. The early republic witnessed a popular displacement of power from the uncommon man, the man of ideas in American politics and religion. It is the intent of this study to tell at least part of this complicated story: how ordinary folk came to distrust leaders of genius and talent and to defend the right of common people to shape their own faith and submit to leaders of their own choosing.

This story also provides new insight into how America became a liberal, competitive, and market-driven society. In an age when most ordinary Americans expected almost nothing from government institutions and almost everything from religious ones, popular religious ideologies were perhaps the most important bellwethers of shifting worldviews. The passion for equality during these years equaled the passionate rejection of the past. Rather than looking backward and clinging to an older moral economy, insurgent religious leaders espoused convictions that were essentially modern and individualistic. These convictions defied elite privilege and vested interests and anticipated a millennial dawn of equality and justice. Yet, to achieve these visions of the common good, they favored means inseparable from the individual's pursuit of spiritual and temporal well-being. They assumed that the leveling of aristocracy, root and branch, would naturally draw people together in harmony and equality. In this way, religious movements eager to preserve the supernatural in everyday life had the ironic effect of accelerating the break-up of traditional society and the advent of a social order of competition, self-expression, and free enterprise. In this moment of democratic aspiration, religious leaders could not foresee that their assault upon mediating structures could produce a society in which grasping entrepreneurs could erect new forms of tyranny in religious, political, and economic institutions. . . .

While all of Christian history is, in some sense, a dialectic between atomization and authority, the early republic was the most centrifugal epoch in American church history. It was a time when the momentum of events pushed toward the periphery and subverted centralized authority and professional expertise. Yet the white-hot intensity of early Disciples, Methodists, Baptists, and Mormons grew cool over time. Cultural alienation gave way to a pilgrimage toward respectability. By 1840 populist dissent had diminished in American Christianity, but the democratic revolution had left a permanent imprint on the denominational landscape. . . .

Religious populism has remained a creative, if unsettling, force at the fringes of major Protestant denominations. More than lawyers or physicians, American clergy have remained subject to democratic forces. In the first third of the nineteenth century, a stiff democratic challenge shattered the professional monopoly of educated elite over law, medicine, and the church. State laws permitted almost anyone to practice law, and various brands of medical practice were allowed to compete for the public's attention. Yet in the twentieth century, doctors and lawyers have reasserted their professional prerogatives. The American Medical Association and the American Bar Association now serve as powerful monopolies. A free-market economy continues in the field of religion, however, and credentialing, licensing, or statutory control is absent. This hands-off position is sacrosanct because of fixed notions about the separation of church and state and because of the long-standing voluntary principle within churches.

The rise of democratic Christianity in the early United States is riddled with irony, unrealistic hope, and unfulfilled expectations. A central theme . . . is the unintended results of people's actions. Attempting to erase the difference between leaders and followers. Americans opened the door to religious demagogues. Despite popular acclaim, these leaders could exercise tyranny unimagined by elites in the more controlled environment of the colonial era. Likewise, a deep sensitivity to audience resulted in values of the audience shaping the message's contours. The quest for unity that drove people to discard formal theology for the Scriptures drove them further asunder. Yet Americans continue to maintain their right to shape their own faith and to submit to leaders they have chosen. Over the last two centuries, an egalitarian culture has given rise to a diverse array of powerful religious leaders, whose humble origins and common touch seem strangely at odds with the authoritarian mantle that people allow them to assume. The tapestry of American Protestantism is richly colored with interwoven strands of populist strength and authoritarian weakness.

◀ *F U R T H E R   R E A D I N G*

Robert H. Abzug, *Cosmos Crumbling: American Reform and the Religious Imagination* (1994).

Sydney E. Ahstrom, *A Religious History of the American People* (1972).

Barbara Leslie Epstein, *The Politics of Domesticity: Women, Evangelism, and Temperance in Nineteenth-Century America* (1981).

Paul Goodman, *Of One Blood: Abolitionism and the Origins of Racial Equality* (1998).

Steven Mintz, *Moralists and Modernizers: America's Pre–Civil War Reformers* (1995).

David J. Rothman, *Discovery of the Asylum: Social Order and Disorder in the New Republic* (1971).

Ronald G. Walters, *American Reformers, 1815–1860* (1978).

C H A P T E R
10

Women, Men, and the
Family at Midcentury

*In the summer of 1848, a group of some three hundred men and women met at
the Woman's Rights Convention in Seneca Falls, New York. Led by Elizabeth Cady
Stanton, Lucretia Mott, and Lucy Stone, the convention protested the situation in
which women in antebellum America found themselves. The Declaration of Sentiments, which came out of the convention, indicted American society for the injustices
suffered by women. Modeled on the Declaration of Independence, it argued that "all
men and women are created equal." These reformers obviously were aware of the
legal, political, and economic handicaps faced by women in nineteenth-century
America. Unlike white men, women could not vote. Women were effectively barred
from professional schools, and few were able to attend colleges of any sort. They therefore typically gained status by entering into marriage. Yet when a woman married,
she lost legal control over her property and wages, and she could not sign contracts.
If she was dissatisfied with married life, divorce was illegal in all but a few states.
Spousal abuse was still lawful in some states provided that the husband beat his wife
with "a reasonable instrument."*

*Despite these obstacles, however, the dizzying changes in antebellum society
profoundly influenced the roles of women and men, and the families in which
they lived. Increasing urbanization, for example, changed the patterns of work.
Whereas work and home had once been located in the same place, people increasingly left home to go to work. The home began to be seen as the woman's domain,
a refuge from the hurly-burly of the outside world, which was dominated by men.
As a result, an ideology of "domesticity" was forged that paired women with the
home and men with the world. Sentimental paeans were written celebrating the
refuge that was the home and woman's role as mother and wife. In addition to
their maternal and wifely roles, however, many women were active in reform
movements. And as women joined groups that sought to bring about social change,
they began to understand with greater clarity the inequities of their position in
society. Women's widespread activism in antislavery and abolitionist movements
ultimately led them to a nascent feminism that questioned their place in society
and fostered ambitions to improve it. This era of change, in short, altered the world*

of both women and men. The question that has plagued historians for some time is what was the direction of change.

One cannot speak, however, of a monolithic "woman's experience." Women lived not only as middle-class wives in northeastern cities, but also as slaves on plantations, in squalid urban immigrant neighborhoods, and on small farms in the western states. Whereas urban middle-class men left home to go to work, male farmers worked together with their families. Whereas some northern women perceived marriage to be a form of oppression, slaves were unable legally to marry. As we remain mindful of this diversity of experience, which is addressed in the following chapters on northern and southern society, we must also focus on the kaleidoscopic change experienced by all men and women in this era. And we should note that women who did not belong to the middle classes were also drawn into the antebellum women's movement. Female factory workers protested their condition, as did women who had lived in slavery. Among the most powerful texts surviving from the nineteenth century is Sojourner Truth's fusion of the wrongs endured by slaves and women. Born in slavery in 1827, Sojourner Truth recounted her field labors and asked rhetorically, "Ain't I a woman?"

QUESTIONS TO THINK ABOUT

Would you characterize the antebellum era as a time when women's place in society improved or deteriorated? Why do you think European visitors assessed the American family differently from the way Americans did? Given the many contexts in which women lived in this era, is it possible to speak of "a woman's experience" in antebellum America?

DOCUMENTS

The first two documents illustrate the comparisons between Europe and the United States made by Europeans visiting the United States. In Document 1, Alexis de Tocqueville in 1831 observes what he calls the "influence of democracy" on the family. Harriet Martineau, in Document 2, compares the patterns of marriage in the United States and England. Document 3, written by Catherine Beecher in 1841, maintains that the principles of democracy and Christianity have influenced the place of women in the United States. In Document 4, the significance of the mother in instructing her children is emphasized. The next two documents provide a very different perspective. In Document 5, Elizabeth Cady Stanton, in a speech delivered at the Seneca Falls Convention, attacks the notion that men are intellectually, morally, or physically superior to women. Document 6 is the Declaration of Rights and Sentiments that was adopted by the Seneca Falls Convention in 1848. Note how it is modeled on the Declaration of Independence and the demands that "one-half the people" be enfranchised. Document 7, which is a paean to woman's place in the home written in 1850, illustrates that not all women agreed with Stanton and the people at the convention. Sojourner Truth, in Document 8, provides a powerful expression of the relationships between women's rights and abolitionism. Document 9 is a marriage contract that shows that both women and men were aware that marriage created impediments for the rights of women.

1. Alexis de Tocqueville Considers the Influence of Democracy on the Family, 1831

I have just been considering how among democratic peoples, particularly America, equality modifies the relations between one citizen and another.

I want to carry the argument further and consider what happens within the family. I am not trying to discover new truths, but to show how known facts have a bearing on my subject.

Everyone has noticed that in our time a new relationship has evolved between the different members of a family, that the distance formerly separating father and son has diminished, and that paternal authority, if not abolished, has at least changed form.

Something analogous, but even more striking, occurs in the United States.

In America the family, if one takes the word in its Roman and aristocratic sense, no longer exists. One only finds scattered traces thereof in the first years following the birth of children. The father then does, without opposition, exercise the domestic dictatorship which his sons' weakness makes necessary and which is justified by both their weakness and his unquestionable superiority.

But as soon as the young American begins to approach man's estate, the reins of filial obedience are daily slackened. Master of his thoughts, he soon becomes responsible for his own behavior. In America there is in truth no adolescence. At the close of boyhood he is a man and begins to trace out his own path.

It would be wrong to suppose that this results from some sort of domestic struggle, in which, by some kind of moral violence, the son had won the freedom which his father refused. The same habits and principles which lead the former to grasp at independence dispose the latter to consider its enjoyment as an incontestable right.

So in the former one sees none of these hateful, disorderly passions which disturb men long after they have shaken off an established yoke. The latter feels none of those bitter, angry regrets which usually accompany fallen power. The father has long anticipated the moment when his authority must come to an end, and when that time does come near, he abdicates without fuss. The son has known in advance exactly when he will be his own master and wins his liberty without haste or effort as a possession which is his due and which no one seeks to snatch from him. . . .

When the state of society turns to democracy and men adopt the general principle that it is good and right to judge everything for oneself, taking former beliefs as providing information but not rules, paternal opinions come to have less power over the sons, just as his legal power is less too.

Perhaps the division of patrimonies which follows from democracy does more than all the rest to alter the relations between father and children.

When the father of a family has little property, his son and he live constantly in the same place and carry on the same work together. Habit and necessity bring them together and force them all the time to communicate with each other. There is bound,

---

Excerpt from Alexis de Tocqueville, *Democracy in America* (New York: Doubleday Anchor Books, 1969), 584–585, 587–589. Reprinted by permission of HarperCollins Publishers, Inc.

then, to be a sort of intimate familiarity between them which makes power less absolute and goes ill with respectful formalities.

Moreover, in democracies those who possess these small fortunes are the very class which gives ideas their force and sets the tone of mores. Both its will and its thoughts prevail everywhere, and even those who are most disposed to disobey its orders end by being carried along by its example. I have known fiery opponents of democracy who allowed their children to call them "thou."

So at the same time as aristocracy loses its power, all that was austere, conventional, and legal in parental power also disappears and a sort of equality reigns around the domestic hearth.

I am not certain, generally speaking, whether society loses by the change, but I am inclined to think that the individual gains. I think that as mores and laws become more democratic the relations between father and sons become more intimate and gentle; there is less of rule and authority, often more of confidence and affection, and it would seem that the natural bond grows tighter as the social link loosens. . . .

Democracy too draws brothers together, but in a different way.

Under democratic laws the children are perfectly equal, and consequently independent; nothing forcibly brings them together, but also nothing drives them apart. Having a common origin, brought up under the same roof, and treated with the same care, as no peculiar privilege distinguishes or divides them, the affectionate and frank intimacy of childhood easily takes root among them. . . .

This gentleness of democratic manners is such that even the partisans of aristocracy are attracted by it, and when they have tasted it for some time, they are not at all tempted to return to the cold and respectful formalities of the aristocratic family. They gladly keep the family habits of democracy provided they can reject its social state and laws. . . .

I think that I may be able to sum up in one phrase the whole sense of this chapter and of several others that preceded it. Democracy loosens social ties, but it tightens natural ones. At the same time as it separates citizens, it brings kindred closer together.

2. Harriet Martineau Remarks on Marriage and "True Love" in America, 1837

If there is any country on earth where the course of true love may be expected to run smooth, it is America. It is a country where all can marry early, where there need be no anxiety about a worldly provision, and where the troubles arising from conventional considerations of rank and connexion ought to be entirely absent. It is difficult for a stranger to imagine beforehand why all should not love and marry naturally and freely, to the prevention of vice out of the marriage state, and of the common causes of unhappiness within it. The anticipations of the stranger are not, however, fulfilled: and they never can be while the one sex overbears the other. Marriage is in America more nearly universal, more safe, more tranquil, more fortunate than in England: but

Harriet Martineau, *General Treatise on Money and Property Rights of Wives* (1837). Obtained from http://xroads.virginia.edu/~HYPER/DETOC/FEM/marriage.htm.

it is still subject to the troubles which arise from the inequality of the parties in mind and in occupation. It is more nearly universal, from the entire prosperity of the country: it is safer, from the greater freedom of divorce, and consequent discourage-ment of swindling, and other vicious marriages: it is more tranquil and fortunate from the marriage vows being made absolutely reciprocal; from the arrangements about property being generally far more favorable to the wife than in England; and from her not being made, as in England, to all intents and purposes the property of her husband. The outward requisites to happiness are nearly complete, and the insti-tution is purified from the grossest of the scandals which degrade it in the Old World: but it is still the imperfect institution which it must remain while women continue to be ill-educated, passive, and subservient: or well educated, vigorous, and free only upon sufferance.

3. Catherine Beecher Sees Linkages Between Democracy and Women's Rights, 1841

There are some reasons, why American women should feel an interest in the support of the democratic institutions of their Country, which it is important that they should consider. The great maxim, which is the basis of all our civil and political institu-tions, is, that "all men are created equal," and that they are equally entitled to "life, liberty, and the pursuit of happiness."

But it can readily be seen, that this is only another mode of expressing the funda-mental principle which the Great Ruler of the Universe has established, as the law of His eternal government. "Thou shalt love thy neighbor as thyself;" and "Whatsoever ye would that men should do to you, do ye even so to them," are the Scripture forms, by which the Supreme Lawgiver requires that each individual of our race shall regard the happiness of others, as of the same value as his own; and which forbid any in-stitution, in private or civil life, which secures advantages to one class, by sacrificing the interests of another.

The principles of democracy, then, are identical with the principles of Christianity. . . .

The tendencies of democratic institutions, in reference to the rights and inter-ests of the female sex, have been fully developed in the United States; and it is in this aspect, that the subject is one of peculiar interest to American women. In this Country, it is established, both by opinion and by practice, that woman has an equal interest in all social and civil concerns; and that no domestic, civil, or political, institution, is right, which sacrifices her interest to promote that of the other sex. But in order to secure her the more firmly in all these privileges, it is decided, that, in the domestic relation, she take a subordinate station, and that, in civil and political concerns, her interests be intrusted to the other sex, without her taking any part in voting or in making and administering laws. . . .

[As Tocqueville writes] ". . . They [the Americans] admit, that, as Nature has appointed such wide differences between the physical and moral constitutions of

---

Catherine Beecher, *A Treatise on Domestic Economy, for the Use of Young Ladies at Home and at School,* rev. ed. (New York: Harper & Bros., 1846). This document can also be found in David Hollinger and Charles Capper, eds., *The American Intellectual Tradition* (New York: Oxford University Press, 1997), pp. 255–269.

man and woman, her manifest design was, to give a distinct employment to their various faculties; and they hold, that improvement does not consist in making beings so dissimilar do pretty nearly the same things, but in getting each of them to fulfil their respective tasks, in the best possible manner. The Americans have applied to the sexes the great principle of political economy, which governs the manufactories of our age, by carefully dividing the duties of man from those of woman, in order that the great work of society may be the better carried on. . . .

"Thus the Americans do not think that man and woman have either the duty, or the right, to perform the same offices, but they show an equal regard for both their respective parts; and, though their lot is different, they consider both of them, as beings of equal value. They do not give to the courage of woman the same form, or the same direction, as to that of man; but they never doubt her courage: and if they hold that man and his partner ought not always to exercise their intellect and understanding in the same manner, they at least believe the understanding of the one to be as sound as that of the other, and her intellect to be as clear. Thus, then, while they have allowed the social inferiority of woman to subsist, they have done all they could to raise her, morally and intellectually, to the level of man; and, in this respect, they appear to me to have excellently understood the true principle of democratic improvement.

"As for myself, I do not hesitate to avow, that, although the women of the United States are confined within the narrow circle of domestic life, and their situation is, in some respects, one of extreme dependence, I have nowhere seen women occupying a loftier position; and if I were asked, now I am drawing to the close of this work, in which I have spoken of so many important things done by the Americans, to what the singular prosperity and growing strength of that people ought mainly to be attributed, I should reply,—*to the superiority of their women.*" . . .

In civil and political affairs, American women take no interest or concern, except so far as they sympathize with their family and personal friends; but in all cases, in which they do feel a concern, their opinions and feelings have a consideration equal, or even superior, to that of the other sex.

In matters pertaining to the education of their children, in the selection and support of a clergyman, in all benevolent enterprises, and in all questions relating to morals or manners, they have a superior influence. In such concerns, it would be impossible to carry a point, contrary to their judgment and feelings; while an enterprise, sustained by them, will seldom fail of success. . . .

The success of democratic institutions, as is conceded by all, depends upon the intellectual and moral character of the mass of the people. If they are intelligent and virtuous, democracy is a blessing; but if they are ignorant and wicked, it is only a curse, and as much more dreadful than any other form of civil government, as a thousand tyrants are more to be dreaded than one. It is equally conceded, that the formation of the moral and intellectual character of the young is committed mainly to the female hand. The mother forms the character of the future man; the sister bends the fibres that are hereafter to be the forest tree; the wife sways the heart, whose energies may turn for good or for evil the destinies of a nation. Let the women of a country be made virtuous and intelligent, and the men will certainly be the same. The proper education of a man decides the welfare of an individual; but educate a woman, and the interests of a whole family are secured. . . .

. . . American women have a loftier position, and a more elevated object of enterprise, than the females of any other nation, [but] so it will appear, that they have greater trials and difficulties to overcome, than any other women are called to encounter. . . .

. . . [T]he flow of wealth, among all classes, is constantly increasing the number of those who live in a style demanding much hired service, while the number of those, who are compelled to go to service, is constantly diminishing. Our manufactories, also, are making increased demands for female labor, and offering larger compensation. In consequence of these things, there is such a disproportion between those who wish to hire, and those who are willing to go to domestic service, that, in the non-slaveholding States, were it not for the supply of poverty-stricken foreigners, there would not be a domestic for each family who demands one. . . . For, just in proportion as wealth rolls in upon us, the number of those, who will give up their own independent homes to serve strangers, will be diminished.

The difficulties and sufferings, which have accrued to American women, from this cause, are almost incalculable. There is nothing, which so much demands system and regularity, as the affairs of a housekeeper, made up, as they are, of ten thousand desultory and minute items; and yet, this perpetually fluctuating state of society seems forever to bar any such system and regularity. The anxieties, vexations, perplexities, and even hard labor, which come upon American women, from this state of domestic service, are endless. . . .

But the second, and still greater difficulty, peculiar to American women, is, a delicacy of constitution, which renders them early victims to disease and decay. . . .

There are many causes operating, which serve to perpetuate and increase this evil. It is a well-known fact, that mental excitement tends to weaken the physical system, unless it is counterbalanced by a corresponding increase of exercise and fresh air. Now, the people of this Country are under the influence of high commercial, political, and religious stimulus, altogether greater than was ever known by any other nation; and in all this, women are made the sympathizing companions of the other sex. At the same time, young girls, in pursuing an education, have ten times greater an amount of intellectual taxation demanded, than was ever before exacted. . . .

No women on earth have a higher sense of their moral and religious responsibilities, or better understand, not only what is demanded of them, as housekeepers, but all the claims that rest upon them as wives, mothers, and members of a social community. . . .

In the first place, the physical and domestic education of daughters should occupy the principal attention of mothers, in childhood; and the stimulation of the intellect should be very much reduced. . . .

In addition to this, much less time should be given to school, and much more to domestic employments, especially in the wealthier classes. A little girl may begin, at five or six years of age, to assist her mother; and, if properly trained, by the time she is ten, she can render essential aid. From this time, until she is fourteen or fifteen, it should be the principal object of her education to secure a strong and healthy constitution, and a thorough practical knowledge of all kinds of domestic employments. . . .

It is in this point of view, that the dearth of good domestics in this Country may, in its results, prove a substantial blessing. If all housekeepers, who have the means, could secure good servants, there would be little hope that so important a revolution, in the domestic customs of the wealthy classes, could be effected. . . .

A second method of promoting the same object, is, to raise the science and practice of Domestic Economy to its appropriate place, as a regular study in female seminaries. . . .

The third method of securing a remedy for the evils pointed out, is, the endowment of female institutions, under the care of suitable trustees, who shall secure a proper course of education. . . .

Parents are little aware of the immense waste incurred by the present mode of conducting female education. In the wealthy classes, young girls are sent to school, as a matter of course, year after year, confined, for six hours a day, to the schoolhouse, and required to add some time out of school to learning their lessons. Thus, during the most critical period of life, they are for a long time immured in a room, filled with an atmosphere vitiated by many breaths, and are constantly kept under some sort of responsibility in regard to mental effort. Their studies are pursued at random, often changed with changing schools, while book after book (heavily taxing the parent's purse) is conned awhile, and then supplanted by others. . . .

The writer believes that the actual amount of education, permanently secured by most young ladies from the age of ten to fourteen, could all be acquired in one year, at the Institution described, by a young lady at the age of fifteen or sixteen. . . .

. . . [E]very American woman, who values the institutions of her Country, and wishes to lend her influence in extending and perpetuating such blessings, may feel that she is doing this, whenever, by her example and influence, she destroys the aristocratic association, which would render domestic labor degrading.

4. A Guidebook Instructs Women on the Role of Mother, 1845

It takes a long time for the world to grow wise. Men have been busying themselves these six thousand years nearly to improve society. They have framed systems of philosophy and government, and conferred on their own sex all the advantages which power, wealth and knowledge could bestow. They have founded colleges and institutions of learning without number, and provided themselves teachers of every art and science; and, after all, the mass of mankind are very ignorant and very wicked. Wherefore is this? Because the *mother,* whom God constituted the first teacher of every human being, has been degraded by men from her high office; or, what is the same thing, been denied those privileges of education which only can enable her to discharge her duty to her children with discretion and effect. God created the woman as a *help-meet* for man in every situation; and while he, in his pride, rejects her assistance in his intellectual and moral career, he never will succeed to improve his nature and reach that perfection in knowledge, virtue and happiness, which his faculties are constituted to attain.

If half the effort and expense had been directed to enlighten and improve the minds of females which have been lavished on the other sex, we should now have a very different state of society. Wherever a woman is found excelling in judgment and knowledge, either by natural genius or from better opportunities, do we not see her

"Maternal Instruction," *Godey's Lady's Book,* 1845.

children also excel? Search the records of history, and see if it can be found that a great and wise man ever descended from a weak and foolish mother. So sure and apparent is this maternal influence, that it has passed into an axiom of philosophy, it is acknowledged by the greatest and wisest of men; and yet, strange to say, the inference which ought to follow, namely, that in attempting to improve society, the first, most careful and continued efforts should be to raise the standard of female education, and qualify woman to become the educator of her children, has never yet been acted upon by any legislators, or acknowledged and tested by any philanthropists.

What is true of the maternal influence respecting sons is, perhaps, more important in the training of daughters. The fashionable schools are a poor substitute for such example and instruction as a thoroughly educated and right principled mother would bestow on her daughters. The best schools in the world will not, in and of themselves, make fine women. The tone of *family education* and of society needs to be raised. This can never be done till greater value is set on the cultivated female intellect. Young ladies must be inspired with high moral principles, noble aims, and a spirit of self-improvement to become what they ought to be. Maternal instruction is the purest and safest means of opening the fountain of knowledge to the young mind.

5. Elizabeth Cady Stanton Demands Women's Right to Vote, 1848

[W]e are assembled to protest against a form of government existing without the consent of the governed to declare our right to be free as man is free, to be represented in the government which we are taxed to support, to have such disgraceful laws as give man the power to chastise and imprison his wife, to take the wages which she earns, the property which she inherits, and, in case of separation, the children of her love; laws which make her the mere dependent on his bounty.

It is to protest against such unjust laws as these that we are assembled today, and to have them, if possible, forever erased from our statute books, deeming them a shame and a disgrace to a Christian republic in the nineteenth century. We have met

> To uplift woman's fallen divinity
> Upon an even pedestal with man's.

And, strange as it may seem to many, we now demand our right to vote according to the declaration of the government under which we live.

This right no one pretends to deny.

We need not prove ourselves equal to Daniel Webster to enjoy this privilege, for the ignorant Irishman in the ditch has all the civil rights he has.

We need not prove our muscular power equal to this same Irishman to enjoy this privilege, for the most tiny, weak, ill-shaped stripling of twenty-one has all the civil rights of the Irishman.

Elizabeth Cady Stanton, Address at the First Women's-Rights Convention, Seneca Falls, July 19, 1848. Obtained from http://www.undelete.org/library/library003.html.

We have no objection to discuss the question of equality, for we feel that the weight of argument lies wholly with us, but we wish the question of equality kept distinct from the question of rights, for the proof of the one does not determine the truth of the other.

All white men in this country have the same rights, however they may differ in mind, body, or estate.

The right is ours. The question now is: how shall we get possession of what rightfully belongs to us?

We should not feel so sorely grieved if no man who had not attained the full stature of a Webster, Clay, Van Buren, or Gerrit Smith could claim the right of the elective franchise.

But to have drunkards, idiots, horse-racing, rum-selling rowdies, ignorant foreigners, and silly boys fully recognized, while we ourselves are thrust out from all the rights that belong to citizens, it is too grossly insulting to the dignity of woman to be longer quietly submitted to.

The right is ours.

Have it, we must.

Use it, we will.

The pens, the tongues, the fortunes, the indomitable wills of many women are already pledged to secure this right.

The great truth that no just government can be formed without the consent of the governed we shall echo and re-echo in the ears of the unjust judge, until by continual coming we shall weary him.

There seems now to be a kind of moral stagnation in our midst.

Philanthropists have done their utmost to rouse the nation to a sense of its sins. War, slavery, drunkenness, licentiousness, gluttony, have been dragged naked before the people, and all their abominations and deformities fully brought to light, yet with idiotic laugh we hug those monsters to our breasts and rush on to destruction.

Our churches are multiplying on all sides, our missionary societies, Sunday schools, and prayer meetings and innumerable charitable and reform organizations are all in operation, but still the tide of vice is swelling, and threatens the destruction of everything, and the battlements of righteousness are weak against the raging elements of sin and death.

Verily, the world waits the coming of some new element, some purifying power, some spirit of mercy and love.

The voice of woman has been silenced in the state, the church, and the home, but man cannot fulfill his destiny alone, he cannot redeem his race unaided. There are deep and tender chords of sympathy and love in the hearts of the downfallen and oppressed that woman can touch more skillfully than man.

The world has never yet seen a truly great and virtuous nation, because in the degradation of woman the very fountains of life are poisoned at their source. It is vain to look for silver and gold from mines of copper and lead. It is the wise mother that has the wise son.

So long as your women are slaves you may throw your colleges and churches to the winds. You can't have scholars and saints so long as your mothers are ground to powder between the upper and nether millstone of tyranny and lust. How seldom, now, is a father's pride gratified, his fond hopes realized, in the budding genius of his son!

The wife is degraded, made the mere creature of caprice, and the foolish son is heaviness to his heart. Truly are the sins of the fathers visited upon the children to the third and fourth generation.

God, in His wisdom, has so linked the whole human family together that any violence done at one end of the chain is felt throughout its length, and here, too, is the law of restoration, as in woman all have fallen, so in her elevation shall the race be recreated.

6. The Seneca Falls Convention Declares Women's Rights, 1848

When in the course of human events it becomes necessary for one portion of the family of man to assume among the people of the earth a position different from that which the laws of nature and of nature's God entitle them, a decent respect to the opinions of mankind requires that they should declare the causes that impel them to such a course.

We hold these truths to be self-evident; that all men and women are created equal; that they are endowed by their Creator with certain inalienable rights; that among these are life, liberty, and the pursuit of happiness; that to secure these rights governments are instituted, deriving their just powers from the consent of the governed. Whenever any form of government becomes destructive of these ends, it is the right of those who suffer from it to refuse allegiance to it, and to insist upon the institution of a new government, laying its foundation on such principles, and organizing its powers in such form as to them shall seem most likely to effect their safety and happiness. Prudence, indeed, will dictate that governments long established should not be changed for light and transient causes; and accordingly, all experience hath shown that mankind are more disposed to suffer, while evils are sufferable, than to right themselves by abolishing the forms to which they are accustomed. But when a long train of abuses and usurpation, pursuing invariably the same object, evinces a design to reduce them under absolute despotism, it is their duty to throw off such government, and to provide new guards for their future security. Such has been the patient sufferance of the women under this government, and such is now the necessity which constrains them to demand the equal station to which they are entitled.

The history of mankind is a history of repeated injuries and usurpation on the part of man toward woman, having in direct object the establishment of an absolute tyranny over her. To prove this, let facts be submitted to a candid world.

He has never permitted her to exercise her inalienable right to the elective franchise.

"Declaration of Rights and Sentiments," adopted by the Seneca Falls Convention, July 19–20, 1848.

He has compelled her to submit to laws, in the formation of which she has no voice.

He has withheld from her rights which are given to the most ignorant and degraded men—both natives and foreigners.

Having deprived her of this first right of a citizen, the elective franchise, thereby leaving her without representation in the halls of legislation, he has oppressed her on all sides.

He has made her, if married, in the eye of the law, civilly dead.

He has taken from her all right in property, even to the wages she earns.

He has made her, morally, an irresponsible being, as she can commit many crimes with impunity, provided they be done in the presence of her husband. In the covenant of marriage, she is compelled to promise obedience to her husband, he becoming, to all intents and purposes, her master—the law giving him power to deprive her of liberty, and to administer chastisements.

He has so framed the laws of divorce, as to what shall be the proper causes of divorce; in case of separation, to whom the guardianship of the children shall be given; as to be wholly regardless of the happiness of women—the law, in all cases, going upon the false supposition of the supremacy of man, and giving all powers into his hands.

After depriving her of all rights as a married woman, if single and the owner of property, he has taxed her to support a government which recognizes her only when her property can be made profitable to it.

He has monopolized nearly all the profitable employments, and from those she is permitted to follow, she receives but a scanty remuneration.

He closes against her all the avenues to wealth and distinction, which he considers most honorable to himself. As a teacher of theology, medicine, or law, she is not known.

He has denied her the facilities for obtaining a thorough education, all colleges being closed against her.

He allows her in Church, as well as State, but a subordinate position, claiming Apostolic authority for her exclusion from the ministry, and, with some exceptions, from any public participation in the affairs of the Church.

He has created a false public sentiment, by giving to the world a different code of morals for men and women, by which moral delinquencies which exclude women from society, are not only tolerated but deemed of little account in man.

He has usurped the prerogative of Jehovah himself, claiming it as his right to assign for her a sphere of action, when that belongs to her conscience and her God.

He has endeavored, in every way that he could to destroy her confidence in her own powers, to lessen her self-respect, and to make her willing to lead a dependent and abject life.

Now, in view of this entire disfranchisement of one-half the people of this country, their social and religious degradation—in view of the unjust laws above mentioned, and because women do feel themselves aggrieved, oppressed, and fraudulently deprived of their most sacred rights, we insist that they have immediate admission to all the rights and privileges which belong to them as citizens of these United States.

In entering upon the great work before us, we anticipate no small amount of misconception, misrepresentation, and ridicule; but we shall use every instrumentality within our power to effect our object. We shall employ agents, circulate tracts, petition the State and national Legislatures, and endeavor to enlist the pulpit and the press in our behalf. We hope this Convention will be followed by a series of Conventions embracing every part of the country.

7. Lydia Sigourney Sentimentalizes Women in the Home, 1850

Home!—sweet word and musical!—keytone of the heart, at whose melody, as by the harp of Orpheus, all the trees in its garden are moved, holy word! refuge from sadness, and despair, best type of that eternal rest, for which we look, when the journey of life is ended!

Home,—blessed spot!—for which the sick yearn, and the stranger sigheth, among people of a strange speech, where none taketh him by the hand, who seeth casements glimmer through the evening storm, and firesides sparkle,—but not for him! . . .

Blessed Bride,—thou art about to enter this sanctuary, and to become a priestess at its altar. When thy foot first presseth its threshold, ask in thy secret soul, wisdom from above, to make the place of thy rest, fair and holy.

Bring with thee the perennial flowers of a pure affection; and however humble may be thine abode, beautify it by neatness, and order, and the ministries of love. Desire that it shall be thine own, and choose not to dwell under the roof of another, that thou mayest avoid care.

In the thronged hotel, a married man hath not his true pre-eminence. At the table of another, he misseth the honor that belongeth unto the head of a household. He is subordinate, and may not show that hospitality which God commendeth.

For his sake, therefore, acquaint thyself with the knowledge that appertaineth unto a wife and a housekeeper. If thou art deficient in this knowledge, rest not, till thou hast acquired it. It cometh readily to an attentive mind, and groweth with experience.

He, who chose thee, above all others, to bear his name, and to share his fortunes, hath a right to expect of thee such knowledge. Defraud him not, by continuing in ignorance, nor make thy beloved a stranger to the comforts of home, that thou mayst fold thy hands in indolence.

For the Apostle hath said, that "no man liveth unto himself." More especially should a woman, when she hath promised to be no longer her own, renounce self, as the aim of her existence. . . .

Consider the sphere in which thou art placed, as the one in which God willeth thee to be; and show kindness, and do good to all, according to thine ability.

Count thy husband's relatives as thy own; and if he hath parents show them the respect and tenderness of a true daughter. Be grateful to them for the culture of his virtue, whose fruits thou art gathering, and under the shadow of whose branches thou dost repose in peace.

Lydia Sigourney, "Home" (1850).

Should his, or thine own parents, reside under the same roof with thee, give thanks for the privilege. For so thou mayest have opportunity to repay some portion of the affection of their cradle-watchings, and tender care, and patience of hope.

Whatever service their feeble years may require, render willingly, and with a cheerful countenance. Covet their prayers more than gold; and by filial piety, win their blessing. . . .

Forgive me, Oh Bride, if in the time of thy joy, I have spoken too gravely unto thee of life's cares. Yet in these very cares lies the secret of woman's happiness, more than in the haunts of pleasure, or the giddiness of mirth.

And in thy faithful efforts to make home beautiful and holy, the wings of guardian spirits shall enfold thy bosom, and give thee strength from above.

8. Sojourner Truth Links Women's Rights to Antislavery, 1851, 1853

I

Well, children, where there is so much racket there must be something out of kilter. I think that 'twixt the negroes of the South and the women at the North, all talking about rights, the white men will be in a fix pretty soon. But what's all this here talking about?

That man over there says that women need to be helped into carriages, and lifted over ditches, and to have the best place everywhere. Nobody ever helps me into carriages, or over mud-puddles, or gives me any best place! And ain't I a woman? Look at me! Look at my arm! I have ploughed and planted, and gathered into barns, and no man could head me! And ain't I a woman? I could work as much and eat as much as a man—when I could get it—and bear the lash as well! And ain't I a woman? I have borne thirteen children, and seen them most all sold off to slavery, and when I cried out with my mother's grief, none but Jesus heard me! And ain't I a woman?

Then they talk about this thing in the head; what's this they call it? [Intellect, someone whispers.] That's it, honey. What's that got to do with women's rights or negro's rights? If my cup won't hold but a pint, and yours holds a quart, wouldn't you be mean not to let me have my little half-measure full?

Then that little man in black there, he says women can't have as much rights as men, 'cause Christ wasn't a woman! Where did your Christ come from? Where did your Christ come from? From God and a woman! Man had nothing to do with Him.

If the first woman God ever made was strong enough to turn the world upside down all alone, these women together ought to be able to turn it back, and get it right side up again! And now they is asking to do it, the men better let them.

Obliged to you for hearing me, and now old Sojourner ain't got nothing more to say.

Sojourner Truth, (I) speech given at a women's convention in Akron, Ohio, 1851, and (II) speech delivered at a women's rights convention in New York City, 1853, as reprinted in Fredrick M. Binder and David M. Reimers, *The Way We Lived* (Boston: Houghton Mifflin, 1988), 258–260.

II

Is it not good for me to come and draw forth a spirit, to see what kind of spirit people are of? I see that some of you have got the spirit of a goose, and some have got the spirit of a snake. I feel at home here. I come to you, citizens of New York, as I suppose you ought to be. I am a citizen of the State of New York; I was born in it, and I was a slave in the State of New York; and now I am a good citizen of this State. I was born here, and I can tell you I feel at home here. I've been lookin' round and watchin' things, and I know a little mite 'bout Woman's-Rights, too. I come forth to speak 'bout Woman's Rights, and want to throw in my little mite, to keep the scales a-movin'. I know that it feels a kind o' hissin' and ticklin' like to see a colored woman get up and tell you about things, and Woman's Rights. We have all been thrown down so low that nobody thought we'd ever get up again; but we have been long enough trodden now; we will come up again, and now I am here.

I was a-thinkin', when I see women contendin' for their rights, I was a-thinkin' what a difference there is now, and what there was in old times. I have only a few minutes to speak; but in the old times the kings of the earth would[n't] hear a woman. There was a king in the Scriptures; and then it was the kings of the earth would kill a woman if she come into their presence; but Queen Esther come forth, for she was oppressed, and felt there was a great wrong, and she said I will die or I will bring my complaint before the king. Should the king of the United States be greater, or more crueler, or more harder? But the king, he raised up his sceptre and said: "Thy request shall be granted unto thee—to the half of my kingdom will I grant it to thee!" Then he said he would hang Haman on the gallows he had made up high. But that is not what women come forward to contend. The women want their rights as Esther. She only wanted to explain her rights. And he was so liberal that he said, "the half of my kingdom shall be granted to thee," and he did not wait for her to ask, he was so liberal with her.

Now, women do not ask half of a kingdom, but their rights, and they don't get 'em. When she comes to demand 'em, don't you hear how sons hiss their mothers like snakes, because they ask for their rights; and can they ask for anything less? The king ordered Haman to be hung on the gallows which he prepared to hang others; but I do not want any man to be killed, but I am sorry to see them so short-minded. But we'll have our rights; see if we don't; and you can't stop us from them; see if you can. You may hiss as much as you like, but it is comin'. Women don't get half as much rights as they ought to; we want more, and we will have it. Jesus says: "What I say to one, I say to all—watch!" I'm a-watchin'. God says: "Honor your father and your mother." Sons and daughters ought to behave themselves before their mothers, but they do not. I can see them a-laughin', and pointin' at their mothers up here on the stage. They hiss when an aged woman comes forth. If they'd been brought up proper they'd have known better than hissin' like snakes and geese. I'm 'round watchin' these things, and I wanted to come up and say these few things to you, and I'm glad of the hearin' you give me. I wanted to tell you a mite about Woman's Rights, and so I came out and said so. I am sittin' among you to watch; and every once and awhile I will come out and tell you what time of night it is.

9. A Marriage Contract Protests the Contemporary Laws Relating to Marriage, 1855

It was my privilege to celebrate May day by officiating at a wedding in a farm-house among the hills of West Brookfield, [Massachusetts]. The bridegroom was a man of tried worth, a leader in the Western Anti-Slavery Movement; and the bride was one whose fair name is known throughout the nation; one whose rare intellectual qualities are excelled by the private beauty of her heart and life.

I never perform the marriage ceremony without a renewed sense of the iniquity of our present system of laws in respect to marriage; a system by which "man and wife are one, and that one is the husband." It was with my hearty concurrence, therefore, that the following protest was read and signed, as a part of the nuptial ceremony; and I send it to you, that others may be induced to do likewise.

REV. THOMAS WENTWORTH HIGGINSON

While acknowledging our mutual affection by publicly assuming the relation of husband and wife, yet in justice to ourselves and a great principle, we deem it a duty to declare that this act on our part implies no sanction of, nor promise of voluntary obedience to such of the present laws of marriage, as refuse to recognize the wife as an independent, rational being, while they confer upon the husband an injurious and unnatural superiority, investing him with legal powers which no honorable man would exercise, and which no man should possess. We protest especially against the laws which give to the husband:

1. The custody of the wife's person.
2. The exclusive control and guardianship of their children.
3. The sole ownership of her personal, and use of her real estate, unless previously settled upon her, or placed in the hands of trustees, as in the case of minors, lunatics, and idiots.
4. The absolute right to the produce of her industry.
5. Also against laws which give to the widower so much larger and more permanent an interest in the property of his deceased wife, than they give to the widow in that of the deceased husband.
6. Finally, against the whole system by which "the legal existence of the wife is suspended during marriage," so that in most States, she neither has a legal part in the choice of her residence, nor can she make a will, nor sue or be sued in her own name, nor inherit property.

We believe that personal independence and equal human rights can never be forfeited, except for crime; that marriage should be an equal and permanent partnership, and so recognized by law; that until it is so recognized, married partners should provide against the radical injustice of present laws, by every means in their power.

Marriage Contract Between Lucy Stone and Henry B. Blackwell (1855), in Elizabeth Cady Stanton et al., eds. *History of Woman Suffrage* (Rochester, N.Y.: Published for Susan B. Anthony, 1877), I: 260–261.

We believe that where domestic difficulties arise, no appeal should be made to legal tribunals under existing laws, but that all difficulties should be submitted to the equitable adjustment of arbitrators mutually chosen.

Thus reverencing law, we enter our protest against rules and customs which are unworthy of the name, since they violate justice, the essence of law.

HENRY B. BLACKWELL

LUCY STONE

☞ E S S A Y S

Historians have puzzled over the status of women in antebellum America for some time. Some scholars have argued that women's status declined in this period as sex roles hardened and work was separated from the home. Others contend that women's status improved as women gained certain rights and as female activism increased. The following two essays agree that women's status improved in this era, but they differ on the reasons why this improvement occurred. Nancy F. Cott of Yale University concentrates on the bonds that women forged from the ideology of domesticity. Although the family was inherently unequal and the domestic ideal contributed to that inequality, women forged bonds among themselves that laid the foundation for activism in society. In contrast, Ellen Carol DuBois, who teaches history at UCLA, focuses on the political battles fought by women in the public sphere. Because many women were deeply involved in social movements such as abolitionism, they were able to translate the content of these crusades into concerns for women's rights and female suffrage. Rather than stemming from the home, the change in women's status, DuBois argues, followed activism in the world over issues such as women's right to vote.

Feminism and the Private World of Women

NANCY F. COTT

"Thine in the bonds of womanhood" Sarah M. Grimké signed the letters to Mary Parker which she published in Boston in 1838 as *Letters on the Equality of the Sexes and the Condition of Women.* Grimké had left behind the South Carolina plantation of her birth and become one of the first women to speak publicly against slavery. "Bonds" symbolized chattel slavery to her. 'She must have composed her phrase with care, endowing it intentionally with the double meaning that womanhood bound women together even as it bound them down.

It is a central purpose of mine to explain why an American feminist of the 1830s would have seen womanhood in that dual aspect. . . .

. . . Recent historical research which has discovered shifts in family and sexual patterns in the late eighteenth century encouraged me to begin in that period. For the case of the United States . . . the period between 1780 and 1830 was a time of wide- and deep-ranging transformation, including the beginning of rapid intensive

Nancy F. Cott, *The Bonds of Womanhood: "Woman's Sphere" in New England, 1780–1835,* 2nd ed. (New Haven, Conn.: Yale University Press, 1997), 1, 3, 5–9, 64–70, 77–81, 163–168, 194–196. Copyright © 1977, 1997. Reprinted by permission of Yale University Press.

economic growth, especially in foreign commerce, agricultural productivity, and the fiscal and banking system; the start of sustained urbanization; demographic transition toward modern fertility patterns; marked change toward social stratification by wealth and growing inequality in the distribution of wealth; rapid pragmatic adaptation in the law; shifts from unitary to pluralistic networks in personal association; unprecedented expansion in primary education; democratization in the political process; invention of a new language of political and social thought; and—not least—with respect to family life, the appearance of "domesticity." . . .

It is fitting to begin with the decade of the 1830s in view although it is the end point of this study, for it presents a paradox in the "progress" of women's history in the United States. There surfaced publicly then an argument between two seemingly contradictory visions of women's relation to society: the ideology of domesticity, which gave women a limited and sex-specific role to play, primarily in the home; and feminism, which attempted to remove sex-specific limits on women's opportunities and capacities. Why that coincidence? Objectively, New England women in 1835 endured subordination to men in marriage and society, profound disadvantage in education and in the economy, denial of access to official power in the churches that they populated, and virtual impotence in politics. A married woman had no legal existence apart from her husband's: she could not sue, contract, or even execute a will on her own; her person, estate, and wages became her husband's when she took his name. Divorce was possible—and, in the New England states, available to wives on the same terms as husbands—but rare. Women's public life generally was so minimal that if one addressed a mixed audience she was greeted with shock and hostility. No women voted, although all were subject to the laws. Those (unmarried or widowed) who held property had to submit to taxation without representation.

This was no harsher subordination than women knew in 1770, but by 1835 it had other grievous aspects. When white manhood suffrage, stripped of property qualifications, became the rule, women's political incapacity appeared more conspicuous than it had in the colonial period. As occupations in trade, crafts, and services diversified the agricultural base of New England's economy, and wage earning encroached on family farm production, women's second-class position in the economy was thrown into relief. There was only a limited number of paid occupations generally open to women, in housework, handicrafts and industry, and school-teaching. Their wages were one-fourth to one-half what men earned in comparable work. The legal handicaps imposed by the marriage contract prevented wives from engaging in business ventures on their own, and the professionalization of law and medicine by means of educational requirements, licensing, and professional societies severely excluded women from those avenues of distinction and earning power. Because colleges did not admit women, they could not enter any of the learned professions. For them, the Jacksonian rhetoric of opportunity had scant meaning.

The 1830s nonetheless became a turning point in women's economic participation, public activities, and social visibility. New textile factories recruited a primarily female labor force, and substantial numbers of young women left home to live and work with peers. In the mid-1830s occurred the first industrial strikes in the United States led and peopled by women. "One of the leaders mounted a pump," the Boston *Evening Transcript* reported during the first "turn-out" in Lowell, Massachusetts, to protest wage reductions, "and made a flaming Mary Woolstonecraft [*sic*] speech on the rights of women." Middle-class women took up their one political tool, the petition, to demand legislation enabling wives to retain rights to their property and earnings. So many women pursued the one profession open to them, primary-school teaching, that their entry began to look like a takeover, although (or, to be accurate, because) they consistently commanded much lower salaries than men. Secondary schools and academies which could prepare young women to teach multiplied. Women's growing literacy, owed in part to the employment of some as teachers of girls, swelled the audience for female journalists and fiction writers. While it had been unprecedented for Hannah Adams to support herself by her writing in the first decade of the nineteenth century, that possibility came within more women's reach. Several ladies' magazines began publication during the decade, thereby increasing the editorial and publication possibilities for women authors and causing a female audience to coalesce.

Women also entered a variety of reform movements, to pursue objects in their own self-interest as well as to improve their society. Health reformers spotlighted women's physical condition. "Moral reformers" attacked the double standard of sexual morality and the victimization of prostitutes. Mothers formed societies to consult together on the rearing of children. Even larger numbers of women joined Christian benevolent associations, to reform the world by the propagation of the faith. An insistent minority of women became active in the antislavery movement, where they practiced tactics of recruitment, organization, fund raising, propagandizing, and petitioning—and initiated the women's rights movement in the United States, when some of them took to heart the principles of freedom and human rights. Although the Seneca Falls Convention of 1848 usually marks the beginning of organized feminism in this country, there were clearly feminist voices in the antislavery movement by the late 1830s.

At the same time, an emphatic sentence of domesticity was pronounced for women. Both male and female authors (the former mostly ministers) created a new popular literature, consisting of advice books, sermons, novels, essays, stories, and poems, advocating and reiterating women's certain, limited role. That was to be wives and mothers, to nurture and maintain their families, to provide religious example and inspiration, and to affect the world around by exercising private moral influence. The literature of domesticity promulgated a Janus-faced conception of women's roles: it looked back, explicitly conservative in its attachment to a traditional understanding of woman's place; while it proposed transforming, even millennial results. One might assume that this pervasive formulation was simply a reaction to—a conservative defense against—expansion of women's nondomestic pursuits. But women's educational, reform, labor force, and political activities were just beginning to enlarge in the 1830s when the concept of domesticity crystallized. Several decades' shift in the allotment of powers and functions inside and outside the household had created the constellation of ideas regarding women's roles that we call domesticity. It was hardly a *deus ex machina.* The particularization and professionalization taking place in the occupational structure between 1780 and 1835 affected women's domestic occupation as well as any other; and concomitant subtle changes in women's view of their domestic role established a substructure for their nondomestic pursuits and self-assertion. The ideology of domesticity may seem to be contradicted functionally and abstractly by feminism, but historically—as they emerged in the United States—the latter depended on the former. . . .

The central convention of domesticity was the contrast between the home and the world. Home was an "oasis in the desert," a "sanctuary" where "sympathy, honor, virtue are assembled," where "disinterested love is ready to sacrifice everything at the altar of affection." In his 1827 address on female education a New Hampshire pastor proclaimed that "It is at home, where man . . . seeks a refuge from the vexations and embarrassments of business, an enchanting repose from exertion, a relaxation from care by the interchange of affection: where some of his finest sympathies, tastes, and moral and religious feelings are formed and nourished;—where is the treasury of pure disinterested love, such as is seldom found in the busy walks of a selfish and calculating world." The ways of the world, in contrast, subjected the individual to "a desolation of feeling," in the words of the *Ladies Magazine;* there "we behold every principle of justice and honor, and even the dictates of common honesty disregarded, and the delicacy of our moral sense is wounded; we see the general good, sacrificed to the advancement of personal interest, and we turn from such scenes, with a painful sensation. . . ."

The contradistinction of home to world had roots in religious motives and rhetoric. Christians for centuries had depreciated "the world" of earthly delights and material possessions in comparison to Heaven, the eternal blessings of true faith. In the 1780s and 1790s British Evangelicals doubled the pejorative connotation of "the world," by preferring bourgeois respectability above the "gay world" of aristocratic fashion. Living in an era of eroding public orthodoxy, they considered family transmission of piety more essential than ever to the maintenance of religion; consequently they conflated the contrasts of Heaven versus "the world" and bourgeois virtue versus the "gay world" with the contrast between the domestic fireside and the world outside. In that tradition, when Esther Grout wrote in her diary, "oh how sweet is retirement. The pleasantest & I think some of the most profitable moments of my life have been spent in retirement," she was referring to her withdrawal from the world in solitary religious devotion and *also* to her repose *at home.*

The rhetorical origins of the contrast between home and world demand less interpretation than the canon of domesticity built upon it. That contrast infused the new literature because, in simplest terms, it seemed to explain and justify material change in individual's lives. Between the Revolution and the 1830s New England's population became more dense and more mobile, its political system more representative and demanding of citizens, its social structure more differentiated and its economic structure more complex than in earlier years when the business of "the world" had mostly taken place in households. Economic growth and rationalization and the entry of the market mechanism into virtually all relations of production fostered specialized and standardized work and a commercial ethic. Because of regional division of production and marketing, agricultural production itself became more specialized and more speculative. The farmer's success was not in his own hands when he produced for distant markets. In handicrafts the functional differentiation of wholesale merchant, retail merchant, contractor or "boss," and pieceworker replaced the unified eighteenth-century pattern in which an artisan made and sold his wares from his residence. Masters (now employers) and their journeymen or apprentices no longer assumed a patriarchal relationship; wages and prices defined their relationship to one another and to the merchants above them. Trends such as the decline of traditional determinants of deference, the assertion of an individualist ethos, increasing extremes of wealth and poverty, and replacement of unitary association networks by pluralistic ones, indicated deep change in social relations. Differentiation and specialization characterized this transformation of society. These were portrayed and symbolized most powerfully in the separation of production and exchange from the domestic arena—the division between "world" and "home."

The canon of domesticity encouraged people to assimilate such change by linking it to a specific set of sex-roles. In the canon of domesticity, the home contrasted to the restless and competitive world because its "presiding spirit" was woman, who was "removed from the arena of pecuniary excitement and ambitious competition." Woman inhabited the "shady green lanes of domestic life," where she found "pure enjoyment and hallowed sympathies" in her "peaceful offices." If man was the "fiercest warrior, or the most unrelenting votary of stern ambition," "toil-worn" by "troubled scenes of life," woman would "scatter roses among the thorns of his appointed track." In the "chaste, disinterested circle of the fireside" only—that is, in the hearts and minds of sisters, wives, and mothers—could men find "reciprocated humanity . . . unmixed with hate or the cunning of deceit." The spirit of business and public life thus appeared to diverge from that of the home chiefly because the two spheres were the separate domains of the two sexes.

In accentuating the split between "work" and "home" and proposing the latter as a place of salvation, the canon of domesticity tacitly acknowledged the capacity of modern work to desecrate the human spirit. Authors of domestic literature, especially the female authors, denigrated business and politics as arenas of selfishness, exertion, embarrassment, and degradation of soul. These rhetoricians suggested what Marx's analysis of alienated labor in the 1840s would assert, that "the worker . . . feels at ease only outside work, and during work he is outside himself. He is at home when he is not working and when he is working he is not at home." The canon of domesticity embodied a protest against that advance of exploitation and pecuniary values. Nancy Sproat, a pious wife and mother who published her own family lectures in 1819, warned that "the air of the world is poisonous. You must carry an antidote with you, or the infection will prove fatal." (A latter-day Calvinist, she clearly gave "the world" dual meaning, opposing it to both "home" and "Heaven." Her antidote, likewise, was a compound, of domestic affection and religious faith.) No writer more consistently emphasized anti-pecuniary bias of the domestic rhetoric than Sarah Josepha Hale, influential editor of the Boston *Ladies' Magazine* from 1828 to 1836 and subsequently of *Godey's Lady's Book* in Philadelphia. "Our men are sufficiently money-making," Hale said. "Let us keep our women and children from the contagion as long as possible. To do good and to communicate, should be the motto of Christians and republicans." She wished "to remind the dwellers in this 'bank-note world' that there are objects more elevated, more worthy of pursuit than wealth." "Time is money" was a maxim she rejected, and she urged mothers to teach their children the relative merits of money and of good works.

Yet the canon of domesticity did not directly challenge the modern organization of work and pursuit of wealth. Rather, it accommodated and promised to temper them. The values of domesticity undercut opposition to exploitative pecuniary standards in the work world, by upholding a "separate sphere" of comfort and compensation, instilling a morality that would encourage self-control, and fostering the idea that preservation of home and family sentiment was an ultimate goal. Family affection, especially maternal affection, was portrayed as the "spirit indefatigable, delighting in its task," which could pervade and "regenerate" society. Furthermore, women, through their reign in the home, were to sustain the "essential elements of moral government" to allow men to negotiate safely amid the cunning, treachery, and competition of the marketplace. If a man had to enter the heartless and debasing world, his wife at home supplied motive and reward for him, to defuse his resentment:

> O! what a hallowed place home is when lit by the smile of such a being; and enviably happy the man who is the lord of such a paradise. . . . When he struggles on in the path of duty, the thought that it is for *her* in part he toils will sweeten his labors. . . . Should he meet dark clouds and storms abroad, yet sunshine and peace await him at home; and when his proud heart would resent the language of petty tyrants, "dressed in a little brief authority," from whom he receives the scanty remuneration for his daily labors, the thought that she perhaps may suffer thereby, will calm the tumult of his passions, and bid him struggle on, and find his reward in her sweet tones, and soothing kindness, and that the bliss of home is thereby made more apparent.

The literature of domesticity thus enlisted women in their domestic roles to absorb, palliate, and even to redeem the strain of social and economic transformation. In the home, women symbolized and were expected to sustain traditional values and practices of work and family organization. The very shrillness of the *cri de coeur* against modern work relations, in the canon of domesticity, meant that women's role in the home would be inflexibly defined. . . .

As long as the wife's legal subordination persisted, in combination with romantic love ideals that stressed personal attraction and emotional motivation for both partners, women faced an overwhelming irony: they were to choose their bondage. "In America the independence of woman is irrecoverably lost in the bonds of marriage," noticed Alexis de Tocqueville, among other visitors to the United States in the early nineteenth century, but she "voluntarily and freely enters upon this engagement," in full knowledge of her destiny. "She has learned by the use of her independence to surrender it without a struggle and without a murmur when the time comes for making the sacrifice." Not wholly accurate—he probably exaggerated both the young unmarried woman's independence and the wife's willingness to bend to subordination—but nevertheless perspicacious, Tocqueville seized on a central paradox of domesticity, that women were expected to make a voluntary choice amounting to self-abnegation. That "sacrifice" was impossible for some. Eliza Perkins Cabot recalled of her adolescence in the early nineteenth century, "My mother thought any of her daughters were fools to marry anybody. They had all they wanted at home." The great majority, of course, found it possible. But what tensions complicated that choice, which was also the most important one a woman would make? "The contract is so much more important in its consequences to females than to males," a young man in 1820, a law student, wrote, comparing the significance of marriage to the two sexes, "for besides leaving everything else to unite themselves to one man they subject themselves to his authority—they depend more upon their husband than he does upon the wife for society & for the happiness & enjoyment of their lives—he is their all—their only relative—their only hope—but as for him—business leads him out of doors, far from the company of his wife . . . & then it is upon his employment that he depends almost entirely for the happiness of his life."

The canon of domesticity and its enveloping social circumstances freighted women's marriage choice with unprecedented meaning. Marrying meant beginning a vocation imbued with significance for society, as well as fitting one's neck to a "yoke" that could not be broken (in accord with conventional propriety); and the separation of the home from "the world" isolated women in their roles as wives and mothers. All this followed the "romantic" acceptance of a husband. Young women's awareness of the conflict between romantic and economic elements in the marriage choice, and of the heavy social consequences of marriage (probably compounded by the contrast between single and married women's lives), seems to have resulted in an emotional reaction or "marriage trauma" in the minds of some by the 1820s and 1830s. Women who sincerely envisioned *beaux ideals* and neither found them in reality nor would settle for less refused ever to marry. The "marriage trauma" may have also enhanced the sense of fulfillment of those who found seemingly perfect partners, whether consciously anticipated or not. But the most frequent manifestation of the "marriage trauma," I suspect, was a withdrawal of emotional intensity from the too-burdened marriage choice, and also from the marital relationship. . . .

Literature of the period gave unprecedented attention to sensibility and "improvement of the heart." Frank L. Mott quotes from the *Christian's, Scholar's and Farmer's Magazine* of 1789 a view representative of American magazine literature: "Everyone boasts of having a heart tender and delicate, and even those who know themselves deficient therein, endeavor to persuade others that they possess these qualities." This valuation of the heart at once seemed to raise esteem of women and to justify no change in their assigned role. Excellence in "heart" was their essential and their sufficient endowment. Another magazine contributor acclaimed women for possessing "all the virtues that are founded in the sensibility of the heart. . . . Pity, the attribute of angels, and friendship, the balm of life, delight to dwell in the female breast. What a forlorn, what a savage creature would man be without the meliorating offices of the gentle sex!"

Prescriptions of women's duties and promises of praise for them, both religious and secular, identified women with qualities of heart. There are occasional explicit references to the reign of this attitude in parents' upbringing of daughters, as well. Mary Lee, in a letter to her sister about the latter's children, distinguished the sons' need for book-learning from a daughter's different requirements: "you wish her heart to be more richly cultivated than the head, and this cannot be under any one's tuition so well as yours. A mother alone can do this, I believe." A wealthy Maine lawyer had clear preferences for his teenaged daughter's education in 1801: "She has enough [intellect], and too much to make her exactly what I wish her to be. I mean only that her thurst [*sic*] for reading will probably obstruct the attainment of those amiable, condescending, and endearing manners, without which a woman is, in my estimation, but a poor piece of furniture." Eulogies of women unfailingly focused on their hearts, regardless of their other substantial achievements. An obituary notice for historian and religious controversialist Hannah Adams declared, "Indeed, literary claims are perhaps among the last that . . . present themselves to the minds of her friends. The virtues and excellences of her character, her blameless life, her sensibility, the warmth of her affections, her sincerity and candor, call forth a flow of feeling that cannot be restrained."

The heart's ruling purpose was to express affections, sympathies, consideration and tenderness toward others—in short, to love. Sarah Connell, at eighteen, believed she understood her own character when she confided to her diary, "To love, is necessary to my very existence." The identification of woman with the heart meant that she was defined *in relation to* other persons. "A true woman's heart never grows cold," wrote the female author of *Girlhood and Womanhood,* "even the most isolated of my sex will ever find some object, upon which her affections will expend themselves." Women's appropriate motivation was "affiliation" rather than "achievement" (to borrow psychologist David McClelland's terms); their cardinal goal was to establish positive affective relationships. Didactic works on sex-roles and marriage from the late eighteenth through the nineteenth century named a woman's "stations" in life according to her personal relationships as daughter, sister, loved one, wife, and mother, not in terms of her discrete individual status or aims. . . .

When they privately assessed their own characters, women used the same standard. "My happiness consists in feeling that I deserve the love of my friends," Sarah Connell went on in her diary, "in studying to make their life pass pleasantly, and in cherishing their esteem. I could not exist in a state of indifference. Nature never formed me for it." Nancy Hyde hoped that the students whom she taught in a female academy in Connecticut would be admired for "the excellent qualities of their hearts, and . . . for diffusing around them that happiness, which is the inseparable concomitant of virtue," as well as for their literary accomplishments. Catherine Sedgwick affirmed, even after she achieved fame as a novelist, that her true happiness derived "from the dearest relations of life," and that her "author existence" was "accidental, extraneous & independent of my inner self." Another woman whose literary aims were not so well rewarded as Sedgwick's consoled herself with the thought that "the heart, that is formed for friendship and affection, is in itself an inexhaustible storehouse of happiness, and the true secret of being happy is to love as many of human kind as possible."

In truth, the identification of women with "the heart" was a gloss on the inequality of the sexes. The need for and inspiration of affiliative motives in women derived from their dependent status. "A woman of fine feelings cannot be insensible that *her constitutional condition is secondary and dependent among men,*" said the Reverend Amos Chase of Litchfield, Connecticut, in 1791, "nor can she long want conviction that the sure way to avoid any evil consequence . . . is to yield the front of battle to a hardier sex." If women were considered dependent on others (men) for protection and support, self-preservation itself demanded skill in personal relationships. . . . To identify women with the heart was to imply that they conducted themselves through life by engaging the affections of others. The cultural metonymy by which the nurturant maternal role stood for the whole of woman's experience further confirmed that "heartfelt" caring was woman's characteristic virtue.

Although it was intended to stress the complementary nature of the two sexes while keeping women subordinate, the identification of women with the heart also implied that they would find truly reciprocal interpersonal relationships only with other women. They would find answering sensibilities only among their own sex. The sex-role division of the eighteenth century impelled women toward friendship and sisterhood with one another for two corollary reasons. Women characterized by "heart" presumably would seek equivalent sympathies in their friends. And just as women were viewed as inferior to men in rationality, men could not be expected to respond in kind to women's feelings. "Who but a woman can know the heart of a woman?" Daniel Dana put the question in 1804. In their actual friendships women answered him: no one. . . .

Sisterhood expressed in an affective way the gender identification—the consciousness of "womanhood"—so thickly sown and vigorously cultivated in contemporary social structure and orthodoxy. Women's reliance on each other to confirm their values embodied a new kind of group consciousness, one which could develop into a political consciousness. The "woman question" and the women's rights movement of the nineteenth century were predicated on the appearance of women as a discrete class and on the concomitant group-consciousness of sisterhood. Both the feminists who began to expose and to protest women's oppression in the 1830s and the educators, writers, and social reformers who intended more conservatively to improve women's status took for granted this double-headed assumption. All of them recognized gender as the most important determinant of the shape of their lives. Feminists moved from acknowledging that to sensing the disabilities imposed by gender roles. In the year of the Seneca Falls Convention, for example, Elizabeth Cady Stanton looked toward the achievement of women's rights and declared, "Woman herself must do this work—for woman alone can understand the height, and the depth, the length and the breadth of her own degradation and woe. Man cannot speak for us—because he has been educated to believe that we differ from him so materially, that he cannot judge of our thoughts, feelings and opinions by his own."

If political feminists viewed women's allotment as inequitable and debasing and—perhaps more offensive—imposed on them without their consent, most women were willing to accept a sphere they saw as different but equal. To strengthen women's position within that sphere by reaffirming their powers of moral suasion vis-à-vis men, by improving their educational opportunities, and by enhancing the social role implicit in their child-rearing duties, seemed sufficient reform. The growth of women's schools, publications, and associations during the 1830s showed progress toward these aims. But in the same decade, confrontation with voices of incipient feminism (such as those of antislavery speakers Angelina and Sarah Grimké) clarified the fact that the ideology of woman's sphere had inherently limited utility to reform woman's lot. . . . For the duration of the nineteenth century, nonetheless, most women honored their separate sphere, especially when they had sisterhood to secure it. They had little objective reason and still less subjective cause to envision advancement (or even comfort) outside it.

Feminism and the Public Demands for Suffrage

ELLEN CAROL DUBOIS

For many years before 1848, American women had manifested considerable discontent with their lot. They wrote and read domestic novels in which a thin veneer of sentiment overlaid a great deal of anger about women's dependence on undependable men. They attended female academies and formed ladies' benevolent societies,

Ellen Carol DuBois, *Feminism and Suffrage: The Emergence of an Independent Women's Movement in America, 1848–1869* (Ithaca, N.Y.: Cornell University Press, 1978), 21–24, 28–33, 35–37, 40, 45–47, 50–52. Copyright © 1978 Cornell University. Used by permission of the publisher, Cornell University Press.

in which they pursued the widest range of interests and activities they could imagine without calling into question the whole notion of "woman's sphere." In such settings, they probed the experiences that united and restrained them—what one historian has called "the bonds of womanhood." Yet women's discontent remained unexamined, implicit, and above all, disorganized. Although increasing numbers of women were questioning what it meant to be a woman and were ready to challenge their traditional position, they did not yet know each other.

The women's rights movement crystallized these sentiments into a feminist politics. Although preceded by individual theorists like Margaret Fuller, and by particular demands on behalf of women for property rights, education, and admission to the professions, the women's rights movement began a new phase in the history of feminism. It introduced the possibility of social change into a situation in which many women had already become dissatisfied. It posed women, not merely as beneficiaries of change in the relation of the sexes, but as agents of change as well. As Elizabeth Cady Stanton said at the meeting that inaugurated the movement, "Woman herself must do the work." The pioneers of women's rights pointed the way toward women's discontent organized to have an impact on women's history.

The women's rights movement developed in the dozen years before the Civil War. It had two sources. On the one hand, it emerged from women's growing awareness of their common conditions and grievances. Simultaneously, it was an aspect of antebellum reform politics, particularly of the antislavery movement. The women who built and led the women's rights movement combined these two historical experiences. They shared in and understood the lives of white, native-born American women of the working and middle classes: the limited domestic sphere prescribed for them, their increasing isolation from the major economic and political developments of their society, and above all their mounting discontent with their situation. Women's rights leaders raised this discontent to a self-conscious level and channeled it into activities intended to transform women's position. They were able to do this because of their experience in the antislavery movement, to which they were led, in part, by that very dissatisfaction with exclusively domestic life. Female abolitionists followed the course of the antislavery movement from evangelicism to politics, moving from a framework of individual sin and conversion to an understanding of institutionalized oppression and social reform. This development is what enabled them and other women's rights pioneers to imagine changing the traditional subservient status of women. Borrowing from antislavery ideology, they articulated a vision of equality and independence for women, and borrowing from antislavery method, they spread their radical ideas widely to challenge other people to imagine a new set of sexual relations. Their most radical demand was enfranchisement. More than any other element in the women's rights program of legal reform, woman suffrage embodied the movement's feminism, the challenge it posed to women's dependence upon and subservience to men.

The first episode of the women's rights movement was the 1848 Seneca Falls Convention, organized by Elizabeth Cady Stanton, Lucretia Mott, and several other women. As befitted an enterprise handicapped by the very injustices it was designed to protest, the proceedings were a mixture of womanly modesty and feminist militancy. When faced with the task of composing a manifesto for the convention, the organizers, in Stanton's words, felt "as helpless and hopeless as if they had been suddenly asked to construct a steam engine." Nor was any woman willing to chair the meeting, and the office fell to Lucretia Mott's husband. Yet the list of grievances which the organizers presented was comprehensive. In retrospect, we can see that their Declaration of Sentiments and Resolutions anticipated every demand of nineteenth-century feminism. To express their ideas about women's rights and wrongs, they chose to rewrite the Preamble of the Declaration of Independence around "the repeated injuries and usurpations on the part of man towards woman." On the one hand, this decision reflected their need to borrow political legitimacy from the American Revolution. On the other, it permitted them to state in the clearest possible fashion that they identified the tyranny of men as the cause of women's grievances.

The Seneca Falls Convention was consciously intended to initiate a broader movement for the emancipation of women. For the women who organized the convention, and others like them, the first and greatest task was acquiring the skills and knowledge necessary to lead such an enterprise. In Elizabeth Cady Stanton's words, they had to transform themselves into a "race of women worthy to assert the humanity of women." Their development as feminists, as women able to bring politics to bear on the condition of their sex, had as its starting point the experience they shared with other women. While many accounts of this first generation of feminist activists stress what distinguished them from other women—their bravery and open rebellion—it is equally important to recognize what they had in common with nonfeminists: lack of public skills; lives marked by excessive domesticity; husbands and fathers hostile to their efforts; the material pressures of housekeeping and childrearing; and the deep psychological insecurity bred by all these factors. A movement is a process by which rebellion generates more rebellion. The women's rights pioneers did not begin their political activities already "emancipated," freed from the limitations that other women suffered. Many of the personal and political resources they drew on to challenge the oppression of women were developed in the course of mounting the challenge itself. . . .

. . . [T]he major resource on which women's rights activists drew to support themselves and advance their cause was one another. Like many nineteenth-century women, they formed intense and lasting friendships with other women. Frequently these were the most passionate and emotionally supportive relationships that they had. While feminists' mutual relationships were similar to other female friendships in emotional texture, they were different in their focus on the public and political concerns that made their lives as women unique. The most enduring and productive of these friendships was undoubtedly that of Elizabeth Cady Stanton and Susan B. Anthony, which began in 1851. The initial basis of their interdependency was that Anthony gave Stanton psychological and material support in domestic matters, while Stanton provided Anthony with a political education. In an episode repeated often in their first decade together, Anthony called on Stanton when she found herself unable to write a speech for a New York teachers' convention: "For the love of me and for the saving of the reputation of womanhood, I beg you, with one baby on your knee, . . . and four boys whistling, buzzing, hallooing 'Ma, Ma,' set yourself about the work. . . . I must not and will not allow these schoolmasters to say, 'See, these women can't or won't do anything when we do give them a chance."

Antoinette Brown and Lucy Stone were also bound by an intense friendship, formed when they were both students at Oberlin. They turned to each other to fortify their common feminism against the assaults of friends and teachers, and, as Brown remembered it, "used to sit with our arms around each other . . . and talk of our friends and our homes and of ten thousand subjects of mutual interest until both our hearts felt warmer and lighter." Their relationship continued to sustain them after they left Oberlin and became abolitionists and women's rights agitators. When Stone was subject to particularly intense harassment for wearing bloomers, Brown offered her support. "Tonight I could nestle closer to your heart than on the night when I went through the dark and the rain and Tappan Hall and school rules—all to feel your arm around me," she wrote, "and to know that in all this wide world I was not alone."

An important aspect of these relationships was overtly political. Given the strength of men's commitment to maintaining their political monopoly, the few women who were fortunate enough to have acquired a political education had to share their skills and knowledge with others. Stanton's contribution to Anthony's political development has already been noted. When Brown and Stone first met, they organized six other women students into "an informal debating and speaking society" to provide the oratorical experience they were denied in Oberlin's "ladies" course. They were so afraid of official intervention that they met in a black woman's home "on the outskirts of town," and occasionally in the woods, with a guard posted "against possible intruders." When Brown returned home to Michigan for a year, she organized another group to discuss women's sphere and women's rights. "We are exceedingly careful in this matter and all move on together step by step," she wrote to Stone. "Some will undoubtedly shrink back when they come to find where they stand and believe they must have been mistaken . . . and a few I hope and believe will go out into the world pioneers in the great reform which is about to revolutionize society."

There were limits, however, to the support women's rights pioneers could offer one another. One such constraint was physical distance. As reformers they traveled to a degree unheard of among pre–Civil War women and, when unmarried, could scarcely be said to have a home. They were usually alone. In addition, the attacks on them for stepping outside women's sphere were constant, severe, and beyond the power of friends to halt or counteract. Brown described for Stone the response she elicited from the townspeople of Oberlin: "Sometimes they warn me not to be a Fanny Wright man, sometimes believe I am joking, sometimes stare at me with amazement and sometimes seem to start back with a kind of horror. Men and women are about equal and seem to have their mouths opened and their tongues loosed to about the same extent." Surrounded on all sides by hostility, women's rights agitators had to work most of the time without the companionship and sisterhood they so prized. "You know we used to wish sometimes that we could live on and have no need of the sympathy of anyone," Brown reminded Stone, after she had left Oberlin, "I have learned to feel so." "What hard work it is to stand alone!" she wrote a few years later. "I am forever wanting to lean over onto somebody but nobody will support me." . . .

The abolitionist movement provided the particular framework within which the politics of women's rights developed. From the 1837 clerical attack on the Grimké sisters, through the 1840 meeting of Lucretia Mott and Elizabeth Cady Stanton at the World's Anti-Slavery Convention, to the Civil War and Reconstruction, the development of American feminism was inseparable from the unfolding of the antislavery drama. In tracing the sources of the women's rights movement, Stanton and Anthony cited abolitionism "above all other causes." Mistaking political rhetoric for histori-cal process, historians commonly identify the connection between the two move-ments as women's discovery of their own oppression through its analogy with slavery. Certainly women's rights leaders made liberal use of the slave metaphor to describe women's oppression. Yet women's discontent with their position was as much cause as effect of their involvement with the antislavery movement. What American women learned from abolitionism was less that they were oppressed than what to do with that perception, how to turn it into a political movement. Aboli-tionism provided them with a way to escape clerical authority, an egalitarian ideol-ogy, and a theory of social change, all of which permitted the leaders to transform the insights into the oppression of women which they shared with many of their contemporaries into the beginnings of the women's rights movement.

Women's involvement in abolitionism developed out of traditions of pietistic fe-male benevolence that were an accepted aspect of women's sphere in the early nine-teenth century. The feminist militance of Sarah and Angelina Grimké and the women who succeeded them was rooted in this common soil. The abolitionist movement was one of the many religious reforms that grew out of evangelical Protestantism. For the movement's first half-decade, the role women had in it was consistent with that in other benevolent religious efforts such as urban missionary activities and moral re-form. Women organized separate antislavery auxiliaries, in which they worked to support men's organizations and gave particular attention to the female victims and domestic casualties of slavery. The Grimkés entered abolitionism on these terms. Unlike other pious activisms, however, abolition had an unavoidably political thrust and a tendency to outgrow its evangelical origins. As the movement became secular-ized, so did the activities of benevolent women in it. "Those who urged women to become missionaries and form tract societies . . . have changed the household utensil to a living, energetic being," wrote domestic author and abolitionist Lydia Maria Child, "and they have no spell to turn it into a broom again."

The emergence of the Garrisonian wing of the abolitionist movement embodied and accelerated these secularizing processes. In 1837 William Lloyd Garrison was converted by utopian John Humphrey Noyes to the doctrine of perfectionism, which identified the sanctified individual conscience as the supreme moral standard, and corrupt institutions, not people, as the source of sin. In particular, Garrisonians turned on their churchly origins and attacked the Protestant clergy for its perversion of true Christianity and its support of slavery. Garrisonians' ability to distinguish religious institutions from their own deeply-felt religious impulses was an impres-sive achievement for evangelicals in an evangelical age. . . .

Women in the Garrisonian abolitionist movement not only absorbed its anti-clericalism, but also drew on its principle of the absolute moral equality of all human beings. Because the Garrisonian abolitionists' target was Northern racial prejudice and their goal the development of white empathy for the suffering slave, they focused their arguments on convincing white people of their basic identity with black people. The weakness of this emphasis on the ultimate moral identity of the races was its inability to account for their historical differences. Garrisonians did not develop an explanation for the origins and persistence of racism, and as a result many abolition-ists continued to believe that there were biological causes for the inferior position of black people. Instead, Garrisonian abolitionism stressed the common humanity of blacks and whites. Garrisonians formulated this approach as a moral abstraction, but its basis was the concrete demands of the agitational task they faced as abolitionists.

Abolitionist feminists appropriated this belief and applied it to women. The philosophical tenet that women were essentially human and only incidentally female liberated them from the necessity of justifying their own actions in terms of what was appropriate to women's sphere. In other words, Garrisonianism provided an ideology of equality for women to use in fighting their way out of a society built around sexual difference and inequality. The degree to which abolitionist feminists ignored the demands of women's sphere is particularly remarkable because they did so at the same time that the ideology of sexual spheres was being elaborated by benevolent women, in other ways very much like them. To the Congregational clergy's demand that she return "to the appropriate duties and influence of women," Sarah Grimké responded: "The Lord Jesus defines the duties of his followers in his Sermon on the Mount . . . without any reference to sex or condition . . . never even referring to the distinction now so strenuously insisted upon between masculine and feminine virtues. . . . Men and women are CREATED EQUAL! They are both moral and accountable beings and whatever is right for man to do is right for woman." . . . The Grimkés were followed by other Garrisonian feminists who also refused to justify their efforts in terms of women's sphere. "Too much has already been said and written about woman's sphere," Lucy Stone said in 1854. "Leave women, then, to find their sphere." The 1851 women's rights convention resolved that: "We deny the right of any portion of the species to decide for another portion . . . what is and what is not their 'proper sphere'; that the proper sphere for all human beings is the largest and highest to which they are able to attain." . . .

From the beginning, gaining the franchise was part of the program of the women's rights movement. It was one of a series of reforms that looked toward the elimination of women's dependent and inferior position before the law. The women's rights movement demanded for married women control over their own wages, the right to contract for their own property, joint guardianship over their children, and improved inheritance rights when widowed. For all women, the movement demanded the elective franchise and the rights of citizenship. Compared to legal reforms in women's status articulated before 1848, for instance equal right to inherit real property, the women's rights program was very broadly based, and intentionally so. In particular, the right to control one's earnings and the right to vote were demands that affected large numbers of women—farm women, wives of urban artisans and laborers, millgirls and needlewomen. . . .

. . . [T]he demand that women be included in the electorate was not simply a stage in the expansion and democratization of the franchise. It was a particularly feminist demand, because it exposed and challenged the assumption of male authority over women. To women fighting to extend their sphere beyond its traditional domestic limitations, political rights involved a radical change in women's status, their emergence into public life. The right to vote raised the prospect of female autonomy in a way that other claims to equal rights could not. Petitions to state legislatures for equal rights to property and children were memorials for the redress of grievances, which could be tolerated within the traditional chivalrous framework that accorded women the "right" to protection. In 1859 the *New York Times* supported the passage of the New York Married Women's Property Act by distinguishing the "legal protection and fair play to which women are justly entitled" from "the claims to a share of political power which the extreme advocates of Women's Rights are fond of advancing." By contrast, the suffrage demand challenged the idea that women's interests were identical or even compatible with men's. As such, it embodied a vision of female self-determination that placed it at the center of the feminist movement. "While we would not undervalue other methods," the 1851 national women's rights convention resolved, "the Right of Suffrage for Women is, in our opinion, the corner-stone of this enterprise, since we do not seek to protect women, but rather to place her in a position to protect herself."

The feminist implications of the suffrage demand are further evident in the reverberations it sent through the ideology of sexual spheres, the nineteenth-century formulation of the sexual division of labor. Most obviously, woman suffrage constituted a serious challenge to the masculine monopoly of the public sphere. Although the growing numbers of women in schools, trades, professions, and wage-labor were weakening the sexual barriers around life outside the family, most adult women remained at home, defined politically, economically, and socially by their family position. In this context, the prospect of enfranchisement was uniquely able to touch all women, offering them a public role and a relation to the community unmediated by husband or children. While the suffrage demand did not address the domestic side of the nineteenth-century sexual order directly, the connections between public and private spheres carried its implications into the family as well. In particular, the public honor of citizenship promised to elevate women's status in the home and raised the specter of sexual equality there. Women's rights leaders were relatively modest about the implications of the franchise for women's position in the family, anticipating reform of family law and improvement in the quality of domestic relations. Their opponents, however, predicted that woman suffrage would have a revolutionary impact on the family. "It is well known that the object of these unsexed women is to overthrow the most sacred of our institutions . . . ," a New York legislator responded to women's rights petitions. "Are we to put the stamp of truth upon the libel here set forth, that men and women, in the matrimonial relation, are to be equal?" In the introduction to the *History of Woman Suffrage,* Elizabeth Cady Stanton penetrated to the core of this antisuffrage response. "Political rights, involving in their last results equality everywhere," she wrote, "roused all the antagonism of a dominant power, against the self-assertion of a class hitherto subservient." . . .

Prewar women's rights agitation had an impact on a large number of women who were not ready to speak or act publicly but were convinced that the position of their sex demanded reform. A friend of her sister's invited Antoinette Brown to visit her "to introduce you to my friends here and let them see that you have not got horns. . . . I think I see more and more clearly that the Lord has a work for females to do that they have not understood," she continued, "and I am glad that there are some that are willing to learn and to do what He requires of them." Anthony reported to Stanton that she had been to dinner with Mrs. Finney, the wife of the president of Oberlin. After her husband denounced women's rights, "Mrs. Finney took me to another seat and with much earnestness inquired all about what we were doing and the growth of our movement. . . . Said she you have the sympathy of a large proportion of the educated women with you. In my circle I hear the movement much talked of and earnest hopes for its spread expressed—but these women dare not speak out their sympathy."

Women's rights agitators barely knew how many women they were affecting, much less how to encourage their halting sympathies.

Ironically, the Garrisonian politics and abolitionist alliance that had enabled the women's rights movement to develop in the first place were beginning to restrain its continued growth. Like the abolitionists before them, women's rights activists saw themselves as agitators, stirring up discontent. However, they had no way to consolidate the feminist sentiment that their agitation was beginning to create. Once the level of their discontent was raised, there was nothing for most women to do with it. Women's rights activities were organized around a small group who were politically skilled, willing to shoulder the opprobrium of "strong-mindedness," and able to commit a great deal of their energies to the movement. Women who were just beginning to develop political skills and sensibilities could not normally find an active role to play. The limitations to growth inherent in the agitational focus of prewar women's rights were embodied in the movement's organizational underdevelopment. There were no national or state organizations. Annual conventions were planned by an informal and constantly changing coordinating committee. Speaking tours and legislative campaigns were highly individualistic matters, which put a premium on personal initiative and bravery. The movement's close political relationship with abolitionism further restrained its organizational growth, in that its ability to rely on the organizational resources of the American Anti-Slavery Society meant that it did not develop its own. Women's rights articles were published in antislavery newspapers, and its tracts were printed with antislavery funds. The surrogate political coherence that abolitionism provided women's rights permitted the movement's leaders to indulge their propensities for individualism without risking the entire women's rights enterprise. The 1852 national convention rejected a proposal for a national women's rights society on the grounds that formal organizations "fetter and distort the expanding mind."

Above all, the prewar women's rights movement depended on abolitionism for its constituency. It is impossible to estimate how many women were touched by women's rights, and how many of these were abolitionists. Still, the movement's strongest, most reliable, and most visible support came from abolitionist ranks, particularly from the women. This dependence on an organized constituency borrowed from abolitionism was particularly marked on the national level. The call for the first national women's rights convention was timed to coincide with the annual meeting of the American Anti-Slavery Society. Abolitionist women provided women's rights with an audience well suited to its first, highly controversial years. Their antislavery activity had already put them outside the pale of respectable womanhood, where they were less likely to be frightened by public hostility. However, the availability of an audience among antislavery women kept feminist leaders from a systematic effort to reach the many women who were not reformers. At the worst, it gave them a kind of disdain for the nonpolitical preoccupations of most women. The fearlessness of female abolitionists sheltered the women's rights movement from a confrontation with the very real fears of male opposition and public disapproval that lay between it and the mobilization of large numbers of women.

Although primarily a source of strength, the relation of women's rights to abolitionism was thus a potential liability as well. The partnership was unequal, with women's rights dependent on abolitionism for essential resources and support. The

basic precepts, strategic methods, and organizational forms of Garrisonian abolitionism had sustained the women's rights movement through its first dozen years.
On this basis, feminist leaders were able to transform insights into the oppression
of women that they shared with many other women into a social movement strong
enough to have a future. This achievement raised other political problems—the
extent of the movement's reforming ambitions, the nature of its constituency, the
organizational form it would take, and above all, its relation to abolitionism. The
resolution of these matters was interrupted by the outbreak of the Civil War. Women's
rights activists subordinated all other interests to the fate of slavery, and suspended
feminist activity for the length of the war. When they returned, four years later, to
consider the future of women's rights, the political context within which they did
so had been completely altered.

FURTHER READING

Karen Haltunnen, *Confidence Men and Painted Women: A Study of Middle-Class Culture in
    America, 1830–1870* (1986).
Joan M. Jensen, *Loosening the Bonds: Mid-Atlantic Farm Women, 1750–1850* (1986).
Linda K. Kerber, *No Constitutional Right to Be Ladies: Women and the Obligations of
    Citizenship* (1999).
Steven Mintz and Susan Kellogg, *Domestic Revolutions: A Social History of the American
    Family* (1988).
Mary P. Ryan, *Cradle of the Middle Class: The Family in Oneida County, New York,
    1790–1865* (1981).
Christine Stansell, *City of Women: Sex and Class in New York City, 1789–1860* (1986).
Brenda E. Stevenson, *Life in Black and White: Family and Community in the Slave South*
    (1997).

C H A P T E R
11

Commercial Development and Immigration in the North at Midcentury

In the thirty years before the Civil War, society in the northern states was transformed in a variety of ways. For one thing, there was a huge migration westward, effectively redistributing the population of the nation. Between 1830 and 1860, the white population of the Old Northwest (the states of Ohio, Michigan, Indiana, Illinois, and Wisconsin) grew from 1.5 million to nearly 7 million. In 1860, one-quarter of the nation's population, most of whom toiled on the land, lived in these northwestern states. As millions of people moved westward, others migrated to the cities. By 1860, there were thirty-five cities in the United States with more than 25,000 inhabitants; New York City had more than one million inhabitants. Most of these cities were located in the northern states. Many city dwellers labored for wages in factories or mills. Many of the early workers were young women who left their rural homes to labor in the factories.

Cloth manufacturing changed radically when a factory in Waltham, Massachusetts, was built that mechanized all the stages in the production of cloth and brought the whole process under one roof. The evolution of cloth factories was complemented by innovations in the use of interchangeable parts that enabled manufacturers to develop complex assembly plants that produced clocks and guns, among other products. By 1860, nearly 300,000 workers toiled in northern industries, and population densities in the city reached up to 150 people per acre. As time went on, immigrants from Europe replaced many of the young female workers in the factories and also labored on western farms. Immigration, which was a mere 150,000 in the 1820s, swelled to over 1.5 million in the 1840s and 2.2 million in the 1850s. Mainly from the German states or Ireland, these immigrants often lived in poverty in urban slums and worshipped in Roman Catholic churches. They illustrated to many Americans the dangers of urbanization, commercialization, and mechanization in the North.

In short, these vast changes created grave challenges for northern society, especially in its growing cities. Densely settled neighborhoods became increasingly unhealthy. Workers strove to organize trade unions that would improve wages and *working conditions. But wages often lagged and workers fell victim to the financial crashes in 1837 and 1857, which increased unemployment and uncertainty. Some northerners began to fear that they would become "wage slaves," people who would never be freed of their need to labor in order to stay alive. To make matters worse, the cultural differences within the cities created tensions that occasionally exploded in violence. Riots in New York, Boston, and Philadelphia, and in rural areas as well, pitted the native born against the immigrant. Immigrants often were scapegoats, and their allegiance to Roman Catholicism only made them more suspect to citizens in a largely Protestant nation.*

Despite these challenges, many northerners remained optimistic that their world of commerce, farming, and manufacturing was the direction in which the United States should head. In particular, they were certain that their society was superior to the slave society in the South. As a result, they developed ideologies that explained their predicament and celebrated their society. Although some northerners feared "wage slavery," others applauded the economic mobility that workers were offered. Free laborers, so the argument went, could improve their condition through their own hard work and could ultimately become economically independent. As Abraham Lincoln observed, "The man who labored for another last year, this year labors for himself, and next year he will hire others to labor for him." This notion of mobility had deep roots in the northern mind; Benjamin Franklin had said essentially the same thing long before Lincoln made this observation. The sum total of free individuals working to improve themselves created a mobile society and a growing economy. "The desire of bettering one's condition," wrote newspaper editor Horace Greeley, "is the mainspring of effort." A key element supporting the system of free labor, however, was the availability of the vast tracts of land in the West. People could move up as they moved West. By forsaking an urban occupation, so the argument went, they relieved the pressures that built up in the city. The West was a necessary "safety valve." It is no coincidence that the Republican Party, a political organization founded in the 1850s whose membership came almost entirely from the northern states, would proclaim that it was the party of "Free Labor, Free Soil, and Free Men."

Q U E S T I O N S   T O   T H I N K   A B O U T

In what ways was economic and geographical mobility central to the experience and ideologies of northerners? Why do you think northerners were so sensitive to terms like *wage slavery* and *white slavery*? In what ways did immigration create a more volatile northern society when it increased dramatically in the decades after 1830?

D O C U M E N T S

Document 1 is a memoir written by Harriet Hanson Robinson, a woman who toiled in the textile mills in Lowell, Massachusetts, in the early 1830s. Robinson focuses on the long hours of toil and the labor unrest that ultimately drove American-born women from work in the mills. Alexis de Tocqueville, in Document 2, observes that although Americans are among the freest and best-educated people in the world, they are unhappy. He attributes this oddity to the desire for mobility that stems from that very freeness. The next two documents grapple with the condition of the working class in northern cities. In Document 3, Orestes Brownson offers a scathing critique of the status of workers in the North in 1840. He goes so far as to suggest that the plight of these "wage slaves" is worse than that of slaves in the South. Document 4, taken from an article in *The United States Democratic Review* in 1842, argues that "white slavery" might take root in the United States. As a solution, it urges Americans to look to the land in the West. The next three documents illustrate the ethnic and racial diversity of the northern states. In Document 5, a Swedish immigrant reflects on life in Wisconsin in 1841 and 1842; he enjoys an independence not available in his homeland. Although he finds Americans different from his people, he does appreciate the republican form of government. Frederick Douglass, in Document 6, illustrates the perils of being a black man working in the city of Baltimore. In Document 7, George Templeton Strong describes in his diary the impact of European immigrants on New York City. Note how Strong, who is no friend to immigrants, compares the Irish with the Chinese. In Document 8 Congressman James Bowlin recounts the opportunities in the West. He sees them as the basis for American freedom and argues that they can solve many of the ills in the urban northeast.

1. Harriet Hanson Robinson, a "Lowell Girl," Describes Her Labor in a Textile Mill, 1831

In 1831, under the shadow of a great sorrow, which had made her four children fatherless,—the oldest but seven years of age,—my mother was left to struggle alone; and, although she tried hard to earn bread enough to fill our hungry mouths, she could not do it, even with the help of kind friends. . . .

Shortly after this my mother's widowed sister, Mrs. Angeline Cudworth, who kept a factory boarding-house in Lowell, advised her to come to that city.

I had been to school constantly until I was about ten years of age, when my mother, feeling obliged to have help in her work besides what I could give, and also needing the money which I could earn, allowed me, at my urgent request (for I wanted to earn *money* like the other little girls), to go to work in the mill. I worked first in the spinning-room as a "doffer." The doffers were the very youngest girls, whose work was to doff, or take off, the full bobbins, and replace them with the empty ones. . . .

. . . When not doffing, we were often allowed to go home, for a time, and thus we were able to help our mothers in their housework. We were paid two dollars a week; and how proud I was when my turn came to stand up on the bobbin-box, and write my name in the paymaster's book, and how indignant I was when he asked me if I could "write." "Of course I can," said I, and he smiled as he looked down on me.

The working-hours of all the girls extended from five o'clock in the morning until seven in the evening, with one-half hour for breakfast and for dinner. Even the doffers were forced to be on duty nearly fourteen hours a day, and this was the greatest hardship in the lives of these children. . . .

I do not recall any particular hardship connected with this life, except getting up so early in the morning, and to this habit, I never was, and never shall be, reconciled, for it has taken nearly a lifetime for me to make up the sleep lost at that early age. But

---

Harriet Hanson Robinson, *Loom and Spindle or Life Among the Early Mill Girls* (New York: T. Y. Crowell, 1898; reprint, Press Pacifica, 1976), 16–22, 37–43, 51–53.

in every other respect it was a pleasant life. We were not hurried any more than was for our good, and no more work was required of us than we were able easily to do.

Most of us children lived at home, and we were well fed, drinking both tea and coffee, and eating substantial meals (besides luncheons) three times a day. We had very happy hours with the older girls, many of whom treated us like babies, or talked in a motherly way, and so had a good influence over us. . . .

I cannot tell how it happened that some of us knew about the English factory children, who, it was said, were treated so badly, and were even whipped by their cruel overseers. . . .

In contrast with this sad picture, we thought of ourselves as well off, in our cosey corner of the mill, enjoying ourselves in our own way, with our good mothers and our warm suppers awaiting us when the going-out bell should ring.

When I look back into the factory life of fifty or sixty years ago, I do not see what is called "a call" of young men and women going to and from their daily work, like so many ants that cannot be distinguished one from another; I see them as individuals, with personalities of their own. This one has about her the atmosphere of her early home. That one is impelled by a strong and noble purpose. The other,— what she is, has been an influence for good to me and to all womankind.

Yet they were a class of factory operatives, and were spoken of (as the same class is spoken of now) as a set of persons who earned their daily bread, whose condition was fixed, and who must continue to spin and to weave to the end of their natural existence. Nothing but this was expected of them, and they were not supposed to be capable of social or mental improvement. . . .

In 1831 Lowell was little more than a factory village. Several corporations were started, and the cotton-mills belonging to them were building. Help was in great demand; and stories were told all over the country of the new factory town, and the high wages that were offered to all classes of work-people,—stories that reached the ears of mechanics' and farmers' sons, and gave new life to lonely and dependent women in distant towns and farmhouses. . . .

But the early factory girls were not all country girls. There were others also, who had been taught that "work is no disgrace." There were some who came to Lowell solely on account of the social or literary advantages to be found there. They lived in secluded parts of New England, where books were scarce, and there was no cultivated society. They had comfortable homes, and did not perhaps need the *money* they would earn; but they longed to see this new "City of Spindles." . . .

It must be remembered that at this date woman had no property rights. A widow could be left without her share of her husband's (or the family) property, a legal "incumbrance" to his estate. A father could make his will without reference to his daughter's share of the inheritance. . . .

The law took no cognizance of woman as a money-spender. She was a ward, an appendage, a relict. Thus it happened, that if a woman did not choose to marry, or, when left a widow, to re-marry, she had no choice but to enter one of the few employments open to her, or to become a burden on the charity of some relative.

In almost every New England home could be found one or more of these women, sometimes welcome, more often unwelcome, and leading joyless, and in many instances unsatisfactory, lives. The cotton-factory was a great opening to these lonely and dependent women. From a condition approaching pauperism they were at once placed above want; they could earn money, and spend it as they pleased; and could gratify their tastes and desires without restraint, and without rendering an account to anybody. . . .

One of the first strikes of cotton-factory operatives that ever took place in this country was that in Lowell, in October, 1836. When it was announced that the wages were to be cut down, great indignation was felt, and it was decided to strike, *en masse.* . . .

One of the girls stood on a pump, and gave vent to the feelings of her companions in a neat speech, declaring that it was their duty to resist all attempts at cutting down the wages. This was the first time a woman had spoken in public in Lowell, and the event caused surprise and consternation among her audience.

Cutting down the wages was not their only grievance, nor the only cause of this strike. Hitherto the corporations had paid twenty-five cents a week towards the board of each operative, and now it was their purpose to have the girls pay the sum; and this, in addition to the cut in wages, would make a difference of at least one dollar a week. It was estimated that as many as twelve or fifteen hundred girls turned out, and walked in procession through the streets. . . .

It is hardly necessary to say that so far as results were concerned this strike did no good. The dissatisfaction of the operatives subsided, or burned itself out, and though the authorities did not accede to their demands, the majority returned to their work, and the corporation went on cutting down the wages.

And after a time, as the wages became more and more reduced, the best portion of the girls left and went to their homes, or to the other employments that were fast opening to women, until there were very few of the old guard left; and thus the *status* of the factory population of New England gradually became what we know it to be to-day.

2. Alexis de Tocqueville Considers the Mobile Northern Society, 1831

In certain remote corners of the Old World you may sometimes stumble upon little places which seem to have been forgotten among the general tumult and which have stayed still while all around them moves. The inhabitants are mostly very ignorant and very poor; they take no part in affairs of government, and often governments oppress them. But yet they seem serene and often have a jovial disposition.

In America I have seen the freest and best educated of men in circumstances the happiest to be found in the world; yet it seemed to me that a cloud habitually hung on their brow, and they seemed serious and almost sad even in their pleasures.

The chief reason for this is that the former do not give a moment's thought to the ills they endure, whereas the latter never stop thinking of the good things they have not got.

It is odd to watch with what feverish ardor the Americans pursue prosperity and how they are ever tormented by the shadowy suspicion that they may not have chosen the shortest route to get it.

Alexis de Tocqueville, *Democracy in America*, Vol. 2 (Boston: Little & J. Brown, 1841), 536–538.

Americans cleave to the things of this world as if assured that they will never die, and yet are in such a rush to snatch any that come within their reach, as if expecting to stop living before they have relished them. They clutch everything but hold nothing fast, and so lose grip as they hurry after some new delight.

An American will build a house in which to pass his old age and sell it before the roof is on; he will plant a garden and rent it just as the trees are coming into bearing; he will clear a field and leave others to reap the harvest; he will take up a profession and leave it, settle in one place and soon go off elsewhere with his changing desires. If his private business allows him a moment's relaxation, he will plunge at once into the whirlpool of politics. Then, if at the end of a year crammed with work he has a little spare leisure, his restless curiosity goes with him traveling up and down the vast territories of the United States. Thus he will travel five hundred miles in a few days as a distraction from his happiness.

Death steps in in the end and stops him before he has grown tired of this futile pursuit of that complete felicity which always escapes him.

At first sight there is something astonishing in this spectacle of so many lucky men restless in the midst of abundance. But it is a spectacle as old as the world; all that is new is to see a whole people performing in it.

The taste for physical pleasures must be regarded as the first cause of this secret restlessness betrayed by the actions of the Americans, and of the inconstancy of which they give daily examples.

A man who has set his heart on nothing but the good things of this world is always in a hurry, for he has only a limited time in which to find them, get them, and enjoy them. . . .

When all prerogatives of birth and fortune are abolished, when all professions are open to all and a man's own energies may bring him to the top of any of them, an ambitious man may think it easy to launch on a great career and feel that he is called to no common destiny. But that is a delusion which experience quickly corrects. The same equality which allows each man to entertain vast hopes makes each man by himself weak. His power is limited on every side, though his longings may wander where they will.

Not only are men powerless by themselves, but at every step they find immense obstacles which they had not at first noticed.

They have abolished the troublesome privileges of some of their fellows, but they come up against the competition of all. . . .

No matter how a people strives for it, all the conditions of life can never be perfectly equal. Even if, by misfortune, such an absolute dead level were attained, there would still be inequalities of intelligence which, coming directly from God, will ever escape the laws of man. . . .

Among democratic peoples men easily obtain a certain equality, but they will never get the sort of equality they long for. That is a quality which ever retreats before them without getting quite out of sight, and as it retreats it beckons them on to pursue. Every instant they think they will catch it, and each time it slips through their fingers. They see it close enough to know its charms, but they do not get near enough to enjoy it, and they will be dead before they have fully relished its delights.

3. Orestes Brownson Condemns
the Plight of "Wage Slaves," 1840

No one can observe the signs of the times with much care, without perceiving that a crisis as to the relation of wealth and labor is approaching. . . .

In this coming contest there is a deeper question at issue than is commonly imagined, a question which is but remotely touched in your controversies about United States Banks and Sub-Treasuries, chartered Banking and free Banking, free trade and corporations, although these controversies may be paving the way for it to come up. . . .

What we would ask is, throughout the Christian world the actual condition of the laboring classes, viewed simply and exclusively in their capacity of laborers? They constitute at least a moiety of the human race. We exclude the nobility, we exclude also the middle class, and include only actual laborers, who are laborers and not proprietors, owners of none of the funds of production, neither houses, shops, nor lands, nor implements of labor, being therefore solely dependent on their hands. . . .

. . . We are not ignorant of the fact, that the merchant, who is literally the common carrier and exchange dealer, performs a useful service, and is therefore entitled to a portion of the proceeds of labor. But make all necessary deductions on his account, and then ask what portion of the remainder is retained, either in kind or in its equivalent, in the hands of the original producer, the workingman? All over the world this fact stares us in the face, the workingman is poor and depressed, while a large portion of the non-workingmen, in the sense we now use the term, are wealthy. It may be laid down as a general rule, with but few exceptions, that men are rewarded in an inverse ratio to the amount of actual service they perform. . . .

In regard to labor two systems obtain; one that of slave labor, the other that of free labor. Of the two, the first is, in our judgement, except so far as the feelings are concerned, decidedly the least oppressive. If the slave has never been a free man, we think, as a general rule, his sufferings are less than those of the free laborer at wages. As to actual freedom one has just about as much as the other. The laborer at wages has all the disadvantages of freedom and none of its blessings, while the slave, if denied the blessings, is freed from the disadvantages. We are no advocates of slavery, we are as heartily opposed to it as any modern abolitionist can be; but we say frankly that, if there must always be a laboring population distinct from proprietors and employers, we regard the slave system as decidedly preferable to the system at wages. It is no pleasant thing to go days without food, to lie idle for weeks, seeking work and finding none, to rise in the morning with a wife and children you love, and know not where to procure them a breakfast, and to see constantly before you no brighter prospect than the almshouse. Yet these are no unfrequent incidents in the lives of our laboring population. . . . It is said there is no want in this country. There may be less than in some other countries. But death by actual starvation in this country is we apprehend no uncommon occurrence. The sufferings of a quiet, unassuming but useful class of females in our cities, in general sempstresses, too proud to

---

Orestes Brownson, "The Laboring Classes," *Boston Quarterly Review,* 1840.

beg or to apply to the almshouse, are not easily told. They are industrious; they do all they can find to do; but yet the little there is for them to do, and the miserable pittance they receive for it, is hardly sufficient to keep soul and body together. . . .

We pass through our manufacturing villages; most of them appear neat and flourishing. The operatives are well dressed, and we are told, well paid. They are said to be healthy, contented, and happy. This is the fair side of the picture; the side exhibited to distinguished visitors. There is a dark side, moral as well as physical. Of the common operatives, few, if any, by their wages, acquire a competence. A few of what Carlyle terms not inaptly the *body-servants* are well paid, and now and then an agent or an overseer rides in his coach. But the great mass wear out their health, spirits, and morals, without becoming one whit better off than when they commenced labor. . . . We know no sadder sight on earth than one of our factory villages presents, when the bell at break of day, or at the hour of breakfast, or dinner, calls out its hundreds or thousands of operatives. We stand and look at these hard working men and women hurrying in all directions, and ask ourselves, where go the proceeds of their labors? The man who employs them, and for whom they are willing as so many slaves, is one of our city nabobs, revelling in luxury; or he is a member of our legislature, enacting laws to put money in his own pocket; or he is a member of Congress, contending for a high Tariff to tax the poor for the benefit of the rich; or in these times he is shedding crocodile tears over the deplorable condition of the poor laborer, while he docks his wages twenty-five per cent; building miniature log cabins, shouting Harrison and "hard cider."—And this man too would fain pass for a Christian and a republican. He shouts for liberty, stickless for equality, and is horrified at a Southern planter who keeps slaves.

One thing is certain; that of the amount actually produced by the operative, he retains a less proportion than it costs the master to feed, clothe, and lodge his slave. Wages is a cunning device of the devil, for the benefit of tender consciences, who would retain all the advantages of the slave system, without the expense, trouble, and odium of being slave-holders.

Messrs. Thome and Kimball, in their account of the emancipation of slavery in the West Indies, establish the fact that the employer may have the same amount of labor done 25 per ct. cheaper than the master. What does this fact prove, if not that wages is a more successful method of taxing labor than slavery? We really believe our Northern system of labor is more oppressive, and even more mischievous to morals, than the Southern. We, however, war against both. We have no toleration for either system. We would see a slave a man, but a free man, not a mere operative at wages. This he would not be were he now emancipated. Could the abolitionists effect all they propose, they would do the slave no service. Should emancipation work as well as they say, still it would do the slave no good. He would be a slave still, although with the title and cares of a freeman. If then we had no constitutional objections to abolitionism, we could not, for the reason here implied, be abolitionists.

The slave system, however, in name and form, is gradually disappearing from Christendom. It will not subsist much longer. But its place is taken by the system of labor at wages, and this system, we hold, is no improvement upon the one it supplants. Nevertheless the system of wages will triumph. It is the system which in name sounds honester than slavery, and in substance is more profitable to the master.

It yields the wages of iniquity, without its opprobrium. It will therefore supplant slavery, and be sustained—for a time.

4. *The United States Democratic Review* Argues That "White Slavery" Threatens the Urban North, 1842

The main question discussed in all the works on political economy that have been issued from the press within the last twenty years, relates to the best means of ameliorating the condition of the laboring population; . . . while wealth has increased in certain quarters, poverty has not been proportionately diminished in others. . . .

. . . The poverty to which we allude, is that wholesale pestilence, which is now considered as a natural grade in society, and which makes perpetual calls on the legislator and the magistrate to satisfy its ceaseless cravings. It is the sure inheritance of the *White Slave* of the factory and of the coal-mine, who in the midst of the most dazzling social improvements and political ameliorations, still continues to trudge on from morning till night for the bare privilege of living—without even so much as a prospective termination to the period of his revolting bondage. . . .

It is fortunate that that great body corporate, styled a nation—a vast assemblage of human beings, knit together by laws and arts and customs, by the necessities of the present and the memory of the past—offers in this country, through these its vigorous and enduring members, a more substantial and healthy frame-work than falls to the lot of other nations. . . . And this very constitution which has secured order, has, consequently, promoted civilisation; and the almost unbroken tide of progressive amelioration has made us the freest, and may yet make us the wealthiest and most refined society of modern ages. But still the condition of the peasantry and the laboring population of the manufacturing districts is yet strongly susceptible of improvement. The present clamors of the Whig party to favor and foster the factory system among us are fraught with direful mischief. With the high price of labor that exists in the United States—with our scanty supply of moneyed capital—with our unlimited range of uncultivated or half-improved soil—it is almost a crime against society to divert human industry from the fields and the forests to iron forges and cotton factories. Nature has pointed out the course which we ought to pursue for perhaps half a century to come, till the plough and the spade have followed the axe of the woodcutter into their "primeval wilderness of shade," and till happy plantations shall have been formed on the deserted domains of the Indian huntsman from the Atlantic to the Ohio, and from the Mississippi to the Pacific. She has directed us to cling to the bosom of mother Earth, as to the most fertile source of wealth, and the most abundant reward of labor. She has told us to remain planters, farmers, and wood-cutters—to extend society and cultivation to new regions—to practise and improve the arts of the builder, the carpenter, and the naval architect—to facilitate every means of internal communication—to promote every branch of internal trade—to encourage every variety of landed produce, but not to waste the energies of our labor; or to interrupt the course of our prosperity, by forcing at home the manufacture of articles which foreigners could supply at half the price for which they could be made in America. . . .

"White Slavery," *The United States Democratic Review* 11, no. 52 (September 1842): 260–261, 269–271.

... [W]e are well aware that in point of humane treatment, rate of wages, and moral restrictions, our factory system is far superior to that which is the shame and degradation of England:—we are also willing to acknowledge that there are occasionally startling instances of prosperity and happiness growing out of early initiation into these dens of toil and trouble: but it does not require a great deal of penetration to perceive that, notwithstanding these negative advantages, the principles of WHITE SLAVERY are gradually taking root in the very midst of us. . . .

There is a class of writers, who, of late years, have undertaken a crusade against Adam Smith and his followers, averring that the modern school of political economy is based on erroneous principles, that the system of protective duties established by our ancestors was the consummation of human wisdom,—and that it is not merely the right, but the duty, of a state to determine in what channels capital should flow, and toward what objects industry should be directed. . . .

. . . Protection and monopolies are not only evils, but they are evils that love to perpetuate themselves. To establish them is easy enough; but to remove them has been the most difficult task that modern statesmen have had to encounter.

5. Gustof Unonius, a Swedish Immigrant, Reflects on Life in the United States, 1841–1842

Milwaukee, Wisconsin, 13 October 1841

The soil here is the most fertile and wonderful that can be found and usually consists of rich black mold. Hunting and fishing will provide some food in the beginning, but they must be pursued sparingly, otherwise time which could more profitably be spent in cultivating the soil is wasted. I beg the emigrant to consider all these factors carefully and closely calculate his assets before he starts out. . . . he will have to suffer much in the beginning, limit himself considerably, and sacrifice much of what he was accustomed to in Europe. . . . I caution against all exaggerated hopes and golden air castles; cold reality will otherwise lame your arm and crush your courage; both must be fresh and active.

As far as we are concerned, we do not regret our undertaking. We are living a free and independent life in one of the most beautiful valleys the world can offer; and from the experiences of others we see that in a few years we can have a better livelihood and enjoy comforts that we must now deny ourselves. If we should be overcome by a longing for the fatherland (and this seems unlikely), we could sell our farm which in eight years will certainly bring ten or twelve dollars per acre. . . . But I believe that I will be satisfied in America.

I am partial to a republican form of government, and I have realized my youthful dream of social equality. Others may say what they will, but there are many attractive things about it. It is no disgrace to work here. Both the gentleman and the day laborer work. No epithets of degradation are applied to men of humble toil; only those whose conduct merits it are looked down upon. . . . Liberty is still stronger in my affections than the bright silver dollar that bears her image. . . .

Gustof Unonius, "Letters from a Swedish Man," in H. Arnold Barton, ed., *Letters from the Promised Land: Swedes in America, 1840–1914* (Minneapolis: University of Minnesota Press, 1975).

Pine Lake, Wisconsin, 25 January 1842

. . . I admit that I am no friend of the big city of New York. The shopkeeper's spirit is too prevalent, but to judge the American national character from that is incorrect. I have found the Americans entirely different. We live in an industrial era and it is true that the American is a better representative of that than any other nationality. Despite this fact, there is something kindly in his speculation for profit and wealth, and I find more to admire in his manner than in that of the European leaders. The merchant here is withal patriotic; in calculating his own gain he usually includes a share for his country. . . . the universities and other educational institutions, homes for the poor, and other institutions of value to society are dependent on and supported by the American merchants. Canals, railroads, etc., are all financed by companies composed of a few individuals whose collective fortunes serve the public for its common benefit and profit. One must, therefore, overlook an avariciousness which sometimes goes to extremes.

It is true that the American is a braggart. . . . During the struggles which rend and agitate the countries of the Old World he sees in the progress of his peaceful fatherland the results of liberty and equality which he considers impossible to obtain under any other conditions. Even though I do not wish to blame him for this, yet I do not deny that his resulting self-satisfaction expresses itself in a highly ridiculous fashion in trivial matters.

6. Frederick Douglass Encounters Racist Animosity in a Northern City, 1845

In a few weeks after I went to Baltimore, Master Hugh hired me to Mr. William Gardner, an extensive ship-builder, on Fell's Point. I was put there to learn how to calk. It, however, proved a very unfavorable place for the accomplishment of this object. Mr. Gardner was engaged that spring in building two large man-of-war brigs, professedly for the Mexican government. The vessels were to be launched in the July of that year, and in failure thereof, Mr. Gardner was to lose a considerable sum; so that when I entered, all was hurry. There was no time to learn any thing. Every man had to do that which he knew how to do. In entering the ship-yard, my orders from Mr. Gardner were, to do whatever the carpenters commanded me to do. This was placing me at the beck and call of about seventy-five men. I was to regard all these as masters. Their word was to be my law. My situation was a most trying one. At times I needed a dozen pair of hands. I was called a dozen ways in the space of a single minute. Three or four voices would strike my ear at the same moment. . . . "Come here!—Go there!—Hold on where you are! Damn you, if you move, I'll knock your brains out!"

This was my school for eight months; and I might have remained there longer, but for a most horrid fight I had with four of the white apprentices, in which my left eye was nearly knocked out, and I was horribly mangled in other respects. The facts in the case were these: Until a very little while after I went there, white and black

Frederick Douglass, *Narrative of the Life of Frederick Douglass, an American Slave* (1845), 91–93.

ship-carpenters worked side by side, and no one seemed to see any impropriety in it. All hands seemed to be very well satisfied. Many of the black carpenters were freemen. Things seemed to be going on very well. All at once, the white carpenters knocked off, and said they would not work with free colored workmen. Their reason for this, as alleged, was, that if free colored carpenters were encouraged, they would soon take the trade into their own hands, and poor white men would be thrown out of employment. They therefore felt called upon at once to put a stop to it. And, taking advantage of Mr. Gardner's necessities, they broke off, swearing they would work no longer, unless he would discharge his black carpenters. Now, though this did not extend to me in form, it did reach me in fact. My fellow-apprentices very soon began to feel it degrading to them to work with me. They began to put on airs, and talk about the "niggers" taking the country, saying we all ought to be killed; and, being encouraged by the journeymen, they commenced making my condition as hard as they could, by hectoring me around, and sometimes striking me. I, of course, kept the vow I made after the fight with Mr. Covey, and struck back again, regardless of consequences; and while I kept them from combining, I succeeded very well; for I could whip the whole of them, taking them separately. They, however, at length combined, and came upon me, armed with sticks, stones, and heavy handspikes. One came in front with a half brick. There was one at each side of me, and one behind me. While I was attending to those in front, and on either side, the one behind ran up with the handspike, and struck me a heavy blow upon the head. It stunned me. I fell, and with this they all ran upon me, and fell to beating me with their fists. I let them lay on for a while, gathering strength. In an instant, I gave a sudden surge, and rose to my hands and knees. Just as I did that, one of their number gave me, with his heavy boot, a powerful kick in the left eye. My eyeball seemed to have burst. When they saw my eye closed, and badly swollen, they left me. With this I seized the handspike, and for a time pursued them. But here the carpenters interfered, and I thought I might as well give it up. It was impossible to stand my hand against so many. All this took place in sight of not less than fifty white ship-carpenters, and not one interposed a friendly word; but some cried, "Kill the damned nigger! Kill him! kill him! He struck a white person." I found my only chance for life was in flight. I succeeded in getting away without an additional blow, and barely so; for to strike a white man is death by Lynch law,—and that was the law in Mr. Gardner's ship-yard; nor is there much of any other out of Mr. Gardner's ship-yard.

I went directly home, and told the story of my wrongs to Master Hugh; and I am happy to say of him, irreligious as he was, his conduct was heavenly, compared with that of his brother Thomas under similar circumstances. He listened attentively to my narration of the circumstances leading to the savage outrage, and gave many proofs of his strong indignation at it. The heart of my once overkind mistress was again melted into pity. My puffed-out eye and blood-covered face moved her to tears. . . . As soon as I got a little the better of my bruises, he took me with him to Esquire Watson's, on Bond Street, to see what could be done about the matter. Mr. Watson inquired who saw the assault committed. Master Hugh told him it was done in Mr. Gardner's ship-yard, at midday, where there were a large company of men at work. "As to that," he said, "the deed was done, and there was no question as to who did it." His answer was, he could do nothing in the case, unless some white man would come forward and testify. He could issue no warrant on my word.

If I had been killed in the presence of a thousand colored people, their testimony combined would have been insufficient to have arrested one of the murderers. Master Hugh, for once, was compelled to say this state of things was too bad. Of course, it was impossible to get any white man to volunteer his testimony in my behalf, and against the white young men. Even those who may have sympathized with me were not prepared to do this. It required a degree of courage unknown to them to do so; for just at that time, the slightest manifestation of humanity toward a colored person was denounced as abolitionism, and that name subjected its bearer to frightful liabilities. The watchwords of the bloody-minded in that region, and in those days, were, "Damn the abolitionists!" and "Damn the niggers!" There was nothing done, and probably nothing would have been done if I had been killed. Such was, and such remains, the state of things in the Christian city of Baltimore.

7. George Templeton Strong Berates the Immigrants in His Midst, 1838–1857

November 6 [1838].   It was enough to turn a man's stomach—to make a man adjure republicanism forever—to see the way they were naturalizing this morning at the *Hall*. Wretched, filthy, bestial-looking Italians and Irish, and creations [creatures] that looked as if they had risen from the lazarettos of Naples for this especial object; in short, the very scum and dregs of human nature filled the clerk of C[ommon] P[leas] office so completely that I was almost afraid of being poisoned by going in. A dirty Irishman is bad enough, but he's nothing comparable to a nasty French or Italian loafer. . . .

April 28 [1848].   Orders given to commence excavating in Twenty-first Street Wednesday night. . . . Hibernia came to the rescue yesterday morning; twenty "sons of toil" with prehensile paws supplied them by nature with evident reference to the handling of the spade and the wielding of the pickaxe and congenital hollows on the shoulder wonderfully adapted to make the carrying of the hod a luxury instead of a labor. . . .

November 13 [1854].   Met a prodigious Know-Nothing [nativist political party] procession moving uptown, as I omnibussed down Broadway to the vestry meeting; not many banners and little parade of any kind, but a most emphatic and truculent demonstration. Solid column, eight or ten abreast, and numbering some two or three thousand, mostly young men of the butcher-boy and *prentice* type . . . marching in quick time, and occasionally indulging in a very earnest kind of hurrah. They looked as if they might have designs on St. Patrick's Cathedral, and I think the Celts of Prince and Mott Streets would have found them ugly customers. . . .

July 7 [1857].   Yesterday morning I was spectator of a strange, weird, painful scene. Certain houses of John Watts DePeyster are to be erected on the northwest corner of this street and Fourth Avenue, and the deep excavations therefore are in progress. Seeing a crowd on the corner, I stopped and made my way to a front place. The earth had caved in a few minutes before and crushed the breath out of a

Allan Nevins and Milton H. Thomas, eds., *The Diary of George Templeton Strong* (New York: Macmillan, 1952), 1: 94, 318, and 2: 197, 348.

pair of ill-starred Celtic laborers. They had just been dragged, or dug, out, and lay white and stark on the ground where they had been working, ten or twelve feet below the level of the street. Around them were a few men who had got them out, I suppose, and fifteen or twenty Irish women, wives, kinfolk or friends, who had got down there in some inexplicable way. The men were listless and inert enough, but not so the women. I suppose they were "keening"; all together were raising a wild, unearthly cry, half shriek and half song, wailing as a score of daylight Banshees, clapping their hands and gesticulating passionately. Now and then one of them would throw herself down on one of the corpses, or wipe some trace of defilement from the face of the dead man with her apron, slowly and carefully, and then resume her lament. It was an uncanny sound to hear. . . . Our Celtic fellow citizens are almost as remote from us in temperament and constitution as the Chinese.

8. James Bowlin, a Congressman, Marvels at the Possibilities of Western Lands, 1846

. . . The public lands were a trust fund in our hands for the benefit of the people—not to be held up by prohibitory, nor squandered by corrupt legislation; but to be so disposed of, as would secure to them the greatest benefits—whether that was in promoting correct principles, increasing the revenue, or in advancing the general prosperity of the country.

Land being the true basis of all individual and national prosperity, its disposition, and the tenure by which it is held, has in every age of the world, and in every civilized nation, engaged the most ardent attention of the statesman. There is no subject in the whole range of political science, that so nearly and directly interests the great body of the people, as that of the right of soil. Its disposition is not only a question of mere utility—that changes with the passing hour—but it is one involving great and important principles, upon which may hang the fate of man and governments. So intimately identified is it with the forms and systems of government, and the political rights and privileges of men, that we are frequently enabled to read the history of a nation, either for weal or for wo, for glory or shame, in the mere regulations of her land systems. That government, no matter by what name it may be called, whose lands are scattered amongst the great body of her people, and are left unfettered by law, to pass in their natural course, from generation to generation, preserving and perpetuating an independent yeomanry, must forever enjoy a high state of political freedom. Whilst such a system is preserved, there is no focus around which to rally political power to oppress. The rays of power are scattered, and can only be concentrated over the ruins of the system itself. Upon the contrary, that government which adopts a system, and pursues a policy, tending to concentrate its soil in the hands of a few, to the detriment of the many, fettering its free passage from man to man, no matter what name it may bear, its ultimate destiny is the destruction of every vestige of equality and liberty. It is the inevitable destiny of nations to be controlled by the proprietors of the soil, and the government is free or despotic, just in

---

James Bowlin, speech in Congress, *The Congressional Globe*, July 6, 1846, pp. 1059–1060.

proportion to the number of its rulers, or participants in political privileges. If you wish to preserve and perpetuate its democratic form, you must pursue a policy tending to disseminate the lands amongst the largest possible number of the people of the state. Hence the great principle that lies at the foundation of any system for the disposition of the public lands we may see proper to adopt. . . .

The celebrated feudal system of more modern times was but a cunningly devised scheme to rob the great body of the people of their just and legitimate interest in the landed estate of the country, and thereby build up an aristocracy upon the ruins of popular liberty. It was but a scheme to perpetuate political power in the hands of the few to the detriment of the many; to make serfs of the people and lords of their rulers. . . . It is this land system that constitutes the props to uphold the monarchies of the Old World. . . .

. . . [L]et us now turn our attention for a moment to the policy adopted by the European nations in colonizing this continent, and its natural and legitimate consequences; for it is a notorious fact, attested to in almost every page of American history, that they pursued a policy diametrically opposed to the system of policy adopted at home. The monarchs of England, France, and Spain, the three great colonizing nations of Europe, donated their lands to the emigrants in the newly-discovered countries—the two latter in the most liberal manner. The policy of this measure was to encourage emigration and settlement in the New World. The effect of it was to inculcate ideas of independence in the great body of the people, elevating their moral sentiments, and arousing their innate love of liberty, until it resulted in stretching a line of republics from the St. Lawrence to the Rio de la Plata. Their day-dreams of empire in the New World all dissolved at the touch of the magic wand of freedom, inculcated and nourished in the breast of the people by the fact that they were the free occupants of their own soil, and ate the bread of their own industry. . . .

. . . [W]e ask no special favors to aid us in our march; we only ask that you place no obstacle in our way—that you leave our action free; and the enterprise, energy, and industry of the same people who subdue forests in their march, and make the wilderness to yield abundant harvests, will make the country prosper. The rich soil, the magnificent rivers, the mild and genial climate of the great West, all contribute to invite emigration amongst us, and that policy would be suicidal that would obstruct or retard it. The West needs population to develop its great resources; and it will be one of the blessings of this great measure that it will contribute to its increase, without impairing the best interests of other portions of the Confederacy. . . .

But the new States have another interest at stake, which appeals strongly to the magnanimity of this Government in behalf of this measure; and that is an interest which almost as deeply concerns the whole Confederacy as the new States—and that was, their interest in bringing these lands into general occupancy and cultivation, so that they might yield a revenue in support of the Government. Under the present system the public lands are not taxed; and the States in which they lie, and from the labor of whose citizens they derive value, can exact no revenue from them. In the hands of individuals they would be taxable, and liable to be made, like other lands, tributary to the support and improvement of the State.

The changing northern world created a variety of challenges for its residents in the antebellum era. Not only was migration to and within the region increasingly important, but the way people worked and where they lived was changing as well. The majority of northerners still lived on farms. However, the proportion of northern Americans that lived in cities and fed their families through work for wages was larger than that in the South, and also larger than it had been in the past. The following two essays ponder the meaning of these changes and how they were used by political parties to mobilize their voters. David R. Roediger, a historian at the University of Illinois, concentrates on the uses of the terms *white slavery* and *wage slavery* among northern Americans. He notes that these concerns were utilized in particular by leaders of the Democratic Party not only to discuss the struggles of the northern worker, but also to connect workers in the North to slaveholders in the South. In contrast, John Ashworth, who teaches history at the University of East Anglia, scrutinizes the rise of the Republican Party. This party, Ashworth argues, was more comfortable with ideas of wage labor. Unlike earlier ideologues, who connected independence with control over property, this new group saw the possibilities of social mobility in toiling for wages. As such, these Americans were more comfortable with the new economy of wage work.

White Slaves, Wage Slaves, and Free White Labor in the North

DAVID R. ROEDIGER

In 1836, supporters of New York City's journeymen tailors papered the city with handbills featuring a coffin. The tailors had just lost a conspiracy case and with it their right to organize. The handbill encouraged protest and demanded redress in strong republican language familiar since the Revolution. It appealed to "Freemen" and to the power of "Mechanics and workingmen." But confidence that the cause of independence would prevail was at an ebb. The coffin signified that the "Liberty of the workingmen [would] be interred!" at the sentencing of the tailors. "Tyrant *masters*" had the upper hand, and the handbill's authors made a direct comparison that had been unthinkable even a decade before: "Freemen of the North are now on a level with the slaves of the South."

The "coffin handbill" shows both the new ease and the continuing hesitancy with which white workers in Jacksonian America began to describe themselves as slaves. Its unqualified North–South comparison is most striking, but the document also suggests some of the ways in which white workers remained beyond comparison with slaves. The whites, if slaves, were also simultaneously "freemen." If "tyrant *masters*" had prevailed, according to one line of the handbill, another line settled for invoking the fear of "would-be masters." Nor was it clear that the "slavery" of the tailors was "wage slavery." They were cast as slaves not because they were "hirelings" but because the state had deprived them of the freedoms necessary for defending

David R. Roediger, *The Wages of Whiteness: Race and the Making of the American Working Class* (New York: Verso, 1991), 65–73, 75–77. Reprinted by permission of Verso.

their rights. The emphasis on the "slavery" of the tailors in fact proved rather short-lived. After hearing of a more favorable court decision in another conspiracy case upstate, "the journeymen's fury abated."

Other instances of comparison between wage labor and chattel slavery between 1830 and 1860 were likewise both insistent and embarrassed. They could not have been otherwise. Labor republicanism inherited the idea that designing men perpetually sought to undermine liberty and to "enslave" the people. Chattel slavery stood as the ultimate expression of the denial of liberty. But republicanism also suggested that long acceptance of slavery betokened weakness, degradation and an unfitness for freedom. The Black population symbolized that degradation. Racism, slavery and republicanism thus combined to require comparisons of hirelings and slaves, but the combination also required white workers to distance themselves from Blacks even as the comparisons were being made.

Chattel slavery provided white workers with a touchstone against which to weigh their fears and a yardstick to measure their reassurance. An understanding of both the stunning process by which some white workers came to call themselves slaves and the tendency for metaphors concerning white slavery to collapse thus takes us to the heart of the process by which the white worker was made. It also furnishes us with an excellent vantage point from which to view the vexed relations between the labor movement and movements to abolish slavery.

The Winding Road to *White Slavery*

Use of terms like *white slavery* and *slavery of wages* in the 1830s and 1840s presents an intriguing variation on the theme of American exceptionalism. US labor historians are usually pressed to explain why American workers have historically lacked the class consciousness said to have existed elsewhere in the industrializing world. But if the antebellum US labor movement was exceptional in its rhetoric, it was exceptionally militant as it critiqued evolving capitalist social relations as a kind of slavery. France, with a revolutionary tradition that forcefully used metaphors regarding slavery to press republican attacks on political oppression, apparently saw but slight use of phrases such as *wage slavery* before the Revolution of 1848. The German states, though they produced a great popularizer of the concept of wage slavery, likewise did not witness frequent use of the term. Only Britain, where the metaphoric term *wage slavery* apparently originated in the second decade of the nineteenth century, rivalled the US in producing a discourse that regarded white hirelings as slaves. But since the spread of the metaphor in Britain was as much associated with the Tory radical politician Richard Oastler as with its use by working class Chartists, one might regard the antebellum US labor movement as exceptional in being the world leader in militant criticisms of wage work as slavery.

Of course, concern over "slavery" was very much in the air in Jacksonian America, whose citizens worried variously that Catholics, Mormons, Masons, monopolists, fashion, alcohol and the national bank were about to enslave the republic. Nonetheless, the use of the white slave metaphor for wage workers ought not be dismissed as merely another example of the "paranoid" style of antebellum politics. It might instead be profitable to view the paranoid style itself as a republican tradition much enlivened by the horrific example of chattel slavery and fears engendered by the growing failure of the American republic to produce a society of independent farmers and mechanics among whites.

By the Age of Jackson, several changes had created the setting in which white workers would begin to make and press, as well as deny and repress, comparisons between themselves and slaves. The rise, after 1829, of a highly visible movement to abolish slavery evoked reexamination of the line between slavery and freedom. Since free Blacks and slave rebels played so central a role in the Black freedom movement, the tendency to equate blackness and servility was likewise called into question. If abolitionism did not recruit more than a minority of white workers, it did make clear that equations between race and fitness for liberty were not eternal truths but objects of political debate.

Meanwhile, the experiences of the white artisans themselves encouraged the consideration of white slavery as a possible social category. In a nation agonizing over the fate of the Republic as the last of its revolutionary generation passed from the scene, urban craftsmen fought monumental struggles, concentrated between 1825 and 1835, for a ten-hour working day. Linking these struggles to time for self-education and full citizenship, the growing labor movement advocated the ten-hour system as the key to workers' independence and to the nation's. Seeking the immediate freedom of being less bossed by increasingly profit-driven masters—and ultimately to be free from having a boss—artisans who undertook concerted actions contrasted the fetters they felt and the liberty they longed for at every possible turn. The workers who gained the ten-hour day in the great 1835 Philadelphia general strike, for example, massed in Independence Square, marched to fife and drum and carried ten-hour banners alongside others proclaiming "LIBERTY, EQUALITY AND THE RIGHTS OF MAN."

The responses of employers tended to sharpen the artisans' sense that a great contest between freedom and its opposite was unfolding and encouraged them to raise the issue in terms of white slavery. In some cases, employers made the initial comparison of free US labor with British "slaves" and with Black slaves. They insisted that the ten-hour system could not function in the United States because the nation had to compete with Britain. The response of the *Working Man's Advocate* to this argument in 1832 reflected labor's view of the British system as utterly degrading. "Are we to slave thirteen or fourteen hours a day," the *Advocate* asked, "because the Manchester spinner or the Birmingham blacksmith so slaves?" As ten-hour struggles continued, US workers learned more about British resistance to long hours and answered employers' objections that British competition must be met in new ways that challenged the idea that only British workplaces encouraged servility. The *New England Artisan* wondered in 1834, "If the poor and oppressed but gallant working men of Great Britain have the daring hardihood to declare that they will work but eight hours . . . , how should the comparatively free . . . American working citizen feel?" In the midst of the shorter hours campaigns of the 1830s, some immigrant US workers also came to maintain that work in America was harder than it had been in Britain. When it was later argued that the ten-hour system could not prevail in Northern states because workplaces on that schedule could not match the production of Southern slave labor, the extent of the republican freedom of the white worker was still more sharply called into question.

Opposed to these substantial reasons for white workers to at least entertain comparisons of themselves and slaves was the continuing desire *not* to be considered anything like an African-American. Not only was the verb *slave* used, as we have seen, to indicate the performance of work in ways unbecoming to whites, but new and negative phrases such as *white nigger* (that is, "drudge") and *work like a nigger* (that is, "to do hard drudging work") came into American English in the 1830s, at roughly the same time that the term *white slavery* became prominent. Richard Henry Dana's searing indictment of the oppression of antebellum sailors in *Two Years before the Mast* took care to quote an irate captain screaming at his crew: "You've got a driver over you! Yes, a *slave-driver,—a nigger driver!* I'll see who'll tell me he isn't a NIGGER slave!"

Such usages, which should give considerable pause to those who believe race and class are easily disentangled, remind us that comparing oneself to a slave or to any Black American could not be lightly undertaken in the antebellum United States. Moreover, it should be obvious that for all but a handful of committed abolitionists/labor reformers, use of a term like *white slavery* was not an act of solidarity with the slave but rather a call to arms to end the inappropriate oppression of whites. Critiques of white slavery took form, after all, alongside race riots, racially exclusive trade unions, continuing use of terms like *boss* and *help* to deny comparison with slaves, the rise of minstrel shows, and popular campaigns to attack further the meager civil rights of free Blacks.

In such a situation, it is not surprising that labor activists rather cautiously backed into making comparisons between white workers and slaves. Many of the earliest comparisons emphasized not that whites were enslaved but rather that they were threatened with slavery. In Dover, New Hampshire in 1828, leaders of four hundred striking women textile workers both connected and disconnected themselves to chattel slavery by asking who among them could "ever bear the shocking fate of slaves to share?" In 1833, male and female members of the Manayunk (Pennsylvania) Working People's Committee refused a wage cut because it would, as they put it, "rivet our chains still closer" and, over time, "terminate, if not resisted, in slavery." In 1834 Lowell's female strikers permitted themselves considerable ambiguity. In a single paragraph they cast themselves as virtually in "bondage," as threatened with *future* slavery by the "oppressing hand of avarice" and as the "daughters of freemen" still. Two years later protesting Lowell women sang:

> Oh! I cannot be a slave;
> I will not be a slave.
> For I'm so fond of liberty
> That I cannot be a slave.

For male artisans, who led the first labor movement, the rise of a small sector of full-fledged factory production both symbolized threats to independence and offered the possibility to experiment with application of the slavery metaphor to white (often child and female) factory workers without necessarily applying it to *themselves.* The factory system tended to confine and discipline workers to an unprecedented extent, at least by the 1840s. Moreover, it was identified with the degrading, antirepublican labor said to be required in Europe, a comparison that gave force to labor leaders' branding of it as a "gaol" or a "Bastille."

That US textile factories employing large workforces of single women (and smaller ones employing whole families) justified their management practices as paternalistic ones only sharpened suspicions of them. Blacklists and the whipping of workers in some small mills likewise provoked outrage. In the 1834 textile strike in Dover, one complaint of the women workers was the management called them "their *slaves*." Perhaps the managers meant to refer to their own paternal responsibilities in adopting this usage, or perhaps to their dictatorial powers. In any case, they hit just the wrong note. Quitting and other forms of informal protest far outdistanced strikes among early mill workers, but for male artisans contemplating the new industrial system the issue of permanent "factory slavery" was a fearsome one.

Many early references to white slavery thus focused on so identifying British manufacturing workers and on adding that women and children in the United States were, or were about to be, so enslaved. "The Factory Girl," an abominable piece of British verse that was in the US perhaps the most widely reprinted of the early treatments of white slavery, combined the ideas that the British workers, and women workers in textiles, were in bondage. It portrayed the sad end of a female British worker:

> That night a chariot passed her
> While on the ground she lay;
> The daughters of her master
> An evening visit pay—
> Their tender hearts were sighing,
> As negroes' wrongs were told;
> While the white slave was dying,
> Who gained their fathers' gold.

This highly sentimental pressing of the comparison with chattel slavery ran through much antebellum writing on white female and child workers by male activists. Seth Luther's stirring 1832 *Address to the Workingmen of New England*, for example, does not refer to American male journeymen as slaves, but it does find factory women in bondage and does quote sentimental verse describing child laborers as "little sinless slaves."

Once made, comparisons to slaves could of course be extended, and artisans sometimes did come to be included in them. By 1835, for example, Luther was helping to write the "Ten-Hour Circular," which bitterly castigated "slavery among [white] mechanics." Stephen Simpson, intellectual leader and first Congressional candidate of the Philadelphia Working Men's party, began his 1831 *Working Man's Manual* by arguing that factory slavery had taken root in Britain where a "serf class" worked in manufacturing but that it could never grow in the US, which had disconnected the age-old links among "slavery, labor [and] degradation" and had made work the province of a "community of FREEMEN." Simpson then proceeded to take virtually all other possible positions. He noted the presence of huge numbers of slaves in the South, where he admitted that "labour shares in . . . disgrace, because it is a part of the slave." Within a few lines the US was characterized as a society sustained by a "mixture of slavery and labor." White women and children suffered special exploitation because "custom . . . classed them with slaves and servants." And, for that matter, Simpson argued, all Northern workers faced a situation in which "capital [was] the Master" and in which employers calculated wages in a manner like that of the "lords of the South [who oppress] sable herds of brutalized humanity."

Some workers, usually in factories, did describe themselves and their peers as already and fully enslaved. As early as 1831, Vermont operatives protested that they were "slaves in every sense of the word," while Lynn shoemakers of the 1840s saw themselves as having "masters—aye, masters" and as being "slaves in the strictest sense of the word." Lowell textile women echoed the Vermont millhands, describing themselves as slaves to long hours, as slaves to the "powers that be" and as "slaves in every sense of the word."

However, radical artisans remained more comfortable discussing the "slavery" of others than that of themselves. George Henry Evans, the printer, labor leader and land reformer who probably did more than anyone else to popularize the terms *white slavery* and *slavery of wages,* could be direct and sweeping in describing even male artisans as, if landless, then unequivocally enslaved. "Stealing the man away from his land, or his land away from the man," he argued, "alike produces slavery." Even Evans's individual writings did not tend to discuss the "slavery" of artisans but instead to concentrate on that of tenant farmers, the unskilled, women workers and child laborers. Though eloquent and expressive of the real fears of white workers, comparisons with slaves did not automatically lead to sustained self-examination among those groups of "hirelings" who were most active in organized labor in the antebellum years. . . .

Slavery of wages came to be used alongside *white slavery* by land reformers and utopian socialists in the last half of the 1840s, often in dialogue with abolitionists. Its wording raised the old issue of whether hireling labor and republican independence could coexist. But its very precision and directness raised problems. Many of those being described as slaves were not wage-earners. Thus, tenant farmers and those imprisoned for debt were frequently discussed, but the problem of the latter was precisely that they could not enter the wage labor market. Most early labor activists remained tied to one of the major political parties, usually the Democrats, and sought unity among the "producing classes," including small employers. To refer to such employers as "masters, aye masters," made sense in terms of fleshing out the metaphor of slavery of wages, but it did not make political sense. Moreover, many masters were simply self-employed workers or men who sporadically employed others while depending mainly on their own labor. Many failed and again became wage-earners. Some evidence suggests that small employers paid better than manufacturers with larger workshops, and clearly merchant capitalists often pressured masters to maintain tough labor policies. Journeymen *aspired* to run a small shop of their own. "Men must be masters," Whitman wrote, "under themselves."

Metaphors regarding the slavery of wages thus confronted the problem that, if the worker could be called a *slave,* the wage-paying master could not, except in the heat of labor conflict, really be regarded as a *slavemaster.* One stopgap solution was to hold that the master himself was a "slave." Boston's "Ten-Hour Circular" thus argued:

> We would not be too severe on our employers [for] they are slaves to the Capitalists, as we are to them. . . . But we cannot bear to be the servant of servants and slaves to oppression, let the source be where it may.

Evans, in keeping with his emphasis on land and rent, similarly maintained that small manufacturers in Lynn were mastered by landlords who owned their shops, while the New York *Mechanic* complained of the "capitalists . . . bossing all the mechanical trades."

The advantages of the phrase *white slavery* over *wage slavery* or *slavery of wages* lay in the former term's vagueness and in its whiteness, in its invocation of *herrenvolk* republicanism. *White slavery* was particularly favored by radical Democratic politicians for a time because it could unite various elements of their coalition—wage workers, debtors, small employers and even slaveholders—without necessarily raising the issue of whether the spread of wage labor was always and everywhere antirepublican. Abolitionists, free Blacks, bankers, factory owners and prison labor could, in sundry combinations, be cast as villains in a loose plot to enslave white workers. Moreover, *white slavery* did not necessarily require a structure solution— arrest of the spread of hireling labor. Although some who employed the term did go on to argue that all long-term wage dependency was bondage, *white slavery* itself admitted solutions short of an attack on the wage system. White workers could be *treated* better—reforms could occur, as they did in the "coffin handbill" case—and the comparison with slavery could be exorcised.

White slavery also served well because it did not call into question chattel slavery itself, an issue that sharply divided the labor movement, the Jacksonians and the nation. . . .

. . . One of the slave South's most eloquent defenders during the 1830s congressional debates over whether to accept petitions from abolitionists was Ely Moore, the nation's first labor Congressman, first president of the National Trades' Union and editor of the *National Trades' Union* newspaper. Moore denounced abolition not only as a "blind, reckless, feverish fanaticism" but also as a plot to rob whites of their independence. These charges found substantial echoes, though also some opposition, in the early labor press. The ex-Chartist Philadelphia typesetter, bookseller and labor reformer John Campbell followed his 1848 book, *A Theory of Equality,* three years later with *Negromania,* a cranky and vicious early attempt to popularize racist pseudo-science. Both the books were pleas for white unity inside the Democratic party. *America's Own and Fireman's Journal,* a labor paper of the 1850s, approvingly republished Las Casas's "A Plea for Slavery."

In the New York City labor movement, despite George Henry Evans's tempering influence, the tendency to indict white slavery and to support Black slavery was especially strong. . . . Walsh's wild popularity from the early forties to the early fifties stemmed from the resonance of his freewheeling attacks on what he called "white wages slavery" with the accent on both of the adjectives. "You are slaves," he thundered to his followers, "and none are better aware of the fact than the heathenish dogs who call you freemen," while outspokenly supporting Southern slavery and even its extension into Kansas and Nebraska. Walsh's bitterest factional opponent within New York City's artisan Democracy, the lockmaker Levi Slamm, echoed this combination of proslavery and attacks on "black-hearted tyrants" who held "white slaves." Slamm, editor of *The Plebeian,* organized the "coffin handbill" protest whose dramatic characterization of white workers as slaves begins this [essay]. John Commerford, the New York chairmakers' leader who . . . may have been the most popular Jacksonian labor leader, joined a number of trade unionists and radical Democrats who excoriated white slavery and gave political support to the South's premier proslavery politician, John C. Calhoun.

The proslavery affinities of those who denounced white slavery have attracted some passing notice from historians, who have offered various explanations. The fear of job competition with emancipated Blacks has received emphasis—perhaps even overemphasis, in that only a minority of proslavery indictments of white slavery raised the issue of job competition and that it was then usually raised in combination with broader fears of amalgamation. Labor's animosity to "middle class" and moralistic abolitionist leaders has also been mentioned. So have the necessity to guard the Republic from potentially fatal divisions over slavery and the need to preserve the Democracy as the party of reform, even at the cost of conciliating slaveholders. John Ashworth's work offers the most forceful recent restatement of the old, much debated view of the Jacksonian Democrats as (among whites) a party of political egalitarianism and social leveling. Surely the Democrats' positions on such issues as free trade, banking, imprisonment for debt, prison labor and, to an extent, land reform, gave some substance to their populism. Ashworth adds an inventive twist that makes the radical labor/proslavery position seem less anomalous, arguing that because Jacksonians could imagine no citizenship but full, equal citizenship they were less able to imagine emancipation of Blacks than more elitist parties. Other historians have even held that Yankee labor radicals were engaged in a sophisticated attempt to exploit splits within the ruling class by allying for a time with proslavery Southerners. This last position probably credits the labor radicals with more acumen than they in fact had, but it may describe what a particularly cerebral radical like Orestes Brownson thought he was doing for a time.

However great the value of existing explanations for the considerable coming together of radical labor and proslavery, these explanations deserve to be supplemented by a simpler one: the very structure of the argument against white slavery typically carried proslavery implications. As Eric Foner has recently observed, radical labor's comparisons of "white" and Black slavery often found the latter less oppressive than the former. Radicals argued, on shreds of evidence, that Southern masters worked their Black slaves far fewer hours per day—perhaps only half the number required by Northern employers. They computed rates of exploitation that putatively showed that a much greater proportion of the value produced by a Black slave was returned to him or her than was returned to the white slave in the North. Even writers who argued that white and Black slavery were roughly equal nonetheless showed a sharp tendency to cite only comparisons favorable to this latter. For example, a comparison of the two labor systems in the *Mechanics' Free Press* in 1830—probably the first such direct and significant one made by organized labor—set out to show that the two differed only "in name." But it then compared the life of a free laborer, full of the threat of starvation, over-exertion, deprived children and uncomforted sickness, with that of the slave with a "master interested in prolonging his life." Even Evans, who strove for balance, found that the "slave to the Land-Lord and capitalist class is in a worse, aye a *worse* condition than the slave who has a master of his own" and reprinted arguments that emancipation without land reform would worsen Black slaves' positions tenfold.

Artisan radical and early historian John Finch cited the "well-known fact that the blacks of the South enjoy more leisure time and liberty and fare quite as well as the operatives in the northern or eastern manufacturing districts." He added that the same comparison more or less applied to whites in "other mechanical pursuits."

Orestes Brownson, who at times found white workers closer to freedom than Blacks, could at other junctures argue that slave labor is "except so far as feelings are concerned . . . decidedly the least oppressive. . . . The laborer at wages has all the disadvantages of freedom and none of its blessings, while the slave, if denied the blessings, is freed from the disadvantages."

The most common comparison, repeated by Walsh and several others, was that the "poor negro" was a "farm horse" with one master who would protect him when he could "toil no more," while the "poor white man" was a "horse in a livery stable" hired to many masters and therefore overworked by all and without protection when infirmed. Chattel slavery was, in this view, better than white slavery, a point fraught with proslavery paternalist implications and not lost on the Southern editors who reprinted articles carrying such opinions.

Free Labor and Wage Labor in the North

JOHN ASHWORTH

Historians have recently started once again to place emphasis on economic transformations, in particular on the implications of what is now termed the market revolution that swept over the United States in the decades following the Peace of Ghent. As yet, however, no consensus exists on the chronology of this development or even on its precise character. While an increasing number of Americans were clearly spending more of their working lives engaged in producing for the market, such changes were almost certainly not unique to the mid-nineteenth century. And what actually constitutes a market revolution? How does its impact on a slave society differ from that on a society committed to free labor? How did it affect the cluster of values and ideals that historians now refer to as constituting the ideals of republicanism? These issues—and many others too—are still largely unresolved.

It is little more than a truism that the market revolution had a transforming effect on American politics. One can trace the profound effects of economic change on political ideology in any decade of the antebellum era. By concentrating, however, on a single decade, the 1850s, and a single party, the Republicans, it may nevertheless be possible to refine our understanding of the processes at work, and to shed some light on the political consequences of the market revolution. . . .

We cannot understand the political universe in which the Republicans flourished without first considering some of the opinions of the patron saint of American democracy, Thomas Jefferson. Jefferson defined the American democratic creed and the values of republicanism in his struggle with the Federalists in the 1790s. Although the Republican party of the 1850s constantly harked back to Jefferson and indeed claimed inspiration from such Jeffersonian triumphs as the Northwest Ordinance of 1787, the Republican victory of 1860 in fact marked the overthrow of the Jeffersonian system. Under the impact of the economic changes associated with

John Ashworth, "Free Labor, Wage Labor, and Slave Power: Republicanism and the Republican Party in the 1850s," in Melvyn Stokes and Stephen Conway, eds., *The Market Revolution in America: Social, Political, and Religious Expressions, 1800–1880* (Charlottesville: University Press of Virginia, 1996), 128, 133–143. Reprinted courtesy of the University Press of Virginia.

the market revolution, the Republicans redefined the American democratic tradition and, in their triumph over the South in the Civil War, destroyed the regime established in 1776 and reconstituted by the Jeffersonian triumph of 1800.

Jefferson's agrarianism, his belief in states' rights, his commitment to limited government—indeed all the major tenets of the Jeffersonian political faith—are all too well known to require any rehearsal here. Nevertheless, it is worth recalling his view of agriculture. This received its most eloquent expression in the *Notes on Virginia,* where Jefferson explained that the farmers' independence and moral purity made them "the chosen people of God, if ever He had a chosen people." In the 1820s the Jeffersonian mantle was picked up by those who rallied to Andrew Jackson. And as the principles of Jacksonian Democracy were defined in the course of Jackson's two administrations, especially under the impact of the struggle with the Bank of the United States, they came increasingly to resemble those of John Taylor of Caroline, high priest of Jeffersonian Democracy. Once again, praise was heaped on agriculture and on the landed interest. Thus, in 1839 the *Democratic Review,* semiofficial magazine of the party, did precisely as Jefferson had done a half-century earlier and compared city and country. The conclusion was a quintessentially Jeffersonian one:

> The farmer is naturally a Democrat—the citizen may be so, but it is in spite of many obstacles. In the country a more healthy moral atmosphere may be said to exist, untainted by the corruptions and contagions of the crowded city, analogous to its purer breezes which the diseased and exhausted denizen of the latter is from time to time compelled to seek for the renovation of his jaded faculties of mind and body. In the city men move in masses. . . . In the country, on the other hand, man enjoys an existence of a healthier and truer happiness, a nobler mental freedom, a higher native dignity—for which a poor equivalent is found in that superficial polish produced by the incessant mutual attrition, and that more intense life, if we may so speak, excited by the perpetual surrounding stimulus that belong to cities. He is thrown more on himself. Most of his labors are comparatively solitary, and of such kind as to leave his mind meanwhile free for reflection. Every thing around him is large, open, free, unartificial, and his mind insensibly, to a greater or less extent, takes a corresponding tone from the general character of the objects and associations in the midst of which he lives and moves and has his being. He is less dependent on the hourly aid of others, in the regular routine of his life, as likewise on their opinions, their example, their influence. The inequalities of social distinctions, the operation of which is attended with equal moral injury to the higher and the lower, affect less his more simple and independent course of life. He is forced more constantly to think and act for himself, with reference to those broad principles of natural right, of which all men alike, when unperverted by artificial circumstances, carry with them a common general understanding. And to live he must labor: all the various modes by which, in great congregations of men, certain classes are ingeniously able to appropriate to themselves the fruits of the general toil of the rest, being to him alike unknown and impracticable. Hence does he better appreciate the true worth and dignity of labor, and knows how to respect, with a more manly and Christian sympathy of universal brotherhood, those oppressed masses of the laboring poor, whose vast bulk constitutes the basis on which alone rests the proud apex of the social pyramid. In a word, he is a more natural, a more healthy, a more independent, a more genuine *man,*—and hence, as we have said above, the farmer is naturally a democrat; the citizen may be so, but it is in spite of many obstacles. We have here briefly, in passing, alluded to the reasons for our preference of the political support of the country over that of the city; and to the causes

of the fact that, as a general rule, the former has always been found to be the true home of American democracy; while in the latter, and in their circumradiated influence, has usually been found the main strength of that party by which, under one form and name or another, the progress of the democratic principle has, from the outset, been so bitterly and unremittingly opposed.

For Jefferson and the Jacksonians alike, the farmer who was most estimable was not the tenant, but the freeholder. He it was who enjoyed the independence that was so necessary to participation in a democratic government.

One can argue that Jeffersonian and Jacksonian Democracy provided a considerable measure of covert support for slaveholders, whose plantations were, in Democratic rhetoric, smoothly assimilated into the farm. But what this tradition could not easily accommodate was the wage laborer. This is less surprising than might be thought. It is too easily forgotten that for most of human history the status of the wage laborer has been a humble one indeed. Americans were heirs to a long and venerable tradition of hostility to wage labor. From Aristotle to the English revolution and beyond, one prominent political thinker after another stressed that the wage worker was akin to a slave. As Aristotle put it, "No man can practise virtue who is living the life of a mechanic or labourer."

These attitudes survived in Europe for hundreds of years. They were evident in the utterances of the Levellers and the Diggers during the English revolution, for example. And they reemerged in the United States to inform both Jeffersonian and Jacksonian views of wage labor. Not surprisingly, a party that was unhappy with the dependence entailed by tenant farming was unenthusiastic about the relationship between employer and worker. In fact, those who were most implacable in their hostility to the banking system—the key political issue of the 1830s—tended also to be the most distrustful of wage labor. At the furthest reaches of the Democratic party was Orestes Brownson, who, as is well known, in 1840 proposed that the party prohibit the inheritance of property. Less well known, however, is the view of wages that he expressed at the same time. Brownson's goal was to "combine labor and capital in the same individual," and he argued that it was agriculture, more than any other pursuit, that could achieve this. But even in the agricultural sector the situation was deteriorating, since "the distance between the owner of the farm, and the men who cultivate it" was "becoming every day greater and greater." Yet this problem shrank into insignificance when compared with the scene in the towns and manufacturing villages, where "the distinction between the capitalist and the proletary" was "as strongly marked as it is in the old world." For Brownson the ultimate threat to individual autonomy was the wages system. Wages were "the cunning device of the devil," and the wage system had to be eliminated, "or else one half of the human race must forever be the virtual slaves of the other."

Brownson was an unusual Democrat and an erratic partisan. More measured in his utterances was New York Senator Silas Wright, who was known to speak for the Van Burenites, in the late 1830s and early 1840s the dominant group within the party. Wright focused attention on manufacturing and complained of "the great power which the manufacturing capitalist must hold over the employee, and, by necessary consequence, over the living, the comfort, and the independence of the laborer." Similarly, Amos Kendall, one of Andrew Jackson's closest collaborators, urged the sons of farmers to remain on the farm rather than to seek employment in factories.

For Kendall the worthy citizen was either a farmer or an "independent mechanic." Here he perhaps left the way open for a modest amount of wage labor. What did he mean by *independent?* Unfortunately, it is difficult to answer this question. An independent mechanic, according to Kendall, was one who could refuse "to sell his services to any man on other conditions than those of perfect equality—both as citizens and men." Kendall may have meant here the self-employed craftsman, who sold his services not to an employer, but instead to the consumer. Or he may have meant a wage worker, whose terms of employment were not such as to produce large inequalities of wealth, power, and esteem. How were such terms to be attained? Kendall did not specify.

Other Democrats had trouble with wage labor. Like Kendall they believed that independence was essential, and like him they were unsure whether it was compatible with employment for wages. The Washington *Globe* referred approvingly to, in effect, two kinds of mechanic or artisan and had no difficulty in defining the first. He was none other than the self-employed craftsman. But a string of subordinate clauses was necessary to offer even an approximate definition of the second. The newspaper spoke of "the healthy mechanic or artisan, who works for himself at his own shop, or if he goes abroad, returns home to his meals every day, and sleeps under his own roof every night; whose earnings are regulated by the wants of the community at large, not by the discretion of a pernicious master; whose hours of labor depend on universal custom; who, when the sun goes down, is a freeman until he rises again, who can eat his meals in comfort, and sleep as long as nature requires." The problem was that the *Globe,* like Kendall and like other Democrats, did not explain how the conditions necessary for acceptable forms of wage labor were to be obtained.

In these circumstances, it was not surprising that the northern Democrats in the 1850s did not extol the wage labor system of the North. Although they were quite certain that free labor was superior to slave labor, they did not glorify wage labor. From the mid-1840s onward, of course, the nation's economy revived, and the resulting prosperity weakened Democratic radicalism. Some of it, nevertheless, persisted into the 1850s. Thus Theophilus Fisk claimed that free-soilism and abolition distracted northern workers from "their own grievous wrongs and intolerable oppressions." More significant, Fernando Wood, campaigning for Breckinridge in 1860, insisted that "until we have provided and cared for the oppressed laboring man in our own midst, we should not extend our sympathy to the laboring men of other states." As mayor of New York city in 1857, Wood set out a view of the condition of northern labor that both revived Democratic radicalism of previous decades and revealed a jaundiced view of the condition of northern wage workers: "In the days of general prosperity they [the working classes] labor for a mere subsistence whilst other classes accumulate wealth, and in the days of general depression they are the first to feel the change, without the means to avoid or endure reverses. Truly it may be said that in New York those who produce everything get nothing, and those who produce nothing get everything. They labor without income, whilst surrounded by thousands living in affluence and splendor who have income without labor."

These views were distinctly uncommon within the Democratic party in the 1850s. They were more common, however, than the celebrations of wage labor in which Republicans (as we shall see) frequently indulged. A prevalent view was simply to record the condition of the wage worker and to argue that he had no cause for complaint. Unlike that of the Republicans, Democratic rhetoric in no way privileged the role of the wage laborer or the relationship between employer and worker. Such had not been Democratic practice in the past; such was not Democratic practice in the 1850s.

In fact, most Democrats abstained from a close analysis of the northern labor system. Republicans, however, did not. While it is true that their rhetoric emphasized free labor, it is equally true that all who listened knew that Republicans had not merely reconciled themselves to wage labor, but had instead come to view it as a key element in the social order, the cement of the northern social system. Freedom, equality, the Union, American democracy itself—all depended, in Republicans' eyes, on the existence of wage labor. This view distinguished them sharply from northern Democrats; it was this, above all, that separated the two parties in the 1850s.

The importance of wage labor in the thinking of Republicans is implicit or explicit in some of the speeches of Charles Sumner. Prior to the election of 1860, Sumner began to adopt a shorthand phrase to refer to southern slavery. He began to call it "labor without wages," confident, it would seem, that this phrase would convey to his listeners the injustice inherent in the master-slave relation. In June 1860, all the evil effects of slavery were traced to its "single object of compelling men to work without wages." This, he repeated a month later, was its "single motive," its "single object." For the greater part of human history labor has been done without wages, and for much of that time, as we have seen, it would have been grounds for complaint if a system had compelled men to work *with* wages. On the same occasion, Sumner employed a familiar argument against slavery when he claimed that it was contrary to God's intentions for mankind. Less familiar, however, was his assumption about wages. "When God created man in his own image," he declared, "and saw that his work was good, he did not destine his fellow creature for endless ages to labor without wages, compelled by the lash." The rhythm of this sentence seems to require that a heavy emphasis be placed upon "without wages," perhaps as heavy as "compelled by the lash." The implication is surely that God approves of wage labor.

Sumner's attitude was made even more explicit in a rhetorical question that he put to the Senate in 1860. Speaking of "the slaveholder," he asked, "How can he show sensibility for the common rights of fellow citizens who sacrifice daily the most sacred right of others merely to secure *labor without wages?* With him a false standard is necessarily established, bringing with it a blunted moral sense and clouded perceptions, so that, when he does something intrinsically barbarous or mean, he does not blush at the recital." Here, then, is the reason Sumner believed that to refer to slavery as "labor without wages" could convey the enormity of the evil. He seems to have viewed wage labor, properly rewarded, as an anchor of morality. The passage makes no sense unless it is assumed that the wage laborer is worthy of respect or esteem. Gone is the old hostility.

Sumner, of course, was a spokesman for Radical Republicanism and represented Massachusetts, the state with the most developed economy in the Union. By contrast, Lincoln was a moderate and came from a far more agricultural state, albeit one whose economy was advancing rapidly in the 1850s. Although his social thought has often been analyzed, the significance and novelty of his view of wage labor have not been fully appreciated. In one respect, however, his views were entirely traditional: he remained somewhat critical of the worker who remained, for the duration of his working life, a wage earner. As he told a Milwaukee audience in 1859, "If any continue through life in the condition of the hired laborer," it was "because of either a dependent nature which prefers it, or improvidence, folly or singular misfortune." In the same vein, Lincoln tended to repel southern charges of wage slavery not by defending the status of the wage earner as a wage earner, but instead by pointing to his opportunities to cease to work for wages. Thus in 1856 he noted that many southerners were claiming that their slaves were "far better off than northern freemen." Lincoln did not take the modern view and reject the comparison by denying the dependence of the wage earner. Instead he charged southerners with an egregious error: "What a mistaken view do these men have of northern laborers! They think that men are always to remain laborers here—but there is no such class. The man who labored for another last year, this year labors for himself, and next year he will hire others to labor for him." Thus mobility legitimated wage labor. Lincoln also took pleasure in recording how small a proportion of the labor of the North was done for wages. At Cincinnati in 1859, he remarked that the wage system entailed "a relation of which I make no complaint." But, he added, "I do insist that the relation does not embrace more than one-eighth of the labor of the country." Though this estimate was almost certainly far wide of the mark, it may be more important to note Lincoln's defensive tone here. Clearly he was glad that wage earners did not constitute a larger proportion of the northern workforce.

At the same time, however, Lincoln glorified the wage labor—and not merely the free labor—system of the North. We can perhaps best understand this by looking at his view of mobility. More than any previous president, Lincoln emphasized social mobility. As early as 1856, he was attributing American greatness to the fact that in the United States "every man can make himself." For Jefferson and Jackson, freedom and equality had necessitated an agrarian society in which the freeholding farmer would, whether or not he went to the West, remain a freeholding farmer for his entire life, gradually acquiring a "competence" for his old age. Such a society would be characterized by an equality of conditions rather than merely an equality of opportunity. Indeed, inequalities of outcome, while inevitable, would present a danger; they would in no sense be necessary to the functioning of the economy. For Lincoln, however, the citizens of the United States, or at least those of the northern states, were engaged in "a race of life." Unequal outcomes are implicit in—indeed the very purpose of—a race. In 1864 he told an Ohio regiment that they were fighting "to secure such an inestimable jewel" as "equal privileges in the race of life." Lincoln's other favorite metaphor was also one that conveyed the idea of mobility and, more specifically, upward mobility. This involved the image of weights being lifted from shoulders. In February 1861, he told a Philadelphia audience that the unity of the nation had hitherto been maintained by "something in that Declaration [of Independence] giving liberty not alone to the people of this country, but hope to the world for all future time." This was the promise "that in due time the weights should be lifted from the shoulders of all men, and that all should have an equal chance." In his special session message of July 4, 1861 he again used both this image and the race-of-life metaphor to explain the purpose of the struggle. The Union itself was now explicable in terms of social mobility.

Mobility had also subtly narrowed the Jacksonian view of equality and liberty so that both were now understood in terms of equality of opportunity. Addressing another Ohio regiment in 1864, the President declared that "nowhere in the world is presented a government of so much liberty and equality." As if to define his terms, he immediately added, "To the humblest and poorest among us are held out the highest privileges and positions." If opportunities were equal and plentiful, then Americans were free and equal. Little wonder, then, that Lincoln invited Americans to internalize the goal social mobility, as he himself had done. "I hold [that] the value of life," he once said, is "to improve one's condition."

How was mobility to be secured? Lincoln held that "when one starts poor, as most do in the race of life, free society is such that he knows he can better his condition; he knows that there is no such fixed condition of labor, for his whole life." It was this that distinguished free labor, "which has the inspiration of hope," from slave labor, "which has no hope." For "the power of hope upon human exertion, and happiness, is wonderful." Yet, just as free labor was essential for social mobility, so, for Lincoln, were wages essential to free labor. And just as mobility legitimated wage labor, so was wage labor essential for mobility. In all Lincoln's descriptions of mobility the need for wage labor was either explicit or implicit. On one occasion free labor was actually defined in terms of the individual's progress from the rank of wage laborer to that of employer. Thus at Milwaukee in 1859 he spoke of "the prudent, penniless beginner in the world," who "labors for wages awhile, saves a surplus with which to buy tools or land for himself, then labors on his own account another while, and at length hires another new beginner to help him." The conclusion was significant: "This say its advocates, is *free* labor [emphasis added]—the just and generous and prosperous system, which opens the way for all—gives hope to all, and energy, and progress, and improvement of condition to all." Finally, and even more explicitly, at Cincinnati the same year he announced that the very purpose of American democracy was to facilitate the progress of the wage laborer: "This progress, by which the poor, honest, industrious, and resolute man raises himself, that he may work on his own account, and hire somebody else, is that progress that human nature is entitled to, is that improvement in condition that is intended to be secured by those institutions under which we live, is the great principle for which this government was really formed." Thus, for Lincoln democracy, the Union, freedom, equality, even the Declaration of Independence could not be understood except in terms of mobility, free labor, and wages.

Lincoln was not alone in these opinions. In New York City the *Times,* an exponent of conservative Republican thought, while the economy was in recession in 1857, replied to southern critics of northern society. "Our best answer," it claimed, "is that the majority of those who suffer from a panic here are by the time the next one comes around in a position not to fear it." For "the Northern artisans of 1837 . . . are the merchants, traders, farmers and statesmen of 1856 and 1857." This was thanks to "free labor," which was "our glory and our safeguard." Thus, for the *Times,* the stability of the northern social system depended on free labor and social mobility. And free labor clearly required wage labor.

There was thus a marked difference between Republican and northern Democratic perceptions of the northern social order. While both groups did not doubt that, so far as the North was concerned, free labor was superior to slavery, the Republicans enthused about the relationship between employer and wage earner, while the Democrats did not. In 1859, the *Chicago Times* neatly illustrated this difference when it chided Lincoln after one of his speeches and claimed that he had misrepresented the condition of northern workers, only 10 percent of whom could become employers. The Republicans and the Democrats saw free labor and the contrast with slavery differently. Essentially Republicans saw slavery and free labor (with its foundation in the wages system) as the bases for divergent social systems; northern Democrats perceived them rather as distinct interests.

What does it mean to say that certain values formed the core of a party's beliefs? One possible answer might be that these values were those that the party's spokesmen most often articulated. In this eventuality, it would be possible to determine which were the key Republican values by counting the references made to the slave power, to free labor, and to wage labor. In this contest it is entirely possible that the slave power would emerge the winner, wage labor a poor third. But such an analysis would be profoundly unsatisfactory.

It is frequently the case that the various components of an ideology or a worldview are interdependent, with each reinforcing, and reinforced by, many of the others. It is also, however, frequently the case that such interdependence is asymmetrical; some components give rise to others, but are less dependent upon them. So it was with wage labor and the slave power in Republican thought. Republicans saw a slave power where Democrats did not, because their faith in the northern social system was so great that they could explain the success of slavery in the South and even (to some extent) in the West only by claiming that normal democratic processes had been subverted or overturned. Since the free labor and wage labor system of the North was deemed "natural," it followed that a slave power was required to explain its failure to take hold in the South and the attempts to spread an alternative system into the West and even the North. Hence the Republicans' preference for a wage labor system can explain their references to the slave power. But this interdependence was asymmetrical: in no sense did a belief in the slave power give rise to Republican perceptions of wage labor.

There is, moreover, additional cause to emphasize the importance of wage labor. For such an emphasis immediately opens up a connection with the dominant economic processes of the mid-nineteenth century. In 1800 only about 10 percent of the American workforce was employed for wages; by 1860 the figure was about 40 percent, heavily concentrated, of course, in the North. The Democratic party, with its strength increasingly concentrated in the South, could not develop a wage labor or even a free labor ideology; indeed, it was all northerners could do to prevent their southern colleagues from placing a proslavery plank in the party platform. Finally, of course, the party split in 1860 over precisely this issue. But for some years before this Democrats in the North had experienced great difficulty in engaging with the dominant economic processes of their time. Perhaps if the panic of 1857 had lasted, a revival of the antibank and anticommercial sentiment of the 1830s and early 1840s might have solved this problem. But it did not. In these circumstances, northern Democrats were impelled to fall back on an appeal to the ethnocultural values that they had always espoused, but now without the economic and social underpinning they had previously had. In this sense, therefore, theirs was an increasingly dislocated ideology.

Here is an additional reason why the Silbey interpretation of Republicanism is unsatisfactory. Not only were the Republicans profoundly divided on all the ethnocultural questions that did not involve slavery; they knew, as most southerners knew, that the slavery question transcended issues like rum and Romanism. It raised too many vital questions about the nation's political economy to be treated in the way that the parties had treated the ethnocultural issues. A society's labor system—the question whether it should be based upon slavery or wages—is simply more important than the decision whether to introduce laws on temperance. Most partisans and observers in the 1850s knew that this was so. Of course the northern Democrats would have liked nothing more than to have subsumed slavery under the heading of "cultural politics," since they would then have had a more potent appeal to the electorate. But the history of the 1850s is, in a sense, the history of the frustration of these hopes.

In the longer view, the Republican achievement was momentous. The election of Lincoln and the victory of the North in the Civil War meant that a fundamental—indeed revolutionary—change in American politics had occurred. The American democratic tradition, forged by Jefferson and by Jackson, had given covert support to the slaveholder by assimilating the slaveholding plantation into the farm. The American democratic tradition as reconstituted in the political upheavals of the 1850s and 1860s would instead rest American democracy upon the relationship between employer and employee, between capitalist and worker, a relationship now hailed as a quintessential characteristic of a "free" society. There it remains to this day.

F U R T H E R   R E A D I N G

Ray Allen Billington, *The Protestant Crusade 1800–1860: A Study of the Origins of American Nativism* (1938).

Stuart W. Bruchey, *Enterprise: The Dynamic Economy of a Free People* (1990).

John Mack Farragher, *Sugar Creek: Life on the Illinois Prairie* (1986).

James O. Horton and Lois E. Horton, *In Hope of Liberty: Culture, Community and Protest Among Northern Free Blacks, 1700–1860* (1996).

John F. Kasson, *Civilizing the Machine: Technology and Republican Values in America, 1776–1900* (1976).

Kerby A. Miller, *Emigrants and Exiles: Ireland and the Irish Exodus to North America* (1985).

Stephan Thernstrom, *Poverty and Progress: Social Mobility in a Nineteenth Century City* (1964).

Sean Wilentz, *Chants Democratic: New York City and the Rise of the American Working Class, 1788–1850* (1984).

C H A P T E R
12

Agricultural Development
and Slavery in the
South at Midcentury

The cotton gin (short for "cotton engine") was a very simple device that had revolutionary implications. Patented by Eli Whitney in 1794, it was able to remove the seeds from short-staple cotton without damaging the fibers. Because short-staple cotton, unlike its long-staple counterpart, did not require wet, semitropical climates, it could be grown throughout much of the antebellum South. The cotton gin, then, played a central role in reinvigorating the southern economy and solidifying the slave system. Already by 1800, cotton and slavery together were spreading westward. Between 1815 and 1840, cotton output jumped from 200,000 to 1.35 million bales, each of which weighed four hundred pounds. Another cotton boom began in 1849, when output reached 2.85 million bales, and lasted until 1860, when 4.8 million bales were produced. Southern planters confidently proclaimed that "cotton was king."

By 1860, some four million people lived and worked as slaves on a belt of land stretching from Virginia into Texas. Slavery and race, moreover, influenced almost every aspect of southern society. Although most white people considered slave owning a source of economic mobility and social status and gave political deference to the wealthy planters, more than two-thirds of white families in the region owned no slaves. These non-slaveowning whites often found themselves pushed off the better land by affluent cotton, sugar, or rice entrepreneurs. Thus slavery also had its costs for many white people. Although not all black people in the South were enslaved, the "free people of color," some quarter of a million people, found their position in southern society increasingly circumscribed. As the nineteenth century wore on and the status of slave increasingly came to be equated with African ancestry, "free people of color" faced growing legal disadvantages. The rise of the cotton South, in sum, created a curious combination of opulence and misery.

Southerners justified, condemned, and accommodated themselves to the slave system in a variety of ways. Many white southerners became increasingly aware that slavery was being criticized as a system of labor whose time had passed. As Americans in the North and Europeans worked to abolish the system, the white

359

South both developed ideologies that justified slavery and increased its vigilance over enslaved people. The master class advanced a myth of paternalism like that discussed in Chapter 2. They presented themselves as custodians of the welfare of a grateful and harmonious slave society. Some went so far as to argue that slavery was "a positive good" rather than simply a necessary evil. All societies contained a working class, they argued, and enslaved people were better off than the "wage slaves" of the North because the slaveowner truly cared for his people. As apologists for slavery made these arguments, however, the South also developed increasingly harsh "slave codes" that reflected a growing fear of slave revolts incited by abolitionists. The North Carolina law prohibiting slaves to read and write, for example, contended that literacy "has a tendency to excite dissatisfaction in their minds."

In fact, laws against literacy were one among many factors that excited dissatisfaction among slaves. After toiling from sunrise to sundown, slaves were nonetheless vulnerable to complaints—supplemented by physical punishment—that they had not worked well enough. If white women could object to slavery because of illicit relationships between their men and their slaves, slave women were obviously at even greater risk. Perhaps most disheartening was the fact that an imperious master might separate slaves from their loved ones through sale.

Slaves were not powerless, of course. They used the paternalist ideology to illustrate the inherent contradictions between the ideal of a benevolent master and the reality of cruelty in slave life. Slaves also developed strategies within their own community to temper the cruelties of enslavement. The family served as an arena in which children were socialized. Christian belief likewise was a powerful resource that simultaneously allowed slaves to look to a better life after death and criticize the system of slavery in which they were set. How one might be both a slaveowner and a Christian was a telling question that few could adequately answer.

☞ QUESTIONS TO THINK ABOUT

How might southern apologists for slavery have used the northern "wage slave" discussed in the last chapter to justify slavery? To what extent do you agree with this argument? How did slaves use religious belief and kinship to temper their plight? Did this strategy play into the hands of slaveholders? How were non-slaveholding whites and "free people of color" affected by the institution of slavery?

☞ DOCUMENTS

These documents illustrate the deep imprint that slavery and plantation agriculture made on southern society. Document 1 is a North Carolina law that prohibits teaching slaves to read or write. Slave revolts and knowledge of the growing abolitionist movement in the North, many white southerners feared, would be furthered through literacy. If slaveholders feared unrest, they nonetheless developed explanations for the system of slavery. Document 2 is a good example of the argument that slavery was a "necessary evil." In this selection, the slaves are portrayed as happy people whose situations are improved by their masters. Poor whites in the South might be neither slaveholders nor slaves, as Document 3 shows, but they were nonetheless affected by the slave system. This document recounts the situation of poor whites living in Georgia. Another method used by whites in the South to describe the behavior of slaves was to attribute it to medical conditions. Document 4 is a bizarre account by a physician that describes certain diseases that are peculiar to African Americans, such as running away. If some whites deemed slavery a necessary evil, others began to see it as a "positive good," as Document 5 illustrates. In this selection, George Fitzhugh praises the peace and quiet of the South in comparison with the North. The next three documents illustrate that slaves had a different view of slavery from that of Fitzhugh. Josiah Henson, in Document 6, describes the punishments that slaves encountered and, worse yet, the divisions of family and friends that occurred when slaves were sold. Document 7 is some reminiscences about slave life by aged African Americans, recorded in the 1930s. Note how these recollections are written in the ex-slaves' dialect, which differs from the more formal accounts in the documents that precede and follow. In Document 8, Harriet Jacobs describes her trials as a young woman living in slavery. Jacobs argues that female slaves were in particular jeopardy because of the actions of powerful male slaveowners. Whereas Jacobs scolds white mistresses who did not protect female slaves, Mary Boykin Chestnut's diary in Document 9 provides us with the perspective of a slave mistress who comes close to blaming women slaves for making the plantation similar to a harem. In Document 10, Frederick Law Olmsted concludes that the slave economy as a whole is not profitable.

1. A North Carolina Law Prohibits Teaching Slaves to Read or Write, 1831

Whereas the teaching of slaves to read and write, has a tendency to excite dissatisfaction in their minds, and to produce insurrection and rebellion, to the manifest injury of the citizens of this State: Therefore, *Be it enacted by the General Assembly of the State of North Carolina, and it is hereby enacted by the authority of the same,* That any free person, who shall hereafter teach, or attempt to teach, any slave within the State to read or write, the use of figures excepted, or shall give or sell to such slave or slaves any books or pamphlets shall be liable to indictment in any court of record in this State having jurisdiction thereof, and upon conviction, shall, at the discretion of the court, if a white man or woman, be fined not less than one hundred dollars, nor more than two hundred dollars, or imprisoned; and if a free person of color, shall be fined, imprisoned, or whipped, at the discretion of the court, not exceeding thirty nine lashes, nor less than twenty lashes.

Be it further enacted, That if any slave shall hereafter teach, or attempt to teach, any other slave to read or write, the use of figures excepted, he or she may be carried before any justice of the peace and on conviction thereof, shall be sentenced to receive thirty nine lashes on his or her bare back.

2. John Pendleton Kennedy, a Southern Man, Romanticizes Slavery and the Life of Slaves, 1832

Nothing more attracted my observation than the swarms of little negroes that basked on the sunny sides of these cabins, and congregated to gaze at us as we surveyed their haunts. They were nearly all in that costume of the golden age which I have heretofore described; and showed their slim shanks and long heels in all varieties

"A North Carolina Law Forbidding the Teaching of Slaves to Read and Write" (1831), as reprinted in Joy Hakim, *A History of the U.S.: Sourcebook and Index* (New York: Oxford University Press, 1999), 108.

John Pendleton Kennedy, *Swallow Barn, or A Sojourn in the Old Dominion,* rev. ed. (New York: George P. Putnam, 1851), 449–459. Originally published in 1832.

of their grotesque natures. Their predominant love of sunshine, and their lazy, list-less postures, and apparent content to be silently looking abroad, might well afford a comparison to a set of terrapins luxuriating in the genial warmth of summer, on the logs of a mill-pond.

And there, too, were the prolific mothers of this redundant brood,—a number of stout negro-women who thronged the doors of the huts, full of idle curiosity to see us. And, when to these are added a few reverend, wrinkled, decrepit old men, with faces shortened as if with drawing-strings, noses that seemed to have run all to nostril, and with feet of the configuration of a mattock. . . .

Meriwether, I have said before, is a kind and considerate master. It is his custom frequently to visit his slaves, in order to inspect their condition, and, where it may be necessary, to add to their comforts or relieve their wants. His coming amongst them, therefore, is always hailed with pleasure. He has constituted himself into a high court of appeal, and makes it a rule to give all their petitions a patient hearing, and to do justice in the premises. This, he tells me, he considers as indispensably necessary;—he says, that no overseer is entirely to be trusted: that there are few men who have the temper to administer wholesome laws to any population, however small, without some omissions or irregularities; and that this is more emphatically true of those who administer them entirely at their own will. On the present occasion, in almost every house where Frank entered, there was some boon to be asked; and I observed, that in every case, the petitioner was either gratified or refused in such a tone as left no occasion or disposition to murmur. Most of the women had some bargains to offer, of fowls or eggs or other commodities of household use, and Meriwether generally referred them to his wife, who, I found, relied almost entirely on this resource, for the supply of such commodities; the negroes being regularly paid for whatever was offered in this way.

One old fellow had a special favour to ask,—a little money to get a new padding for his saddle, which, he said, "galled his cretur's back." Frank, after a few jocular passages with the veteran, gave him what he desired, and sent him off rejoicing.

"That, sir," said Meriwether, "is no less a personage than Jupiter. He is an old bachelor, and has his cabin here on the hill. He is now near seventy, and is a kind of King of the Quarter. He has a horse, which he extorted from me last Christmas; and I seldom come here without finding myself involved in some new demand, as a con-sequence of my donation. Now he wants a pair of spurs which, I suppose, I must give him. He is a preposterous coxcomb, and Ned has administered to his vanity by a present of a *chapeau de bras*—a relic of my military era, which he wears on Sundays with a conceit that has brought upon him as much envy as admiration—the usual condition of greatness."

The air of contentment and good humor and kind family attachment, which was apparent throughout this little community, and the familiar relations existing be-tween them and the proprietor struck me very pleasantly. I came here a stranger, in great degree, to the negro character, knowing but little of the domestic history of these people, their duties, habits or temper, and somewhat disposed, indeed, from prepossessions, to look upon them as severely dealt with, and expecting to have my sympathies excited towards them as objects of commiseration. I have had, therefore, rather a special interest in observing them. The contrast between my preconceptions of their condition and the reality which I have witnessed, has brought me a most aggreable surprise. I will not say that, in a high state of cultivation and of such self-dependence as they might possibly attain in a separate national existence, they might not become a more respectable people; but I am quite sure they never could become a happier people than I find them here. . . . [N]o tribe of people have ever passed from barbarism to civilization whose middle stage of progress has been more secure from harm, more genial to their character, or better supplied with mild and beneficient guardianship, adapted to the actual state of their intellectual feebleness, than the negroes of Swallow Barn. And, from what I can gather, it is pretty much the same on the other estates in this region.

3. A Southerner Observes the Life of Poor Whites in Georgia, 1849

It was morning when I left Tallula, and before nightfall I had ridden thirty miles. No pleasant villages, with neat white cottages and ornamented gardens, so many of which one sees in a day's ride through New-England, greeted my vision; but the log-cabins of the "squatters" scattered here and there, with an occasional frame-house of the rudest construction, were seen.

I met no one walking: all ride, however poor. Sometimes two are seen on the same animal; a man and woman, perhaps, on one poor doleful-looking mule, or on some antiquated horse, more cadaverous looking than themselves. I met also large wagons, canvass covered, drawn by four or six mules, and driven by negroes. As night approached, I saw the camp-fires of these drivers, they sitting about the fire, on the ground, cooking "hog and hominy," cracking rude jokes, singing "corn songs" and laughing their loud "Yah! yah!" as the whiskey-bottle passed among them.

Being anxious to see how the poorest class of people lived in the interior, at night I stopped at the door-way of a very small and rudely-constructed hut, and inquired if I could "get stay" for the night. At first I was refused; but upon representing myself a stranger in the country, and fearing to go farther, as there were "forks in the road" and "creeks to cross" before reaching another house, they finally consented to my staying.

The cabin contained but one room, with no windows; the chimney, built of mud and stones, was, as is usual in the South, outside the house. The furniture of the house was scanty in the extreme: a roughly-constructed frame, on which was laid a corn-shuck mattress, a pine table, and a few shuck-bottomed "cha'rs."

I had not been long in this place, before preparations for supper commenced. An iron vessel—a "spider," so called—was brought and set over the fire; in this dish was roasted some coffee; afterward, in the same dish, a "corn cake" was baked, and still again some rank old ham was fried, and the corn-cake laid in the ashes to have it "piping hot." This constituted our supper, which, being placed on the table, three of us sat down to partake, of, while Cynthia, the youngest daughter, held a blazing light-wood knot for us to see by, and the "gude woman" sat in the corner "rubbing

Eugene L. Schwaab, ed., *Travels in the Old South* (Lexington: University Press of Kentucky, 1973). Reprinted with permission of The University Press of Kentucky.

snuff," or "dipping," with her infant in her arms. A pet deer stalked in through the open door-way, and helped himself from the table without molestation.

Bed-time coming, one by one the family retired to the corner, and all lay together on the corn-shucks, sleeping as soundly as on "downy couch." Taking my saddle-bags for a pillow, and wrapping my blanket around me, I laid down before the fast dying embers, and was soon in the embrace of "tired nature's sweet restorer." Morning came, and as I was to leave early, all were up "by sun." I asked the hostess for a wash, and the vessel which had served for roasting, baking and frying in the evening previous was now brought; and, "'tis true, 'tis pity, and pity 'tis 'tis true," I washed myself in the dish out of which twelve hours before I had eaten a hearty supper. I paid them well, and thanked them kindly, for they had given me the best they had. Destitute as they were, they seemed contented and happy: "Where ignorance is bliss, 'tis folly to be wise."

4. Dr. Cartwright, a Southern Doctor, Theorizes About the Peculiar Diseases of Slaves, 1851

MISCELLANEOUS DEPARTMENT.

1.—DISEASES AND PECULIARITIES OF THE NEGRO RACE.

By Dr. Cartwright of New-Orleans—(Concluded.)

DRAPETOMANIA, OR THE DISEASE CAUSING NEGROES TO RUN AWAY.

Drapetomania is from δραπέτης, a runaway slave, and μανια, *mad or crazy*. It is unknown to our medical authorities, although its diagnostic symptom, the absconding from service, is . . . well known to our planters and overseers. . . . The cause, in the most of cases, that induces the negro to run away from service, is as much a disease of the mind as any other species of mental alienation, and much more curable, as a general rule. With the advantages of proper medical advice, strictly followed, this troublesome practice that many negroes have of running away, can be almost entirely prevented, although the slaves be located on the borders of a free state, within a stone's throw of the abolitionists. . . .

To ascertain the true method of governing negroes, so as to cure and prevent the disease under consideration, we must go back to the Pentateuch, and learn the true meaning of the untranslated term that represents the negro race. In the name there given to that race, is locked up the true art of governing negroes in such a manner that they cannot run away. The correct translation of that term declares the Creator's will in regard to the negro; it declares him to be the submissive knee-bender. In the anatomical conformation of his knees we see *"genu flexit"* written in his physical structure, being more flexed or bent, than any other kind of man. If the white man attempts to oppose the Deity's will, by trying to make the negro anything

Dr. Cartwright, "Diseases and Peculiarities of the Negro Race," *De Bow's Review* 2, no. 3 (September 1851): 331–332, 334–336.

else than *"the submissive knee-bender,"* (which the Almighty declared he should be,) by trying to raise him to a level with himself, or by putting himself on an equality with the negro; or if he abuses the power which God has given him over his fellow-man, by being cruel to him, or punishing him in anger, or by neglecting to protect him from wanton abuses of his fellow-servants and all others, or by denying him the usual comforts and necessaries of life, the negro will run away; but if he keeps him in the position that we learn from the Scriptures he was intended to occupy, that is, the position of submission; and if his master or overseer be kind and gracious in his bearing towards him, without condescension, and at the same time ministers to his physical wants, and protects him from abuses, the negro is spell-bound, and cannot run away. . . .

When left to himself, the negro indulges in his natural disposition to idleness and sloth, and does not take exercise enough to expand his lungs and to vitalize his blood, but dozes out a miserable existence in the midst of filth and uncleanliness, being too indolent, and having too little energy of mind to provide for himself proper food and comfortable lodging and clothing. The consequence is, that the blood becomes so highly carbonized and deprived of oxygen, that it not only becomes unfit to stimulate the brain to energy, but unfit to stimulate the nerves of sensation distributed to the body. A torpor and insensibility pervades the system; the sentient nerves distributed to the skin lose their feeling in so great a degree, that he often burns his skin by the fire he hovers over without knowing it, and frequently has large holes in his clothes, and the shoes on his feet burnt to a crisp, without having been conscious of when it was done. This is the disease called dysæsthesia. . . .

The complaint is easily curable, if treated on sound physiological principles. . . . Any kind of labor will do that will cause full and free respiration in its performance, as lifting or carrying heavy weights, or brisk walking; the object being to expand the lungs by full and deep inspiration and expirations, thereby to vitalize the impure circulating blood by introducing oxygen and expelling carbon. . . .

According to unaltered physiological laws, negroes, as a general rule to which there are but few exceptions, can only have their intellectual faculties awakened in a sufficient degree to receive moral culture and to profit by religious or other instructions, when under the compulsatory authority of the white man; because, as a general rule to which there are but few exceptions, they will not take sufficient exercise, when removed from the white man's authority, to vitalize and decarbonize their blood by the process of full and free respiration, that active exercise of some kind alone can effect. . . .

. . . The dysæsthesia æthiopica adds another to the many ten thousand evidences of the fallacy of the dogma that abolitionism is built on; for here, in a country where two races of men dwell together, both born on the same soil, breathing the same air, and surrounded by the same external agents—liberty, which is elevating the one race of people above all other nations, sinks the other into beastly sloth and torpidity; and the slavery, which the one would prefer death rather than endure, improves the other in body, mind and morals; thus proving the dogma false, and establishing the truth that there is a radical, internal or physical difference between the two races, so great in kind, as to make what is wholesome and beneficial for the white man, as liberty, republican or free institutions, etc., not only unsuitable to the negro race, but actually poisonous to its happiness.

5. George Fitzhugh Argues That Slavery Is a Positive Good That Improves Society, 1854

At the slaveholding South all is peace, quiet, plenty and contentment. We have no mobs, no trade unions, no strikes for higher wages, no armed resistance to the law, but little jealousy of the rich by the poor. We have but few in our jails, and fewer in our poor houses. We produce enough of the comforts and necessaries of life for a population three or four times as numerous as ours. We are wholly exempt from the torrent of pauperism, crime, agrarianism, and infidelity which Europe is pouring from her jails and alms houses on the already crowded North. Population increases slowly, wealth rapidly. In the tide water region of Eastern Virginia, as far as our experience extends, the crops have doubled in fifteen years, whilst the population has been almost stationary. In the same period the lands, owing to improvements of the soil and the many fine houses erected in the country, have nearly doubled in value. This ratio of improvement has been approximated or exceeded wherever in the South slaves are numerous. We have enough for the present, and no Malthusian* spectres frightening us for the future. Wealth is more equally distributed than at the North, where a few millionaires own most of the property of the country. (These millionaires are men of cold hearts and weak minds; they know how to make money, but not how to use it, either for the benefit of themselves or of others.) High intellectual and moral attainments, refinement of head and heart, give standing to a man in the South, however poor he may be. Money is, with few exceptions, the only thing that ennobles at the North. We have poor among us. But none who are over-worked and under-fed. We do not crowd cities because lands are abundant and their owners kind, merciful and hospitable. The poor are as hospitable as the rich, the negro as the white man. Nobody dreams of turning a friend, a relative, or a stranger from his door. The very negro who deems it no crime to steal, would scorn to sell his hospitality. We have no loafers, because the poor relative or friend who borrows our horse, or spends a week under our roof, is a welcome guest. The loose economy, the wasteful mode of living at the South, is a blessing when rightly considered; it keeps want, scarcity and famine at a distance, because it leaves room for retrenchment. The nice, accurate economy of France, England and New England, keeps society always on the verge of famine, because it leaves no room to retrench, that is to live on a part only of what they now consume. Our society exhibits no appearance of precocity, no symptoms of decay. A long course of continuing improvement is in prospect before us, with no limits which human foresight can descry. Actual liberty and equality with our white population has been approached much nearer than in the free States. Few of our whites ever work as day laborers, none as cooks, scullions, ostlers, body servants, or in other menial capacities. One free citizen does not lord it over another; hence that feeling of independence and equality that distinguishes us; hence that pride of character, that self-respect, that give us ascendancy when we come in contact with Northerners. It is a distinction to be a Southerner, as it was once to be a Roman citizen.

George Fitzhugh, *Sociology for the South, or the Failure of Free Society* (Richmond, Va.: A. Morris, 1854), Appendix, pp. 253–255.

*Reverend Thomas Malthus was a British economic philosopher who, in 1798, argued that there was a tendency in nature for populations to exceed their means of subsistence and resources, resulting in disease, famine, and other suffering.

6. Josiah Henson Portrays the Violence and Fears in Slave Life, 1858

I was born June 15th, 1789, in Charles County, Maryland. . . . My mother was a slave of Dr. Josiah McPherson, but hired to the Mr. Newman to whom my father belonged. The only incident I can remember which occurred while my mother continued on Mr. Newman's farm, was the appearance one day of my father with his head bloody and his back lacerated. He was beside himself with mingled rage and suffering. The explanation I picked up from the conversation of others only partially explained the matter to my mind; but as I grew older I understood it all. It seemed the overseer had sent my mother away from the other field hands to a retired place, and after trying persuasion in vain, had resorted to force to accomplish a brutal purpose. Her screams aroused my father at his distant work, and running up, he found his wife struggling with the man. Furious at the sight, he sprung upon him like a tiger. In a moment the overseer was down, and, mastered by rage, my father would have killed him but for the entreaties of my mother, and the overseer's own promise that nothing should be said of the matter. The promise was kept—like most promises of the cowardly and debased—as long as the danger lasted. . . .

. . . The authorities were soon in pursuit of my father. The fact of the sacrilegious act of lifting a hand against the sacred temple of a white man's body . . . this was all it was necessary to establish. And the penalty followed: one hundred lashes on the bare back, and to have the right ear nailed to the whipping-post, and then severed from the body. . . .

The day for the execution of the penalty was appointed. The Negroes from the neighboring plantations were summoned, for their moral improvement, to witness the scene. A powerful blacksmith named Hewes laid on the stripes. Fifty were given, during which the cries of my father might be heard a mile, and then a pause ensued. True, he had struck a white man, but as valuable property he must not be damaged. Judicious men felt his pulse. Oh! he could stand the whole. Again and again the thong fell on his lacerated back. His cries grew fainter and fainter, till a feeble groan was the only response to his final blows. His head was then thrust against the post, and his right ear fastened to it with a tack; a swift pass of a knife, and the bleeding member was left sticking to the place. Then came a hurrah from the degraded crowd, and the exclamation, "That's what he's got for striking a white man." A few said, "it's a damned shame"; but the majority regarded it as but a proper tribute to their offended majesty. . . .

. . . [F]rom this hour he became utterly changed. Sullen, morose, and dogged, nothing could be done with him. The milk of human kindness in his heart was turned to gall. . . . No fear or threats of being sold to the far south—the greatest of all terrors to the Maryland slave—would render him tractable. So off he was sent to Alabama. What was his fate neither my mother nor I have ever learned. . . .

Our term of happy union as one family was now, alas! at an end. Mournful as was [Dr. McPherson's] death to his friends it was a far greater calamity to us. The estate and the slaves must be sold and the proceeds divided among the heirs. We were but property—not a mother, and the children God had given her.

Josiah Henson, *Uncle Tom's Story of His Life: An Autobiography of the Rev. Josiah Henson* (London, 1877).

Common as are slave-auctions in the southern states, and naturally as a slave may look forward to the time when he will be put upon the block, still the full misery of the event—of the scenes which precede and succeed it—is never understood till the actual experience comes. The first sad announcement that the sale is to be; the knowledge that all ties of the past are to be sundered; the frantic terror at the idea of being "sent south"; the almost certainty that one member of a family will be torn from another; the anxious scanning of purchasers' faces; the agony at parting, often forever, with husband, wife, child—these must be seen and felt to be fully understood. Young as I was then, the iron entered into my soul. The remembrance of breaking up of McPherson's estate is photographed in its minutest features in my mind. The crowd collected around the stand, the huddling group of Negroes, the examination of muscle, teeth, the exhibition of agility, the look of the auctioneer, the agony of my mother—I can shut my eyes and see them all.

My brothers and sisters were bid off first, and one by one, while my mother, paralyzed by grief, held me by the hand. Her turn came, and she was bought by Isaac Riley of Montgomery County. Then I was offered to the assembled purchasers. My mother, half distracted by the thought of parting forever from all her children, pushed through the crowd, while the bidding for me was going on, to the spot where Riley was standing. She fell at his feet and clung to his knees, entreating him in tones that a mother only could command, to buy her baby as well as herself, and spare to her one, at least of her little ones. Will it, can it be believed that this man, thus appealed to, was capable not merely of turning a deaf ear to her supplication, but of disengaging himself from her with such violent blows and kicks, as to reduce her to the necessity of creeping out of his reach, and mingling the groan of bodily suffering with the sob of a breaking heart? As she crawled away from the brutal man I heard her sob out, "Oh, Lord Jesus, how long, how long shall I suffer this way!" I must have been then between five and six years old. I seem to see and hear my poor weeping mother now. This was one of my earliest observations of men; an experience which I only shared with thousands of my race.

7. Former Slaves Recall Their Lives in Slavery, 1850s

Sarah Gudger
Age When interviewed: 121

. . . I sure has had a hard life. Just work and work and work. I never know nothin' but work. . . .

My pappy, he lived with Joe Gudger. He old and feeble, I 'members. He depend on my pappy to see after everythin' for him. He always trust my pappy. One mornin' he follow Pappy to de field. Pappy he stop his work and ole Marse Joe, he say: "Well, Smart (Pappy, he name Smart), I'se tired, worried, and troubled. All dese years I work for my chillen. Dey never do de right thing. Dey worries me, Smart. I

Norman R. Yetman, *Life Under the "Peculiar Institution": Selections from the Slave Narrative Collection* (New York: Holt, Rinehart and Winston Inc., 1970), 150–153, 256–259.

tell, you, Smart, I'se a good mind to put myself away. I'se a good mind to drown myself right here. I terrible worried, Smart."

Pappy, he take hold Old Marse Joe and lead him to de house. "Now Marse Joe, I wouldn't talk such talk iffen I'se you. You been good to you family. Just you content yo'self and rest." But a few days after dat, Ole Marse Joe was found a-hangin' in de barn by de bridle. Old Marse had put heself away. . . .

De rich white folks never did no work; dey had darkies to do it for dem. In de summer we had to work outdoors, in de winter in de house. I had to card and spin till ten o'clock. Never get much rest, had to get up at four de next mornin' and start again. Didn't get much to eat, neither, just a li'l corn bread and 'lasses. Lordy, you cain't know what a time I had. . . .

I members when my ole mammy die. She lived on Reems Creek with other Hemphills. She sick long time. One day white man come to see me. He say: "Sarah, did you know you mammy was dead?" "No," I say, "but I wants to see my mother afore dey puts her away." I went to de house and say to Ole Missie: "My mother she die today. I wants to see my mother afore dey puts her away," but she look at me mean and say: "Get on out of here, and get back to you work afore I wallop you good." So I went back to my work, with the tears streamin' down my face, just a-ringin' my hands, I wanted to see my mammy so. . . .

I was getting along smartly in years when de War come. . . .

. . . Many de time we get word de Yankees comin'. We take our food and stock and hide it till we sure dey's gone. We weren't bothered much. . . .

When de War was over, Marse William he say: "Did yo' all know yo'all's free. You free now." I chuckle, 'memberin' what de ole woman tell us about freedom, and no learnin'. Lots o' men want me to go to foreign land, but I tell 'em I go live with my pappy, long as he live. I stay with de white folks about twelve months, den I stay with my pappy long as he live.

Ferebe Rogers
Age When interviewed: 100+

I 'members a whole heap about slavery times. When freedom come I had five chillen. Five chillen and ten cents. Dey says I'm a hundred and eight or nine years old, but I don't think I'm quite as old as dat. I knows I'se over a hundred, though. I was bred and born on a plantation on Brier Creek in Baldwin County. My old marster was Mr. Sam Hart. He owned my mother. She had thirteen chillen. I was de oldest, so I took devil's fare.

My daddy was a old-time free nigger. He was a good shoemaker and could make as fine shoes and boots as every you see. But he never would work till he was plumb out o' money—den he had to work. But he quit just soon as he made a little money. . . . De old-time free niggers had to tell how dey make day livin', and if dey couldn't give satisfaction about it, dey was put on de block and sold to de highest bidder. Most of 'em sold for three years for fifty dollars. My daddy brought one hundred dollars when he was sold for three or four years.

I was on de block twice myself. When de old head died dey was so many slaves for de chillen to draw for, we was put on de block. Mr. John Bagget bought me den, and said I was a good breedin' woman. . . .

I was a field hand myself. I come twixt de plow handles. I weren't de fastest one with a hoe, but I didn't turn my back on nobody plowin'. My marster had over a thousand acres o' land. He was good to us. We had plenty to eat, like meat and bread and vegetables. We raised everything on de plantation—wheat, corn, potatoes, peas, hogs, cows, chickens, sheep—just everything.

. . . My husband was Kinchen Rogers. His marster was Mr. Bill Golden, and he lived about four miles from where I stayed on de Hart plantation. . . . I went to church Sundays, and dat's where I met my husband. I been married just one time. He de daddy o' all my chillen. I had fifteen in all.

Young marster was fixin' to marry us, but he got cold feet, and a nigger by name o' Enoch Golden married us. He was what we called a "double-headed nigger"— he could read and write, and he knowed so much. On his dyin' bed he said he been de death o' many a nigger 'cause he taught so many to read and write.

Me and my husband couldn't live together till after freedom 'cause we had different marsters. When freedom come, Marster wanted all us niggers to sign up to stay till Christmas. After dat we worked on shares on de Hart plantation; den we farmed four-five years with Mr. Bill Johnson.

I'm goin' to tell you de truth. I don't tell no lies. Dese has been better times to me. I think it's better to work for yourself and have what you make dan to work for somebody else and don't get nothin' out of it. Slavery days was mighty hard. My marster was good to us (I mean he didn't beat us much, and he give us plenty plain food), but some slaves suffered awful. My aunt was beat cruel once, and lots de other slaves. When dey got ready to beat you, dey'd strip you stark mother naked and dey'd say, "Come here to me, God damn you! Come to me clean! Walk up to dat tree, and damn you, hug dat tree!" Den dey tie your hands round de tree, den tie you feets; den dey'd lay de rawhide on you and cut your buttocks open. Sometimes dey'd rub turpentine and salt in de raw places, and den beat you some more. Oh, it was awful! And what could you do? Dey had all de advantage of you. . . .

I had my right arm cut off at de elbow if I'd tried to learn to read and write. If dey found a nigger what could read and write, dey'd cut your arm off at de elbow, or sometimes at de shoulder.

George Rogers
Age When interviewed: 94

George Rogers is the name I has carried for ninety-four years and over. I will be ninety-five the first day of this comin' August. . . .

. . . My marster was a good man. We had no church on the plantation, but we had prayer meeting in our houses. He allowed dat and when dey had a big meeting, he made us all go. We had dances or anything else we wanted to at night. We had corn shuckings, candy pullings, and all the whiskey and brandy we wanted. My daddy didn't do nothin' but still for him. Whiskey was only ten cents a quart den.

I have never seen him really whip a slave any more dan he whipped his own chillens.

8. Harriet Jacobs Deplores Her Risks
in Being a Female Slave, 1861

During the first years of my service in Dr. Flint's family, I was accustomed to share some indulgences with the children of my mistress. Though this seemed to me no more than right, I was grateful for it, and tried to merit the kindness by the faithful discharge of my duties. But I now entered on my fifteenth year—a sad epoch in the life of a slave girl. My master began to whisper foul words in my ear. Young as I was, I could not remain ignorant of their import. I tried to treat them with indifference or contempt. The master's age, my extreme youth, and the fear that his conduct would be reported to my grandmother, made him bear this treatment for many months. He was a crafty man, and resorted to many means to accomplish his purposes. Sometimes he had stormy, terrific ways, that made his victims tremble; sometimes he assumed a gentleness that he thought must surely subdue. . . . He peopled my young mind with unclean images, such as only a vile monster could think of. I turned from him with disgust and hatred. But he was my master. I was compelled to live under the same roof with him—where I saw a man forty years my senior daily violating the most sacred commandments of nature. He told me I was his property; that I must be subject to his will in all things. . . . No matter whether the slave girl be as black as ebony or as fair as her mistress. In either case, there is no shadow of law to protect her from insult, from violence, or even from death. . . . The mistress, who ought to protect the helpless victim, has no other feelings towards her but those of jealousy and rage. The degradation, the wrongs, the vices, that grow out of slavery, are more than I can describe. They are greater than you would willingly believe. Surely, if you credited one half the truths that are told you concerning the helpless millions suffering in this cruel bondage, you at the north would not help to tighten the yoke. You surely would refuse to do for the master, on your own soil, the mean and cruel work which trained bloodhounds and the lowest class of whites do for him at the south. . . .

I once saw two beautiful children playing together. One was a fair white child; the other was her slave, and also her sister. When I saw them embracing each other, and heard their joyous laughter, I turned sadly away from the lovely sight. I foresaw the inevitable blight that would fall on the little slave's heart. I knew how soon her laughter would be changed to sighs. The fair child grew up to be a still fairer woman. From childhood to womanhood her pathway was blooming with flowers, and overarched by a sunny sky. Scarcely one day of her life had been clouded when the sun rose on her happy bridal morning.

How had those years dealt with her slave sister, the little playmate of her childhood? She, also, was very beautiful; but the flowers and sunshine of love were not for her. She drank the cup of sin, and shame, and misery, whereof her persecuted race are compelled to drink.

Harriet Jacobs, *The Trials of Girlhood* (1861), as reprinted in Erik Brunn and Jay Crosby, eds., *Our Nation's Archive* (New York: Black Dog and Leventhal Publishers, 1999), 291–293.

In view of these things, why are ye silent, ye free men and women of the north? Why do your tongues falter in maintenance of the right? Would that I had more ability! But my heart is so full, and my pen is so weak! There are noble men and women who plead for us, striving to help those who cannot help themselves. God bless them! God give them strength and courage to go on! God bless those, every where, who are laboring to advance the cause of humanity!

9. Mary Chestnut Describes Her Hatred of Slavery from a White Woman's View, 1861

I wonder if it be a sin to think slavery a curse to any land. Men and women are punished when their masters and mistresses are brutes, not when they do wrong. Under slavery, we live surrounded by prostitutes, yet an abandoned woman is sent out of any decent house. Who thinks any worse of a Negro or mulatto woman for being a thing we can't name? God forgive us, but ours is a monstrous system, a wrong and an iniquity! Like the patriarchs of old, our men live all in one house with their wives and their concubines; and the mulattoes one sees in every family partly resemble the white children. Any lady is ready to tell you who is the father of all the mulatto children in everybody's household but her own. Those, she seems to think, drop from the clouds. My disgust sometimes is boiling over. Thank God for my country women, but alas for the men! They are probably no worse than men everywhere, but the lower their mistresses, the more degraded they must be. . . .

I hate slavery. You say there are no more fallen women on a plantation than in London, in proportion to numbers; but what do you say to this? A magnate who runs a hideous black harem with its consequences under the same roof with his lovely white wife, and his beautiful and accomplished daughters? He holds his head as high and poses as the model of all human virtues to these poor women whom God and the laws have given him. From the height of his awful majesty, he scolds and thunders at them, as if he never did wrong in his life. Fancy such a man finding his daughter reading "Don Juan." "You with that immoral book!" And he orders her out of his sight. You see, Mrs. Stowe did not hit the sorest spot. She makes Legree a bachelor.

Someone said: "Oh, I know half a Legree [villain in *Uncle Tom's Cabin*], a man said to be as cruel as Legree. But the other half of him did not correspond. He was a man of polished manners, and the best husband and father and church member in the world." "Can that be so?" "Yes, I know it. And I knew the dissolute half of Legree. He was high and mighty, but the kindest creature to his slaves; and the unfortunate results of his bad ways were not sold. They had not to jump over ice blocks. They were kept in full view, and were provided for, handsomely, in his will. His wife and daughters, in their purity and innocence, are supposed never to dream of what is as plain before their eyes as the sunlight. And they play their parts of unsuspecting angels to the letter. They profess to adore their father as the model of all earthly goodness."

"Well, yes. If he is rich, he is the fountain from whence all [blessings] flow."

Mary Boykin Chestnut, *A Diary from Dixie* (1861), ed. Ben Ames Williams (Boston: Houghton Mifflin, 1949), 21–22, 122–123, 162.

"The one I have in my eye, my half of Legree, the dissolute half, was so furious in his temper, and so thundered his wrath at the poor women that they were glad to let him do as he pleased if they could only escape his everlasting fault-finding and noisy bluster." . . .

". . . The make-believe angels were of the last century. . . . Women were brought up not to judge their fathers or their husbands. They took them as the Lord provided, and were thankful." . . .

"You wander from the question I asked. Are Southern men worse because of the slave system, and the facile black women?"

"Not a bit! They see too much of them. The barroom people don't drink, the confectionary people loathe candy. Our men are sick of the black sight of them!" . . .

Martha Adamson is a beautiful mulattress, as good looking as they ever are to me. I have never seen a mule as handsome as a horse, and I know I never will; no matter how I lament and sympathize with its undeserved mule condition. She is a trained sempstress, and "hired her own time, as they call it; that is, the owner pays doctor's bills, finds food and clothing, and the slave pays his master five dollars a month, more or less, and makes a dollar a day if he pleases. Martha, to the amazement of everybody, married a coal-black Negro, the son of Dick the Barber, who was set free fifty years ago for faithful services rendered Mr. Chestnut's grandfather. She was asked: How could she? She is so nearly white. How could she marry that horrid Negro? It is positively shocking! She answered that she inherits the taste of her white father, that her mother was black.

10. Frederick Law Olmsted Depicts the Economic Costs of Slavery, 1861

One of the grand errors out of which this rebellion has grown came from supposing that whatever nourishes wealth and gives power to an ordinary civilized community must command as much for a slaveholding community. The truth has been overlooked that the accumulation of wealth and the power of a nation are contingent not merely upon the primary value of the surplus of productions of which it has to dispose, but very largely also upon the way in which the income from its surplus is distributed and reinvested. Let a man be absent from almost any part of the North twenty years, and he is struck, on his return, by what we call the "improvements" which have been made: better buildings, churches, schoolhouses, mills, railroads, etc. In New York city alone, for instance, at least two hundred millions of dollars have been reinvested merely in an improved housing of the people; in labour-saving machinery, waterworks, gasworks, etc., and much more. It is not difficult to see where the profits of our manufacturers and merchants are. Again, go into the country, and there is no end of substantial proof of twenty years of agricultural prosperity, not alone in roads, canals, bridges, dwellings, barns and fences, but in books and furniture, and gardens, and pictures, and in the better dress and evidently higher education of the people. But where will the returning traveller see the accumulated

Frederick Law Olmsted, *The Cotton Kingdom; A Traveler's Observations on Cotton and Slavery in the American Slave States* (New York: Mason Brothers, 1861), 1: 24–26.

cotton profits of twenty years in Mississippi? Ask the cotton-planter for them, and he will point in reply, not to dwellings, libraries, churches, schoolhouses, mills, rail-roads, or anything of the kind; he will point to his negroes—to almost nothing else. Negroes such as stood for five hundred dollars once, now represent a thousand dollars. We must look then in Virginia and those Northern Slave States which have the monopoly of supplying negroes for the real wealth which the sale of cotton has brought to the South. But where is the evidence of it? where anything to compare with the evidence of accumulated profits to be seen in any Free State? If certain portions of Virginia have been a little improving, others unquestionably have been deteriorating, growing shabbier, more comfortless, less convenient. The total increase in wealth of the population during the last twenty years shows for almost nothing. One year's improvements of a Free State exceed it all.

It is obvious that to the community at large, even in Virginia, the profits of sup-plying negroes to meet the wants occasioned by the cotton demand have not compen-sated for the bar which the high cost of all sorts of human service, which the cotton demand has also occasioned, has placed upon all other means of accumulating wealth; and this disadvantage of the cotton monopoly is fully experienced by the negro-breeders themselves, in respect to everything else they have to produce or obtain.

ESSAYS

The contradictions of a world of slaves and slaveholders in a nation that prided itself on individual freedom and rights have long occupied historians. Scholars have considered how slaves could use these contradictions to carve out greater power in what by all accounts was a brutal institution. The two essays in this chapter illustrate how historians have stressed various aspects of the incongruities of freedom and slavery. Eugene D. Genovese, Distinguished Scholar-in-Residence at the University Center in Atlanta, Georgia, stresses the role of paternalism in creating links between slaves and slave-holders. Because masters felt it necessary to justify the morality of slavery through paternalism, slaves won a moral victory that they could use to their advantage. James Oakes, who teaches history at Northwestern University, stresses the contradictions be-tween the liberal world of slaveholders and the system of slavery. Rather than focusing on the tensions within a paternalist ethic, Professor Oakes stresses the contradictions that arose when slaveholders used notions of rights to justify slavery. Slavery could not exist without sanction from the government, but this justification ultimately regulated and restricted the rights of slaveholders.

The Paternalist World of the Slave South

EUGENE D. GENOVESE

Cruel, unjust, exploitative, oppressive, slavery bound two peoples together in bitter antagonism while creating an organic relationship so complex and ambivalent that neither could express the simplest human feelings without reference to the other. Slavery rested on the principle of property in man—of one man's appropriation of

Eugene D. Genovese, *Roll, Jordan, Roll: The World the Slaves Made* (New York: Vintage Books, 1972), 3–7, 87–93. Copyright © 1972, 1974 by Eugene D. Genovese. Used by permission of Pantheon Books, a division of Random House, Inc.

another's person as well as of the fruits of his labor. By definition and in essence it was a system of class rule, in which some people lived off the labor of others. American slavery subordinated one race to another and thereby rendered its fundamental class relationships more complex and ambiguous; but they remained class relationships. The racism that developed from racial subordination influenced every aspect of American life and remains powerful. But slavery as a system of class rule predated racism and racial subordination in world history and once existed without them. Racial subordination, as postbellum American developments and the history of modern colonialism demonstrate, need not rest on slavery. Wherever racial subordination exists, racism exists; therefore, southern slave society and its racist ideology had much in common with other systems and societies. But southern slave society was not merely one more manifestation of some abstraction called racist society. Its history was essentially determined by particular relationships of class power in racial form.

The Old South, black and white, created a historically unique kind of paternalist society. To insist upon the centrality of class relations as manifested in paternalism is not to slight the inherent racism or to deny the intolerable contradictions at the heart of paternalism itself. Imamu Amiri Baraka captures the tragic irony of paternalist social relations when he writes that slavery "was, most of all, a paternal institution" and yet refers to "the filthy paternalism and cruelty of slavery." Southern paternalism, like every other paternalism, had little to do with Ole Massa's ostensible benevolence, kindness, and good cheer. It grew out of the necessity to discipline and morally justify a system of exploitation. It did encourage kindness and affection, but it simultaneously encouraged cruelty and hatred. The racial distinction between master and slave heightened the tension inherent in an unjust social order.

Southern slave society grew out of the same general historical conditions that produced the other slave regimes of the modern world. The rise of a world market—the development of new tastes and of manufactures dependent upon non-European sources of raw materials—encouraged the rationalization of colonial agriculture under the ferocious domination of a few Europeans. African labor provided the human power to fuel the new system of production in all the New World slave societies, which, however, had roots in different European experiences and emerged in different geographical, economic, and cultural conditions. They had much in common, but each was unique.

Theoretically, modern slavery rested, as had ancient slavery, on the idea of a slave as *instrumentum vocale*—a chattel, a possession, a thing, a mere extension of his master's will. But the vacuousness of such pretensions had been exposed long before the growth of New World slave societies. The closing of the ancient slave trade, the political crisis of ancient civilization, and the subtle moral pressure of an ascendant Christianity had converged in the early centuries of the new era to shape a seigneurial world in which lords and serfs (not slaves) faced each other with reciprocal demands and expectations. This land-oriented world of medieval Europe slowly forged the traditional paternalist ideology to which the southern slaveholders fell heir.

The slaveholders of the South, unlike those of the Caribbean, increasingly resided on their plantations and by the end of the eighteenth century had become an entrenched regional ruling class. The paternalism encouraged by the close living of masters and slaves was enormously reinforced by the closing of the African slave trade, which compelled masters to pay greater attention to the reproduction of their labor force. Of all the slave societies in the New World, that of the Old South alone maintained a slave force that reproduced itself. Less than 400,000 imported Africans had, by 1860, become an American black population of more than 4,000,000.

A paternalism accepted by both masters and slaves—but with radically different interpretations—afforded a fragile bridge across the intolerable contradictions inherent in a society based on racism, slavery, and class exploitation that had to depend on the willing reproduction and productivity of its victims. For the slaveholders paternalism represented an attempt to overcome the fundamental contradiction in slavery: the impossibility of the slaves' ever becoming the things they were supposed to be. Paternalism defined the involuntary labor of the slaves as a legitimate return to their masters for protection and direction. But, the masters' need to see their slaves as acquiescent human beings constituted a moral victory for the slaves themselves. Paternalism's insistence upon mutual obligations—duties, responsibilities, and ultimately even rights—implicitly recognized the slaves' humanity.

Wherever paternalism exists, it undermines solidarity among the oppressed by linking them as individuals to their oppressors. A lord (master, *padrone, patron, padrón, patrão*) functions as a direct provider and protector to each individual or family, as well as to the community as a whole. The slaves of the Old South displayed impressive solidarity and collective resistance to their masters, but in a web of paternalistic relationships their action tended to become defensive and to aim at protecting the individuals against aggression and abuse; it could not readily pass into an effective weapon for liberation. Black leaders, especially the preachers, won loyalty and respect and fought heroically to defend their people. But despite their will and considerable ability, they could not lead their people over to the attack against the paternalist ideology itself.

In the Old South the tendencies inherent in all paternalistic class systems intersected with and acquired enormous reinforcement from the tendencies inherent in an analytically distinct system of racial subordination. The two appeared to be a single system. Paternalism created a tendency for the slaves to identify with a particular community through identification with its master; it reduced the possibilities for their identification with each other as a class. Racism undermined the slaves' sense of worth as black people and reinforced their dependence on white masters. But these were tendencies, not absolute laws, and the slaves forged weapons of defense, the most important of which was a religion that taught them to love and value each other, to take a critical view of their masters, and to reject the ideological rationales for their own enslavement.

The slaveholders had to establish a stable regime with which their slaves could live. Slaves remained slaves. They could be bought and sold like any other property and were subject to despotic personal power. And blacks remained rigidly subordinated to white. But masters and slaves, whites and blacks, lived as well as worked together. The existence of the community required that all find some measure of self-interest and self-respect. Southern paternalism developed as a way of mediating irreconcilable class and racial conflicts; it was an anomaly even at the moment of its greatest apparent strength. But, for about a century, it protected both masters and slaves from the worst tendencies inherent in their respective conditions. It mediated, however unfairly and even cruelly, between masters and slaves, and it disguised, however imperfectly, the appropriation of one man's labor power by another. Paternalism in any historical setting defines relations of superordination and subordination. Its strength as a prevailing ethos increases as the members of the community accept—or feel compelled to accept—these relations as legitimate. Brutality lies inherent in this acceptance of patronage and dependence, no matter how organic the paternalistic order. But southern paternalism necessarily recognized the slaves' humanity—not only their free will but the very talent and ability without which their acceptance of a doctrine of reciprocal obligations would have made no sense. Thus, the slaves found an opportunity to translate paternalism itself into a doctrine different from that understood by their masters and to forge it into a weapon of resistance to assertions that slavery was a natural condition for blacks, that blacks were racially inferior, and that black slaves had no rights or legitimate claims of their own.

Thus, the slaves, by accepting a paternalistic ethos and legitimizing class rule, developed their most powerful defense against the dehumanization implicit in slavery. Southern paternalism may have reinforced racism as well as class exploitation, but it also unwittingly invited its victims to fashion their own interpretation of the social order it was intended to justify. And the slaves, drawing on a religion that was supposed to assure their compliance and docility, rejected the essence of slavery by projecting their own rights and value as human beings. . . .

Charles Pettigrew, a large planter in North Carolina, made the point in his will in 1806 when he declared: "It is a pity that agreeably to the nature of things, Slavery & tyranny must go together—and that there is no such thing as having an obedient & useful slave without painful exercise of undue & tyrannical authority." William Elliott of South Carolina spoke with much truth when he said that masters were generally kind but added, " Against *insubordination alone,* we are severe." Elliott probably did not know the Akan proverb and would not have quoted it if he had: "One does not acquire a slave in order to be affronted by him."

"Absolute obedience and subordination to the lawful authority of the master," the Supreme Court of Alabama announced in 1861, "are the duty of the slave." The centrality of this demand to the lives and thought of the slaveholders appeared in the will of Stephen Henderson of Louisiana. He wished to free his slaves but inveighed against abolitionist fanatics and troublemakers. While still slaves, his people were to receive kind treatment, details of which he carefully spelled out; but, "There must be strict discipline." Andrew Jackson, whose 150 to 200 slaves made him one of the biggest slaveholders in Tennessee, cried out, "I could not bear the idea of inhumanity to my poor negroes." He saw no more incompatibility in the juxtaposition of that sentiment and his frequent and severe use of the whip to punish impertinence and violations of discipline than in that which characterized his relationship to the troops under his firm command.

The problems inherent in the contradiction in the slave's legal existence as man and thing constantly emerged. Those who demanded absolute obedience were trying to reduce the slave to an extension of the master's will, which the best of the slaveholders took for granted as humane and just. But the effort could not be sustained even when supported by terror and the greatest violence. At law and in the community, limitations everywhere arose, in no small part because the slaves fought to impose them. Solomon Northup recalled a decent master's remonstrating with a brutal one: "This is no way of dealing with them, when first brought into the country. It will have a pernicious influence and set them all running away. The swamps will be full of them."

The humanity of the slave implied his action, and his action implied his will. Hegel was therefore right in arguing that slavery constituted an outrage, for, in effect, it has always rested on the falsehood that one man could become an extension of another's will. If one man could so transform himself, he could do it only by an act of that very will supposedly being surrendered, and he would remain so only while he himself chose to. The clumsy attempt of the slaveholders to invoke a religious sanction did not extricate them from this contradiction. The Christian tradition, from the early debates over the implications of original sin through the attempts of Hobbes and others to secularize the problem, could not rationally defend the idea of permanent and total submission rooted in a temporally precise surrender of will. The idea of man's surrender to God cannot be equated with the idea of man's surrender to man, but even if it could, the problem would remain. The Catholic and Arminian struggle for constant rededication to God as an act of free will avoided the difficulty, and only the extreme forms of antinomianism took the plunge into a doctrine of continuous and permanent submission. By so doing—the politically radical ramifications not withstanding—antinomianism passed into a hysterical abnegation of humanity. But apart from the ultras among the South's predestinarian Regular Baptists, and by no means always among them, the southern versions of Protestantism did not take that road, Moreover, the slaveholders perceived the revolutionary political dangers in such a doctrine, as their mounting attacks on northern "religious fanaticism" reveal. Hence, their attempt to justify slavery philosophically contradicted their increasing need for a moderate theology, no matter how fundamentalist its dress. They ended, therefore, with no reply at all to the liberal challenge, epitomized in Hegel's critique, and had to fall back on the assertion of naked power. And at that, they ruined themselves, for their recognition of the slaves' right to life, explicitly endorsed in the laws against the murdering of slaves, both exposed the absurdity of the assertion of a doctrine of total surrender of will and registered their own inability to justify even to themselves the unlimited use of force.

Why, then, did the slaveholders so often reiterate their demand for absolute obedience while repudiating its theoretical foundation explicitly in their courts and implicitly in their daily behavior? Because in no other way could they justify themselves to themselves. Because in no other way could they see themselves as morally responsible beings who are doing their duty. We must therefore accept the naiveté of Mrs. Schoolcraft as an ideological position essential to the self-esteem, self-confidence, and moral strength of her class. Commenting on Trollope's observation that slaves love their masters in the same way that dogs do, she agreed, but with a difference. "The slave," she told herself, "can never be treated with the hardness of heart that poor white operators are, because the fact of his being dependent makes his master love to patronize him." And more sharply, "How thankful I am to God that the slave, who seems given up to the will of his master, should have the very strongest passion of that master's heart enlisted to protect him and provide for his every want."

The slaveholders found themselves trapped by the exigencies of their untenable view of their relationship to their slaves. Their position suffered the more from an awareness of dependency upon their slaves' labor, which necessarily transformed a doctrine of absolute property and absolute will into a doctrine of reciprocity. Everard Green Baker of Panola, Mississippi, a thoughtful young man and perhaps a model master, wrestled with the problem in his diary and vowed to avoid waste. "A man," he explained, "should not squander what another accumulates with the exposure of health & the wearing out of the physical powers, & is not that the case with the man who needlessly parts with that which the negro by the hardest labor & often undergoing what he in like situation would call the greatest deprivation?" The slave's body, he added later, "has been worn out in hard service for us [so] that the decrepitude of age [must] receive our tenderest notice, since the vigor of life—the buoyancy of spirit, & strength of arm has worn itself away with many a hard year's labor—through suns & tempests, to enable us to indulge in the comforts & niceties of this world. . . ." A few years later, he wrote on Christmas Day: "I have endeavored too to make my Negroes joyous and happy—& am glad to see them enjoying themselves with such a contented hearty good will. . . . Thus I commenced another year under favorable auspices as far as my domestic affairs are concerned—I did all I could to make their hollidays pleasant to them & they seem to appreciate my endeavors."

Insisting that a master had a duty to provide a slave with legal counsel, Judge Starnes of the State Supreme Court of Georgia explained that this duty must be understood as being "in return for the profit of the bondman's labor." Yet he ruled in the case at issue that unless the master's punishment aimed to kill, the slave must submit and had no right to make a judgment on its severity. The slaves saw this attitude in their masters' behavior. Robert McKinley, an ex-slave of North Carolina, remembered a local slaveholder who explained his kindness toward his slaves as a necessary return to people whose hard work made his own easier life possible. Louise Jones, an ex-slave of Virginia, described how her master had enjoyed himself at his slaves' Christmas balls, which his wife hated:

> Den ole Missus say to Marsa, "I b'lieve you lak dem niggers better'n you do me." Den Marsa say, "Sho, I lak my niggers. Dey works hard an' makes money fo' me, an' I'm goin' to see dat dey have a good time. You go back to de house ef you don' wanna stay here. I'se gwine stay an' see dat my niggers have a good time."

The slaves understood these impulses in their masters and seized the significant concession they implied. Unable to challenge the system as such—unable to resist it frontally except on desperate occasions and then with little hope of success—they accepted what could not be avoided. In its positive aspect this accommodation represented a commitment, shared by most peoples, however oppressed, to the belief that a harsh and unjust social order is preferable to the insecurities of no order at all. It also represented an awareness that the masters required their affection, or at least the appearance of it, in order to curb their own tendencies toward cruelty and even greater injustice. Slaveholders had the great advantage over colonizers of being an intrinsic part of their society rather than marginal men who were imposing themselves on a conquered country. Thus, they could reverse the assumption that those who conquer and dominate others must hate them if they are to justify themselves as Christians and human beings. The slaveholders struggled to reverse the pattern and to "love" those whom they made suffer. They could deny to themselves that in fact they did cause suffering and could assert that their domination liberated the slaves from a more deprived existence. Such a view demanded the doctrine of reciprocal duties implicit and sometimes explicit in their defense of their regime and their own lives. Inherent in this doctrine were dangerously deceptive ideas of "gratitude," "loyalty," and "family." Inherent also was an intimacy that turned every act of impudence and insubordination—every act of unsanctioned self-assertion—into an act of treason and disloyalty, for by repudiating the principle of submission it struck at the heart of the master's moral self-justification and therefore at his self-esteem. Nothing else, apart from personal idiosyncrasy, can explain the ferocity and cruelty of masters who normally appeared kind and even indulgent. The slaves accepted the doctrine of reciprocity, but with a profound difference. To the idea of reciprocal duties they added their own doctrine of reciprocal rights. To the tendency to make them creatures of another's will they counterposed a tendency to assert themselves as autonomous human beings. And they thereby contributed, as they had to, to the generation of conflict and great violence.

This paternalism of the masters toward their slaves influenced and was in turn reinforced by the relationship of the planters to middle-class and lower-class whites. Those nonslaveholders who lived as farmers and herdsmen in the up country and well back of the plantation districts had only minimal contact with the great planters and created a world of their own, presenting to the slaveholders' regime a complex of problems beyond the scope of this discussion. Those nonslaveholders who lived in the interstices of the plantation districts further divided into strata: solid yeomen; respectable sub-subsistence farmers who supplemented their incomes by working as day laborers; skilled and semiskilled mechanics; and dissolute, déclassé "poor white trash." The relationship between the planters and these several strata varied in time and place and requires discrete analysis, but a few generalizations of special importance may be risked here. Each of these strata had its own stake in slavery, however much the slaveholders' regime, considered as social system, may have oppressed them. The yeomen who raised a little cotton often relied on the planters to gin and market it for them. Those who raised primarily corn and pork found their market in the nearby plantations and planter-dominated towns. The day laborers and mechanics worked for these same planters, and the poor whites depended to some extent on their charity as well as on their patronage for such odd jobs as hunting runaway slaves. The economic relationship of the upper and lower classes, in short, bound them together without economic exploitation. If anything, the planters proved generous in dealings with surrounding whites. Slavery as a system did oppress the nonslaveholders but in a disguised and impersonal way, while creating personal bonds across class lines. A full analysis of these bonds would have to go well beyond economics and take account of kinship patterns and social intercourse. A single family, defined in this quasi-traditional society as extending to fourth or fifth cousins, often had members among the richest and poorest strata of a given county. And any planter with social pretensions or a modest spirit of neighborliness, not to mention political ambitions, would periodically throw a big barbecue for the whole community, white and black.

Thus, the paternalist spirit readily extended beyond the black-white relationship and impinged upon the relationship of rich to poorer whites. As such, it reinforced the paternalism of the master-slave relationship itself. The slaves saw proud, free white men willingly defer to the great and powerful planters. This wider paternalism—or rather, pseudopaternalist element in a complex system of class relations—ran into strong countertendencies. The meanest whites could participate in the political process, claim equality with the rich, and thumb their noses at the high and mighty. The social relationships of poorer to richer whites involved much more than a pattern of deference. Rather, that pattern provided one element in a contradictory and potentially explosive whole. For present purposes, however, it is enough that that element existed, fortified plantation paternalism, and strengthened the impulse of both masters and slaves to see paternalism as the normal and proper form of class relations.

The Liberal World of the Slave South

JAMES OAKES

We cannot say why Lydia, the slave John Mann had hired for the year, refused to accept her master's punishment. She comes to us from records that give her no last name, much less assign her motives. Perhaps she had been abused too often before; perhaps she had one of those "saucy" dispositions of which so many slaveowners complained. But whatever her reasons, sometime in the late 1820's, Lydia did something for which Mann sought to "chastise her" and "in the act of doing so the slave ran off." Mann then "called upon [the slave] to stop, which being refused, he shot at and wounded her." Mann was indicted for committing a battery upon the slave and the case went all the way to the North Carolina Supreme Court.

A few years later another North Carolina slave whose last name we do not know also turned and walked away rather than accept chastisement, and was also shot in the back. But this time the slave, Will, kept walking, and the overseer who had shot him pursued him for several minutes. When he caught up with Will, the slave physically resisted and finally pulled a knife, stabbing the overseer, Richard Baxter, in three different places. That evening Baxter bled to death. Will was subsequently indicted for murder, convicted, and sentenced to die. He, too, appealed his conviction to the state supreme court.

Both cases began when a slave refused to accept the most basic precept of human bondage: total subordination to the master. The refusal need not have grown out of any seething resentments or from any well-formulated conviction that slavery itself had to be challenged. Lydia and Will did what slaves across the South did all the time—they got angry and refused to accept punishment. Theirs were among the thousands of acts of refusal so commonplace in slavery that historians refer to them as "day-to-day" resistance. . . .

. . . Having made their way to the North Carolina Supreme Court, their cases produced two of the most intriguing decisions in the history of southern slave law. *State* v. *Mann* and *State* v. *Will* were classic instances of the ordinary becoming extraordinary. Lydia and Will, in their simple acts of resistance to a master's authority, had forced the courts to confront the intrinsic nature of slavery and its place in a liberal political system. In so doing the slaves helped provoke a significant revision of the law of slavery, one that threatened to redefine the balance of power in the

James Oakes, *Slavery and Freedom: An Interpretation of the Old South* (New York: Vintage, 1990), 137–139, 155–159, 174–176, 178–181. Copyright © 1990 by James Oakes. Used by permission of Alfred A. Knopf, a division of Random House, Inc.

master-slave relationship. Add up all the similar cases, accumulate the relevant precedents, and the history of slavery in the Old South comes steadily into view.

How could this happen? How could a system that demanded the total subordination of the slave, that was virtually defined by the slave's exclusion from politics, become so sensitive to the political consequences of seemingly trivial and isolated acts of slave resistance? . . . [T]he slaveholders had helped create the liberal institutions within which they exercised their power; in the face of an independent yeomanry, the slaveholders reinforced rather than weakened their commitment to liberal government; in the face of an increasingly hostile North the slaveholders relied ever more insistently on the protections afforded them by the liberal state. And yet liberalism, in the end, provided the slaves with the crack into which their acts of resistance drove the decisive wedge. . . .

. . . Masters knew that the slaves could not influence American politics with their votes, petitions, speeches, and editorials. But as the decades passed it was becoming apparent that slaves could affect the political system by intruding themselves into it as runaways, criminals, victims, or even witnesses. Any action that forced the legal system to recognize the slave as in any way independent of the master represented an implicit threat to the principle of total subordination. Grounded in the presumption of universal, inviolable rights, the American political system at once defined the slaves as rightless and yet risked undermining slavery every time it recognized the legal personality of the slave.

The American political system also limited the master's capacity to contain the consequences of slave resistance. As a legal entity, the master-slave relationship was defined by slave codes passed in representative legislatures, protected by state constitutions, and interpreted by local and national judiciaries. Yet not one of those political structures was determined by or dependent upon slavery. Quite the reverse: the slaveholders' legal survival depended on political institutions that slavery did not create, and in the end this put the master class at a fatal disadvantage. For the slaveholders' domination of liberal political institutions had the paradoxical effect of legitimizing the same government structures that would ultimately be used to destroy slavery.

Slavery's dependence on the state exposed still another paradox, one that was common to all slave systems but whose significance was transformed in a liberal political culture: the fact that slaves were "totally" subordinate to the masters did not mean that the master's power over the slave was absolute. On the contrary, the state formally (and the community informally) regulated the master's power in a variety of ways—even in the United States where the law gave masters unusually wide leeway. For this reason, John Codman Hurd defined slavery "as that condition of a natural person, in which, by the operation of law, the application of his physical and mental powers depends, as far as possible, upon the will of another *who is himself subject to the supreme power of the state.*"

How much power did the state have? Beyond simply calling slavery into existence, the government's role in regulating and maintaining the master-slave relationship was essential, nowhere more so than in the determination of who could be legally enslaved. Here the state's power was nothing less than overwhelming, for if it could say who was or was not rightfully enslaved, it could theoretically enslave everyone or abolish slavery in effect even when constitutionally prohibited from doing so. . . .

The slaveholders never seriously questioned the state's right to say who was a slave, and the reason for their silence was undoubtedly the consensus southern legislatures operated within when they addressed this issue: slaves should be Negroes and Negroes should be slaves. Thomas Cobb summarized the logic in his treatise on the law of slavery: "White persons may not be enslaved. . . . The presumption of freedom arises from the color." Since "all the negroes introduced into America were brought as slaves," Cobb explained, "the black color of the race raises the presumption of slavery." This was the universal supposition by the eighteenth century, and it served to mask the awesome implications of the authority the state exercised when it codified that presumption.

Yet over and over again the southern legislatures went further than this. They had to. What, after all, was a "Negro"? All the pseudo-scientific flimflam produced by men like Samuel Cartwright and Josiah Nott could not alter the fact that "race" was a cultural construction rather than a biological reality. Consider the problems raised by miscegenation, the fact that whites and blacks could together produce children whose "race" was instantly problematical. Genetics inevitably failed the racial theorists, though it took a century for it to do so. In the meantime, the law stepped in to provide official sanction as well as clarification for a powerful cultural proposition. "Every person who has one-fourth, or other larger part, of negro blood, shall be deemed a mulatto," the Kentucky legislature decreed in 1852, "and the word negro, when used in any statute, shall be construed to mean mulatto as well as negro." In these and many other areas the state exercised its prerogative to determine who was legitimately a slave.

The government also decided whether and under what circumstances a master could free a slave. It specified how slaves were to be distributed among contending heirs whenever a master died intestate. The state even reserved the right to take slaves away from masters for a variety of reasons. It could expropriate a slave if the master did not pay his taxes, if he was convicted of a criminal offense, or if it was determined that he was simply too cruel. The state of Louisiana reserved the right to free any slave it chose. After piously declaring that "no master of slaves shall be compelled, either directly or indirectly, to enfranchise" his slaves, the legislature went on to make a huge exception "in cases where the enfranchisement shall be made for services rendered to the State, by virtue of an act of the Legislature."

Finally, the state required that the masters observe minimum standards of humane treatment. Premeditated and unprovoked murder of a slave was illegal in the South by the end of the eighteenth century. Some states—Alabama, for instance— charged every master to "treat his slave with humanity, and . . . not inflict upon him any cruel punishment; he must provide him with a sufficiency of healthy food and necessary clothing; cause him to be properly attended during sickness, and provide for his necessary wants in old age." As of 1830 Kentucky law provided that "slaves, if inhumanely treated, shall be taken from their masters and sold to others." The fact that such laws were common to slave societies throughout history suggests that they were vague enough to encompass sadistic beatings and near-starvation at least as often as they ensured genuine kindness and concern.

The law, of course, is not a reliable guide to everyday practice. And it is worth remembering that restricting the power of the masters, even to the point that slaves could be taken from them for mistreatment, had no liberating implications for those who were unfree. Once again, the fact that the master's power was less than absolute did not imply that the slave's subordination was less than total. The Kentucky law, like most of its kind, provided only that expropriated slaves be sold to other, presumably more humane, masters.

Still, the law restrained the slaveholders in important ways. Masters could not enslave anybody they wanted, they could not free a slave under any circumstances, and their slaves could be expropriated for a variety of reasons, including gross mistreatment. Yet the slaveholders were the last to acknowledge that the state had such tremendous powers. After all, the discipline imposed on masters by the law of slavery was, at least in part, self-discipline. Slaveholders wrote these laws and almost always held clear majorities in the legislatures that enacted them. Hence the powers granted to the state in the southern slave codes must be taken as in some manner an expression of the slaveholders' assumptions. The prosecution of a sadistic master, for example, could actually serve the larger interests of the slaveholding class by demonstrating the masters' willingness to abide by the standards of decency upheld in the rule of law. Thus state power posed no threat when governmental authorities were called upon to distinguish the commonplace brutality of the system from the wanton murder of a helpless slave.

But the power of the state, once legitimized, was not easily controlled. It was the arbitration of difficult cases, those in which the boundaries of acceptable behavior were put to the test, that raised the power of the state from a theoretical to a practical concern. Those boundaries were usually at issue in the most important judicial cases concerning slavery in the Old South. In some ways it was an ordinary legal problem: where do you draw the line? In this case, where did the state's power end and the individual master's begin? But the intrinsic ambiguity of slave law—the total subordination of the slave to a master who himself owed allegiance to the state—transformed a simple problem into a profound dilemma. For it was all but impossible for a liberal political culture to place limits on the master's power without implicitly granting rights to slaves.

This made the jurisprudence of slavery intrinsically subversive. Thomas Cobb sought to evade the problem by declaring that the rights accorded slaves were not really "rights" at all, but merely procedural guarantees granted by the state for pragmatic reasons. For some, this was a critical point: the guarantee of certain legal procedures for accused slaves was not the same as the vesting of rights in slaves. But for others, the distinction was far too delicate since it was difficult, perhaps impossible, to separate the legal (and social) consequences of procedural guarantees from inherent rights. How else can rights be implemented in the real world, critics wondered, except as procedural guarantees? As Hurd pointed out, "every recognition of rights in the slave, independent of the will of the owner or master, which is made by the state to which he is subject, diminishes in some degree the essence of that slavery by changing it into a relation between legal persons."

Slave law, therefore, had to maintain a delicate balance. The state's right to regulate slavery was implicit in the very nature of the master-slave relationship. Slavery could not survive without some legal recognition of its existence, some legal determination of who was and was not a slave, some rudimentary definition of slavery itself. At the same time, extensive regulation that restricted the master's power over the slave necessarily "diminished" the essence of slavery. . . .

Slave resistance thus contributed to the ideological war that was forcing the slaveholders into ever more explicit defenses of their social order. The long period of "agitation" over the slavery issue, a New Orleans newspaper noted in late 1860, "has evolved the true principles on which the institution of slavery is based. It has convinced all Southern men of the moral right, the civil, social and political benefit of slavery." In their final form proslavery principles reflected the influence within the South of the wider intellectual universe of the nineteenth century. Reactionaries invoked the themes of romantic anti-modernism. Theologians ran the gamut from anti-rationalist conservatism to evangelical individualism. Radical democrats transformed eighteenth-century republicanism into proslavery racism. Whiggish advocates of commercial development joined slavery to the language of nineteenth-century boosterism, whereas the most conservative proslavery ideologues reiterated the critiques of urban industrial society pouring forth from disgruntled artisans, reform-minded novelists, parliamentary committees, and revolutionary socialists. In each case, cultural traditions that had little to do with slavery were drafted into the service of southern slave society and in the process were dramatically transformed into a complex and highly developed body of proslavery thought.

If proslavery ideology reflected the increasingly powerful revolt against liberalism, it is worth remembering that the revolt matured even as liberalism reached its greatest achievements and widest influence. It is no surprise, therefore, that in the liberal-capitalist world the southern masters inhabited, proslavery thought focused most often on the primacy of rights—with particular fidelity to the right of property. The political structure of the liberal state placed an added burden on the slaveholders as they formulated their defense of human bondage. For in the context of the protracted tensions between upcountry yeomen and black-belt planters, the voting power of the South's slaveless farmers compelled the master class to emphasize still other features of their distinctive social order: the political equality of all white men and the absence of aristocratic barriers to slaveownership.

Each of these influences was at work as the slaveholders turned to the North in answer to the rising chorus of denunciation against them. Each and all were readily visible in the works of leading proslavery intellectuals—and still more so in the final defense of slavery put forward by the advocates of secession. Slavery's apologists were pushed to the limits of liberal ideology, and in some of the most interesting cases beyond those limits. As most of them searched for a justification of a social order that systematically inverted liberalism's fundamental precepts, they found themselves trapped, by cultural inheritance and political circumstances, within the language of liberalism itself. Nevertheless, the debate over slavery in the nineteenth century provoked sharp, categorical analyses of the relative merits of an agricultural society grounded in the labor of slaves and an urbanizing, industrializing society grounded on wage labor.

In his influential analysis of the debate over slavery in the Virginia legislature during 1831–1832, for example, Thomas R. Dew came close to suggesting that the very nature of the master-slave relationship contradicted the rancorous competition endemic to liberalism. "We do not find among [the slaveholders] that cold, contracted, calculating *selfishness,* which withers and repels everything around it," Drew argued, "and lessens or destroys all the multiplied enjoyments of social intercourse." Nevertheless, Dew's argument against the gradual emancipation and colonization of

Virginia's slaves rested on the force of economic self-interest, the very thing he later claimed slavery diminished. Citing bourgeois economists from Adam Smith to Thomas Malthus, Dew slammed repeatedly at the economic impracticality of emancipation schemes, bemoaning "the intrusion, in this matter, of those who have no interest at stake." As proof against all claims that slave labor was inferior to free, he pointed to the high price a slave commanded on the open market. This, he claimed, was "an evidence of his value with every one acquainted with the elements of political economy."

At the core of Dew's argument rested the simplest of all liberal assumptions: the right of property. "We take it for granted that the right of the owner to his slave is to be respected," he wrote. For the "great object of government is the protection of property." Beginning from this premise, Dew launched a Madisonian attack on the tyranny of the majority in language that anticipated Calhoun's theory of the "concurrent majority," yet did not forsake the liberal presumption of fundamental rights. "The fact is, it is always a most delicate and dangerous task for one set of people to legislate for another, without any community of interests," Dew explained. "It is sure to destroy the great principle of responsibility, and in the end to lay the weaker at the mercy of the stronger. It subverts the very end for which all governments are established, and becomes intolerable, and consequently against the fundamental rights of man." . . .

The increasingly inflated claims about the physical well-being and creature comforts of the slave quarters exposed yet again the depths of the slaveholders' immersion in the culture of liberal capitalism. If the ethic of consumption was beginning to transform the way Americans talked about freedom, it could not help but transform the way they talked about slavery. Critics of slavery held that the superiority of capitalism was proved by the unprecedented levels of wealth it generated and by the widespread opportunities it offered men and women to partake of that wealth. Masters answered not by rejecting the standards to which they were being held but by claiming that those standards were more fully satisfied in the South than anywhere else—that the South was wealthier than the North and that the slaves benefited from that wealth even more than the wage earners of industrial society.

The more insistently the slaveholders defended their "treatment" of the slaves, however, the more clearly they revealed the totality of their power over the lives of others. At issue in the master-slave relationship was not whether slaveholders exercised their power responsibly but the intrinsic injustice of their power to begin with, not whether the slaves were overworked but the terms under which they were compelled to work, not whether slave families existed but whether they were secure against the masters' power to destroy them. With every new detail the slaveholders added to the argument that they treated their slaves kindly, they succeeded only in exposing the extremity of their power—the very thing the slaves so deeply resented and so consistently resisted.

Not all of slavery's defenders followed this train of logic. As we have seen, John C. Calhoun was developing a powerful alternative to the doctrine of individual rights. By the 1850's it was possible for the slaveholders to go still further by transforming the critique of wage labor into a fundamental rejection of liberalism. They could begin, as George Fitzhugh did, with a vision of an ideal society grounded on the labor of slaves rather than on the primacy of rights. Far more explicitly than had

William Harper, Fitzhugh equated slavery with feudalism. He littered his analysis of master-slave relations with references to reciprocity and organicism, language more reminiscent of the Middle Ages than the nineteenth century. He had nothing to say about the social death of the slaves, about their kinlessness, or about the way they were systematically dishonored—all the things that made slavery a distinct form of subordination. Nor did he acknowledge any of capitalism's influence on the way slave labor was driven in the South. Instead, Fitzhugh rather innocently supposed that it was capitalism whose vitality depended on slavery rather than the other way around.

But if Fitzhugh's characterization of the workings of slave society was considerably more romanticized than Calhoun's had been, his critique of liberalism was far more trenchant. The most thoroughly reactionary of all proslavery ideologues, Fitzhugh zeroed in on the core of liberal ideology and explicitly repudiated it. He pronounced "Locke's theory of the social contract" a catastrophic "heresy . . . pregnant with mischief." But where many others had merely rejected the doctrine that rights were "natural," Fitzhugh went on to dispute the great liberal postulate that rights, whether grounded in nature or secured by mankind, should take precedence over the interests of society. Man "has no rights whatever, as opposed to the interests of society; and that society may very properly make any use of him that will redound to the public good. Whatever rights he has are subordinate to the good of the whole," Fitzhugh concluded, "and he has never ceded rights to it, for he was born its slave, and had no rights to cede." From these premises the conclusion followed almost automatically that slavery, not freedom, was the "natural" form of social organization.

Yet both Fitzhugh and Calhoun faced a similar dilemma. Their impulse to defend slavery had pushed them outside the confines of liberalism, forcing them to blaze a trail that few of their fellow Southerners saw fit to follow. For by the 1850's it was also possible for the slaveholders to take from American political culture its fear of centralized government, its racism, its republican disdain for dependency, and its consumerism—and to fashion from these another defense of slavery grounded not in the vision of an alternative society but on the sanctity of private property.

The historical circumstances within which the masters developed their defense of slavery all but assured that they would choose the latter path. The great issues that had nationalized the debate over slavery—its expansionism and the intractable problem of runaways—tended to lead the slaveholders into an ever more resolute defense of the rights of property. The forums in which they presented their arguments (the Supreme Court and the United States Congress, for example) could hardly accommodate a proslavery ideology that repudiated the philosophical premises upon which those political institutions operated. And the yeomen farmers who finally had to be convinced that secession was the only way to protect southern slavery were hardly receptive to assaults on the very idea of free society.

So, forced by the expansion of slavery and the resistance of slaves to engage in a debate they would have preferred to avoid, the slaveholders overwhelmingly fell back on the rhetoric of constitutional rights and the security of private property. Citing the North's "Personal Liberty Bills and such legal 'aid and comfort,'" a Kentucky editor predicted that runaways would slowly drain the state of its slaves unless it joined the Confederacy. In "the present Union" there were "no *efficient* provisions for the protection of Southern rights and property," he warned in December

1860. "That Congress has no power to interfere with slavery in the States is admitted," another editor explained earlier in the year.

> The fugitive slave law providing for the rendition of slaves escaped into other States, perfects the remedial protection to the institution as it exists in the States. In the Territories slave property is equally well guarded against invasion. It is now decided that neither the Federal nor Territorial government has the power to interpose between the slave holder and his property, either to wrest it from him or impair his rights.—More than this, it is decided to be the duty of both these governments to secure every species of property, including slaves, all needful protection. And here arises the only political issue which now divides parties.

Constitutional rights. Property rights. States' rights. Southern rights. The language of liberalism permeated the rhetoric secessionists. Even as slave resistance hurled southern jurists into an excruciating controversy over the anomaly of "slave rights," the slaveholders asserted more firmly than ever their commitment to the primacy of rights. On the eve of a bloody war between the North and the South, southern slave society remained trapped within the ideological conventions of American political culture.

FURTHER READING

Catherine Clinton, *The Plantation Mistress: Woman's World in the Old South* (1982).
Eugene D. Genovese, *The Slaveholders' Dilemma: Freedom and Progress in Southern Conservative Thought, 1820–1860* (1992).
Herbert G. Gutman, *The Black Family in Slavery and Freedom, 1750–1925* (1976).
Lawrence W. Levine, *Black Culture and Black Consciousness* (1977).
Stephanie McCurry, *Masters of Small Worlds: Yeoman Households, Gender Relations, and the Political Culture of the Antebellum South Carolina Low Country* (1995).
Albert Raboteau, *Slave Religion* (1978).
Gavin Wright, *The Political Economy of the Cotton South* (1978).

Careening Toward Civil War

For many Americans, the signing of the Treaty of Guadelupe Hidalgo on February 2, 1848, was a moment of fulfillment and a cause for jubilation. The United States had just won a war against Mexico and had gained title to some 500,000 square miles of land. Although in retrospect we may see the Mexican-American War as a war of aggression by the United States, many Americans at the time saw it as the realization of manifest destiny. The nation now encompassed nearly three million square miles; in some seventy years, the United States had become a transcontinental colossus. Ironically, however, this fulfillment of manifest destiny planted the seeds for civil war. As Americans celebrated their military victory, they had to determine politically the ways in which the newly acquired lands would be developed. For nearly thirty years, American politicians had attempted to create a balance between slave and free states. Now the issue of how or if slavery would be extended westward became the question of the day. As politicians endeavored to deal with the question, Americans of various stripes became actively engaged in the debate and increasingly illustrated the fact that perhaps this was not an issue that had a political solution.

Politicians, both before the 1840s and afterward, typically attempted to arrive at compromise. Because there were two strong national political parties vying for power in Washington, it was in their interests to maintain a spirit of compromise between North and South. Accordingly, after bitter debate, Congress passed the Compromise of 1850, which purportedly solved the problem. One part of the compromise admitted California as a free state, thus forever creating an imbalance between free and slave states. Another component of the compromise was the Fugitive Slave Act, which empowered slaveowners to go to court to recapture people who had escaped northward. Alleged fugitives were denied the right of trial by jury, and white people in the North were required to abet efforts to recapture fugitive slaves. As Americans soon found out, however, this time compromise did not solve the problem; in fact, it may have worsened it.

A level of distrust among Americans multiplied in the 1850s, in part because of the failure of the attempts at compromise. The abolitionist movement grew in the North, in part because of the publication of Uncle Tom's Cabin, a novel by Harriet Beecher Stowe that powerfully indicted slavery and the Fugitive Slave Act. Many northerners contended that their region, with its growing population, flourishing industry, and "free labor," was the best model for America's future. They worried about a "slave power conspiracy" that seemingly controlled the national government and was intent on spreading slavery westward, to the detriment of white farmers

*who also wanted to farm the available western lands. At the same time, white people
in the South became increasingly distrustful of northerners. In the southern view,
northerners were promoting abolitionism and thus endangering the system of
plantation slavery, which from their perspective was what created an ordered and
stable society.*

*As these divisions grew, the strains on the political party systems became so great
that a political crisis developed in the 1850s. First the Whig Party, then the newly
formed American Party, and finally the Democratic Party were unable to address the
concerns of their constituents. These failures were compounded by further attempts
to address the question of slavery. The Kansas-Nebraska Act in 1854 resulted in de
facto civil war in Kansas Territory shortly after its passage; the* Dred Scott *decision
in 1857 convinced many northerners that the Supreme Court was proslavery; and
John Brown's raid in 1859 persuaded many white southerners that northern abolitionists were intent on fomenting slave rebellion. In 1860, when Abraham Lincoln
became the first candidate of the Republican Party to be elected president, he received
only 39 percent of the popular vote and only a little over 1 percent of the vote in slave
states. Many white southerners considered Lincoln to represent not just the North,
but the incendiary abolitionist elements of northern society. Within five weeks of
Lincoln's election, seven legislatures of the Lower South had called for elections to consider secession. By February 22, they had formed a new nation, written a constitution,
and inaugurated their new president, Jefferson Davis. Ten days remained before
Lincoln would take office. The United States was on the brink of its bloodiest war.*

QUESTIONS TO THINK ABOUT

Was the Civil War inevitable? Can you think of ways in which compromises might
have forestalled the division between the North and the South? Of the documents you
have read in this chapter, which is most conciliatory toward the other side? Which is
most antagonistic?

DOCUMENTS

After author Henry David Thoreau spent a night in jail for protesting the Mexican-
American War, which he believed was a war to extend slavery, he wrote *Civil Disobedience,* an excerpt of which is Document 1. In this essay, he advocates withdrawal of
support for government if it acts incorrectly or immorally. During the debate that ended
in the Compromise of 1850, Senator John C. Calhoun in Document 2 warns about the
divisions that have grown between the sections. He argues that these divisions will increase as the disequilibrium between North and South in the national government grows.
In Document 3, Frederick Douglass powerfully depicts the hypocrisy of celebrating
American freedom on the Fourth of July as long as slavery exists. In Document 4, a
series of letters written in "bleeding Kansas" in 1856, a southerner recounts the violence
between southerners and "Yankees" that existed in the territory following the Kansas-
Nebraska Act. The violence in Kansas ultimately was duplicated on the floors of Congress. Senator Charles Sumner's speech, delivered in May of 1856, about the "crime
against Kansas," Document 5, was viewed by many white southerners as excessive.
Sumner was attacked some days later by a relative of Senator Butler, who is vilified in
the speech. Document 6 is Chief Justice Roger Taney's decision in *Dred Scott* v. *Sanford,*
which was hailed by proslavery southerners and condemned by antislavery northerners.

Among other things, Taney held that neither slaves nor free black people could sue in court because they were not citizens and that no law could be passed to prohibit slavery in the territories. In Document 7, Abraham Lincoln and Stephen Douglas debate the future of slavery and the legality of slavery in the territories. Although Lincoln and Douglas were running for a U.S. Senate seat from Illinois, they replayed the debate two years later when they ran for president. In Document 8, Senator William Seward celebrates the system of free labor and argues that conflict between societies based on free and slave labor is irrepressible. After John Brown led a raid into the South in hopes of fostering a slave revolt, he became a hero to many northerners, and his calm speech (Document 9) in the face of execution, denying any intentions of violence, only served to increase his popularity. Finally, in Document 10, just eight months before Lincoln's election, the *Charleston Mercury* argues that slavery must be protected in the territories because the spread of the American nation westward and southward is all but inevitable.

1. Henry David Thoreau Protests Against Slavery and the Mexican War, 1846

I heartily accept the motto, "That government is best which governs least"; and I should like to see it acted up to more rapidly and systematically. . . . Government is at best but an expedient; but most governments are usually, and all governments are sometimes, inexpedient. The objections which have been brought against a standing army, and they are many and weighty, and deserve to prevail, may also at last be brought against a standing government. . . .

This American government, what is it but a tradition . . . ? . . . It is excellent, we must all allow. Yet this government never of itself furthered any enterprise, but by the alacrity with which it got out of its way. . . .

. . . Can there not be a government in which majorities do not virtually decide right and wrong, but conscience?—in which majorities decide only those questions to which the rule of expediency is applicable? Must the citizen ever for a moment, or in the least degree, resign his conscience to the legislator? Why has every man a conscience, then? I think that we should be men first, and subjects afterward. . . .

The mass of men serve the state thus, not as men mainly, but as machines, with their bodies. They are the standing army, and the militia, jailers, constables, *posse comitatus*, etc. In most cases there is no free exercise whatever of the judgment or of the moral sense. . . .

How does it become a man to behave toward this American government today? I answer that he cannot without disgrace be associated with it. I cannot for an instant recognize that political organization as *my* government which is the *slave's* government also. . . .

. . . There are thousands who are *in opinion* opposed to slavery and to the war, who yet in effect do nothing to put an end to them; who, esteeming themselves children of Washington and Franklin, sit down with their hands in their pockets, and say that they know not what to do, and do nothing; who even postpone the question of

Henry David Thoreau, "Civil Disobedience," in *A Yankee in Canada, with Anti-Slavery and Reform Papers* (1866). This document can also be found in *Walden and Civil Disobedience: Complete Texts with Introduction, Historical Contexts, Critical Essays*, ed. Paul Lauter (Boston: Houghton Mifflin, 2000), 17, 18, 19, 20, 21–22, 23, 24, 25, 36.

freedom to the question of free trade, and quietly read the prices-current along with the latest advices from Mexico, after dinner, and, it may be, fall asleep over them both. What is the price-current of an honest man and patriot today? . . .

It is not a man's duty, as a matter of course, to devote himself to the eradication of any, even the most enormous wrong; he may still properly have other concerns to engage him; but it is his duty, at least, to wash his hands of it, and, if he gives it no thought longer, not to give it practically his support. . . .

. . . Those who, while they disapprove of the character and measures of a government, yield to it their allegiance and support, are undoubtedly its most conscientious supporters, and so frequently the most serious obstacles to reform. Some are petitioning the State to dissolve the Union, to disregard the requisitions of the President. Why do they not dissolve it themselves—the union between themselves and the State—and refuse to pay their quota into its treasury? . . .

. . . Action from principle, the perception and the performance of right, changes things and relations; it is essentially revolutionary, and does not consist wholly with anything which was. It not only divides States and churches, it divides families; ay, it divides the *individual,* separating the diabolical in him from the divine. . . .

I do not hesitate to say, that those who call themselves Abolitionists should at once effectually withdraw their support, both in person and property, from the government of Massachusetts, and not wait till they constitute a majority of one, before they suffer the right to prevail through them. I think that it is enough if they have God on their side, without waiting for that other one. . . .

The authority of government . . . is still an impure one: to be strictly just, it must have the sanction and consent of the governed. It can have no pure right over my person and property but what I concede to it. . . . I please myself with imagining a State at last which can afford to be just to all men, and to treat the individual with respect as a neighbor; which even would not think it inconsistent with its own repose if a few were to live aloof from it, not meddling with it, nor embraced by it, who fulfilled all the duties of neighbors and fellow-men. A State which bore this kind of fruit, and suffered it to drop off as fast as it ripened, would prepare the way for a still more perfect and glorious State, which also I have imagined, but not yet anywhere seen.

2. Senator John C. Calhoun Proposes Ways to Preserve the Union, 1850

I have, Senators, believed from the first that the agitation of the subject of slavery would, if not prevented by some timely and effective measure, end in disunion. . . . [T]he Union is in danger. You have thus had forced upon you the greatest and the gravest question that can ever come under your consideration: How can the Union be preserved? . . .

The first question, then, . . . is: What is it that has endangered the Union?

To this question there can be but one answer: That the immediate cause is the almost universal discontent which pervades all the States composing the southern section of the Union. . . .

John C. Calhoun, "Proposal to Preserve the Union": Speech on the Compromise of 1850.

. . . What is the cause of this discontent? It will be found in the belief of the people of the southern States, as prevalent as the discontent itself, that they cannot remain, as things now are, consistently with honor and safety, in the Union. The next question to be considered is: What has caused this belief?

One of the causes is, undoubtedly, to be traced to the long-continued agitation of the slave question on the part of the North, and the many aggressions which they have made on the rights of the South during the time. . . .

There is another, lying back of it, with which this is intimately connected, that may be regarded as the great and primary cause. That is to be found in the fact that the equilibrium between the two sections in the Government, as it stood when the Constitution was ratified and the Government put in action has been destroyed. . . . [A]s it now stands, one section has the exclusive power of controlling the Government, which leaves the other without any adequate means of protecting itself against its encroachment and oppression. . . .

[The] great increase of Senators, added to the great increase of the House of Representatives and the electoral college on the part of the North, which must take place under the next decade, will effectually and irretrievably destroy the equilibrium which existed when the Government commenced. . . .

As . . . the North has the absolute control over the Government, it is manifest that on all questions between it and the South, where there is a diversity of interests, the interests of the latter will be sacrificed to the former, however oppressive the effects may be. . . .

If the agitation goes on, the same force, acting with increased intensity, as has been shown, will finally snap every cord, when nothing will be left to bind the States together except force. . . .

How can the Union be saved? To this I answer, there is but one way by which it can be, and that is by adopting such measures as will satisfy the States belonging to the southern section that they can remain in the Union consistently with their honor and their safety.

3. Frederick Douglass Asks How a Slave Can Celebrate the Fourth of July, 1852

Fellow-citizens, pardon me, allow me to ask, why am I called upon to speak here to-day? What have I, or those I represent, to do with your national independence? Are the great principles of political freedom and of natural justice, embodied in that Declaration of Independence, extended to us? and am I, therefore, called upon to bring our humble offering to the national altar, and to confess the benefits and express devout gratitude for the blessings resulting from your independence to us?

Would to God, both for your sakes and ours, that an affirmative answer could be truthfully returned to these questions! Then would my task be light, and my burden easy and delightful. For who is there so cold, that a nation's sympathy could not warm him? Who so obdurate and dead to the claims of gratitude, that would not thankfully

Frederick Douglass, Fourth of July Oration (1852), in Philip S. Foner, *The Life and Writings of Frederick Douglass,* Vol. 2, *Pre-Civil War Decade, 1850–1860* (New York: International Publishers Col, Inc, 1950). Obtained from http://www.pbs.org/wgbh/aia/part4/4h2927t.html.

acknowledge such priceless benefits? Who so stolid and selfish, that would not give his voice to swell the hallelujahs of a nation's jubilee, when the chains of servitude had been torn from his limbs? I am not that man. In a case like that, the dumb might eloquently speak, and the "lame man leap as an hart."

But such is not the state of the case. I say it with a sad sense of the disparity between us. I am not included within the pale of glorious anniversary! Your high independence only reveals the immeasurable distance between us. The blessings in which you, this day, rejoice, are not enjoyed in common. The rich inheritance of justice, liberty, prosperity and independence, bequeathed by your fathers, is shared by you, not by me. The sunlight that brought light and healing to you, has brought stripes and death to me. This Fourth July is yours, not mine. . . .

What, to the American slave, is your 4th of July? I answer; a day that reveals to him, more than all other days in the year, the gross injustice and cruelty to which he is the constant victim. To him, your celebration is a sham; your boasted liberty, an unholy license; your national greatness, swelling vanity; your sounds of rejoicing are empty and heartless; your denunciation of tyrants, brass fronted impudence; your shouts of liberty and equality, hollow mockery; your prayers and hymns, your sermons and thanksgivings, with all your religious parade and solemnity, are, to Him, mere bombast, fraud, deception, impiety, and hypocrisy—a thin veil to cover up crimes which would disgrace a nation of savages. There is not a nation on the earth guilty of practices more shocking and bloody than are the people of the United States, at this very hour.

Go where you may, search where you will, roam through all the monarchies and despotisms of the Old World, travel through South America, search out every abuse, and when you have found the last, lay your facts by the side of the everyday practices of this nation, and you will say with me, that, for revolting barbarity and shameless hypocrisy, America reigns without a rival.

4. Axalla John Hoole, a Southerner, Depicts the Situation in "Bleeding Kansas," 1856

Kansas City, Missouri, Apl. 3d., 1856

My Dear Brother . . .

The Missourians (all of whom I have conversed with, with the exception of one who, by the way, I found out to be an Abolitionist) are very sanguine about Kansas being a slave state & I have heard some of them say it *shall* be. I have met with warm reception from two or three, but generally speaking, I have not met with the reception which I expected. Everyone seems bent on the Almighty Dollar, and as a general thing that seems to be their only thought. . . .

. . . Give my love to [the immediate family] and all the Negroes. . . .

Your ever affectionate brother, Axalla.

William Stanley Hoole, ed., "A Southerner's Viewpoint of the Kansas Situation" (1856–1857), *Kansas Historical Quarterly* 3 (1934).

Lecompton, K. T., Sept. 12, 1856

My dear Mother . . .

You perceive from the heading of this that I am now in Lecompton, almost all of the Proslavery party between this place and Lawrence are here. We brought our families here, as we thought that we would be better able to defend ourselves when altogether than if we scattered over the country.

Lane came against us last Friday (a week ago to-day). As it happened we had almost 400 men with two cannon—we marched out to meet him, though we were under the impression at the time that we had 1,000 men. We came in gunshot of each other, but the regular soldiers came and interferred, but not before our party had shot some dozen guns, by which it is reported that five of the Abolitionists were killed or wounded. We had strict orders from our commanding officer (Gen'l Marshall) not to fire until they made the attack, but some of our boys would not be restrained. I was a rifleman and one of the skirmishers, but did all that I could to restrain our men though I itched all over to shoot. . . .

. . . I am more uneasy about making money than I am about being killed by the Yankees. . . .

Your Affectionate Son.

Douglas, K. T., July the 5th., 1857

Dear Sister

I fear, Sister, that coming here will do no good at last, as I begin to think that this will be made a Free State at last. 'Tis true we have elected Proslavery men to draft a state constitution, but I feel pretty certain, if it is put to the vote of the people, it will be rejected, as I feel pretty confident they have a majority here at this time. The South has ceased all efforts, while the North is redoubling her exertions. . . .

One of our most staunch Proslavery men was killed in Leavensworth a few days ago. It is hard to ascertain the facts in relation to the murder correctly, but as far as I can learn, there was an election for something. The man who was killed (Jas. Lyle) went up to the polls and asked for a ticket. An Abolitionist handed him one which he, Lyle, tore in two. The other asked him why he did that; he replied he did all such tickets that way. The Abolitionist told him he had better not do so again, when Lyle told him if he would give him another he would. It was given him, and he tore it also, at which the Abolitionist drew a bowie knife and stabbed Lyle to the heart, then ran a few paces, drew a revolver, and commenced firing at the dying man. The fellow was taken prisoner and eighty men were sent from Lawrence that night, by Jim Lane, to keep Lyle's friends from hanging him. Gov. Walker put out for Leavensworth on Friday to have the prisoner carried to the fort, in order to keep the Abolitionists from rescuing him, or prevent Lyle's friends from hanging him by mob law. . . .

You must give my love to all. . . . Tell all the Negroes a hundred Howdies for us. . . .

Your Affectionate Brother, Axalla.

5. Senator Charles Sumner Addresses the "Crime Against Kansas," 1856

MR. PRESIDENT:

You are now called to redress a great transgression. Seldom in the history of nations has such a question been presented. . . .

Take down your map, sir, and you will find that the Territory of Kansas, more than any other region, occupies the middle spot of North America. . . . A few short months only have passed since this spacious and mediterranean country was open only to the savage who ran wild in its woods and prairies; and now it has already drawn to its bosom a population of freemen larger than Athens. . . .

Against this Territory, thus fortunate in position and population, a crime has been committed, which is without example in the records of the past. . . .

. . . It is the rape of a virgin Territory, compelling it to the hateful embrace of Slavery; and it may be clearly traced to a depraved longing for a new slave State, the hideous offspring of such a crime, in the hope of adding to the power of slavery in the National Government. . . .

. . . The strife is no longer local, but national. Even now, while I speak, portents hang on all the arches of the horizon threatening to darken the broad land, which already yawns with the mutterings of civil war. The fury of the propagandists of Slavery, and the calm determination of their opponents, are now diffused from the distant Territory over widespread communities, and the whole country. . . .

. . . [A] madness for Slavery which would disregard the Constitution, the laws, and all the great examples of our history; also a consciousness of power such as comes from the habit of power; a combination of energies found only in a hundred arms directed by a hundred eyes; a control of public opinion through venal pens and a prostituted press; an ability to subsidize crowds in every vocation of life—the politician with his local importance, the lawyer with his subtle tongue, and even the authority of the judge on the bench; and a familiar use of men in places high and low, so that none, from the President to the lowest border postmaster, should decline to be its tool; all these things and more were needed, and they were found in the slave power of our Republic. There, sir, stands the criminal, all unmasked before you—heartless, grasping, and tyrannical. . . .

. . . I must say something of a general character, particularly in response to what has fallen from Senators who have raised themselves to eminence on this floor in championship of human wrongs. I mean the Senator from South Carolina (Mr. Butler), and the Senator from Illinois (Mr. Douglas). . . . The Senator from South Carolina has read many books of chivalry, and believes himself a chivalrous knight, with sentiments of honor and courage. Of course he has chosen a mistress to whom he has made his vows, and who, though ugly to others, is always lovely to him; though polluted in the sight of the world; is chaste in his sight. I mean the harlot, Slavery. For her, his tongue is always profuse in words. Let her be impeached in character, or any proposition made to shut her out from the extension of her

Senator Charles Sumner, speech in the U.S. Senate on the "Crime Against Kansas," delivered May 19–20, 1856, reprinted in *Evening Journal,* Albany, N.Y., May 22–23, 1856.

wantonness, and no extravagance of manner or hardihood of assertion is then too great for this Senator. The frenzy of Don Quixote, in behalf of his wench, Dulcinea del Toboso, is all surpassed. The asserted rights of Slavery, which shock equality of all kinds, are cloaked by a fantastic claim of equality. If the slave States cannot enjoy what, in mockery of the great fathers of the Republic, he misnames equality under the Constitution in other words, the full power in the National Territories to compel fellowmen to unpaid toil, to separate husband and wife, and to sell little children at the auction block then, sir, the chivalric Senator will conduct the State of South Carolina out of the Union! Heroic knight! Exalted Senator! A second Moses come for a second exodus!

. . . [T]he Senator in the unrestrained chivalry of his nature, has undertaken to apply opprobrious words to those who differ from him on this floor. He calls them "sectional and fanatical"; and opposition to the usurpation in Kansas he denounces as "an uncalculating fanaticism." . . . He is the uncompromising, unblushing representative on this floor of a flagrant sectionalism, which now domineers over the Republic, and yet with a ludicrous ignorance of his own position unable to see himself as others see him . . . , he applies to those here who resist his sectionalism the very epithet which designates himself. . . .

. . . [T]he Senator from Illinois (Mr. Douglas) is the Squire of Slavery, its very Sancho Panza, ready to do all its humiliating offices. . . . Standing on this floor, the Senator issued his rescript, requiring submission to the Usurped Power of Kansas; and this was accompanied by a manner—all his own—such as befits the tyrannical threat. Very well. Let the Senator try. I tell him now that he cannot enforce any such submission. The Senator, with the slave power at his back, is strong; but he is not strong enough for this purpose. . . .

The Senator dreams that he can subdue the North. He disclaims the open threat, but his conduct still implies it. How little that Senator knows himself or the strength of the cause which he persecutes! He is but a mortal man; against him is an immortal principle. With finite power he wrestles with the infinite, and he must fall. Against him are stronger battalions than any marshalled by mortal arm[:] the inborn, ineradicable, invincible sentiments of the human heart against him is nature in all her subtle forces; against him is God. Let him try to subdue these.

6. Chief Justice Roger Taney Determines the Legal Status of Slaves, 1857

The question is simply this: Can a negro, whose ancestors were imported into this country, and sold as slaves, become a member of the political community formed and brought into existence by the Constitution of the United States, and as such become entitled to all the rights, and privileges, and immunities, guarantied by [the Constitution] to the citizen? One of which rights is the privilege of suing in a court of the United States in the cases specified in the Constitution. . . .

. . . We think they [negroes] are not, and that they are not included, and were not intended to be included, under the word "citizens" in the Constitution, and can

---

Roger Taney, opinion in *Dred Scott* v. *Sanford* (1857).

therefore claim none of the rights and privileges which [it] . . . secures to the citizens of the United States. On the contrary, they were at the time considered as a subordinate and inferior class of beings, who had been subjugated by the dominant race, and, whether emancipated or not, yet remained subject to their authority, and had no rights or privileges but such as those who held the power and the Government might choose to grant them. . . .

In discussing this question, we must not confound the rights of citizenship which a State may confer within its own limits, and the rights of citizenship as a member of the Union. It does not by any means follow, because he has all the rights and privileges of a citizen of a State, that he must be a citizen of the United States. . . .

The question then arises, whether the provisions of the Constitution, in relation to the personal rights and privileges to which the citizen of a State should be entitled, embraced the negro African race, at that time in this country, or who might afterwards be imported, who had then or should afterwards be made free in any State; and to put it in the power of a single State to make him a citizen of the United States. . . .

The court think the affirmative of these propositions cannot be maintained. And if it cannot, the plaintiff in error could not be a citizen of the State of Missouri . . . and consequently, was not entitled to sue in its courts. . . .

It is difficult at this day to realize the state of public opinion in relation to that unfortunate race, which prevailed in the civilized and enlightened portions of the world at the time of the Declaration of Independence, and when the Constitution of the United States was framed and adopted. But the public history of every European nation displays it in a manner too plain to be mistaken.

They had for more than a century been regarded as beings of an inferior order, and altogether unfit to associate with the white race, either in social or political relations; and so far inferior, that they had no rights which the white man was bound to respect; and that the negro might justly and lawfully be reduced to slavery for his benefit. . . .

And in no nation was this opinion more firmly fixed or more uniformly acted upon than by the English Government and English people. . . .

The opinion thus entertained and acted upon in England was naturally impressed upon the colonies they founded on this side of the Atlantic. And accordingly, a negro of the African race was regarded by them as an article of property, and held, and bought and sold . . . in every one of the thirteen colonies. . . .

[Laws passed in the thirteen colonies] show that a perpetual and impassable barrier was intended to be erected between the white race and the one which they had reduced to slavery, and governed as subjects with absolute and despotic power. . . .

[T]here are two clauses of the Constitution which point directly to the negro race as a separate class of persons, and show clearly that they were not regarded as a portion of the people or citizens of the Government then formed.

One of these clauses reserves to each of the thirteen States the right to import slaves until the year 1808. . . . And by the other provision the States pledge themselves to each other to maintain the right of property of the master, by delivering up to him any slave who may have escaped from his service, and be found within their respective territories. . . .

The only two provisions [of the Constitution] which point to [slaves] and include them, treat them as property, and make it the duty of the Government to protect it; no other power, in relation to this race, is to be found in the Constitution. . . .

[T]he court is of the opinion, that, upon the facts stated in the plea of abatement, Dred Scot was not a citizen of Missouri within the meaning of the Constitution of the United States, and not entitled as such to sue in its courts.

7. Abraham Lincoln and Stephen Douglas Debate Their Positions on Slavery, 1858

Mr. Douglas' Opening Speech

At half past two, Mr. Douglas took the front of the platform. . . .

Mr. Douglas said—Ladies and gentlemen. I appear before you to-day for the purpose of discussing the leading political topics which now agitate the public mind. . . .

. . . Mr. Lincoln here says that our government cannot endure permanently in the same condition in which it was made by its framers. It was made divided into free States and slave States. Mr. Lincoln says it has existed for near eighty years thus divided; but he tells you that it cannot endure permanently on the same principles and in the same conditions relatively in which your fathers made it. ["Neither can it."—*Times*] Why can't it endure divided into free and slave States? Washington, as the President of the Convention, Franklin, and Madison, and Hamilton, and Jay, and the patriots of that day, made this government divided into free States and slave States, leaving each State perfectly free to do as it pleased on that subject of slavery. ["Right, right."—*Times*] Why can't it exist upon the same principles upon which our fathers made it. ["It can."—*Times*] Our fathers knew when they made this government that in a country as wide and broad as this with such a variety of climate, of interests, of productions, as this that the people necessarily required different local laws and local institutions in certain localities from those in other localities. They knew that the laws and regulations that would suit the granite hills of New Hampshire would be unsuited to the rice plantations of South Carolina. ["right, right,"—*Times*] Hence, they provided that each State should retain its own Legislature and its own sovereignty, with the full and complete power to do as it pleased within its own limits in all that was local and not national. [Applause.—*Times*] One of the reserved rights of the States was that of regulating the relation between master and slave, or the slavery question. . . . I therefore say that uniformity in the local laws and local legislations of the different States was neither possible nor desirable. If any uniformity had been adopted, it must inevitably have been the uniformity of slavery everywhere, or the uniformity of negro citizenship and negro equality everywhere.

. . . Now, I ask you, are you in favor of conferring upon the negro the rights and privileges of citizenship? ["No, no."—*Times*] Do you desire to strike out of our State Constitution that clause which keeps slaves and free negroes out of the State, and allow the free negro to flow in ["never,"—*Times*] and cover our prairies with his settlements. Do you desire to turn this beautiful State into a free negro colony. . . . I believe that this government was made on the white basis. ["Good,"—*Times*] I believe it was made by white men for the benefit of white men and their posterity forever, and I am in favor of confining the citizenship to white men—men

Abraham Lincoln and Stephen Douglas, *The Lincoln-Douglas Debates of 1858* (New York: Oxford University Press, 1965), 45, 53–56, 59, 61–63, 77.

of European birth and European descent, instead of conferring it upon Negroes and Indians, and other inferior races. . . .

. . . I do not believe the Almighty ever intended the negro to be the equal of the white man. ["Never, never."—*Times*] If he did he has been a long time demonstrating the fact. [Laughter.—*Tribune;* Cheers.—*Times*] For six thousand years the negro has been a race upon the earth, and during that whole six thousand years—in all latitudes and climates wherever the negro has been—he has been inferior to whatever race adjoined him. The fact is he belongs to an inferior race and must occupy an inferior position. . . .

. . . What shall be done for the free negro? . . . [W]e must leave each and every other State to decide for itself beyond our limits. . . .

Mr. Lincoln's Reply

. . . Mr. Lincoln then came forward and was greeted with loud and protracted cheers from fully two-thirds of the audience. . . .

. . . [L]et me say I think I have no prejudice against the Southern people. They are just what we would be in their situation. If slavery did not now exist amongst them, they would not introduce it. If it did now exist amongst us, we should not instantly give it up. . . .

When southern people tell us they are no more responsible for the origin of slavery, than we; I acknowledge the fact. When it is said that the institution exists, and that it is very difficult to get rid of it, in any satisfactory way, I can understand and appreciate the saying. I surely will not blame them for not doing what I should not know how to do myself. If all earthly power were given me, I should not know what to do, as to the existing institution. My first impulse would be to free all the slaves, and send them to Liberia,—to their own native land. But a moment's reflection would convince me, that whatever of high hope (as I think there is) there may be in this, in the long run, its sudden execution is impossible. If they were all landed there in a day, they would all perish in the next ten days; and there are not surplus shipping and surplus money enough in the world to carry them there in many times ten days. What then? Free them all, and keep them among us as underlings? Is it quite certain that this betters their condition? . . . What next? Free them, and make them politically and socially, our equals? My own feelings will not admit of this; and if mine would, we well know that those of the great mass of white people will not. . . . We can not, then, make them equals. It does seem to me that systems of gradual emancipation might be adopted; but for their tardiness in this, I will not undertake to judge our brethren of the south.

When they remind us of their constitutional rights, I acknowledge them, not grudgingly, but fully, and fairly; and I would give them any legislation for the reclaiming of their fugitives, which should not, in its stringency, be more likely to carry a free man into slavery, than our ordinary criminal laws are to hang an innocent one.

But all this; to my judgment, furnishes no more excuse for permitting slavery to go into our own free territory, than it would for reviving the African slave trade by law. The law which forbids the bringing of slaves *from* Africa; and that which has so long forbid the taking them *to* Nebraska, can hardly be distinguished on any moral principle; and the repeal of the former can find quite as plausible excuses as that of the latter. . . .

. . . I have no purpose directly or indirectly, to interfere with the institution of slavery in the states where it exists. I believe I have no lawful right to do so, and I have no inclination to do so. I have no disposition to introduce political and social equality between the white and the black races. There is a physical difference between the two, which in my judgment will probably forever forbid their living together on terms of respect, social and political equality, and . . . I . . . am in favor of the race to which I belong having the superior position; but I hold that because of all this there is no reason at all furnished why the negro after all is not entitled to all that the declaration of independence holds out, which is, "life, liberty, and the pursuit of happiness." . . .

. . . When he [Douglas] is saying that the negro has no share in the Declaration of Independence, he is going back to the year of our revolution, and, to the extent of his ability, he is muzzling the cannon that thunders its annual joyous return. When he is saying, as he often does, that if any people want slavery they have a right to have it, he is blowing out the moral lights around us. When he says that he don't care whether slavery is voted up or down, then, to my thinking, he is, so far as he is able to do so, perverting the human soul and eradicating the light of reason and the love of liberty on the American continent.

8. William Seward Warns of an Irrepressible Conflict, 1858

Our country is a theatre, which exhibits, in full operation, two radically different political systems; the one resting on the basis of servile or slave labor, the other on the basis of voluntary labor of freemen.

The laborers who are enslaved are all negroes, or persons more or less purely of African derivation. But this is only accidental. The principle of the system is, that labor in every society, by whomsoever performed, is necessarily unintellectual, groveling and base; and that the laborer, equally for his own good and for the welfare of the state, ought to be enslaved. The white laboring man, whether native or foreigner, is not enslaved, only because he cannot, as yet, be reduced to bondage. . . .

. . . One of the chief elements of the value of human life is freedom in the pursuit of happiness. The slave system is not only intolerable, unjust, and inhuman, towards the laborer, whom, only because he is a laborer, it loads down with chains and converts into merchandise, but is scarcely less severe upon the freeman, to whom, only because he is a laborer from necessity, it denies facilities for employment, and whom it expels from the community because it cannot enslave and convert him into merchandise also. . . . The free-labor system conforms to the divine law of equality, which is written in the hearts and consciences of man, and therefore is always and everywhere beneficent.

The slave system is one of constant danger, distrust, suspicion, and watchfulness. It debases those whose toil alone can produce wealth and resources for defense, to the lowest degree of which human nature is capable. . . .

The free-labor system educates all alike, and by opening all the fields of industrial employment, and all the departments of authority, to the unchecked and

William Seward, "The Irrepressible Conflict," speech given at Rochester, New York, October 25, 1858, in *The Works of William H. Seward,* ed. George Baker (Boston: Houghton, Mifflin, and Company, 1884), 4 (new edition): 289–302.

402   *Major Problems in American History*

equal rivalry of all classes of men, at once secures universal contentment, and brings into the highest possible activity all the physical, moral and social energies of the whole state. . . .

Hitherto, the two systems have existed in different states, but side by side within the American Union. This has happened because the Union is a confederation of states. But in another aspect the United States constitute only one nation. Increase of population, which is filling the states out to their very borders, together with a new and extended net-work of railroads and other avenues, and an internal commerce which daily becomes more intimate, is rapidly bringing the states into a higher and more perfect social unity or consolidation. Thus, these antagonistic systems are continually coming into closer contact, and collision results. . . .

Shall I tell you what this collision means? . . . It is an irrepressible conflict between opposing and enduring forces, and it means that the United States must and will, sooner or later, become either entirely a slaveholding nation, or entirely a free-labor nation. . . .

. . . In the field of federal politics, slavery, deriving unlooked-for advantages from commercial changes, and energies unforeseen from the facilities of combination between members of the slaveholding class and between that class and other property classes, early rallied, and has at length made a stand, not merely to retain its original defensive position, but to extend its sway throughout the whole Union. . . . The plan of operation is this: By continued appliances of patronage and threats of disunion, they will keep a majority favorable to these designs in the senate, where each state has an equal representation. Through that majority they will defeat, as they best can, the admission of free states and secure the admission of slave states. Under the protection of the judiciary, they will, on the principle of the Dred Scott case, carry slavery into all the territories of the United States now existing and hereafter to be organized. By the action of the president and the senate, using the treaty-making power, they will annex foreign slaveholding states. In a favorable conjecture they will induce congress to repeal the act of 1808, which prohibits the foreign slave trade, and so they will import from Africa, at the cost of only twenty dollars a head, slaves enough to fill up the interior of the continent. . . . When the free states shall be sufficiently demoralized to tolerate these designs, they reasonably conclude that slavery will be accepted by those states themselves. . . .

I think, fellow citizens, that I have shown you that it is high time for the friends of freedom to rush to the rescue of the constitution, and that their very first duty is to dismiss the democratic party from the administration of the government.

9. John Brown Makes His Last Statement to the Court Before Execution, 1859

I have, may it please the Court, a few words to say. In the first place, I deny everything but what I have all along admitted: of a design on my part to free slaves. I intended certainly to have made a clean thing of that matter, as I did last winter, when I went into Missouri and there took slaves without the snapping of a gun on either side,

---

John Brown, Last Statement to the Virginia Court (1859).

moving them through the country, and finally leaving them in Canada. I designed to have done the same thing again on a larger scale. That was all I intended. I never did intend murder, or treason, or the destruction of property, or to exercise or incite slaves to rebellion, or to make insurrection.

. . . Had I interfered in the manner which I admit, and which I admit has been fairly proved—for I admire the truthfulness and candor of the greater portion of the witnesses who have testified in this case—Had I so interfered in behalf of the rich, the powerful, the intelligent, the so-called great, or in behalf of any of their friends, either father, mother, brother, sister, wife or children, or any of that class, and suffered and sacrificed what I have in this interference, it would have been all right. Every man in this Court would have deemed it an act worthy of reward rather than punishment.

This Court acknowledges, too, as I suppose, the validity of the law of God. I see a book kissed, which I suppose to be the Bible, or at least the New Testament, which teaches me that all things whatsoever I would that men should do to me, I should do even so to them. It teaches me, further, to remember them that are in bonds as bound with them. I endeavored to act up to that instruction. I say I am yet too young to understand that God is any respecter of persons. I believe that to have interfered as I have done, as I have always freely admitted I have done, in behalf of His despised poor, I did no wrong, but right. Now, if it is deemed necessary that I should forfeit my life for the furtherance of the ends of justice, and mingle my blood further with the blood of my children and with the blood of millions in this slave country whose rights are disregarded by wicked, cruel, and unjust enactments, I say, let it be done.

Let me say one word further. I feel entirely satisfied with the treatment I have received on my trial. Considering all the circumstances, it has been more generous than I expected. But I feel no consciousness of guilt. I have stated from the first what was my intention, and what was not. I never had any design against the liberty of any person, nor any disposition to commit treason or incite slaves to rebel or make any general insurrection. I never encouraged any man to do so, but always discouraged any idea of that kind.

10. The *Charleston Mercury* Argues That Slavery Must Be Protected, 1860

The right to have [slave] property protected in the territory is not a mere abstraction without application or practical value. In the past there are instances where the people of the Southern States might have colonized and brought new slave States into the Union had the principle been recognized, and the Government, the trustee of the Southern States, exercised its appropriate powers to make good for the slaveholder the guarantees of the Constitution. . . . When the gold mines of California were discovered, slaveholders at the South saw that, with their command of labor, it would be easy at a moderate outlay to make fortunes digging gold. The inducements to go there were great, and there was no lack of inclination on their part. But, to make the emigration profitable, it was necessary that the [slave] property of

"Prospects of Slavery Expansion," *Charleston Mercury,* February 28, 1860.

Southern settlers should be safe, otherwise it was plainly a hazardous enterprise, neither wise nor feasible. Few were reckless enough to stake property, the accumulation of years, in a struggle with active prejudices amongst a mixed population, where for them the law was a dead letter through the hostile indifference of the General Government, whose duty it was, by the fundamental law of its existence, to afford adequate protection—executive, legislative, and judicial—to the property of every man, of whatever sort, without discrimination. Had the people of the Southern States been satisfied they would have received fair play and equal protection at the hands of the Government, they would have gone to California with their slaves. . . . California would now have been a Slave State in the Union. . . .

What has been the policy pursued in Kansas? Has the territory had a fair chance of becoming a Slave State? Has the principle of equal protection to slave property been carried out by the Government there in any of its departments? On the contrary, has not every appliance been used to thwart the South and expel or prohibit her sons from colonizing there? . . . In our opinion, had the principle of equal protection to Southern men and Southern property been rigorously observed by the General Government, both California and Kansas would undoubtedly have come into the Union as Slave States. The South lost those States for the lack of proper assertion of this great principle. . . .

New Mexico, it is asserted, is too barren and arid for Southern occupation and settlement. . . . Now, New Mexico . . . teems with mineral resources. . . . There is no vocation in the world in which slavery can be more useful and profitable than in mining. . . . [Is] it wise, in our present condition of ignorance of the resources of New Mexico, to jump to the conclusion that the South can have no interest in its territories, and therefore shall waive or abandon her right of colonizing them? . . .

We frequently talk of the future glories of our republican destiny on the continent, and of the spread of our civilization and free institutions over Mexico and the Tropics. Already we have absorbed two of her States, Texas and California. Is it expected that our onward march is to stop here? Is it not more probable and more philosophic to suppose that, as in the past, so in the future, the Anglo-Saxon race will, in the course of years, occupy and absorb the whole of that splendid [but] ill-peopled country, and to remove by gradual process, before them, the worthless mongrel races that now inhabit and curse the land? And in the accomplishment of this destiny is there a Southern man so bold as to say, the people of the South with their slave property are to consent to total exclusion . . . ? Our people will never sit still and see themselves excluded from all expansion, to please the North.

✒ E S S A Y S

Historians have long debated the causes of the Civil War. Some scholars have argued that the war could have been avoided, that a generation of blundering politicians had ineptly maneuvered the nation into war. Other historians have agreed with William Seward, a statesman from New York who served in President Lincoln's cabinet, that the war was an "irrepressible conflict." The following two essays reflect these two views. In the first essay, the late David M. Potter, former professor of history at Stanford University, explains the four basic positions—already in place following the Mexican-American War—that politicians could take to solve the question of slavery in the territories. Although politicians strove to deal with the issue for the next fifteen years, the "sectional shears" ultimately bisected the nation. Michael F. Holt, professor of history at the University of Virginia, in contrast, concentrates on the political causes of the Civil War. The divisions between North and South had existed for decades, Professor Holt argues, but it was only when the political process broke down that Americans were led down the road to the Civil War. Rather than blaming a blundering generation, however, Professor Holt focuses on the breakdown of the political system itself.

The Sectional Divisions That Led to Civil War

DAVID M. POTTER

If American sectionalism entered a new phase in 1846, it was neither because North and South clashed for the first time nor because the issue of slavery for the first time assumed importance. As early as the Confederation, North and South had been at odds over the taxation of imports and exports, over the degree of risk to be run in seeking navigation rights at the mouth of the Mississippi, and over the taxation of slave property. Once the government under the Constitution went into effect, bitter sectional conflicts raged over the assumption of state debts, the chartering of a central bank, and other matters. This sectional rivalry tended to become institutionalized in the opposing Federalist and Jeffersonian Republican organizations, and it became so serious that Washington issued a solemn warning against sectionalism in his Farewell Address. Later, as the Jeffersonians enjoyed a quarter-century of domination in national politics, they became more nationalistic in their outlook, while Federalist nationalism withered. But no matter which region embraced nationalism and which particularism, sectional conflict remained a recurrent phenomenon.

From the outset, slavery had been the most serious cause of sectional conflict. In the constitutional convention, questions of taxing slave property and of counting it in the basis of representation had engendered intense friction. These quarrels were adjusted, if not resolved, by the three-fifths compromise and other provisions of the Constitution. But more often than not, sectional disagreements were adjourned rather than reconciled. If friction did decrease, it was less because of sectional agreement on the moral question of slavery than because of the general understanding that slavery was primarily a state problem rather than a federal one. Minor contests, sometimes very stubbornly fought, took place over slavery in the District of Columbia, suppression of the international slave trade, and rendition of fugitive slaves. Later, similar battles were fought over the disposition of antislavery petitions in Congress and the annexation of Texas as a slave state.

But these were marginal affairs. On the central issue of slavery itself, the locus of decision was the states, which had abolished slavery throughout New England and the Middle Atlantic region while perpetuating it from Delaware south. In the late twentieth century, when federal authority seems to reach everywhere and to be invoked for every purpose, it is difficult to realize that during much of the nineteenth century, state government rather than federal government symbolized public authority for most citizens. Thus, for several decades after the founding of the Republic, the question of slavery did not naturally come within the federal orbit, and it was only by some special contrivance that even an aspect of it could be brought into the congressional arena. It was this fact and not any agreement on the substantive question that drew the fuse of the explosive issue.

There was one contingency, however, which did transfer the slavery question at once and inescapably to the federal level. This was when the federal government held jurisdiction over western lands, not yet organized or admitted as states, in which the status of slavery was indeterminate. There had been such lands in 1787, but Congress had decided, with only a minimum of sectional disagreement, to exclude slavery from the Northwest Territory by the Ordinance of 1787. South of the Ohio River, Kentucky entered the Union as a slave state without ever being a federal territory, and the western lands that constituted most of the Southwest Territory, or later the Alabama and Mississippi territories, were ceded by North Carolina and Georgia with stipulations that Congress must not disturb the existing status of slavery in those areas. Thus Congress was deprived of what might have been a discord-breeding authority, and the status of slavery was settled throughout the then existing area of the United States.

The disruptive potentialities of territory in an indeterminate status did not become fully apparent until 1820. Missouri had applied for admission as a slave state, thus raising the question of slavery for the whole area of the Louisiana Purchase and presenting the imminent possibility that slave states would outnumber free states in the Union. A violent political convulsion followed, ending with a compromise that settled the territorial issue for another quarter of a century. During that interval, the bitterness over the gag rule against antislavery petitions and the decade-long struggle over the annexation of Texas (which, like Kentucky, skipped the territorial phase) showed what disruptive forces were ready to burst forth. But the potentiality did not again become an actuality until the prospect of acquiring land from Mexico revived the issue of slavery in the territories, thus returning the problem of slavery to the federal level and making Congress the area of combat for the whole complex of sectional antagonisms. As this situation developed, everyone in politics needed a defined position on the territorial status of slavery, even more than he needed a position on slavery itself. Militants on both sides wanted arguments to justify complete restriction or complete nonrestriction, as the case might be, while those politicians seeking to preserve a measure of national harmony needed formulas to prevent complete victory for either side.

For fifteen years between 1846 and 1861, countless speeches, resolutions, editorials, and party platforms set forth a wide variety of proposals for resolving the territorial issue. But essentially there were four basic positions. Significantly, all four were put forward within sixteen months after the territorial question reemerged to prominence in 1846. For more than a decade thereafter they remained the fixed rallying points of a shifting political warfare. Sometimes opportunists followed a weaving path among the available choices, and in the election of 1848 both major parties contrived to evade them. But sooner or later, almost everyone in public life committed himself to one of the four basic formulas.

The first of these was David Wilmot's—that Congress possessed power to regulate slavery in the territories and should use it for the total exclusion of the institution.

This free-soil formula was, in a sense, older than the Constitution, having received its first sanction in the Jefferson-inspired Ordinance of 1787, which declared: "There shall be neither slavery nor involuntary servitude in the said territory, otherwise than in the punishment of crimes whereof the party shall have been duly convicted." This was the language which Wilmot adopted, and so it has sometimes been said that Thomas Jefferson was the real author of the Wilmot Proviso.

Once the Northwest Ordinance was adopted under the Confederation, it remained the basic policy for the Old Northwest under the Constitution. Congress reaffirmed it on August 2, 1789, and again as the successive territories of the region were erected—Indiana (1800), Michigan (1805), Illinois (1809), and Wisconsin (1836). Thus Presidents Washington, John Adams, Jefferson, Monroe, and Jackson all assented to the principle that Congress possessed a constitutional power to prohibit slavery in the territories.

But not everyone who believed that the power existed believed also that it ought to be exercised. Some political leaders embraced the view that the power of Congress should be used in a way that would recognize the claims of both sections. Accordingly, Congress accepted cessions of western land from North Carolina in 1790 and from Georgia in 1802, with the condition that "no regulation made or to be made, by Congress, shall tend to emancipate slaves." It organized the Southwest Territory (out of the North Carolina cession) in 1791 and the Mississippi Territory (originally the northern zone of West Florida, to which the Georgia cession was later added) in 1798, both without restrictions upon slavery. Meanwhile, it admitted Kentucky (separated from Virginia) as a slave state in 1792. In sum, the federal government did not maintain a uniform policy concerning slavery in the territories, but instead practiced a kind of partition by which the Ohio River became a boundary between free territory to the north and slave territory to the south.

At first this practice was more an expedient or a reflex than a deliberate policy, but it assumed a formal character at the time of the Missouri crisis, which resembled the crisis of the late 1840s in more ways than one. In each case, a free-state congressman offered a motion in the House to exclude slavery from some part of the trans-Mississippi West. Both motions caused divisions along strictly sectional lines; both passed the House and failed to pass the Senate. Each precipitated a crisis that was not settled until a later session of Congress. Each inspired the formulation of an alternative plan making some kind of territorial adjustment between proslavery and antislavery interests. In 1820, Congress adopted the compromise proposed by Senator Jesse Thomas of Illinois, admitting Missouri as a slave state and dividing the rest of the Louisiana Purchase (except the state of Louisiana, already admitted) along latitude 36° 30', with slavery prohibited north of that line. By 1846, this compromise formula had become both familiar and traditional, and within a few minutes after Wilmot introduced his proviso, Representative William W. Wick of Indiana offered a resolution to extend the 36° 30' line into the prospective Mexican cession.

This principle of territorial division had thus become the second basic formula, and the sanction of solemn agreement between opposing parties was later claimed for it. Actually, it was adopted only because Henry Clay and other compromisers skillfully used two separate majorities to get it passed—one a solid bloc of southerners, with a sprinkling of northern support, to defeat restrictions on slavery in Missouri; the other a solid bloc of northerners, together with slightly more than half of the southern members, to exclude slavery north of 36° 30′ in the remainder of the Louisiana Purchase. But despite the lack of a clear mandate which would have been necessary to a real covenant, and despite the limitation of this settlement to the Louisiana Purchase, the Compromise had brought peace, and consequently the line 36° 30′ later took on a certain aura of sanctity. It was probably for this reason that Wick put it forward so promptly on the night of the Wilmot Proviso.

In the four years between 1846 and 1850, the proposal to extend the Missouri Compromise received a large measure of influential support. The administration rallied to it: Polk, as party leader, urged Democrats in Congress to support it; and the secretary of state, James Buchanan, made it his primary issue in a bid for the Democratic nomination in 1848. In Congress, southern Democrats, although questioning its constitutionality, voted repeatedly to apply it as a basis of settlement, and Stephen A. Douglas, later a champion of popular sovereignty, became its sponsor in the Senate. In July 1848, the 36° 30′ line almost became the basis of a compromise proposed by John M. Clayton of Delaware, which had the backing of all the forces of conciliation. To many people in both parties and both sections, the Missouri Compromise seemed to offer the best hope of peaceable adjustment.

To a surprising degree, historians have overlooked the strength of the movement to extend the Missouri Compromise line, and it has become, in a sense, the forgotten alternative of the sectional controversy. History has made heroes of the free-soilers like Lincoln. Douglas has had a body of admirers who argue that popular sovereignty offered the most realistic way of restricting slavery without precipitating civil war. And Calhoun has been accorded much respect for the intellectual acumen with which he saw through the superficialities of compromise. But the champions of 36° 30′ are forgotten, and even James Buchanan's biographers scarcely recognize his role as an advocate of the Missouri Compromise principle.

No doubt this neglect arises primarily from the fact that the proposal to divide the new territory, like the old, along a geographical line was the first of the four alternatives to be discarded in the late 1840s. Perhaps, too, historians have felt that as a simple, unadulterated bargain by which both parties would have given up part of what they believed in, it lacked the ideological rationale to make it interesting. But in a situation in which there were apparently no rational solutions acceptable to both sides, it had already proved to be a remarkably effective irrational solution. If in the end it failed to provide either a nonviolent answer to the slavery question or an enduring peace, no other alternative succeeded better. With it, for more than thirty years, the country had avoided the twin dangers of disruption and war.

Whatever its philosophical defects, the Missouri formula had one ostensible merit that proved more disadvantageous than all its faults. It was free of ambiguity; it spelled out clearly what each side would gain and lose. Thus it did not offer either side the hope of gaining ground by favorable construction of ambiguous language.

While President Polk was supporting the Missouri Compromise plan, the chief aspirant to the presidential succession came forward with a proposal possessing all the charms of ambiguity. The aspirant was Lewis Cass of Michigan, and his "Nicholson letter" of December 1847 formulated the doctrine of what was later called popular sovereignty as a third major position on the territorial question. Without taking a decisive stand on the question of whether Congress possessed power to regulate slavery in the territories, Cass held that if such power existed, it ought not to be exercised, but that slavery should be left to the control—at a stage not clearly specified—of the territorial government. His doctrine was based upon the plausible and thoroughly democratic premise that citizens of the territories had just as much capacity for self-government as citizens of the states. If it was consistent with democracy to permit the citizens of each state to settle the slavery question for themselves, it would be equally consistent with democracy to permit the citizens of a territory also "to regulate their own internal concerns in their own way." For good measure, this was not only a matter of sound policy, but also of constitutional obligation: Cass did "not see in the Constitution any grant of the requisite power [to regulate slavery] to Congress," and he believed that such regulation would be "despotic" and of "doubtful and invidious authority."

On its face, this position seemed simple and enticing: by invoking the principle of local self-government, against which no one would argue, it promised to remove a very troublesome question from Congress and to make possible a consensus within the badly divided Democratic party. It seemed impartial, in that it challenged both northern and southern partisans to accept the verdict of the local majority.

But either by contrivance or by chance, the popular sovereignty formula held a deeply hidden and fundamental ambiguity: it did not specify at what stage of their political evolution the people of a territory were entitled to regulate slavery. If they could regulate while still in the territorial stage, then there could be "free" territories, just as there were "free" states; but if they could regulate only when framing a constitution to apply for statehood, then slavery would be legal throughout the territorial period, and the effect would be the same as legally opening the territory to slavery. Cass's letter lent itself to the inference that territorial legislatures might exclude slavery during the territorial stage. But his statement that he favored leaving to the people of a territory "the right to regulate it [slavery] for themselves, under the general principles of the Constitution," said far less than it appeared to say, for all that it amounted to ultimately was a proposal to give the territorial governments as much power as the Constitution would allow, without specifying what the extent of this power might be. Cass did state that he saw nothing in the Constitution which gave Congress power to exclude slavery, and this statement implicitly raised a question whether Congress could confer upon territorial legislatures powers that it did not itself possess. But Cass refrained from exploring this implication also. The doctrine of congressional non-intervention, as he first formulated it, was more a device to get the territorial question out of Congress than a solution to place it definitely in the hands of the territorial legislatures.

The doctrine of popular sovereignty need not have been so ambiguous. To give it a clearer meaning, Cass needed only to do at the outset what both he and Douglas did later—that is, to assert his belief in the constitutionality as well as the desirability of a system by which the territorial legislatures, rather than Congress, would regulate slavery in the territories. But for nearly two years, Cass avoided this clarification and preserved the ambiguity. This equivocation made the doctrine especially enticing to politicians, for it allowed northern Democrats to promise their constituents that popular sovereignty would enable the pioneer legislatures to keep the territories free, while southern Democrats could assure proslavery audiences that popular sovereignty would kill the Wilmot Proviso and would give slavery a chance to win a foothold before the question of slavery exclusion could arise at the end of the territorial period.

Each wing of the party, of course, understood what the other was up to, condoned it as a political expedient for getting Democrats elected, and hoped to impose its own interpretation after the elections were won. But two years beyond each election there was always another election, and a clear confrontation of the meaning of popular sovereignty was repeatedly avoided. The territorial issue, difficult at best and badly needing to be faced with candor and understanding on both sides, thus remained for more than a decade an object of sophistry, evasion, and constitutional hair-splitting, as well as of disagreement.

While middle-ground alternatives to the Wilmot Proviso were being developed by the administration and by Cass, leaders within the slave states had already formulated a fourth major position which was the logical antithesis of the free-soil position. This was the contention that Congress did not possess constitutional power to regulate slavery in the territories and, therefore, that slavery could not be excluded from a territory prior to admission to statehood. Like all major southern doctrines for more than a generation, this one was more effectively stated by John C. Calhoun than by anyone else. Thus, the accepted formulation appeared in a set of resolutions which Calhoun introduced in the Senate on February 19, 1847. Essentially, these resolutions argued that the territories of the United States were the common property of the several states, which held them as co-owners; that citizens of any given state had the same rights under the Constitution as the citizens of other states to take their property—meaning slaves—into the common territories, and that discrimination between the rights of the citizens of various states in this respect would violate the Constitution; therefore, any law by Congress (or by a local legislature acting under authority from Congress) which impaired the rights of citizens to hold their property (slaves) in the territories would be unconstitutional and void.

According to this reasoning, the Wilmot Proviso would be unconstitutional, and so, for that matter, would the exercise of popular sovereignty by a territorial legislature. These implications, Calhoun intended. But further, his argument plainly meant that the Missouri Compromise was unconstitutional also, since it embodied a congressional act depriving citizens of the right to carry slaves into the territories north of 36° 30′. This challenge to the constitutionality of the compromise of 1820 was not new. In fact a substantial number of southerners—especially strict constructionists from Virginia—had voted against the act for constitutional reasons when it was originally adopted. But despite his theory, Calhoun was only half-hearted in challenging the 36° 30′ line. Embarrassing evidence was brought to light that he had himself supported it in 1820, as a member of Monroe's cabinet, and in any case he regarded it as a fair operating arrangement. In fact, the twenty-ninth Congress witnessed the odd spectacle of Calhoun's loyal follower, Armistead Burt, proposing the extension of the Missouri line in the House, at almost the same time when Calhoun himself was enunciating a doctrine which implicitly challenged the line's constitutionality in the Senate. At this point, he would have been willing to abandon consistency and accept the Missouri line, if the North had been prepared to extend it. But as he saw the Burt proposal voted down by a solid northern majority, his position hardened, and he later became adamant in his insistence that the South must accept nothing less than the full recognition of its literal rights in all the territories. By 1848, many southerners were asserting that they would never lend their support to a presidential candidate or to a party which advocated any federal law affecting "mediately or immediately" the institution of slavery.

Calhoun never pressed his resolutions to a vote, and indeed he had no reason to, for they were certain to be defeated. He had no way of knowing that ten years later, long after any hope of their adoption in Congress had been abandoned, they would be adopted, in somewhat modified form, by the Supreme Court in the Dred Scott decision. What he sought primarily was to state a southern position which would serve as a counterpoise, to unify the South, as the free-soil position was already unifying the North. Historians have not taken sufficient note of the fact that in this effort, Calhoun gained one of the few clear-cut successes of his career. Most of his life was spent in attempts to create political solidarity among southerners, and most of these attempts failed. But the doctrine that Congress could neither exclude slavery from a territory itself nor grant power to a territorial government to do so became one of the cardinal tenets of southern orthodoxy and operated as one of the key elements of southern unity in the crises that were to follow.

The four doctrines championed by Wilmot, Buchanan, Cass, and Calhoun soon became so many converters to be used by men who needed to discuss the slavery question in terms of something other than slavery. In their legal subtleties and constitutional refinements, these doctrines appear today as political circumlocutions, exercises in a kind of constitutional scholasticism designed to concentrate attention upon slavery where it did not exist and to avoid contact with the real issue of slavery in the states. But Thomas Hart Benton characterized two of the doctrines in a figure of speech which illuminated their functional reality and their historical importance: Wilmot's doctrine and Calhoun's doctrine, he said, were like the two blades of a pair of shears: neither blade, by itself, would cut very effectively; but the two together could sever the bonds of Union.

Buchanan's proposal and Cass's concept were intended to prevent the cutting action of the two blades, and for some years they did so. But in all the prolonged and involved legislative battles that embittered the years between 1846 and 1861, the devices to inhibit sectionalism never succeeded for very long. Time and again, the forces which were trying to resist sectional polarization temporarily rallied their followers under the banner of the Missouri Compromise or of popular sovereignty. But invariably the divisions returned, after a while, to the polarities of free soil and of Calhoun's doctrine. The shears continued to cut, deeper and deeper. Thus, although the dispute was to be waged with many variations and many diversionary thrusts, the contest always came back to one of these four doctrinal bases. The dialectic of the crisis of 1860 had been articulated by December of 1847.

The Political Divisions That Contributed to Civil War

MICHAEL F. HOLT

The Civil War represented an utter and unique breakdown of the normal democratic political process. When one section of the country refused to accept the decision of a presidential election, secession and the ensuing war became the great exception to the American political tradition of compromise. The rending of the nation was

Michael F. Holt, *The Political Crisis of the 1850s* (New York: W. W. Norton & Company, 1983), 1–6, 12–16. Reprinted by permission of the author.

the one time that conflict seemed too irrepressible, too fundamental, to be contained within common consensual boundaries. Because the war was such an anomaly, both participants and later historians have been fascinated with its causes since the shooting started.

The literature on the causation of the Civil War is vast and requires no detailed review here. Basically historians have been divided into two camps, although there have been a number of variations in each. Because the war pitted one section against another, many insist that a fundamental and intensifying conflict between the North and South brought it on. Members of this group have differed about the sources of sectional division, but most have argued that irreconcilable differences over Negro slavery inexorably ruptured one national institution after another between 1830 and 1860 until those differences produced war in 1861. In reply revisionist historians have minimized the internal solidarity of both the North and the South and the serious-ness of the disputes between them. They have blamed the war instead on the mis-takes of political leaders and the efforts of agitators such as the abolitionists and Southern fire-eaters. Despite the variations of the debate, the central issue has always been the role of slavery in causing the war, and recently the fundamentalists have won the larger audience. Historians like Eugene Genovese and Eric Foner have es-tablished beyond cavil the reality and gravity of ideological, economic, and political conflict between the free labor society of the North and the slave-based plantation society of the South. Slavery and irreconcilable views about the desirability of slavery's expansion lay at the base of that sectional clash, they argue, and the unwill-ingness of either section to tolerate the triumph of the other's values produced the war. Thus we have returned to an older view that sectional conflict over Negro slavery caused the Civil War.

Without disputing the reality of sectional conflict between North and South, one can still point out that the sectional conflict interpretation leaves certain crucial questions about the breakup of the nation unanswered. For one thing, to delineate the factors that divided North from South does not by itself explain why the slave states behaved so differently from each other during the secession crisis. When se-cession first occurred and the Confederacy was formed, only seven states in the Deep South withdrew, yet eight other slave states chose to remain in the Union. True, four more states joined the Confederacy once Abraham Lincoln called up troops after the firing on Fort Sumter, but resistance to overt federal coercion was far dif-ferent from secession in anticipation of a Republican administration. If a desire to protect or extend black slavery caused Southerners to break up the nation, why didn't all the slave states react the same way in the initial crisis?

More important, the argument that an escalating sectional conflict between North and South before April 1861 produced war between them after that date does not really explain why a conflict of long duration produced war then and not at some other time. The problem is how a basic conflict between sectional interests and values that had long been carried on in peaceful channels such as politics abruptly became a shooting war after smoldering for decades, and why it did so at one time instead of at another. What produced the sectional hostility, in other words, was not necessarily what caused armed conflict in 1861. Ideological differ-ences, after all, do not always produce wars. . . . [T]here most certainly was sectional conflict between North and South over slavery-related matters, yet that conflict, or cold war, had existed at least since the Constitutional Convention of 1787. Can a conflict that lasted almost three-fourths of a century explain why war broke out in 1861 and not earlier? If slavery or even the slavery extension issue caused the war, for example, why not in 1820 or 1832 or 1846 or 1850 or 1854? The basic problem concerning the war, in short, has less to do with the sources of sectional conflict than with the war's timing. The important question is not what divided North from South, but how the nation could contain or control that division for so long and then allow it suddenly to erupt into war.

This [essay] argues that the answers to these questions about varying Southern behavior and the timing of the Civil War lie in the political crisis of the 1850s. The key to Civil War causation is to be found in the reasons why the American political system could no longer contain the sectional conflict, not in the conflict itself. The [essay] differs from those of the fundamentalists by focusing less on the intensifying conflict than on the capacity of politicians and political structures to confine it to normal political channels. It argues that the change in that capacity had less to do with the explosiveness of the slavery issue *per se* than with a whole range of political developments, some of which created and others of which were responses to a crisis of confidence in the normal political process. Moreover, while I agree with revisionists that the individual decisions of politicians were important in exacerbating the situation, my emphasis is less on their ineptitude or the fanaticism of agitators than it is on the mechanics or dynamics of the political system itself.

The political crisis of the 1850s had two interrelated dimensions. The first was a fundamental reshaping of the nature of party competition. A national two-party system of Whigs and Democrats, which had functioned superbly for twenty years in all parts of the country and had helped contain the sectional conflict, collapsed. A realignment of voters followed between 1853 and 1856 in which a Democratic majority was replaced by an anti-Democratic majority in the North, even as the Democrats assumed an unassailable position in the South. Finally, new parties were organized, and out of the turmoil of the late 1850s the anti-Southern Republican party emerged triumphant. Because Southern secession was a direct response to the victory of the Republican party in the presidential election of 1860, there was a direct causal link between those political developments and the outbreak of war. One cannot account for Southern secession without accounting for the political events in the North that drove the South out of the Union. The political reorganization and realignment that replaced the national competition between Whigs and Democrats with a sectional competition between the Northern Republican party and a predominantly Southern Democracy was a major factor in the disruption of the Union.

More was involved in the collapse of the old two-party system, however, than merely the disappearance of national parties with affiliations across sectional lines. An equally crucial development took place at the state and local level. There, in the political arenas closest to the people, older frameworks of competition also dissolved. Voters with local needs and grievances that were every bit as important, if not more important, to them than national issues no longer had familiar party alternatives through which to seek political action. In this vacuum they tried to form new parties to meet their immediate needs, and much of the story of the political reorganization of the 1850s that led to civil war is to be found in those efforts. Local and state politics were just as crucial as national developments in shaping the political crisis of the 1850s.

The second aspect of the political crisis of the 1850s has received far less notice from historians, but it was just as critical as the first. This [essay] will attempt to demonstrate that the collapse of the old framework of two-party rivalry aggravated and in part reflected a loss of popular faith in the normal party political process to meet the needs of voters, to redress personal, group, and sectional grievances. Malignant distrust of politicians as self-centered and corrupt wirepullers out of touch with the people spread like an epidemic during the 1850s. So, too, did dissatisfaction with political parties as unresponsive and beyond popular control. Americans grew impatient with the inefficacy of traditional political methods and institutions. Widespread disgust with politics as usual engendered cries for reform that helped to destroy the old parties, propel voters to new affiliations, and shape new parties as ways were sought to return power to the people.

Underlying and intensifying the sense of crisis in the 1850s was a deep-seated republican ideology that had suffused American politics since the time of the Revolution. To Americans of the antebellum period, republicanism meant a number of things, and different Americans emphasized different parts of the creed. But to most white Americans who perceived political developments through the framework of republicanism, it meant, in Lincoln's words, government by and for the people, a government whose power over the people was restrained by law, and whose basic function was to protect the equality and liberty of individuals from aristocratic privilege and concentrations of arbitrary or tyrannical power. When Americans differed with each other politically, it was not so much over the desirability of republican government as over their perceptions of what most threatened its survival. . . .

Most Americans, North and South, therefore, were concerned with the same thing in the 1850s: the need to reform the political process in order to preserve republicanism and return political power to the people. Where they differed was in the way they defined the antirepublican plot and in the steps they took to combat it. Some saw the political pretensions of the hierarchical Catholic Church, directed by the Pope, as the major subverter of the American republic, and they formed a new political organization that promised to restore government to the people and to purify the corrupt political process by insisting that native-born Protestant Americans rule America. Others claimed with justice that this new anti-Catholic organization was itself a menace to republicanism. Yet the somewhat paradoxical result was that those on opposing sides regained confidence that they could do battle for republicanism within the party political process.

The common fear for the republic also fed the fire of sectional antagonism. Northerners and Southerners both identified powerful and hostile groups in the other section who would destroy their liberty and reduce them to an unequal status. This was made politically possible, even likely, because the collapse of the old two-party system in the early 1850s had been accompanied by a resurgence and exacerbation of naked sectional conflict between North and South. One of the reasons that conflict became so emotional, in turn, was that each section began to view the other as the subverter of republicanism, as a lawless and usurping tyrant bent on perverting the traditional basis of society and government. Hence the secessionist impulse in the Deep South was another manifestation of the national sense of crisis, of disgust with politicians and the old political process, and of the search for reform to save republicanism. Whatever else secession represented, it was a rejection of the normal political process that other Americans by 1860 were still content to work through, a refusal not only to tolerate the election of Lincoln but also to believe that the system could neutralize whatever threats he represented.

Like other Americans in the 1850s, Southerners had lost faith in politics as usual. Unlike Americans elsewhere, however, men from the Deep South never regained their faith in the efficacy of party politics. Thus they proved more receptive to the message that secession itself was necessary to restore republicanism. I will argue, in other words, that sectional extremism flourished in the Deep South precisely because no new framework of two-party competition had appeared there—as it had in the North and upper South—to help restore public confidence that republicanism could once again be secured by normal political methods. . . .

Politicians had long recognized that group conflict was endemic to American society and that the vitality of individual parties depended on the intensity of their competition with opposing parties. Thomas Jefferson had perceived in 1798 that "in every free and deliberating society, there must, from the nature of man, be opposite parties, and violent dissensions and discords." "Seeing that we must have somebody to quarrel with," he wrote John Taylor, "I had rather keep our New England associates for that purpose, than to see our bickerings transferred to others." Even more explicit in their recognition of what made parties work were the founders of New York's Albany Regency in the 1820s. They deplored the lack of internal discipline and cohesion in the Jeffersonian Republican party once the Federalists disappeared, and they moved quickly to remedy it. Although any party might suffer defeats, they realized, "it is certain to acquire additional strength . . . by the attacks of adverse parties." A political party, indeed, was "most in jeopardy when an opposition is not sufficiently defined." During "the contest between the great rival parties [Federalists and Jeffersonians] each found in the strength of the other a powerful motive of union and vigor." Significantly, those like Daniel Webster who deplored the emergence of mass parties in the 1820s and 1830s also recognized that strife was necessary to perpetuate party organization and that the best way to break it down was to cease opposition and work for consensus. Politicians in the 1840s and 1850s continued to believe that interparty conflict was needed to unify their own party and maintain their voting support. Thus an Alabama Democrat confessed that his party pushed a certain measure at the beginning of the 1840 legislative session explicitly as "the best means for drawing the party lines as soon as possible" while by 1852, when opposition to the state's Democracy appeared to disintegrate, another warned perceptively, "I think the only danger to the Democratic party is that it will become too much an omnibus in this State. We have nothing to fear from either the Union, or Whig party or both combined. From their friendship and adherence much." Many of the important decisions in the 1840s and 1850s reflected the search by political leaders for issues that would sharply define the lines between parties and thus reinvigorate the loyalty of party voters.

If conflict sustained the old two-party system, what destroyed it was the loss of the ability to provide interparty competition on *any* important issue at *any* level of the federal system. Because the political system's vitality and legitimacy with the voters depended on the clarity of the definition of the parties as opponents, the blurring of that definition undid the system. What destroyed the Second Party System was consensus, not conflict. The growing congruence between the parties on almost all issues by the early 1850s dulled the sense of party difference and thereby eroded voters' loyalty to the old parties. Once competing groups in society decided that the party system no longer provided them viable alternatives in which they could carry on conflict with each other, they repudiated the old system by dropping out, seeking third parties that would meet their needs, or turning to nonpartisan or extrapolitical action to achieve their goals. Because the collapse of the Second Party System was such a vital link in the war's causation, therefore, one arrives at a paradox. While the Civil War is normally viewed as the one time when conflict prevailed over consensus in American politics, the prevalence of consensus over conflict in crucial parts of the political system contributed in a very real way to the outbreak of war in the first place.

One of the reasons the Second Party System functioned for so long despite the presence of sectional antagonism was the federal system. Historians of the politics of the 1840s and 1850s, indeed, of most periods, have not adequately assessed the impact of the federal system on parties. They have assumed that forces operating at one level of political activity caused developments at all levels. Historians of the prewar period have especially been obsessed with national events. If slavery ruptured the national parties in Congress, if the speeches and correspondence of national leaders were filled with remarks about slavery, slavery must have destroyed the old parties and shaped political developments. As the new voting studies show, however, this assumption may be unwarranted.

Yet even grass-roots voting studies frequently neglect the most crucial arena of political activity in the nineteenth century—the states. Most of the legislation that affected the everyday lives of people was enacted at state capitals and not at Washington. State parties formed the core of the political system, not the flimsy national organizations that came together once every four years to contest the presidency. To voters and politicians, therefore, control of a state's government was often more important than electing men to Congress; consequently, within an individual state, the competitiveness of a party in gubernatorial and legislative elections was often more influential in determining its longevity than national affairs. Attention has been inordinately focused on Washington, but the real story of the political reorganization of the 1850s is to be found in individual states with their varying conditions. In accounting for the demise of the Second Party System, for example, one must be careful to distinguish between the sectional divisions within national parties and the death of state parties within each section. The old Whig party disintegrated, the Democratic party was reshaped, and voters realigned not in presidential elections where national party cohesion mattered, but in state and local elections where parties in each section could go their own way. Similarly, the pace at which the new Republican party arose, the nature of its coalition, and the emergence of a new two-party framework in the South varied from state to state according to conditions within them. Only by recognizing the complexity caused by the division of powers within the federal system can one arrive at a more accurate portrayal of the political antecedents of war.

For a long while the federal system was a key to the health of the Second Party System. Because both parties functioned at different levels, politicians had the luxury of saying different things in different parts of the country. They could define for home audiences lines of interparty conflict that did not necessarily apply to the country as a whole. Many voters, probably the vast majority, learned of national and even state issues only what their local politicians and newspapers told them. In this situation politicians could make issues that hurt their parties at one level help them at another. Issues involving slavery that disrupted the parties along sectional lines in Congress, for example, were often debated along party lines in the states. New York Whigs and Georgia Whigs could have diametrically opposed views on a matter involving slavery, but at home they could use their divergent positions to strengthen themselves against the common Democratic foe. Before a home audience what mattered most was not that the Whigs disagreed with each other in Congress, but that they differed from the Democrats in their state. The ability of the old system to provide party alternatives on slavery-related matters at the state level, indeed, was the major reason why the Second Party System managed the sectional conflict for so long, even when national parties were divided by it.

The advantages of the federal system went beyond even this important mechanism. State parties battled over more than national issues. There was a whole range of state issues over which they could conflict, issues they could use to reinforce the image of party difference or often to divert attention from disrupting national matters. At the local level, moreover, parties could add parochial concerns to the list of state and national questions over which they contended. Although national and state parties might eschew clear party positions on temperance or religion, for example, local party newspapers could adopt opposing stands to attract voters interested in one side or the other of those issues. At some level or other of the multitiered federal government structure, almost every issue that entered the political arena could be fought on party lines. Multilevel party competition thus normally reinforced the voters' faith in existing parties as vehicles for competing ethnic, economic, religious, and regional groups in the society at large. Only when the image of party difference disappeared at all levels and when, as a result, faith in the parties waned, did the political conditions develop in the North and South that led to the breakup of the nation.

FURTHER READING

William L. Barney, *The Secessionist Impulse: Alabama and Mississippi in 1860* (1974).

David Donald, *Charles Sumner and the Coming of the Civil War* (1960).

Eric Foner, *Free Soil, Free Labor, Free Men: The Ideology of the Republican Party Before the Civil War* (1970).

Lacy K. Ford, Jr., *Origins of Southern Radicalism: The South Carolina Upcountry, 1800–1860* (1988).

William E. Gienapp, *The Origins of the Republican Party, 1852–1856* (1986).

Bruce Levine, *Half Slave and Half Free: The Roots of the Civil War* (1992).

Kenneth M. Stampp, *America in 1857: A Nation on the Brink* (1991).

CHAPTER
14

The Civil War

Events moved quickly after Abraham Lincoln assumed the presidency on March 4, 1861. When Lincoln attempted to resupply Fort Sumter, an outpost in the harbor of Charleston, South Carolina, that was still controlled by Union forces, the Confederate Army shelled the fort; the federal troops surrendered on April 13, 1861. This brief bombardment began a long civil war from which a second revolution would be forged.

When the war began, few expected that it would last four horrifying years. Confederate leaders believed that the world's need for cotton would lead other nations to support their cause. They realized that the Union armies would have to conquer the Confederacy, and they expected that most northerners would tire of war before this could be achieved. Strategists for the Union advocated the "anaconda plan," which coupled a blockade of southern port cities with a military thrust down the Mississippi River valley to divide the Confederacy. In theory, this plan would squeeze the economic life out of the Confederacy, causing its citizenry to sue for peace.

The war went badly for the Union in the early campaigns, particularly in the eastern theater. Indecisive Union generals failed to take advantage of their superior military strength, while able Confederate military leaders, such as Robert E. Lee and "Stonewall" Jackson, befuddled the Union armies. The tide turned in mid-1863 when the Union won two battles in rapid succession, at Vicksburg in the western theater and at Gettysburg in the east. Under the leadership of Ulysses S. Grant and William Tecumseh Sherman, the Union forces took advantage of their numerical strength. These two formerly obscure generals utilized an idea of "total war," which meant that they were willing to wage war against the civilian population as well as against the army and government of their enemy. Shortly after Lincoln's reelection in 1864, Sherman began his "march to the sea," which devastated Georgia. By December 21, 1864, his army had reached the sea at Savannah. Within four months, General Lee surrendered.

The war was revolutionary on many levels. In some ways it might be called the world's first modern war. For the first time, armies engaged in trench warfare. Using rifles that could fire up to five hundred yards, soldiers killed people they could not see. Railroads were used to transfer armies; ironclad ships faced one another in naval combat. As a result, the loss of life suffered by the armies was frightening. In all, 620,000 men died as a result of battle and disease. One out of every six white males in the southern states aged thirteen to forty-three in 1860 was dead five years later. An additional half million men were maimed during the war, and yet another half million spent some time in overcrowded and unsanitary prison camps. People throughout the world observed the war with wonderment and horror. This was what future wars would be like.

In part because of these horrors, American society was transformed. Northern society was not unified behind the war effort, and dissent grew when the government suspended the right of habeus corpus and introduced a draft. The result was riots in northern cities and a heightened distrust of Lincoln's leadership. Basic questions of rights during war thus plagued society. Women's roles expanded as well, in part because men were at war, but also because women actively sought ways, such as participation in the Sanitary Commission, to support the war effort. In the Confederacy, the exigencies of war forced its leader to consider measures that had been unthinkable prior to the war. A confederacy formed on the rights of states found that it needed to centralize its government during war. A culture based on the splendor of a rural world had to foster industrialization in order to fight a war. And a society based on slavery ultimately considered arming slaves to fight in the Confederate Army. As the war destroyed southern society, all Americans had to ponder how that society would be reconstructed following the war's conclusion. One monumental change became clear by 1863: the Emancipation Proclamation signaled the end of slavery in the South. African Americans throughout the United States mobilized to end slavery. Whether fighting for the Union Army or fleeing their plantation homes to provide aid to invading forces, black people were instrumental in turning the war into a conflict to end slavery. By 1864, Lincoln had come to agree. In his Second Inaugural Address, he imagined that the war would continue "until every drop of blood drawn from the lash shall be paid by another drawn from the sword." Americans nevertheless would continue to ponder how much this national cleansing would alter the trajectory of the nation.

QUESTIONS TO THINK ABOUT

What advantages did the Confederacy have at the outset of the Civil War? What were the Union's advantages? Why did the Union ultimately win the war? How did war strain and change the societies in both North and South? Which questions about the future of the United States were answered by the Civil War? Which questions were not?

DOCUMENTS

The first three documents illustrate the varied opinions during the early years of the Civil War. In Document 1, Senator Robert Toombs, in a speech given just days after Lincoln was elected, describes how he is an outlaw in the North and how secession resembles the Declaration of Independence in 1776. In contrast, Frederick Douglass, in Document 2, looks to the future and demands the emancipation of the slaves. Freed slaves, he assures his readers, will conduct themselves well in a "natural order of human relations." In Document 3, *Debow's Review*, a southern periodical, does not mince words when it describes the war as a "bastard begotten of power and arrogance." The next three documents depict the lives of people who lived through the war. Document 4 is a letter to President Lincoln from James Henry Gooding, a black soldier. Gooding pleads to be treated—and paid—like a real soldier rather than a mere laborer. In Document 5, Tally Simpson, a Confederate soldier, in a letter home, describes the battle of Gettysburg and the devastation of the Confederate troops as a result. Women were active in wartime activities, as Document 6 illustrates. The Sanitary Commission was an organization staffed mainly by women that cared for sick and wounded soldiers. In this document, Mary A. Livermore recalls her work with the Sanitary Commission and poignantly describes the concern many women felt for those living amid the horror of war. The final four documents consider the later years of the war. In Document 7, Abraham Lincoln, in his Gettysburg Address in 1863, succinctly and profoundly addresses a nation at war. In Document 8, Congressman Clement Vallandigham of Ohio focuses on the questions of civil liberty in the North and as such disagrees with Lincoln's characterizations of the war. Vallandigham, a Democrat who opposed the war, condemns actions by Lincoln such as the suspension of the right of habeas corpus as a "reign of terror." In Document 9, his Second Inaugural Address in 1865, Lincoln expresses a desire to "bind up the nation's wounds," but also refers in almost apocalyptic terms to the war as an atonement for the sin of slavery. Finally, in Document 10, Sidney Andrews, a northern journalist, describes the aftermath of Sherman's march to the sea in South Carolina and Georgia. His accounts illustrate the devastation wreaked on the southern states as the war drew to a close.

1. Senator Robert Toombs Compares Secession with the American Revolution, 1860

. . . But we are told that secession would destroy the fairest fabric of liberty the world ever saw, and that we are the most prosperous people in the world under it. The arguments of tyranny as well as its acts, always reenact themselves. The arguments I now hear in favor of this Northern connection are identical in substance, and almost in the same words as those which were used in 1775 and 1776 to sustain the British connection. We won liberty, sovereignty, and independence by the American Revolution—we endeavored to secure and perpetuate these blessings by means of our Constitution. The very men who use these arguments admit that this Constitution, this compact, is violated, broken and trampled underfoot by the abolition party. Shall we surrender the jewels because their robbers and incendiaries have broken the casket? Is this the way to preserve liberty? I would as lief surrender it back to the British crown as to the abolitionists. I will defend it from both. Our purpose is to defend those liberties. What baser fate could befall us or this great experiment of free government than to have written upon its tomb: "Fell by the hands of abolitionists and the cowardice of its natural defenders." If we quail now, this will be its epitaph.

We are said to be a happy and prosperous people. We have been, because we have hitherto maintained our ancient rights and liberties—we will be until we surrender them. They are in danger; come, freemen, to the rescue. If we are prosperous, it is due to God, ourselves, and the wisdom of our State government. We have an executive, legislative, and judicial department at home, possessing and entitled to the confidence of the people. I have already vainly asked for the law of the Federal Government that promotes our prosperity. I have shown you many that retard that prosperity—many that drain our coffers for the benefit of our bitterest foes. I say bitterest foes—show me the nation in the world that hates, despises, villifies, or

Robert Toombs, speech, November 1860, in Frank Moore, ed., *The Rebellion Record, 1862–1863* (Putnam Holt, 1864), Supplement to Vol. I, 367–368. This document can also be found in William W. Freehling and Craig M. Simpson, eds., *Secession Debated: Georgia's Showdown in 1860* (New York: Oxford University Press, 1992), 48–49.

plunders us like our abolition "brethren" in the North. There is none. I can go to England or France, or any other country in Europe with my slave, without molestation or violating any law. I can go anywhere except in my own country, whilom [i.e., at one time] called "the glorious Union"; here alone am I stigmatized as a felon; here alone am I an outlaw; here alone am I under the ban of the empire; here alone I have neither security nor tranquillity; here alone are organized governments ready to protect the incendiary, the assassin who burns my dwelling or takes my life or those of my wife and children; here alone are hired emissaries paid by brethren to glide through the domestic circle and intrigue insurrection with all of its nameless horrors. My countrymen, "if you have nature in you, bear it not." Withdraw yourselves from such a confederacy; it is your right to do so—your duty to do so. I know not why the abolitionists should object to it, unless they want to torture and plunder you. If they resist this great sovereign right, make another war of independence, for that then will be the question; fight its battles over again—reconquer liberty and independence. As for me, I will take any place in the great conflict for rights which you may assign. I will take none in the Federal Government during Mr. Lincoln's administration.

If you desire a Senator after the fourth of March, you must elect one in my place. I have served you in the State and national councils for nearly a quarter of a century without once losing your confidence. I am yet ready for the public service, when honor and duty call. I will serve you anywhere where it will not degrade and dishonor my country. Make my name infamous forever, if you will, but save Georgia.

2. Frederick Douglass Calls for the Abolition of Slavery, 1862

. . . If I were asked to describe the most painful and mortifying feature presented in the prosecution and management of the present war on the part of the United States Government, against the slaveholding rebels now marshalled against it, I should not point to Ball's Bluff, Big Bethel, Bull Run, or any of the many blunders and disasters on flood or field; but I should point to the vacillation, doubt, uncertainty and hesitation, which have thus far distinguished our government in regard to the true method of dealing with the vital cause of the rebellion. We are without any declared and settled policy—and our policy seems to be, to have no policy. . . .

But why, O why should we not abolish slavery now? All admit that it must be abolished at some time. What better time than now can be assigned for that great work—Why should it longer live? What good thing has it done that it should be given further lease of life? What evil thing has it left undone? Behold its dreadful history! Saying nothing of the rivers of tears and streams of blood poured out by its 4,000,000 victims—saying nothing of the leprous poison it has diffused through the life blood of our morals and our religion—saying nothing of the many humiliating concessions already made to it—saying nothing of the deep and scandalous reproach it has brought upon our national good name—saying nothing of all this, and more the simple fact that this monster Slavery has eaten up and devoured the patriotism of

---

Frederick Douglass, "The Future of the Negro People of the Slave States," *Douglass' Monthly* (March 1862).

the whole South, kindled the lurid flames of a bloody rebellion in our midst, invited the armies of hostile nations to desolate our soil, and break down our Government, is good and all-sufficient cause of smiting it as with a bolt from heaven. . . .

But to return. What shall be done with the four million slaves, if emancipated? I answer, deal justly with them; pay them honest wages for honest work; dispense with the biting lash, and pay them the ready cash; awaken a new class of motives in them; remove those old motives of shriveling fear of punishment which benumb and degrade the soul, and supplant them by the higher and better motives of hope, of self-respect, of honor, and of personal responsibility. Reverse the whole current of feeling in regard to them. They have been compelled hitherto to regard the white man as a cruel, selfish, and remorseless tyrant, thirsting for wealth, greedy of gain, and caring nothing as to the means by which he obtains it. Now, let him see that the white man has a nobler and better side to his character, and he will love, honor, esteem the white man.

But it is said that the black man is naturally indolent, and that he will not work without a master. I know that this is a part of his bad reputation; but I also know that he is indebted for this bad reputation to the most indolent and lazy of all the American people, the slaveholders—men who live in absolute idleness, and eat their daily bread in the briny sweat of other men's faces. That the black man in Slavery shirks labor—aims to do as little as he can, and to do that little in the most slovenly manner—only proves that he is a man. . . .

Again, it is affirmed that the Negro, if emancipated, could not take care of himself. My answer to this is, let him have a fair chance to try it. For 200 years he has taken care of himself and his master in the bargain. I see no reason to believe that he could not take care, and very excellent care, of himself when having only himself to support. . . .

It is one of the strangest and most humiliating triumphs of human selfishness and prejudice over human reason, that it leads men to look upon emancipation as an experiment, instead of being, as it is, the natural order of human relations. Slavery, and not Freedom, is the experiment; and to witness its horrible failure we have to open our eyes, not merely upon the blasted soil of Virginia and other Slave States, but upon a whole land brought to the verge of ruin.

We are asked if we would turn the slaves all loose. I answer, Yes. Why not? They are not wolves nor tigers, but men. They are endowed with reason—can decide upon questions of right and wrong, good and evil, benefits and injuries—and are therefore subjects of government precisely as other men are.

3. *Debow's Review,* a Southern Journal, Condemns the Government and Army of the Union, 1862

A government which does not rest upon the consent of the governed, is necessarily an odious and bad government—bad, because even the benefits it may confer are the fruits of usurpation. If the axiom be true, that the power of governing is but the

---

T. W. McMahon, "Cause and Contrast—The American Crisis," *Debow's Review* 32, no. 3 (March–April 1862).

commission of God to the ruler, the trust is sufficiently onerous and responsible, even when willingly acquiesced in by the governed. But for him that usurps power to rule over a people who despise him, there can be no other name than TYRANT. To govern a people against their will is a crime against humanity, and insult to reason, and an outrage upon liberty. Such a ruler must, of necessity, be a conqueror. His jurisdiction is maintained by the remorseless ravage of states—by covering his path with death, terror and desolation—by rendering himself hateful to the virtuous, sacrificing the heroic, and enslaving the free. The bravest of his friends and foes fall together, the victims of his pride, tyranny and usurpation. Having become himself the first violator of public law, his followers will emulate his evil example, until general crime takes the place of regular order, and the fiercer passions of hatred and revenge substitute humanity and sociology. By his influence, commerce and agriculture are ruined—the plastic and mechanic arts sink into decrepitude—science, literature and religion are neglected or forgotten—demoralization becomes contagious—good men are forced, or deluded, into a copartnership of action with the despicable— villainy and profligacy are licensed to invade the sanctuaries of virtue and purity— and while innocence and industry are stripped of armor and shield, indecency and crime stalk abroad gigantic, unchecked and unpunished: for these are inevitable consequences of war. . . .

. . . [S]ince the world began—since war first cursed earth and degraded man—it would be difficult to discover, in the pages of universal history, the record of so unholy and iniquitous a civil strife as that into which Abraham Lincoln has plunged the American states. The war which he wages is a bastard begotten of power and arrogance. He, his advisers, and the section of the old republic to which he belongs, had, during the quarter of a century previous to his inauguration, heaped abuse, and outrage, and wrong, upon the people they are now endeavoring to crush, subjugate and exterminate. They represented that the South hung, like a mill-stone, round the neck of the Union, retarding her progress and blighting her prosperity. They inculcated in all of their moral teachings and political proclamations—some directly and others indirectly—that she would be "let slide," or that slavery should be abolished, ere the North could take her proper place among the nations. And, resolved at length to preserve her institutions, protect her property, and bear the responsibility of her own sins and disadvantages, the South separated herself from what seemed to be a dissatisfied partner; but implored a continuance of peace and friendship in parting. Here the North changed front. She declared that the South should not depart; that she should still remain in the Union, but as an inferior, without the protection guaranteed by the constitution, and stripped of her four thousand millions of dollars worth of slave property. . . .

. . . Twice, within a period of less than a single century, have two different and implacable foes sought the bloody spoliation of the South, by means of servile insurrections. On the 7th day of November, 1775, Lord Dunmore issued, in Virginia, a proclamation similar in spirit and intent to that addressed by General Fremont, in 1861, to the people of Missouri. "You may observe," writes the former three days afterward to General Howe, "that I offer freedom to the blacks of all white rebels that join me, in consequence of which there are two or three hundred already come in, and those I form into corps as fast as they come in, giving them white officers and noncommissioned in proportion. And from this plan I make no doubt of getting men enough *to reduce this colony to a proper sense of their duty."* A Virginia convention indignantly responded to the proclamation; but the final reply was given by George Washington, at the cannon's mouth, before Yorktown, to Lord Cornwallis, in 1781. And how well Missouri has emulated these noble examples, in answering the ordinance of Fremont, let the battles which she fought, and the victories which she won, at Springfield and Lexington, relate: for there is a coincidence of virtue in the deeds of patriots, as there is of baseness in the actions of tyrants. . . .

"I do solemnly swear, that I will faithfully execute the office of President of the States, and will, to the best of my ability, *preserve,* protect, and defend the constitution of the United States"—was the inauguration oath of Abraham Lincoln. That constitution recognizes the sovereign independence of each and every state— guarantees to them separate and free forms of government—renders their laws and possessions exempt from all external influences—upholds them as equal partners of a general agency—gave to congress the power of *regulating* the territories for the mutual advantage of all—and clothed it with absolute and exclusive jurisdiction (except in adjusting what might promote the general welfare) only in a district of ten miles square; but Mr. Lincoln interpreted the constitution, and respected his oath, so as to render state governments mere nullities—political toys—nonentities. He created new offices, and swarmed upon independent states hireling myrmidons [faithful who follow without question] to devour their substance. He raised standing armies without law and without authority. He rendered the military power absolute over the civil. And he made the jurisdiction of the constitution the slave of his will. The right of the Federal authority to make war upon, or coerce a state into obedience, was, in the convention that framed it, indignantly denied to the constitution; but he has undertaken to subjugate and lay waste fourteen states, and to crush their peoples beneath the fiery heel of war.

4. James Henry Gooding, an African American Soldier, Pleads for Equal Treatment, 1863

MORRIS ISLAND, S.C.
SEPTEMBER 28, 1863

YOUR EXCELLENCY, ABRAHAM LINCOLN:

Your Excellency will pardon the presumption of an humble individual like myself, in addressing you, but the earnest solicitation of my comrades in arms besides the genuine interest felt by myself in the matter is my excuse, for placing before the Executive head of the Nation our Common Grievance.

On the 6th of the last Month, the Paymaster of the Department informed us, that if we would decide to receive the sum of $10 (ten dollars) per month, he would come and pay us that sum, but that, on the sitting of Congress, the Regt. [regiment] would, in his opinion, be allowed the other 3 (three). He did not give us any guarantee that

James Henry Gooding to Abraham Lincoln, in Herbert Aptheker, ed., *A Documentary History of the Negro People in the U.S.* (New York: Citadel Press, 1951), 482–484.

this would be, as he hoped; certainly he had no authority for making any such guarantee, and we cannot suppose him acting in any way interested.

Now the main question is, are we Soldiers, or are we Laborers? We are fully armed, and equipped, have done all the various duties pertaining to a Soldier's life, have conducted ourselves to the complete satisfaction of General Officers, who were, if anything, prejudiced against us, but who now accord us all the encouragement and honors due us; have shared the perils and labor of reducing the first strong-hold that flaunted a Traitor Flag; and more, Mr. President, to-day the Anglo-Saxon Mother, Wife, or Sister are not alone in tears for departed Sons, Husbands and Brothers. The patient, trusting descendant of Afric's Clime have dyed the ground with blood, in defence of the Union, and Democracy. Men, too, your Excellency, who know in a measure the cruelties of the iron heel of oppression, which in years gone by, the very power their blood is now being spilled to maintain, ever ground them in the dust.

But when the war trumpet sounded o'er the land, when men knew not the Friend from the Traitor, the Black man laid his life at the altar of the Nation—and he was refused. When the arms of the Union were beaten, in the first year of the war, and the Executive called for more food for its ravenous maw, again the black man begged the privilege of aiding his country in her need, to be again refused.

And now he is in the War, and how has he conducted himself? . . . Obedient and patient and solid as a wall are they. All we lack is a paler hue and a better acquaintance with the alphabet.

Now your Excellency, we have done a Soldier's duty. Why can't we have a Soldier's pay? You caution the Rebel chieftain, that the United States knows no distinction in her soldiers. She insists on having all her soldiers of whatever creed or color, to be treated according to the usages of War. Now if the United States exacts uniformity of treatment of her soldiers from the insurgents, would it not be well and consistent to set the example herself by paying all her soldiers alike?

We of this Regt. were not enlisted under any "contraband" act. But we do not wish to be understood as rating our service of more value to the Government than the service of the ex-slave. Their service is undoubtedly worth much to the Nation, but Congress made express provision touching their case, as slaves freed by military necessity, and assuming the Government to be their temporary Guardian. Not so with us. Freemen by birth and consequently having the advantage of thinking and acting for ourselves so far as the Laws would allow us, we do not consider ourselves fit subjects for the Contraband act.

We appeal to you, Sir, as the Executive of the Nation, to have us justly dealt with. The Regt. do pray that they be assured their service will be fairly appreciated by paying them as American Soldiers, not as menial hirelings. Black men, you may well know, are poor; three dollars per month, for a year, will supply their needy wives and little ones with fuel. If you, as Chief Magistrate of the Nation, will assure us of our whole pay, we are content. Our Patriotism, our enthusiasm will have a new impetus, to exert our energy more and more to aid our Country. Not that our hearts ever flagged in devotion, spite the evident apathy displayed in our behalf, but we feel as though our Country spurned us, now we are sworn to serve her. Please give this a moment's attention.

5. Tally Simpson, a Confederate
Soldier, Recounts the
Battle of Gettysburg, 1863

Bunker's Hill Va
Saturday, July 18th /63

My dear Carrie

It had been a very long time since I received a letter from you when your last arrived, and I'll assure you it afforded me much pleasure.

Ere this reaches its destination you will have heard of the terrible battle of Gettysburg and the fate of a portion of our noble Army. I am a good deal of Pa's nature—extremely hopeful. But I must confess that this is a gloomy period for the Confederacy. One month ago our prospects were as bright as could well be conceived. Gallant Vicksburg, the Gibraltar of the West and the pride of the South, has fallen the victim to a merciless foe. Port Hudson has surrendered unconditionally, and it is now reduced to a fact that cannot be disputed that the Mississippi is already or must very soon be in the possession of the Yankees from its source to its mouth. And what good will the Trans Mississippi be to the Confederacy thus cut off?

A few weeks ago Genl Lee had the finest Army that ever was raised in ancient or modern times—and commanded by as patriotic and heroic officers as ever drew a sword in defence of liberty. But in an unfortunate hour and under disadvantageous circumstances, he attacked the enemy, and tho he gained the advantage and held possession of the battlefield and even destroyed more of the foe than he lost himself, still the Army of the Potomac lost heavily and is now in a poor condition for offensive operations. I venture to assert that one third of the men are barefooted or almost destitute of necessary clothing. There is one company in this regt which has fifteen men entirely without shoes and consequently unfit for duty. This is at least half of the company alluded to. The night we recrossed the river into Virginia, Harry's shoes gave out, and he suffered a great deal marching over rough turnpikes. But when he reached Martinsburg, he purchased a pair of old ones and did very well afterwards.

Tis estimated by some that this Army has been reduced to at least one fifth its original strength. Charleston is closely beset, and I think must surely fall sooner or later. The fall of Vicksburg has caused me to lose confidence in something or somebody, I can't say exactly which. And now that gunboats from the Mississippi can be transferred to Charleston and that a portion of Morris Island has been taken and can be used to advantage by the enemy, I fear greatly the result of the attack. I trust however, if it does fall, its gallant defenders will raze it to the ground that the enemy cannot find a single spot to pitch a tent upon the site where so magnificent a city once raised, so excitingly, its towering head. Savannah will follow, and then Mobile, and finally Richmond.

Guy R. Everson and Edward H. Simpson, Jr., eds. *"Far, Far from Home": The Wartime Letters of Dick and Tally Simpson, Third South Carolina Volunteers* (New York: Oxford University Press, 1994), 256–259.

These cities will be a loss to the Confederacy. But their fall is no reason why we should despair. It is certainly calculated to cast a gloom over our entire land. But we profess to be a Christian people, and we should put our trust in God. He holds the destiny of our nation, as it were, in the palm of his hand. He it is that directs the counsel of our leaders, both civil and military, and if we place implicit confidence in Him and go to work in good earnest, never for a moment losing sight of Heaven's goodness and protection, it is my firm belief that we shall be victorious in the end. Let the South lose what it may at present, God's hand is certainly in this contest, and He is working for the accomplishment of some grand result, and so soon as it is accomplished, He will roll the sun of peace up the skies and cause its rays to shine over our whole land. We were a wicked, proud, ambitious nation, and God has brought upon us this war to crush and humble our pride and make us a better people generally. And the sooner this happens the better for us. . . .

Your ever affec cousin
T. N. Simpson

James is quite well and stands these marches finely. He sends his love to his family and to all the negros generally. He likewise wishes to be remembered to his master and all the white family.

6. Mary A. Livermore, a Northern Woman, Recalls Her Role in the Sanitary Commission, 1863

Organizations of women for the relief of sick and wounded soldiers, and for the care of soldiers' families, were formed with great spontaneity at the very beginning of the war. There were a dozen or more of them in Chicago, in less than a month after Cairo was occupied by Northern troops. They raised money, prepared and forwarded supplies of whatever was demanded, every shipment being accompanied by some one who was held responsible for the proper disbursement of the stores. Sometimes these local societies affiliated with, or became parts of, more comprehensive organizations. Most of them worked independently during the first year of the war, the Sanitary Commission of Chicago being only one of the relief agencies. But the Commission gradually grew in public confidence, and gained in scope and power; and all the local societies were eventually merged in it, or became auxiliary to it. As in Chicago, so throughout the country. The Sanitary Commission became the great channel, through which the patriotic beneficence of the nation flowed to the army. . . .

Here, day after day, the drayman left boxes of supplies sent from aid societies in Iowa, Minnesota, Wisconsin, Michigan, Illinois, and Indiana. Every box contained an assortment of articles, a list of which was tacked on the inside of the lid. . . .

One day I went into the packing-room to learn the secrets of these boxes,— every one an argosy of love,—and took notes during the unpacking. A capacious box, filled with beautifully made shirts, drawers, towels, socks, and handkerchiefs, with

Mary A. Livermore, *My Story of the War: A Woman's Narrative of Four Years Personal Experience* (Hartford: A. D. Worthington and Company, 1889), 135–137.

"comfort-bags" containing combs, pins, needles, court-plaster, and black sewing-cotton, and with a quantity of carefully dried berries and peaches, contained the following unsealed note, lying on top:—

> DEAR SOLDIERS,—The little girls of —— send this box to you. They hear that thirteen thousand of you are sick, and have been wounded in battle. They are very sorry, and want to do something for you. They cannot do much, for they are all small; but they have bought with their own money, and made what is in here. They hope it will do some good, and that you will all get well and come home. We all pray to God for you night and morning. . . .

Another mammoth packing-case was opened, and here were folded in blessings and messages of love with almost every garment. On a pillow was pinned the following note, unsealed, for sealed notes were never broken:—

> MY DEAR FRIEND,—You are not *my* husband nor son; but you are the husband or son of some woman who undoubtedly loves you as I love mine. I have made these garments for you with a heart that aches for your sufferings, and with a longing to come to you to assist in taking care of you. It is a great comfort to me that God loves and pities you, pining and lonely in a far-off hospital; and if you believe in God, it will also be a comfort to *you.* Are you near death, and soon to cross the dark river? Oh, then, may God soothe your last hours, and lead you up "the shining shore," where there is no war, no sickness, no death. Call on Him, for He is an ever-present helper.

7. Abraham Lincoln Speaks About the Meaning of the War, 1863

Fourscore and seven years ago our fathers brought forth, on this continent, a new nation, conceived in Liberty, and dedicated to the proposition that all men are created equal.

Now we are engaged in a great civil war, testing whether that nation, or any nation so conceived, and so dedicated, can long endure. We are met on a great battlefield of that war. We have come to dedicate a portion of that field, as a final resting-place for those who here gave their lives, that that nation might live. It is altogether fitting and proper that we should do this.

But, in a larger sense, we can not dedicate—we can not consecrate—we can not hallow—this ground. The brave men, living and dead, who struggled here, have consecrated it far above our poor power to add or detract. The world will little note, nor long remember what we say here, but it can never forget what they did here. It is for us the living, rather, to be dedicated here to the unfinished work which they who fought here have thus far so nobly advanced. It is rather for us to be here dedicated to the great task remaining before us—that from these honored dead we take increased devotion to that cause for which they here gave the last full measure of devotion—that we here highly resolve that these dead shall not have died in vain—that this nation, under God, shall have a new birth of freedom—and that government of the people, by the people, for the people, shall not perish from the earth.

Abraham Lincoln, Gettysburg Address (1863).

8. Congressman Clement Vallandigham Denounces the Union War Effort, 1863

The men who are in power at Washington, extending their agencies out through the cities and states of the Union and threatening to reinaugurate a reign of terror, may as well know that we comprehend precisely their purpose. I beg leave to assure you that it cannot and will not be permitted to succeed. The people of this country endorsed it once because they were told that it was essential to "the speedy suppression or crushing out of the rebellion" and the restoration of the Union; and they so loved the Union of these states that they would consent, even for a little while, under the false and now broken promises of the men in power, to surrender those liberties in order that the great object might, as was promised, be accomplished speedily.

They have been deceived; instead of crushing out the rebellion, the effort has been to crush out the spirit of liberty. The conspiracy of those in power is not so much for a vigorous prosecution of the war against rebels in the South as against the democracy in peace at home. . . .

. . . Now, if in possession of the purse and the sword absolutely and unqualifiedly, for two years, there be anything else wanting which describes a dictatorship, I beg to know what it is. . . .

I will not consent to put the entire purse of the country and the sword of the country into the hands of the executive, giving him despotic and dictatorial power to carry out an object which I avow before my countrymen is the destruction of their liberties and the overthrow of the Union of these states. . . .

The charge has been made against us—all who are opposed to the policy of this administration and opposed to this war—that we are for "peace on any terms." It is false. I am not, but I am for an immediate stopping of the war and for honorable peace. I am for peace for the sake of the Union of these states. . . .

[A]nd I, unlike some of my own party, and unlike thousands of the Abolition Party, believe still, before God, that the Union can be reconstructed and will be. That is my faith, and I mean to cling to it as the wrecked mariner clings to the last plank amid the shipwreck.

9. Abraham Lincoln Strives to Reunite the Nation, 1865

On the occasion corresponding to this four years ago, all thoughts were anxiously directed to an impending civil-war. All dreaded it—all sought to avert it. While the inaugural address was being delivered from this place, devoted altogether to *saving* the Union without war, insurgent agents were in the city seeking to *destroy* it without war—seeking to dissolve the Union, and divide effects, by negotiation. Both parties deprecated war; but one of them would *make* war rather than let the nation survive; and the other would *accept* war rather than let it perish. And the war came.

One eighth of the whole population were colored slaves, not distributed generally over the Union, but localized in the Southern part of it. These slaves constituted

Clement Vallandigham's Copperhead Dissent (1863), in Clement L. Vallandigham, *Speeches, Arguments, Addresses, and Letters of Clement L. Vallandigham* (New York: J. Walter & Col., 1864), 479–502.

Abraham Lincoln, *Second Inaugural Address* (1865).

a peculiar and powerful interest. All knew that this interest was, somehow, the cause of the war. To strengthen, perpetuate, and extend this interest was the object for which the insurgents would rend the Union, even by war; while the government claimed no right to do more than to restrict the territorial enlargement of it. Neither party expected for the war, the magnitude, or the duration, which it has already attained. Neither anticipated that the *cause* of the conflict might cease with, or even before, the conflict itself should cease. Each looked for an easier triumph, and a result less fundamental and astounding. Both read the same Bible, and pray to the same God; and each invokes His aid against the other. . . . If we shall suppose that American Slavery is one of those offences which, in the providence of God, must needs come, but which, having continued through His appointed time, He now wills to remove, and that He gives to both North and South, this terrible war, as the woe due to those by whom the offence came, shall we discern therein any departure from those divine attributes which the believers in a Living God always ascribe to Him? Fondly do we hope—fervently do we pray—that this mighty scourge of war may speedily pass away. Yet, if God wills that it continue, until all the wealth piled by the bond-man's two hundred and fifty years of unrequited toil shall be sunk, and until every drop of blood drawn with the lash, shall be paid by another drawn with the sword, as was said three thousand years ago, so still it must be said "the judgments of the Lord, are true and righteous altogether."

With malice toward none; with charity for all; with firmness in the right, as God gives us to see the right, let us strive on to finish the work we are in; to bind up the nation's wounds; to care for him who shall have borne the battle, and for his widow, and his orphan—to do all which may achieve and cherish a just, and a lasting peace, among ourselves, and with all nations.

10. Sidney Andrews, a Northern Journalist, Reports on the Devastation of Georgia, 1866

Columbia, September 12, 1865.

The war was a long time in reaching South Carolina, but there was vengeance in its very breath when it did come,—wrath that blasted everything it touched, and set Desolation on high as the genius of the State. "A brave people never before made such a mistake as we did," said a little woman who sat near me in the cars while coming up from Charleston; "it mortifies me now, every day I live, to think how well the Yankees fought. We had no idea they could fight half so well." In such humiliation as hers is half the lesson of the war for South Carolina.

. . . Sherman came in here, the papers used to say, to break up the railroad system of the seaboard States of the Confederacy. He did his work so thoroughly that half a dozen years will nothing more than begin to repair the damage, even in this regard.

The railway section of the route from Charleston lies mostly either in a pine barren or a pine swamp, though after passing Branchville we came into a more open and rolling country, with occasional signs of life. Yet we could not anywhere, after we

---

Sidney Andrews, *The South Since the War: As Shown by Fourteen Weeks of Travel and Observation in Georgia and the Carolinas* (Boston: Ticknor and Fields, 1866), 28–37.

left the immediate vicinity of the city, see much indication of either work or existence. The trim and handsome railway stations of the North, the little towns strung like beads on an iron string, are things unknown here. In the whole seventy-seven miles there are but two towns that make any impression on the mind of a stranger,—Summerville and George's,—and even these are small and unimportant places. . . .

I came up from Orangeburg, forty-five miles, by "stage," to wit, an old spring-covered market-wagon, drawn by three jaded horses and driven by Sam, freedman, late slave,—of the race not able to take care of themselves, yet caring, week in and week out, for the horses and interests of his employer as faithfully and intelligently as any white man could. There were six of us passengers, and we paid ten dollars each passage-money. We left Orangeburg at four, P.M.; drove eight miles; supped by the roadside; drove all night; lunched at sunrise by a muddy brook; and reached Columbia and breakfast at eleven, A.M., thankful that we had not broken down at midnight, and had met only two or three minor accidents. I am quite sure there are more pleasant ways of travelling than by "stage" in South Carolina at the present time. Thirty-two miles of the forty-five lie in such heavy and deep sand that no team can travel faster than at a moderate walk. For the other thirteen miles the road is something better, though even there it is the exception and not the rule to trot your mules. The river here was formerly spanned by an elegant and expensive bridge, but the foolish Rebels burned it; and the crossing of the Congaree is now effected in a ferry, the style and management of which would disgrace any backwoods settlement of the West.

The "Shermanizing process," as an ex-Rebel colonel jocosely called it, has been complete everywhere. To simply say that the people hate that officer is to put a fact in very mild terms. . . .

Certain bent rails are the first thing one sees to indicate the advent of his army. They are at Branchville. I looked at them with curious interest. "It passes my comprehension to tell what became of our railroads," said a travelling acquaintance; "one week we had passably good roads, on which we could reach almost any part of the State, and the next week they were all gone,—not simply broken up, but gone; some of the material was burned, I know, but miles and miles of iron have actually disappeared, gone out of existence."

We rode over the road where the army marched. Now and then we found solitary chimneys, but, on the whole, comparatively few houses were burned, and some of those were fired, it is believed, by persons from the Rebel army or from the neighboring locality. The fences did not escape so well, and most of the planters have had these to build during the summer. This was particularly the case near Columbia. Scarcely a tenth of that destroyed appears to have been rebuilt, and thousands of acres of land of much richness lie open as a common.

There is great scarcity of stock of all kinds. What was left by the Rebel conscription officers was freely appropriated by Sherman's army, and the people really find considerable difficulty not less in living than in travelling. Milk, formerly an article much in use, can only be had now in limited quantities: even at the hotels we have more meals without than with it. There are more mules than horses, apparently; and the animals, whether mules or horses, are all in ill condition and give evidence of severe overwork.

Columbia was doubtless once the gem of the State. . . .

It is now a wilderness of ruins. Its heart is but a mass of blackened chimneys and crumbling walls. Two thirds of the buildings in the place were burned, including, without exception, everything in the business portion. Not a store, office, or shop escaped; and for a distance of three fourths of a mile on each of twelve streets there was not a building left. . . . The residence portion generally escaped conflagration, though houses were burned in all sections except the extreme northeastern.

Every public building was destroyed, except the new and unfinished state-house. This is situated on the summit of tableland whereon the city is built, and commands an extensive view of the surrounding country, and must have been the first building seen by the victorious and on-marching Union army. . . . The poverty of this people is so deep that there is no probability that it can be finished, according to the original design, during this generation at least.

The ruin here is neither half so eloquent nor touching as that at Charleston. This is but the work of flame, and might have mostly been brought about in time of peace. Those ghostly and crumbling walls and those long-deserted and grass-grown streets show the prostration of a community,—such prostration as only war could bring.

. . . Old men and despondent men say it can never be rebuilt. "We shall have to give it up to the Yankees, I reckon," said one of two gentlemen conversing near me this morning. "Give it up!" said the other; "they've already moved in and taken possession without asking our leave." I guess the remark is true. I find some Northern men already here, and I hear of more who are coming.

Of course there is very little business doing yet. The city is, as before said, in the heart of the devastated land. . . .

The women who consider it essential to salvation to snub or insult Union officers and soldiers at every possible opportunity do not seem as numerous as they appeared to be in Charleston; and indeed marriages between soldiers and women of the middle class are not by any means the most uncommon things in the world. . . .

. . . [A] man of much apparent intelligence, informed me that the negroes have an organized military force in all sections of the State, and are almost certain to rise and massacre the whites about Christmas time.

Another had heard, and sincerely believed, that General Grant's brother-in-law is an Indian, and is on his staff, and that the President has issued an order permitting the General's son to marry a mulatto girl whom he found in Virginia.

A woman, evidently from the country districts, stated that there had been a rising of the negroes in Maryland; that a great many whites had been killed; and that some considerable portion of Baltimore and many of the plantations had been seized by the negroes.

And, finally, an elderly gentleman who represented himself as a cotton factor, declared that there would be a terrible civil war in the North within two years; that England would compel the repudiation of our National debt and the assumption of the Confederate debt for her guaranty of protection.

The people of the central part of the State are poor, wretchedly poor; for the war not only swept away their stock and the material resources of their plantations, but also all values,—all money, stocks, and bonds,—and generally left nothing that can be sold for money but cotton, and only a small proportion of the landholders have any of that. Therefore there is for most of them nothing but the beginning anew of life, on the strictest personal economy and a small amount of money borrowed in the city. It would be a benefit of hundred of millions of dollars if the North could be made to practise half the economy which poverty forces upon this people.

They are full of ignorance and prejudices, but they want peace and quiet, and seem not badly disposed toward the general government. Individuals there are who rant and rave and feed on fire as in the old days, but another war is a thing beyond the possibilities of time. So far as any fear of that is concerned we may treat this State as we please,—hold it as a conquered province or restore it at once to full communion in the sisterhood of States. The war spirit is gone, and no fury can reenliven it.

E S S A Y S

The Civil War ended slavery, but historians have debated who was most responsible for the Emancipation Proclamation. James M. McPherson, professor of history at Princeton University, stresses the political genius of Abraham Lincoln, arguing that Lincoln played a crucial role in engineering three revolutions during the Civil War, one of which was the abolition of slavery. Professor McPherson emphasizes the political difficulties that Lincoln faced in bringing about abolition. Although Lincoln moved cautiously during the early years of war, his proclamation of emancipation completely changed the meaning of the war because it proclaimed a revolutionary new aim of the war. A group of scholars led by Ira Berlin, a member of the department of history at the University of Maryland, argues in contrast that the responsibility for the Emancipation Proclamation lies with the slaves themselves. President Lincoln, he contends, entered the Civil War only to save the Union, and Confederate leaders were convinced that slavery would endure. It was the actions of slaves, he argues, that forced Lincoln to come to terms with emancipation. By moving to the Union Army, they not only aided the war effort, but ultimately forced the issue. If he began as a president intent only on saving the Union, Lincoln ultimately became known as the Great Emancipator. But his legacy would not have occurred, Professor Berlin and his colleagues believe, had it not been for African Americans' forcing the issue.

The Role of Abraham Lincoln in the Abolition of Slavery

JAMES M. MCPHERSON

The foremost Lincoln scholar of a generation ago, James G. Randall, considered the sixteenth president to be a conservative on the great issues facing the country, Union and slavery. If conservatism, wrote Randall, meant "caution, prudent adherence to tested values, avoidance of rashness, and reliance upon unhurried, peaceable evolution, [then] Lincoln was a conservative." His preferred solution of the slavery problem, Randall pointed out, was a program of gradual, compensated emancipation with the consent of the owners, stretching over a generation or more, with provision for the colonization abroad of emancipated slaves to minimize the potential for racial conflict and social disorder. In his own words, Lincoln said that he wanted to "stand on middle ground," avoid "dangerous extremes," and achieve his goals through "the spirit of compromise . . . [and] of mutual concession." In essence, concluded Randall, Lincoln believed in evolution rather than revolution, in "planting, cultivating, and harvesting, not in uprooting and destroying." Many historians have agreed with this interpretation. To cite just two of them: T. Harry Williams maintained that "Lincoln was on the slavery question, as he was on most matters, a conservative"; and Norman Graebner wrote an essay entitled "Abraham Lincoln: Conservative Statesman," based on the premise that Lincoln was a conservative because "he accepted the need of dealing with things as they were, not as he would have wished them to be."

Yet as president of the United States, Lincoln presided over a profound, wrenching experience which, in Mark Twain's words, "uprooted institutions that were centuries old, changed the politics of a people, transformed the social life of half the country, and wrought so profoundly upon the entire national character that the influence cannot be measured short of two or three generations." Benjamin Disraeli, viewing this experience from across the Atlantic in 1863, characterized "the struggle in America" as "a great revolution. . . . [We] will see, when the waters have subsided, a different America." The *Springfield* (Mass.) *Republican,* an influential wartime newspaper, predicted that Lincoln's Emancipation Proclamation would accomplish "the greatest social and political revolution of the age." The historian Otto Olsen has labeled Lincoln a revolutionary because he led the nation in its achievement of this result.

As for Lincoln himself, he said repeatedly that the right of revolution, the "right of any people" to "throw off, to revolutionize, their existing form of government, and to establish such other in its stead as they may choose" was "a sacred right—a right, which we may hope and believe, is to liberate the world." The Declaration of Independence, he insisted often, was the great "charter of freedom" and in the example of the American Revolution "the world has found . . . the germ . . . to grow and expand into the universal liberty of mankind." Lincoln championed the leaders of the European revolutions of 1848; in turn, a man who knew something about those revolutions—Karl Marx—praised Lincoln in 1865 as "the single-minded son of the working class" who had led his "country through the matchless struggle for the rescue of an enchained race and the reconstruction of a social world."

What are we to make of these contrasting portraits of Lincoln the conservative and Lincoln the revolutionary? Are they just another example of how Lincoln's words can be manipulated to support any position, even diametrically opposed ones? No. It is a matter of interpretation and emphasis within the context of a fluid and rapidly changing crisis situation. The Civil War started out as one kind of conflict and ended as something quite different. These apparently contradictory positions about Lincoln the conservative versus Lincoln the revolutionary can be reconciled by focusing on this process. The attempt to reconcile them can tell us a great deal about the nature of the American Civil War.

That war has been viewed as a revolution—as the second American Revolution—in three different senses. Lincoln played a crucial role in defining the outcome of the revolution in each of three respects.

The first way in which some contemporaries regarded the events of 1861 as a revolution was the frequent invocation of the right of revolution by southern leaders to justify their secession—their declaration of independence—from the United

States. The Mississippi convention that voted to secede in 1861 listed the state's grievances against the North, and proclaimed: "For far less cause than this, our fathers separated from the Crown of England." . . .

For Lincoln it was the *Union,* not the Confederacy, that was the true heir of the Revolution of 1776. That revolution had established a republic, a democratic government of the people by the people. This republic was a fragile experiment in a world of kings, emperors, tyrants, and theories of aristocracy. If secession were allowed to succeed, it would destroy that experiment. It would set a fatal precedent by which the minority could secede whenever it did not like what the majority stood for until the United States fragmented into a dozen pitiful, squabbling countries, the laughing stock of the world. The successful establishment of a slaveholding Confederacy would also enshrine the idea of inequality, a contradiction of the ideal of equal natural rights on which the United States was founded. "This issue embraces more than the fate of these United States," said Lincoln on another occasion. "It presents to the whole family of man, the question, whether a constitutional republic, or a democracy . . . can, or cannot, maintain its territorial integrity." Nor is the struggle "altogether for today; it is for a vast future. . . . On the side of the Union it is a struggle for maintaining in the world that form and substance of government whose leading object is to elevate the condition of men . . . to afford all an unfettered start, and a fair chance in the race of life."

To *preserve* the Union and *maintain* the republic: these verbs denote a conservative purpose. If the Confederacy's war of independence was indeed a revolution, Lincoln was most certainly a conservative. But if secession was an act of counterrevolution to forestall a revolutionary threat to slavery posed by the government Lincoln headed, these verbs take on a different meaning and Lincoln's intent to conserve the Union becomes something other than conservatism. But precisely what it would become was not yet clear in 1861.

The second respect in which the Civil War is viewed as a revolution was in its abolition of slavery. This was indeed a revolutionary achievement—not only an expropriation of the principal form of property in half the country, but a destruction of the institution that was basic to the southern social order, the political structure, the culture, the way of life in this region. But in 1861 this revolutionary achievement was not part of Lincoln's war aims.

From the beginning of the war, though, abolitionists and some Republicans urged the Lincoln administration to turn the military conflict into a revolutionary crusade to abolish slavery and create a new order in the South. As one abolitionist put it in 1861, although the Confederates "justify themselves under the right of revolution," their cause "is not a revolution but a rebellion against the noblest of revolutions." The North must meet this southern counterrevolution by converting the war for the Union into a revolution for freedom. "WE ARE THE REVOLUTIONISTS," he proclaimed. The principal defect of the first American Revolution, in the eyes of abolitionists, had been that while it freed white Americans from British rule it failed to free black Americans from slavery. Now was the time to remedy that defect by proclaiming emancipation and inviting the slaves "to a share in the *glorious second American Revolution.*" And Thaddeus Stevens, the grim-visaged old gladiator who led the radical Republicans in the House of Representatives, pulled no punches in this regard. "We must treat this [war] as a radical revolution," he declared, and "free every slave—slay every traitor—burn every rebel mansion, if these things be necessary to preserve" the nation.

Such words grated harshly on Lincoln's ears during the first year of the war. In his message to Congress in December 1861 the president deplored the possibility that the war might "degenerate into a violent and remorseless revolutionary struggle." It was not that Lincoln *wanted* to preserve slavery. On the contrary, he said many times: "I am naturally anti-slavery. If slavery is not wrong, nothing is wrong." But as president he could not act officially on his private "judgment [concerning] the moral question of slavery." He was bound by the Constitution, which protected the institution of slavery in the states. In the first year of the war the North fought to preserve this Constitution and restore the Union as it had existed before 1861. Lincoln's theory of the war held that since secession was illegal, the Confederate states were still legally in the Union although temporarily under the control of insurrectionists. The government's purpose was to suppress this insurrection and restore loyal Unionists to control of the southern states. The conflict was therefore a limited war with the limited goal of restoring the status quo ante bellum, not an unlimited war to destroy an enemy nation and reshape its society. And since, in theory, the southern states were still in the Union, they continued to enjoy all their constitutional rights, including slavery.

There were also several political reasons for Lincoln to take this conservative position in 1861. For one thing, the four border slave states of Missouri, Kentucky, Maryland, and Delaware had remained in the Union; Lincoln desperately wanted to keep them there. He would like to have God on his side, Lincoln supposedly said, but he *must* have Kentucky. In all of these four states except Delaware a strong pro-Confederate faction existed. Any rash action by the northern government against slavery, therefore, might push three more states into the Confederacy. Moreover, in the North itself nearly half of the voters were Democrats, who supported a war for the Union but might oppose a war against slavery. For these reasons, Lincoln held at bay the Republicans and abolitionists who were calling for an antislavery war and revoked actions by two of his generals who had proclaimed emancipation by martial law in areas under their command.

Antislavery Republicans challenged the theory underlying Lincoln's concept of a limited war. They pointed out that by 1862 the conflict had become in theory as well as in fact a full-fledged war between nations, not just a police action to suppress an uprising. By imposing a blockade on Confederate ports and treating captured Confederate soldiers as prisoners of war rather than as criminals or pirates, the Lincoln administration had in effect recognized that this was a war rather than a mere domestic insurrection. Under international law, belligerent powers had the right to seize or destroy enemy resources used to wage war—munitions, ships, military equipment, even food for the armies and crops sold to obtain cash to buy armaments. As the war escalated in scale and fury and as Union armies invaded the South in 1861, they did destroy or capture such resources. Willy-nilly the war *was* becoming a remorseless revolutionary conflict, a total war rather than a limited one.

A major Confederate resource for waging war was the slave population, which constituted a majority of the southern labor force. Slaves raised food for the army, worked in war industries, built fortifications, dug trenches, drove army supply wagons, and so on. As enemy property, these slaves were subject to confiscation under the laws of war. The Union Congress passed limited confiscation laws in August 1861 and July 1862 that authorized the seizure of this human property. But pressure mounted during 1862 to go further than this—to proclaim emancipation as a *means* of winning the war by converting the slaves from a vital war resource for the South to allies of the North, and beyond that to make the abolition of slavery a *goal* of the war, in order to destroy the institution that had caused the war in the first place and would continue to plague the nation in the future if it was allowed to survive. By the summer of 1861, most Republicans wanted to turn this limited war to restore the old Union into a revolutionary war to create a new nation purged of slavery.

For a time Lincoln tried to outflank this pressure by persuading the border slave states remaining in the Union to undertake voluntary, gradual emancipation, with the owners to be compensated by the federal government. With rather dubious reasoning, Lincoln predicted that such action would shorten the war by depriving the Confederacy of its hope for the allegiance of these states and thereby induce the South to give up the fight. And though the compensation of slaveholders would be expensive, it would cost much less than continuing the war. If the border states adopted some plan of gradual emancipation such as northern states had done after the Revolution of 1776, said Lincoln, the process would not radically disrupt the social order.

Three times in the spring and summer of 1862 Lincoln appealed to congressmen from the border states to endorse a plan for gradual emancipation. If they did not, he warned in March, "it is impossible to foresee all the incidents which may attend and all the ruin which may follow." In May he declared that the changes produced by his gradual plan "would come gently as the dews of heaven, not rending or wrecking anything. Will you not embrace it? . . . You can not, if you would, be blind to the signs of the times." But most of the border-state representatives remained blind to the signs. They questioned the constitutionality of Lincoln's proposal, objected to its cost, bristled at its veiled threat of federal coercion, and deplored the potential race problem they feared would come with a large free black population. In July, Lincoln once more called border-state congressmen to the White House. He admonished them bluntly that "the unprecedentedly stern facts of the case" called for immediate action. The limited war was becoming a total war; pressure to turn it into a war of abolition was growing. The slaves were emancipating themselves by running away from home and coming into Union lines. If the border states did not make "a decision at once to emancipate *gradually* . . . the institution in your states will be extinguished by mere friction and abrasion—by the mere incidents of the war." In other words, if they did not accept an evolutionary plan for the abolition of slavery, it would be wiped out by the revolution that was coming. But again they refused, rejecting Lincoln's proposal by a vote of twenty to nine. Angry and disillusioned, the president decided to embrace the revolution. That very evening he made up his mind to issue an emancipation proclamation. After a delay to wait for a Union victory, he sent forth the preliminary proclamation on September 22—after the battle of Antietam—and the final proclamation on New Year's Day 1863.

The old cliché, that the proclamation did not free a single slave because it applied only to the Confederate states where Lincoln had no power, completely misses the point. The proclamation announced a revolutionary new war aim—the overthrow of slavery by force of arms if and when Union armies conquered the South.

Of course, emancipation could not be irrevocably accomplished without a constitutional amendment, so Lincoln threw his weight behind the Thirteenth Amendment, which the House passed in January 1865. In the meantime two of the border states, Maryland and Missouri, which had refused to consider gradual, compensated emancipation in 1862, came under control of emancipationists who pushed through state constitutional amendments that abolished slavery without compensation and went into effect immediately—a fate experienced by the other border states, Kentucky and Delaware, along with the rest of the South when the Thirteenth Amendment was ratified in December 1865.

But from the time the Emancipation Proclamation went into effect at the beginning of 1863, the North fought for the revolutionary goal of a new Union without slavery. Despite grumbling and dissent by some soldiers who said they had enlisted to fight for the Union rather than for the "nigger," most soldiers understood and accepted the new policy. A colonel from Indiana put it this way: whatever their opinion of slavery and blacks, his men "desire to destroy everything that gives the rebels strength." Therefore "this army will sustain the emancipation proclamation and enforce it with the bayonet." Soon after the proclamation came out, General-in-Chief Henry W. Halleck wrote to General Ulysses S. Grant near Vicksburg that "the character of the war has very much changed within the last year. There is now no possible hope of reconciliation with the rebels. . . . We must conquer the rebels or be conquered by them. . . . Every slave withdrawn from the enemy is the equivalent of a white man put *hors de combat*." One of Grant's field commanders explained that "the policy is to be terrible on the enemy. I am using negroes all the time for my work as teamsters, and have 1,000 employed."

Lincoln endorsed this policy of being "terrible on the enemy." And the policy soon went beyond using freed slaves as teamsters and laborers. By early 1863 the Lincoln administration committed itself to enlisting black men in the army. Arms in the hands of slaves constituted the South's ultimate nightmare. The enlistment of black soldiers to fight and kill their former masters was by far the most revolutionary dimension of the emancipation policy. And, after overcoming his initial hesitation, Lincoln became an enthusiastic advocate of this policy. In March 1863 he wrote to Andrew Johnson, military governor of occupied Tennessee: "The bare sight of fifty thousand armed, and drilled black soldiers on the banks of the Mississippi, would end the rebellion at once. And who doubts that we can present that sight, if we but take hold in earnest?" By August 1863, when the Union army had organized 50,000 black soldiers and was on the way to enlistment of 180,000 before the war was over, Lincoln declared in a public letter that "the emancipation policy, and the use of colored troops, constitute the heaviest blow yet dealt to the rebellion."

When conservatives complained of the revolutionary nature of these heavy blows, Lincoln responded that the nation could no longer pursue "a temporizing and forbearing" policy toward rebels. "Decisive and extensive measures must be adopted." Conservatives who did not like it should blame the slaveholders and fire-eaters who started the war. They "must understand," said Lincoln in an angry tone, "that they cannot experiment for ten years trying to destroy the government, and if they fail still come back into the Union unhurt." In a metaphor that he used several times, Lincoln said that "broken eggs cannot be mended." The egg of slavery was already broken by 1862; if the South continued fighting it must expect more eggs to be broken, so the sooner it gave up "the smaller [would] be the amount of that which will be beyond mending." Lincoln's fondness for this metaphor is interesting, for modern revolutionaries sometimes use a similar one to justify the use of violence to bring about social change: you cannot make an omelet, they say, without breaking eggs—that is, you cannot make a new society without destroying the old one.

Another way of illustrating how Lincoln came to believe in this revolutionary concept is to quote from his second inaugural address, delivered at a time when the war had gone on for almost four terrible years. On the one hand were the famous words of the second inaugural calling for the binding up of the nation's wounds, with malice toward none and charity for all. With these words Lincoln invoked the New Testament lesson of forgiveness; he urged a soft peace once the war was over. But although he believed in a soft peace, it could be won only by a hard war. This was an Old Testament concept, and for Lincoln's Old Testament vision of a hard war, examine *this* passage from the second inaugural: "American Slavery is one of those offences which, in the providence of God . . . He now wills to remove [through] this terrible war, as the woe due to those by whom the offence came. . . . Fondly do we hope—fervently do we pray—that this mighty scourge of war may speedily pass away. Yet if God wills that it continue, until all the wealth piled by the bondman's two hundred and fifty years of unrequited toil shall be sunk, and until every drop of blood drawn with the lash, shall be paid by another drawn with the sword, as was said three thousand years ago, so still it must be said 'the judgments of the Lord, are true and righteous altogether.'"

This was the language not only of the Old Testament, but also of revolution. In the second respect in which the Civil War has been viewed as a revolution—its achievement of the abolition of slavery—Lincoln fits the pattern of a revolutionary leader. He was a reluctant one at first, to be sure, but in the end he was more radical than Washington or Jefferson or any of the leaders of the first revolution. They led a successful struggle for independence from Britain but did not accomplish a fundamental change in the society they led. Lincoln did preside over such a change. Indeed, as he put it himself, also in the second inaugural, neither side had anticipated such "fundamental and astounding" changes when the war began.

These words introduce the third respect in which the Civil War can be viewed as a revolution: it destroyed not only slavery but also the social structure of the old South that had been founded on slavery, and it radically altered the power balance between the North and the South. It changed the direction of American development. This was what Mark Twain meant when he wrote that the war had "uprooted institutions that were centuries old . . . transformed the social life of half the country, and wrought so profoundly upon the entire national character." It was what Charles A. Beard meant when he wrote . . . that the Civil War was a "social cataclysm . . . making vast changes in the arrangement of classes, in the distribution of wealth, in the course of industrial development."

The war ended seventy years of southern domination of the national government and transferred it to Yankee Republicans who controlled the polity and economy of the United States for most of the next seventy years. It increased northern wealth and capital by 50 percent during the 1860s while destroying 60 percent of southern wealth. The output of southern industry in proportion to that of the North was cut in half by the war; the value of southern agricultural land in relation to that of the North was cut by three-fourths.

These changes occurred because when the Civil War became a total war, the invading army intentionally destroyed the economic capacity of the South to wage war. Union armies ripped up thousands of miles of southern railroads and blew up hundreds of bridges; Confederate cavalry raids and guerrilla operations behind Union lines in the South added to the destruction. More than half of the South's farm machinery was wrecked by the war, two-fifths of its livestock was killed, and one-quarter of its white males of military age—also the prime age for economic production—were killed, a higher proportion than suffered by any European power in World War I, that holocaust which ravaged a continent and spread revolution through many of its countries. . . .

Although Abraham Lincoln was a compassionate man who deplored this destruction and suffering, he nevertheless assented to it as the only way to win the war. After all, he had warned southerners two years earlier that the longer they fought, the more eggs would be broken. Now, in 1864, he officially conveyed to Sheridan the "thanks of the nation, and my own personal admiration and gratitude, for [your] operations in the Shenandoah Valley"; he sent Sherman and his army "grateful acknowledgments" for their march through Georgia. . . .

What conclusions can we draw, then, that make sense of those contrasting pictures of Lincoln the conservative and Lincoln the revolutionary quoted at the beginning of this essay? Although it may seem like an oxymoron, Lincoln can best be described as a conservative revolutionary. That is, he wanted to conserve the Union as the revolutionary heritage of the founding fathers. Preserving this heritage was the *purpose* of the war; all else became a means to achieve this end. As Lincoln phrased it in his famous public letter to Horace Greeley in August 1862, "My paramount object in this struggle *is* to save the Union, and is *not* either to save or to destroy slavery. . . . What I do about slavery and the colored race, I do because I believe it helps to save the Union." By the time he wrote these words, Lincoln had made up his mind that to save the Union he must destroy slavery. The means always remained subordinated to the end, but the means did become as essential to the northern war effort as the end itself. In that sense perhaps we could describe Lincoln as a pragmatic revolutionary, for as a pragmatist he adapted the means to the end. Thus we can agree with the historian Norman Graebner who was quoted earlier as stating that Lincoln "accepted the need of dealing with things as they were, not as he would have wished them to be." But instead of concluding, as Graebner did, that this made Lincoln a conservative, we must conclude that it made him a revolutionary. Not an ideological revolutionary, to be sure—Lincoln was no Robespierre or Lenin with a blueprint for a new order—but he was a pragmatic revolutionary who found it necessary to destroy slavery and create a new birth of freedom in order to preserve the Union.

"The dogmas of the quiet past," Lincoln told Congress in December 1862, "are inadequate to the stormy present. As our case is new, we must think anew, and act anew." It was *the war itself,* not the ideological blueprints of Lincoln or any other leader, that generated the radical momentum that made it a second American revolution. Like most wars that become total wars, the Civil War snowballed into huge and unanticipated dimensions and took on a life and purpose of its own far beyond the causes that had started it. As Lincoln said in his second inaugural address, neither side "expected for the war the magnitude or the duration which it has already attained." Or as he put it on another occasion, "I claim not to have controlled events, but confess plainly that events have controlled me." But in conceding that the war rather than he had shaped the thrust and direction of the revolution, Lincoln was perhaps too modest. For it was his own superb leadership, strategy, and sense of timing as president, commander in chief, and head of the Republican party that determined the pace of the revolution and ensured its success. With a less able man as president, the North might have lost the war or ended it under the leadership of Democrats who would have given its outcome a very different shape. Thus in accepting "the need of dealing with things as they were," Lincoln was not a conservative statesman but a revolutionary statesman.

The Role of African Americans in the Abolition of Slavery

IRA BERLIN, BARBARA J. FIELDS, STEVEN F. MILLER,

JOSEPH P. REIDY, AND LESLIE S. ROWLAND

The beginning of the Civil War marked the beginning of the end of slavery in the American South. At first, most white Americans denied what would eventually seem self-evident. With President Abraham Lincoln in the fore, federal authorities insisted that the nascent conflict must be a war to restore the natural union, and nothing more. Confederate leaders displayed a fuller comprehension of the importance of slavery, which Vice-President Alexander Stephens called the cornerstone of the Southern nation. But if Stephens and others grasped slavery's significance, they assumed that the Confederate struggle for independence would require no change in the nature of the institution. A Southern victory would transform the political status, not the social life, of the slave states; black people would remain in their familiar place. Despite a vigorous dissent from Northern abolitionists, most white people—North and South—saw no reason to involve slaves in their civil war.

Slaves had a different understanding of the sectional struggle. Unmoved by the public pronouncements and official policies of the federal government, they recognized their centrality to the dispute and knew that their future depended upon its outcome. With divisions among white Americans erupting into open warfare, slaves watched and waited, alert for ways to turn the military conflict to their own advantage, stubbornly refusing to leave its outcome to the two belligerents. Lacking political standing or public voice, forbidden access to the weapons of war, slaves nonetheless acted resolutely to place their freedom—and that of their posterity—on the wartime agenda. Steadily, as opportunities arose, they demonstrated their readiness to take risks for freedom and to put their loyalty, their labor, and their lives in the service of the federal government. In so doing, they gradually rendered untenable every Union policy short of universal emancipation and forced the Confederate

---

Ira Berlin, Barbara J. Fields, Steven F. Miller, Joseph P. Reidy, and Leslie S. Rowland, *Slaves No More: Three Essays on Emancipation and the Civil War* (New York: Cambridge University Press, 1992), 3–6, 15–16, 19, 43–44, 46–47, 49–53, 61–64, 69–70, 74–76. Reprinted with permission of Cambridge University Press.

government to adopt measures that severely compromised the sovereignty of the master. On both sides of the line of battle, Americans came to know that a war for the Union must be a war for freedom.

The change did not come easily or at once. At first, Northern political and military leaders freed slaves only hesitantly, under the pressure of military necessity. But, as the war dragged on, their reluctance gave way to an increased willingness and eventually to a firm determination to extirpate chattel bondage. The Emancipation Proclamation of January 1, 1863, and the enlistment of black soldiers into Union ranks in the following months signaled the adoption of emancipation as a fundamental Northern war aim, although that commitment availed little until vindicated by military victory. Even after the surrender of the Confederacy, slavery survived in two border states until the Thirteenth Amendment became part of the United States Constitution in December 1865.

Whereas Union policy shifted in favor of emancipation, Confederate leaders remained determined to perpetuate slavery. But the cornerstone of Southern nationality proved to be its weakest point. Slaves resisted attempts to mobilize them on behalf of the slaveholders' republic. Their sullen and sometimes violent opposition to the Confederate regime magnified divisions within Southern society, gnawing at the Confederacy from within. In trying to sustain slavery while fending off the Union army, Confederate leaders unwittingly compromised their own national aspirations and undermined the institution upon which Southern nationality was founded. In the end, the victors celebrated slavery's demise and claimed the title of emancipator. The vanquished understood full well how slavery had helped to seal their doom.

The war provided the occasion for slaves to seize freedom, but three interrelated circumstances determined what opportunities lay open to them and influenced the form that the struggle for liberty assumed: first, the character of slave society; second, the course of the war itself; and third, the policies of the Union and Confederacy governments. Although none of these operated independently of the others, each had its own dynamic. All three were shaped by the particularities of Southern geography and the chronology of the war. Together, they made the destruction of slavery a varying, uneven, and frequently tenuous process, whose complex history has been obscured by the apparent certitude and finality of the great documents that announced the end of chattel bondage. Once the evolution of emancipation replaces the absolutism of the Emancipation Proclamation and the Thirteenth Amendment as the focus of study, the story of slavery's demise shifts from the presidential mansion and the halls of Congress to the farms and plantations that became wartime battlefields. And slaves—whose persistence forced federal soldiers, Union and Confederate policy makers, and even their own masters onto terrain they never intended to occupy—become the prime movers in securing their own liberty. . . .

In April 1861, within days of Lincoln's call for volunteers to protect the nation's capital and put down the rebellion, the first Northern soldiers arrived in Washington. During the succeeding months, their numbers increased manyfold. As they took up positions around Washington and in the border states, they encountered slaves set in motion by the new disciplinary measures, by the attempts to conscript them into Confederate labor gangs or to refugee them to the interior, and—most importantly—by the desire to be free.

Before long, fugitive slaves began to test their owners' assertions about Yankee abolitionism. Those who ventured into Union army lines early in the war were mostly young men. Camps composed of hundreds of soldiers could be forbidding and dangerous places for women and children, and keeping up with an army on the march was nearly impossible for all but young and healthy adults. Fugitive-slave men also outnumbered women and children because men generally had greater opportunities to leave the home farm or plantation. Slave artisans, wagoners, and boatmen often had permission to move about in the course of their work, and sometimes to seek employment on their own; nearly all of them were men. Moreover, where slave hiring was common—as it was throughout the Upper South—seasonal agricultural labor kept hired men on the move between owner and employer. . . .

Confrontations between slaveholders and soldiers multiplied as the number of Union troops in the slave states increased. In late May 1861, when Virginia voters ratified secession, federal forces crossed the Potomac into the northern part of the state, and disputes between masters and military officers became endemic. The conflicts soon made their way into the press, rousing the ire of abolitionists who were outraged by the use of federal soldiers as slave catchers. In July, antislavery congressmen pushed a resolution through the House of Representatives declaring it "no part of the duty of the soldiers of the United States to capture and return fugitive slaves." Although the resolution had no binding effect, it bolstered antislavery sentiment within the Northern army.

The rumblings of congressional radicals were only one indication of the Lincoln administration's difficulty in sustaining a consistent policy regarding slavery. Orders to return fugitive slaves to their owners—designed to preserve the loyalty of the border states and encourage unionism in the Confederacy—lost their rationale once Northern soldiers encountered slaves whose owners were patently disloyal. . . .

. . . Now their [black laborers'] numbers increased rapidly as federal commanders discovered what Confederate officers had known all along: Slaves and free-black people were the most readily available—sometimes the only—source of military labor. Nearly every army post, supply depot, and wood yard acquired a contingent of black men to clear camps, build roads, construct fortifications, chop wood, and transport supplies. Few naval vessels lacked a handful of black men who handled the dirty and difficult business of coaling. Union commanders also found that black men, free and slave, possessed a variety of skills and were knowledgeable wagoners, scouts, and pilots. White workers—Northern and Southern—disdained certain kinds of labor as "nigger work," but black men and women stood able and often willing to take up the task—particularly if it would assure their liberty. The generally accepted notion that white people could not labor in tropical climates further increased reliance on black workers as the Union army marched south. . . .

Former slaves who labored for the Union army or took refuge in the contra-band camps did not remain satisfied with their own escape from slavery. Almost as soon as they reached the safety of federal lines, they began plotting to return home and liberate families and friends. Some traveled hundreds of miles into the Confederate interior, threading their way through enemy lines, eluding Confederate pickets, avoiding former masters, and outrunning the slave catchers hired to track them down. Not all succeeded, but when they did, their courage helped hundreds escape bondage and informed still others of the possibility of freedom. Occasionally, these brave men and women received assistance from sympathetic Union soldiers and commanders, who accompanied former slaves back to the old estates or provided material assistance to those intent upon returning to free others. The bargain seemed mutually beneficial—the Union army gained additional laborers, and the former slaves secured the liberty of their loved ones.

The growing importance of black labor increased support for emancipation in the North. Abolitionists publicized the role of black laborers, arguing that their service to the Union made them worthy of freedom and citizenship. Other Northerners, indifferent or even hostile to the extension of civil rights to black people, also saw value in the exchange of labor for freedom. Expropriation of the slaveholders' property seemed condign punishment for treason. And they noted that by doing the army's dirty work, black laborers freed white soldiers for the real business of war. Samuel J. Kirkwood, governor of Iowa, was appalled to learn that one of his state's regiments had "*sixty men on extra duty* as teamsters &c. whose places could just as well be filled with *niggers.*" He urged the military authorities to employ additional black laborers to do such "*negro work.*" Indicating the drift of Northern opinion, Governor Kirkwood added a few words on the subject of enlisting black men as soldiers: "When this war is over & we have summed up the entire loss of life it has imposed on the country I shall not have any regrets if it is found that a part of the dead are *niggers* and that *all* are not white men."

Cynical though they were, such sentiments strengthened the hand of abolitionists, white and black, who urged the arming of black men with muskets as well as shovels. They had long maintained that enlisting black soldiers would enhance the military might of the Union, while also securing emancipation and pushing the nation toward racial equality. Their earlier efforts to introduce black men into military service had been peremptorily dismissed, sometimes with sharp rebuke. But as public opinion turned against slavery, the proponents of black enlistment met with increasing success. In the summer and fall of 1862, the first black soldiers entered Union ranks in the Sea Islands of South Carolina, in southern Louisiana, and in Kansas. . . .

On New Year's Day, 1863, . . . the Emancipation Proclamation fulfilled his [Lincoln's] pledge to free all slaves in the states still in rebellion. Differences between the preliminary proclamation of September and the final pronouncement of January suggest the distance Lincoln and other Northerners had traveled in those few months. Gone were references to compensation for loyal slaveholders and colonization of former slaves. In their place stood the determination to incorporate black men into the federal army and navy. As expected, the proclamation applied only to the seceded states, leaving slavery in the loyal border states untouched, and it exempted Tennessee and the Union-occupied parts of Louisiana and Virginia. Nonetheless, its simple, straightforward declaration—"that all persons held as slaves" within the rebellious states "are, and henceforward shall be, free"—had enormous force.

As Lincoln understood, the message of freedom required no embellishment. However deficient in majesty or grandeur, the President's words echoed across the land. Abolitionists, black and white, marked the occasion with solemn thanksgiving that the nation had recognized its moral responsibility, that the war against slavery had at last been joined, and that human bondage was on the road to extinction. But none could match the slaves' elation. With unrestrained—indeed, unrestrainable—

joy, slaves celebrated the Day of Jubilee. Throughout the South—even in areas exempt from the proclamation—black people welcomed the dawn of a new era.

In announcing plans to accept black men into the army and navy, the Emancipation Proclamation specified their assignment "to garrison forts, positions, stations, and other places, and to man vessels"—evidently proposing no active combat role and, in fact, advancing little beyond the already established employment of black men in a variety of quasi-military positions. Nonetheless, black people and their abolitionist allies—who viewed military service as a lever for racial equality, as well as a weapon against slavery—seized upon the President's words and urged large-scale enlistment. Despite continued opposition from the advocates of a white man's war, the grim reality of mounting casualties convinced many Northerners of the wisdom of flexing the sable arm. Moreover, once the Emancipation Proclamation had made the destruction of slavery a Union war aim, increasing numbers of white Northerners thought it only fitting that black men share the burden of defeating the Confederacy. . . .

As black soldiers joined white soldiers in expanding freedom's domain, the Union army became an army of liberation. Although the Emancipation Proclamation implied an auxiliary role, black soldiers would not permit themselves to be reduced to military menials. They longed to confront their former masters on the field of battle, and they soon had their chance. The earliest black regiments acquitted themselves with honor at the battles of Port Hudson, Milliken's Bend, and Fort Wagner in the spring and summer of 1863, and black soldiers thereafter marched against the Confederacy on many fronts. Meanwhile, scores of black regiments served behind the lines—protecting railroads, bridges, and telegraph lines; manning forts; and fending off guerrillas and rearguard rebel attacks. Their services became essential to the Union war effort as Northern armies advanced deep into Confederate territory, lengthening the lines of communication and supply. The subversive effect of black soldiers on slavery, first demonstrated on the South Atlantic coast and in southern Louisiana, increased with the number of black men in federal ranks. By war's end, nearly 179,000—the overwhelming majority slaves—had entered the Union army, and another 10,000 had served in the navy.

Military service provided black men with legal freedom and more. In undeniable ways, it countered the degrading effects of Southern slavery and Northern discrimination. Soldiering gave black men, free as well as slave, a broader knowledge of the world, an acquaintance with the workings of the law, access to some rudimentary formal education, and a chance to demonstrate their commitment to freedom for themselves and their people. Battlefield confrontations with the slaveholding enemy exhilarated black soldiers by proving in the most elemental manner the essential equality of men. In their own eyes, in the eyes of the black community, and, however reluctantly, in the eyes of the nation, black men gained new standing by donning the Union blue.

Large-scale enlistment of black soldiers deepened the federal government's commitment to all former slaves. Although black men contributed to the Northern cause both as laborers and as soldiers, it seemed more difficult to deny support to the families of those who shouldered muskets than to the families of those who wielded shovels. When the army mustered black soldiers from the Confederate states, it implicitly—and sometimes explicitly—agreed to protect and provide for their families and friends. Adjutant General Thomas understood the relationship between recruiting soldiers and caring for their families as fully as any federal officer. When he began recruiting black regiments in the Mississippi Valley, he organized contraband camps as he established recruitment stations; often the two were the same. Commanders in other parts of the Union-occupied Confederacy followed a similar course, though their efforts never kept pace with the number of black refugees. . . .

The deterioration of slavery in the Union-occupied Confederacy had no immediate effect on the institution in the Union's own slave states. Having stood by the old flag when the other slave states seceded, Delaware, Maryland, Kentucky, and Missouri were not included in the Emancipation Proclamation. Insistent upon slavery's full legal standing under the federal constitution, slaveholders in the border states rejected Lincoln's repeated urgings that they adopt some plan of gradual, compensated emancipation. Indeed, their minority position as slaveholders in the Union seemed only to stiffen their resolve. Rather than bend to the winds of change, they deployed old defenses of their right to human property and fashioned new ones. Border-state legislatures bolstered antebellum slave codes, which were rigorously enforced by local officials. State courts not only upheld these laws and sustained the rights of slaveholders, but also entertained suits against anyone who interfered with slavery, including officers of the United States army.

The legality of slavery narrowed the avenues to freedom in the border states, but slaves hazarded them nonetheless. From the earliest months of the war, many of them had found refuge with Northern regiments, and some gained employment as military laborers. In Missouri, especially along the Kansas border, a virtual civil war within the Civil War provided slaves with opportunities to leave their owners, and in Maryland, proximity to the District of Columbia afforded fugitive slaves a safe haven. The slaves' persistence and the receptivity of federal troops and army quartermasters forced border-state slaveholders into rearguard actions that undermined their unionist credentials. By the end of 1863, exasperated army officers and federal officials had tired of feuding with masters who appeared to care more for their property than for the Union. As Lincoln had predicted, the "friction and abrasion" of war were eroding slavery in the border states. . . .

Still, slavery did not give way in the border states until black men began entering the Union army in large numbers. In the summer of 1863, with the enlistment of black men already proceeding in the North and in the Union-occupied Confederacy, federal authorities inaugurated black recruitment in Maryland and Missouri. Reluctant to offend slaveholding unionists, President Lincoln and the War Department at first authorized the enlistment only of free blacks and of slaves whose owners were disloyal. But black men—including the slaves of loyal owners—volunteered so enthusiastically that it proved nearly impossible to restrict enlistment. This was particularly true once nonslaveholding white men recognized that black recruits reduced conscription quotas that they would otherwise have to fill. Nonslaveholders demanded that slaves be enlisted as well as—and sometimes instead of—free blacks. In Maryland, where nonslaveholding farmers feared that the enlistment of free-black men would diminish their work force while leaving that of the slaveholders intact, this demand reached its highest pitch. In all the border states, antislavery partisans united in urging the elimination of distinctions between slaves of the loyal and those of the disloyal. With the ready compliance of black volunteers, recruiters stepped up enlistment, circumventing regulations regarding the status of the recruits or the politics of their owners. . . .

With slavery in shambles and Northern victory increasingly sure, unionists in much of the occupied South concluded the business of emancipation. Federal officials and army commanders turned on their slaveholding allies and made it clear that the liquidation of slavery was prerequisite for readmission to the Union. Antislavery unionists, previously stymied by slaveholding loyalists, took control of the unionist coalitions and pressed for immediate abolition. Early in 1864, Arkansas loyalists enacted constitutional changes ending slavery. Unionists in states partly or wholly exempt from the Emancipation Proclamation followed suit, in Louisiana late in 1864 and in Tennessee early in 1865. As Lincoln had hoped, these new state constitutions placed emancipation upon firmer ground, beyond the reach of judicial challenge to the confiscation acts or the Emancipation Proclamation.

Union military success also strengthened the North's own commitment to freedom. Sherman's triumph at Atlanta helped Lincoln beat back a challenge for the presidency by George B. McClellan, the former general-in-chief. The previous spring, with reelection in doubt, congressional support for emancipation had faltered. The Senate had approved a constitutional amendment abolishing slavery, but when it came before the House, the Democratic opposition had denied it the two-thirds majority required for passage. In January 1865, with Lincoln reelected and the Republicans securely in power, the House approved the amendment and forwarded it to the states for ratification. As the state legislatures opened their debates, the President and the Congress turned in earnest to the task of postwar reconstruction. In early March, Lincoln signed legislation creating the Bureau of Refugees, Freedmen, and Abandoned Lands (or Freedmen's Bureau, as it became known) to supervise the transition from slavery to freedom. A joint resolution adopted the same day liberated the wives and children of black soldiers, regardless of their owners' loyalty, and thereby provided a claim to freedom for tens of thousands of border-state slaves whose bondage had been impervious to law or presidential edict. . . .

After the war, freedpeople and their allies—some newly minted, some of long standing—gathered periodically to celebrate the abolition of slavery. They spoke of great deeds, great words, and great men, praising the Emancipation Proclamation and the Thirteenth Amendment and venerating their authors. A moment so great needed its icons. But in quieter times, black people told of their own liberation. Then there were as many tales as tellers. Depending upon the circumstances of their enslavement, the events of the war, and the evolution of Union and Confederate policy, some recounted solitary escape; others, mass defections initiated by themselves or the Yankees. Many depicted their former owners in headlong flight, and themselves left behind to shape a future under Union occupation. Others told of forced removals from home and family to strange neighborhoods and an enslavement made more miserable by food shortages, heightened discipline, and bands of straggling soldiers. Still others limned a struggle against slaveholders whose unionist credentials sustained their power. More than a few black people shared the bitter memory of escaping slavery only to be reenslaved when the Northern army retreated or they ventured into one of the Union's own slave states. Some recalled hearing the news of freedom from an exasperated master who reluctantly acknowledged the end of the old order; others, from returning black veterans, bedecked in blue uniforms with brass buttons. Those who had escaped slavery during the war often had additional stories to relate. They told of serving the Union cause as cooks, nurses, and laundresses: as teamsters and laborers; as spies, scouts, and pilots; and as sailors and soldiers. Even those who had remained under the dominion of their owners until the defeat of the Confederacy and had been forced to labor in its behalf knew that their very presence, and often their actions, had played a part in destroying slavery.

These diverse experiences disclosed the uneven, halting, and often tenuous process by which slaves gained their liberty, and the centrality of their own role in the evolution of emancipation. The Emancipation Proclamation and the Thirteenth Amendment marked, respectively, a turning point and the successful conclusion of a hard-fought struggle. But the milestones of that struggle were not the struggle itself. Neither its origins nor its mainspring could be found in the seats of executive and legislative authority from which the great documents issued. Instead, they resided in the humble quarters of slaves, who were convinced in April 1861 of what would not be fully affirmed until December 1865, and whose actions consistently undermined every settlement short of universal abolition.

Over the course of the war, the slaves' insistence that their own enslavement was the root of the conflict—and that a war for the Union must necessarily be a war for freedom—strengthened their friends and weakened their enemies. Their willingness to offer their loyalty, their labor, and even their lives pushed Northerners, from common soldiers to leaders of the first rank, to do what had previously seemed unthinkable: to make property into persons, to make slaves into soldiers, and, in time, to make all black people into citizens, the equal of any in the Republic. White Southerners could never respond in kind. But they too came to understand the link between national union and universal liberty. And when the deed was done, a new truth prevailed where slavery had reigned: that men and women could never again be owned and that citizenship was the right of all. The destruction of slavery transformed American life forever.

F U R T H E R   R E A D I N G

Shelby Foote, *The Civil War: A Narrative (three vols.)* (1958–1974).
Joseph T. Glatthaar, *Forged in Battle: The Civil War Alliance of Black Soldiers and White Officers* (1989).
James M. McPherson, *Battle Cry of Freedom: The Civil War Era* (1988).
Mark E. Neely, Jr., *The Fate of Liberty: Abraham Lincoln and Civil Liberties* (1992).
Stephen B. Oates, *With Malice Toward None: A Life of Abraham Lincoln* (1977).
Phillip S. Paludan, *"A People's Contest": The Union and the Civil War, 1861–1865* (1989).
Emory M. Thomas, *The Confederate Nation, 1861–1865* (1979).

CHAPTER
15

Reconstruction, 1865–1877

Even before the Civil War was over, President Lincoln and congressional leaders began to puzzle over how best to reintegrate the people of the South into the Union. Before he was assassinated, President Lincoln proposed the "10 percent plan," which would have allowed a state government to reestablish itself once one-tenth of those who had voted in 1860 took an oath of loyalty to the United States. Radicals in Congress were appalled by the leniency of Lincoln's plan and pushed through their own bill, which increased to one-half the proportion of the voters who were required to swear that they had never supported secession. Lincoln's assassination cut short this increasingly vituperative debate, but it did not end the controversy over Reconstruction, a controversy that would engross the nation for nearly fifteen years. Significantly, political disagreements over Reconstruction policy were vast, and the strategies advocated were so varied that Reconstruction took a crooked path. As approaches to rebuilding the South shifted, the hopes among some of transforming southern society grew and then were dashed. Ultimately, despite important legal precedents that were set in the era, many of the social, political, and economic conventions that had characterized antebellum society endured after Reconstruction ended.

Although people differed on what was the best policy for Reconstruction, everyone agreed that the Confederate states were in dire straits. The war had devastated the South: entire cities lay in ruins; two-thirds of the southern railroads had been destroyed; and at least one-third of the South's livestock had disappeared. Likewise, the abolition of slavery unalterably transformed southern society at the same time that it gave hope to people freed from their bondage (known as freedmen). Following Lincoln's death, many believed that Andrew Johnson, who succeeded Lincoln as president, would advocate a severe form of Reconstruction. Instead, Johnson engineered a plan that seemed to many northerners to be much too charitable. Although he distrusted the southern elite, Johnson nonetheless pardoned many of the Confederate leaders, who in turn were instrumental in creating new state legislatures that did not seem sufficiently contrite to many northerners. When some reconstructed legislatures passed "black codes" in 1865, which among other things forced freedmen to carry passes and prohibited them from owning land, Johnson did not oppose them. In the years that followed, Johnson's behavior became increasingly partisan. He opposed the Fourteenth Amendment (which gave freed slaves citizenship and guaranteed them due process of law), and he campaigned against the Republican Party in the election of 1866. Ironically, Johnson's course of action, combined with the intransigence of unrepentant southern leaders, was a major factor in bringing about the era of Radical Reconstruction beginning in 1866. Because he was so impolitic, Johnson strengthened the resolve of Congress to enact a more radical policy.

The Republican Party won such a resounding victory in the elections of 1866 that it did not need to fear vetoes from Johnson. When Congress reconvened in 1867, it set a much harsher and more radical plan of Reconstruction. It passed the Reconstruction Act of 1867, which created military districts in the South, guaranteed male freedmen the right to vote in state elections, and disfranchised Confederate leaders. Congress later passed and sent to the states the Fifteenth Amendment, which gave black men the right to vote. As a consequence of its conflict with Johnson, Congress impeached him and nearly removed him from office. As much of a departure as Radical Reconstruction was from Johnson's plan, however, it was not as radical as many political leaders would have liked. Freedmen received political rights, but Congress did not radically expand public education or confiscate the land owned by Confederate sympathizers, as some of its members had advocated. As a result, freedmen were denied the economic independence that a grant of "forty acres and a mule" would have provided.

If Reconstruction was engineered in Washington, new social conventions were forged in the South that would be extremely important in the future. The lives of former slaves were dramatically changed, and freedmen expressed their understanding of freedom in a variety of ways. Most immediately, they hoped to be independent of the control of white people, which was the most obvious expression of freedom. Yet freedom was observed in a variety of ways. Many attempted to reunite families that had been rent asunder by sale; others celebrated by conducting religious services independent of white control; and still others fostered schools to educate their children, an education they had been denied in slavery. For some time, these efforts were advanced by governmental institutions. The Freedman's Bureau, for example, was an agency established in 1865 that assisted freedmen in finding employment and establishing schools. More importantly, many African Americans played important roles in the new Republican Party of the South, and by 1868 black men were seated for the first time in southern state legislatures. African Americans' influence grew to such an extent that between 1869 and 1877, more than 600 black men served in state legislatures, six served as lieutenant governors, fourteen were members of the U.S. House of Representatives, and two were U.S. senators.

These political gains, however, were short-lived. In spite of the electoral successes of African Americans, the Democratic Party enjoyed increasing political success as former Confederates eventually had their political rights restored. As early as 1870, the governors of Alabama and Georgia were Democrats. These electoral victories were complemented by extralegal violence. The Ku Klux Klan, a secretive terrorist organization, successfully intimidated Republicans—and especially black Republicans—beginning in 1866. Of those black people who had been delegates to state constitutional conventions in 1867, for example, at least one-tenth were attacked and seven were killed. Changes in the electorate in conjunction with intimidation shifted the trajectory of Reconstruction once again as radical transformation was replaced with a movement toward "redemption," white southerners' term for reclaiming the world they had known before the Civil War.

The end of Reconstruction was hastened by events in the North as well as the South. Ulysses S. Grant, elected president in 1868, was a better general than politician, and his administration became mired in scandal shortly after he took office. In 1873, the nation was rocked by a financial panic that led to a depression lasting six years. The scandals and the economic depression weakened the Republican Party.

Meanwhile Congress, in part because of the resurgence of the Democratic Party, and the Supreme Court were weakening in their resolve to continue a strict policy of Reconstruction. The death knell for Reconstruction was the national election of 1876, when it became clear that the North was no longer willing to pursue its earlier goals. The election of the Democratic candidate for president was avoided only by a deal in 1877 wherein Rutherford B. Hayes would be declared president if he promised to withdraw federal troops from those states in the South where they still remained. The deal was made. Reconstruction was over.

QUESTIONS TO THINK ABOUT

What were the failures of Reconstruction and what were its successes? Why did it collapse? Did Reconstruction come to an end primarily because it was abandoned by the North, opposed by the white South, or undermined by a lack of unity within the Republican Party at the local level?

DOCUMENTS

The South was in a state of astonishing flux after the collapse of the Confederacy. Document 1 consists of reminiscences of former slaves about the coming of freedom and the challenges they faced in the early years of Reconstruction. These hazards were heightened by the "black codes" enacted in many southern states, one of which is given in Document 2. This example from Louisiana in 1865 illustrates the many ways in which the rights of "freedom" were abridged. The next three documents illustrate the many viewpoints on how the federal government should reconstruct the South in the years immediately after the war. In Document 3, President Andrew Johnson argues against black suffrage because he fears that "the subjugation of the States to negro domination would be worse than the military despotism under which they are now suffering." In contrast, Thaddeus Stevens, a Radical representative in Congress, argues for passage of the Reconstruction Act of 1867 in Document 4 because he believes that only an unfaltering federal presence will prevent "traitors" from ruling the South. The radical implications of the debate on Reconstruction had an impact in other arenas of political debate, as Document 5 shows. Elizabeth Cady Stanton argues that the very radicals who are pushing for increased rights for freed slaves are deferring the issue of women's suffrage. Document 6 is the text of the Fourteenth Amendment, which among other things provides the due process of law for all citizens advocated by Stevens in Document 4. As radical as these measures were, their successful implication was made difficult by conditions in the United States, as the final three documents show. Document 7 is a recollection by a freedman in 1871 of a visit in the night by the Ku Klux Klan. Consider how difficult it would be to retain one's political leanings in the face of such threats. In Document 8, Carl Schurz, a senator from Missouri, concludes in 1872 that federal oversight of the South has been a failure. Schurz, who advocated suffrage for African American men in 1865, now believes that many of the Reconstruction policies—including black suffrage—were mistaken and he advocates a retreat in Reconstruction policy. Finally, in Document 9, L. Q. C. Lamar, a representative from Mississippi, denounces Reconstruction in the South. Lamar's speech, given in 1874, was a signal of the direction of Reconstruction. Within three years, the South would be "redeemed."

1. African Americans Talk About Their Personal Experiences of Newfound Freedom, c. 1865

FELIX HAYWOOD From San Antonio, Texas. Born in Raleigh, North Carolina. Age at Interview: 88

The end of the war, it come just like that—like you snap your fingers. . . . How did we know it! Hallelujah broke out—

> Abe Lincoln freed the nigger
>   With the gun and the trigger;
> And I ain't going to get whipped any more.
>   I got my ticket,
> Leaving the thicket,
>   And I'm a-heading for the Golden Shore!

Soldiers, all of a sudden, was everywhere—coming in bunches, crossing and walking and riding. Everyone was a-singing. We was all walking on golden clouds. Hallelujah!

> Union forever,
>   Hurrah, boys, hurrah!
> Although I may be poor,
>   I'll never be a slave—
> Shouting the battle cry of freedom.

Everybody went wild. We felt like heroes, and nobody had made us that way but ourselves. We was free. Just like that, we was free. It didn't seem to make the whites mad, either. They went right on giving us food just the same. Nobody took our homes away, but right off colored folks started on the move. They seemed to want to get closer to freedom, so they'd know what it was—like it was a place or a city. Me and my father stuck, stuck close as a lean tick to a sick kitten. The Gudlows started us out on a ranch. My father, he'd round up cattle—unbranded cattle—for the whites. They was cattle that they belonged to, all right; they had gone to find water 'long the San Antonio River and the Guadalupe. Then the whites gave me and my father some cattle for our own. My father had his own brand—7 B)—and we had a herd to start out with of seventy.

We knowed freedom was on us, but we didn't know what was to come with it. We thought we was going to get rich like the white folks. We thought we was going to be richer than the white folks, 'cause we was stronger and knowed how to work, and the whites didn't, and they didn't have us to work for them any more. But it didn't turn out that way. We soon found out that freedom could make folks proud, but it didn't make 'em rich.

Did you ever stop to think that thinking don't do any good when you do it too late? Well, that's how it was with us. If every mother's son of a black had thrown 'way his hoe and took up a gun to fight for his own freedom along with the Yankees, the war'd been over before it began. But we didn't do it. We couldn't help stick to our masters. We couldn't no more shoot 'em than we could fly. My father and me used to talk 'bout it. We decided we was too soft and freedom wasn't going to be much to our good even if we had a education.

WARREN MCKINNEY, From Hazen, Arkansas. Born in South Carolina. Age at Interview: 85.

I was born in Edgefield County, South Carolina. I am eighty-five years old. I was born a slave of George Strauter. I remembers hearing them say, "Thank God, I's free as a jay bird." My ma was a slave in the field. I was eleven years old when freedom was declared. When I was little, Mr. Strauter whipped my ma. It hurt me bad as it did her. I hated him. She was crying. I chunked him with rocks. He run after me, but he didn't catch me. There was twenty-five or thirty hands that worked in the field. They raised wheat, corn, oats, barley, and cotton. All the children that couldn't work stayed at one house. Aunt Mat kept the babies and small children that couldn't go to the field. He had a gin and a shop. The shop was at the fork of the roads. When the war come on, my papa went to build forts. He quit Ma and took another woman. When the war close, Ma took her four children, bundled 'em up and went to Augusta. The government give out rations there. My ma washed and ironed. People died in piles. I don't know till yet what was the matter. They said it was the change of living. I seen five or six wooden, painted coffins piled up on wagons pass by our house. Loads passed every day like you see cotton pass here. Some said it was cholera and some took consumption. Lots of the colored people nearly starved. Not much to get to do and not much houseroom. Several families had to live in one house. Lots of the colored folks went up North and froze to death. They couldn't stand the cold. They wrote back about them dying. No, they never sent them back. I heard some sent for money to come back. I heard plenty 'bout the Ku Klux. They scared the folks to death. People left Augusta in droves. About a thousand would all meet and walk going to hunt work and new homes. Some of them died. I had a sister and brother lost that way. I had another sister come to Louisiana that way. She wrote back.

I don't think the colored folks looked for a share of land. They never got nothing 'cause the white folks didn't have nothing but barren hills left. About all the mules was wore out hauling provisions in the army. Some folks say they ought to done more for the colored folks when they left, but they say they was broke. Freeing all the slaves left 'em broke.

That reconstruction was a mighty hard pull. Me and Ma couldn't live. A man paid our ways to Carlisle, Arkansas, and we come. We started working for Mr. Emenson. He had a big store, teams, and land. We liked it fine, and I been here fifty-six years now. There was so much wild game, living was not so hard. If a fellow could get a little bread and a place to stay, he was all right. After I come to this state, I voted some. I have farmed and worked at odd jobs. I farmed mostly. Ma went back to her old master. He persuaded her to come back home. Me and her went back and run a farm four or five years before she died. Then I come back here.

LEE GUIDON, From South Carolina. Born in South Carolina. Age at Interview: 89.

Yes, ma'am, I sure was in the Civil War. I plowed all day, and me and my sister helped take care of the baby at night. It would cry, and me bumping it [in a straight chair, rocking]. Time I git it to the bed where its mama was, it wake up and start crying all over again. I be so sleepy. It was a puny sort of baby. Its papa was off at war. . . .

After freedom a heap of people say they was going to name theirselves over. They named theirselves big names, then went roaming round like wild, hunting cities. They changed up so it was hard to tell who or where anybody was. Heap of 'em died, and you didn't know when you hear about it if he was your folks hardly. Some of the names was Abraham, and some called theirselves Lincum. Any big name 'cepting their master's name. It was the fashion. I heard 'em talking 'bout it one evening, and my pa say, "Fine folks raise us and we gonna hold to our own names." That settled it with all of us. . . .

I reckon I do know 'bout the Ku Kluck. I knowed a man named Alfred Owens. He seemed all right, but he was a Republican. He said he was not afraid. He run a tanyard and kept a heap of guns in a big room. They all loaded. He married a Southern woman. Her husband either died or was killed. She had a son living with them. The Ku Kluck was called Upper League. They get this boy to unload all the guns. Then the white men went there. The white man give up and said, "I ain't got no gun to defend myself with. The guns all unloaded, and I ain't got no powder and shot." But the Ku Kluck shot in the houses and shot him up like lacework. He sold fine harness, saddles, bridles—all sorts of leather things. The Ku Kluck sure run them outen their country. They say they not going to have them round, and they sure run them out, back where they came from. . . .

For them what stayed on like they were, Reconstruction times 'bout like times before that 'cepting the Yankee stole out and tore up a scandalous heap. They tell the black folks to do something, and then come white folks you live with and say Ku Kluck whup you. They say leave, and white folks say better not listen to them old Yankees. They'll git you too far off to come back, and you freeze. They done give you all the use they got for you. How they do? All sorts of ways. Some stayed at their cabins glad to have one to live in and farmed on. Some running round begging, some hunting work for money, and nobody had no money 'cepting the Yankees, and they had no homes or land and mighty little work for you to do. No work to live on. Some going every day to the city. That winter I heard 'bout them starving and freezing by the wagon loads.

I never heard nothing 'bout voting till freedom. I don't think I ever voted till I come to Mississippi. I votes Republican. That's the party of my color, and I stick to them as long as they do right. I don't dabble in white folks' business, and that white folks' voting is their business. If I vote, I go do it and go on home. . . .

When I owned most, I had six head mules and five head horses. I rented 140 acres of land. I bought this house and some other land about. The anthrax killed nearly all my horses and mules. I got one big fine mule yet. Its mate died. I lost my house. My son give me one room, and he paying the debt off now. It's hard for colored folks to keep anything. Somebody gets it from 'em if they don't mind.

The present times is hard. Timber is scarce. Game is about all gone. Prices higher. Old folks cannot work. Times is hard for younger folks too. They go to town too much and go to shows. They going to a tent show now. Circus coming, they say. They spending too much money for foolishness. It's a fast time. Folks too restless. Some of the colored folks work hard as folks ever did. They spends too much. Some folks is lazy. Always been that way.

I signed up to the government, but they ain't give me nothing 'cepting powdered milk and rice what wasn't fit to eat. It cracked up and had black something in it. A lady said she would give me some shirts that was her husband's. I went to get them, but she wasn't home. These heavy shirts give me heat. They won't give me the pension, and I don't know why. It would help me buy my salts and pills and the other medicines like Swamp Root. They won't give it to me.

TOBY JONES, From Madisonville, Texas. Born in South Carolina. Age at Interview: 87.

I worked for Massa 'bout four years after freedom, 'cause he forced me to, said he couldn't 'ford to let me go. His place was near ruint, the fences burnt, and the house would have been, but it was rock. There was a battle fought near his place, and I taken Missy to a hideout in the mountains to where her father was, 'cause there was bullets flying everywhere. When the war was over, Massa come home and says, "You son of a gun, you's supposed to be free, but you ain't, 'cause I ain't gwine give you freedom." So I goes on working for him till I gits the chance to steal a hoss from him. The woman I wanted to marry, Govie, she 'cides to come to Texas with me. Me and Govie, we rides that hoss 'most a hundred miles, then we turned him a-loose and give him a scare back to his house, and come on foot the rest the way to Texas.

All we had to eat was what we could beg, and sometimes we went three days without a bite to eat. Sometimes we'd pick a few berries. When we got cold we'd crawl in a brushpile and hug up close together to keep warm. Once in awhile we'd come to a farmhouse, and the man let us sleep on cottonseed in his barn, but they was far and few between, 'cause they wasn't many houses in the country them days like now.

When we gits to Texas, we gits married, but all they was to our wedding am we just 'grees to live together as man and wife. I settled on some land, and we cut some trees and split them open and stood them on end with the tops together for our house. Then we deadened some trees, and the land was ready to farm. There was some wild cattle and hogs, and that's the way we got our start, caught some of them and tamed them.

I don't know as I'spected nothing from freedom, but they turned us out like a bunch of stray dogs, no homes, no clothing, no nothing, not 'nough food to last us one meal. After we settles on that place, I never seed man or woman, 'cept Govie, for six years, 'cause it was a long ways to anywhere. All we had to farm with was sharp sticks. We'd stick holes and plant corn, and when it come up we'd punch up the dirt round it. We didn't plant cotton, 'cause we couldn't eat that. I made bows and arrows to kill wild game with, and we never went to a store for nothing. We made our clothes out of animal skins.

2. Louisiana Black Codes Reinstate Provisions of the Slave Era, 1865

SECTION 1. *Be it therefore ordained by the board of police of the town of Opelousas,* That no negro or freedman shall be allowed to come within the limits of the town of Opelousas without special permission from his employers, specifying the object of his visit and the time necessary for the accomplishment of the same. . . .

SECTION 2. *Be it further ordained,* That every negro freedman who shall be found on the streets of Opelousas after 10 o'clock at night without a written pass or permit from his employer shall be imprisoned and compelled to work five days on the public streets, or pay a fine of five dollars.

SECTION 3. No negro or freedman shall be permitted to rent or keep a house within the limits of the town under any circumstances, and any one thus offending shall be ejected and compelled to find an employer or leave the town within twenty-four hours. . . .

SECTION 4. No negro or freedman shall reside within the limits of the town of Opelousas who is not in the regular service of some white person or former owner, who shall be held responsible for the conduct of said freedman. . . .

SECTION 5. No public meetings or congregations of negroes or freedmen shall be allowed within the limits of the town of Opelousas under any circumstances or for any purpose without the permission of the mayor or president of the board. . . .

SECTION 6. No negro or freedman shall be permitted to preach, exhort, or otherwise declaim to congregations of colored people without a special permission from the mayor or president of the board of police. . . .

SECTION 7. No freedman who is not in the military service shall be allowed to carry firearms, or any kind of weapons, within the limits of the town of Opelousas without the special permission of his employer, in writing, and approved by the mayor or president of the board of police. . . .

SECTION 8. No freedman shall sell, barter, or exchange any articles of merchandise or traffic within the limits of Opelousas without permission in writing from his employer or the mayor or president of the board. . . .

SECTION 9. Any freedman found drunk within the limits of the town shall be imprisoned and made to labor five days on the public streets, or pay five dollars in lieu of said labor.

Condition of the South, Senate Executive Document No. 2, 39 Cong., 1 Sess., pp. 92–93.

SECTION 10. Any freedman not residing in Opelousas who shall be found within the corporate limits after the hour of 3 p.m. on Sunday without a special permission from his employer or the mayor shall be arrested and imprisoned and made to work. . . .

SECTION 11. All the foregoing provisions apply to freedmen and freedwomen, or both sexes. . . .

E. D. ESTILLETTE,
President of the Board of Police.
JOS. D. RICHARDS, *Clerk.*

Official copy:

J. LOVELL,
Captain and Assistant Adjutant General.

3. President Andrew Johnson Denounces Changes in His Program of Reconstruction, 1867

It is manifestly and avowedly the object of these laws to confer upon negroes the privilege of voting and to disfranchise such a number of white citizens as will give the former a clear majority at all elections in the Southern States. This, to the minds of some persons, is so important that a violation of the Constitution is justified as a means of bringing it about. The morality is always false which excuses a wrong because it proposes to accomplish a desirable end. We are not permitted to do evil that good may come. But in this case the end itself is evil, as well as the means. The subjugation of the States to negro domination would be worse than the military despotism under which they are now suffering. It was believed beforehand that the people would endure any amount of military oppression for any length of time rather than degrade themselves by subjection to the negro race. Therefore they have been left without a choice. Negro suffrage was established by act of Congress, and the military officers were commanded to superintend the process of clothing the negro race with the political privileges torn from white men.

The blacks in the South are entitled to be well and humanely governed, and to have the protection of just laws for all their rights of person and property. If it were practicable at this time to give them a Government exclusively their own, under which they might manage their own affairs in their own way, it would become a grave question whether we ought to do so, or whether common humanity would not require us to save them from themselves. But under the circumstances this is only a speculative point. It is not proposed merely that they shall govern themselves, but that they shall rule the white race, make and administer State laws, elect Presidents and members of Congress, and shape to a greater or less extent the future destiny of the whole country. Would such a trust and power be safe in such hands?

Andrew Johnson, "Third Annual Message," December 3, 1867, in *A Compilation of Messages and Papers of the Presidents, 1789–1897*, ed. James D. Richardson (Washington, D.C.: Bureau of National Literature and Art, 1899), Vol. VI, pp. 564–565.

The peculiar qualities which should characterize any people who are fit to decide upon the management of public affairs for a great state have seldom been combined. It is the glory of white men to know that they have had these qualities in sufficient measure to build upon this continent a great political fabric and to preserve its stability for more than ninety years, while in every other part of the world all similar experiments have failed. But if anything can be proved by known facts, if all reasoning upon evidence is not abandoned, it must be acknowledged that in the progress of nations negroes have shown less capacity for government than any other race of people. No independent government of any form has ever been successful in their hands. On the contrary, wherever they have been left to their own devices they have shown a constant tendency to relapse into barbarism. In the Southern States, however, Congress has undertaken to confer upon them the privilege of the ballot. Just released from slavery, it may be doubted whether as a class they know more than their ancestors how to organize and regulate civil society.

4. Congressman Thaddeus Stevens Demands a Radical Reconstruction, 1867

. . . It is to be regretted that inconsiderate and incautious Republicans should ever have supposed that the slight amendments [embodied in the pending Fourteenth Amendment] already proposed to the Constitution, even when incorporated into that instrument, would satisfy the reforms necessary for the security of the Government. Unless the rebel States, before admission, should be made republican in spirit, and placed under the guardianship of loyal men, all our blood and treasure will have been spent in vain. I waive now the question of punishment which, if we are wise, will still be inflicted by moderate confiscations, both as a reproof and example. Having these States, as we all agree, entirely within the power of Congress, it is our duty to take care that no injustice shall remain in their organic laws. Holding them "like clay in the hands of the potter," we must see that no vessel is made for destruction. Having now no governments, they must have enabling acts. The law of last session with regard to Territories settled the principles of such acts. Impartial suffrage, both in electing the delegates and ratifying their proceedings, is now the fixed rule. There is more reason why colored voters should be admitted in the rebel States than in the Territories. In the States they form the great mass of the loyal men. Possibly with their aid loyal governments may be established in most of those States. Without it all are sure to be ruled by traitors; and loyal men, black and white, will be oppressed, exiled, or murdered. There are several good reasons for the passage of this bill. In the first place, it is just. I am now confining my argument to negro suffrage in the rebel States. Have not loyal blacks quite as good a right to choose rulers and make laws as rebel whites? In the second place, it is a necessity in order to protect the loyal white men in the seceded States. The white Union men are in a great minority in each of those States. With them the blacks would act in a body; and it is believed that in each of said States, except one, the two united

Thaddeus Stevens, Speech in the House, January 3, 1867, *Congressional Globe,* 39 Cong., 2 Sess., Vol. 37, pt. 1, pp. 251–253. This document can also be found in Harold M. Hyman, ed., *Radical Republicans and Reconstruction* (Bobbs-Merrill, 1967), pp. 373–375.

would form a majority, control the States, and protect themselves. Now they are the victims of daily murder. They must suffer constant persecution or be exiled. The convention of southern loyalists, lately held in Philadelphia, almost unanimously agreed to such a bill as an absolute necessity.

Another good reason is, it would insure the ascendancy of the Union party. Do you avow the party purpose? exclaims some horror-stricken demagogue. I do. For I believe, on my conscience, that on the continued ascendancy of that party depends the safety of this great nation. If impartial suffrage is excluded in rebel States then every one of them is sure to send a solid rebel representative delegation to Congress, and cast a solid rebel electoral vote. They, with their kindred Copperheads of the North, would always elect the President and control Congress. While slavery sat upon her defiant throne, and insulted and intimidated the trembling North, the South frequently divided on questions of policy between Whigs and Democrats, and gave victory alternately to the sections. Now, you must divide them between loyalists, without regard to color, and disloyalists, or you will be the perpetual vassals of the free-trade, irritated, revengeful South. For these, among other reasons, I am for negro suffrage in every rebel State. If it be just, it should not be denied; if it be necessary, it should be adopted; if it be a punishment to traitors, they deserve it.

But it will be said, as it has been said, "This is negro equality!" What is negro equality, about which so much is said by knaves, and some of which is believed by men who are not fools? It means, as understood by honest Republicans, just this much, and no more: every man, no matter what his race or color; every earthly being who has an immortal soul, has an equal right to justice, honesty, and fair play with every other man; and the law should secure him those rights. The same law which condemns or acquits an African should condemn or acquit a white man. The same law which gives a verdict in a white man's favor should give a verdict in a black man's favor on the same state of facts. Such is the law of God and such ought to be the law of man. This doctrine does not mean that a negro shall sit on the same seat or eat at the same table with a white man. That is a matter of taste which every man must decide for himself. The law has nothing to do with it.

5. Elizabeth Cady Stanton Questions Abolitionist Support for Female Enfranchisement, 1868

To what a depth of degradation must the women of this nation have fallen to be willing to stand aside, silent and indifferent spectators in the reconstruction of the nation, while all the lower stratas of manhood are to legislate in their interests, political, religious, educational, social and sanitary, moulding to their untutored will the institutions of a mighty continent. . . .

While leading Democrats have been thus favorably disposed, what have our best friends said when, for the first time since the agitation of the question [the enfranchisement of women], they have had an opportunity to frame their ideas into statutes to amend the constitutions of two States in the Union.

Elizabeth Cady Stanton, "Who Are Our Friends?" *The Revolution,* 15 (January 1868).

Charles Sumner, Horace Greeley, Gerrit Smith and Wendell Phillips, with one consent, bid the women of the nation stand aside and behold the salvation of the negro. Wendell Phillips says, "one idea for a generation," to come up in the order of their importance. First negro suffrage, then temperance, then the eight hour movement, then woman's suffrage. In 1958, three generations hence, thirty years to a generation, Phillips and Providence permitting, woman's suffrage will be in order. What an insult to the women who have labored thirty years for the emancipation of the slave, now when he is their political equal, to propose to lift him above their heads. Gerrit Smith, forgetting that our great American idea is "individual rights," in which abolitionists have ever based their strongest arguments for emancipation, says, this is the time to settle the rights of races; unless we do justice to the negro we shall bring down on ourselves another bloody revolution, another four years' war, but we have nothing to fear from woman, she will not revenge herself! . . .

Horace Greeley has advocated this cause for the last twenty years, but to-day it is too new, revolutionary for practical consideration. The enfranchisement of woman, revolutionizing, as it will, our political, religious and social condition, is not a measure too radical and all-pervading to meet the moral necessities of this day and generation.

Why fear new things; all old things were once new. . . . We live to do new things! When Abraham Lincoln issued the proclamation of emancipation, it was a new thing. When the Republican party gave the ballot to the negro, it was a new thing, startling too, to the people of the South, very revolutionary to their institutions, but Mr. Greeley did not object to all this because it was new. . . .

And now, while men like these have used all their influence for the last four years, to paralyze every effort we have put forth to rouse the women of the nation, to demand their true position in the reconstruction, they triumphantly turn to us, and say the greatest barrier in the way of your demand is that "the women themselves do not wish to vote." What a libel on the intelligence of the women of the nineteenth century. What means the 12,000 petitions presented by John Stuart Mill in the British Parliament from the first women in England, demanding household suffrage? What means the late action in Kansas, 10,000 women petitioned there for the right of suffrage, and 9,000 votes at the last election was the answer. What means the agitation in every State in the Union? In the very hour when Horace Greeley brought in his adverse report in the Constitutional Convention of New York, at least twenty members rose in their places and presented petitions from every part of the State, demanding woman's suffrage. What means that eloquent speech of George W. Curtis in the Convention, but to show that the ablest minds in the State are ready for this onward step?

6. The Fourteenth Amendment Grants Citizenship and Due Process of Law to African Americans, 1868

Section 1. All persons born or naturalized in the United States, and subject to the jurisdiction thereof, are citizens of the United States and of the State wherein they reside. No State shall make or enforce any law which shall abridge the privileges or

---

U.S. Constitution, amend. 14.

immunities of citizens of the United States; nor shall any State deprive any person of life, liberty, or property, without due process of law; nor deny to any person within its jurisdiction the equal protection of the laws.

Section 2. Representatives shall be apportioned among the several States according to their respective numbers, counting the whole number of persons in each State, excluding Indians not taxed. But when the right to vote at any election for the choice of electors for President and Vice-President of the United States, Representatives in Congress, the executive and judicial officers of a State, or the members of the legislature thereof, is denied to any of the male inhabitants of such State, being twenty-one years of age, and citizens of the United States, or in any way abridged, except for participation in rebellion, or other crime, the basis of representation therein shall be reduced in the proportion which the number of such male citizens shall bear to the whole number of male citizens twenty-one years of age in such State.

Section 3. No person shall be a Senator or Representative in Congress, or elector of President and Vice-President, or hold any office, civil or military, under the United States or under any State, who, having previously taken an oath as a member of Congress, or as an officer of the United States, or as a member of any State legislature, or as an executive or judicial officer of any State, to support the Constitution of the United States, shall have engaged in insurrection or rebellion against the same, or given aid or comfort to the enemies thereof. But Congress may, by a vote of two-thirds of each house, remove such disability.

Section 4. The validity of the public debt of the United States, authorized by law, including debts incurred for payment of pensions and bounties for services in suppressing insurrection or rebellion, shall not be questioned. But neither the United States nor any State shall assume or pay any debt or obligation incurred in aid of insurrection or rebellion against the United States, or any claim for the loss or emancipation of any slave; but all such debts, obligations, and claims shall be held illegal and void.

Section 5. The Congress shall have power to enforce, by appropriate legislation, the provisions of this article.

7. Elias Hill, an African American Man, Recounts a Nighttime Visit from the Ku Klux Klan, 1871

On the night of the 5th of last May, after I had heard a great deal of what they had done in that neighborhood, they came. It was between 12 and 1 o'clock at night when I was awakened and heard the dogs barking, and something walking, very much like horses. As I had often laid awake listening for such persons, for they had been all through the neighborhood, and disturbed all men and many women, I supposed that it was them. . . . Some one then hit my door. It flew open. One ran in the house, and stopping about the middle of the house, which is a small cabin, he turned around, as it seemed to me as I lay there awake, and said, "Who's here?" Then I knew they would take me, and I answered, "I am here." He shouted for joy, as it seemed, "Here

Report to the Joint Select Committee to Inquire into the Condition of Affairs in the Late Insurrectionary States, 42 Cong., 2 Sess., December 4, 1871–June 10, 1872, Vol. I, Serial 1483, pp. 44–46.

he is! Here he is! We have found him!" and he threw the bedclothes off of me and caught me by one arm, while another man took me by the other and they carried me into the yard between the houses, my brother's and mine, and put me on the ground beside a boy. The first thing they asked me was, "Who did that burning? Who burned our houses?"—gin-houses, dwelling-houses and such. Some had been burned in the neighborhood. I told them it was not me; I could not burn houses; it was unreasonable to ask me. Then they hit me with their fists, and said I did it, I ordered it. They went on asking me didn't I tell the black men to ravish all the white women. No, I answered them. They struck me again with their fists on my breast, and then they went on, "When did you hold a night-meeting of the Union League, and who were the officers? Who was the president?" I told them I had been the president, but that there had been no Union League meeting held at that place where they were formerly held since away in the fall. This was the 5th of May. They said that Jim Raney, that was hung, had been at my house since the time I had said the League was last held, and that he had made a speech. I told them he had not, because I did not know the man. I said, "Upon honor." They said I had no honor, and hit me again. They went on asking me hadn't I been writing to Mr. A. S. Wallace, in Congress, to get letters from him. I told them I had. They asked what I had been writing about? I told them, "Only tidings." They said, with an oath, "I know the tidings were d—d good, and you were writing something about the Ku-Klux, and haven't you been preaching and praying about the Ku-Klux?" One asked, "Haven't you been preaching political sermons?" Generally, one asked me all the questions, but the rest were squatting over me—some six men I counted as I lay there. Said one, "Didn't you preach against the Ku-Klux," and wasn't that what Mr. Wallace was writing to me about. "Not at all," I said. "Let me see the letter," said he; "what was it about?" I said it was on the times. They wanted the letter. I told them if they would take me back into the house, and lay me in the bed, which was close adjoining my books and papers, I would try and get it. They said I would never go back to that bed, for they were going to kill me—"Never expect to go back; tell us where the letters are." I told them they were on the shelf somewhere, and I hoped they would not kill me. Two of them went into the house. My sister says that as quick as they went into the house they struck the clock at the foot of the bed. I heard it shatter. One of the four around me called out, "Don't break any private property, gentlemen, if you please; we have got him we came for, and that's all we want." I did not hear them break anything else. They staid in there a good while hunting about and then came out and asked me for a lamp. I told them there was a lamp somewhere. They said "Where?" I was so confused I said I could not tell exactly. They caught my leg—you see what it is—and pulled me over the yard, and then left me there, knowing I could not walk nor crawl, and all six went into the house. I was chilled with the cold lying in the yard at that time of night, for it was near 1 o'clock, and they had talked and beat me and so on until half an hour had passed since they first approached. After they had staid in the house for a considerable time, they came back to where I lay and asked if I wasn't afraid at all. They pointed pistols at me all around my head once or twice, as if they were going to shoot me, telling me they were going to kill me; wasn't I ready to die, and willing to die? Didn't I preach? That they came to kill me—all the time pointing pistols at me. This second time they came out of the house, after plundering the house, searching for letters, they came at me with these pistols, and asked if I was ready to die. I told them that I was not exactly ready; that I would rather live; that I hoped they would not kill me that time. They said they would; I had better prepare. One caught me by the leg and hurt me, for my leg for forty years has been drawn each year, more and more year by year, and I made moan when it hurt so. One said "G-d d——n it, hush!" He had a horsewhip, and he told me to pull up my shirt, and he hit me. He told me at evey lick, "Hold up your shirt." I made a moan every time he cut with the horsewhip. I reckon he struck me eight cuts right on the hip bone; it was almost the only place he could hit my body, my legs are so short—all my limbs drawn up and withered away with pain. I saw one of them standing over me or by me motion to them to quit. They all had disguises on. I then thought they would not kill me. One of them then took a strap, and buckled it around my neck and said, "Let's take him to the river and drown him." "What course is the river?" they asked me. I told them east. Then one of them went feeling about, as if he was looking for something, and said, "I don't see no east! Where is the d——d thing?" as if he did not understand what I meant. After pulling the strap around my neck, he took it off and gave me a lick on my hip where he had struck me with the horsewhip. One of them said, "Now, you see, I've burned up the d——d letter of Wallace's and all," and he brought out a little book and says, "What's this for?" I told him I did not know; to let me see with a light and I could read it. They brought a lamp and I read it. It was a book in which I had keep an account of the school. I had been licensed to keep a school. I read them some of the names. He said that would do, and asked if I had been paid for those scholars I had put down. I said no. He said I would now have to die. I was somewhat afraid, but one said not to kill me. They said "Look here! Will you put a card in the paper next week like June Moore and Sol Hill?" They had been prevailed on to put a card in the paper to renounce all republicanism and never vote. I said, "If I had the money to pay the expense, I could." They said I could borrow, and gave me another lick. They asked me, "Will you quit preaching?" I told them I did not know. I said that to save my life. They said I must stop that republican paper that was coming to Clay Hill. It has been only a few weeks since it stopped. The republican weekly paper was then coming to me from Charleston. It came to my name. They said I must stop it, quit preaching, and put a card in the newspaper renouncing republicanism, and they would not kill me; but if I did not they would come back the next week and kill me. . . .

[Satisfied that he could no longer live in that community, he had written to make inquiry about the means of going himself to Liberia.]

8. Missouri Senator Carl Schurz Admits the Failures of Reconstruction, 1872

. . . But the stubborn fact remains that they [Southern black voters and officeholders] *were* ignorant and inexperienced; that the public business *was* an unknown world to them, and that in spite of the best intentions they *were* easily misled, not infrequently by the most reckless rascality which had found a way to their confidence. Thus their political rights and privileges were undoubtedly well calculated, and even

Carl Schurz, Speech in the Senate, January 30, 1872, in *Speeches, Correspondence, and Political Papers of Carl Schurz,* ed. Frederic Bancroft (New York: G. P. Putnam's & Co., 1913), pp. 326–327.

necessary, to protect their rights as free laborers and citizens; but they were not well calculated to secure a successful administration of other public interests.

I do not blame the colored people for it; still less do I say that for this reason their political rights and privileges should have been denied them. Nay, sir, I deemed it necessary then, and I now reaffirm that opinion, that they should possess those rights and privileges for the permanent establishment of the logical and legitimate results of the war and the protection of their new position in society. But, while never losing sight of this necessity, I do say that the inevitable consequence of the admission of so large an uneducated and inexperienced class to political power, as to the probable mismanagement of the material interests of the social body, should at least have been mitigated by a counterbalancing policy. When ignorance and inexperience were admitted to so large an influence upon public affairs, intelligence ought no longer to so large an extent have been excluded. In other words, when universal suffrage was granted to secure the equal rights of all, universal amnesty ought to have been granted to make all the resources of political intelligence and experience available for the promotion of the welfare of all.

But what did we do? To the uneducated and inexperienced classes—uneducated and inexperienced, I repeat, entirely without their fault—we opened the road to power; and, at the same time, we condemned a large proportion of the intelligence of those States, of the property-holding, the industrial, the professional, the tax-paying interest, to a worse than passive attitude. We made it, as it were, easy for rascals who had gone South in quest of profitable adventure to gain the control of masses so easily misled, by permitting them to appear as the exponents and representatives of the National power and of our policy; and at the same time we branded a large number of men of intelligence, and many of them of personal integrity, whose material interests were so largely involved in honest government, and many of whom would have cooperated in managing the public business with care and foresight—we branded them, I say, as outcasts, telling them that they ought not to be suffered to exercise any influence upon the management of the public business, and that it would be unwarrantable presumption in them to attempt it.

I ask you, sir, could such things fail to contribute to the results we read to-day in the political corruption and demoralization, and in the financial ruin of some of the Southern States? These results are now before us. The mistaken policy may have been pardonable when these consequences were still a matter of conjecture and speculation; but what excuse have we now for continuing it when those results are clear before our eyes, beyond the reach of contradiction?

9. Mississippi Congressman L. Q. C. Lamar Denounces Reconstruction, 1874

When, in order to consummate your policy, you divided the southern country into military districts, your military commanders, distrusting the purposes of the southern people and knowing the negroes were incompetent to manage the affairs of government, called to their aid and installed into all the offices of the States, from the

From L. Q. C. Lamar, Speech in the House, June 8, 1874, *Congressional Record,* 43 Cong., 1 Sess., Vol. 2, pt. 6, p. 429.

highest to the lowest, a set of men from the North who were strangers to our people, not possessing their confidence, not elected by them, not responsible to them, having no interest in common with them, and hostile to them to a certain extent in sentiment.

I am not going to characterize these men by any harshness of language. I am speaking of a state of things more controlling than ordinary personal characteristics. Even if it were true that they came to the South for no bad purposes, they were put in a position which has always engendered rapacity, cupidity corruption, grinding oppression, and taxation in its most devouring form. They were rulers without responsibility, in unchecked control of the material resources of a people with whom they had not a sentiment in sympathy or an interest in common, and whom they habitually regarded and treated as rebels who had forfeited their right to protection. These men, thus situated and thus animated, were the fisc of the South. They were the recipients of all the revenues, State and local. Not a dollar of taxes, State or local, but what went into their pockets. The suffering people on whom the taxes were laid could not exercise the slightest control, either as to the amount imposed or the basis upon which they were laid. The consequence was that in a few short years eight magnificent Commonwealths were laid in ruins. This condition of things still exists with unabated rigor in those Southern States. For when, by your reconstruction measures, you determined to provide civil governments for these States, the machinery by which these men carried their power over into those civil governments was simple and effectual. Under your policy generally—I repeat, my purpose to-day is not arraignment—under that policy you disfranchised a large portion of the white people of the Southern States. The registration laws and the education laws in the hands of these men kept a still larger proportion away.

But there was an agency more potent still.

By persistent misrepresentation a majority in Congress was made to believe that the presence of the United States Army would be necessary not merely to put these governments in force, but to keep them in operation and to keep them from being snatched away and worked to the oppression and ruin of the black race and the few loyal men who were there attempting to protect their rights. Thus was introduced into those so-called reconstructed civil governments the Federal military as an operative and predominant principle. Thus, with a quick, sudden, and violent hand, these men tore the two races asunder and hurled one in violent antagonism upon the other, and to this day the negro vote massed into an organization hostile to the whites is an instrument of absolute power in the hands of these men. These governments are in external form civil, but they are in their essential principle military. They are called local governments, but in reality they are Federal executive agencies. Not one of them emanates from the uncontrolled will of the people, white or black; not one which rests upon the elective principle in its purity. They have been aptly styled by a distinguished statesman and jurist in Mississippi, (Hon. W. P. Harris,) State governments without States, without popular constituencies. For they are as completely insulated from the traditions, the feelings, the interests, and the free suffrages of the people, white and black, as if they were outside the limits of those States. Where is the public sentiment which guides and enlightens those to whom is confided the conduct of public affairs? Where is the moral judgment of a virtuous people to which they are amenable? Where is the moral indignation which falls like the scathing lightning upon the delinquent or guilty public officer? Sir, that class and race in which reside these great moral agencies are prostrated, their interests, their prosperity jeopardized, their protests unheeded, and every murmur of discontent and every effort to throw off their oppression misrepresented here as originating in the spirit which inaugurated the rebellion. Sir, the statement that these southern governments have no popular constituencies is true, but they nevertheless have a constituency to whom they bear a responsibility inexorable as death. It is limited to the one point of keeping the State true and faithful to the Administration; all else is boundless license. That constituency is here in Washington; its heart pulsates in the White House. There is its intelligence and there is its iron will. I do not exaggerate when I say that every one of these governments depends, every moment of their existence, upon the will of the President. That will makes and unmakes them. A short proclamation backed by one company determines who is to be governor of Arkansas. A telegram settles the civil magistracy of Texas. A brief order to a general in New Orleans wrests a State government from the people of Louisiana and vests its control in the creatures of the Administration.

E S S A Y S

The collapse of Reconstruction had enormous costs for the African American populations of the South. Arguably, its failure also postponed the economic and social recovery of the entire region until well into the twentieth century. Historians have long debated the meaning of Reconstruction and particularly the reasons for its abandonment. In the first essay, Thomas Holt of the University of Chicago argues that in spite of many obstacles, advocates of Reconstruction had a fighting chance. It was lost to them partly because of their own political miscalculations, and especially because of the enormous difficulty in achieving Republican Party unity in the South. Not only did race divide white and black Republicans, but class differences divided "freemen" and "freedmen" as well. Eric Foner of Columbia University takes a somewhat different tack, emphasizing the tremendous odds against success. White southerners violently opposed reform, and over time northerners became fatigued by the struggle. Political expediency (and anger at President Andrew Johnson) drove Reconstruction at the federal level from the first, and when the reforms became inexpedient, the policy died out.

Social Class Divides Negro State Legislators in South Carolina, Impeding Reconstruction

THOMAS HOLT

Reconstruction was "a frightful experiment which never could have given a real statesman who learned or knew the facts the smallest hope of success." Daniel H. Chamberlain, the last Republican governor of South Carolina, wrote this post-mortem a quarter of a century after he had been driven from office by a violent and fraudulent campaign to restore native whites to power in the fall and winter of 1876–77. Undoubtedly his view was colored by the social milieu of America at the

Thomas C. Holt, "Negro State Legislators in South Carolina During Reconstruction," in *Southern Black Leaders of the Reconstruction Era,* ed. Howard N. Rabinowitz (Urbana: University of Illinois Press), pp. 223–226, 229–230, 233–234, 236–244. Copyright 1982, Board of Trustees of the University of Illinois. Used by permission of the University of Illinois Press.

turn of the century, when racism of the most virulent type had become the intellectual orthodoxy. On the other hand, these later reflections do not differ much from his assessment just two months after he had been forced to relinquish his office. In June 1877 he explained to William Lloyd Garrison that "defeat was inevitable under the circumstances of time and place which surrounded me. I mean here exactly that the uneducated negro was too weak, no matter what his numbers, to cope with the whites." In later years he described that weakness more explicitly: blacks were "an aggregation of ignorance and inexperience and incapacity."

The story of Reconstruction in South Carolina and elsewhere has been considerably revised since Chamberlain presented his analysis of its failure; yet, his basic premise is still shared by many revisionists. "The failure of the Radical government . . . was due not so much to its organization as to its personnel," Francis B. Simkins and Robert H. Woody wrote in 1932. Given the armed support of the federal establishment and the overwhelming black majority in South Carolina, the failure of the Republican regime could only have been caused by the venality, ignorance, and corruption of the leadership. Northern adventurers, mediocre scalawags, and uneducated, "excitable" freedmen constituted a legislature so guilty of mismanagement and fraud that the white minority rose up in justifiable wrath to put it down. Simkins and Woody were more charitable to the achievements of the Reconstruction regime than Chamberlain, but they leave little doubt that the inexperienced, undisciplined ex-slaves were the weak link in the Republican coalition.

While Simkins and Woody read the supposed incapacities of the slave into the failures of Reconstruction, a recent revisionist history of slavery reverses the process: the failures of the postemancipation political order help confirm a controversial description of the slave regime. Eugene Genovese, in *Roll, Jordan, Roll,* evokes a seminal, sometimes brilliant picture of the slave's worldview; but the essence of his argument is that that worldview was conditioned by a basically paternalistic master-slave relationship. Furthermore, the long-term consequence of that paternalism on blacks was to transform "elements of personal dependency into a sense of collective weakness." Although the slaves were able to manipulate the masters' paternalism in ways that reaffirmed their individual manhood, "they could not grasp their collective strength as a people and act like political men." This "political paralysis," this absence of "a stern collective discipline," not only accounts for their failure to mount significant slave revolts or to take advantage of their masters' strategic weakness to strike for freedom during the Civil War, but also explains their failure to "organize themselves more effectively in politics" after the war. In short, the behavior of the freedman confirms the conditioning of the slave.

But it is difficult to reconcile any of these views with events in South Carolina during Reconstruction. Certainly the cause of its failure cannot be laid to the political incapacity and inexperience of the black masses. They were uneducated. They were inexperienced. But they overcame these obstacles to forge a formidable political majority in the state that had led the South into secession. During the Reconstruction era 60 percent of South Carolina's population was black. This popular majority was turned into a functioning political majority as soon as Reconstruction legislation was put into effect with the registration for the constitutional convention in 1867. Despite violence and economic intimidation, the black electorate grew rather than declined between 1868 and 1876. The only effective political opposition before the election of 1876 came from so-called reform tickets, especially in 1870 and 1874. On these occasions, black and white Republican dissidents fused with Democrats to challenge the regular Republican party. But the strength of these challenges was generally confined to the predominantly white up-country counties and Charleston with its large white plurality and freeborn Negro bourgeoisie. Indeed, many observers condemned the unflinching, "blind" allegiance of black Republicans as evidence of their lack of political sophistication. But given the political alternatives and the records of so-called reform and fusion candidates, the black electorate could just as easily be credited with a high degree of political savvy. For South Carolina certainly, Frederick Douglass was right: the Republican party—despite its weaknesses and inadequacies—was the deck, all else the sea. . . .

Activities other than partisan politics also demonstrate the freedmen's capacity for collective political action. For example, in the lowland rice-growing areas, cash-poor planters instituted a system wherein their workers were paid in scrip rather than currency. The scrip or "checks" could be redeemed only at designated stores in exchange for goods priced significantly above normal retail items. Although the legislature made some attempts in 1872 and again in 1875 to reform and control the system, its essential features remained unchanged: the workers exchanged low-paid labor for high-priced goods. Since their political representatives appeared to be unable to correct this problem, in July 1876 the workers took matters into their own hands. They struck. The strike was widespread and involved considerable violence against nonstrikers. Governor Chamberlain sent in the militia and had the strike leaders jailed. He also sent Negro Congressman Robert Smalls to convince the strikers to renounce violence and concede scabs their right to work. Smalls reported to the governor that he had succeeded in his mission, but subsequent reports of continued violence suggest that the right-to-work principle was attended more in the breach than in the observance. Eventually the planters capitulated and abolished the scrips system. . . .

Ultimately the failures of South Carolina Republicans must be laid not to their black ex-slave constituents but to the party leadership. Thus Simkins and Woody are partly right when they blame the personnel of the South Carolina government, but they are wrong to the extent that they find venality, corruption, ignorance, and inexperience as the primary causal factors. Surely there were venal men. Clearly corruption was rife. But there were corrupt Democrats before, during, and after Reconstruction, including the architects of the Democratic campaign of 1876, Martin W. Gary and M. C. Butler. Republican corruption merely offered a propagandistic advantage in the Democratic efforts to discredit the Radical regime. With the possible exception of the land-commission frauds, corruption was secondary to the major failures of that regime while in office and to its ability to sustain office. Very likely native whites viewed the fact that blacks wielded political power as itself a form of corruption of governmental process.

South Carolina was unique among American state governments in that blacks enjoyed control over the legislature and many other political entities. Of the 487 men elected to various state and federal offices between 1867 and 1876, 255 were black. While it is true that they never succeeded in elevating any of their number to the U.S. Senate, they did fill nine of the state's fifteen congressional terms between 1870 and 1876, including four of the five seats available from 1870 to 1874. J. J. Wright was elected to one of the three positions on the state supreme court in 1870, which he held until 1877. However, no black was ever even nominated for the governorship, and all of the circuit judges, comptrollers general, attorneys general, and superintendents of education during this period were white. Only a handful of blacks served in the important county offices of sheriff, auditor, treasurer, probate judge, and clerk of court. More commonly blacks were elected to such local offices as school commissioner and trial justice; but even among these they were not a majority.

Clearly blacks enjoyed their greatest power in the General Assembly. Their membership averaged from just over one-third during the first five sessions of the Senate to about one-half during the last five; but in the House of Representatives they were never less than 56 percent of the membership. . . . More important than their membership was their growing control of key committees and leadership posts in both branches of the General Assembly. Samuel J. Lee became the first black Speaker of the House in 1872; he was succeeded by Robert B. Elliott from 1874 to 1876. The president pro tem of the Senate was a black after 1872, as was the lieutenant governor, who presided over that body. Better than two-thirds of the respective committee chairmanships were held by blacks in the House after 1870 and in the Senate after 1872. Furthermore, in both houses the key committees—those controlling money bills or the flow of major legislation—generally had black chairmen.

Little wonder then that former slaveholders viewed the new order with alarm. Indeed, the displaced local whites often became hysterical in their denunciations of the new order. For example, when William J. Whipper was elected to a judgeship in the important Charleston circuit, the *News and Courier* ran a banner headline declaring its "Civilization In Peril." As a deliberate Republican policy, the judicial system had been kept inviolately white and conservative. The election of a black radical to fill one of the most important of these posts was the first step toward the creation of "an African dominion," indeed "a new Liberia." Here, as elsewhere in the South, to involve blacks in the political process was "to Africanize" the social system.

The biographical profile of the Negro leadership justifies neither the fears of white contemporaries nor the charges of many historians of that era. While the overwhelming majority of their constituents were black, illiterate, and propertyless ex-slave farmworkers, most of the political leadership was literate, a significant number had been free before the Civil War, many were owners of property, and most were employed in skilled or professional occupations after the war. At least one in four of the 255 Negroes elected to state and federal offices between 1868 and 1876 were of free origins. Indeed, counting only those for whom information is available, one finds that almost 40 percent had been free before the Civil War. Of those whose educational attainments are known, 87 percent were literate, and the 25 identifiable illiterates approximately matched the number who had college or professional training. Information on property ownership is available for little more than half the legislators. Seventy-six percent of these men possessed either real or taxable personal property, and 27 percent of them were worth $1,000 or more. Indeed, one in four held over $1,000 in real property alone. . . .

Thus, while there were differences in their respective social and economic backgrounds, neither the freeborn nor ex-slave legislators conform to the traditional stereotype of ignorant, pennyless sharecroppers rising from cotton fields to despoil the legislature and plunder the state. In truth, most of the freeborn and many of the slaveborn were a "middle" class of artisans, small farmers, and shopkeepers located on the social spectrum somewhere between the vast majority of Negro sharecroppers and the white middle and upper classes. Indeed, because of their education, class position, and general aspirations, they were more likely to embrace than reject the petty bourgeois values of their society.

But while their political opponents have distorted the social and economic backgrounds of the Negro leadership, charges that they were politically inexperienced can scarcely be denied. Northern as well as southern blacks had few if any opportunities to gain experience in partisan politics during the antebellum period. Most could not vote in the state in which they resided, and they were unlikely to hold office in any state. In various ways, employees of the missionary societies and churches, the army, and the Freedmen's Bureau gained experience in public life and in serving and mobilizing constituents. Between 1865 and 1868 about one-fourth of the black elected officials had been affiliated with one or more of these institutions, as also had more than 37 percent of those who served in the first Republican government in 1868. But, of course, while these affiliations could help prepare men for public service, they were no substitute for direct legislative and partisan political experience.

The black legislator's lack of prior political experience was further exacerbated by the likelihood of an abbreviated service for most of their number. The high turnover in the House of Representatives suggests the volatility of that body. Only two black members, William M. Thomas of Colleton and Joseph D. Boston of Newberry, served the entire four terms of the Reconstruction period. Eight other men served three terms; but 61 percent of the 212 blacks elected to the House between 1868 and 1876 were one-term members. Only 15 of these advanced to higher elective offices in the state senate or executive branch or at the federal level. Clearly, for the most of its sessions, the House of Representatives was composed of a disproportionate number of freshmen legislators.

It is difficult to evaluate the political impact of this rather high turnover in membership. Generally, a low turnover rate is evidence of significant institutionalization in a legislature that is reflected in strong party leadership and discipline. Conversely the relatively weak party discipline of the South Carolina Republican party would appear to be congruent with the high turnover of its members. Certainly the evidence of intraparty dissension and weak leadership among Republican legislators is formidable by almost any standard. The index of relative cohesion developed by sociologist Stuart Rice in the 1920s provides one way of measuring unity or conflict within a party or subgroup. On the Rice scale a score of 100 indicates unanimity of the group, while a score of 0 indicates a perfect split, half of the members voting for a measure and half against it. Throughout the Reconstruction era, Democrats voted together more consistently than did Republicans. While the Democrats' average score was never less than 68, the Republicans never exceeded 50. . . .

Although no single bloc or segment of the Republican party was solely responsible for its weakness, there were political differences within the party that diminished its strength. Evidence suggests that the lack of party solidarity revealed on legislative roll calls reflected differences in aspirations and ideological orientations of various subgroups within the party. From the beginning of Reconstruction there had been conflict between white and Negro Republicans and between Negroes with roots in the freeborn mulatto bourgeoisie and the black ex-slaves. During the early meetings between 1865 and 1868, Negro aspirations for greater representation and power clashed with white efforts to maintain political control, and the demands for universal manhood suffrage and land reform articulated by black ex-slaves did not always resonate with the policy objectives and ideological orientation of their freeborn colleagues. At the end of the Reconstruction era, such differences in interests, perceptions, and orientation still undermined party unity. The cohesion indices for all ten legislative sessions and the agreement scores for the 1876 session generally reflect these conflicts. For instance, by calculating the average number of times a given subgroup voted with other Republicans, one can uncover the breaks in the party's ranks. In 1876 the average agreement score for white Republicans was 37.3 as compared with 44.6 for Negroes. Similarly, black former slaves scored 46.9 as compared with 38.7 for mulattoes of free origin. Clearly, what little political stability Republicans could lay claim to was provided not by the better educated and more experienced whites or by the brown bourgeoisie, but by the blacks of slave origin. . . .

It is not surprising that white Republican legislators did not see eye to eye with their black colleagues; there was ample evidence of distrust and animosity between these segments of the party. During the early years of Reconstruction, whites actively discouraged blacks from seeking their appropriate share of offices and power. On several occasions during the first two years of Republican rule, whites tried to exclude blacks from major state executive offices, congressional seats, judgeships, and even key party leadership posts. During the 1870 campaign Negroes rebelled against this policy and demanded their fair share of state and party offices. Nevertheless, during the final year of Republican rule, the party again would be split badly by the governor's effort to deny an important judicial post to William J. Whipper, a northern black lawyer.

Such conflicts cannot be traced solely to racial animosities, but there is evidence that racism was a contributing factor. For example, in 1868 Franklin J. Moses, Jr., Speaker of the House and governor of the state from 1872 to 1874, advised Governor Robert K. Scott to appoint only native whites to state judicial posts. In 1871 State Representative T. N. Talbert was even more explicit. "My policy," he wrote the governor, "is to get as many of the native whites of the state to unite with us as we can and try and induce Northern men to come and settle among us. There is not enough virtue and intelligence among the Blacks to conduct the government in such a way as will promote peace and prosperity."

Given the nation's racial climate it is not surprising, perhaps, that tensions would develop between Negro and white Republicans or that they would often perceive policy issues differently; but there was no reason to expect that Negro legislators would be so much less cohesive among themselves than their Democratic rivals. For much of the Reconstruction period a unified Negro leadership could have dominated the legislature. Their overwhelming majority in the House together with a consistently large plurality in the Senate should have enabled Negroes, given inevitable absenteeism and defections among white Republicans and Democrats, to attain most of their major legislative objectives. But in fact Negro leaders were often at odds on legislative objectives, political policies, and ideology. Furthermore, the nature of their disunity followed a consistent pattern from the earliest political meetings and is best explained by reference to differences in their socioeconomic status and antebellum experience.

The most visible, though not necessarily most significant, divisions were between the black ex-slaves and those mulattoes who had been free before the war. The number of freeborn brown officeholders was far out of proportion to their share of the state's population, especially in the early conventions and legislative sessions, and their control of leadership positions was even more striking. In the 1868–70 House of Representatives, for example, half the committee chairmanships held by Negroes were filled by freeborn mulattoes. Between 1868 and 1876, over half the Negro state senators were drawn from this class and their average term of service was longer than that of black freedmen. Five of the seven Negroes elected to the state executive branch were freeborn brown men as well as four of the state's seven Negro congressmen.

Obviously, free brown men successfully offered themselves as prominent leaders of a predominantly black ex-slave electorate, but their very success aroused jealousy and political divisiveness within the party. In 1871 black leader Martin R. Delany complained to Frederick Douglass about mulatto dominance of patronage positions. In 1870 William H. Jones, Jr., black representative from Georgetown, publicly ridiculed Joseph H. Rainey, his mulatto rival for the state Senate, because of his extremely light complexion. State Senator William B. Nash, a black ex-slave, once referred to his mulatto colleagues as "simply mongrels."

It is misleading, however, to consider these intraracial tensions as merely a consequence of differences in skin color and antebellum origins. The fact is that among South Carolina Negroes a light complexion and free origins correlated very strongly with other indicators of bourgeois class status; mulattoes and those who had been free before the war were more likely to own property and thus to enjoy higher status than black ex-slaves, who were more likely to be propertyless. These general patterns were reflected in the General Assembly, where legislators of free origins were generally better educated than the freedmen, more likely to own property, and more likely to be employed as artisans or in a profession rather than as farmworkers. These objective differences, as minor as they might have appeared to whites, generated not only consciousness of class differences but social institutions that confirmed and reinforced those differences. The Brown Fellowship Society was one such institution. Founded in 1790, the society limited its members to free brown men, providing them with a variety of financial services as well as social connections. At least three legislators belonged to the Brown Fellowship Society, and several others were members of social clubs with a similar orientation though less prestige. Church affiliation was another indicator of status aspirations if not class position. Thomas W. Cardozo, brother of Francis L. Cardozo and a representative of the American Missionary Association in 1865, complained to his superiors that he could not "worship intelligently with the colored people [meaning black freedmen]" and urged the formation of a separate missionary church for himself and his teachers. The pattern of religious affiliation among Negro legislators suggests that Cardozo's prejudices were not uncommon. Of the legislators whose religious affiliations can be identified, all but one of the freeborn were Catholic, Presbyterian, or Episcopalian, while 70 percent of the former slaves were either Methodist or Baptist.

It appears that these differences in social background and status produced differing perspectives on public policy. During the 1868 Constitutional Convention, for example, black ex-slave delegates voted with other Negro delegates an average of 72 percent of the time, while freeborn mulatto delegates averaged 67.9 percent. The differences in voting behavior were more dramatic when sensitive issues of land reform and confiscation were debated. Robert C. De Large's resolution to halt the disfranchisement of ex-Confederates and the confiscation of their property was one early test of radical and conservative tendencies in the convention. Although De Large's motion was opposed by a majority of the Negro delegates, it drew its heaviest support from mulatto delegates who had been free before the war, about 40 percent of whom supported the resolution, and its heaviest opposition from those blacks who had been slaves, about 75 percent of whom opposed it. Debates on whether to impose literacy and poll-tax requirements for voting reveal similar divisions. Delegates from the antebellum free class argued strenuously, though unsuccessfully, that illiterates and persons failing to pay a poll tax should not be allowed to vote. . . .

A closer examination of two issues, education and labor legislation, suggests the political difference that social class differences made in South Carolina. The establishment of an educational system was one of the most striking successes of the Republican regime. The system did not function as well as its founders had hoped, but its creation firmly established the principle of free public education in a state that had not had such a system before the war. It also provided the infrastructure on which later systems could be based. The freedmen enthusiastically took advantage of the new opportunity, and their leaders endorsed public schooling as a major goal of the postwar period. A resolution passed at one of the early conventions declared, "Knowledge is power." Curiously, in the view of some leaders, the endorsement of education as a major objective for the new black citizens served also to set off the uneducated as degraded and unfit to participate in public life. Thus convention delegates who advocated literacy and poll-tax qualifications for suffrage, all of whom were freeborn brown men of well-to-do backgrounds, were motivated by a desire to encourage education among the masses. According to this view, uneducated adults would be encouraged to go to school to avoid disfranchisement and the poll taxes levied on registered voters would pay the costs of maintaining the school system. As we have seen, the black freedmen in the convention as well as those in Chaplain Noble's class perceived the issue differently. A literacy requirement would be political suicide for a largely illiterate black electorate, so they decided they "had better not wait for eddication."

Despite their differences, legislators were successful in passing laws establishing schools for all. But their efforts to regulate the evolving free-labor market were much less productive. Two of the scores of bills introduced on labor subjects serve to illustrate the differing perceptions among Republicans. One, introduced by James Henderson, a Negro farmer from Newberry County, on January 8, 1870, would have established labor-contract agents to directly supervise and monitor relations between planters and workers. Several days later a substitute bill was introduced by George Lee, a Negro lawyer from Charleston. Lee's bill relied on the regular court system to settle contract disputes and gave the laborer a ninety-day lien on the crop at harvest. Thus, rather than direct state intervention to resolve labor disputes, the disputants had to assume the initiative and expense of litigation themselves. Normally the planter was better situated to undertake such risks than was the worker.

Clearly, many of the legislators preferred a laissez-faire approach to regulating the labor market. John Feriter, a white native Republican, declared that the "law of supply and demand must regulate the matter"; and Reuben Tomlinson, a white northern Republican and former abolitionist, insisted, "I don't believe it is in the power of the General Assembly to do anything except to give them [farmworkers] equal rights before the law." Apparently a majority of both white and black legislators agreed with Feriter and Tomlinson; they voted for Lee's bill, which approached this laissez-faire ideal, and against Henderson's bill, which advocated state regulation. However, the minority voting for Henderson's bill included 48 percent of the ex-slaves as compared with only 11 percent of the freeborn, and 35 percent of the blacks in contrast with only 18 percent of the mulattoes. It would appear then that those whose origins were closer to the masses of the electorate saw labor problems differently than their colleagues from more privileged backgrounds.

The 1876 legislative session was the last opportunity Republicans had to ensure economic justice for their constituents. Elected by a very close margin in 1874, Governor Daniel Chamberlain moved openly to build a political coalition of conservative Republicans and Democrats. His "reform" policies won general approval among Democrats. Chamberlain sought to cut government spending by reducing social services and education programs. He removed Republicans from important local offices and replaced them with Democrats. These policies won Democratic support but alienated and demoralized Republicans. J. W. Rice's despondent letter to Chamberlain protesting the appointment of several Democrats to Laurens County offices formerly held by Republicans was typical of the governor's correspondence during this period: "I am at last discouraged and thinking about resigning." Generally, the party morale declined and dissension increased. During the spring of 1876, Democrats watched gleefully as Republican conventions often tottered on the brink of physical violence. As A. P. Aldrich told a cheering audience, the Democrats planned "to keep Chamberlain and some of the carpetbaggers fighting, till they eat each other up all but the tails, and that he would keep the tails jumping at each other, until Southern raised gentlemen slide into office and take the reins of government."

Aldrich proved a true prophet. Both Wade Hampton, the Democratic gubernatorial candidate, and Daniel Chamberlain, the Republican, claimed victory after the November election that year, but only the Democrats possessed the unity and strength to enforce their claim. For five months there were two governments in South Carolina competing for control of the state and recognition by federal authorities. Although Republicans controlled the state house and the machinery of government, years of intraparty strife and rivalry had finally taken their toll. Unfavorable decisions by Republican-elected judges and defections and resignations of Republican officeholders weakened Chamberlain's authority, while Hampton grew more formidable as the crisis stretched from weeks into months. Hampton's unofficial militia of red-shirted gunmen imposed bloody curfews on blacks in much of the countryside, while Chamberlain's militia was disarmed and ineffective. Hampton collected $100,000 in state taxes, while Chamberlain was unable to command the allegiance of taxpayers or tax collectors. By March newly elected Republican President Rutherford B. Hayes had decided already to concede the disputed elections in the

South in exchange for the presidency, but it is doubtful that he could have decided otherwise in South Carolina even had he wanted to. By that time only a massive show of federal force could have saved the Republican regime; probably, such action was not politically feasible in 1877, nor is it clear that it could have been more than a temporary expedient.

The failure of South Carolina's Reconstruction then was not caused by a weak and ignorant electorate. Despite the economic threats and physical terrors of the 1876 campaign, black freedmen turned out in force and delivered a record vote to Republican candidates. True, there was "political paralysis," an absence of "stern collective discipline," and a failure of will; but these were shortcomings of the Republican leadership, not of the masses of black voters. Divisions among the leaders—between white and black and among Negroes themselves—diminished the power these voters had entrusted to them and betrayed the aspirations they had clearly articulated. The freedmen made an amazing transformation after the Civil War; slaves became political men acting forcefully to crush the most cherished illusions of their former masters. The tragedy of Reconstruction is that they received so much less than they gave.

The Odds Against the Success of Reconstruction Were Great

ERIC FONER

At first glance, the man who succeeded Abraham Lincoln seemed remarkably similar to his martyred predecessor. Both knew poverty in early life, neither enjoyed much formal schooling, and in both deprivation sparked a powerful desire for fame and worldly success. During the prewar decades, both achieved material comfort, Lincoln as an Illinois corporation lawyer, Andrew Johnson rising from tailor's apprentice to become a prosperous landowner. And for both, antebellum politics became a path to power and respect.

In terms of sheer political experience, few men have seemed more qualified for the Presidency than Andrew Johnson. Beginning as a Greenville, Tennessee, alderman in 1829, he rose to the state legislature and then to Congress. He served two terms as governor, and in 1857 entered the Senate. Even more than Lincoln, Johnson gloried in the role of tribune of the common man. His speeches lauded "honest yeomen" and thundered against the "slaveocracy"—a "pampered, bloated, corrupted aristocracy." The issues most closely identified with Johnson's prewar career were tax-supported public education, a reform enacted into law during his term as governor, and homestead legislation, which he promoted tirelessly in the Senate. . . .

In the weeks following Lincoln's assassination, leading Radicals met frequently with the new President to press the issue of black suffrage. Yet Johnson shared neither the Radicals' expansive conception of federal power nor their commitment to political equality for blacks. Despite his own vigorous exercise of authority as military governor, Johnson had always believed in limited government and a strict construction of the Constitution. In Congress, he even opposed appropriations to pave Washington's muddy streets. His fervent nationalism in no way contradicted his respect for the rights of the states. Individual "traitors" should be punished, but the states had never, legally, seceded, or surrendered their right to govern their own affairs. . . .

The definitive announcement of Johnson's plan of Reconstruction came in two proclamations issued on May 29, 1865. The first conferred amnesty and pardon, including restoration of all property rights except for slaves, upon former Confederates who pledged loyalty to the Union and support for emancipation. Fourteen classes of Southerners, however, most notably major Confederate officials and owners of taxable property valued at more than $20,000, were required to apply individually for Presidential pardons. Simultaneously, Johnson appointed William W. Holden provisional governor of North Carolina, instructing him to call a convention to amend the state's prewar constitution so as to create a "republican form of government." Persons who had not been pardoned under the terms of the first proclamation were excluded from voting for delegates, but otherwise, voter qualifications in effect immediately before secession (when the franchise, of course, was limited to whites) would apply. Similar proclamations for other Southern states soon followed. . . .

Johnson's pardon policy reinforced his emerging image as the white South's champion. Despite talk of punishing traitors, the President proved amazingly lenient. No mass arrests followed the collapse of the Confederacy. Jefferson Davis spent two years in federal prison but was never put on trial; his Vice President, Alexander H. Stephens, served a brief imprisonment, returned to Congress in 1873, and ended his days as governor of Georgia. Some 15,000 Southerners, a majority barred from the general amnesty because of their wealth, filed applications for individual pardons. Soon they were being issued wholesale, sometimes hundreds in a single day. By 1866, over 7,000 had been granted. . . .

With Johnson's requirements fulfilled, the South in the fall of 1865 proceeded to elect legislators, governors, and members of Congress. In a majority of the states, former Whigs who had opposed secession swept to victory. . . . The vast majority of the new Senators and Congressmen had opposed secession, yet nearly all had followed their states into the rebellion. Active Unionists were resoundingly defeated. Probably the most closely watched contest occurred in North Carolina, where Jonathan Worth, a Unionist Whig and Confederate state treasurer, defeated Governor Holden. Once in office, Worth quickly restored the old elite, whose power Holden had to some extent challenged, to control of local affairs. The result confirmed the power of wartime political leadership in a state with a large population of non-slaveholding yeomen.

All in all, the 1865 elections threw into question the future of Presidential Reconstruction. Johnson himself sensed that something had gone awry: "There seems, in many of the elections," he wrote at the end of November, "something like defiance, which is all out of place at this time." The stark truth was that outside the Unionist mountains, Johnson's policies had failed to create a new political leadership to replace the prewar slaveocracy. If the architects of secession had been repudiated, the South's affairs would still be directed by men who, while Unionist in 1860, formed part of the antebellum political establishment. Their actions would do much to determine the fate of Johnson's Reconstruction experiment. . . .

As the new legislatures prepared to convene, the Southern press and the private correspondence of planters resounded with calls for what a New Orleans newspaper called "a new labor system . . . prescribed and enforced by the State." The initial response to these demands was embodied in the Black Codes, a series of state laws crucial to the undoing of Presidential Reconstruction. Intended to define the freedmen's new rights and responsibilities, the codes authorized blacks to acquire and own property, marry, make contracts, sue and be sued, and testify in court in cases involving persons of their own color. But these provisions were secondary to the attempt to stabilize the black work force and limit its economic options. Henceforth, the state would enforce labor agreements and plantation discipline, punish those who refused to contract, and prevent whites from competing for black workers.

Mississippi and South Carolina enacted the first and most severe Black Codes toward the end of 1865. Mississippi required all blacks to possess, each January, written evidence of employment for the coming year. Laborers leaving their jobs before the contract expired would forfeit wages already earned, and, as under slavery, be subject to arrest by any white citizen. A person offering work to a laborer under contract risked imprisonment or a fine of $500. To limit the freedmen's economic opportunities, they were forbidden to rent land in urban areas. Vagrancy—a crime whose definition included the idle, disorderly, and those who "misspend what they earn"—could be punished by fines or involuntary plantation labor; other criminal offenses included "insulting" gestures or language, "malicious mischief," and preaching the Gospel without a license. South Carolina's Code required blacks to pay an annual tax from $10 to $100 if they wished to follow any occupation other than farmer or servant (a severe blow to the free black community of Charleston and to former slave artisans). . . .

Although blacks protested all these measures, their most bitter complaints centered on apprenticeship laws that obliged black minors to work without pay for planters. These laws allowed judges to bind to white employers black orphans and those whose parents were deemed unable to support them. The former owner usually had preference, and the consent of the parents was not required. Blacks pleaded with the Freedmen's Bureau for help in releasing their own children or those of deceased relatives. "I think very hard of the former oners," declared one freedman, "for Trying to keep My blood when I kno that Slavery is dead." As late as the end of 1867, Bureau agents and local justices of the peace were still releasing black children from court-ordered apprenticeships. . . .

Throughout these months [summer and fall of 1865] letters passed back and forth among leading Radicals, lamenting Johnson's policies and promising to organize against them. But an unmistakable note of gloom pervaded this correspondence. "I hope you will do all that can be done for the protection of the poor negroes," Sen. Henry Wilson wrote Freedmen's Bureau Commissioner Howard, since "this nation seems about to abandon them to their disloyal masters." . . .

When the Thirty-Ninth Congress convened early in December, Johnson's position remained impressive. The President sincerely claimed to have created a new political order in the South, controlled by men loyal to the Union. He simply could not believe, one suspects, that Northern Republicans would jettison his program over so quixotic an issue as the freedmen's rights. The door stood open for Johnson to embrace the emerging Republican consensus that the freedmen were entitled to civil equality short of the suffrage and that wartime Unionists deserved a more prominent role in Southern politics.

Those close to Johnson, however, knew he was not prone to compromise. Indeed, they relished the prospect of a political battle over Reconstruction. "A fight between the Radicals and the Executive is inevitable," declared Harvey Watterson. "Let it come. The sooner the better for the whole country." . . .

As the split with the President deepened, Republicans grappled with the task of embedding in the Constitution, beyond the reach of Presidential vetoes and shifting political majorities, the results of the Civil War. At one point in January, no fewer than seventy constitutional amendments had been introduced. Not until June, after seemingly endless debate and maneuvering, did the Fourteenth Amendment, the most important ever added to the Constitution, receive the approval of Congress. Its first clause prohibited the states from abridging equality before the law. The second provided for a reduction in a state's representation proportional to the number of male citizens denied suffrage. This aimed to prevent the South from benefiting politically from emancipation. Before the war, three-fifths of the slaves had been included in calculating Congressional representations; now, as free persons, all would be counted. Since Republicans were not prepared to force black suffrage upon the South, they offered white Southerners a choice—enfranchise the freedmen or sacrifice representation in Congress. The third clause barred from national and state office men who had sworn allegiance to the Constitution and subsequently aided the Confederacy. While not depriving "rebels" of the vote, this excluded from office most of the South's prewar political leadership, opening the door to power, Republicans hoped, for true Unionists. The Amendment also prohibited payment of the Confederate debt and empowered Congress to enforce its provisions through "appropriate" legislation.

Because it implicitly acknowledged the right of states to limit voting because of race, Wendell Phillips denounced the amendment as a "fatal and total surrender." Susan B. Anthony, Elizabeth Cady Stanton, and others in the women's suffrage movement also felt betrayed, because the second clause introduced the word "male" into the Constitution. Alone among suffrage limitations, those founded on sex would not reduce a state's representation.

Ideologically and politically, nineteenth-century feminism had been tied to abolition. Feminists now turned Radical ideology back upon Congress. If "special claims for special classes" were illegitimate and unrepublican, how could the denial of women's rights be justified? Should not sex, like race, be rejected as an unacceptable basis for legal distinctions among citizens? Rather than defining Reconstruction as "the negro's hour," they called it, instead, the hour for change: Another generation might pass "ere the constitutional door will again be opened." The dispute over the Fourteenth Amendment marked a turning point in nineteenth-century reform. Leaving feminist leaders with a deep sense of betrayal, it convinced them, as Stanton put it, that woman "must not put her trust in man" in seeking her rights. Women's leaders now embarked on a course that severed their historic alliance with abolitionism and created a truly independent feminist movement.

The Fourteenth Amendment, one Republican newspaper observed, repudiated the two axioms on which the Radicals "started to make their fight last December: dead States and equal suffrage." Yet it clothed with constitutional authority the principle Radicals had fought to vindicate: equality before the law, overseen by the national government. For its heart was the first section, which declared all persons born or naturalized in the United States both national and state citizens and prohibited the states from abridging their "privileges and immunities," depriving any person of life, liberty, or property without "due process of law," or denying them "equal protection of the laws."

For more than a century, politicians, judges, lawyers, and scholars have debated the meaning of this elusive language. But the aims of the Fourteenth Amendment can be understood only within the political and ideological context of 1866: the break with the President, the need to find a measure able to unify all Republicans, and the growing party consensus in favor of strong federal action to protect the freedmen's rights, short of the suffrage. During many drafts, changes, and deletions, the Amendment's central principle remained constant: a national guarantee of equality before the law. This was "so just," a moderate Congressman declared, "that no member of this House can seriously object to it." In language that transcended race and region, the Amendment challenged legal discrimination throughout the nation and changed and broadened the meaning of freedom for all Americans. . . .

The Republicans who gathered in December 1866 for the second session of the Thirty-Ninth Congress considered themselves "masters of the situation." Johnson's annual message, pleading for the immediate restoration of the "now unrepresented States," was ignored. The President, declared the New York *Herald,* his erstwhile supporter, "forgets that we have passed through the fiery ordeal of a mighty revolution, and that the pre-existing order of things is gone and can return no more—that a great work of reconstruction is before us, and that we cannot escape it."

Black suffrage, it soon became clear, was on the horizon. In mid-December, Trumbull told the Senate that Congress possessed the authority to "enter these States and hurl from power the disloyal element which controls and governs them," an important announcement that moderates intended to overturn the Johnson governments. In January 1867, a bill enfranchising blacks in the District of Columbia became law over the President's veto. Then, Congress extended manhood suffrage to the territories. Even more radical proposals were in the air, including widespread disenfranchisement, martial law for the South, confiscation, the impeachment of the President. A *Herald* editorial writer apologized to Johnson for the paper's advocacy of his removal: Its editor always went with the political tide, and the tide now flowed toward the Radicals. . . .

Throughout these deliberations, Johnson remained silent. Toward the end of February, New York *Evening Post* editor Charles Nordhoff visited the White House. He found the President "much excited," certain "the people of the South . . . were to be trodden under foot 'to protect niggers.'" Nordhoff had once admired the President; now he judged him a "pig-headed man" governed by one idea: "bitter opposition to universal suffrage." Gone was the vision of a reconstructed South controlled by loyal yeomen. "The old Southern leaders . . . ," declared the man who had once railed against the Slave Power, "must rule the South." When the Reconstruction bill reached his desk on March 2, Johnson returned it with a veto, which Congress promptly overrode. Maryland Sen. Reverdy Johnson was the only member to break party ranks. Whatever its flaws, he declared, the bill offered the South a path back into the Union, and the President should abandon his intransigence and accede to the plainly expressed will of the people. Reverdy Johnson's was the only Democratic vote in favor of any of the Reconstruction measures of 1866–67.

In its final form, the Reconstruction Act of 1867 divided the Confederate states, except Tennessee, into five military districts under commanders empowered to employ the army to protect life and property. And without immediately replacing the Johnson regimes, it laid out the steps by which new state governments could be created and recognized by Congress—the writing of new constitutions providing for manhood suffrage, their approval by a majority of registered voters, and ratification of the Fourteenth Amendment. Simultaneously, Congress passed the Habeas Corpus Act, which greatly expanded citizens' ability to remove cases to federal courts.

Like all the decisions of the Thirty-Ninth Congress, the Reconstruction Act contained a somewhat incongruous mixture of idealism and political expediency. The bill established military rule, but only as a temporary measure to keep the peace, with the states assured a relatively quick return to the Union. It looked to a new political order for the South, but failed to place Southern Unionists in immediate control. It made no economic provision for the freedmen. Even black suffrage derived from a variety of motives and calculations. For Radicals, it represented the culmination of a lifetime of reform. For others, it seemed less the fulfillment of an idealistic creed than an alternative to prolonged federal intervention in the South, a means of enabling blacks to defend themselves against abuse, while relieving the nation of that responsibility.

Despite all its limitations, Congressional Reconstruction was indeed a radical departure, a stunning and unprecedented experiment in interracial democracy. In America, the ballot not only identified who could vote, it defined a collective national identity. Democrats had fought black suffrage on precisely these grounds. "Without reference to the question of equality," declared Indiana Sen. Thomas Hendricks, "I say we are not of the same race; we are so different that we ought not to compose one political community." Enfranchising blacks marked a powerful repudiation of such thinking. In some ways it was an astonishing leap of faith. Were the mass of freedmen truly prepared for political rights? Gen. E. O. C. Ord, federal commander in Arkansas, believed them "so servile and accustomed to submit" to white dictation that they would "not dare to present themselves at the polls." Even some Radicals harbored inner doubts, fearing that "demagogues" or their former masters would control the black vote, or that political rights would prove meaningless without economic independence.

In the course of Reconstruction, the freedmen disproved these somber forecasts. They demonstrated political shrewdness and independence in using the ballot to affect the conditions of their freedom. However inadequate as a response to the legacy of slavery, it remains a tragedy that the lofty goals of civil and political equality were not permanently achieved. And the end of Reconstruction came not because propertyless blacks succumbed to economic coercion, but because a tenacious black community, abandoned by the nation, fell victim to violence and fraud.

"We have cut loose from the whole dead past," wrote Wisconsin Sen. Timothy Howe, "and have cast our anchor out a hundred years." His colleague, Waitman T. Willey of West Virginia, adopted a more cautious tone: "The legislation of the last two years will mark a great page of history for good or evil—I hope the former. The crisis, however, is not yet past." . . .

Violence had been endemic in large parts of the South since 1865. But the advent of Radical Reconstruction stimulated its expansion. By 1870 the Ku Klux Klan and kindred organizations like the Knights of the White Camelia and the White Brotherhood were deeply entrenched in nearly every Southern state. The Klan, even in its heyday, did not possess a well-organized structure or clearly defined regional leadership. But the unity of purpose and common tactics of these local organizations make it possible to generalize about their goals and impact and the challenge they posed to the survival of Reconstruction. In effect, the Klan was a military force serving the interests of the Democratic party, the planter class, and all those who desired the restoration of white supremacy. Its purposes were political in the broadest sense, for it sought to affect power relations, both public and private, throughout Southern society. It aimed to destroy the Republican party's infrastructure, undermined the Reconstruction state, reestablish control of the black labor force, and restore racial subordination in every aspect of Southern life.

Violence was typically directed at Reconstruction's local leaders. As Emanuel Fortune, driven from Jackson County, Florida, by the Klan, explained: "The object of it is to kill out the leading men of the republican party . . . men who have taken a prominent stand." Jack Dupree, victim of a particularly brutal murder in Monroe County, Mississippi—assailants cut his throat and disemboweled him, all within sight of his wife, who had just given birth to twins—was "president of a republican club" and known as a man who "would speak his mind." Countless other local leaders fled their homes after brutal whippings. And many blacks suffered merely for exercising their rights as citizens. Alabama freedman George Moore reported how, in 1869, Klansmen came to his home, administered a beating, "ravished a young girl who was visiting my wife," and wounded a neighbor. "The cause of this treatment, they said, was that we voted the radical ticket." Nor did white Republicans escape the violence. Klansmen murdered three scalawag members of the Georgia legislature and drove ten others from their homes. The Klan in western North Carolina settled old scores with wartime Unionists, burned the offices of the Rutherford *Star*, and brutally whipped Aaron Biggerstaff, a Hero of America and Republican organizer. . . .

The issues of white supremacy, low taxes, and control of the black labor force dominated the Democratic campaigns of the mid-1870s. And their appeal became evident in 1873 and 1874 as Democrats solidified their hold on states already under their control and "redeemed" new ones. Texas Democrat Richard Coke defeated Gov. Edmund J. Davis in 1873 by a margin of better than two to one. Meanwhile, Virginia Democrats jettisoned the moderate Republicans with whom they had cooperated in 1869 and carried the state with a "straight-out" ticket and a platform of "race against race." The 1874 Southern elections proved as disastrous for Republicans as those in the North. Democrats won over two-thirds of the region's House seats, redeemed Arkansas, and gained control of Florida's legislature.

In these campaigns, which mostly took place in states where blacks comprised a minority of the population, Democratic victories depended mainly on the party's success at drawing the political color line. In Louisiana and Alabama, however, the brutality of white-line politics came to the fore. Louisiana's White League, organized in 1874, was openly dedicated to the violent restoration of white supremacy. It targeted local Republican officeholders for assassination, disrupted court sessions, and drove black laborers from their homes. In Red River Parish, the campaign degenerated into a violent reign of terror, which culminated in August in the cold-blooded murder of six Republican officials. In September 1874 3,500 leaguers, mostly Civil War veterans, overwhelmed an equal number of black militiamen and Metropolitan Police under the command of Confederate Gen. James Longstreet and occupied the city hall, statehouse, and arsenal. They withdrew only upon the arrival of federal troops, ordered to the scene by the President. A similar campaign of violence helped "redeem" Alabama for the Democrats in the elections of 1874.

The Crisis of 1875

By the time the Forty-Third Congress reassembled in December, the political landscape had been transformed. As a result of the Democratic landslide, this session would be the last time for over a decade that Republicans controlled both the White House and Congress. With political violence erupting in many parts of the South, and their party's hegemony in Washington about to expire, Benjamin Butler and other Stalwarts devised a program to safeguard what remained of Reconstruction. Their proposals included the Civil Rights Bill, a new Enforcement Act expanding the President's power to suppress conspiracies aimed at intimidating voters, a two-year army appropriation (to prevent the incoming Democratic House from limiting the military's role in the South), a bill expanding the jurisdiction of the federal courts, and a subsidy for the Texas & Pacific Railroad. The package embodied the idealism, partisanship, and crass economic advantage typical of Republican politics. Civil rights was the program's spearhead, and to make it more palatable, Butler dropped the bill's controversial clause requiring integrated schools.

Events in Louisiana disrupted the already tenuous party unity necessary to enact such a program. Having suppressed the New Orleans insurrection of September 1874, Grant, newly determined to "protect the colored voter in his rights," ordered Gen. Philip H. Sheridan to use federal troops to counteract violence and sustain the administration of Gov. William P. Kellogg. On January 4, 1875, when Democrats attempted to seize control of the state assembly by forcibly installing party members in five disputed seats, a detachment of troops entered the legislative chambers and escorted out the five claimants.

If, for Reconstruction's critics, South Carolina epitomized the evils of corruption and "black rule," Louisiana now came to represent the danger posed by excessive federal interference in local affairs. The spectacle of soldiers "marching into the Hall . . . and expelling members at the point of the bayonet" aroused more Northern opposition than any previous federal action in the South. In Boston a

large body of "highly respectable citizens" gathered at Faneuil Hall to demand Sheridan's removal and compare the White League with the founding fathers as defenders of republican freedom. Wendell Phillips was among those present. Four decades earlier, Phillips had launched his abolitionist career in this very hall, when he reprimanded a speaker who praised the murderers of antislavery editor Elijah P. Lovejoy. Then, his eloquence converted the audience. Now, as he rebuked those who would "take from the President . . . the power to protect the millions" the nation had liberated from bondage, he heard only hisses, laughter, and cries of "played out, sit down." "Wendell Phillips and William Lloyd Garrison," commented the *New York Times,* "are not exactly extinct from American politics, but they represent ideas in regard to the South which the majority of the Republican party have outgrown." The uproar over Louisiana made Republicans extremely wary of further military intervention in the South. . . .

The full implications of the "let alone policy" became clear in the 1875 political campaign in Mississippi. White Mississippians interpreted the 1874 elections as a national repudiation of Reconstruction. Although the Democratic state convention adopted a platform recognizing the civil and political rights of blacks, the campaign quickly became a violent crusade to destroy the Republican organization and prevent blacks from voting. Democratic rifle clubs paraded through the black belt, disrupting Republican meetings and assaulting local party leaders. Unlike crimes by the Ku Klux Klan's hooded riders, those of 1875 were committed in broad daylight by undisguised men, as if to underscore the impotence of local authorities and Democrats' lack of concern about federal intervention. . . .

Appeals for protection poured into the offices of Governor Ames. "They are going around the streets at night dressed in soldiers clothes and making colored people run for their lives . . . ," declared a petition by black residents of Vicksburg. "We are intimidated by the whites. . . . We will not vote at all, unless there are troops to protect us." Convinced "the power of the U.S. alone can give the security our citizens are entitled to," Ames early in September requested Grant to send troops to the state. From his summer home on the New Jersey shore, the President dispatched instructions to Attorney General Edwards Pierrepont. One widely quoted sentence came to epitomize the North's retreat from Reconstruction: "The whole public are tired out with these annual autumnal outbreaks in the South . . . [and] are ready now to condemn any interference on the part of the Government." Pierrepont sent an aide to the state, who in October arranged a "peace agreement" whereby the only two active militia companies were disbanded and whites promised to disarm. But Democrats, as black state senator Charles Caldwell reported, held the agreement "in utter contempt." On election eve, armed riders drove freedmen from their homes and threatened to kill them if they tried to vote. The next day, Democrats destroyed the ballot boxes or replaced Republican votes with their own. "The reports which come to me almost hourly are truly sickening . . . ," Ames reported to his wife. "The government of the U.S. does not interfere." The result was a Democratic landslide. Nor did this conclude Mississippi's "Redemption." In plantation counties where Republicans still held local positions, violence continued after the election, with officials forced to resign under threat of assassination and vigilante groups meting out punishment to blacks accused of theft and other violations of plantation discipline. On Christmas Day, Charles Caldwell, "as brave a man as I

ever knew," according to one associate, was shot in the back in Clinton after being lured to take a drink with a white "friend." When the legislature assembled, it impeached and removed from office black Lieut. Gov. Alexander K. Davis and then compelled Gov. Ames to resign and leave the state rather than face impeachment charges himself. . . .

All in all, from the inability of the Forty-Third Congress in its waning days to agree on a policy toward the South to Grant's failure to intervene in Mississippi, 1875 marked a milestone in the retreat from Reconstruction. As another Presidential election approached, it seemed certain that whoever emerged victorious, Reconstruction itself was doomed. . . .

More than any other state, national attention in 1876 focused on South Carolina, whose political climate was transformed by an event in the tiny town of Hamburg. What came to be known as the Hamburg Massacre began with the black militia's celebration of the July 4th centennial. When the son and son-in-law of a local white farmer arrived on the scene and ordered the militiamen to move aside for their carriage, harsh words were exchanged, although militia commander Dock Adams eventually opened his company's ranks and the pair proceeded on their way. Four days later, the black militia again gathered in Hamburg, as did a large number of armed whites. After Adams refused a demand by Gen. Matthew C. Butler, the area's most prominent Democratic politician, to disarm his company, fighting broke out, about forty militiamen retreated to their armory, and Butler made for Augusta, returning with a cannon and hundreds of white reinforcements. As darkness fell, the outnumbered militiamen attempted to flee the scene. Hamburg's black marshal fell mortally wounded and twenty-five men were captured; of these, five were murdered in cold blood. After the killings, the mob ransacked the homes and shops of the town's blacks.

Among the affair's most appalling features was the conduct of Gen. Butler, who either selected the prisoners to be executed (according to black eyewitnesses) or left the scene when the crowd began "committing depredations" (his own, hardly more flattering, account). In either case, Butler's conduct underscored the utter collapse of a sense of paternalist obligation, not to mention common decency, among those who called themselves the region's "natural leaders." Certainly, no one could again claim that the South's "respectable" elite disdained such violence, for in one of its first actions, South Carolina's Redeemer legislature in 1877 elected Butler to the U.S. Senate. . . .

With so much at stake, the 1876 campaign became the most tumultuous in South Carolina's history and the one significant exception to the Reconstruction pattern that cast blacks as the victims of political violence and whites as the sole aggressors. In September, black Republicans assaulted Democrats of both races leaving a Charleston meeting; several were wounded and one white lost his life. A month later a group of blacks began firing at a "joint discussion" at Cainhoy, a village near the city, resulting in the deaths of five whites and one black.

But the campaign of intimidation launched by [Democratic candidate Gen. Wade] Hampton's supporters far overshadowed such incidents. Rifle clubs disrupted Republican rallies with "violent and abusive tirades." A reign of terror reminiscent of Ku Klux Klan days swept over Edgefield, Aiken, Barnwell, and other Piedmont

counties, with freedmen driven from their homes and brutally whipped, and "leading men" murdered. The belief that they need not fear federal intervention gave Democrats a free hand. Former slave Jerry Thornton Moore, president of an Aiken County Republican club, was told by his white landlord that opponents of Reconstruction planned to carry the election "if we have to wade in blood knee-deep." "Mind what you are doing," Moore responded, "the United States is mighty strong." Replied the landlord: "but, Thornton, . . . the northern people is on our side."

South Carolina's election, a Democratic observer acknowledged, "was one of the grandest farces ever seen." Despite the campaign of intimidation, [the incumbent Republican governor Daniel H.] Chamberlain polled the largest Republican vote in the state's history. But Edgefield and Laurens County Democrats carried out instructions to vote "early and often" and prevent blacks from reaching the polls, thereby producing massive majorities that enabled their party to claim a narrow statewide victory.

Early returns on election night appeared to foretell a national Democratic victory. [New York governor Samuel J.] Tilden carried New York, New Jersey, Connecticut, and Indiana, more than enough, together with a solid South, to give him the Presidency. *New York Times* editor George F. Jones even wired Hayes announcing his defeat. But in the early hours of the morning, someone at Republican headquarters noticed that if Hayes carried South Carolina, Florida, and Louisiana, where the party controlled the voting machinery, he would have a one-vote Electoral College majority. Both Gen. Daniel E. Sickles and William E. Chandler later claimed to have made this discovery and to have sent telegrams, over the signature of the sleeping party chairman, Zachariah Chandler, urging Republican officials to hold their states for Hayes. Soon after he awakened, Chandler announced: "Hayes has 185 electoral votes and is elected." . . .

Among other things, 1877 marked a decisive retreat from the idea, born during the Civil War, of a powerful national state protecting the fundamental rights of all American citizens.

FURTHER READING

Eric Anderson and Alfred Moss, eds., *The Facts of Reconstruction* (1991).
Michael Les Benedict, *A Compromise of Principle: Congressional Republicans and Reconstruction* (1974).
Laura Edwards, *Gendered Strife and Confusion: The Political Culture of Reconstruction* (1997).
Eric Foner, *Nothing but Freedom: Emancipation and Its Legacy* (1983).
Leon Litwack, *Been in the Storm So Long: The Aftermath of Slavery* (1979).
Nell Irvin Painter, *Exodusters: Black Migration to Kansas After Reconstruction* (1977).
Michael Perman, *The Road to Redemption* (1984).
Jonathan Wiener, *Social Origins of the New South* (1978).